HANS KREBS

MONOGRAPHS ON THE HISTORY AND PHILOSOPHY OF BIOLOGY

Editors
RICHARD BURIAN
RICHARD BURKHARDT, JR.
RICHARD LEWONTIN
JOHN MAYNARD SMITH

HANS KREBS

The Formation of a Scientific Life
1900–1933

Volume I

FREDERIC LAWRENCE HOLMES

New York   Oxford
OXFORD UNIVERSITY PRESS
1991

Oxford University Press

Oxford   New York   Toronto
Delhi   Bombay   Calcutta   Madras   Karachi
Petaling Jaya   Singapore   Hong Kong   Tokyo
Nairobi   Dar es Salaam   Cape Town
Melbourne   Auckland

and associated companies in
Berlin   Ibadan

Copyright © 1991 by Oxford University Press, Inc.

Published by Oxford University Press, Inc.,
200 Madison Avenue, New York, New York 10016

Oxford is a registered trademark of Oxford University Press

Library of Congress Cataloging-in-Publication Data
Holmes, Frederic Lawrence.
Hans Krebs / Frederic L. Holmes.
p.   cm. — (Monographs on the history and philosophy of biology)
Includes bibliographical references and index.
Contents: v. 1. The formation of a scientific life, 1900-1933.
ISBN 0-19-507072-0
1. Krebs, Hans Adolf, Sir.
2. Biochemists—Germany—Biography.
I. Title.   II. Series.
QP511.8.K73H65   1991   574.19'2'092—dc20
[B]   91-2201

1 3 5 7 9 8 6 4 2

Printed in the United States of America
on acid-free paper

For Harriet

FOREWORD

To the privilege and pleasure afforded by Professor Holmes's invitation to prepare these prefatory remarks, I must add my thanks for the opportunity to acknowledge my personal debt to an Krebs. We first met in about 1938, after the great researches described in these volumes, and when his place among the leaders in the development of biochemistry was assured. However, the awe inspired by these achievements was quickly dispelled by the kind of warm encouragement that all aspiring young scientists hope to receive from their distinguished elders. During the succeeding years, I visited Krebs in Sheffield and in Oxford, he came to Yale, and we conducted a lively correspondence. When we talked about biochemical matters, there were occasional disagreements, but instead of weakening our collegial friendship these differences of opinion appeared to strengthen it. Above all, I continued to receive from Krebs boosts to my morale in the research conducted in my laboratory, in my efforts as a teacher of biochemistry, and later in my venture into the history of this discipline. I valued his praise, as well as his criticism, all the more as, with the passing years, I came to appreciate better the exacting standards he set for himself and expected of others.

Among my many fond memories of Krebs, two may be mentioned here. In July 1952, my wife (Sofia Simmonds) and I were his guests in Sheffield. His laboratory there was located in a few very crowded rooms in a rather shabby building. However, even a brief visit was sufficient to show that what these rooms may have lacked in spaciousness, fancy furniture, or shiny apparatus was more than compensated for by the spirit of enthusiastic inquiry that Krebs evoked from all his junior associates. The other occasion was in November 1953, when Krebs lectured at Yale, and an overflow audience expressed its joy at the announcement, a few weeks earlier, that he was to receive a Nobel Prize in Physiology or Medicine.

At one of our last encounters in Oxford, I told Krebs about my friend Larry Holmes, who had expressed a desire to meet him in order to discuss the possibility of a close examination, based on Krebs's recollections and his research notebooks, of the sequence of thought and experiment in his great discoveries of the 1930s. As I had grown accustomed to his courteous reserve, it would not have surprised me if Krebs had declined, so it was a source of delight to learn from Holmes that Krebs had agreed to embark on this project, and also to receive a letter (14 April 1978) in which Krebs wrote me that their contacts "have been very happy ones." From their association, and from the historical insight and meticulous scholarship Holmes had previously displayed in his seminal writings about Claude Bernard and Antoine Lavoisier, there has emerged this admirable book.

Joseph S. Fruton

NOTES ON SOURCES

Documents designated "KC" (Krebs Collection), were, at the time I used them, in the personal possession of Sir Hans Krebs. They were grouped by categories in boxes, but were not formally organized. They have since then been catalogued and deposited in the Sheffield University Library. I have not had the opportunity to visit this archive in order to identify the catalogue entries under which the individual documents can now be found in that collection. Readers who wish to examine these materials should be able to locate them with facility by means of the comprehensive *Catalogue of the Papers and Correspondence of Sir Hans Adolf Krebs FRS (1900–1981)*, compiled by Jeannine Alton and Peter Harper. Enquiries concerning the catalogue and the collection should be addressed to The Librarian, Sheffield University, Sheffield S10 2TN, UK. For documents that I consulted after the collection had been catalogued in Oxford, I have included the entry numbers.

I have referred to the laboratory notebooks of Hans Krebs by numbers that he and I affixed to their covers during the course of my visits to Oxford so that he could easily retrieve those that I wished to examine further. These numbers do not coincide with the numbering system adopted in the *Catalogue of the Papers and Correspondence*. They can most easily be identified with the *Catalogue* entries through the dates covered by each notebook.

References to transcribed conversations are given according to the participants, in the form "person interviewed-FLH," the date of the conversation, the number of the tape, and the page number of the taped transcription. Because there are some irregularities in the latter numbers some ambiguities result, and these references are given only as an informal guide to those who may wish to consult the transcripts. Microfilms of most, but not all, of the transcripts are on deposit in the Sheffield archive. The complete set of transcripts is presently in my possession.

All translations from published and unpublished sources originally written in German, including Hans Krebs's laboratory notebooks, are my own.

During the period covered by this work, the notations for organic compounds were less standardized than they have since become. I have, in general reproduced the representations of structural formulas originally used by the authors whose writings I cite, rather than to modernize them.

In the footnotes the following abbreviations are used for titles of journals repeatedly cited:

Ann. Chem.	Annalen der Chemie und Pharmacie
Arch. exp. Path.	Archiv für experimentelle Pathologie und Pharmakologie
Arch. ges. Physiol.	Pflüger's Archiv für die gesammte Physiologie des Menschen und der Thiere
Arch. mikros. Anat.	Archiv für mikroskopische Anatomie
Arch. Pharm.	Naunyn-Schmiedeberg's Archiv für Pharmakologie und experimentelle Pathologie
Beitr. chem. Physiol.	Beiträge zur chemischen Physiologie und Pathologie
Ber. chem. Ges.	Berichte der deutschen chemischen Gesellschaft
Biochem. J.	Biochemical Journal
Biochem. Z.	Biochemische Zeitschrift
C. r. Soc. Biol.	Comptes rendus de la Société de Biologie
Erg. Physiol.	Ergebnisse der Physiologie
J. Biol. Chem.	Journal of Biological Chemistry
Journ. de physiol.	Journal de physiologie et de pathologie générale
J. Gen. Physiol.	The Journal of General Physiology
J. Physiol.	The Journal of Physiology
J. prakt. Chem.	Journal für praktische Chemie
Klin. Woch.	Berliner Klinische Wochenschrift
Physiol. Rev.	Physiological Reviews
Skand. Arch. Physiol.	Skandinavisches Archiv für Physiologie
Z. Biol.	Zeitschrift für Biologie
Z. exp. Med.	Zeitschrift für die gesamte experimentelle Medizin
Z. physiol. Chem.	Hoppe-Seyler's Zeitschrift für physiologischen Chemie

ACKNOWLEDGMENTS

Many people have helped me generously along the road that led to this book and its sequel. That my deepest gratitude is owed to their subject himself should be self-evident. The sudden death of Sir Hans Krebs in 1981 was a great personal loss to me, as it was to his numerous colleagues, students, and friends.

I have received from the beginning to the end of this project crucial support from Joseph S. Fruton. It was only after discussing the idea with him in the early spring of 1976 that I felt bold enough to contact Krebs. An opportune visit that Fruton made to Oxford just before the arrival of my initial letter to Krebs undoubtedly conditioned the welcoming response that my letter received. His meticulous reading of each chapter as I finished it was immensely valuable to me.

During the course of my research I interviewed a number of people who had known Krebs during his early years. All responded helpfully and warmly to the questions I asked them. Some of them became afterward my good friends. Those among them whose recollections have been incorporated into this first volume include: Theodor Benzinger, Hermann Blaschko, Heinz Fuld, Ursula Leitner, David Nachmansohn, Erich Stern, and Hans Weil-Malherbe. It was a special pleasure to come to know Hans's brother, E. W. Krebs, whose memories of their shared childhood were crucial to my reconstruction of Hans's early life. Hans Weil-Malherbe and Wolf Krebs each read most of the chapters in this volume and provided important corrections.

Another special pleasure, reflected less directly in the book itself, was to come to know the members of Krebs's research "team" during the years I visited Oxford. Reginald Hems, Patricia Lund, and Dermot Williamson particularly made me feel at home in the laboratory which, like similar laboratories that enter the present story, remained always at the core of Krebs's professional life.

While this project was in a late stage, the papers of Hans Krebs were organized and catalogued at the Contemporary Archives Centre in Oxford. The director of this center, Jeannine Alton, and her assistant, Peter Harper, graciously helped me to examine documents that I had not seen during Krebs's lifetime.

I began this work while I was a member of the Faculty of the University of Western Ontario. The research was made possible by a grant from the Hannah Institute for the History of Medicine. I acknowledge with special thanks the generous offer by the Hannah Institute to continue supporting the project after I left Ontario to establish the Section of the History of Medicine at the Yale University School of Medicine.

At Western, Linda Gretzinger began the lengthy task of transcribing the taped interviews that I brought back with me from Oxford and elsewhere. At Yale Gail Sacco continued that work for several years. Selda Lippa has finished the transcribing, typed all of the manuscript, and contributed in many other ways to the completion of the project. Patricia Johnson organized my research trips and managed my other professional responsibilities so efficiently that I was freed to concentrate much more of my time than would otherwise have been possible on what proved to be a lengthier process of research and writing than I had ever imagined.

Although she will enter the story itself only near the end of Volume II, Lady Margaret Krebs has already entered very much into the experiences that have made my work on the life of her husband rewarding. Coming to know her has made me appreciate why meeting her in 1936 was among the most fortunate events in the life of Hans Krebs.

While I have been working on this book, my wife, Harriet, began a book about her grandfather. It has been especially nice to share with her some of our common problems and rewards in reconstructing in words the lives of people we have known.

Since I began work on what has become these two volumes, our daughters, Catherine, Susan, and Rebecca, have grown up and begun lives of their own; but it has still been heartening when they asked, on their visits home, "How is your book coming, Dad?"

CONTENTS

INTRODUCTION

Born in 1900, Hans Adolf Krebs measured his years by those of the century. Before he died at 81, he had become a revered figure for several generations of biochemists. For nearly 50 years he had stood at or near the forefront of the large subfield of biochemistry known as intermediary metabolism. His two most prominent discoveries—the ornithine cycle of urea synthesis and the citric acid (or TCA) cycle—were viewed as foundations on which much of the modern structure of intermediary metabolism has been erected. Thousands of other people who were not biochemists, but had taken at least an elementary biology course, had encountered the Krebs cycle. Some of them resented the name, because they associated it with having to memorize the formulas of the compounds involved in the cycle.

These volumes tell the story of the early scientific life of Hans Krebs. It begins with his birth, and ends shortly after the discovery of the citric acid cycle in 1937. Those were the years in which both his life and his life work were formed. For those years it provides an exceptionally detailed picture of the investigative, professional, and personal world of a great scientist. My principal aim has been to portray Krebs's activity at the intimate level of the daily interaction of thought and operation from which, I believe, the characteristic patterns of scientific creativity can best be retrieved.

This is the third study of the creative activity of an individual scientist that I have attempted, and in some ways the most difficult. My previous studies of Claude Bernard and Antoine Lavoisier reconstructed selected aspects of the research pathways of two outstanding scientists of the deeper past.[1] Their investigative lives were intense and prolonged. To portray even portions of their work in close detail, and to situate it within the context of the science of their time, required lengthy narratives. For a twentieth century scientist the situation that must be described is even more complex. The prior history of the fields they entered is longer and more intricate. The interactions of the individual with other scientists are more numerous. The documentary record available is apt to be more extensive. Twentieth century conditions typically permit the scientist to perform, either alone or with associates, a greater volume of scientific work, to collect more massive quantities of data than was possible for their predecessors of earlier eras. In my efforts to cope with these factors, I have felt that the approach that I developed in my earlier studies has been pressed to its limits. Only readers can judge whether this approach has in fact been stretched beyond these limits.

This study resembles those on Bernard and Lavoisier in that its account of Krebs's scientific work is structured around a set of surviving laboratory notebooks that trace his daily experimental activities. It differs from them in that it also incorporates information that I was able to acquire through extended conversations with Hans Krebs.

In May 1976, I wrote to Krebs in Oxford to say that I had become interested in the possibility of writing a historical study of his early biochemical research. "The feasibility of carrying out such a plan," I suggested, "would depend upon two conditions. First, that your research records for the period still exist and that I might obtain access to them; and second, that I could spend some time discussing with you your recollections of that period."

With a promptness that I later learned was characteristic, Krebs replied:

I am very much interested in your proposal and I shall be glad to co-operate. I am myself engaged on autobiographical writing but as far as I can judge this would not seriously overlap with anything you might undertake. Naturally your approach would be much more objective than mine could possibly be. My research records are extant and I shall be glad to make them available to you. How useful they might prove I am not at all clear about. A preliminary inspection of the material might help to clarify this aspect.

So I would welcome an exploratory visit from you. Are you already in a position to suggest an approximate date?

I arrived in Oxford in August, with a tape recorder in my briefcase, some knowledge of Krebs's early scientific papers, and little further idea about how to proceed. When Krebs met me on a Sunday afternoon, he was carrying three or four of his old laboratory notebooks in a sack, and he left them with me to examine whether they would be useful. Only then did I realize that he was still, at the age of 76, actively directing the research of his scientific group in the Metabolic Research Laboratory at the Radcliffe Infirmary. The next morning he set me up at a bench in a vacant nearby laboratory, and came by to answer my "questions" when he could find a break from his daily routines. At first this turned out to be for about 30 minutes in the morning, with another similar session at mid-afternoon. After 2 days we agreed that the project was feasible. I stayed for 2 weeks, and returned two or three times each year for the next five years.

Gradually over the course of my visits, additional laboratory notebooks turned up, until I had available a complete set dating from 1926, the year he became an assistant in the laboratory of Otto Warburg, until after the discovery of the citric acid cycle in 1937. Krebs also made available to me many other letters and documents that he had saved. True to his word, he cooperated fully, warmly, and trustingly. At first uncertain about what I wanted to learn in our interviews, he soon came to enjoy them and always asked, at the end of a stay, when I planned to come again. He sometimes referred to our interaction as a "collaboration"; but he did not seek to control the direction of the enterprise. I spent the time between interviews preparing questions, and he answered, as best he could without prior preparation, whatever I asked. The topics we covered ranged from his childhood and family, to the systematic examination of many pages out of his laboratory notebooks; from comments on his scientific style and those of colleagues, to literature, music, and much else.

The contents of the answers to the questions I asked Krebs during the 130 hours of our recorded conversations are, I believe, rich and illuminating. They have not, however, transformed the project into an oral history. The narrative backbone rests on the dense collection of contemporary sources—laboratory notebooks, published papers, correspondence, and so on—that documents his life and work.

As in my previous studies, I regard the present volume both as a story about the scientific life of one person and as part of a broader inquiry into the fine structure of creative scientific activity. Some of the patterns that I have discerned in Krebs's work remind me of patterns that I had encountered in the work of Bernard or of Lavoisier. Other patterns have appeared to contrast with the ways in which they had investigated and thought. This is to be expected. The accumulation of studies such as these can enable us to refine what we knew already: that highly successful scientists share some characteristics within a range of the possible modes of creative investigation, but that each is also unique in important ways.

More than in my previous efforts, I have tried to weave together in this story the scientific investigative pathway with the professional and personal life of the investigator. This is in part because I have had the opportunity to learn more about the life and personality of Hans Krebs than I knew about Bernard or Lavoisier. I believe also, however, that I have enlarged my conception of the scope of creative scientific activity. Although it is in most cases not possible to draw tight connections between stages in Krebs's investigative pathway and stages in his career, or other developments within his professional or personal environment, I believe that it is relevant to that pathway to know what else was going on concurrently in his life. Success in scientific investigation is not a matter of reason and experimentation alone. Howard Gruber has stressed that a scientist who is able to sustain productive activity does so through the way he organizes his life.[2] Krebs himself felt that he succeeded not so much through the qualities of his intellect as through his commitment to scientific research, and his determination not to be diverted from his central purposes. If these factors are important, then it is important to know what pressures or opportunities impinged on the scientist's life from outside his laboratory; what in his background, his personality, or other factors in his life either assisted him in or threatened his ability to maintain such purposes.

Often, Krebs carried out more than one line of investigation at a time, or moved back and forth between ongoing lines of investigation, or interrupted continuing investigations to try out new ideas. That characteristic of his work poses the problem of whether it is better to follow him chronologically through the resulting digressions, or to reorganize his research trail so as to bring out in more coherent form the trajectories of the various problems he pursued. In general, I have chosen the first alternative. This choice sometimes makes it more difficult to follow the thread of particular investigative lines whose history is presented in dispersed segments; it is, I believe, truer to the scientific style of the investigator. To follow these digressions is to follow the scientist as he really worked. Moreover, lines of investigation branch out from one another, merge or partially merge, and separate again, so that a clean analytical division cannot always be made. The coincidence in time of developments in different lines of investigation sometimes affects the way in which the investigator treats one or another line, and can sometimes account for a move that cannot be explained through the internal dynamic within the line itself. Again, the interval of time in which he allows a particular line to lie fallow sometimes influences the direction in which the investigator proceeds when he returns to it. The investigative life of a scientist unfolds in an order that I have felt it best to preserve, even at the expense of the extra demands placed on the reader.

I had initially intended to utilize my conversations with Hans Krebs only as sources of information about the events in his earlier life that I planned to reconstruct. Recognizing that recollections are inevitably colored by the passage of time, I expected that through the ordinary exercise of historical judgment I would be able to distinguish the effects of hindsight, of selective memory filters, and other biases, to isolate usable evidence concerning the past. As I began to write, however, I came to perceive the processes of the older scientist looking back on himself, his later attitudes toward earlier events, or his efforts to reconstruct his own former states of mind as matters of considerable intrinsic interest. I could not incorporate them into the narrative itself, yet to leave them out meant to lose valuable insights. To circumvent this dilemma I have broken into the narrative at various points, inserting excerpts from my conversations with Krebs. In most cases I have indicated these discussions with asterisks. Collectively these sections may be viewed as a secondary theme woven into this book, illustrating some of the qualities of memory.

Gerald Holton has suggested that to understand an *event* in science we must describe the intersections between several time trajectories, including those of the "state of shared knowledge," and of the "largely 'private' path of the individual investigator."[3] Applied to the present case that would involve describing, in addition to the research pathway of Hans Krebs, the development of much of the field of intermediary metabolism during the first third of this century. I have struggled with the problem of describing two such complicated trajectories within a single narrative, and have concluded that a comprehensive history of intermediary metabolism must await separate treatment. In Chapter 1, I have compressed an overview of some of the central strands in the development of that field up until the time that Krebs entered it. Many particular developments relevant to certain phases of his work had to be left out of that chapter, however, and I have described them separately at those points at which they impinged on his investigative trail. The resulting picture of the field is less coherent than I would have wished, but that problem appears insurmountable to me. As historians of science we have only begun to confront the magnitude of the task of situating the work of twentieth century scientists within the complexities of a modern specialty field.

In constructing the narrative of Krebs's life and work until 1937 I have, with few exceptions, avoided foreshadowing at any point events that then lay still in the future. I have done so in the belief that, except to the extent that the individuals involved anticipate the future, it does not influence the present, whereas all that has already happened may be part of the explanation for what is currently happening. A story should retain its meaning up until any point to which it has been told, even if we imagine that it had historically been interrupted at that point. I intend for the story to unfold, insofar as possible, "as it happened." I am conscious of at least two drawbacks to this narrative style. Readers often find it easier to wade through the details, particularly of scientific investigations, if they can sense in advance where they are "heading"; and historians are tempted to point out that events that may appear trivial or small as they occur are significant because they will turn out afterward to have been starting points for what became important through further developments. Nevertheless, such forward projections tend to spoil the historical coherence of the situations that existed at a particular time, and to "give away" so much of the story that by the time readers have reached those later developments they are anticlimactic. Like a traditional novel, a historical narrative should maintain some degree of suspense.

I am aware also of the artifice entailed in this approach. The historian knows in advance the general outcome of the story, and in the case of major scientists such as Hans Krebs, so do many of the readers. I agree with the view recently espoused by Robert Richards, that a narrative is inevitably teleological. The historian is writing "toward an ending," and selects the events and details of events to be described with foreknowledge of how they will contribute toward or pose obstacles to the denouements in the story.[4] Nevertheless, to withhold references to the ending until it arrives is not to sustain a pure illusion. Unless one adopts an extreme deterministic view of history, the ending was not inevitable before it historically occurred, and the historian can legitimately preserve space in his or her narrative for possible outcomes other than those that eventually appear.

* * *

As far as I know, these volumes represent the first effort to reconstruct the unbroken investigative pathway of a major twentieth century scientist from the time at which he first entered a laboratory until he made the discovery for which he is best known. It has been possible to do so because there exists an essentially complete record of the experiments that Hans Krebs performed over that period. The task is difficult because Krebs's work habits and his methods enabled him to carry out one or more sets of experiments nearly every working day. The total number of relevant experiments is, therefore, immense. I have not described every experiment. Along portions of his research trail during which he appeared to be mainly consolidating results already attained, or following routine strategies, I have sometimes condensed, summarized, or omitted. Otherwise, however, I have tried to include every meaningful step in the course of his ongoing research, especially during the seven crucial years after he began to carry on experiments on his own in 1930.

Modern readers are less tolerant of detail than were readers of earlier times. They now prefer stories to be streamlined and synoptic, and regard the author who does not accommodate that preference as unselective, unable to extract the larger picture from the trivia. These are, however, often preferences of convenience rather than of principle, and we should not automatically acquiesce in them. We must contemplate carefully at what level of detail we can approach most closely the elusive reality of events, at what level we can reach the maximum clarity. The broad picture is sometimes a mosaic inseparable from the many details that compose it. We cannot grasp the richness of a complex musical composition by playing only its main themes, even though we may gain understanding by analyzing its themes after we have heard it. This book should be read and understood similarly. I do not expect readers to assimilate all of the details in this story on a first reading, any more than one would expect to appreciate every note in a symphony at first hearing. On a scientific research trail, the closest things to "unit events"—the "notes" of the composition—are the individual experiments. Whenever I have tried to lump similar experiments into generic descriptions, or select out certain examples as "representative," I have caught myself falling into imprecise interpretations. Similar though many of the experiments recounted in these volumes are, there are rarely any that are identical in every respect. The subtle nuances differentiating them reflect the subtle nuances in the thinking of the investigator. I have, of course, attempted to elicit from these details broader patterns. On first encountering these books, readers might well scan the descriptive details rather lightly, and return later to scrutinize some sections at closer range. My conclusions are not the only ones to be extracted from these details, and I believe it important that readers have available the evidence on which I have based my own generalizations. I am hopeful that this work can serve not only as a coherent, autonomous narrative, but as a repository of case material for historians, philosophers, cognitive scientists, and others wishing to examine the processes of scientific creativity from perspectives different from my own. I am heartened that Herbert Simon and his associates have already found parts of the manuscript of this book useful as a source for their studies of the heuristics of experimental scientific discovery.[5] The rarity of close accounts of individual creative scientific activity is evident to them, and will be to others who turn their attention to such problems.

Detailed treatments are particularly troublesome to historians of science because so much of the detail is technical; yet, unlike the scientist, the historian of science does not aim to communicate mainly with fellow specialists in the technical area in question. Along with other humanists, historians of science hope to reach diverse audiences; but we are confronted with the dilemma that, in providing discussions and descriptions specific enough to satisfy readers knowledgeable in the scientific field, we are in danger of alienating the general reader. There is no easy way out of this difficulty; nevertheless, it can be eased if author and reader alike take to heart the current point of view in literary criticism, that any text has multiple levels of potential meaning, and that these meanings are a joint product of the performance of the writer and the reader. In this book, as in any book, it is not necessary that all readers focus their attention on the same levels or absorb the same degree of detail.

1

Intermediary Metabolism in the First Third of the Twentieth Century

The field of intermediary metabolism, in which Hans Krebs became a leading investigator during the 1930s, had coalesced into a well-defined subfield of biochemistry during the three decades preceding his entry into that area. This chapter is intended to provide a panoramic view of developments during the period that shaped the general problems that Krebs took up. Although the themes discussed here do not become immediately pertinent to the account of Krebs's professional life until Chapter 7, it is convenient to group them together at the beginning. Later chapters will make reference to portions of this chapter as they come to bear on successive stages of Krebs's work, and some of the more specialized aspects of the prior history of intermediary metabolism will be treated in the places at which Krebs encountered them. Some readers may prefer to postpone reading this chapter until after the chapters on his early life and training.

The central problem in the early history of intermediary metabolism was to discover the stages by which foodstuffs are broken down in the animal body until they form the final end products that are either excreted or breathed out from the lungs. The chemical boundaries of this problem were directly traceable to the theory of respiration proposed at the end of the eighteenth century by Antoine Lavoisier. Between 1777 and 1790 Lavoisier showed that animals burn carbon and hydrogen to form carbonic acid and water, that this process maintains animal heat, and that it is somehow connected with the mechanical work an animal performs.[1] From that time onward chemists and biologists contended with several fundamental questions, which took on different forms with progressive changes in the state of knowledge and of the technical methods available for investigations. They asked where the combustions take place, what is the nature of the compounds that contain the carbon and hydrogen while they are undergoing respiratory oxidation, and why substances that require a much higher temperature to burn outside the organism can be oxidized within it at normal body temperature.

During the early nineteenth century advances in knowledge about organic compounds of biological origin led to the generalization that there are three main classes of foodstuffs — carbohydrates, fats, and "albuminoid bodies," or as the latter were called later in the century, proteins — each of which is decomposed by combining with oxygen to form simple end products.[2] Eventually it became possible to describe these overall reactions in terms of specific chemical equations. Thus, the oxidation of the physiologically most significant carbohydrate, glucose, was expressed as:

$$C_6 H_{12} O_6 + 6 O_2 \rightarrow 6 CO_2 + H_2O$$

For protein the situation was complicated by the presence of a fourth element, nitrogen, that was not completely oxidized but excreted in the form of urea. From the time of Justus Liebig's influential *Animal Chemistry* of 1842 onward, however, it was generally assumed that at an early stage in their degradation, proteins are split into a nitrogenous portion that is excreted, and a nonnitrogenous portion that is further oxidized in a manner similar to the nonnitrogenous foodstuffs.[3] By the 1860s physiologists were developing methods capable of measuring precisely the food intake, the excretions, and the respiratory exchanges of animals and humans.[4] With these methods they were able to establish the quantitative proportions of each of the three classes of foodstuffs metabolized under varied physiological and pathological conditions.

The same chemical advances that enabled physiologists to deal so effectively with the overall process of respiratory oxidation persuaded them that in between its initial and final stages lay an extended hidden sequence of intervening steps. By the 1830s chemists could induce, in organic compounds in the laboratory, controlled partial oxidations that gave rise to multiple compounds containing progressively higher proportions of oxygen before reaching the ultimate breakdown products. Those who applied the growing knowledge of the chemistry of organic compounds to physiological questions inferred that equivalent series of step-by-step oxidations must occur within organisms, especially within animals.[5] Until near the end of the century, however, these intermediate stages, thought by then to occur within the minute cells of the tissues, seemed inaccessible to direct investigation.

In the last decade of the century and the first decade of the new century, physiological chemists began to probe more persistently the problem of what takes place between the starting and the end points of metabolism. Stimulated in part by new knowledge of the structural formulas and reaction mechanisms of biologically important compounds, they were able to propose more imposing theoretical reaction sequences to test experimentally. The work of Emil Fischer and others began to reveal the molecular architecture of polysaccharides and proteins, showing them to be made up of small units linked through characteristic types of readily hydrolyzable bonds.[6] As strong evidence emerged that the foodstuffs are dissociated into these smaller molecules during digestion, the main thrust of investigations of metabolic processes could be transferred, as Frederick Gowland Hopkins put it, from "complex substances which elude ordinary chemical methods" to "simple substances undergoing comprehensible reactions."[7] Further encouragement to the study of these reactions came from Eduard Buchner's discovery of cell-free fermentation.[8] In the early years of this century biochemists optimistically hoped that the reactions comprising cellular respiratory oxidations too could be investigated by ordinary chemical methods in materials extracted from organized tissue. During those years the term *intermediary metabolism* began to appear with increasing frequency as the visible sign of a newly emerging specialty area.

During the 30 years prior to Hans Krebs's entry into this field, intermediary metabolism was an active area of investigation, pursued by some of the most eminent individuals within the expanding science of biochemistry. Successes did not come as easily as those at the turn of the century might have expected, however, and by 1930 there was still no definitive theoretical framework to integrate what biochemists had been able to learn about the compounds and reactions involved in the intermediate steps of the respiratory oxidation of foodstuffs. Investigators had, however, accumulated a promising array of methods and of viewpoints concerning the types of mechanisms that must be involved. They had identified certain organic compounds as nodal substrates in these processes. There were established theoretical and methodological assumptions that channeled research into well-outlined directions, and that delimited the range of acceptable interpretations of particular experimental results. The following section will not attempt to summarize the intricate chronological evolution of the field over these 30 years, but to survey how prior developments in that field might have looked to someone finding his place in it in 1933.

I

In general discussions of respiratory oxidation the study of what were later called *metabolic pathways* was ordinarily not treated during the 1920s as a distinct subfield, but embedded within the broader subject of "the mechanism of physiological [or biological] oxidation processes." The dominant problem considered under this heading was still the old question of "why foodstuffs, which are generally not attacked by molecular oxygen at lower temperatures, are burned with the greatest ease to their final end products within the organism."[9] In view of recent historical claims that the modern science of biochemistry took shape in the first decade of the century around the enzyme theory,[10] we might expect that this question would have been framed entirely within the bounds of that theory. In fact, there still existed up until the beginning of the fourth decade of the century at least three competing general approaches. In addition to theories revolving around the question of whether there was a particular type of enzyme, such as an oxidase or a peroxidase, involved in the oxidation of metabolic substrates, there were prominent theories based on the conception that the central agents in biological oxidations were heavy metal catalysts, and theories that also invoked the catalytic action of membrane surfaces within the cells. During the 1920s debate fixed particularly on two rival theories identified with Heinrich Wieland and Otto Warburg. In 1912 and 1913 Wieland had clarified and supported experimentally the view that biological oxidations do not consist of successive additions of oxygen directly to the substrate molecules, as had commonly been assumed until then, but of the removal of pairs of hydrogen atoms, which afterward combine with oxygen to form water. The critical catalytic action required for this process to occur in organisms, Wieland maintained, was the "activation" of the hydrogen. This activation he attributed to a class of enzymes, specific to the individual substrate molecules, which he named *dehydrases*, (afterward called dehydrogenases). In 1924, Warburg showed that certain iron–heme compounds can partially oxidize various biologically significant molecules, and that the reaction is inhibited by substances such as hydrogen cyanide (HCN)that were known to poison cellular respiration. Warburg inferred that there is in cells an *Atmungsferment*, containing iron, that "activates" molecular oxygen, alternately combining with it and transferring it to the substrate molecules. Warburg adamantly rejected Wieland's theory, and the controversy between them and their respective supporters took on during this period a sharply polemical tone.[11]

Wieland and Warburg both investigated the oxidation of molecules they considered representative of substrates that are oxidized in cells, but they were both more interested in elucidating the general mechanism of oxidations than in the particular sequences of oxidation reactions that might comprise the integrated metabolic processes. Some of the biochemists who dealt with cellular respiration in these decades, however, directed their main efforts toward the working out of such sequences. The strongest advocate of the latter approach throughout the period was Franz Knoop. While working as a student in the laboratory of Franz Hofmeister, in the first years of the century, Knoop had formed as the central goal of his career, to acquire "a knowledge of the course of the decompositions and oxidations of the building materials and nutrient substances in the animal organism which would leave no gaps." Quickly he achieved a major success in this direction, when he was able to provide convincing evidence in 1904, by feeding dogs aromatic analogues of fatty acids, that these major building materials of the organism are decomposed by the successive removal of two carbon atoms at a time. He named the process *β-oxidation*. Subsequently, other biochemists confirmed Knoop's theory using organ perfusion methods, and β-oxidation soon became generally accepted as the principal, if not the exclusive, pathway of fatty acid degradation.[12]

Knoop's initial advance toward his stated scientific goal turned out also to be his most important contribution toward it. Although he provided a few years later the first strong evidence that amino acids are oxidatively deaminated to form keto acids,[13] he did not develop an approach broadly applicable to the search for further metabolic reaction steps. In later years he contented himself mainly with general overviews of the subject, sometimes in the form of lectures that were published afterward, in which he tried to integrate the current state of knowledge about biological oxidations into the viewpoint he had from the outset advocated. In 1931 he maintained, as staunchly as ever, that "the final goal of physiological chemistry" is to "present a scheme that puts together an unbroken series of equations of all of the reactions from the foodstuffs which continuously supply to the organism its energy needs, all the way to the slag that again leaves the organism as energyless final oxidation products." The problem had proven so difficult, however, he acknowledged 30 years after he had taken it up, that one could still provide only an "a priori conception of what such a scheme would have to look like."[14]

The major obstacle that researchers faced in their study of intermediary metabolism was that the intermediate substances they sought to identify rarely appeared among the excretory products, or even in the blood, of animals. Except when one succeeded with some special trick, as when Knoop fed dogs aromatic analogues of the fatty acids the animals normally decompose completely, and found partial decomposition products of the former in the urine, one could learn very little about the intermediate steps by experiments on whole animals. From the very absence of these intermediates, however, investigators inferred something important about the character of metabolic processes. Intermediates must not normally accumulate, but be further decomposed as rapidly as they are formed. That was what one would, in any case, expect if the intermediate substances formed reaction chains leading step-by-step from the foodstuffs to the final excretory products.[15]

In principle the most obvious way to make the elusive intermediates appear would be to interfere with the metabolic processes within an animal somewhere along the way, so that an intermediate normally removed by further decomposition is instead excreted. To do so without killing the animal in the process was, however, no easy task. During the 1870s, investigators sometimes attempted to limit the access of oxygen to the tissues, without cutting it off entirely, hoping that foodstuffs might be then only partially oxidized. They attained in this way no decisive results.[16] A more promising approach appeared to be to exploit naturally occurring pathological conditions in animals or humans, in which they failed to metabolize fully their nutrients. One such situation was already well recognized. Since early in the century, the diagnostic indicator for diabetes was the excretion of sugar in the urine. During the 1860s, Max Pettenkofer and Carl Voit began studies of the quantitative metabolism of diabetes, which led eventually to the conclusion that diabetics excrete sugar because they are unable to oxidize it.[17] Since sugar was one of the starting points in a chain of respiratory oxidations, that knowledge did not in itself directly aid in the search for intermediates; but, in the 1880s, Oscar Minkowski and others showed that in the extreme condition called acidosis, diabetics also excreted β-hydroxybutryic acid ($CH_3CHOHCH_2COOH$), acetoacetic acid ($CH_3\overset{\text{O}}{\overset{\|}{C}}CH_2COOH$) and acetone ($CH_3\overset{\text{O}}{\overset{\|}{C}}CH_3$).[18] These compounds, referred to collectively as the *ketone bodies*, were soon regarded as intermediate products of metabolism, that organisms normally oxidize further. That interpretation was strengthened when Georg Rosenfeld found in 1885 that one could induce healthy humans to excrete ketone bodies by removing carbohydrate from their diets.[19] Because the presence of carbohydrates seemed to prevent the ketone bodies from appearing, the former were classified as *antiketogenic* substances. Large quantities of fat in the diet were found, on the other hand, to be ketogenic.[20]

The ketogenic effects of fat received a theoretical explanation when Knoop proposed his theory of β-oxidation. Naturally occurring fats were composed characteristically of fatty acids that contain an even number of carbon atoms. Successive removal of the atoms, two at a time, would eventually leave a four-carbon fatty acid that could readily be supposed to give rise, during the course of the oxidation of its next β-carbon atom, to β-hydroxybutryic or acetoacetic acid. Between 1906 and 1908 Gustav Embden brought the method of perfusing surviving isolated livers of dogs with a continuous supply of arterial blood to bear on this interpretation. When he added even-numbered fatty acids to the blood entering the organ, he could detect a large increase in the quantity of ketone bodies in the perfused fluid, whereas the odd-numbered acids had no such effect. With similar methods he showed that β-hydroxybutryic acid gives rise to acetoacetic acid.[21] By solidifying Knoop's theory of β-oxidation itself, and linking it up with the ketone bodies, Embden's fundamental investigation appeared to move a long way toward the goal of an unbroken series of metabolic equations. Moreover, his results held the promise that organ perfusion methods might enable biochemists to track down the intermediate reactions that evaded detection in animal feeding experiments.

To complete this picture, one would need to know how the ketone bodies themselves are normally further decomposed. Embden also took up that question. The natural intermediate to suspect was acetic acid (CH_3COOH), because it was readily metabolized when fed to animals, and it would be the expected product of one further β-oxidation of β-hydroxybutryic or acetoacetic acid. In this case, however, Embden was unable to obtain conclusive evidence. He left the question with the prediction that "through the proof of the formation of acetic acid from acetoacetic acid, the formation of acetic acid in the organism will be brought into clear relationship with the decomposition of fat and proteins."[22]

Through these investigations acetic acid was acquiring a special place within the sketchy outlines of intermediary pathways that were beginning to emerge. As a breakdown product of amino acids, as a product of the fermentation of sugar, and as the assumed two-carbon piece split off from fatty acids in β-oxidation as well as the residue of the last β-oxidation, acetic acid was coming to appear as a common connecting link in the sequences of all three of the major classes of foodstuffs. From feeding experiments of the preceding century it had long been clear that animals must be able to convert either carbohydrate or protein, or both, to fat; but little was known of the mechanisms of such transformations, and biochemists still tended to think of the step-by-step decompositions of fats, proteins, and carbohydrates, respectively, as separate parallel sequences, leading by progressive additions of oxygen gradually but directly from the starting points to the end products. The suggestion that acetic acid probably appears in all three pathways offered the first concrete picture of three pathways that did not run independently of one another, but converged upon a single, relatively simple intermediary compound.

The centrality of acetic acid brought to the fore another complication, how to account for its own further oxidation. Because of the simplicity of its composition there were very few compounds capable, in theory, of serving as intermediates between it and the final end products, carbon dioxide and water. Neither of the two obvious choices, oxalic acid (COOHCOOH) or glycolic acid (CH$_2$OHCOOH) appeared to be metabolized by organisms. This paradox led Otto Porges to postulate, in 1910, that acetic acid is not further oxidized, but enters into some unknown synthetic reaction.[23] Thus, the general patterns expected of metabolic pathways took on additional complexity. Not only might the oxidative sequences for the three classes of foodstuffs be connected together, but the degradation series themselves might be interrupted by synthetic detours.

In the first decade of the twentieth century, outlines of some paths of intermediary metabolism seemed to be coming rapidly into view. Details of the picture filled in much more slowly during the next two decades. The perfusion methods proved cumbersome as well as expensive and time consuming, and the problems they could solve were limited by the difficulty in detecting or measuring quantitatively the minute concentrations of intermediary products searched for in the perfusion fluid by the classical analytical methods of organic chemistry. Despite continued investigation of these problems, biochemists' understanding of the relationships between the long-chain fatty acids, the ketone bodies, and acetic acid remained, in 1930, very nearly what it had been in 1910. They assumed that β-oxidations led somehow to β-hydroxybutryic acid, acetoacetic acid, and acetic acid, but were uncertain of the order in which any of these three compounds were converted to the others, and still did not know the further fates of these compounds.[24]

Less satisfying still was the state of the question of the antiketogenic effect of glucose and related substances. During the 1920s investigators still fell back on colorfully vague statements made at the turn of the century, such as "fats burn in the fire of carbohydrates," while they persisted in the search for a more definite mechanism.[25]

II

If, as nearly everyone accepted by the beginning of this century, the respiratory oxidations took place within the cells of the tissues, then it might appear evident that to study the process most directly one ought to examine it in tissues isolated from the organism. Physiologists had, in fact, repeatedly observed the respiration of isolated tissues during the nineteenth century, but had been able to attain only very low overall rates compared with the rate of an animal as a whole. In 1906, Federico Battelli and Lina Stern in Switzerland, and Thorsten Thunberg in Sweden, began almost simultaneously to study respiration in isolated tissues under more advantageous conditions. In 1907 Battelli and Stern expressed the broad objective of such studies:

> The problem of combustions in the animal organism is extremely complex. To attempt to resolve it, one must simplify it. We have thought that one could hope to obtain some information by studying the elementary respiration of tissues separated from the body, while varying the experimental conditions as much as possible.[26]

Battelli and Stern used minced muscle preparations, in which they believed the cell structures were mostly intact, suspended in blood or saline media. They measured the oxygen consumption by connecting the flasks containing the respiring tissues to simple U-shaped manometers. They attained respiratory rates approaching those of normal warm-blooded animals by maintaining the flasks in a constant temperature bath and agitating them continuously by means of a mechanically shaken platform. The simplicity of their apparatus allowed them to carry out multiple experiments easily, and consequently to test extensively the effects on the respiratory rate of varied media, of toxic substances, and of the addition of substances that the cells might be able to oxidize.[27] Thunberg utilized a more complicated, less adaptable apparatus, but one that enabled him to make more precise measurements.[28] Although his initial assumptions and objectives differed markedly from those of Battelli and Stern, their respective research programs converged during the next 3 years. After systematically testing the effects of a large number of organic acids on the respiratory rate, Thunberg discovered, in 1909, that malic acid ($COOHCHOHCH_2COOH$), citric acid ($COOHCH_2COHCOOHCH_2COOH$), and succinic acid ($COOHCH_2CH_2COOH$) increased the quantity of carbon dioxide formed, without raising the consumption of oxygen. The effect of succinic acid was the most marked.[29] Learning of Thunberg's results, Battelli and Stern found that in their system succinic acid dramatically increased the overall respiration rate. The succinic acid was not completely decomposed, however, but only oxidized, as they thought, to malic acid ($C_4H_6O_4 + O = C_4H_6O_5$, as they expressed the reaction). Apparently, they had been able to identify one of the discrete, single steps within the pathways of respiratory oxidation, but were very cautious about drawing inferences concerning the nature of the broader process in which this step might fit. Subsequently they showed that citric, malic, and fumaric acid ($COOHCH = CHCOOH$) are totally oxidized.[30] "The oxidation of these acids," they asserted in 1910, "is the first example of well-defined compounds which undergo a direct and complete combustion through isolated animal tissues."[31]

Battelli and Stern's discovery was not immediately accepted as of capital importance, because the compounds in question — three small dicarboxylic acids and a tricarboxylic acid — were not regarded as metabolically important substances. They were not chemically related in any evident direct manner to the three classes of foodstuffs whose oxidative decomposition was the central object of intermediary metabolism.[32] Nevertheless, the fact that, of the many compounds tested, only these four conspicuously raised the respiration of isolated tissue could not in the long run be overlooked. During the next 20 years the question of their role often attracted and puzzled biochemists. The oxidation of succinic acid stood out as an especially significant reaction, not only because of its high activity, but because the conditions under which the reaction could be carried out suggested that it was activated by a particularly stable enzyme system. In the 1920s a number of biochemists, including especially Dorothy Needham, investigated the mechanism and quantitative relations of this oxidation in close detail.[33]

For reasons that are not entirely clear, biochemists of this period did not follow up the general experimental approach of investigating respiratory oxidations in surviving isolated tissues, despite the promising results that Thunberg, Battelli, and Stern had achieved. Nevertheless, their early work remained conspicuous in the scientific literature of the subject as the 1920s opened.

III

From the traditional perspective that the principal object of intermediary metabolism consists of the successive stages in the oxidation of foodstuffs, the case of carbohydrates posed in 1930 a paradox. As Knoop put it in his review *Oxidations in the Animal Body* in 1931, "The oxidative decomposition of the carbohydrates, which appears to the chemist to offer so many more points of attack than the fatty acids, normally begins, remarkably enough, not through oxidations at all."[34] The interpretation generally accepted in this period, as stated for example, by Hans von Euler in 1928, was that "normal respiration, for which the consumption of molecular oxygen is characteristic, is composed of two phase groups, an anaerobic, and a subsequent oxidative one into which the consumption of oxygen is concentrated."[35] Much more was known about the anaerobic than about the aerobic stage; yet it was evident that the former released only a small portion of the total energy available from the complete oxidation of carbohydrates. About the crucial, oxidative steps, little was certain beyond the hypothesis that it may begin with the oxidation of lactic acid to

pyruvic acid ($CH_3CHOHCOOH \rightarrow CH_3\overset{\overset{\displaystyle O}{\displaystyle \|}}{C}COOH$). "With this reaction," Knoop lamented, "we are unfortunately at the limit of our exact knowledge."[36]

If knowledge of the anaerobic phase of the decomposition of carbohydrates, or glycolysis as it was commonly called, had advanced further than knowledge of the aerobic phase, that was in large part due to the close similarity perceived between this phase in animal tissue — especially in muscle — and the process of alcoholic fermentation in yeast. Edward Buchner's success in producing cell-free fermentation had stimulated intensive investigation of this process during the early years of the century, with special attention to the intermediate stages that might account for the chemically complex transformation of a sugar to alcohol. Moreover, one could also study fermentation in intact yeast cells, which, as microorganisms, were already equivalent to isolated cells of animal tissue, far more easily than one could at the time track down intermediary processes within animals.

None of the schemes proposed between 1900 and 1910 for the intermediate steps in alcoholic fermentation by Buchner himself, by Alfred Wohl,[37] and others, won general acceptance. In the course of developing and criticizing them, however, the investigators in this field established some general criteria for reasoning about and testing such theories that set precedents for the whole field of intermediary metabolism. The reaction sequences suggested included some intermediates that were suspected because they either appeared in the fermentation solution or, if added to it, diminished during the course of the reaction. The schemes also typically incorporated compounds inferred from reaction mechanisms familiar to organic chemistry. Some of these intermediates were, in fact, only hypothetical molecules constructed to fit a plausible series of molecular rearrangements. The reactions proposed were expected to fit certain rules, such as that the same organic groups — especially H, OH, CHO, or COOH groups — within different organic compounds undergo the same types of reaction; or that the particular type of reaction most likely to happen in a given situation is influenced by the presence of a negative element such as Cl or O at a nearby position in the molecule. It was deemed legitimate to establish that a particular reaction mechanism is probably operative by eliminating all the theoretical alternatives. Reaction sequences were built up from the repetition of certain reactions considered typical of biological processes, in particular the rearrangement of H and OH groups within a molecule by successive removals and additions of water. Reaction mechanisms established for simpler molecules, where only one or two theoretical alternatives were possible, could be applied to analogous reactions of more complicated molecules.[38] The most critical and mysterious chemical transformation involved in fermentation, the cleavage of the six-carbon sugar into smaller molecules, Wohl explained in 1904 as a reversal of the familiar reaction between two aldehyde or ketone molecules, known as an aldol condensation. Wohl assumed that this reversed condensation reaction splits the sugar into two three-carbon molecules. Nearly all subsequent theories of fermentation and of muscle glycolysis incorporated this feature.[39]

The most crucial investigative norm that emerged in these years was the test to which one must subject a suspected intermediate. Buchner had asserted in 1904 that lactic acid is an intermediate of alcoholic fermentation because it sometimes appeared in, and at other times disappeared from, the media in which he carried out fermentation.[40] Arthur Slator, who developed methods for measuring quantitative rates of fermentation over short periods, contended that such observations were inadequate grounds for the conclusion. An intermediate must be consumed as rapidly as it is formed, otherwise it would accumulate. Therefore, Slator argued convincingly, if a substance is to be regarded as an intermediate it "must be fermented at least as rapidly as glucose is."[41] Although Wohl and others presented cogent theoretical arguments against this rule,[42] it was generally accepted within a few years. The power of the rule was mainly heuristic. It provided a pragmatic guide toward narrowing down the theoretical possibilities. Eventually the rule acquired the status of an axiom, scarcely questioned by those who investigated not only fermentation, but any other intermediary process in which the experimental procedure was to add suspected intermediates to a medium in which a process was taking place whose overall rate could be measured quantitatively. The axiom could be the more readily accepted because it could also be broken, when there were compelling reasons to do so, by ascribing the failure of a substrate to meet this standard to its inability to penetrate the cell membranes.

In 1913 Carl Neuberg offered a theory of the intermediate steps in alcoholic fermentation that resembled in some of its general characteristics the proposals already made by others, but that soon dominated the field. He outlined five successive stages:[43]

1. $C_6H_{12}O_6$ -H_2O = $C_6H_8O_4$
   sugar   methylglyoxal-aldol

2. $C_6H_8O_4$ = 2 CH_2=C(OH)CHO (or 2 CH_3COCOH)
         methylglyoxal

3. CH_2=C(OH)COH H_2 $CH_2OHCHOHCH_2OH$
                 + | =   glycerol
   CH_2=C(OH)CHO   O CH_2=C(OH)COOH
   2 methylglyoxal   water   enol pyruvic acid

4. CH_3COOOH = CO_2 + CH_3COH
   pyruvic acid   acetaldehyde

5. CH_3COCOH O $CH_3COCOOH$
   methyl glyoxal | pyruvic acid
               + | =
   CH_3COH H_2 CH_3CH_2OH
   acetaldehyde   ethyl alcohol

The pyruvic acid left at the end of reaction five reenters reaction 4, therefore, the end products are the alcohol of reaction 5 and the CO_2 formed in reaction 4. Part of this scheme was based on two capital discoveries in which Neuberg had played a major part. In 1911, almost simultaneously with Otto Neubauer, he had found that pyruvic acid can be fermented; soon afterward he could make it ferment as rapidly as glucose.[44] Pyruvic acid was thus the first compound found that could meet Slator's stringent criterion for an intermediate. Neuberg showed in addition that in the process acetaldehyde and CO_2 are formed. This reaction he could explain by the simple equation

$$CH_3COCOOH \rightarrow CO_2 + CH_3CHO$$

The CO_2 had been released by splitting the carboxyl group off from this α-keto acid. The enzyme Neuberg assumed to have caused the reaction he designated a "carboxylase," emphasizing that it was the prototype for a general class of enzymatic decarboxylations.[45] In addition to identifying a type of reaction that might account for the shortening of a carbon chain in various metabolic situations, Neuberg brought the exceptionally reactive pyruvic acid into the center of attention.   In the following decades pyruvic acid came to appear increasingly, like acetic acid, as a nodal substrate expected to occupy the crossroads connecting various metabolic pathways.

In contrast to the strong experimental evidence that Neuberg could adduce for pyruvic acid and acetaldehyde as intermediates, he had retrieved methylglyoxal from the scheme proposed by Wohl in 1904, even though it had since then repeatedly failed the test of fermentability.   The inducement for Neuberg to overturn this experimental criterion was not only that methylglyoxal fit smoothly into his reaction sequence in accordance with known organic reactions, but that his theory treated the compound as undergoing a special reaction whose potential biological significance had recently attracted strong interest.   In 1911 Battelli and Stern, and a few months later Jakob Parnas, had found that several aldehydes, in the presence of animal tissue extracts, can enter a reaction in which half of their molecules are oxidized to the corresponding carboxylic acids, while the other half are reduced to the corresponding alcohols.   Parnas recognized the reaction as a biological manifestation of one that Stanislao Cannizzaro had discovered in 1858, and it soon became known as the *Cannizzaro reaction*.   As Parnas pointed out, the reaction was particularly significant because it suggested a specific chemical mechanism for explaining biological oxidations that can take place without molecular oxygen.   The oxidation is achieved through a balanced oxidation and reduction, in which the oxygen of a water molecule oxidizes one molecule while its hydrogen reduces another molecule.   Such coupled reactions were soon referred to in general as *oxido-reductions*, this particular type being designated a *dismutation*.[46]   In Neuberg's fermentation scheme two molecules of methylglyoxal (or pyruvic aldehyde as it can also be named) take part in the dismutation in reaction 3, whereas in reaction 5 one molecule of methylglyoxal and one of acetaldehyde enter the same type of transformation.

Incorporating the most exciting new developments in the field, and backed by his growing authority in biochemistry, Neuberg's fermentation theory was generally accepted by the early 1920s, and was still the dominant theory in 1930. Fritz Lipmann, F.F. Nord, and H. Waelsch recalled in 1956, concerning his conception of alcoholic fermentation, that Neuberg's "interpretation of metabolic events in terms of organic reactions created the pattern of inquiry into the mechanisms of intermediary metabolism."[47]   Their opinion was in part a eulogistic tribute; but, as the most successful effort of its time to lay out the steps in the process whose investigation had led the way into the problems and the promise of intermediary metabolism, Neuberg's scheme certainly did exert a broad impact on the manner in which biochemists treated other problems in the field.

Ever since the early nineteenth century, physiological chemists had viewed alcoholic fermentation as the model for understanding processes within animal tissues that were not yet as clearly defined.[48]   The discovery of other fermentations that, as Pasteur had shown by 1860, were produced by specific microorganisms, reinforced the view that fermentations were a widespread class of processes that could account for many of the chemical changes occurring within plants and animals. A special connection between the *Stoffwechsel* within animals and lactic acid fermentation grew out of the evidence that animal tissues and fluids, and particularly muscle tissue, contain lactic acid.[49] During the decades after 1850 Claude Bernard, Ludimar Hermann, Felix Hoppe-Seyler, and others asserted that some of the decomposition processes within animals that had been regarded exclusively as respiratory oxidations were, instead, fermentations.[50] German physiologists, in particular, associated the formation of lactic acid with muscular activity. During the period in which Liebig's opinion that muscular work derives from the breakdown of its nitrogenous constituents held sway, they were constrained to regard this lactic acid as formed from proteins. When opinion shifted during the 1860s to the view that nonnitrogenous foodstuffs are a major source of the energy consumed in muscular work, however, it became natural to regard the lactic acid formed in muscle as derived from sugar, or from its precursor glycogen, and therefore, to be closely parallel to the lactic acid fermentation of microorganisms. Through the rest of the century physiological chemists worked to establish correlations between the consumption of carbohydrate in animals or their muscle tissue, the formation of lactic acid, and muscular activity. Although they attained suggestive supporting evidence,[51] there were also results contrary to what they expected,[52] and the issue long remained in doubt. Finally, in 1907, Frederick Gowland Hopkins and Walter Fletcher elegantly resolved part of the question by showing that lactic acid forms anaerobically in muscles when they contract, but disappears again in the presence of oxygen.[53] The evidence that this lactic acid arises from carbohydrates, however, remained equivocal. Gustav Embden believed that he had proven "the conversion of carbohydrate into lactic acid in the animal organism" in 1904, when he showed that lactic acid appeared in the fluid with which he perfused a liver that contained glycogen, but did not appear if the liver was free of glycogen. In 1912, he strengthened his proof by correcting some technical faults in his earlier analytical procedures.[54] Others did not regard his proof as decisive, however, and sought alternative demonstrations using ground tissue, tissue extracts, and leukocytes. Most of these results appeared suspect because it was difficult to assure that the conditions were strictly aseptic and that the lactic acid that appeared had not been formed by bacteria.[55] In other respects also those who investigated muscle glycolysis had not yet reached the experimental standards that had been achieved over the preceding years in the study of yeast fermentation. Conditions did not yet permit accurate measurements of the rate of the reaction, so that it was not possible to apply directly the criterion for an intermediate that was expected by then in the study of alcoholic fermentation. Faced with these uncertainties, the biochemists who studied carbohydrate metabolism continued to rely on the conviction that sugar must be decomposed in animals in a manner similar to its decomposition in fermentation. Embden expressed the prevailing attitude in 1912 when he wrote that "one is more and more persuaded that the fate of carbohydrates during their biological decompositions...are extraordinarily similar to one another throughout the entire living world." These decomposition processes are obviously most accessible in the effects of bacteria and yeast on sugars, in contrast to the animal organism, for which similarly well established points along "the paths of intermediary carbohydrate metabolism are not yet recognized."[56]

This viewpoint prompted biochemists to apply immediately to the carbohydrate metabolism of animals the new knowledge about the intermediates of alcoholic fermentation that Neuberg and his school discovered in 1911 and the following years. When pyruvic acid proved to be fermented rapidly by yeast, workers in his laboratory and elsewhere began looking for evidence that it also forms, and is further decomposed, in animals. Similarly they tried to show that methylglyoxal can disappear in animal tissues. They were able, in the years before World War I, to obtain some suggestive results for these reactions,[57] but their confidence that pyruvic acid and methylglyoxal are intermediates in animal glycolysis rested mainly on their belief that the process must be just like alcoholic fermentation except for some late step that diverts the path to lactic acid instead of alcohol.

In his studies of yeast fermentation Neuberg had shown that oxaloacetic acid ($COOHCH_2COCOOH$) is fermented to acetaldehyde and CO_2 in a similar manner to pyruvic acid, and had speculated that pyruvic acid might itself be an intermediate step in that reaction:

$$COOHCH_2COCOOH = CO_2 + CH_3COCOOH$$
oxaloacetic acid   pyruvic acid
$$CH_3COCOOH = CO_2 + CH_3CHO$$ [58]

In 1914 Paul Mayer found, in Neuberg's laboratory, that finely minced rabbit muscle or liver tissue mixed with oxaloacetic acid in the absence of oxygen yielded twice as much CO_2 as did oxaloacetic acid in solution by itself. Drawing on Neuberg's theory of the reaction in fermentation, Mayer inferred that in this case also, oxaloacetic acid was transformed to pyruvic acid. The result suggested to him a mechanism generally applicable to the step-by-step decompositions of animal combustion, in which α-keto acids give rise by decarboxylation to the corresponding α-keto acids containing one less carbon atom. As in the case of the β-oxidation scheme for fatty acids, an outline for a general mode of successive decompositions of the carbon chains of the oxidizable substances in animals seemed to be emerging. Because, as Otto Neubauer had recently demonstrated, the "first step" in the transformation of amino acids in the organism appeared to be their conversion to α-keto acids, this carboxylase mechanism promised to subsume carbohydrate and protein metabolism in a common path.[59] For the next 20 years, however, it proved difficult here also to advance from such conjectures to connected descriptions of established reaction steps.

During the 1920s, Otto Meyerhof dominated the investigation of muscle metabolism. Utilizing precise manometric methods that Otto Warburg had developed, Meyerhof measured the rates of respiration of isolated muscles small enough to be supplied by oxygen by diffusion. He measured the quantities of lactic acid that formed anaerobically in the active and resting states of the muscle and its disappearance aerobically. By showing that the acid appears during the same time periods that a muscle is stimulated to contract, he tightened the long supposed connection between the formation of the acid and mechanical work. Because the respiratory quotient for resting muscles in his experiments was approximtely 1.0, he concluded that carbohydrate is the principal, if not the only, substance oxidized in muscle respiration. By measuring the decrease in the content of glycogen in muscles contracted anaerobically, he could show that carbohydrate was also the probable source for all of the lactic acid formed. Meyerhof began with the commonly accepted conception that lactic acid is an intermediate in the respiratory oxidation of the carbohydrate, produced during the anaerobic phase and decomposed in the subsequent aerobic phase. When he measured the quantity of oxygen consumed, however, he found to his surprise that it was only one third to one sixth of the quantity required to oxidize the lactic acid that disappeared in this phase. From this anomaly he constructed the theory that the energy released through the oxidation of this fraction of the lactic acid is used to reconvert the remainder anaerobically to carbohydrate. From indirect evidence that the intermediates in this resynthesis of carbohydrate were different from those of the glycolysis itself, he came to view the process not as a reversible reaction, but a cycle, that he depicted as follows:

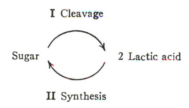

I Cleavage

Sugar   2 Lactic acid

II Synthesis

By 1930, this scheme was widely known as the "lactic acid cycle," or the "Meyerhof cycle."[60]

In these experiments, carried out mainly between 1919 and 1925 on intact isolated muscle tissue, Meyerhof set rigorous quantitative standards. He ascertained, for example, not only that carbohydrate decreased when lactic acid appeared, but that the decrease in the amount of the former present in the muscle was sufficient to account for the increase of the latter. He also utilized effectively the general method of blocking a stage in an overall pathway to cause an intermediate to accumulate. Thus, with HCN, a known inhibitor of respiratory oxidation, he could induce lactic acid to appear in the presence of oxygen, just as it does under anaerobic conditions. Afterward he demonstrated the same relationships between carbohydrate and lactic acid, glycolysis, and respiration, in minced muscle tissue. Finally, he obtained a cell-free muscle extract that, when combined with a heat-labile activator from yeast juice that he named *hexokinase*, could decompose carbohydrate to lactic acid just as in intact muscle tissue. He, thereby, made muscle glycolysis finally as accessible to direct chemical investigation as alcoholic fermentation had been for a quarter of a century. With this extract he confirmed an earlier observation by Embden that, if one blocks the formation of lactic acid with fluoride, a phosphate ester of the sugar accumulates.[61]

In spite of this important support for the view that glycolysis, like fermentation, includes a stage in which the carbohydrate combines with phosphate, Meyerhof did not systematically test for other intermediate steps, even though the carbohydrate-free muscle extract he prepared afforded newly favorable circumstances for doing so. He was content to adapt Neuberg's theory of alcoholic fermentation — "the scheme that at present should be regarded as being experimentally best supported" he stated in 1930 — to muscle glycolysis by assuming that the two processes are identical up to the stage at which methylglyoxal forms, but that the latter is then converted to lactic acid in muscle by the simple addition of water.[62] For his purposes Meyerhof needed only to deal with the stages marking the boundaries of glycolysis and of respiration: that is the appearance and disappearance of carbohydrate and lactic acid. Thus, although he contributed powerfully to knowledge of "The Chemical Processes in Muscle," as he entitled the monograph summarizing his work, he did so by fixing his attention narrowly on certain problems characteristic of the special function of muscles. For Meyerhof the goal of muscle physiology was not to establish the unbroken series of reactions leading from foodstuffs to oxidative end products, but "to answer the question how the chemical processes in the organism perform mechanical work."[63]

IV

Far as they were from the goal of filling in the complete series of reaction steps between foodstuffs and final oxidation products, biochemists nevertheless felt during the 1920s that they were progressing toward a clear understanding of the general types of reactions that make up these series. Implicit in most discussions was the assumption that metabolic pathways are composed of a few basic reactions that repeat themselves in analogous situations. Thus, after Neuberg discovered the decarboxylation of pyruvic acid in yeast, he and others inferred that an indefinite number of α-keto acids can split off a carboxyl group in a similar manner, in animal tissue as well as in plants. The Cannizzaro dismutation was similarly expected to apply metabolically to a variety of aldehydes. The β-oxidation mechanism was assumed to operate for all of the fatty acids that occur naturally in fats. Wieland applied the mechanism of dehydrogenation to any substrate molecule from which two hydrogen atoms can be removed. All amino acids were expected to be deaminated in a similar manner. Except for some special situations, such as the reversed aldol condensation reaction invoked to explain the cleavage of hexose carbon chains, sequences made up from these several mechanisms, interspersed with additions or removals of the elements of water as needed, were expected to account for whatever the specific steps of the gradual decompositions might turn out to be.

The rationale underlying these anticipations was the experience gained from nineteenth century organic chemistry that the same groups attached to the carbon chains of different organic compounds tended to behave similarly. Biochemists generally supposed in addition that these compounds undergo in biological processes the same types of reactions that occur in the laboratory. Knoop, in fact, had to defend his theory of β-oxidation repeatedly from the objection that fatty acids were not decomposed in this way according to the "known rules" of pure chemistry.[64]

As the influence of the enzyme theory grew after 1910, biochemists associated each of the types of metabolic reaction they identified with an enzyme. Neuberg named the enzyme he supposed to split off the carboxyl groups from α-keto acids *carboxylase*. The Cannizzaro reaction was attributed to *mutase*. The removal of hydrogen atoms was due to *dehydrase*, or as it was later named, *dehydrogenase*. In the 1920s investigators studied intently the properties of such enzymatic reactions. One of the central questions they confronted was whether there was just one enzyme for each type of reaction; whether every individual substrate that undergoes such a reaction has its own enzyme; or whether a single enzyme might catalyze the reaction for closely similar molecules, but that more dissimilar molecules require distinct enzymes. Methods for isolating enzymes had not reached a stage in which one could be confident that the enzyme present in any given preparation was pure, so that in most cases the issue remained in doubt. A particularly controversial question during the decade was whether or not the mutase that caused the Cannizzaro reaction was identical to the "Schardinger" enzyme in milk that converts hypoxanthine to xanthine.[65]

Beyond the question of the specificity of the enzymes of intermediary metabolism lay subtler implications concerning the organization of the pathways themselves. How specific and tightly defined were they? Did every species of a given type of foodstuff pass through an identical pathway? Or were there variant versions of the same general sequence, along which homologous or analogous members of the same family of organic compounds traversed only the same succession of reaction mechanisms, each step resulting in homologous or analogous versions of the same intermediate? Or were the pathways still looser, so that there might be multiple possible routes connecting critical points? Such questions were never drawn out in so clear a manner, for the general statements made about the still unknown steps in intermediary metabolism were ordinarily vague enough to include any of these possibilities. In the way in which biochemists handled particular problems, however, we can sometimes find hints about which of these patterns they anticipated finding. When Julius Pohl fed methyl alcohol to an animal, in 1893, hoping to infer from its partially oxidized products the likely steps in the oxidation of ethyl alcohol,[66] he was evidently assuming the second of these alternatives, as did Knoop when he deduced the mechanism of the oxidation of ordinary aliphatic fatty acids from the results of feeding dogs analogous phenyl-substituted acids. On the other hand, the identification of acetic acid and pyruvic acid as ubiquitous intermediates would seem to imply that at some stage in the pathways all metabolizable substances have been reduced to the same common forms.

Another aspect of the organization of intermediary metabolism in higher animals that remained in doubt during the first third of the century was the distribution of its processes within the organs of their bodies. The growth of the cell theory during the nineteenth century had settled the older question of whether the respiratory oxidations take place in the fluids or the tissues. As the elementary vital units of the organism, all living cells must respire. It was not so evident, however, that all stages of respiration are repeated in all cells in the same way. The variety of fermentation products obtainable from different microorganisms made it obvious that at least the anaerobic phases of the decomposition of foodstuffs could be carried out in different ways. If, as the quotation from Embden in 1912 illustrates, biochemists were, on the one hand, coming to believe that the basic decomposition processes were "extraordinarily similar" in all organisms and tissues, the fact that yeast produces alcohol where muscle produces lactic acid fixed attention also on the strategic variations. Nor was it necessarily true that all steps in a process common to an organism are carried out in all its tissues. Some investigators, such as Hans Euler, explored the possibility that sugar in the animal body is not entirely decomposed in any one organ, but that the decomposition "proceeds step-by-step in several organs." In keeping with this view he searched for the organ that might cleave pyruvic acid; that is, for the organ that might contain Neuberg's enzyme carboxylase.[67] Such an organization would confer great advantages on the methods of perfusing individual organs and on experiments with isolated tissues, because one could hope that the intermediate products of the step carried out by a given organ would appear spontaneously in the perfused fluid or tissue medium. It soon became clear that metabolic processes were not divided up in this neat fashion. Nevertheless, there could still be significant variations in the specific metabolites that different tissues can consume, in the completeness of the pathways within them, in their rates, in the relative importance of glycolysis and aerobic respiration, and in other details. The question of which tissues to use in studying a particular problem, therefore, remained crucial from a theoretical, as well as a practical standpoint.

V

Of all of the prominent investigators of intermediary metabolism up until 1930, Thorsten Thunberg came the closest to putting together what was known about reaction mechanisms and about specific "combustible substances" into a coherent picture of the way in which metabolic oxidative pathways might be organized. In 1913 Thunberg already believed that "the oxidative processes in the living cell must be thought of as forming chain reactions, a series of reactions connected to one another in such a way that, by and large, none of the links in the reaction chain can proceed more rapidly than the others."[68] He was still casting about, however, for an effective means to identify these links. By 1916 he had found his starting point. In 1914 Hans Einbeck, seeking to confirm Battelli and Stern's discovery that succinic acid is oxidized to malic acid in tissues, found instead that fumaric acid is produced.[69] To Thunberg the conversion of succinic acid ($COOHCH_2CH_2COOH$) to fumaric acid ($COOHCH=CHCOOH$) suggested that Wieland's theory that in biological oxidations two hydrogen atoms are removed from substrate molecules, was applicable to this first link in the chain of cellular oxidations to be identified experimentally. To test his interpretation, Thunberg devised a method to carry out the reaction anaerobically, in an evacuated test tube containing the dye methylene blue to act as an acceptor for the hydrogen atoms that should be released according to the theory. When he mixed these substances with an extract from muscle tissue, the solution turned colorless, an indication that the dye had been reduced to the leuco-form by absorbing hydrogen. "The biological oxidation of succinic acid," he concluded, "must take place in the following way. First the succinic acid is dehydrogenated through the action of the muscle enzyme. If oxygen is then present, it exerts an oxidizing action on the hydrogen. But the hydrogen can also be transported to other substances which readily accept hydrogen."[70]

Quickly following up his success with succinic acid, Thunberg systematically tested dozens of fatty, dicarboxylic, keto, hydroxy, and amino acids, as well as sugars and alcohols, to identify other substances that might be links in the oxidative metabolic chains. At first none of them, except citric acid, reduced methylene blue. After working for 3 years to refine his method, however, he was able to show that the same four acids that had accelerated the respiration of isolated tissues in the earlier experiments that he and Battelli and Stern had carried out — that is, succinic, fumaric, malic, and citric acids — all reacted strongly in his new system. In addition the ordinary fatty acids, formic, acetic, butyric, and caproic were "unequivocal activators," as well as lactic, α-hydroxyglutaric, and tartronic acid. Of the amino acids, glutamic acid stood out as the only one to possess a strong activating power.[71]

In a long paper that became the standard point of reference for the study of oxidative intermediary metabolism for the next decade, Thunberg reported these results in 1920, and set forth the principles that he believed should guide future endeavors to construct out of such results the sequences of the oxidative reaction chains. The substances he had studied act on methylene blue, he emphasized, only when tissue extracts are included. The reactions are, therefore, enzymatic, biological oxidations. Strongly committed by now to the enzyme theory in its most specific form, Thunberg asserted, and supported with evidence from the temperatures of inactivation of the reactions, that each reaction is catalyzed by its own individual dehydrogenase. The fact that a cell *can* oxidize a given substance does not necessarily prove, however, that the substance is part of a normal metabolic pathway. To justify the inference that the substances he could identify as oxidizable probably *are* metabolites, Thunberg invoked a general principle of economy and simplicity that he probably obtained from the well-known discussion on this subject by Frederick Gowland Hopkins. Behind the methods of intermediary metabolism, Thunberg wrote, "lies the conception, explicit, or more often unspoken, that the power respectively of the organism or tissue to transform the substances supplied to it is limited, and that it possesses a distinct transforming power only in relation to substances that in reality it normally transforms."[72]

In spite of this concept, Thunberg did not automatically regard the substances that reduced methylene blue in his system as participants in the metabolic chains. To narrow down the multiple possibilities, he invoked two other theoretical guidelines. "Great weight must be attached," he claimed, "to the test of whether a substance appearing as an activator leads, by its transformation, to the formation of substances which, for their part, prove then to be acted on by the machinery of the cell."[73] That is, if the product of the dehydrogenation reaction was itself a compound likely to undergo a further reaction in the oxidative chain, that was presumptive evidence that the initial compound is probably a metabolite. At this stage such a test had to be made on theoretical grounds, however, because Thunberg's experiments showed only that a compound in question reduces methylene blue. He did not determine by direct analysis the products of the reactions that took place in his evacuated tubes. To provide further theoretical restrictions on the allowable links, he postulated that, because methylene blue acquires two hydrogen atoms when it is reduced, the metabolic dehydrogenation steps must, in every case, remove two hydrogen atoms at once from any given substrate.[74]

Applying these principles to the particular substances he had found to reduce methylene blue, Thunberg inferred the reactions that could meet his criteria. Malic acid, for example, must give rise either to oxaloacetic or oxyfumaric acid.[75]

$$COOHCHOHCH_2COOH \quad -2H \rightarrow COOHCOCH_2COOH$$

malic acid   oxaloacetic acid

$$or \quad COOHCOH=CHCOOH$$

oxyfumaric acid

For the case of acetic acid, Thunberg's guidelines led him to an unusual and highly significant conclusion. Its activity in his system reinforced the existing view of its importance as an intermediate. Yet the elimination of two of its hydrogen atoms could yield only a non-existent compound, CHCOOH. He proposed instead "a reaction in which two acetate molecules are simultaneously each deprived of one hydrogen atom, with the joining of their carbon atom chains into one. The substance which must thereby form is succinic acid.

$$
\begin{array}{ccc}
CH_3\text{-}COOH & -H & CH_2\text{-}COOH \\
 & = & | \\
CH_3\text{-}COOH & -H & CH_2\text{-}COOH
\end{array}
\quad +H_2
$$

The transformaton of acetic acid would in this way slip into the pathway opened by the conversion of succinic acid, with the powerful enzyme which acts first on it and then on fumaric acid."[76] Noting the difficulties biochemists had long felt over how acetic acid can be further decomposed, and Porges's earlier opinion that it must instead undergo a synthesis, Thunberg thought that he could now explain the difficulty and identify the synthetic reaction. Beyond that, he was clearly beginning to connect links into segments of a reaction chain.

In Thunberg's methylene blue experiments citric acid proved to be as conspicuously active as it had been in the earlier respiration experiments. Nevertheless, he treated that compound only parenthetically in his discussion. "Finally, as to the citric acid," he wrote, "it is hard to see how a simple dehydrogenation reaction can take place. By merely eliminating hydrogen atoms from its formula one arrives at impossible products." The only plausible interpretation he could think of was to assume that the constituents of water immediately replace the hydrogen atoms, giving hydroxy-citric acid. Thunberg depicted the reaction without further comment.[77] It obviously suggested to him no further connections with other steps in possible reaction chains.

Thunberg justified relying on his new method in place of further respiration experiments on isolated tissues mainly in terms of the greater simplicity and convenience of the methylene blue test, and because he regarded it as more sensitive than measurements of the effects of a substance on the respiration rates.[78] His confidence in his method was undoubtedly strengthened by the fact that it singled out the same four di- or tricarboxylic acids that had most prominently accelerated the respiration of tissues. We can see, however, that Thunberg's approach lent itself to judgments concerning the probability that a substance is a substrate that could differ markedly from conclusions based on the older method. In place of the quantitative criteria on which the tissue respiration methods rested, the methylene blue method favored a combination of semiquantitative judgments and theoretical preferences. The divergent outcomes of the conclusions to which the two approaches might lead is most obvious in the case of citric acid. If assessed on the basis of its capacity to increase cellular respirations, citric acid ought to have been placed at center stage as a potential intermediate. Because its chemical structure did not lend itself to a satisfying interpretation within Thunberg's conceptual framework, however, it was much easier, in accord with the methodological precepts that he introduced, to relegate citric acid to the theoretical background.

Thunberg was not ready, in 1919, to construct an extended scheme representing the chains of oxidative metabolism. He did, however, conclude his pathfinding paper with a general vision of how the substances identified as probable substrates would eventually be linked together by means of the several types of mechanism that he and others now believed must make up the steps of the reaction chains.

The simple substances, such as glucose, fats, and amino acids, which are offered to the cells as nourishment, pass through a whole series of intermediate stages before they reach the final state of decomposition. An earlier step in the reaction chain is transformed into a later one through indirect oxidation, or "dehydrogenation." Combined in certain cases with the uptake of water, the dehydrogenation causes the formation of products respectively poorer in hydrogen and richer in oxygen. In combination with the splitting off of carbon dioxide it causes a shortening of the carbon chain. In both of these types of reaction a whole series of dehydrogenases, or more generally expressed, hydrogen transfer enzymes, are active. They are distinctly specific for the various intermediate steps. The hydrogen removed from a particular substance can either be combined with oxygen, through which an indirect oxidation is achieved, or it can be applied to the hydrogenation of other substances.[79]

Within 3 years of the appearance of Thunberg's paper, three biochemists took up the challenge to erect on his methodological principles a comprehensive scheme of the reaction chains of intermediary metabolism. One of these responses came from a student in Thunberg's laboratory, and undoubtedly reflected Thunberg's own thinking. Increasing still further the sensitivity of the methylene blue method, Gunnar Ahlgren added more organic acids to the list of hydrogen donators, including four ketoacids — pyruvic, α-ketoglutaric, acetoacetic, and oxaloacetic — that were already expected to play significant metabolic roles. Acetaldehyde was also an activator. Reporting these results in 1923, Ahlgren proposed that oxaloacetic acid is decarboxylated to pyruvic acid, which loses a second carboxyl group to yield acetaldehyde. If acetaldehyde were next hydrated, then a following dehydrogenation would form acetic acid. Although he did not explicitly say so, Ahlgren was drawing into Thunberg's framework the reactions established by Neuberg in fermentation, interjecting the carboxylase mechanism to extend the chain formed by dehydrogenations. With these assumptions in place, Ahlgren presented a grand hypothesis that transformed the partial sequences already identified, into a closed system:

> If one sets out from the hypothesis formulated by Thunberg, according to which succinic acid is formed through the [de]hydrogenation of acetic acid (2 molecules of acetic acid -H = 1 molecule of succinic acid) one can imagine the following circulation within the decomposition process:

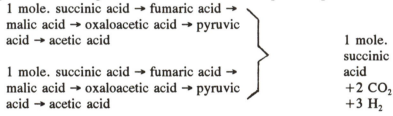

> 1 mole. succinic acid → fumaric acid →
> malic acid → oxaloacetic acid → pyruvic
> acid → acetic acid
>
> 1 mole. succinic acid → fumaric acid →
> malic acid → oxaloacetic acid → pyruvic
> acid → acetic acid
>
> 1 mole.
> succinic
> acid
> +2 CO₂
> +3 H₂

The preceding results, based on experiments, furnish, as one can see, a certain support for such reasoning.[80]

Behind Ahlgren's somewhat awkward representation we can see that the hypothesis accounted for the complete oxidation of succinic acid, shown in overall form on the right, by a continuous chain of reactions. This chain joined Thunberg's theoretical synthesis of succinic acid from acetic acid with Battelli and Stern's respiratory oxidation of succinic acid, as modified by Einbeck, extending the chain through dehydrogenations and dehydrations to include all four of the closely related dicarboxylic acids. Then, by means of successive decarboxylations the hypothesis brought the hitherto isolated phenomenon of the respiratory activity of these acids into the broad picture of the decomposition of foodstuffs, by linking the former with the two acids that had come to be regarded as pivotal to the intersecting paths of carbohydrate and fatty acid metabolism. Ahlgren specified that the connection to the β-oxidation mechanism for fatty acids was probably through acetoacetic acid, an activator in the methylene blue system, which he thought could be divided by hydrolysis into two molecules of acetic acid. "We see here, consequently, the junction of the pathway: butyric acid → crotonic acid → β-hydroxybutryic acid → acetoacetic acid, with the grand route of decomposition which passes by way of succinic acid."[81]

The form of the reaction chain Ahlgren proposed did not fit the common expectation that successive, gradual oxidations would lead in direct lines from the building blocks of the three classes of foodstuffs to their final end products. There was, as Ahlgren termed it, a *circulation*. That is, the net oxidation of succinic acid was achieved through a series of seven reactions that formed a closed cycle, returning over and over, without using reversible reactions, to the same starting point. This form probably did not surprise Thunberg, however, because very early in his study of respiratory oxidation he had deduced from general considerations concerning the kinetics of respiration that some of the intermediary processes would have to be cyclic.[82]

At nearly the same time that Ahlgren published this hypothesis, Knoop included a nearly identical series of reactions in a more general theoretical discussion of the mechanisms of intermediary metabolism. Whether Knoop knew directly of the scheme as it emerged from the school in Lund, or converged on the same set of conversions independently, his starting point was clearly the framework established in both the 1920 paper and the specific argument of Thunberg for the synthesis of succinic acid from acetic acid. In Knoop's treatment the cyclic pattern did not emerge distinctly. Rather, he stressed that the interconnections between this and other paths of decomposition could account for the oxidation of acetic acid, the interconversions of acetic and pyruvic acid, the central position of pyruvic acid, and the capacity of animals to compensate for the continual variations in their food supply by synthesizing, from the breakdown products of one class of foodstuff, their requirements for another.[83]

Heinrich Wieland apparently also independently drew from Thunberg's 1920 paper the same inferences that Ahlgren and Knoop reached. In a review of the mechanisms of oxidation published in 1922, Wieland summarized the "beautiful work" of Thunberg that had connected "fatty acid decomposition with the dehydrogenation theory." After discussing the synthesis of succinic acid and the formation of fumaric acid from succinic, Wieland added "The path of the further decomposition would then be characterized through the stages of fumaric, malic, oxaloacetic, and pyruvic acid, acetaldehyde, and acetic acid."[84] Wieland left the matter with this bare statement at the time, but in 1925, in the standard German biochemical handbook edited by Carl Oppenheimer, he presented a clear representation of an integrated scheme for the oxidation of succinic acid by dehydrogenation that resembled closely the Thunberg-Ahlgren scheme.

The five steps leading from succinic acid to acetaldehyde and CO_2 Wieland regarded as unproblematic:

$HOOCCH_2CH_2COOH$ + methylene → $HOOCCH=CHCOOH$ + leuco-
succinic acid   blue   fumaric acid   methylene
                                                                                  blue

$$+H_2O$$
$HOOCCH=CHCOOH → HOOCCHOHCH_2COOH$
                        malic acid
$$-2H$$
$HOOCCHOHCH_2COOH → HOOCCOCH_2COOH$
                        oxaloacetic acid

$HOOCCOCH_2COOH$ → $HOOCCOCH_3$ + CO_2
                        pyruvic acid

$HOOCCOCH_3$ → $O=CHOCH_3$ + CO_2
                        acetaldehyde

These reactions, he asserted, make the decomposition of a normal cellular constituent "chemically transparent through the principle of dehydrogenation." The remaining steps were, in Wieland's view not yet established. "In what way the path goes further, whether by way of acetic acid, which is, in fact, dehydrogenated by tissues, through the molecular dehydrogenation of which succinic acid can again form,

$$-2H$$
2 $COOHCH_3$ → $HOOCCH_2CH_2COOH$, which then undergoes once more the decomposition described [above]...is still uncertain."[85]

Thus, whether by simultaneous convergent reasoning or by reacting to one another's ideas in an order we cannot specify, three of the leading biochemists of the day had, by 1925, suggested essentially the same series of reactions. To the series, however, each attached a different significance. For Thunberg and Ahlgren the synthesis of succinic acid was the starting point for a cyclic process that formed the mainstream of oxidative decomposition. Knoop embedded the same reactions less conspicuously within a broader network of decomposition and synthetic pathways. Wieland focused on the five reactions beginning with succinic acid, as a biological manifestation of his dehydrogenation mechanism, relegating the synthesis of succinic acid to an uncertain and subordinate position. In spite of these differences of emphasis, contemporaries merged the three versions into a common hypothesis known as the Thunberg–Knoop–Wieland scheme. During the rest of the decade biochemists who directed themselves toward the goal of filling in the steps in the chains of intermediary metabolism were strongly attracted to this scheme.

VI

The investigations of Joachim Kühnau in Wiesbaden on the decomposition of β-hydroxybutryic acid, one of the ketone bodies studied repeatedly since the 1880s, were typical of research on the paths of intermediary metabolism during the late 1920s. First he tried "model" experiments, seeking chemical agents that would act on the acid in a similar manner to oxygen in living cells. He was unsuccessful in this attempt, as he was also when he tested the action of yeast on the same acid. Then, however, he was able to produce a cell-free extract of liver tissue in which, when he added β-hydroxybutryic acid, a substantial portion of the latter disappeared. In keeping with the increasingly dominant enzyme theory, he considered the extract to contain an "enzyme complex," which he designated the *hydroxybutyroclastic system*. He studied various expected properties of this system, and established that dimethyldihydroresorcin acted as an inhibitor. By additional precipitation procedures he separated from the enzyme complex a component enzyme that he regarded as an aldehydemutase. His central interest, however, was to determine the "decomposition steps" of β-hydroxybutyric acid by identifying the compounds contained in the tissue extract several hours after he had added that acid. Depending on the conditions of the experiment, he was able to isolate or otherwise "prove" the presence of aldol, acetoacetic acid, 1-3,butyleneglycol, acetaldehyde, succinic, fumaric, and malic acid, and traces of acetic and pyruvic acid.[86]

Kühnau's experimental contribution was representative of numerous efforts in this period to characterize the reactions of substances that had long been suspected to be important metabolic substrates. He was unusual, however, in the extent to which he attempted to fit his results into the ongoing stream of investigation to provide a broadly integrated scheme of intermediary metabolism. His scheme was eclectic, probably reflecting directions of thought and discussion common within the field at the time; but he was bold enough to explicate in published form the overall picture into which the pieces he and others were examining were likely to fit.

To build his scheme Kühnau drew on the reaction mechanisms commonly assumed to recur throughout the paths of intermediary metabolism. Having found acetoacetic acid (CH_3COCH_2COOH) and acetaldol ($CH_3CHOHCH_2CHO$) among the products in his extract, he claimed that they were, respectively, the oxidative and reductive products of a Cannizzaro dismutation of β-hydroxybutyric acid. He allowed for an alternative pathway through acetaldehyde, which would also undergo a dismutation. The formation of pyruvic acid and acetic acid he accounted for by the action of a carboxylase in the enzyme complex. The presence of acetic acid and the dicarboxylic acids in his reaction mixture enabled him to link up his path for β-hydroxybutryic acid with the Thunberg-Wieland–Knoop scheme for the former substances. Summarizing the evidence for the reactions included in this scheme provided by Thunberg, Battelli and Stern, Einbeck, Neuberg, and others, including Juda Quastel's studies of bacterial metabolism, Kühnau confronted the still unconfirmed synthesis of succinic acid from acetic acid by arguing that acetic acid is the only plausible source for succinic acid, which is "a normal constituent" of muscle and liver tissue. Because β-hydroxybutryic acid was itself regarded as a product of the β-oxidation of fatty acids, Kühnau believed that his scheme could finally provide the mechanism to resolve the frequently debated question of whether animals can convert fats to carbohydrates.[87]

"Our results" Kühnau concluded, "permit the establishment of a detailed scheme for the decomposition of a β-hydroxybutryic acid. We find that *the destruction of the ketone bodies in the organism in principle proceeds over the same intermediary steps, as the oxidative carbohydrate- and protein-decomposition.* Acetaldehyde and acetic acid as the initial and final members of a closed cycle are the control centers of the transformations in metabolism."[88]

Tabelle I.

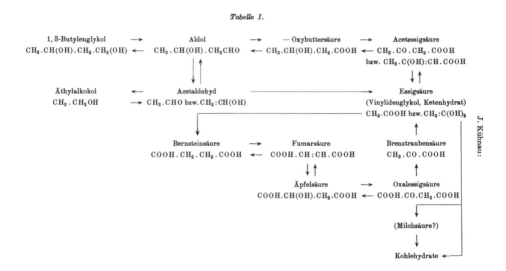

This scheme was not merely a theoretical deduction from the reaction mechanisms of organic chemistry. The compounds included in it had all been identified in biological material, and the majority of the reactions had been observed under conditions that made it reasonable to infer that they were enzymatic reactions. The strength of the experimental evidence varied considerably from one step to another. Most firmly established was the sequence from succinic to malic acid, which had been investigated frequently and recently demonstrated quantitatively by Dorothy Needham. The reactions Kühnau himself provided had less definitive support. The yields of none of the compounds in his reaction mixture were large enough to account for all of the β-hydroxybutryic acid that disappeared, and the connection to acetic acid was based on only traces of a volatile acid too small to be identified specifically. Finally, in the absence even of qualitative evidence for the conversion of acetic acid to succinic acid, he had to fall back on the coherence of the overall scheme to support a reaction that had no direct experimental underpinnings. Speculative though the complete scheme was, the growing body of results about its components seemed compatible with it, and biochemists had grounds to hope that further investigations would confirm those portions of it that still had to be propped up through theoretical connections. If Kühnau's scheme, or a variant of it, were to be validated, then the investigators in this field would have moved a long way toward Knoop's goal of an unbroken series of reactions between foodstuffs and end products — and the closed cycle would become a central organizing feature of metabolic pathways.

Not everyone accepted Thunberg's methylene blue reduction system as an adequate means to establish the reactions of oxidative metabolism. From Moscow, Aleksei Bakh and David Mikhlin reported, in January 1927, that succinic acid added to washed muscle tissue caused it to absorb 300 times as much oxygen as would be equivalent to the quantity of methylene blue that the tissue reduced anaerobically during the same time. HCN inhibited the oxidation but not the reduction of methylene blue, and changes in pH influenced the former differently than it did the latter. The oxidation of succinic acid, and the reduction of methylene blue by succinic acid were, according to Bakh and Mikhlin "two entirely independent processes, evoked by different enzymes."[89]

In Munich, Amandus Hahn believed that Thunberg's methylene blue experiments provided "a strong support for the Wieland dehydrogenation theory."[90] The criticisms of Bakh persuaded Hahn, however, that the cellular reactions Thunberg had inferred from the decolorizing action of "certain substances" required firmer experimental evidence. Thunberg had, in fact, observed only that these substances caused the blue color of the methylene blue to disappear, and had deduced the products of the reactions from chemical theory. In 1927, Hahn and W. Haarmann embarked on a program to establish these reactions by attempting to isolate and identify directly the metabolic products. Starting with succinic acid, they added from 8 to 10 g of the substance to between 1,000 and 2,000 g of finely divided muscle tissue containing methylene blue. After allowing these mixtures to incubate for several hours in the absence of oxygen, they were able to isolate fumaric acid and malic acid totaling up to 20 per cent of the initial succinic acid. Control mixtures without succinic acid yielded no fumaric or malic acid. Having disposed of Bakh and Mikhlin's objections to Thunberg's interpretation of this reaction, Hahn and Haarmann pursued the question of "how the further decomposition of malic acid is carried out." Guided by the series Thunberg had already proposed, they sought mainly to support the view that malic acid is converted to oxaloacetic acid, which is then decomposed to pyruvic acid by splitting off carbon dioxide. By early 1928 they were able to show that when they added either malic or oxaloacetic acid to finely divided muscle tissue with methylene blue, the preparation disengaged anaerobically many times as much carbon dioxide as did their controls. Six months later they had strengthened their demonstration by "trapping" the oxaloacetic acid formed, as a semicarbazide, before it could be further decomposed. In addition they showed that malic acid increased the quantity of pyruvic acid that they could isolate as a phenylhydrazone from a similar muscle–methylene blue system.   Subsequently, they duplicated these observations in anaerobic systems without the methylene blue, proving, they thought, that muscle tissue contains its own natural hydrogen acceptors.   By 1930, Hahn and Haarmann had accumulated enough evidence to demonstrate convincingly that Thunberg's reaction sequence from succinic acid as far as pyruvic acid actually occurs within muscle tissue.[91]

Hahn and Haarmann did not restrict themselves, however, to reactions that fit into the mainstream of the Thunberg–Wieland–Knoop scheme.   In 1928 they showed that lactic acid also gives rise to pyruvic acid through

$$-2\,H$$

a dehydrogenation reaction ($CH_3CHOHCOOH \rightarrow CH_3COCOOH$).   In 1929 they established that citric acid yields the same product, although in this case they offered no equation for the reaction involved.   In 1930 they added propionic acid, glycerophosphoric acid, and fructose diphosphate to the list of substances that could be converted to pyruvic acid in dehydrogenation reactions.[92] Summarizing their progress at that time, they depicted the dehydrogenation processes they had demonstrated to take place in muscles as follows:

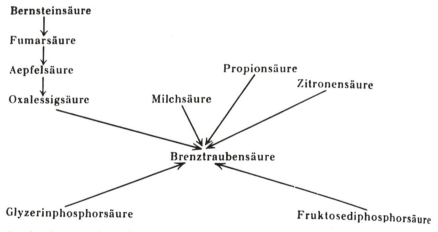

In the long series of papers published between 1927 and 1931, Hahn was silent about the further pathway that Thunberg and Ahlgren had suggested for pyruvic acid via acetic acid back to succinic acid.   He suggested, in fact, nothing about the decomposition of the pyruvic acid, which he had shown to arise from so many sources.   Perhaps he simply did not include that stage in his research program, or had not found a way to demonstrate the succeeding steps.   His scheme was not incompatible with the full Thunberg–Wieland–Knoop scheme, but he chose not to link the two together as Kühnau had linked his scheme with it.   Neither was Hahn's scheme dependent on the validity of the reactions that had not yet received experimental support comparable to what he and Haarmann had provided for a portion of the scheme.   As Figure 1.2 suggests, Hahn connected certain stages of several reaction series through the dehydrogenation mechanism operative in them and through the common participation of pyruvic acid in each of them. He did not integrate this scheme into more comprehensive unbroken chains leading from foodstuffs to final products or completing closed circles. One might say that Hahn simply fixed his attention on a central intersection of intermediary metabolism, putting aside the examination of the pathways that this junction linked together. In any case, the work of Hahn and Haarmann made pyruvic acid more prominent than ever as one of the fulcrums around which future theories of both the anaerobic and aerobic phases of intermediary metabolism must revolve.

During the years that Hahn was narrowing his focus to the paths leading to pyruvic acid, Erich Toennissen, in Erlangen, was centering on the further decomposition of that same key intermediate. Toennissen built his research career during the 1920s on experiments designed to verify or modify the current mainstream theories of carbohydrate metabolism. While proposing new versions of metabolic schemes based on the work of Neuberg, Meyerhof, and Thunberg, Toennissen showed himself flexible enough to shift readily his own theoretical position.

Like many others during this period, Toenniessen entered the field of carbohydrate metabolism through its connection with diabetes. The discovery by Banting and Best, in 1921, of the pancreatic hormone they named insulin, and of the dramatic effect of that substance in restoring the capacity of severe diabetic patients to metabolize sugar,[93] stimulated investigators of intermediary metabolism to repeated efforts to find out where insulin acts along the pathway of carbohydrate decomposition. Toenniessen approached this question by comparing the actions on accepted intermediates, such as lactic acid, of tissue *breis* made from pancreas, liver, and muscle, and from combinations of these tissues. He was also fascinated with the more general question of defining at what point along the path of carbohydrate decomposition "the true oxidations begin." In 1923 he assumed that the first oxidative step was the conversion of lactic acid to pyruvic acid. When he could not detect pyruvic acid in his tissue extracts several hours after adding lactic acid to them, however, he decided that "pyruvic acid is not a physiological intermediate in the decomposition of carbohydrate in mammals." It had, after all, only been inferred to belong there because of the general expectation that animal glycolysis was similar to fermentation, where Neuberg had established its important role. After satisfying himself that an oxidation of lactic acid to pyruvic acid could be "excluded," he concluded that lactic acid must be decomposed directly to acetaldehyde (thus bypassing the pyruvic acid step in Neuberg's fermentation scheme). After finding that an aldehyde did form in the combined *brei* of pancreas and muscle tissue, Toenniessen thought that his theory was "probable." Now he believed that "carbohydrate decomposition is carried out as far as acetaldehyde without oxidation." Further experiments convinced him that it was the decomposition of lactic acid to acetaldehyde that required insulin.[94]

By 1926 Toenniessen had reversed himself about pyruvic acid, regarding it now as "highly probable that pyruvic acid is an important intermediate product in the decomposition of sugar." Naturally, he then wanted to see what influence insulin exerted on the further decomposition of pyruvic acid. Having apparently returned to the fold of Neuberg's fermentation scheme, Toenniessen expected to investigate the effects of insulin on the conversion of pyruvic acid to acetaldehyde. When he searched for the latter substance in the *brei* of tissues to which he had added the former, however, he found none. Instead, he "proved" that acetic acid had been formed, by identifying a silver salt corresponding to silver acetate. Removing acetaldehyde from its purported place in the process even as he restored the place of pyruvic acid, he believed that he had established that in mammals "pyruvic acid is decomposed by means of an oxidation to acetic acid." Insulin turned out not to be involved in this oxidation, for when he added insulin to a mixture of pyruvic acid and tissue *brei* the quantity of the pyruvic acid increased. Insulin, he inferred, inhibits the oxidation. It must promote not a decomposition, but a synthesis of glycogen from pyruvic acid.[95] Later in this same year he "proved" that methylglyoxal forms from fructose diphosphate added to a mixture of muscle and pancreas *brei*. He thus verified, he thought, that the key intermediate in Neuberg's fermentation scheme was also central to carbohydrate metabolism in animals. Once again he relocated the boundary between anaerobic and aerobic metabolism. The "oxidation of carbohydrates" surely "starts at methylglyoxal." Under anaerobic conditions, on the other hand, methylglyoxal gives rise to lactic acid, which enters the "lactic acid cycle" of Meyerhof.[96]

By the time Toenniessen found that acetic acid formed from pyruvic acid in his own experiments, the advent of the Thunberg–Knoop–Wieland hypothesis provided a new framework within which to fit his discovery. He, therefore, set out to provide the experimental proof for Thunberg's "purely theoretical conception" that the acetic acid is further transformed to succinic acid and back again to pyruvic acid. In experiments with ground muscle tissue he and E. Prell were able to confirm that pyruvic acid is decomposed into acetic acid and formic acid. Then, after subcutaneously injecting pyruvic acid into rabbits, they obtained from the urine a salt corresponding in its properties to the silver salt of succinic acid. At the meeting of the German Society for Internal Medicine in 1927, Toenniessen declared that "the ring is closed."[97] In 1928 he provided further proof that he had connected the elements of the Thunberg scheme by perfusing the lower extremities of a rabbit with a fluid containing pyruvic acid and detecting succinic acid afterward in that fluid.[98]

Sometime after announcing these results, Toenniessen encountered a rude setback. The decomposition of pyruvic acid to acetic acid that he had reported in 1926 had not been carried out by the muscle tissue, as he had thought, but by *staphylococcus* bacteria that had contaminated his preparation. When he repeated the experiment under stricter sterile conditions, the reaction did not take place, whereas controls containing the bacteria alone were able to carry it out. Toenniessen now viewed as "completely unresolved" the question "in what manner pyruvic acid is oxidatively further decomposed." By 1930, however, he had come up with an answer.[99]

With E. Brinkmann, Toenniessen carried out a new series of perfusion experiments on the lower extremities of rabbits. After adding pyruvic acid to the perfusing fluid, they examined both the fluid and the perfused muscle tissue for acetic, formic, and succinic acids. In those experiments in which they kept the perfusion fluid continuously oxidized, they detected none of these substances, except for very small quantities of formic acid, in either the fluid or the tissue, even though the quantity of pyruvic acid diminished. If, however, they added oxygen only intermittently to the fluid, they regularly found succinic acid in the musculature in greater amounts than could be accounted for by the normal presence of that substance according to the earlier analyses of Einbeck and others. The pyruvic acid is, therefore, Toenniessen inferred, converted to succinic acid; but he could "with certainty exclude" the possibility that this conversion "proceeds by way of acetic acid," since that substance did not appear in any of these experiments. How then did pyruvic acid become succinic acid? Clearly no simple reaction step could connect two such different compounds. Having already ruled out acetaldehyde as a step in the decomposition of carbohydrates, Toenniessen had no familiar compounds available to consider as the intermediates. He opted for an immediate oxidative synthesis instead of an intervening further decomposition of pyruvic acid. A polymerization of two molecules of pyruvic acid would form α-β-diketoadipic acid, which would then quickly decompose to yield succinic and formic acid:

$$CH_3COCOOH + CH_3COCOOH \xrightarrow{-2H} COOHCOCH_2CH_2COCOOH$$

$$COOHCOCH_2CH_2COCOOH + 2 H_2O \rightarrow COOHCH_2CH_2COOH + 2 HCOOH$$

Acknowledging that α-β-diketoadipic acid had never been isolated from muscle tissue, Toenniessen used a familiar argument to explain away its absence; the polymerization product would decompose "very quickly (or at least more quickly than it is formed)."[100]

Having already established to his satisfaction that methylglyoxal connects hexosediphosphate to pyruvic acid in the earlier stages of carbohydrate metabolism, and with Hahn and Haarmann's investigations having established the reactions connecting succinic acid with pyruvic acid, Toenniessen could now state that "through the conversion of pyruvic acid to succinic acid established by us, the ring of successive steps in the decomposition of glucose is closed without gaps, at least for one path, perhaps even for the main path of carbohydrate combustion."[101] This was a grand assertion. For the central case of carbohydrate metabolism, Toenniessen claimed to have reached the goal that Knoop and others had set forth as the long-term objective of biochemistry. Considering how often Toenniessen had changed his mind about which substances he had "proven" to be intermediates in carbohydrate metabolism and which ones he had been able to "exclude" from that process, contemporaries undoubtedly did not accept his claim at face value. Nevertheless, his new results were taken to be a serious challenge to the original Thunberg–Wieland–Knoop scheme. By 1930 it was becoming conspicuous that, whereas all the reactions in the scheme from succinic acid to pyruvic acid had been demonstrated to occur in animal tissue, no one had been able to verify Thunberg's critical theoretical reaction, the synthesis of succinic acid from acetic acid. Toenniessen's scheme, which obviated that step by forming the succinic acid from a condensation of pyruvic acid that apparently did occur in animal tissue, appeared, therefore, at the least, as a viable alternative hypothesis.

More lay at stake in the competition between Toenniessen and Brinkmann's theory and the Thunberg-Wieland-Knoop scheme than a simple choice between two possible routes from pyruvic acid to succinic acid. It had been the inclusion of acetic acid in the older scheme that had enabled Ahlgren, Knoop, and later Kühnau, to link together the metabolism of carbohydrates and fats. The Toenniessen-Brinkmann route provided no such link. Toenniessen was well aware of this feature, and pointed out its implication for the long-standing controversy over whether animals can, in fact, convert fats to carbohydrates.[102] If Thunberg's reaction had been proven to occur, he noted, that would have shown that fatty acids can be transformed to carbohydrates. His investigation proved, on the contrary, he said, that at least in muscle tissue this transformation does not take place.[103]

If the Toenniessen-Brinkmann scheme differed significantly from the scheme that had formed its point of departure, it was nevertheless conceived within the broad framework of Thunberg's "circulation" centered around succinic acid, as the mainstream of oxidative metabolic decomposition. By 1930 it appears that the basic pattern of a "closed ring" of reactions had taken sufficient hold in the minds of biochemists to survive experimental failures to confirm specific details of cyclic reaction schemes.

Connecting individual reactions into extended unique reaction chains, whether cyclic, linear, or branched, was not the only way that biochemists sought to order the paths of intermediary metabolism during the 1920s. They also looked for analogous sequences: that is, for a repetition of the same three or four reaction steps linking a group of compounds related in the same way as the individual compounds of an analogous group. When the unsaturated monocarboxylic crotonic acid ($CH_3CH=CHCOOH$) proved to decolorize methylene blue, although only weakly, Ahlgren offered the hypothesis that it "occupies in the oxidation of butyric acid to β-hydroxybutryic acid the same intermediate place that fumaric acid occupies in the oxidation of succinic acid to malic acid." Because the further oxidation of a β-hydroxybutryic acid produced acetoacetic acid, which was already thought to decompose to acetic acid, Ahlren could suggest a junction between this series and the main succinic acid series.[104] Biochemists looked for corresponding series, even when they could see no obvious way to join them together. The view that such parallel series would be found seems to have been a natural extension of the expectation that the same mechanisms for single reaction steps would appear repeatedly in the metabolic paths.

Not even the concept of parallel reaction series could comfortably encompass citric acid within the expected metabolic patterns. In 1930 this substance remained as anomalous as it had been since 1910. As we have seen, none of the reaction schemes proposed during the 1920s found room for it, except for Hahn and Haarmann's multiple paths converging on pyruvic acid, and they gave no clue about how the six-carbon citric acid could decompose to three-carbon pyruvic acid. Nor could one readily accommodate citric acid into a standard Wieland dehydrogenation reaction, because, as Thunberg pointed out in 1920, unless one assumed a simultaneous addition of water, the products were impossible. In 1929 he finally proposed a hypothetical reaction mechanism for citric acid in which he avoided the latter consequence by accepting the former condition. In it water is added first:

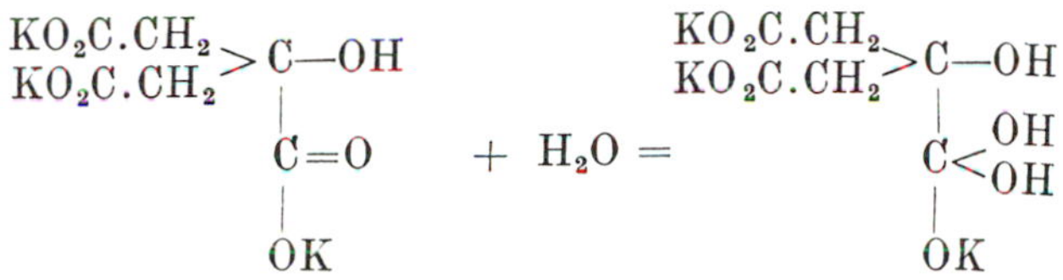

$$
\begin{array}{c}
\mathrm{KO_2C.CH_2} \\
\mathrm{KO_2C.CH_2}
\end{array}\!\!\!>\!\!\mathrm{C-OH} \quad\quad
\begin{array}{c}
\mathrm{KO_2C.CH_2} \\
\mathrm{KO_2C.CH_2}
\end{array}\!\!\!>\!\!\mathrm{C-OH}
$$
$$
\underset{\mathrm{OK}}{\overset{}{\mathrm{C}=\mathrm{O}}} \quad + \; \mathrm{H_2O} = \quad \underset{\mathrm{OK}}{\overset{}{\mathrm{C}}}\!\!<^{\mathrm{OH}}_{\mathrm{OH}}
$$

Next the citrico-dehydrogenase enzyme activates two hydrogen atoms and transfers them to an acceptor. The freed valences on the two oxygen atoms from which the hydrogens are removed combine with the valences of the carbon chain, splitting the molecule into one molecule of potassium carbonate and one molecule of acetonedicarboxylic acid:[105]

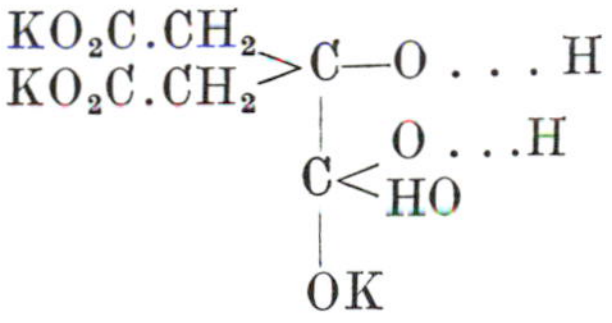

$$
\begin{array}{c}
\mathrm{KO_2C.CH_2} \\
\mathrm{KO_2C.CH_2}
\end{array}\!\!\!>\!\!\mathrm{C-O\ldots H}
$$
$$
\underset{\mathrm{OK}}{\overset{}{\mathrm{C}}}\!\!<^{\mathrm{O\ldots H}}_{\mathrm{HO}}
$$

Thunberg was making use of the traditional rules, applied since the time of Baeyer to biological processes, to construct reaction theories by adding and subtracting water as needed, and forming ephemeral intermediates to explain difficult chemical transformations. Even then the theoretical product, acetonedicarboxylic acid, did not offer any obvious bridge to the main metabolic pathways currently under discussion. Citric acid remained dangling — experimentally too important, to be discarded, yet theoretically too recalcitrant to find its place within the conceptual frameworks that were taking shape.

* * *

If we look again at Franz Knoop's admission in 1931 that biochemists could not yet provide more than an a priori concept of what an unbroken series of reactions connecting foodstuffs with end products would eventually look like, we can now see that this a priori conception had by then taken on a very concrete form. Although no complete reaction chains were firmly established in detail, the outlines to which they would have to conform were specified in a number of ways that closely restricted the acceptable solutions to the remaining unsolved problems. The starting and end points of the chains had long been fixed. It was now generally accepted that the intermediate stages must pass by way of certain compounds such as lactic, pyruvic, and acetic acid, the ketone bodies, and the dicarboxylic acids. Certain sequences, such as the progressive β-oxidation of fatty acids, the dicarboxylic acid series, the cleavage of hexoses into one of several possible three-carbon compounds, of which the heavily favored candidate was methylglyoxal, and the early deamination of amino acids, were taken for granted, as was the application of a small set of recurring reaction mechanisms to order the links in the metabolic chains. In his synthetic overview of 1931, Knoop pointed out certain broader architectural features of the reaction pathways that must apply no matter what the details turned out to be. The ability of organisms to compensate for variations in their food supply by converting one form of foodstuff to another was a basic premise that must be explained in terms of specific bridges connecting the pathways of carbohydrate, fat, and protein decomposition. On general chemical grounds it was evident that six-carbon sugars, long-chain fatty acids, and amino acids could not be directly interconverted, therefore, they must be linked through the simple products common to their deeper stages of decomposition.[106] The combination of all these considerations left little room for theoretical maneuver. Unless in their long search biochemists had somehow overlooked an entire route, or class of organic reactions, the main task still facing them would appear to be to determine which of the few available alternatives for building the necessary bridges between the established pieces of the metabolic picture were the correct ones.

In principle the standards by which these decisions were to be made were clear. Since the first decade of the century biochemists had generally accepted that, because intermediates do not accumulate, an intermediate must be shown to decompose as rapidly in a respiring biological system as the overall process took place. Only in the study of yeast fermentation and of bacterial metabolism, however, did investigators regularly measure these rates. In studying animal metabolism they had not much pursued during the 1920s the approach with which Battelli and Stern and Thunberg had made auspicious beginnings by 1910. With the organ perfusion, methylene blue, and tissue extract methods on which they had come to rely, they were limited mainly to qualitative or semiquantitative indications that a suspected metabolic step or stage takes place. Along the way they developed very useful methods for "trapping" with chemical agents an intermediate product that would normally be further decomposed. The evidence that the reactions they inferred from such investigations really took place within organs — that they were enzymatic rather than spontaneous chemical decompositions — was often quite strong; but until they could find means to meet more consistently that stringent quantitative criterion that biochemists had so far honored only when it was convenient to do so, they could seldom be certain whether the reactions they studied lay along the main metabolic pathways, or were physiologically insignificant side reactions.

In recent years, it has become fashionable to contrast the bold theoretical style of molecular biology with an allegedly "staid empirical style" of the older biochemistry.[107] The foregoing account should make it clear that such a contrast is largely mythological. The biochemists of the early twentieth century were driven by a simple but profound theoretical vision that guided them, as it had guided their predecessors for nearly a century, through a myriad of dense experimental thickets toward the distant goal of an unbroken account of the chemical reactions connecting the foodstuffs that enter an organism with the end products that leave it. They were sustained also by the fundamental conviction that when they understood these processes they could also understand how the organism utilizes the energy stored in its foodstuffs to produce heat and mechanical work.

Not all biologists through this long era accepted this point of view; but from the mid-nineteenth century it was sufficiently evident to enough of those who sought chemical explanations for vital phenomena that such series of gradual decomposition reactions *must* exist, so that they took up the quest for these steps over and over, sometimes putting it aside when there seemed no immediate hope for advancing toward the goal, but always returning to it when other developments revived the hope. When they were not yet in a position to describe these processes literally, they sometimes expressed them metaphorically — as Thunberg did in 1909, quoting Schönbein 50 years before him, when he wrote of metabolism as "a chemical drama consisting of many acts."[108] By 1930 biochemists must have felt that the vision was much closer than ever before to emerging in full view. They had come further toward delineating its critical features during the previous 10 years than during any preceding time. Yet they were also faced with baffling contradictions. No scheme that they had been able to propose could meet the theoretical requirements for a full set of reaction steps without relaxing accepted standards for experimental verification. Some, such as Kühnau and Toenniessen, boldly trusted their theoretical intuitions to fill in the gaps where what others would demand for decisive proof was still missing. More skeptical observers who regarded such schemes only as suggestive,[109] nevertheless recognized their heuristic value.[110] The situation in intermediary metabolism as the 1930s began was simultaneously fluid and rigidly fixed. It was fluid in that none of the plethora of partial solutions that were coming forth for a long-standing set of problems was fully satisfactory. It was rigid in that the openings through which one might move toward more perfect solutions seemed tightly guarded by premises concerning the structure that all such theories must exhibit.

2

Boyhood in Hildesheim

Hans Adolf Krebs was born on August 25, 1900, in a modest house on the *Zingel*, a broad street bordering the beautiful inner city of Hildesheim, in Hanover. His father chose the name Hans in the mistaken belief that it was a characteristically Germanic one. Hans was given the middle name Adolf after his maternal grandfather, but the spelling was modernized.[1]

Six weeks later the Krebs family moved to a larger house on the other side of the same street, at Zingel 9. Anticipating that a second child would require more room, Georg Krebs had already purchased the house at Zingel 9, and had had an extension built across the back to accommodate an office and a surgical operating room for his medical practice.[2]

The space on the first floor in the new Krebs home that was not designated for Dr. Krebs's professional use contained the bedrooms. Family life centered on the second floor, where the sitting and dining rooms were, and where there was a *Kinderzimmer* in which Hans must have spent much of his first years. Large windows gave the house a bright, open feeling. The household into which Hans entered was secure and well ordered. His mother, Alma Davidson Krebs, managed it with quiet efficiency and the assistance of a cook and a housemaid. The restrained manner in which his parents cared for their child, with little outward show of emotion, was leavened by the presence of a warm and lively sister, 6 years older, who acted sometimes as a second mother. When Hans was an infant Lise often took him out in his baby carriage, and when he grew old enough she took him for walks. Sometimes she bought him sweets, a treat not often accorded him in the austere regimen prevailing at home.[3]

When Hans was 2 years old, he acquired a younger brother. The new arrival was named Wolfgang, after Georg Krebs's favorite composer, Mozart, and his favorite author, Goethe.[4] From the beginning he was called Wolf. As small children Hans and Wolf played together in the *Kinderzimmer* and in the spacious garden that extended along the south side of the house and behind it. The Zingel had been one of the first *Villenstrasse* developed outside the boun-

Figure 2.1 Georg and Alma Krebs at the time of their wedding.

Figure 2.2 Wolf, Hans, and Lisa Krebs with their mother, in their garden.

Figure 2.3 The Krebs home at Zingel 9.

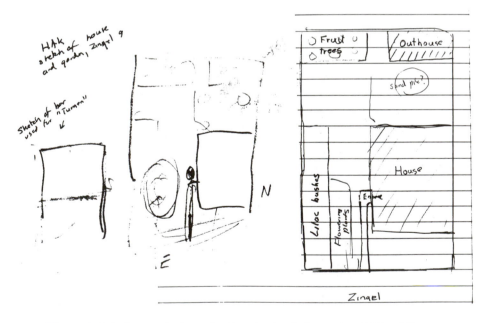

Figure 2.4 Left: Sketch drawn by Hans Krebs, in December 1979, while describing arrangement of his childhood home and garden. Right: Interpretation of sketch by author.

dary of the old city — it occupied a portion of what had once been the moat — and the houses built along it were semidetached or separate, with individual private gardens. The luxuriant, well-maintained Krebs garden contained apple, pear, and lime trees, a ginkgo tree, strawberry, raspberry, and gooseberry bushes, flower beds in which Georg Krebs often rearranged the plantings, and a long border of lilac bushes. The Krebs children found much to do here. For their play there was a sandbox and an exercise bar, and at the back a large outbuilding in which garden equipment and much else was stored.[5]

As the older and more dominant brother, Hans usually chose their activities. Wolf was a gentle child who normally accommodated himself to whatever Hans wanted to do.[6] He was not, however, always the one to follow behind. Though Hans was more industrious, Wolf was physically bolder, and would venture into situations in which Hans hung timidly back. As a small child Wolf once startled his mother by climbing so high in a tree standing close to the house that he appeared outside a second floor window. On the whole Hans and Wolf got along well together, and became each other's best childhood friends. Once when they were lying awake in the *Kinderzimmer* instead of falling asleep, Hans made up a little story based on a Hanoverian folk tale about a button that snapped off a pair of trousers. Wolf was so absorbed by the story that he asked Hans the next night for another installment, and Hans was imaginative enough to think up a new episode each night for a long while.[7]

The home life into which Hans, his brother and his sister had to fit was materially austere. Although Georg Krebs probably enjoyed a substantial income by the time Hans was born, the family maintained a frugal existence characteristic of many middle-class professional German families. They believed that income should not be spent on immediate luxuries, but put aside for future needs such as the education of their children and their own old ages. Consequently the children were not indulged with excessive clothes or toys, and they were served plain meals. They were also required to eat everything that was placed before them.[8] That this rule was enforced with consideration for their preferences, however, is suggested by an incident that occurred once when Hans was invited out to dinner. He was served something that he ordinarily hated to eat. He consumed it without complaining, however, and when he returned home his mother asked him what he had had. When she heard, she said "But you don't like that." Hans replied "In other people's houses, one eats everything" [*Bei fremden Leuten ißt man alles*].[9] The incident also suggests that the children were well schooled in the behavior expected of them outside their own home.

The rhythm of daily activity at Zingel 9 was organized around Georg Krebs's professional life, and the children had to conform to his schedule. He held office hours at home every morning, and Hans became accustomed early to the presence of his father's patients in the waiting room downstairs. Around midday he left for the nearby Sankt Bernward *Krankenhaus*, returning by 2 PM for the noontime meal. In customary German fashion that was the main meal of the day. The children were expected to appear for the meal exactly on time;

Figure 2.5 Hans and Wolf Krebs about 1905.

but on the days when their father performed a major operation at the hospital he might well arrive late, and they would have to wait for him. Afterward the children were strictly ordered to be quiet while their father took his afternoon nap. He saw patients again at home until about 6 PM. Then he relaxed and the family gathered for a cold supper.[10]

On Sundays the Krebs's often went to dinner at the home of one of their relatives, or relatives in turn ate with them. Alma Krebs was the daughter of a Hildesheim banker who had died when she was 14. The Davidson family had been settled in the area for centuries, and there were many aunts, uncles, cousins, and more distant relations living in or near the city. The family was close-knit enough so that it maintained a fund to aid any members of it who might fall on times of need. The regular Sunday visits sustained these connections, and provided the children with an enlarged family circle of adults with whom they could be comfortable and of other children with whom they could play.[11]

As soon as they were old enough to do so, the Krebs children were required to participate in another fixture of German family life, the Sunday walk. Hildesheim was surrounded on three sides by wooded hills. A short walk to the eastern edge of the city took one to the foot of the *Galgenberg*, from which one could ascend along a broad gravel pathway through stands of tall trees, picturesque slopes and well-kept lawns. Outlooks along the way afforded spacious views of the steeples and rooftops of the city to the west and the broad plain to the north. After a leisurely half hour one reached a characteristic large, ornate restaurant at which Sunday hikers could refresh themselves. It was a typical German setting for an outing that was both beautiful and orderly. On the western side of the city the *Steinberg* offered a similar walk, lacking a terminal restaurant, but penetrating more deeply into a stately forest through which one might occasionally see deer loping. Georg Krebs stopped frequently along the way to point out to his children the names of the wildflowers bordering the paths. Hans developed a strong interest in these flowers; but he sometimes chafed at the necessity to hike along compliantly in the family group, on outings that sometimes lasted all day. Perhaps it also tried the childrens' patience to sit for half an hour at a crowded restaurant over tea or coffee, and listen to typical German band music.[12]

I

When he was 7 years old, Hans began school at the *Evangelische Knabenmittels-chule*. Although Lutheran in orientation, the *Mittelschule* was not administered by the church. A gradual transfer of power from church to public authorities had been completed by 1904. As in most German cities, there were two types of primary school: *Volkschule* for those who were expected to leave school at age 14, and the *Mittelschule*, recently founded in Hildesheim, for those who would either continue to 16 or compete after 3 years to enter the *Gymnasium*.[13] For members of the *gebildete*, or educated classes, such as the Krebs family, the *Mittelschule* was the obvious choice.

On the first day of school in the fall of 1907 Hans's mother took him the very short distance to the *Mittelschule*, which was almost across the street from their home. To ease the transition he was given a bag of sweets and other treats. School started early and finished by 1 PM, so Hans was home in time for the noontime meal. Each morning began with a prayer and readings from the Bible. The other subjects he had in his first days at school were reading, writing, arithmetic, and singing. He and the other pupils began their writing not on paper, but on slates.[14]

After a week his teacher noticed that Hans could not read what was written on the blackboard, and recommended to his parents that he have an eye examination. Hans turned out to be near-sighted. When told that he would have to wear glasses, at first he was very distressed. He soon realized, however, that

Figure 2.6 Mittelschule attended by Hans Krebs.

the glasses were little problem, and that some other children also had to wear them.[15]

Like other German schools, the *Mittelschule* fostered a competitive spirit among pupils by such devices as seating them according to their class standing. Discipline was tight. The pupils had to stand up when the teacher entered, and to be orderly throughout the day. Nevertheless it was dangerous for anyone to appear to try harder than the rest, or to ingratiate the teacher. He risked being called a *Streber* by the other boys. Hans made sure to be just naughty and disrespectful enough to avoid being a *Streber*; but he enjoyed learning. He absorbed information readily, and did not mind the large amount of memorization of Biblical passages, verses, and *Sentenzes* (maxims) that was required.[16]

At the end of the first term Hans was ranked first in a class of 38 boys. That does not mean that he obtained top marks. German schools did not dispense praise easily, and few pupils were led by their report cards to believe that they had done as well as they could. Hans received the highest mark of "1" only for "orderliness." In "conduct," "attentiveness," and "industriousness," as well as for his "achievement" in each of his four subjects he obtained "2s". With minor variations the same pattern persisted through his three years at the *Mittelschule*. Although he improved his marks in conduct, attentiveness, and industriousness, he received almost entirely "2s" in his subjects. Nevertheless he was always first in his class. In athletics, which began in the middle of his second year, he clearly did not excel. He began with a "4," which he was subsequently able to raise only to a "3."[17]

Hans's early education was not limited to what he studied in school. The broad German concept of *Bildung*, of learning that formed one's whole personality, pervaded both his family and his surroundings. At home his father was the dominant intellectual influence. Georg Krebs was a widely cultivated man who read avidly on many subjects, enjoyed clever conversation embroidered with literary quotations or allusions, and was strongly interested in the arts. He played the piano reasonably well, occasionally sang ballads, and attended the theater or a concert once a week. Mozart operas were his particular favorites. At family celebrations he contributed witty original verses, and sometimes expressed his feelings in odes written to his wife. He and six or seven relatives and friends gathered each week for a *Kunstgeschichtliche Abend*, at which one of them gave a little talk on an artist or work of art.[18]

Georg Krebs had a small library of books, many of them on history. In addition he belonged to a group of about 20 people who subscribed jointly each month to a book that they passed from house to house. Hans took advantage of the wide variety of books available in his house to read extensively on many topics. He often browsed through the encyclopedia. Among the books he read early were historical novels by Felix Dahn, which portrayed the ancient Germanic people in romanticized heroic tones.[19]

Hildesheim was itself a veritable repository of German cultural history. Founded as a bishopric in 815 AD, it had flourished as a religious and artistic center under the inspiration of the forceful princely bishop Bernward. Later it became a thriving commercial center; but it suffered greatly during the seventeenth century in the 30 years war, and was for the next 200 years a provincial backwater. One of the consequences of this long stagnation was that the inner city remained at the end of the nineteenth century much as it had been at its peak, a harmonious blend of late medieval and early modern architecture. The dominating structure remained the massive *Dom*, with its many treasures, of which the most renowned was the *Bernwardstür*, a pair of large bronze doors at the main entrance to the cathedral adorned with beautiful relief figures depicting Biblical events. Also famous was the *Tausendjährigen Rosenstock*, a rose bush growing up the wall of the choir of the cathedral, that had been in that place since the founding of the town. There were four other major cathedrals in Hildesheim and numerous small churches. They dominated an inner city that retained almost intact the appearance it had had since the seventeenth century.[20]

As Hans grew old enough to explore the streets of Hildesheim on his own, he became fascinated by the beauty and variety of its houses and public buildings. He had only to walk to the first street corner from his house, turn left and go a few hundred yards farther to reach the spacious town square, dominated by the magnificent late medieval butchers-guild house. The first four floors of this ornate wooden structure overhung each other, so that the building became progressively wider for half its height. Two further floors were constrained by the converging lines of its enormous steeply pitched red-tile roof. Opposite the guild house was the stately city hall. The other buildings surrounding the square

Figure 2.7 Market square in Hildesheim, with *Knochenhaueramtshaus*, c. 1925–30. Photo courtesy of Roemer Museum, Hildesheim.

were varied but harmonious. Hans never ceased to admire the overall beauty of this square. Elsewhere he could wander through street after street of similar picturesque buildings, the oldest of them in half-timbered late medieval Gothic style, the later ones in the more classic lines of the Renaissance. Children in Hildesheim were routinely taught to distinguish the styles and periods of their architectural heritage.[21]   Grand edifices and humble dwellings alike were similar enough to form a coherent impression, yet endlessly varied in their dimensions, inexact in their vertical and horizontal lines, with roofs, gables, dormers, and chimneys protruding in every direction.

Imposing though its largest buildings were, the scale of Hildesheim, its streets, and its many old houses was intimate enough not to overwhelm a child. The facades were often decorated in bright colors, and woodcutters from centuries past had embellished the timbers with many carvings, often invitingly humorous. There were also verses and maxims inscribed everywhere in the woodwork. Hans particularly enjoyed these sayings, and learned his favorite ones by heart.

Attentive to cultural values, the city fathers took measures by the late nineteenth century to protect the old city from changes that would destroy its historical integrity. They acted also to enhance the cultural life of the city by establishing museums that were remarkable for a city of modest size. The Krebs children were familiar with the plants, stuffed animals, and geological specimens at the Römer natural history museum. They were present also when the *Pelizaeusmuseum*, housing a fine Egyptological collection gathered by a former city councillor, reopened in 1911 in a new building.[22]

Theater and music were regarded in Hildesheim not as entertainment, but as "a measure of the *Bildungsstand* of a city." In 1909 a stately *Stadttheatre* was completed at the corner of *Zingel* and *Theaterstraße*, only a few minutes away from the Krebs household. Hans was very impressed with the new building, and keen to see performances there. He was not taken often, except to the annual Christmas children's play, because his parents thought that he was not ready for the adult theater. But when he did go he was thrilled. He and Wolf often heard chamber music in a concert hall in the *Rathaus*.[23]

Educated German families generally believed that they ought to provide for their children the opportunity to learn to play music themselves. Hans and Wolf began together to take piano lessons in 1910 or 1911. There were some obstacles to overcome besides the intrinsic ones, for they were not allowed to disturb their father by playing the piano, which was in the sitting room, when he was there. Both were eager to learn to play, however, and practiced diligently whenever he was away.[24]

Despite the beauty preserved from its past, Hildesheim was far from a static museum. Sharing in the strong economic development of the decades after German unification, the city had grown from a population of 20,000 in 1870 to 50,000 in 1910. The northeast sector acquired a number of medium-size industries, and a distinct working class emerged.[25] Hans and Wolf saw ample early evidence that they had been born into a changing world. While they were small children the cobblestones of Zingel were torn up and tracks laid for the first trolley car lines in Hildesheim. Soon they could board one of the cars of the *elektrische Straßenbahn*, drop a *Pfennig* in the fare box, and travel across town. Not long afterward the stoves used to heat the rooms in their house gave way to a central heating system, and the gas lights were gradually replaced by electric bulbs. Once an aeroplane flew from Hamburg to Hildesheim, tilted its wings to interested onlookers, and flew away again. In 1910 it was announced that a Zeppelin would land at Hildesheim. Hans, Wolf, and their father joined the throng that gathered on the *Galgenberg*, but were only able to see the huge lighter-than-air craft pass by at a distance. Not long afterward Hildesheim received one of the first self-dialing telephone systems. All around the young Krebs boys were highly visible manifestations that they were entering an era of rapid technological progress.[26]

Equally visible to Hans and his family was the prominent role of the army in German life. The 79th Prussian infantry regiment was quartered in barracks not far from the Krebs home,[27] and there were frequent parades on the large parade ground in front of it. Officers wearing their uniforms in the street and at public events were a familiar feature in Hans's youthful world. He often wondered why the officers wore on their arms a medallion with "Gibraltar" inscribed on it. He undoubtedly did not think about the function of the army in imperial Germany as a bulwark of the monarchical regime and of the conservative social establishment; but he did absorb the values of responsibility, reliability, and punctuality that were reinforced by the ubiquitous effects of military life. The practice of awarding minor civil service posts to retired reserve officers spread these values throughout local bureaucratic functions. The post office, the trains, and other services could be counted on. In school, classes began and ended precisely on time. Shops opened exactly at their appointed hours. The paramount importance of responsibility and reliability, and their manifestation in punctuality, became second nature to the young Hans Krebs.[28]

The army uniforms symbolized also the military power of an imperial Germany playing an increasingly prominent part in international events. Hans's father was a patriotic German fully in sympathy with his country's nationalistic aspirations. Keenly interested in politics, Georg Krebs belonged to the National Liberal party that had been able at the time of unification to reconcile its liberalism with support for the conservative architect of unification, Otto von Bismarck.[29] Having grown up in the Bismarck era, he too combined liberal political views with great admiration for the Iron Chancellor, a picture of whom hung in his surgery, with the caption "We Germans fear God but nothing else in the world." Hans absorbed the attitudes of his father without question. Pride in the German victories over France in 1870 was also instilled in school. Even as a small child Hans thought about how lucky he was to be German.[30]

Being German was for the Krebs family not an uncomplicated matter, because they were also Jews. Legally emancipated from old restrictions during the nineteenth century, German Jews were able, by the time Georg Krebs came of age, to pursue a broader range of professional opportunities than ever before, and hoped increasingly that they could become fully integrated into the new German nation. Careers in the higher civil service and the officer corps remained closed to them, however, and the concept of the "Second Reich" as a Christian state stimulated doubts about whether Jews could take their place in such a society while retaining their distinct identity. Some Jewish leaders maintained that liberal freedoms guaranteed individuals the right to hold onto their beliefs without prejudice to their positions as citizens. Some liberal Christians, as well as some Jewish leaders, asserted, however, that the price for integration must be complete assimilation. To acquire their full rights as Germans, the Jews would have to cease being Jews.[31]

Georg Krebs gradually reached the conclusion that assimilation was the best solution. When Lise was small she received some Judaic instruction, but by the time his sons were children he had decided that they should be raised outside of formal Jewish institutions. He explained his position to Hans and Wolf, who passively accepted it. The only religious instruction they received, therefore, was the daily Bible readings and songs in school, from which they learned more about Christian teachings than they knew about the religion from which they had sprung.[32]

Georg Krebs undoubtedly felt confident about his choice of assimilation because, as a highly respected physician whose practice extended well beyond the small Jewish population in Hildesheim, he felt fully accepted in his community. He did not experience the anti-Semitism that was becoming more prominent in some aspects of German life at the turn of the century. As a child Hans also encountered no anti-Semitism directed at him personally.[33]

As Hans and Wolf grew from childhood to boyhood, they continued to share common activities. They played dominoes and other games, and a little later their father, who was an able chess player, introduced them to that challenging pastime. The two brothers approached the game in characteristically different ways. Hans studied his father's book on chess and set out methodically to learn the standard starting and end games. Wolf felt his way more casually into the game, simply trying various moves to see what would happen, and not worrying much about whether he won or lost. Similarly, when they collected stamps, Hans carefully inserted each stamp into its correct place in the book. He learned systematically about the geography of the countries from which the stamps came. Wolf was mainly interested in pretty stamps. To some extent such differences reflect the obvious fact that Hans was two years older, but they were in keeping with traits in their personalities that were more lasting. The industrious Hans viewed his more easy-going brother as lazy; but Wolf was also inventive and clever. It is quite likely that he eventually played better chess than Hans did. Outdoors, Wolf was more likely to take the lead. During one of their rare family holidays, on the coast of Holland, in 1909, when the ocean was rough, Wolf plunged happily into the water breaking over his head while Hans refused to go near it. Wolf viewed his older brother as intellectually dominant, but physically timid.[34]

Their differences in temperament led Hans and Wolf gradually to diverge in their pursuits. Wolf began to engage in outdoor sports and to spend much of his leisure time playing at the homes of cousins and friends. As a boy Hans had no close friends, and he kept himself busy with activities he could do on his own. He read extensively, he spent as much time as he could practicing the piano, and he took up hobbies. His botanical interest having been stirred by his father, he collected and dried wild flowers, pressed them in a herbarium press he had been given, and systematically learned their Latin names. He was also interested in building things. When he was about 10 years old he constructed, out of cardboard and paper, an elaborate device in which a marble placed at one end would roll through a trough, following a pathway that went downward and upward, around curves and through spirals, without stopping or overshooting. Called the "coo coo bahn," Hans's invention made a great impression on the family and on others who saw it.[35]

Hans was not physically inactive. He liked to run, and to enter games when he could. There was a great deal of emphasis on fitness, both at home and at school. At his father's insistence he learned to swim when he was 9 or 10, and afterward he went swimming often. He explored much of Hildesheim on foot, and after he had received a bicycle he rode long distances into the surrounding countryside; but he did not participate actively in group sports. Because he was the smallest person in his school class, he felt vulnerable to attack by local bullies. He did not become involved in schoolboy fights, probably because he carefully avoided them. He was, in short, a loner. Did he also feel lonely? His brother thought so. He himself later recalled that he had thought of himself as "a rather unattractive and unpopular boy"; but he also emphasized that he was "never bored."[36]

As a boy Hans greatly admired his father. Georg Krebs was successful, charming, and witty. He maintained an intellectual atmosphere in the home that his sons found stimulating. At family meals the children were encouraged to take part in lively conversations. He did not, however, devote a large part of his leisure time to them. He spent much of it, by himself, reading or playing cards before supper with several acquaintances. Much as he enjoyed conversational contacts, he did not establish closer bonds with other people. Hans was sometimes awed, or even frightened by his father, and he was convinced that his father was much brighter than he himself was. His confidence was not increased by the many criticisms he received from his father, in whose eyes it seemed that nothing he could do was good enough. His father criticized him for bullying his younger brother, for being untidy, for laughing too much at nonsense rhymes, and not having a sufficiently intellectual wit; and he criticized both boys for their manners and for being shy. The harshness with which the criticisms were delivered made Hans feel that his father was slightly contemptuous of him. Although Hans was strong willed enough not to be cowed, sometimes even enough to argue back, his father's attitude hurt. In his autobiography he wrote rather blandly that "My father's critical comments helped me to be modest in assessing my abilities and potential, but they did not discourage me unduly." In conversation, in 1979, he said more forthrightly that they had made him feel "that I wasn't much good, [that I was] inferior to him." When reminded that his father had criticized him and Wolf for their shyness, he remarked "It was largely he himself who made us shy."[37]

II

There were, in 1910, two high schools for boys in Hildesheim. One of them, the *Andreanische Gymnasium*, traced its origins to the late thirteenth century. The other high school, the *Andreasrealgymnasium*, had just been established.[38] These two institutions embodied, respectively, the two ideals that had dominated educational debate in Germany throughout the nineteenth century. Oriented around Latin, Greek, and classical and modern literature, the *Gymnasium* upheld the humanistic belief in a *Bildung* that shaped the whole personality and intellectual outlook of the individual. Placing more emphasis on modern languages, mathematics, and to some extent the natural sciences, the *Realgymnasium* represented the goal of *Ausbildung*, or practical preparation for adult occupations.

In the Krebs family there was again little doubt about what the educational choice would be. Even in an age more materialistically oriented than the early nineteenth century that had defined the goals of *Bildung*, educated middle-class families such as theirs strongly upheld the humanistic ideal. Hans's maternal grandfather, a banker, and his uncles, all of whom were practical business people, had attended the time-honored "Andreanum." Georg Krebs, with his

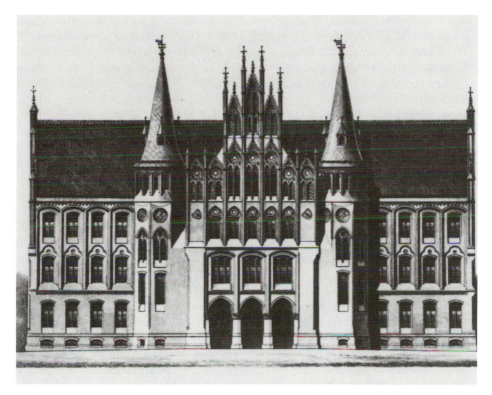

Figure 2.8 Gymnasium Andreanum in Hildesheim.

broad cultural interests, probably had no difficulty deciding to send his sons there; and they had no means or reason to question his judgment.[39]

Despite its ancient heritage, the Andreanum was housed in a modern building completed in 1869.[40] Its large U-shaped structure was ornamented with a turreted neo-Gothic facade. Hans entered the sixth form at the Andreanum in the spring (Easter) term of 1910. He could walk the short distance from his home to school in 5 minutes. School began at 8 AM and ended at 1 PM, so that he could easily return home in time for lunch. Occasionally he even made an extra trip during one of the 15-minute recesses to retrieve something he had forgotten to bring in the morning.[41]

During his first year Hans studied Latin, German, religion, natural history, geography, and arithmetic. He was also graded for his performance in writing, singing, and athletics. He found the discipline strict and the work demanding. His grades at the end of the spring term were rather ordinary. On a scale of 1, very good; 2, good; 3, adequate; 4, deficient; and 5, unsatisfactory, Hans earned "2s" only in religion, natural history, and athletics, with "3s" in the rest of his subjects. He received "good" for his attentiveness, but only "adequate" for his industriousness. His conduct was described as "good," but with the qualification that "his notebooks are untidy." It is a measure of the stern standards maintained at the Gymnasium that such a record was sufficient to rank Hans fifth of 27 pupils. During the 2 years that he spent in the sixth form, his position fluctuated mildly without a clear upward or downward trend. He received further negative comments about his orderliness. In the spring term of 1911 he climbed to second in his class, probably on the strength of a rare "1" in geography; but in 1912 in the fifth form he fell back to eighth despite continued "1s" in that subject. In the spring term of 1912 his teacher noted that his industriousness was "not always adequate."[42] On the whole Hans was doing reasonably well in school; but he did not stand out as he had done in *Mittelschule*, and he did not display special talents in any subject to dispel his father's doubt that he possessed any unusual intellectual capacity.

Wolf had as a boy shown more interest in mechanical activities, such as repairing electrical equipment and plumbing, than in intellectual pursuits. Nevertheless, he followed Hans to the humanistic Andreanum in 1912. Although Wolf was a less conscientious pupil than Hans, it soon became clear that he was unusually good in mathematics. The subject came very easily to him, and he attracted attention to his talent in his first year of geometry when the teacher broke off in the middle of a problem he was working out and asked the class if they could find the solution. While most of the first-year pupils were asking second-year pupils if they could remember the answer from the year before, Wolf came up with a solution different from the one in the textbook. Georg Krebs was especially impressed with Wolf's mathematical and mechanical skills because he himself had no particular aptitude in either area, and he came to regard Wolf as the more gifted of his two sons.[43]

If Hans did not make so auspicious an impression in any subject in his early Gymnasium years, neither did he have serious difficulties in any of them. He could cope well enough in mathematics, even if overshadowed in that area by his younger brother. In subjects that required the pupils to absorb large amounts of information, Hans had the clear advantage. He organized his time more effectively, liked to read, and had an excellent memory. He had no trouble learning by heart the many lines of poetry and prose that had to be memorized. Wolf found it more difficult to commit to memory what he could not think out logically. Languages did not come readily to Hans, and since the eight periods of Latin per week dominated his school day, he had to work hard at it. His German studies were probably less demanding, but made a strong impact on him. Here he was introduced to the classics of German literature, beginning with plays of Schiller, such as *Die Räuber*, *Die Jungfrau von Orleans*, and *Wilhelm Tell*, and the easier works of Goethe, including *Reinicke Fuchs* and *Götz von Berlichingen*. Although too young to appreciate the depth and power of these great German writers, he was undoubtedly absorbed by these stories with their intense evocation of courtly ideals and knightly honor, conflicts between freedom and oppression, battles and heroic deeds, loyalty and betrayal, and devotion to the fatherland.[44]

Figure 2.9 Left: Krebs family in Obersdorf, 1911. Right: Hans and Wolf Krebs with their grandfather Krebs in Silesia.

The Gymnasium teachers assigned substantial amounts of homework. Hans and Wolf normally began to study right after lunch, in their *Kinderzimmer*. Conscientious though he was, Hans was not too disciplined to divert himself sometimes by talking or playing with his brother when they were supposed to be working. Such lapses incurred a risk, because the room was directly above the surgery where their father took his afternoon nap. If the boys became noisy enough to wake him up, Georg Krebs was likely to storm up the stairs to punish them. Hans, being more alert to such impending confrontations than his younger brother, sometimes managed to slip across the hall into the toilet in time to leave Wolf to face alone their father's anger.[45]

During the afternoons Hans and Wolf also took advantage of special handicraft classes offered within the school system of the city to learn paper and wood working, and bookbinding. Both boys enjoyed working with their hands, and they took up bookbinding at home. Wolf converted Hans's flower press into a device to hold the tapes used to tie the groups of sheets together, and they used it often.[46]

When he was 11, Hans developed an intense interest in current events. He began to read regularly the two daily newspapers — one of them probably the *Berliner Tageblatt*, the other an old newspaper called the *Vossische Zeitung* — to which his father subscribed. The catalyst for his interest was apparently the dramatic international events of the year 1911. In April a German gunboat entered a Moroccan port in response to French military actions there. There was an outburst of patriotic feeling in Germany, but the German government quickly backed down when the French ignored its demands. As a result Italy was emboldened to occupy Tripoli, an action that brought it into war with Turkey and encouraged the Balkan states to join together to attack Turkey to wrest that country's remaining European possessions from it. Hans followed all these events avidly, with little awareness of their deeper political significance and no foreboding about their ominous nature.[47]

In the German Gymnasium pupils were grouped not in yearly "grades," but in "forms" in each of which one normally remained for 2 years. In the spring of 1912 Hans moved up to the fourth form. The subjects that he had had in the sixth and fifth form continued, and French, history, and geometry were added. His form master was Prof. Dr. Johannes Gebauer, a remarkable man who was also the town archivist and a scholarly historian, and was writing a history of Hildesheim. Gebauer taught German and Latin as well as history, and he made a strong impression on Hans. A stern, demanding teacher, somewhat militaristic in bearing, Gebauer was critical of his pupils' performances and seldom offered praise. Hans responded, however, to the high standards that Gebauer set, and that he expected of his pupils.[48]

Gebauer taught German history mainly as political events, focusing on rulers and wars. An enthusiastic supporter of German nationalism, he stressed the importance of Luther and the Reformation, the growth of Prussia, which he attributed to the astuteness of its kings, and the unification of Germany under Bismarck. It was probably in part through Gebauer's inspiration that history became Hans's favorite subject. The assigned readings in school were mainly routine textbooks, but there were also some readings in classical historical writings, the highlight for Hans being portions of Thucydides's *History of the Peloponnesian War*. On his own Hans read more broadly in history. His father possessed some volumes by outstanding German historians, including Theodor Mommsen, Heinrich von Treitschke, and Leopold von Ranke, and Hans tackled such ambitious books as Ranke's *History of the Papacy* and Mommsen's *History of the Roman Empire*. He formed no particular historical viewpoint. History simply helped him to satisfy his wide curiosity and his appetite for information.[49]

During the 2 years that Hans spent in the fourth form he earned more "2s" than "3s," and ranked in each term second or third in his class. Perhaps Gebauer inspired him to perform better than usual, or Gebauer may have perceived strengths in the quiet but industrious pupil that his earlier teachers had missed. Gebauer remained his form master for the first year of the third form. At that point arithmetic (probably algebra) and Greek were added to the other subjects continued from the lower forms. Possibly feeling the pressure of

Figure 2.10 Wolf and Hans Krebs, about 1914.

studying three languages at once, Hans obtained only "3s" in French and Latin, and was on the borderline between "3" and "2" in Greek.[50]

In July 1914, Lise, Hans, and Wolf traveled with their mother to the Baltic coast, near the island of Rügen, to spend a 3-week summer holiday. Not too old for childhood beach games, the brothers built sand models of Hildesheim and of a ship that were elaborate enough to attract the attention of a photographer. Their peaceful stay was almost cut short by a letter from their father advising them to come home early because "dark clouds are appearing on the political horizon"; war, he thought, was imminent. A naval officer whom they knew dismissed, however, this idea. Maintaining that he would be among the first to be informed of such a situation, he assured the Krebses that no war was coming.

Nevertheless, as they arrived in Berlin on their way home at the end of the month, the newspapers were announcing the mobilization of France and Russia.[51]

After war was declared, in August 1914, most Germans were excitedly optimistic. A patriotic fervor swept the nation, which was persuaded that the German cause was just and would be vindicated. Hildesheimers shared this feeling. The 79th field regiment was immediately organized to leave for the front, and one of Alma Krebs's cousins was among the reservists called up. When the regiment marched from its barracks to the *Hauptbahnhof* to be loaded onto a train, Hans and his family were in the crowd gathered to see them off. The mood was cheerful. Germany had already invaded Belgium with apparent success, and these Hildesheimers were among the many Germans who looked forward to glorious victories.[52]

By September the celebratory spirit of August had already been shaken by the first casualty lists, which included the cousin that Hans and his family had watched off to war. He was reported missing in action. Soon the German thrust into Belgium stalemated in battles that caused horrendous losses, and the Russians moved into East Prussia.[53] Like other Germans, however, the Krebs family remained steadfastly patriotic and hopeful of an early victory. Georg Krebs volunteered to serve at the military barracks in Hildesheim, where he examined wounded soldiers who had been sent back there, and he published advice on the management of field injuries to the ears and nose. In a lecture on such injuries that he delivered to doctors at the Hildesheim Reserve Barracks in December 1914, he gave expression to his strong nationalistic emotions. Noting that in the Russo-Japanese war parts of soldier's ears had sometimes been bitten off in close combat, Dr. Krebs declared "I would not be surprised if the menagerie of wild people that our enemies, 'the representatives of civilization' lead against us, will act in similar ways."[54] Hans and Wolf accepted their father's view of the war just as they had always accepted his opinions on other questions. Hans followed the war news daily in the newspapers, and kept a map on which he drew the latest battle positions. Otherwise, through 1914 and early 1915 the war had little direct impact on the life of his family.[55]

At the age of 15 Hans decided that he wanted to go into medicine, a choice motivated mainly by his father's example. Georg Krebs's practice was thriving, and he had acquired great respect in Hildesheim. Born in Silesia, and trained as an ear, nose, and throat specialist in Berlin, he had settled in Hildesheim in 1892 in part because of its scenic surroundings, but largely because there was no one in the area at that time practicing his specialty. Dr. Krebs kept up with the latest advances in surgical and diagnostic techniques in an era of rapid medical change. He gave local lectures and published numerous articles in medical journals on the treatment of problems he had encountered in his practice involving, for example, infections of the sinuses and of the inner and outer ear and chronic sore throats.[56]

Hans sometimes watched with interest his father examine sputum under a microscope to check for the characteristic bacillus that might give the first warning of an incipient case of tuberculosis. What most impressed the son, however, was the attitude of patients toward his father. Although Georg Krebs had more the temperament of a surgeon than a physician, saw his patients briefly, and did not inquire into their personal problems, his general competence and his surgical skill gave them great confidence in him. By the time Hans was old enough to appreciate his father's professional standing, Georg Krebs's practice had grown to include not only Hildesheim, but the surrounding countryside. Many came by train to be seen or treated by him. The nearest other specialist in his field, 60 kilometers away in Göttingen, was heard to complain that Dr. Krebs attracted patients all the way from his doorstep. Hans had frequent opportunity to hear from patients filling the waiting room at Zingel 9 the appreciation they felt for his father, and to sense that a doctor's life was a gratifying one. He also knew that his father had to be available in the evenings and on Sundays to see patients who could not come during working hours, and that he had to be ready at any time to respond to emergencies, but that was no deterrent to a boy brought up to esteem discipline, reliability, and service as prime virtues.[57]

When Hans came to the definite conclusion that he would go into medicine, he anticipated that he would follow in his father's footsteps; that is, after completing his medical training he would join his father's practice. He reached these decisions on his own, before discussing them with his father; but he was undoubtedly influenced by his father's frequent admonitions to Wolf and to him that life was very difficult, competition was stiff, and it was not easy to make a living. Aware that sons often joined family businesses or professional practices as a way to gain some advantage in a competitive world, Hans welcomed the idea that he would be more secure working with his father until he could establish himself than he would be if he tried to move out directly on his own.[58]

His plan to follow a course in which his father's success offered him a protected entry into medical practice probably reflected also Hans's modest sense of his own potential that his father's skeptical comments continued to reinforce. Nothing Hans did seemed to persuade his father that his capacities were unusual. Hans managed to get into the "elite" division of his math class, which was given more difficult problems to solve than the rest of the class; but that accomplishment paled in comparison to Wolf, who was easily the best in his form in mathematics. Hans read widely in serious works of history and literature, but his father thought that he read too uncritically and unsystematically. When Hans was about 15, his father criticized him for not having a *Weltanschauung*, something he claimed that other boys of Hans's age had already developed. Hans could not respond to such an expectation, and probably did not understand what his father meant. He looked up some of the writings of Kant and other philosophers but could not make sense of them and thought that he could not produce a philosophy of life, which made him feel that he was very inferior.[59]

How did Georg Krebs really regard his elder son? The filters of time and of incomplete testimony allow us only a partial view. Hans later came to the conclusion that his father had misjudged him because he was in general not a good judge of other people. Wolf later felt that his father's view of Hans was somewhat biased by the fact that Hans was more inclined to argue with his father than Wolf himself was, and that there was, therefore, more friction between them; and also that Georg Krebs comparatively overestimated Wolf's talents because they were in areas he himself did not understand.[60] Hans's feeling that his father treated him with condescension was an effect of his father's actions toward him, but does not give direct insight into the father's intentions. Did Georg Krebs really think that Hans's abilities were ordinary, or did he believe that his criticisms would provoke Hans toward what would be in his view a better use of his talents? Was he slightly contemptuous, as Hans thought, or only insensitive to the way his comments would be taken by a shy adolescent who held him in awe? We have no way to reconstruct the father's side of the picture.

Notwithstanding his father's opinion, Hans was not merely absorbing information indiscriminately. If he did not develop a strong point of view, a distinct line of special interest, or a questioning attitude, he did respond with feeling and enthusiasm to some of his educational experiences. In geometry, for example, relationships such as that the square of the hypotenuse of a triangle is equal to the sum of the squares of the other two sides struck him as a kind of miracle. Much of the time spent on Latin seemed unrewarding to him because after 8 years of study he felt he did not have a command of the language; but when he reached the top form he took a special class on Horace, given by the headmaster, which he found "enthralling." This teacher showed his pupils how the quality of the translation of the Latin into German, the choice of the words that best expressed the aesthetic quality as well as the meaning of the Latin, could reveal the poetic nature of the original. Another high point occurred when Hans read the text of Plato's *Apology* in the original Greek and encountered the famous passage in which Socrates claimed to be wiser than others because he knew that he did not know. Hans was deeply impressed by this acknowledgment that there were limitations on human knowledge itself.[61]

Not all of his educational experiences at the Andreanum were so favorable. After 1914 the departure of most of the younger faculty for wartime service left a shortage of good teachers. Hans and Wolf both took physics from a teacher unqualified in the subject. Although Hans had one science subject in each of his last 4 years in Gymnasium — botany, zoology, chemistry, and physics — there was little time devoted to these subjects in comparison to the humanistic ones from which he derived most of his intellectual stimulation.[62]

The best marks that Hans received during his later Gymnasium years were for the essays that he had to write at frequent intervals. He was somewhat surprised that he did so well on them, because his essays were usually shorter than those of his schoolmates. The reason (he later surmised) that he did so well was that "I didn't say anything that I didn't know anything about." If his later writing style can be extrapolated backward, his school essays were probably also succinct, lucid, and carefully organized. When assigned once to write on a topic selected by himself, Hans discussed the matter with his father and chose the subject "On whom does history convey the title 'The Great'." After looking up the lives of emperors and kings, from Charlemagne to Frederick II, who had been so designated, he concluded that it was not as easy as he had thought to decide on the qualifications.[63]

Hans and Wolf both continued to study the piano through their Gymnasium years. At the local conservatory where they took lessons, their elementary and intermediate instructors had been rather ordinary, but when they reached the advanced level they encountered an inspiring teacher, Richard Gerlt. A fine pianist, Gerlt gave frequent concerts in Hildesheim. He was a strict teacher who demanded that his students learn both correct technique and proper interpretation. He believed in exposing his pupils to many and difficult pieces, each of which he gave them only 1 week to learn. He was also a warm, patient person who taught by example as well as precept. Hans and Wolf responded with enthusiasm to Gerlt and practiced very hard — an hour every day — to meet his standards. They were led through much of the classic repertoire, including all of the Beethoven sonatas, Brahms, and Grieg. Hans spent more time at the piano than at any other activity. He also learned that he had no special musical talent, that no amount of effort could take him past an average level of proficiency. The conservatory recitals in which he had to participate remained always a trial to him, because he never got over stage fright at having to perform in public. Nevertheless, the depth of involvement with music that he could attain through participating actively in it rather than merely listening to performances became very meaningful to him. He was particularly fond of playing the music of Beethoven, because of the broad range of feeling that it expressed to him.[64]

To the Krebs brothers Richard Gerlt was more than an outstanding teacher. He regularly talked to them about many aspects of life, ranging from the war and politics to the aesthetics of dressing well. Perhaps in part because he had come from Berlin, he appeared to them to have a more cosmopolitan outlook than they found elsewhere in their small town environment.[65]

During these years Hans had one friend, the son of another doctor in the neighborhood. He was several years younger than Hans, and went to a different school. Their principal activity in common was to go on long bicycle rides. Once they ventured on an expedition for several days, staying overnight in barns belonging to the patients of the boy's father. They talked mainly about politics and the war. On the whole, however, Hans remained solitary. He did not make close contacts with any of his schoolmates at the Andreanum, and the time left over from study and practice he spent mostly on activities he could carry on by himself or with Wolf. The brothers maintained their interest in bookbinding and collected their sheet music into handsome volumes. They made the covers from canvas that they took from old garden chairs, and paper that Hans had decorated with varied patterns by applying paste dyes with a sponge. Hans derived a particular pleasure from making these patterns. An outdoor activity that Hans and Wolf both took up was tennis, which they played frequently on a court belonging to one of their cousins. As usual, in sports, Wolf became better at tennis than Hans, who did rather poorly; but Hans nevertheless liked the game very much.[66]

III

As the Great War dragged on much longer than anyone had expected, it encroached increasingly on everyday life. One of the first restrictions that Hans and Wolf felt was that they were required to turn in the rubber tires from their bicycles. Hans thus lost the most important means he had had to venture out on his own beyond the immediate confines of his daily routines. In compensation his father permitted him to purchase a small second-hand single-place boat, with covered decks, that one paddled like a kayak. He could carry it to the *Innerste*, a small river winding through the southwest edge of the city, and paddle along its picturesque walls, buildings, and wooded banks.[67]

A cultural loss for the two boys was that the state theater that had opened in 1910 closed during the war just as they were old enough to begin attending it. The most serious deprivation for the Krebs family, as for most Germans, was the rationing of food that began in 1915 and that became more stringent over the next 2 years as shortages became increasingly severe. Georg Krebs might well have been able to obtain extra supplies for his family from patients who came from surrounding farms, but his patriotism did not permit him to seek special privileges. He insisted that they adhere strictly to the allotted rations. To supplement their limited diet the family went regularly to a town soup kitchen across the street for a primitive but filling meal. A legitimate way to improve their nutrition was to produce food for themselves. Installing a wire fence around some decrepit outbuildings that stood at the rear of their property, the family began raising chickens, ducks, and rabbits. This activity provided a welcome addition to their table, though it was a little hard on the boys because they grew fond of the animals.[68]

Then Hans had the idea that they should use the fertilizer the animals produced to grow vegetables. Commandeering some flower boxes, he placed them on the sunny flat roof covering the extension of the house constructed for his father's surgery, and with the aid of chicken manure and the urine that he collected from the rabbits, he grew the best tomatoes his family had ever seen. Expanding his contribution to their nutritional needs, Hans persuaded his somewhat reluctant father to allow him to convert portions of the decorative flower gardens around the house into plots to grow beans and maize. Not knowing that corn must be set out in rows to be pollinated, he planted the seeds between flowers, and grew stalks that bore no ears. Wolf contributed to the maintenance of the family household by repairing the plumbing when no plumbers were available.[69]

To make up for the growing scarcity of farm labor, schoolboys in Hildesheim were asked in the summer of 1917 to "volunteer" on nearby farms. Hans joined a group that weeded potato fields and then returned to harvest the potatoes. It was hard work, but he enjoyed it. For the often solitary boy it was a pleasant new experience to participate in a purposeful group activity. Afterward he was credited with having "achieved good success in agricultural service for the Fatherland."[70]

The later years of the war are usually depicted as ones of deprivation, hardship, and discouragement for the German civilian population. Hans's experience suggests that for a teenage boy in a relatively secure family, such conditions could also have positive effects. The same restrictions that made life less comfortable provided challenges to which he responded constructively and resourcefully.

By 1917 Hans was facing the possibility that if the war continued much longer he might have to take a direct role in it. He saw his older schoolmates called into the army as they reached conscription age, and anticipated his turn approaching. Although he later professed to have been "rather indifferent" about this prospect, there is some contemporary evidence that he felt at the time more positive feelings about his duty to the Fatherland. In August, his sister Lise, who had in the meantime become a Red Cross nurse and worked in a military hospital, sent him a birthday letter from a farm on which she was spending a holiday. In it she wrote, "With all my heart I wish you everything good for the new year, and that you will not have anything further to do with the war, even if you may perhaps count it as a 'good'" [wenn du es vielleicht auch zu dem "Guten" rechnen solltest]. Lise herself had volunteered to serve at the front, but her father had prevented it.[71] It would not be surprising if Hans too — an obedient son of a staunchly patriotic father, and a boy who had himself avidly followed the daily wartime news — should have wanted to do his part.

Soon after his 17th birthday Hans received a notice to report for a medical examination. In November 1917 he was certified, on grounds of his personal character and educational achievement, to be eligible for 1-year voluntary military service in a branch of the army of his choice when he reached military age, provided he was not first called to active duty. In the spring of 1918 he was advanced after 1½ years from the Prima to the top or Oberprima form at the Andreanum, in anticipation that he would be conscripted when he reached the age of 18. At about the time of his birthday he received the expected order to report for duty within 3 weeks. In September special arrangements were made for him to take the Abitur, the final examinations required to complete the Gymnasium, ahead of schedule. On each of several consecutive days he wrote a 3-hour examination. These consisted of translations from Latin, Greek, French, and English into German, essays in history and geography, and tests in mathematics and physics. He obtained six marks of "good" and two of "satisfactory," a performance that exempted him from having to take any oral examinations. He himself thought that he had not done very well, and that he had been graded leniently in consideration of his impending military service.[72]

With his Gymnasium education thus rushed to completion Hans reported with his suitcase in hand to the designated assembly point in Hildesheim and was assigned to a signal corps unit in Hanover. With a group of about 20 other conscriptees who had drawn the same assignment, he was transported the 30 kilometers to the post where his basic training was to begin.[73]

* * *

In his autobiography Hans Krebs expressed puzzlement over the "fatalistic way" in which he and others of his generation had accepted their conscription at this late stage in a war that Germany could no longer win.[74] It is clear, however, that the passage of time had given him a perspective vastly different from that of the young man of 18 who reported for duty in September 1918. When shown the passage quoted above from his sister's letter, he commented "I must have thought...one has to do one's duty and carry on fighting."[75] His original feelings had obviously long vanished from his recollection of himself. It is true that by the time his call came the German position had become hopeless, two of its allies had collapsed, and its own last offensive effort had just failed; but Hans knew none of this at the time (as he noted in his autobiography), because the censored German newspapers he followed so closely did not report the situation objectively. Richard Gerlt had spoken to Hans at his last piano lesson in a "guarded" way about the uselessness of continuing to fight, but no one else either inside or outside his family had expressed to him such a view.[76] Undoubtedly Krebs's later recollection that he had been "indifferent" was correct in the general sense that he had answered the call neither with a sense of grand mission nor of opposition; but a boy whose milieu both at home and in school was imbued with nationalistic pride, to whom reliability and discipline were upheld as cardinal virtues, could not have been entirely unmoved to be about to enter the service that in his society most prominently symbolized those values. A boy anxious to conform to the expectations placed on him could not have been oblivious to the coming test of his capacity to meet his obligations to the Germany to which he felt fortunate to belong. A relatively small, physically timid boy must, however, also have felt some apprehension about how he would fare under the rigors of military training. An imaginative boy who had just had to write out a statement directing that "after death my body be cremated,"[77] could not have avoided some thought about the potential risks that he faced. A boy who had, except for occasional well-protected family holidays, lived his entire life within a radius of his childhood home that he could cover on his bicycle must have had some sense of momentous change as he was transported for the first time toward a life that would separate him from his home and family.

3

Outward Movement

The signals division was an outgrowth of the growing complexity of military communications during the course of the long war. As this function became increasingly important, specialized units were formed to provide it. The Hanover regiment (*Nachrichten Abteilung 10*) that Hans Krebs entered had only recently been established, and a new barracks had been built for it. He found himself, therefore, in exceptionally comfortable living conditions for a trainee.[1]

Plunged immediately into the routines of basic training, Hans learned how to dress properly in his uniform, to drill, to fire a carbine, to fit himself into a rigid system of discipline, and to take orders. Each day he attended lessons in communication skills. He learned Morse code and used it to send messages by telegraph.[2]

Whatever he may have anticipated, Hans apparently adjusted well to this initial phase in army life. He was particularly impressed by the strict procedures followed to ensure that orders were understood and carried out without error. The soldier given an order was required to repeat it in full, identifying himself in the third person by name and rank, and to report back afterward that he had completed the order, repeating it again in full. Hans appreciated the necessity for such elaborate rituals to guarantee reliable performance under the stress of combat, and he was comfortable within a system that permitted no excuses for failure to be totally reliable and punctual. Even the coarse, exaggerated language known as *Kasernen Hochstil* appealed to his sense of humor. He thought it quite funny, for example, when a fellow soldier reported for duty with one of the numerous buttons on his uniform undone and the noncommissioned officer in charge shouted at him "this fellow comes to his duty half-naked."[3]

After he had completed several weeks of basic training, Hans was allowed to live off the post, and stayed with a relative in Hanover. He had a photograph taken of himself in his uniform. The rather formal pose suggests not only confidence, but a quiet sense of pride. All of the earlier surviving photographs of Hans are clearly those of a boy. In his military uniform one can see emerging the features of a handsome young man.[4]

Figure 3.1 Hans Krebs in uniform.

The regiment trained through the month of October with high morale and no information, other than that in the censored newspapers, about the progress of the war. Hans and his fellow soldiers were, therefore, taken by surprise on November 7 or 8 when a noncommissioned officer informed them that a revolution had broken out and that they were to be issued ammunition to combat it. The soldiers waited in readiness for about 2 hours, but no orders were given, because, as they probably learned afterward, their officers had disappeared, slipping away in civilian clothes. Finally a group of sailors appeared, explained to them that they had come from Kiel, where they had taken part in a mutiny against an expected order to engage the British fleet in a last desperate naval battle, and told the soldiers to join the revolution. Apparently no one did. Hans and the others waited for several days, but no one came to tell them what they should do. Finally he and most of the soldiers in his regiment decided to go home.[5]

While still in Hanover Hans encountered Erich Stern, the son of close friends of his parents, who had also been in the army for 2 months, in a field artillery unit stationed in another part of the same city. Less fortunate than Hans, Erich had had to live in an old and dirty barracks. They decided to join forces for the trip to Hildesheim, along with a girl friend and a former classmate of Erich. The trains were not running on schedule, and they had to wait for several hours on the platform to board one headed toward home. When they had traveled about three-fourths of the distance, a group of soldiers stopped the train, and Hans and his companions had to walk the last 6 miles carrying their belongings in their backpacks.[6]

Hans arrived at about the time — November 11, 1918 — that the armistice between Germany and the allies was signed. He found conditions at home about as they had been when he left. Concern over the fragile political situation in Germany was balanced by relief that the protracted war was finally over. By then the newly formed provisional government headed by Friedrich Ebert was acting in cooperation with the army to restore order in the face of uprisings and other signs of national disorganization that appeared to threaten the social fabric. From local perspectives, such as that of Hans Krebs in Hildesheim, a substantial degree of order and discipline still remained. Despite its precarious overall situation the new government retained a sense of responsibility toward those who had served in the nation's armed forces. From the newspapers Hans learned that all military personnel should report back to their posts, where they would receive their discharge papers if they could state that they had other occupations to take up.[7]

The sudden turn of events confronted Hans, who had until a few days before expected to spend at least a year in the army, with the need to decide quickly what he wanted to do next. Since he had already obtained his *Abitur* from the Gymnasium, he was eligible to matriculate to a university. He and Erich Stern talked their situations over and decided that they would both enroll as medical students. Because of the unsettled political circumstances and the unreliability of transportation — the trains were running, but not on time, a relatively chaotic state of affairs by German standards — they chose the nearest major university. The University of Göttingen was only 60 kilometers from Hildesheim. Returning to their respective barracks in Hanover near the end of November, Hans and Erich each stated that he wished to have his discharge in order to become a university student. Their requests were immediately approved.[8]

The winter semester had already begun, as usual, during the last week of October. In recognition of their need to make up lost time, discharged members of the armed forces were permitted to enroll in universities whenever they were ready. Unlike many veterans who had served for several years, Hans and Erich were enabled through this dispensation to begin their university education sooner than they normally would have done. They set off together for Göttingen by train, on December 4. Erich wore his uniform, because he had no other suit left.[9]

Hans's father and his Gymnasium teachers had imparted to him not only the great value of a university education, but the sense that the university years were a time of new freedom and a high point in one's life. As Hans traveled the short distance through the tranquil countryside between Hildesheim and Göttingen, the chilly atmosphere of an unheated train in November undoubtedly did not dampen his high expectations.[10]

I

The first task facing Hans and Erich in Göttingen was to find lodgings. There were lists available of private homes with rooms for rent, and they each obtained one the same day they arrived, but in different parts of the city. Nevertheless they kept in close contact, carrying on much of their initial university activity together. Warm, attractive and outgoing, a direct and engaging conversationalist, Erich appeared to Hans to radiate confidence, to have a special talent for understanding other people, and to establish empathetic rapport quickly and easily. Hans was himself still too shy to say very much in groups; and in social situations Erich usually took the lead.[11] Two weeks after their arrival in Göttingen, Hans's mother wrote him:

> I am glad that you have made friends with Erich Stern and that you often do things together with him. He is a nice, modest young man, he had always pleased me even as a child, when I often met him at the Fränkels. It is only a shame that you live so far from one another.[12]

As a boy Hans had not known Erich well, despite his parents' friendship with Erich's uncle and aunt (the Fränkels), and they had not been classmates because Erich had gone to the Realgymnasium instead of the Andreanum.[13] Now Erich became the first close friend that Hans had ever made. Their association must have eased considerably Hans's early steps toward the new freedom of university life.

Hans enrolled officially as a medical student on December 10. His first preoccupation was with anatomy. Attending his initial lecture in "Systematic Anatomy Pt I," Hans found himself immediately in difficulty. The subject was the larynx; but Hans had never heard even the basic technical terms, such as "epithelium," that Prof. Merkel used in describing the organ. He made a frantic effort to catch up. Outside the lectures themselves, university students were left entirely on their own to organize their studies. Hans quickly bought anatomy textbooks and began reading what he had missed. His capacity to absorb easily large amounts of information now stood him in good stead, and he soon had matters under control. He had also to purchase his own dissection equipment to enter the anatomical laboratory for the traditional first-year medical student's encounter with a cadaver. Here too he must have worked long and hard to overcome his late start. When the winter semester ended, on January 25, 1919, he received the usual certificate attesting his participation, with an additional notation that "the candidate has completed the required number of preparations."[14]

Leaving home did not free Hans from the responsibility to keep in close touch with his family. Like most German families his parents were anxious to receive news from him every few days, despite his protests that he was not good at writing letters. His mother, who handled the return correspondence, had to coax and admonish him to do so, to praise him when he did, and to remind him also not to omit sending birthday letters to his grandmother and other relatives. Connections were also maintained by the fact that, to conserve money, Hans regularly sent his clothes home to be laundered and repaired, and sometimes received a sausage or other extra food in the return package.[15]

The major news from the home front during Hans's first weeks away was that his father had taken "Uncle Arnold" — actually a first cousin of Hans's mother — into his practice. Much younger than his father, Uncle Arnold had practiced the same ear, nose, and throat specialty in Hanover before the war, but had spent the entire war as an army medical officer, and on his return he had to start over. Meanwhile Georg Krebs's practice had continued to grow. Burdened doubly over the past 5 years by the increase in the number of his own patients and his service in the local military hospital, he was by the end of the war fatigued and in need of help. By January 1919, he and Uncle Arnold were practicing together at Zingel 9, and both were kept very busy.[16]

For the benefit of returning veterans German universities inserted, in 1919, a special *Zwischensemester* between the winter semester and the beginning of the normal summer semester. During this concentrated two months Hans continued hearing anatomy lectures and performing dissections. He added lectures in zoology, introduction to inorganic chemistry, and "The most important [aspects] of experimental physics" by Prof. Robert Pohl. All of the lectures seemed very good to Hans, and he attended them faithfully. For the course "bones and tendons" Erich Stern, like many other medical students, acquired a skeleton to learn the details of bone structure. Hans had only a skull, but he spent much time in the anatomical museum studying the bones on display there. Their schedule was demanding. They attended four or five lectures, beginning at 8 AM, each morning 6 days per week. After an hour for lunch they spent the afternoon carrying out their anatomical dissections, with some late afternoon lectures ending at about 6 PM. The evenings were filled with homework.[17] In one of his letters home Hans must have described himself as extremely busy but pleased with what he was doing. His mother answered in February, "You seem not to have time on your hands, and that is good; for '*Arbeit macht das Leben süß*' as the poet says, and especially when your present activity so well suits you."[18]

Continuing shortages made the winter of 1918–1919 uncomfortable for students as for other Germans. To conserve electricity they were required to turn out their lights at 10 PM. The food served by their landladies and at the *Mittagtisch* was often inadequate, and Hans complained in a letter home that he was too cold in his poorly heated room. For him and for others accustomed for several years to wartime deprivations, however, these were minor inconveniences. Hans compensated for the limited reading time available in the evenings by getting up very early to study in the morning light. His family sent him food to supplement what appeared on the table, and he and Erich were able to join a more satisfactory *Mittagtisch* in March for what Hans's mother considered the "unbelievable price" of 1.3 marks per day. His mother did not treat Hans's reports about being cold as a serious problem. "Visit some acquaintances who have a warm room," she counseled him, "or go into a pub, a little glass of beer will not harm you." It is unlikely that Hans followed this last advice. Although he had no objection in principle to the beer drinking which played so prominent a part in German student life, he did not much care for it himself and preferred nonalcoholic beverages whenever they were available.[19]

Coping with material difficulties was made easier by the fact that the situation seemed to be improving. In January Hans's mother wrote that they had had dinner guests two nights before, "for the first time in years...since we just now finally have something to eat." By March she reported that "we have received all sorts of luxuries, such as butter, eggs, and roasts....When you come home in two weeks you will still share in consuming our riches."[20] Hans was also soon able to move to a more satisfactory rooming house in Göttingen. One inconvenience that was not alleviated was the overcrowding in lecture halls and laboratories. The returning veterans made the congestion even worse; but the serious attitude of these mature students and their eagerness to get on with their education reinforced Hans's own industrious habits.[21]

At the end of the *Zwischensemester* Hans and Erich had only a 1-week holiday in Hildesheim before returning to Göttingen to begin the summer semester. Erich continued to take his shy friend "under his wing." They attended lectures and went to their noontime meals together, and when they had time they played tennis or took walks together. Hans still confronted academic subjects for which he felt at first unprepared. At the initial lecture in inorganic chemistry given by the well-known chemist Adolf Windaus, Hans turned to Erich and whispered, "Oh God, I can never learn that [*O'Gott, das lerne ich nie*]." With his Realgymnasium background Erich was initially better prepared than Hans to cope with the sciences; but he soon came to appreciate that Hans overcame the deficits in his prior scientific training by concentrating intently on his studies, and that underneath the quiet exterior was a person with great determination and drive.[22]

Although he took a physics laboratory as well as the chemistry lectures, anatomy continued to dominate Hans's academic activity. Besides gross anatomy he now attended lectures in histology and embryology. In addition he took foundations of botany, microscopic botany, and "botanical demonstrations and excursions," the field trips occurring on weekends under the leadership of the professor of botany Albert Peter. A knowledge of plants was regarded as important in medical education, because the majority of drugs were prepared from herbs and other plant substances; but Hans was motivated more by the special interest in plants he had had ever since his father began identifying flowers for him during family hikes.[23]

The seriousness with which Hans pursued his academic work did not preclude other activities. On their own away from home for the first time, Hans and Erich felt the attraction of expanding horizons. Intellectually they did not limit

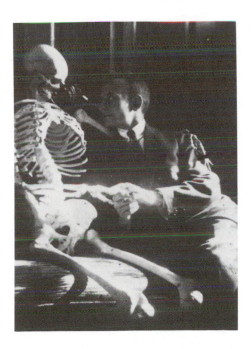

Figure 3.2 Göttingen, 1919. Above, Erich Stern with skeleton. Below, Erich Stern and Hans Krebs.

themselves to the courses required for their medical training, but attended lectures in philosophy, history of art, and other subjects that interested them. The daughter of the landlady in the pension where Erich lived organized social gatherings that sometimes included musical performances or cultural lectures, and Hans and Erich were usually present for them. They and other students talked about all the subjects that young people to whom new worlds are opening up generally do.[24]

Near the end of May Lise wrote Hans from Hildesheim with news of the family and of a recent visit she had made to Berlin. She asked him what friends he was making, and "what sort of 'ladies' you are going out with?"[25] To the latter question Hans could have given no answer. Although he was becoming more sociable, he had at age 19 not yet acquired the interest in women that preoccupied many of his fellow students and probably filled much of the talk he heard. His older sister was, in fact, probably trying to encourage him along. In her view the Krebs's "develop late, but hopefully so much the better."[26]

During his first 6 months away from home Hans surprised and pleased his family by writing frequent humorous, entertaining letters to his parents, his sister while she was in Berlin, and his relatives. During the early summer, however, he gave vent to another side of his temperament — a very limited tolerance for anything he considered a waste of time — when he stated in one of his letters that those he was receiving from home contained too much trivial gossip: that is, news that "so-and-so did this and so-and-so did this."[27] His mother responded with annoyance on July 3:

> Since my letters displease you so, for it is only to these that your letters can refer, I shall spare you from that in the future. But you should not be surprised if you only seldom hear anything from home.[28]

Hans's letter had undoubtedly been tactless, but the sharpness of his mother's reaction probably reflected the fact that, unknown to him, she was becoming seriously depressed. The main cause may have been endogenous, for several other members of her family had experienced deep depressions. Her mental state was probably also exacerbated by undernourishment and weariness left by the prolonged stress of the wartime period. Georg Krebs, overworked and fatigued himself, tried unsuccessfully to comfort her. Wolf, who was still at home and could see that his mother was not behaving normally, was much concerned, but could do little.[29]

By the time Hans approached the end of the summer semester at Göttingen, critical political events had taken place in Germany. The National Assembly in Weimar had drawn up the constitution for a Republic, and the Versailles Treaty had officially ended the state of war. The harshness of the treaty terms evoked bitter reactions in Germany. Drastic forced reductions in the army produced discontents that threatened the authority of the government.[30] Hans and his fellow students must have discussed these events at *Mittagtisch* and elsewhere with great interest and some anxiety. The centers of unrest were, however, mainly in Berlin and to the east, far from their daily lives. Their everyday

world was becoming more regular, the trains were once again reliable,[31] and
it appeared to Hans and Erich now safe to venture further afield for the next
stages of their education.

German students traditionally shifted several times from one university to
another during the course of their education, a process facilitated by the
standardized curricula available at all German-speaking universities. Students
chose to shift in part to hear professors with distinguished reputations lecture in
their special fields, in part to broaden their own social and cultural experiences.
Student conversations and the grapevine were probably the strongest influences
on the choices that most individuals made. Erich decided to move to the
University of Heidelberg for the winter term. He was attracted mainly by the
romantic aura of Heidelberg.[32] Hans had scarcely more specific grounds for
his choice of the University of Freiburg in Baden, in the southwest corner of
Germany. He knew in general that Freiburg had a strong reputation, but what
appealed most to him was the prospect of hiking and skiing in the beautiful
nearby Black Forest. He was motivated also by a desire "to get away from
home and see something else," and Freiburg was "really about the farthest place
I could go."[33] Having tasted the "new freedom," Hans was clearly ready for
more of it. Loyal though he remained to his family, he may well have sensed
a need to distance himself further from its hitherto dominating influence on his
life.

Aside from listening to lectures, German preclinical medical students
normally had no personal contact with their professors. They were not evaluated
in individual courses, and it was left entirely up to them to organize themselves
to learn the subjects in which they would be examined after five semesters in the
Physikum. Under such circumstances it was hard to know where one stood, and
students tended to size up their own progress mainly by comparison with what
other students with whom they talked seemed to know.[34] Quiet as he was,
Hans found that in university for the first time he made friends, in part because
he and many of his fellow students shared the new experience of being away
from home, in part because he met there others with interests similar to his own.
Although he did not establish close ties with anyone beside Erich at Göttingen,
he did become well enough acquainted with another student to visit him at his
home in Lüneberg at the close of the summer semester on the way to a short
holiday at a resort on the Baltic Sea coast.[35]

The shortcomings in his scientific preparation at the Gymnasium that brought
Hans some initial difficulties as a medical student did not provoke him to regret
the humanistic orientation of his prior education. So highly did he value that
form of education that soon afterward — perhaps during his first university year
— he undertook to make up on his own a climactic literary experience that he
had missed by leaving the Andreanum early to enter the army. During their last
year the Gymnasium pupils normally read Goethe's *Faust*, one of the masterpiec-
es of the German cultural tradition. Hans bought a "tiny" volume containing the
text of *Faust* and began to study it carefully. To fill in for the explanations and
exercises that his Gymnasium teacher would have provided, he looked up
commentaries on the poem. The complexity of Goethe's grandest work, with its

many references to Greek and Roman mythology as well as to Christian traditions, was far more than he could take in at once; but, to judge from the importance that *Faust* held for him throughout his adult life, it is safe to surmise that it absorbed him deeply even at his first reading. He was probably impressed even then by Faust's humble declaration at the beginning of the long poem that although he had studied law, medicine, and theology, he was no cleverer than when he began ("Da steh ich nun, ich armer Thor! Und bin so klug als wie zuvor"). He was probably already then moved by the ending in which Faust was redeemed from his pact with the devil because he had never ceased striving ("Gerettet ist das edle Glied/der Geisterwelt von Bösen/Wer immer strebend sich bemüht/Den können wir erlösen"). Perhaps even on his first reading he memorized some of the verses that he could still quote readily 60 years later. To learn passages by heart, as he had been required to do so often in school, was not difficult for Hans, and he liked having a store of quotations to use on fitting occasions. Perhaps in part because he was reticent about expressing his inner emotions directly, he found a special appeal in the writings of the poet with "a unique gift for putting simple and deep feelings into appropriate words."[36]

II

In September 1919, Hans left for Freiburg to find lodgings there. Then, on the 23rd he took the train to Baden-Baden, a fashionable spa near Karlsruhe, to join his family in celebration of his parents 25th wedding anniversary. Georg Krebs had planned this reunion away from home in part to avoid a large gathering of relatives, and in part because he hoped that a holiday would improve his wife's spirits. Wolf took time out from school to come, along with Lise, and they all dined at a luxury hotel, enjoying a quality of food that they had not seen for several years. Hans stayed for a few days and then returned to Freiburg for the winter semester, which started in October, while Georg and Alma Krebs remained several weeks in Baden-Baden.[37]

Soon after this event Lise went to Hamburg to enter an innovative school that had recently been founded to prepare people for social work. About a week later her father asked her to come home temporarily to manage the household, because her mother had become ill. Without hesitation Lise returned and assumed that responsibility.[38] No one expected Hans to alter his educational plans.

At Freiburg, painstakingly detailed anatomical instruction continued to be central to Hans's training and he spent much of his time in the dissecting room. In addition, he was exposed to a larger range of biological questions. Lectures on "bacteriology and the lower funguses" not only served as a practical introduction to the subject, but presented Robert Koch as the founder of bacteriology, and made Hans aware of the great advances in medical diagnosis that had resulted during the previous decades through the progress of that field. Having bypassed physiology at Göttingen because it was not well taught there, Hans was now able to attend lectures on that subject by the well-known

Figure 3.3 Krebs family at silver anniversary of Georg and Alma Krebs, September 1919.

physiologist Johannes von Kries, who had made important discoveries concerning vision. Hans found von Kries's lectures sound and thoughtful, though not very exciting.[39]

In the early twentieth century, bacteriology and physiology were well-established foundations for a "scientific" medicine. Hans's curriculum also included aspects of biology that were less directly connected with practical applications. One of these was a course on evolutionary theory, in which he was introduced to Darwinism, as well as to Ernst Haeckel's famous "biogenetic law" — ontogeny recapitulates phylogeny. Hans's father owned a copy of Darwin's *Origin of Species*, which Hans had probably not yet read through, but that had at least prepared him to appreciate the basic importance of the question of the descent of humans from lower organisms.[40]

At the same time Hans took a zoology course that included lectures and a "microscopic *Prakticum.*" The lecturer was one of the most distinguished biologists in Germany, Hans Spemann. At the height of his career after 25 years of brilliant experimental investigations of the processes that determine the developmental fate of various parts of amphibian embryos, Spemann had recently arrived in Freiburg to become director of the Zoological Institute. Spemann strongly believed that medical students should be familiar with the manifold forms of life, and that zoology must remain a vital part of medical education.

Hans Krebs was impressed by the systematic manner in which Spemann surveyed the morphological diversity of the animal kingdom, but more so by the beautiful drawings that he drafted on the blackboard during his lectures to illustrate their forms.   Spemann also referred frequently to his predecessor August Weismann, so that Hans became familiar with the overarching questions concerning the germ plasm, heredity, and development that Weismann had raised a generation earlier.   Besides all this, Hans took organic experimental chemistry, experimental physics, and ionic theory — ten courses in all, including two laboratories.[41]   It was a demanding schedule even for one who organized his time effectively and concentrated intently on his work.

When Hans had last seen his mother in Baden-Baden she had appeared reasonably well to him, but after her return to Hildesheim Alma Krebs became more severely depressed.   She would not eat regularly, and she steadily lost weight.   For Wolf, who could see his mother's condition worsen from day to day, it was an extremely trying time.   One day when he came home from school she was lying in bed under heavy sedation.   While Wolf, Lise, and her husband stayed with her, she said to them that she had had the best husband and the best children that she could have hoped for.   A few hours later she died.[42]

Hans, who was generally aware that his mother was depressed, but did not realize how serious her condition had become, received the news in a telegram from his father.   It was "a complete shock" to him.   He could not believe it. Summoned home for the funeral, he found his father controlled but very much upset.   Not knowing how he would manage on his own, Georg Krebs asked Lise to stay on in the house, and she unquestioningly gave up her plans to train for social work.[43]

The two sons were not told what had caused their mother's death.   Wolf, who had been close by, felt that she must have made an attempt on her own life.[44] Hans, who was far away, inferred that she had been a victim of the influenza epidemic that had been causing so many sudden deaths in Europe for the past 2 years.   In his autobiography he later stated "I felt I had lost an irreplaceable support."[45]   It is likely that he did not appreciate how much support he received from his mother until she was not there.   Looking back much later on his childhood he maintained that his mother had been relatively uninfluential on his development.[46]   Quiet and delicate, dominated by her husband,[47] Alma Krebs had been responsible for those aspects of a secure home environment that growing children are most apt to take for granted.   As young adults they felt keenly the loss of the unobtrusive presence that had bound them together as a family.

As the youngest member, the "Nestling" of the family, Wolf was probably the most strongly affected by his mother's death.   He, too, experienced a depression, which he was able to overcome by taking refuge in a project — the construction and installation of a burglar alarm in the house — that could fully absorb his attention.[48]   Hans kept his emotions to himself and returned quickly to Freiburg to resume his studies.[49]

In the early stage of his preclinical training Hans applied his strong capacity to absorb information to learn the foundations of what appeared to him as established fields of scientific knowledge; just as he had in earlier years absorbed historical and other types of information without questioning how such knowledge is acquired.   During his first semester at Freiburg he began to appreciate that knowledge is changeable and discoverable.   His first glimpse of this insight came from anatomy lectures in which his teachers repeatedly mentioned that there were many small variations in the details of anatomical structure.   They stressed that if one observed very carefully, and were alert for possible deviations from the norm, such as a nerve in an unusual position, one might even get one's name attached to some new anatomical feature.[50]

More absorbing to Hans were accounts from some of his professors of their own discoveries that they incorporated into their lectures.   Surprisingly Spemann did not discuss his own work; but von Kries dwelt extensively on his.   Von Kries described, among other things, the way in which he had discovered that the rods in the retina are responsible for color vision, the cones for vision in dim light.   Hans found this an intriguing story.   He was also interested in the stories that his anatomy professor Eugen Fischer, whose research discipline was anthropology, told about his field work with South African tribes.   Through such personal accounts Hans began to perceive science not only as the systematic body of knowledge that he found in his textbooks, but as a lively human activity.[51]

His heavy schedule of lectures, laboratories, and studies in Freiburg still left Hans enough time for other activities.   His enthusiasm for theater drew him to see a play or an opera almost every week.   He hiked and cycled in the Black Forest as he had planned to do.   His botanical interests also flourished. Regularly he went along on expeditions to the surrounding areas led by the professor of botany, a native of Hildesheim.   Hans especially enjoyed these field trips because the flora was different from that familiar to him in Hanover, and because the professor's interest in ecology led him to see that there was more to botany than collecting and identifying plants: that plants lived in communities adapted in complex ways to their environments.   During the winter he also took up skiing.[52]

At the end of the winter semester, Hans went home to Hildesheim.   Far from weary of learning, he quickly signed up to attend adult education lectures in botany, history of art, and "the nature of life" at the Hildesheim *Volkshoch- schule*.   At home Lise was managing the household efficiently, and remained very caring toward her younger brothers; but the absence of his mother must have brought home strongly to Hans that the intact family in which he had grown up was irretrievably lost.   His father was weary from overwork and disillusioned by the outcome of the war.   Unlike many bourgeois Germans, however, he did not yearn for the old order.   The former proud nationalist now leaned toward pacifism.   Although alarmed by the left-wing Spartacists and Communists, he supported the new Republic, and he favored the Democratic Party because he believed that it stood for freedom and tolerance.   His children, still much influenced by their father's views, placed their hopes too in a new democratic order.[53]

Figure 3.4 Hans Krebs in 1919.

That democratic order was far from secure in the spring of 1920. The ability of the Social Democratic government to retain the loyalty of the army remained questionable, and the various private armies that sprang up in part to counteract the Bolshevik threat, in part to absorb the many former soldiers left without occupations by the drastic reductions in the regular army forced by the Allies, continuously threatened the stability of a nation struggling to recover from both hardships and the humiliations of defeat. Such events remained most of the time far from the immediate lives of the members of the Krebs family, although Lise had witnessed manifestations of a general strike in Berlin the year before when she visited there.[54] Now, however, a sudden political crisis touched very close to them.

On March 13, while Hans was at home, he and his family heard, along with the rest of the world, that a rightist political organization named the *National Vereinigung* had overthrown the government in Berlin and established a new one headed by a former Prussian civil servant named Wolfgang Kapp. The legitimate government had retreated to Stuttgart and called for a general strike in defence of the republic. German labor unions responded strongly to the call, and in Berlin and other cities all public services came to a halt.[55]

In Hildesheim too the general strike was effective. On Saturday, March 13, the daily presses were shut down, and streetcars and trains, milk deliveries, and the postal and telegraph services stopped. Sunday was quiet, but trouble broke out in the *Godehardplatz* on Monday, due to a rumor that a shipment of weapons and munitions made to the local *Landsratsamt* the previous week was intended to arm reactionary forces. When a local national guard, the *Sarstedt Einwohner-wehr*, entered the city and tried to obtain the weapons, crowds stormed into the *Landsratsamt* building, disarmed some public officials, and attempted to make the weapons unusable. Meanwhile, a rightist military unit, the *Goslar Jäger*, on a march toward Hanover, happened into Hildesheim, surrounded the *Einwohner-wehr*, occupied the railway station and a barracks, and took some legal officials and the executive committee of the union captive. After a relatively calm night, punctured with occasional gun shots, there were further outbreaks the next day, machine gun emplacements appeared, crowds gathered in the streets, and at one point machine guns fired into the crowd, killing six bystanders. By March 20, units of the regular army had restored order and forced the Goslar Jäger to withdraw. Meanwhile in Berlin the inept self-proclaimed Kapp government had already collapsed, and what became known as the "Kapp Putsch" was quickly over.[56]

Much of the disturbance in Hildesheim took place within a few streets of the Krebs home. On the 15th of March, Hans and his family heard shooting directly in front of their house between contingents of the opposing armies lined up on the wide pavement of the Zingel. The incident was quickly over, and Georg Krebs went out into the street to say that any casualties could be brought into his office; but none had resulted from this encounter. Returning from a piano lesson, Wolf had encountered the forces on the south side of Zingel, who would not let him through even though he pleaded that he was only trying to get home. By using a small side street, however, he was able to slip around them unnoticed.[57]

It was disturbing to Hans to witness at close hand the existence of opposed armed forces so ready to engage in open violence. The confrontation had quickly evaporated, however, and, as he later put it, "it was of no importance to my life"[58]; that is, the event did not divert him from his immediate or longer term goals. Soon afterward he returned to Freiburg to begin the summer semester.

III

During the summer semester of 1920 Hans Krebs took more courses than he had during the previous semester, 14 in all. They included a continuation of physiology by Van Kries; general physiology from another lecturer; three anatomy lectures under Fischer, one of them in histology; experimental physics, a chemistry *Prakticum*, and "work in the anatomical laboratory." This last, as well as two lecture courses in embryology he took from Wilhelm von Möllendo-rff, a recently appointed assistant to Fischer, who had already achieved distinction for his work on the vital staining of tissues.[59]

In Möllendorff's embryology course Krebs was among a small group of students who volunteered to demonstrate for other students some of the microscope slides used to observe early stages of development. One of the students to whom he gave such a demonstration was Hermann Blaschko, who had recently transferred to Freiburg after beginning his medical studies part time at the University of Berlin in 1917. Krebs and Blaschko discovered that they shared a stronger interest in the scientific side of their medical education than most of their fellow students, and they began getting together to discuss problems that had been presented in the lectures they attended. The son of an eminent histologist and physician, Blaschko had spent some time during the war as a technician in the laboratory of the distinguished physiologist Nathan Zuntz, who was a friend of his father. Convinced by this experience that he would eventually go into research, Blaschko was nevertheless persuaded by his father that he must first complete his medical training. Soon he and Krebs became good friends.[60]

Less assiduous in attending lectures than Krebs, Blaschko went only to those that interested him. He was most attracted to the physiological lectures of von Kries. For both Blaschko and Krebs the lectures of Franz Knoop in physiologi-cal chemistry also commanded a special attention during the summer semester of 1920. As we have seen in Chapter 1, Knoop had carried out, 16 years earlier, pioneering experiments from which he had derived the β-oxidation theory of fatty acid degradation, still, in 1920, the only well-established sequence of intermediary metabolic reactions; and he had become the strongest advocate of a physiological chemistry whose central object would be to identify all of the reactions connecting foodstuffs with final breakdown products. Knoop oriented his course lectures around this point of view. Knoop took his teaching responsibilities very seriously. He presented his lectures in a free form, from sparse notes; but he prepared carefully for them, even after lecturing for many years on the same subject. He spoke in a controlled, deliberate manner, but with a capacity to portray in vivid language the broad contours of his subject.[61]

From the text of an inaugural lecture as ordinary professor of physiological chemistry that Knoop gave about this time we can sample some of the general views that he probably developed in fuller detail during his course lectures. "No definition of the concept of life," he declared,

Can overlook the significance of the unique chemical capacity of living organisms — there are no vital functions that take place without chemical motion. Alongside the continuity of the morphological substrates that Weismann established 25 years ago for his germ plasm appears the continuity of the chemical motion of this same organic material, which lasts uninterruptedly from the first cell from which we originate and comes to an end only with the death of the individual.... The task of pursuing these finely tuned motions in all their phases, from the most diverse points

Figure 3.5 Franz Knoop. From *Z. physiol. chem.*, 283 (1948). opp p. 1.

of view — that is, of doing *physiological chemistry* — therefore appears unusually exciting.[62]

"The true goal of biochemistry" Knoop probably told his students many times, "is to reduce the chemical transformations to an unbroken series of equations that will permit an overview of all phases of synthesis and decomposition, of the binding of energy and of its release."[63]

In the physiological lectures that Hans had previously heard, and in his physiology textbooks, metabolism had been presented mainly in terms of the quantitative relations between the material intake and output of the body, the steps in between having been treated as almost entirely unknown.[64] Knoop too pointed out that little progress had been made in this direction. "What is the present state of our knowledge?" he asked: "Here we must be modest — very modest — when we evaluate our results and think about the magnitude of the problem"; but he called urgently for greater efforts and a fuller application of chemistry to overcome the difficulties the subject presented.[65]

Knoop devoted a large part of his lectures to his own earlier investigations.[66]
His discovery of β-oxidation and his experiments on the deamination of amino
acids he regarded as models of the approach that could eventually reveal all of
the intermediate stages of oxidative decomposition. He stressed also that the
reaction mechanism he had established for fatty acids "was completely unknown
to pure chemistry." Nature, he asserted, "surely follows some ways that no
laboratory yet knows, and that will usually turn out to be simpler and more
direct - that is why its study is generally so enticing!"[67] Knoop also discussed
in quite personal terms in his lectures the obstacles to a career in his field. He
pointed out, "proudly" it seemed to Hans, that although he had as a young man
made important contributions, he had not received a salaried position until he
was 37 years old.[68]

Franz Knoop had, in fact, given the lectures in physiological chemistry from
1904 until 1909 as an unsalaried *Privatdozent*. In 1909 he was promoted to
unpaid extraordinary professor, but he did receive, on an impermanent basis,
compensation for his service as an assistant in the chemistry laboratory of the
medical faculty. In 1913 he received an offer to join the Rockefeller Institute
in New York, with a laboratory of his own and a salary that was by German
standards very handsome. In return for declining this offer he obtained a regular
salaried post as extraordinary professor and the promise of a future institute.
Despite the ensuing wartime conditions, he was given, in 1915, some recently
vacated space in the Pharmacological Institute to equip for a rather modest
Physiological-Chemistry Institute. In 1919 he was promoted to the irregular
position of "personal ordinary professor," and at the time Krebs and Blaschko
attended his lectures he was utilizing an offer from Leipzig to negotiate for a
regular professorship at Freiburg.[69]

Through these years Knoop had to struggle with his university and with the
Ministry of Culture and Education of Baden for each improvement in his
position, and he felt inadequately supported and compensated. His difficulties
arose in part from the fact that despite his prominent discoveries, he was not
perceived as a highly productive research scientist. In 1911, for example, he
was passed over for a professorship in physiology in Berlin, probably because
"so far as is known here, he has until now published only a limited range of
scientific work."[70] His ability as a lecturer seems to have been more prominent
than his achievements in research. The main obstacle to his advance, even after
the offer from the Rockefeller Institute brought home to his university that he
had international standing, was the subordinate place that physiological chemistry
held in the German university hierarchy. Although it had been made a required
part of the preclinical state medical examination (the *Physikum*), in 1904, the
subject was taught in most universities by an extraordinary professor who was
in fact an assistant to the professor of physiology.[71] Knoop was in such a
position with respect to von Kries until he managed to convert his international
recognition into an exception to this pattern at Freiburg.[72]

Knoop undoubtedly did not delve into these complexities when he made the
claim in his lectures that he had received no pay for his work until he was 37.
The message that Hans absorbed from his lectures was that physiological

chemistry was an absorbing field in which to do research, but that one could not in general expect to make one's living by doing research in a basic science.[73]

IV

The cumulative effects of the descriptions of their own discoveries by teachers such as von Kries and Knoop stirred in Hans a desire to try some research himself. Despite the numerous courses he was taking, he had now made up fully for the initial deficiencies in his preparation, and he found his work, which was mainly memorization, easy enough so that he thought he could afford to spend some extra time in a laboratory. Accordingly he went to Eugen Fischer to see if he could work in the anatomical institute. Fischer referred him to Möllendorff, who invited him to undertake a project involving the histological staining of skeletal muscle tissue.[74]

Möllendorff had himself made a decision to enter the field of anatomy under the influence of teachers he had encountered as a medical student. During the required clinical *Prakticum* year following his medical training, in 1912, he entered the anatomical institute at Greifswald and took up vital staining, that is, the injection of dyes into living animals to elucidate physiological processes by examining the subsequent deposition of the dyes in particular tissues. During the following years he investigated by such means problems related to the function of the kidney tubules.[75] Gradually he came to focus his attention on the method of vital staining itself.

The vital stains most commonly used were synthetic organic molecules, and were divided into two broad classes. Acidic dyes contained a negatively charged group that combined in solution with a positive ion to form a salt. Basic dyes possessed the converse property. Although the chemical constitutions of individual acidic and basic dyes varied widely, the members of each class shared some general characteristics as vital stains. Acidic dyes tended to be absorbed only by certain tissues, whereas basic dyes penetrated more extensively. The majority of histologists, therefore, explained the distribution of dyes within tissues, and within individual cells, in terms of the chemical affinities of the dyes with specific substituents of the cells such as their proteins. Following the lead of Rudolf Höber, Möllendorff developed an alternative "physical" viewpoint, according to which the characteristics of different vital stains depended on their respective degrees of "dispersibility." Measured by the rate at which they diffused through a gel or passed in solution by dialysis across a membrane, the dispersibility of dyes was, Möllendorff came to believe, the most important factor controlling the rapidity with which and extent to which they penetrated into cells; whether they stained the protoplasmic fluid in a diffuse manner or were deposited as granules; and the time that it took for them to be washed out of the cells. Möllendorff found a continuous range of variation in the dispersibility of both acidic and basic dyes, but he grouped them for convenience into the three general categories of high, intermediate, and low dispersibility.[76]

Möllendorff's interpretation of these correlations was influenced by the rapidly growing field of colloid chemistry. The varying dispersibilities of dyes,

Figure 3.6 Wilhelm von Möllendorff. From *Zeitschrift für Zellforschung* Abt. A, 33 (1943): opp. p. 167.

he inferred, was mainly a consequence of the relative sizes of their particles, due in part to the number of atoms in their molecules, and in part to the degree to which the molecules aggregated under varying conditions to form larger particles. At the time Hans Krebs approached him, Möllendorff was about to embark on a new research program in which he would apply the principles he had worked out with vital stains to provide a theoretical foundation for the methods long in use to stain fixed tissue preparations. In his view, the staining techniques that had evolved during the preceding 50 years relied too much on empirical "tricks" practiced by individual histologists and lacking the rational grounding that would enable them to vary their methods purposefully. By comparing the actions of numerous dyes on specific tissues under controlled and systematically varied conditions, he hoped to clarify the relation between the effects observed and the physical or chemical properties both of the dyes and of the tissues.[77]

Möllendorff had extensive teaching responsibilities, but he spent part of every day in the laboratory, and he instructed Hans in the basic histological techniques necessary to begin his research. Hans learned how to make slices from animal tissues, to fix them and embed them in paraffin. Although he was not unusually adept at these operations, he enjoyed working with his hands in the laboratory, just as he had enjoyed handicrafts as a boy. He worked in the laboratory along with Möllendorff's wife Milie, who assisted her husband in his research, and with two or three other students. Möllendorff also provided him with some basic texts that he would need for background information: Martin Heidenhahn's *Plasma und Zelle*, which gave a broad critical review of the cell theory as well as a survey of tissues and histological methods; recent articles in the fields of histology, vital staining, and colloid chemistry; and Möllendorff's own latest review of the methods of vital staining written for Abderhalden's handbook of biological laboratory methods.[78]

Hans's project on the staining of skeletal muscle tissues was one of several parallel studies on various animal tissues begun at this time as part of Möllendorff's new research direction. Hans obtained his muscle tissue from the back and limbs of a 4-week old white mouse. After preparing tissue slices he began testing dyes commonly used in histological work. Using equimolar aqueous solutions of each dye to make his results comparable, he immersed the tissue in the dye for 24 hours, then air dried it on filter paper and treated it further with xylol and Canadian balsam. He tested in all 15 different acidic dyes and 12 basic dyes.[79] There is no record of the time period over which he carried out these tests, but he most likely worked at it until the end of the summer semester of 1920, in late July.

For some time the fledgling investigator simply tested one dye after another, following his standardized procedure, without knowing what he would be able to do with his results. One evening he went to a Wagnerian opera at the Freiburg theater. Afterward, just as he was starting across the square on which the theater stood, it suddenly became clear to him how he should proceed. He had probably already found that although some of the dyes stained certain characteristic bands of the striated muscle tissues more intensely and distinguished them more sharply from the background than other dyes, there was no consistent difference in this regard between the acidic dyes and the basic dyes. The decisive factor, he must have realized now, must not be the chemical constitution, but the physical properties of the respective dyes. Such an insight was hardly surprising, as it reflected the approach that Möllendorff had long pursued, but Hans apparently had to recognize for himself that this viewpoint applied to his particular research problem. He may not at this moment have formulated a detailed idea about the physical factors involved, but he had at least a sense of the direction in which he should think about the question.[80]

Although the end of the summer semester probably interrupted him in the midst of his experiments in Möllendorff's laboratory, for financial reasons Hans had to spend the long summer vacation at home in Hildesheim. He tried to do some more work there, using his father's microscope and some dyes given to him by an industrial firm, but little came of it.[81]

Hans made more progress during the vacation time with his music. Even during the busy school semesters he had kept up his practicing by hiring time on a piano. Back in Hildesheim he resumed his lessons with Richard Gerlt. His teacher assigned him one of the late Beethoven piano sonatas, Opus 110. As he learned to play this tightly structured composition, Opus 110 became his favorite sonata. He enjoyed it in part for its unified structure — the theme begun in the first movement, repeated in intricately varied forms and reappearing in the fugue of the third movement; but the sonata also seemed to express an extraordinary range of emotions, from the gentle, contemplative early sections to the expansive ascending final passage ending in a spirit of optimism. Hans was moved by the fact that even in complete deafness Beethoven could write in a jubilant mood. Wolf was so impressed with Hans's enthusiasm for the work that he too took it up; but Wolf came to prefer Opus 109, with its freer style and more melodic theme and variations. It is tempting, even if risky, to discern in the brothers' differing but similar choices a reflection of their respective temperaments. The importance to Hans of the emotional depth of the music of Beethoven seems at any rate to reflect the depths of feeling beneath his own controlled external behavior.[82]

Hans returned to Freiburg in October 1920, for his final preclinical semester. For the first time he did not have to do any more anatomical dissections. He took laboratory courses in physiology and physics, and lecture courses in experimental pharmacology, plant biochemistry, genetics, and the physiology of the central nervous system. He also took Eugen Fischer's anthropology course, perhaps because the references Fischer had made in the anatomy course to his anthropological field work had so interested him.[83]

Probably throughout this semester Hans continued his research in Möllendorff's laboratory. The idea of connecting the physical properties of the dyes to their staining properties proved to be an effective investigative guide. He found that he could divide the dyes he had tested into three groups, within each of which all the dyes, whether they were acidic or basic, had nearly the same effects. Dyes in the first group stained deeply two of the cross-striations (the Z + I stripe and the M + Qh stripe according to the standard notation of the time), making them stand out strongly against the rest of the tissue. Members of the second group colored the whole tissue diffusely, without differentiating any structures. Those of the third group stained the Z stripe only, and less strongly than did dyes of the first group. The three groups of dyes coincided with the three classes that Möllendorff had identified in accord with their rates of diffusion through a gelatin gel as having low, high, and intermediate dispersibility. Hans carried out additional diffusion experiments on those dyes he had used that Möllendorff had not tested, and found that they fit into the expected positions.[84]

To explain these results Hans theorized that the distribution of the dyes within the components of the skeletal tissue and the intensity of the coloration were conditioned both by the diffusibility of the dye and the differing densities of the structures within the tissue. The dyes with a low degree of dispersibility provided the strongest contrasts, because they penetrated only into the least dense parts of the tissue. The highly dispersible dyes stained evenly, because they spread throughout the tissue. Dyes of intermediate dispersibility expectedly gave an intermediate picture. It is not clear whether Hans thought of this interpretation or Möllendorff suggested it to him, but in any case it was an adaptation of Möllendorff's general views to the particular observations Hans had made on skeletal muscle.[85]

Hans tested his explanation by carrying out further experiments in which he followed the progressive staining of tissues left for varying time intervals in the dye solutions, and regressive staining in which dye previously absorbed into the tissue is partially washed out of it. The results fit into patterns consistent with his interpretation of the previous results.[86] By the time the semester ended in February 1921, Hans had completed a well-defined experimental investigation that had yielded some novel observations lending themselves to a coherent explanatory framework. Möllendorff encouraged him to feel that he had made a scientific contribution and invited him to write up a paper for publication. Both understood that Hans would not have time for further experimental work after he began the clinical stage of his medical training.[87]

His work with Möllendorff provided the only close access to a teacher that Hans had during his preclinical university years. Otherwise, like his fellow students, he had only the distant contact with members of the faculty afforded by large crowded lecture halls. Nor were their performances during these five semesters measured beyond the nominal certification that they complete in each laboratory course the required number of preparations. Like his classmates, Hans could only guess at how well he was doing, but he apparently experienced little anxiety over this uncertainty. Accustomed to do well but not to shine academically, he assumed that he was still not outstanding but that he could manage what was required of him. Now, however, he was approaching a major test of that assumption, the *ärztliche Vorprüfung*, known also as the *Physikum*, in which he would be examined in his knowledge of the required preclinical subjects. On March 7 1921, Hans passed the *Vorprüfung* with grades of "very good" in anatomy, physiology, chemistry, zoology, and botany, and "good" in physics. He was awarded an overall mark of "very good." Hans's capacity to absorb large amounts of information, to recall it accurately, and to state it succinctly undoubtedly underlay what appears, by the grading scales of the time, to have been an exemplary performance.[88]

4

Clinical Years

While Hans Krebs was at home between semesters — it may have been in February or March of 1921 — his father suggested to him and to Wolf that they should make a legal declaration that they had left the Jewish religious community. The idea was a logical culmination of the conviction Georg Krebs had long held that assimilation was the best solution to the Jewish problem in Germany. They should, he explained to his sons, take an active step to show that they believed seriously in assimilation. It is possible that he had contemplated such a move for some time but had not taken it while his wife was alive because she would not like the idea; or he may have felt that he should wait until his sons were of age to do so.[1]

Having been raised entirely outside the faith of their forebears, Hans and Wolf had no difficulty accepting their father's suggestion. The three went together to a Notary to fill out the necessary forms. The document that each of them signed stated that he had *aus dem Judentum ausgetreten*. Henceforth when they filled out forms on which they had to indicate a religious belief they designated themselves *freireligiös*. The step they had taken was a common one among politically liberal nonreligious German Jews. In the Weimar Republic full assimilation appeared to many an attainable goal.[2]

Although he was probably already intending to move on to another university for the clinical years of his medical education, Hans remained in Freiburg for the summer semester of 1921 to hear the lectures of one of the most eminent pathologists in Germany, Ludwig Aschoff. At the age of 55 Aschoff, who had held the chair in pathology at Freiburg since 1907, was at the apex of his career. Energetic and exceptionally skilled at descriptive tissue pathology, Aschoff had made important contributions to the understanding of lesions of the heart associated with rheumatic fever, of the structure and formation of thrombi in thrombosis, of the causes of atherosclerosis and numerous other problems. He had defined the reticuloendothelial system as a family of tissues dispersed within the body but functionally united through its role in phagocytosis and other metabolic processes.[3]

Figure 4.1 Ludwig Aschoff. From *Ludwig Aschoff: ein Gelehrtenleben in Briefen an die Familie* (Freiburg: Hans Ferdinad Schul Verlag, 1966), opp. p. 193.

Aschoff connected his specific pathological investigations to a broad vision of the organization of vital processes. He defined a healthy organism as one "possessing complete powers of adaptability toward the natural exchange of external vital conditions. "Disease, has no autonomous existence, but depends on disturbances of the normal vital functions."[4] In an era dominated by the germ theory, Aschoff's physiological view of disease was probably far from conventional. He sought not only to identify the morphological appearances associated with pathological conditions, but to trace them to underlying metabolic processes. Atherosclerosis, for example, he attributed to the deposit in the vascular walls of cholesterin esters carried in the blood plasma. The various conditions that produce health or disease he classified according to the type of regulatory mechanism through which the body attempts to restore its capacity to adapt to external circumstances.[5]

Aschoff was, to Hans Krebs, an inspiring teacher. Years later Krebs wrote that Aschoff's "lectures on pathology made a deep and lasting impression on his students. The manner in which he treated the great problems of pathology — inflammation, malignancy, etiology — from a general biological point of view influenced decisively our attitude toward the problems of the clinic, the medical and the biological sciences." Aschoff was undoubtedly one of those who instilled in Krebs the viewpoint that "the nature of life is...at the bottom of medicine" and who reinforced in him the desire not merely to memorize medical knowledge, but to "go into the depth of any matter I am studying."[6]

The inspirational leadership that Aschoff exercised reached beyond his professional subject.   As Krebs afterward remembered,

> Aschoff had the desire and the courage to express also on occasion his views concerning general questions about academic life, and beyond the learned man we perceived also a great personality, who did not believe that his responsibilities as an academic teacher ended with representing his discipline, but who viewed it as his task also to discuss with the students general academic and political questions. His idealism in these matters was exemplary.[7]

Warm-hearted and humane, Aschoff was deeply concerned about the condition of Germany and how its people should bear themselves to emerge from their misfortunes. Although he had been in the past a loyal supporter of *Kaiser und Reich*, he firmly rejected the efforts he saw around him to return to old ways that had been forever destroyed. It troubled him to see students drinking, dueling, and waving old banners "as if there had been no unfortunate war and no Versailles treaty." Equally disturbing to him was the tendency of the middle class to indulge in the same expensive luxuries they had enjoyed before the war. Germany could not survive, he believed, if the burdens of its defeat were shifted to the working class. Students who formed societies that excluded socialism as unGerman, and the founders of the new *Vaterlandspartei* as well, were repeating all of the mistakes of the war and prewar period. "I always tell my students" Aschoff wrote his mother-in-law at about the time that Hans was beginning to attend his lectures,

> That you should make certain that all Germans feel as truly German as you do. That is a wonderful responsibility, whose fulfillment alone can save us. But how do we reach this high goal? Certainly not by calling oneself a patriotic German and denying German-ness to all democrats, socialists or communists.

Our students must, he believed, forego traditional pleasures, dedicate themselves to their studies, and contribute toward national unification.   Aschoff foresaw continued hardship for a Germany beset both by internal disruption and the vengeful attitudes of the victorious allies who were just then pressing on the defeated nation a burden of reparation payments that many Germans viewed as intolerable. Nevertheless, he did not lose hope. "I am certain," he wrote, "that our people will again reach the old heights, but it will take a long time."[8]

Views such as these, Aschoff also interjected into the lectures that Hans heard.[9] Much has been written by historians about the reactionary attitudes of German academics during the Weimar period, attitudes that are seen in retrospect as helping to undermine a fragile democracy. However valid such generalizations may be, they should be tempered by noting examples such as Ludwig Aschoff. His generosity of spirit, his message of hope demanding sacrifice must have helped to nurture the optimism and the commitment of students such as Hans Krebs, who did not waste time either in drinking or in clinging to a vanished past, but who sought to build stable futures within a present torn by turmoil.

I

In addition to the courses in special pathology and pathological histology by Aschoff, Hans took Eugen Fischer's course in human genetics and continued with experimental pharmacology. His time was now dominated, however, by participation as a *Praktikant* in the clinics. In the summer semester of 1921 he took "methods of physical examination," "obstetrical and gynecological examination," and "examination of the respiratory passages, the upper digestive tract and ears," and he attended the surgical *Poliklinik*.[10]

Participation in the clinics in the German university system did not mean that the medical students were actively involved in patient care. The clinics were lecture–demonstrations. They seemed unsystematic in the sense that the subject treated on any given day depended on the availability of a suitable patient. The patient was wheeled into the center of a large lecture hall in which 200 to 300 students were seated on the steeply rising semicircular rows of seats arranged so that all could observe the ensuing examination. For each session four students were called down. Sometimes they were asked to take the case history, or the lecturer read parts of a previously assembled case history and asked the students to make a further examination and give an opinion. Sometimes the lecturer treated students who made mistakes through their inexperience rather harshly; but Hans, who was probably called down for his turn two or three times during the semester, fortunately encountered no such chastening experiences. After the examination had been completed the lecturer would discuss the general nature of the disease or other disorder in question.[11]

Although each student had only rare opportunities to participate directly in the examinations, most of them found the demonstrations intensely interesting, and attended them faithfully. Each session lasted several hours, so that Hans was fully occupied with them and the other lectures during the day, and had only evenings left to study more systematically the subject matter treated opportunistically in the clinical demonstrations.[12]

His successful completion of an experimental investigation in Möllendorff's laboratory had strongly reinforced Hans's interest in research. He began to think that he might eventually enter academic medicine, where he could have opportunities to combine clinical and experimental work. No definite plan took shape in his mind, but he did gather from his laboratory experience a clear conviction that he did not know enough basic chemistry to go further. That lesson was amplified by his contact with a family relation in Freiburg — a brother-in-law of the Uncle Arnold now practicing with his father — whom he occasionally visited. This man, a practicing internist, was also working in the university pharmacology department in the hope that he could someday go into research. The pharmacologists there had told him, however, that he had better learn some chemistry before he started, and he was now enrolled in a chemistry course. The message was not lost on Hans that he too should make a special effort to learn more chemistry if he expected to have a future in research.[13]

The nature of his work with Möllendorff also shaped Hans's view of the type of chemistry to which he should give priority. Although it might seem that he ought to have been impressed by the dyes he used with the need to know more about the structures and reactions of organic compounds, the influence of Möllendorff's physical approach to histological staining directed his attention more strongly toward physical chemistry, and especially to its applications in the burgeoning field of colloid chemistry.[14]

Colloids had originally been defined by Thomas Graham in the nineteenth century as substances that, when in solution, would not diffuse through a pergament or animal membrane. By the early twentieth century the colloidal state had come to mean a dispersed two-phase system in which the dispersed phase was comprised of particles intermediate in size between molecules and those visible in an ordinary microscope. Properties of colloids that commanded special attention were their ability to form sols and gels, the influence of the hydrogen ion concentration and of other electrolytes on their precipitation, and particularly the interactions that took place on the surfaces between the two phases. Although inorganic colloids, such as gold sols, were prominently studied, organic colloids were considered more important, and the conviction spread rapidly during the first decade of the century that such colloids played a crucial role in the phenomena of life. The structure and functions of cells in particular were thought to be determined largely by the colloidal character of their constituent proteins and lipids, and by the properties of the surfaces between such structures and the intercellular and intracellular fluids.[15]

Hans saw that the interpretation of his staining experiments on skeletal muscle tissue confronted him with problems in physical and colloidal chemistry for which he had little grounding. It may have been for this reason that despite the demanding schedule of his first clinical semester at Freiburg he also took a course in colloidal chemistry. It is also possible that one of the textbooks he studied in connection with this course was a newly published, lucidly written *Manual of Physical Chemistry, in particular of colloid chemistry, for physicians and biologists* by the distinguished physical chemist Leonor Michaelis. During this time Hans also bought and studied the comprehensive textbook *The Physical*

Chemistry of Cells and Tissues by one of the pioneers in that field, Rudolf Höber. Already accustomed by the German university system to organize his studies on his own, Hans embarked on a reading program intended to supplement the limited exposure to chemistry required for his medical degree with the knowledge he thought would prepare him for opportunities he had yet to identify in the world of experimental medicine.[16]

The clinical lectures that Hans attended afforded him and his fellow medical students dramatic access to the ways in which skilled clinicians responded to real patients, connected specific cases with their own prior experiences, brought broader background knowledge to bear on the situation, and reasoned toward a diagnosis and treatment. This form of education did not provide, however, the practical experience of frequent direct contact with patients so essential for students to learn to do what they observed their teachers doing. As many of his classmates did, Hans partially made up for this lack by spending the long summer vacation as a voluntary junior assistant — known as a *Famulus* — in the general hospital in Hildesheim. He assisted physicians in their physical examinations. He also had the sobering experience of seeing patients who were gravely ill and watching some of them die. He participated regularly in postmortem examinations. He enjoyed a special opportunity to gain further experience by assisting his father during the tonsillectomies and other simple operations that Georg Krebs performed at home.[17]

Hans continued to be influenced in some aspects of his personal life by his sister. As a boy he kept his hair short and simply parted. After their mother's death, however, Lise decided that he would look more handsome if he let it grow longer and combed it straight back. Hans accepted her suggestion, and his appearance changed markedly.[18] Lise was, however, ready to give up her role of holding together the Krebs household. After turning down one proposal of marriage by Adolf Daniel, a somewhat older man, she accepted him in 1921, and after their wedding moved with her husband to Frankfurt on der Oder. Georg Krebs had to hire a housekeeper to manage Zingel 9.[19]

During his summer holiday Hans made up his mind to continue his clinical education at the University of Munich. Already at Freiburg he had heard much about the excellent reputation of the Munich clinical faculty. Among many outstanding clinicians the most famous were the psychiatrist Emil Kraepelin, the author of the modern classification of mental illnesses; the formidable surgeon Ferdinand Sauerbruch; and the great teacher of internal medicine Friedrich von Müller. Back in Hildesheim Hans talked over his plans with Erich Stern, who was also working as an assistant at the general hospital. Erich was interested in Munich, and the two friends decided to rejoin forces. As in their previous choices, Hans and Erich were not motivated solely by academic considerations. The rich cultural life of Munich was a strong inducement, as was the idea of skiing and hiking in the nearby Bavarian Alps. Ever since his family had taken one of its rare holiday trips together to the Alps in 1911, Hans had been enchanted by their beauty. He had been thrilled especially by the rare sight of intensely colored flowers abundant on the high mountain slopes against a back-

Figure 4.2 Hans Krebs in family guest room, 1921.

ground of snow. Vivid recollections of this experience made the prospect of living within easy distance of the Alps very enticing to him.[20]

During Hans's last semester at Freiburg Wolf had completed his Gymnasium education at the Andreanum. His superior talent and preference for mathematics and physics left no question that he would go on to a *Technische Hochschule* to prepare for engineering.[21] Hans, who still viewed his younger brother as unenterprising, was concerned that Wolf would take the simplest route he could, by attending a nearby technical school in Hanover or Braunschweig. He suggested rather forcefully to Wolf that he ought to be more venturesome and that they could both go to Munich, which possessed also an excellent *Technische Hochschule*. Wolf readily agreed, and the plan was also acceptable to their father. In October 1921, Hans, Wolf, and Erich Stern set off together for Bavaria.[22]

As soon as they had entered Bavaria the distinctiveness of this southern German state was evident to the young northerners. When they got off the train at a stop between Nuremberg and Munich, Wolf found the fluid Bavarian dialect so different from the crisp northern German language to which he was accustomed that he could barely understand a word. Having been exposed to another variety of southern German speech in Baden, Hans probably had less difficulty, but with his keen ear for dialects Hans was probably also fascinated with the way Bavarians spoke.[23]

Hans and Wolf found a room together in Munich, but the landlady appeared to be rather hostile toward them, and they soon began to feel that things would not work out there. When she demanded payment for something that they believed they did not owe, she confiscated one of their suitcases that was kept in a locked area of the attic protected by a high fence. The beleaguered Krebs brothers were not above carrying out a covert operation to extricate themselves from their situation. With the help of Erich Stern they ascended to the attic, climbed on a chair and dangled a line with a hook on it from a pole that they reached over the fence. Catching the handle of the suitcase they elevated the pole and escaped with their property. Shortly afterward they moved to another rooming house with a more amenable landlady. They took care to locate a house with a piano, because they were both eager to keep up their practicing.[24]

During the winter semester of 1921–1922 Hans attended the clinics of both Sauerbruch and von Müller, as well as the *Frauenklinik* of Albert Döderlein, a distinguished pioneer in the use of aseptic gynecological and obstetrical procedures.[25] Sauerbruch must have been particularly imposing to Hans and to Erich. Although he regarded himself as a general surgeon, Sauerbruch was best known for the innovative operative techniques he devised for thoracic surgery, making that cavity for the first time as accessible as the abdominal cavity. He was also famous for the number of politically and socially prominent patients he had had. Sauerbruch's clinical lectures attracted many listeners, members of other faculties as well as medical students. Aware that surgeons like himself who tackled difficult operations with great self-confidence were sometimes accused of performing unnecessary or harmful operations, he attempted in his lectures to demonstrate the circumspection with which he weighed all relevant factors, the assumptions with which he approached an operation, and his recognition of the limits on what surgery could achieve. A man of unruly temperament, he was not always methodical in his presentation, but he gripped the attention of his audience with his lucid discussions and the power of his personality.[26]

Impressive though these eminent surgeons may have been to Hans, he probably knew by this time that he would not become a surgeon himself, and was leaning toward internal medicine as his specialty. The II Medical Clinic of Friedrich von Müller must, therefore, have been of central interest to him. Müller was judged by some contemporaries to be the best teacher of internal medicine of his generation. His lectures in Munich regularly attracted 300 to 400 listeners. Müller paid great attention to didactic methods that would afford so large an audience the fullest possible access to what he wished to convey to them. He made certain to be thoroughly familiar in advance with the case history of each patient presented as the subject of a lecture. Because his clinic was intended for students in their first clinical year, he assumed no prior knowledge of pathology on their part, explained basic concepts before

introducing a diagnosis, and used the most ordinary words applicable.   He
thought it was important for the lecturer to develop chemical formulas,
anatomical diagrams, and other visual illustrations step-by-step on the blackboard
rather than to resort to previously prepared drawings or projections.   He went
to great lengths to ensure that when the examinations involved percussion or
auscultation the sounds were audible to the audience.   Anchoring his presentation
in the concrete condition of the patient before him, he drew his listeners
systematically toward the broader implications of the case, leading them through
differences of opinion and into the historical background.   Although he
understood the importance of the personality of the clinical teacher, he tried not
to place himself in the forefront, but to concentrate the attention on the subject.
Aware that he was not educating scholars but training the next generation of
physicians, nevertheless, he perceived his goal not as to impart information but
to teach them to learn: as part of their *allgemeine Bildung*.[27]

Both Hans and Erich admired Müller greatly as a teacher.   Hans valued
particularly the informal yet highly effective way in which Müller first called up
several students to examine the patient at hand, drew out pertinent aspects of the
situation by asking them questions, then went on to talk about the general nature
of the disease that had been identified.[28]

Müller regretted that the large size of the lectures did not permit him to
establish personal contacts with most of the medical students.[29]   Hans and his
fellow students did not expect such contacts or expect to be known to their
teachers.   He was, therefore, surprised one day, while returning in a railroad
compartment from a botanical expedition in the Alps with a bunch of flowers,
when Müller happened to sit down opposite him, recognized his face, and asked
what the flowers were for.   Explaining that he too had had a long-standing
interest in botany, he advised Hans to make certain that he got the whole plant,
including its roots, if he wanted them for a herbarium.   Even though Müller
seemed to him straightforward and unpompous, Hans was probably too shy to
point out that that was just what he had done.[30]

When Müller had become chief of the II Medical Clinic in 1902, it had
become one of his responsibilities to carry on an older tradition maintained by
his predecessors: to offer a series of "evening hour" lectures covering systematically the field of internal medicine.   Müller chose to lecture on his own favorite
subject, metabolic diseases.   He had acquired his interest in that field as a
medical student in Munich two decades earlier, when he spent a year as assistant
to Carl Voit, the leader of the foremost school of metabolism in the nineteenth
century.   Afterward, Müller had applied the quantitative methods he learned
there to measure the effects on carbohydrate, protein, and fat metabolism of such
disorders as typhoid fever, Basedow's disease, and jaundice.   In his lectures
Müller assumed that he must first teach the general chemical foundations of the
subject.   He began with the chemical formulas of the pertinent organic
compounds, discussed Knoop's β-oxidation theory, Neuberg's theory of
fermentation, and contemporary views of amino acid metabolism.   Lecturing
twice a week from 5 to 6 PM, he covered the physiology of metabolism between

the beginning of the winter semester and the Christmas break. From then until the end of the semester he discussed specific metabolic diseases.[31]

After presenting these lectures himself for several years, Müller turned them over to his assistants. By the time Hans attended them they were given by a *Privatdozent*, Siegfried Thannhauser. Before the war Thannhauser had worked in Müller's clinic as a young physician, had taken time out to study chemistry in the laboratory of the famous Adolf von Baeyer, where he earned a PhD in 1913, and had come back to Müller as a private assistant. Thannhauser served throughout the war as a military field doctor, then returned again to Müller's clinic, where at his chief's suggestion he undertook an investigation of the chemistry of gout.[32]

Müller's strong interest in the metabolic foundations of disease and Thannhauser's stimulating lectures furthered the interest in metabolism that Hans had already derived from the lectures of Franz Knoop. Everywhere he found reinforcement for the belief that chemistry was fundamental to the further development of medicine. The research interests of his clinical teachers continually enhanced his desire to engage in research also. By now he was certain that he would not follow in his father's footsteps, and that if he had a research career it would be based somehow on physiological chemistry; but beyond this general orientation he still formed no definite plan.[33]

Although the daily clinics and his self-study now kept him too busy to seek further research opportunities, Hans must have spent considerable time during his first two clinical semesters turning the results of his earlier experiments with Möllendorff into a research paper. Besides reviewing the previous literature relevant to the subject and composing the manuscript, he made 11 drawings of stained skeletal muscle sections.[34]

The first two sections of his paper on "The Staining of Skeletal Muscle with Anilin Dyes" described his methods and results clearly and succinctly. There followed longer sections providing a "critical view of the results" and an "evaluation of our results." With conspicuous confidence Hans stated — using the widely spaced letters in which German scientific papers then customarily placed emphatic assertions — that the most essential result of the work was that:

> The distribution of a dye is dependent to a high degree upon its condition of solution: for dyes of the same dispersibility stain in the same way, whereas on the contrary dyes with different conditions of solubility always act differently. Connections between the chemical constitution of a dye and its distribution in a fixed preparation cannot be established.[35]

Further on in his discussion, when he had connected the different degrees of the staining of the several tissue structures with the densities of the latter, he claimed in the same emphatic style, that "Dyes offer us a reagent for the determination of the density relationships in muscle."[36]

Hans reviewed at length the results of several of the most important earlier workers in the field, stressing the differences between "chemical" theories of staining of which the leading proponent was Martin Heidenhain, and the "physicalist" theory with which he associated himself. He offered physicalist explanations of the results of other investigators and made several strong criticisms of the views of Heidenhain.[37]

Hans Krebs's first scientific paper was remarkably well organized and clearly reasoned, but it was hardly concise. His elaborate discussion extended a relatively minor investigation into a lengthy paper (in published form it filled 24 pages). Undoubtedly in this respect as in its content he emulated the style of his mentor, who customarily incorporated into his scientific writings discussions of the relation between his results and those of other investigators that exceeded the space given to the descriptions of his own investigations.

Hans wrote his paper out in longhand and mailed it off to Möllendorff, probably some time before the end of the winter semester of 1921–1922. He anticipated that Möllendorff would revise it and publish it as a co-authored paper. To his surprise Möllendorff made only a few small changes, mainly to tone down the aggressive language in which Hans had expressed his critique of Heidenhahn, added an introduction relating Hans's paper to the broader investigation in his laboratory of which it comprised the first published results, and submitted it to the *Archiv für mikroskopische Anatomie* under the sole authorship of Hans Adolf Krebs.[38]

In March, 1922 Möllendorff wrote to Hans,

Dear Mr. Krebs,

I have finally prepared your work for printing. I have made some miscellaneous changes in the presentation; some of your assertions were a little too pithy. I have also written an introduction. On the whole I am still very pleased with the outcome and congratulate you on the satisfying result.
How are you, where will you spend the coming semester?
Please let me hear from you again.[39]

Hans's surprise that the paper would appear in his own name reflected the common practice in German laboratories for work produced by subordinates to appear under the name of the professor in charge. Even though Hans had performed the experiments and written nearly every word of the paper, the idea for the project, the techniques, and the interpretative framework he owed to Möllendorff. Möllendorff was, therefore, generous in assigning the whole public credit for the work to the young medical student who had asked him for a project. One reason he probably did so was that he was pleasantly surprised that with no prior experience Hans was able to produce a paper of publishable quality.[40] He must also have intended his action to encourage Hans to see himself as a potentially independent investigator.

Hans, Wolf, and Erich all took full advantage of the unexcelled cultural resources of Munich. Tickets to internationally famous opera and theater performances were very inexpensive, although they had to stand in line for long times to obtain them. They were able to see Bruno Walter conduct Mozart at the Munich Opera House. The music of Richard Strauss enjoyed enormous popularity in Germany then, and they of course saw performances of *Der Rosenkavalier* and other Strauss works. They went often to the *Alte Pinakothek*, the magnificent gallery of pre-1800 paintings collected by Bavarian monarchs. Wolf frequented the *Alte Pinakothek* more than the other two, because it was so close to the *Technische Hochschule* that he could use breaks between lectures to visit it. Coming from a small town with more limited galleries, he was exhilarated by the grandeur of the *Pinakothek* and quickly acquired a taste for art.[41]

The outdoor attractions were no less grand. Often Hans, Wolf, and Erich cycled to the Alps on weekends, and during their first Christmas vacation they went skiing together in the company of a young Bavarian who had skied for many years and gave them instructions. They had to go into Austria to find enough snow. As in other outdoor sports, Wolf soon became more proficient than his older brother, but all three greatly enjoyed the sport and the spectacular slopes on which they pursued it.[42]

At the end of their first semester in Munich Hans and Wolf moved to separate rooming houses. The long distance between the medical buildings where Hans spent most of his time and the *Technische Hochschule* made it convenient for each to find lodgings nearer to his daily activity. Each had also found by now separate circles of students within which to move. They continued, however, to plan common weekend and other activities.[43]

For the summer semester of 1922 Hans moved on to the advanced internal medicine clinic taught by Ernst von Romberg, distinguished as an investigator of the cardiovascular system. In the opinion of Friedrich von Müller his colleague von Romberg lectured more dogmatically than he himself did, giving less attention to foundations in pathological anatomy, and not raising questions or doubts; but the students appreciated that Romberg gave them "precise rules for therapy," providing a firm didactic basis for their future activity as doctors. Hans took four other clinics: in dermatology and sexual disorders under Leo von Zumbusch; in pediatrics under one of the leading pediatricians in Germany, Meinhard von Pfaundler; in ophthalmology under Carl von Hess, who had made important contributions to the comparative physiology of light and color and the accommodation mechanisms of the eyes; and in psychiatry under the great Emil Kraepelin. On the threshold of retirement by then, Kraepelin still made a strong impression in his lectures.[44] Altogether, it must have been academically another richly rewarding semester for Hans.

Hans and Wolf naturally shunned the numerous student social groups devoted mainly to drinking or fencing. Soon after arriving in Munich, however, they joined a more serious student organization known as the *Freie Wissenschaftliche Vereinigung*. Its members included students from all of the university faculties, who met regularly to exchange views on their respective intellectual interests. The discussions were lively, and the two brothers attended eagerly. They came particularly to admire a somewhat older student named Hans

Schwartz, whose maturity and breadth of knowledge they associated with his cosmopolitan upbringing in Berlin. Both were awed by the brilliance with which Schwartz could speak and debate on almost any topic.[45]

Each member of the *Vereinigung* was expected to present a paper at one of its meetings on a topic of his own choice, to be followed by a general discussion. When his turn came, Hans selected the mechanist-vitalist question in biology. He was moved to do so under the stimulus of a lecture he had recently heard on that subject by the renowned embryologist and philosopher Hans Driesch. In preparation for his talk Hans studied Driesch's book *The Science and Philosophy of the Organism*, a comprehensive discussion of his views that Driesch presented originally as a set of lectures in Scotland in 1907 and 1908. Influenced partly by his earlier reading of some of the popular writings of Ernst Haeckel, Hans intended to support the mechanist position. Under the impact of Driesch's closely reasoned case against the possibility of a chemical or mechanical explanation of the phenomena of morphogenesis and in favor of the autonomy of life, however, Hans came to be less sure of his own view. He ended up concluding that it was largely a matter of personal temperament whether one thought that a complete mechanical explanation of life could ultimately be reached.[46]

His interest in such fundamental questions, discussed within the context of the embryological development of organisms such as sea urchins, may appear remote from Hans's current academic concerns in clinical medicine. His appreciation for the significance of these issues derived in part from his previous exposure to the embryological lectures of Spemann and the textbook by Oscar Hertwig that he had studied in Freiburg, in both of which he would have learned about the epoch-making experiment in which Driesch had separated the two blastomeres of a sea urchin egg after its first cleavage division and observed both of them develop into small whole larvae. That the philosophical implications of such experiments seemed immediately pertinent to him in his clinical years is not only a mark of his keen personal interest in them; the traditional value placed on *Wissenschaft* in German universities supported the ethos that the practice of medicine itself is grounded in the nature of life.[47]

For a young man increasingly confident of his academic ability, but still socially shy, it must have been a major step forward to deliver his first paper to a group and to lead the ensuing discussion. Wolf was so intimidated at the prospect of speaking to the group that he managed to avoid giving a paper.[48]

In May the university closed for a week for the Whitsuntide holiday. Hans, Wolf, and six or seven other students organized a long bicycle tour into the Alps. Carrying their clothing and rucksacks and racks installed on their bicycles, the cyclists rode 20 or 30 miles each day, taking enough time out to visit art museums, churches, and other sights along the way. By putting their bicycles on the train for long climbs into the mountains and cycling on downhill portions they were able to cover a large territory. Each evening they sent the boldest negotiator in their group to obtain the least expensive lodgings available. During the rides the adventurous Wolf usually led the way. During the 6 days that the tour lasted the group made their way from Munich into Austria to

Salzburg, then turned westward to Innsbruck and finally back to Munich. They imbibed much mountain air and scenery along the way, and must have returned fit and refreshed for their next round of studies.[49]

During the summer semester of 1922 Hans was, for the first time, strongly attracted to a woman. The 17-year-old granddaughter of his new landlady, she was vivacious, high-spirited, and an excellent piano player. To avoid having letters from her arriving at her grandmother's house, Hans exchanged notes with her through Wolf, who delivered the epistles in person to their respective recipients.[50]

A principal motive for the frugality that had prevailed in the Krebs family before the war had been that, like many middle class professional Germans, Georg Krebs was putting aside money to see his children through their educations. He had himself been impecunious as a student, and he often told his children that he intended for them to have an easier time. German university fees were characteristically low, but there was no scholarship or other public assistance available, and students were typically dependent entirely on their parents to meet their expenses until they had completed their studies.[51]

By the time Hans and Wolf were together in Munich the postwar inflation was already undermining Georg Krebs's plans. Although his practice still flourished, his savings were continually eroded, and it is likely that many of his patients found it difficult to pay fees that he would be forced to raise rapidly.[52] Fortunately basic student expenses, including tuition, room rents, and train fares, remained very low in comparison to most other prices. Up until the early summer of 1922 the two younger Krebs's were probably only constrained to avoid unnecessary expenditures.

The murder of the German foreign minister, Walther Rathenau, in June 1922, caused a crisis of confidence that accelerated the rate of inflation to a dizzying tempo. Like everyone else in Germany, Hans, Wolf, and Erich Stern experienced in Munich the wildly changing prices of everything in sight. The price of a meal could double between the time they entered a restaurant and the time to pay the bill, and the prices of goods in store windows were attached to a "multiplier" that increased hourly.[53]

When their father sent Hans and Wolf their monthly check for living expenses they had to rush immediately to a nearby restaurant to exchange it for meal vouchers before the check had totally lost its value. The vouchers procured for them on each of the following days merely a portion of mince meat. If they wished to have rolls in addition the cost doubled.[54]

Because there was a great disparity during this period between the internal value of the mark and its external exchange rate, foreign currency had enormous purchasing power in Germany. It was this situation that enabled Erich Stern to survive in Munich. His mother, a widow living on fixed income, was among those hardest hit by the inflation. Erich had, however, an uncle in New York who sent him a dollar each month, and that was enough for him to live on. The Krebs brothers only occasionally enjoyed the benefits of this monetary absurdity. Once their father treated a foreign patient who paid him 10 dollars. With it Georg Krebs and Lise came to visit Hans and Wolf in Munich, took them to dinner at an expensive restaurant, went to the theater and still had some money left at the end of the evening.[55]

As is well known, many middle class Germans were devastated by the inflation, some of them suffering irreparable losses of savings and status.[56] Hans and Wolf were relatively fortunate in that the strength of their father's professional practice enabled him to continue to meet their most basic needs. They had to cope each day with the problem of how to get enough to eat with what he could send them. They probably found it difficult also to purchase all of the textbooks they needed. The remainder of their costs remained low, in part because rents could not be raised. Concert and theater tickets remained so cheap that they probably did not have to give up this cultural pleasure. They could continue at no cost to enjoy cycling in the surrounding area. The austerity in their lives was not a great hardship for them because it did not interfere with their main objective, to study and learn. They were, moreover, young and optimistic enough to believe that such topsy-turvy conditions could not continue indefinitely, and that something would be done soon to repair their economic world.[57]

II

During the summer vacation of 1922 Hans again served as a *Famulus* in the Hildesheim general hospital and assisted at his father's operations. For the winter semester of 1922–1923 he decided to study in Berlin. Once again he did so for a blend of academic and nonacademic motives. Berlin was one of the great medical centers of the world, so that he could expect to be exposed to an exceptional quality of instruction. Berlin was also emerging, however, even in the midst of the troubled state of Germany, as the intense center for the new social and cultural freedom released by the open atmosphere of the Weimar Republic. Hans felt sufficiently drawn to these developments to want to see a bit of Berlin along with the further extension of his medical education.[58]

The most notable of the clinics that Hans attended in Berlin was given at the II *medizinische Poliklinik* by its director, Friedrich Kraus. During the course of a long career Kraus had made contributions to metabolic, infectious, cardiac, pulmonary, and blood diseases. He was best known, however, for his peculiar views about the foundations of individuality. The true "governance" of the person derived, according to Kraus from the vegetative system of the body, constituting the "deep person" which he contrasted with the "cortical person." Kraus's ideas were regarded by some, including Hans, as rather crazy. Nevertheless, Hans found Kraus a very interesting lecturer. At the Surgical Clinic Hans heard another eminent lecturer, August Bier, who had among other things introduced lumbar anesthesia into surgery. In addition Hans took a gynecological clinic and one in his father's specialty, otolaryngology.[59]

While Hans studied in Berlin the inflation grew further out of control as the government printed more and more money in denominations so large that its paper value was beyond comprehension while its real value plummeted. Ordinary people were coming to realize that the cause was no longer merely rapidly rising prices: their money was becoming worthless. Hans, who had inherited the modest sum of 2,000 marks from his mother was among those who saw at this time that unless he spent it immediately his savings would completely disappear. His 2,000 marks just sufficed to buy a copy of *Die Philosophie des als Ob* by Hans Vaihinger.[60]

Hans was interested in this book because Vaihinger's view that all areas of human thought, including scientific thought, are grounded in essential fictions was widely discussed in Germany at the time. Sometime during this period Hans had begun to read systematically in introductory philosophical textbooks as well as in fundamental writers such as Kant. His interest in philosophy had been stirred as far back as the Gymnasium through reading Plato and through the attention given to the famous dictum of Descartes, *Cogito ergo sum*. He was influenced also by the perception that educated Germans were expected to have read some philosophical writers on their own. Undoubtedly he felt some satisfaction in being mature enough to take in works that had bewildered him when he tried to read them as a teenager in response to his father's criticisms. He did not become deeply involved in the problems about which he read, however, and he saw no connection between this reading and his scientific aspirations.[61]

Hans's single semester in Berlin was very stimulating, both medically and culturally. Although he thought — perhaps in part because of the impression Kraus made on him — that the medical standards in Berlin were not highly critical, he was greatly attracted by the vitality of the medical activity, the number of outstanding people there, and the vigorous interest in research. He made up his mind that he would try to fulfill his required postdoctoral year of hospital residency there in a department of general medicine (*Innere Medizin*). Hoping to arrange such a position in advance, he sought interviews in various Berlin clinics. Positions with a salary, or even free room and board were very scarce, however, and he was unable to find an opening. Before he left he did line up an unpaid post at the III Medical Clinic of the University of Berlin for the beginning of 1924.[62]

Hans returned to Munich as planned for the summer semester of 1923. Among the courses for which he registered was a clinic for immunology. During the Whitsuntide holiday he and Wolf again participated in an extended cycling expedition, traveling this time from Munich along the foothills of the Alps to Lindau, where they took a boat across Lake Constance. They returned by way of the Danube valley.[63] After the summer vacation spent again in the Hildesheim hospital, he came back to Munich in October to prepare for the climactic event in his education, the final examination or *ärztliche Prüfung*. This ordeal normally lasted for more than 2 months. The students who were ready to take it were divided into groups of four who studied together and were examined together. One week was devoted to each of the required subjects, which included general surgery, internal medicine, urology, psychiatry, ophthalmology, otolaryngology, pharmacology, pathology, obstetrics, and hygiene. The examinations were mainly oral, but the candidates were also required, in each subject, to write a case history and reach a diagnosis of a patient selected for the purpose. During the examinations the four students within each group were permitted to exchange opinions, but not to have contact with any other group, and there was no way to find out in advance what questions might be asked in any subject. The students were simply responsible to be familiar enough with each field to discuss any aspect of it. The examinations themselves occupied only portions of 3 days of the week spent on a subject, and the students used the rest of the time to review.[64]

Hans and Erich were placed in the same group and worked together to get ready for their examinations. They were well prepared for all of their subjects except for hygiene. That field had not interested either of them, and both had to stay up all night to cram for it. The suspense associated with the long period of testing was heightened by the feeling the students had that there was an arbitrary element in the degree of difficulty they would encounter. There was for each field a single examiner; it was well known that some of them were very severe and were feared, while others were overly lenient.[65]

During the weeks that Hans and Erich were occupied in this manner Germany was undergoing some of the most severe of its many postwar crises. Inflation was more extreme than ever. There was widespread loss of confidence in the national government and several attempts or threats to overthrow state and local governments. Fears of Communist uprisings on the left were balanced by apprehension about the moves of right wing groups with their private armies. Some of the most ominous events were taking place right in Munich, where a general state commissioner appointed to oversee public security entered into complicity with such groups and there appeared a possibility that the Bavarian government would join a plot to overthrow the Republic. Meanwhile, however, a strong new federal chancellor, Gustav Streseman was able to suppress revolts in two other states with a show of force and determination sufficient to deter the central figures in Munich from moving against him. Their retreat induced the leader of one of the rightist groups, Adolf Hitler, to act on his own. On November 8, Hitler declared in a Munich beer hall that the government had been overthrown, and marched through central Munich to the *Odeonplatz* the next day with his storm troopers.[66]

Hans was among those who saw notices posted announcing the overthrow of the Bavarian government and stating that Hitler and General Ludendorff were now in power. There was considerable concern among the medical students about what was happening, and they looked to their teachers to comment on where things stood. Attending a lecture by Friedrich von Müller, Hans was surprised that Müller said nothing about it, and wondered whether the reason was that Müller expected the threat to disappear quickly or if he felt that it was too dangerous to speak out. Erich Stern happened to be walking along a street in Munich when he saw a crowd fleeing. The army had just fired on the National Socialist storm troopers, and the leaders of the intended Putsch were quickly jumping into automobiles to get away. Within a few hours everything was over and the medical students could concentrate again on their own problems.[67]

That Hans, Erich, and their fellow students were not diverted for more than a few hours by the critical events occurring during the time that they were taking their examinations is undoubtedly partly a measure of their preoccupation with the process that put all that they had been doing for the past five semesters to the test. It is also, however, a sign that, for this German generation, living normal lives in the midst of general crisis was not unusual. Ever since they had been old enough to be aware of the outside world theirs had been in a state of crisis.

On December 13, 1923, Hans and Erich completed their examinations. The examining commission awarded Hans an overall mark of "very good"[68] — the highest possible in the understated German scale of formal educational achievement.

Precarious as the external circumstances were when Hans and Erich completed their medical education, it was still an exciting time to be entering medicine. Historians and physicians of today often look back on the medicine of that period as relatively powerless, but that is a retrospective view based on the knowledge that the 1920s belong to the preantibiotic era. Physicians then were well aware of the narrow limits on their ability to cure or arrest disease. Like their predecessors over the centuries they frequently had to look on helplessly while their patients died. It was also a period, however, in which recent developments had given them a few therapeutic means of unprecedented power, with the promise of more to come. Bacteriology and the germ theory of disease were still new enough so that the ability to make precise diagnoses of infectious diseases seemed to be the prelude to the capacity to control them. If the only effective antitoxin so far to emerge from these developments was that for diphtheria, that was itself a potent weapon against one of the most devastating illnesses of childhood and a success that gave hope for similar future antitoxins against other diseases. The discovery by Paul Ehrlich of salvarsan, a chemical agent able to arrest syphilis, appeared as the harbinger of other future "magic bullets." New knowledge about hormones provided means to deal with endocrine disorders, and progress in the identification of vitamins enabled physicians to cope with deficiency diseases. Cancer remained a mysterious scourge, but the eminent biochemist in Berlin, Otto Warburg, was known to be engaged in studies of the respiration of isolated cancer tissue that might soon unveil some of its secrets. Even as Hans and Erich were finishing their studies in Munich, physicians around the world were beginning to receive supplies of a new drug called insulin, through which they could control the dreaded diabetes, and even retrieve patients in advanced states of deterioration from imminent death. Insulin was not only a miracle, but dramatic evidence of the emerging power of medicine to combat disease. Hans had good reason to feel that he would be able to participate in further advances along these hopeful lines.[69]

When Hans told his father that he would not follow him into otolaryngology, but planned to enter academic medicine so that he could do research, his father accepted his decision with disappointment. He warned Hans that science was not an occupation at which one could make a living, and that Hans must not rely on him for financial support. Hans understood that he could not support himself through research. He saw that many of his teachers were able to combine research with lucrative private practices, and he hoped that he too could somehow combine clinical and experimental activity. He did not have a clear idea of how he would manage it, but just hoped for the best.[70]

While Hans was finishing his studies in Munich, Wolf was nearby completing the second year of his electrical engineering course. Now entirely occupied with the subjects that most interested him, Wolf excelled in his studies. On visits home, however, Wolf saw that his father was very lonely in the empty Krebs household, and he decided to leave Munich to be nearer to him. His first choice was an excellent *Technische Hochschule* in Hanover, but he was unable to transfer there on short notice, so he enrolled for the summer semester of 1924 in Brunswick. From there he could come home every weekend to keep his father company. It is unlikely that Wolf's more single-minded older brother would have sacrificed his own plans for such a reason, even if he had been as sensitive to his father's need. Hans probably thought that Wolf moved to Brunswick simply because once he himself had left Munich his little brother was unambitious enough to want to live close to home.[71]

III

On January 2, 1924, Hans Krebs began his required year of clinical hospital service at the III Medical Clinic of the University of Berlin. The clinic was located in the heart of the central city, on the north bank of the River Spree next to the Monjibou Palace. Krebs found a room three to four miles to the west, and often cycled back and forth, riding along the shaded paths through the beautiful Berlin *Tiergarten* and past the Brandenburg gate or the *Reichstag*.[72]

The director of the clinic, Alfred Goldscheider, was another in the galaxy of distinguished figures who headed the major institutions of this capital medical center. Earlier in his long career he had made important contributions to nerve physiology, showing in particular that heat, cold, and pain are sensed at different points on the skin. He had also helped to lay the foundations for the field of physical therapy. Now nearing retirement, Goldscheider still gave his clinical lectures 5 days a week. The resident physicians were expected to attend along with medical students. Since, as in the clinics Krebs had earlier attended, the lectures were based on individual case histories, he found he had still much to learn from them. Outside the lectures he had little contact with Goldscheider, most of whose time was occupied by his large private practice in internal medicine.[73]

Krebs was assigned clinical duties in the outpatient department, attached to the service of a Dr. Mosler, a specialist in cardiac diseases. Krebs performed preliminary examinations, decided whether X-rays or other laboratory tests were necessary, then presented the patients to a senior physician on duty for a final decision on what should be done.[74]

Like other medical institutions within the university, the III Medical Clinic encouraged its junior medical staff to engage themselves in research, and those who chose to spend their practical year in university clinics without pay often did so because of the research opportunities. After he had taken a few weeks to acquaint himself with the hospital routines and its personnel, Krebs found that he could spare about half his time to work in the laboratory. Mosler was uninterested in research, but the head of the clinical section in which Krebs worked, Dr. Annelise Wittgenstein, supported his interest enthusiastically and arranged for the facilities he needed to get started. In addition to space in one of the laboratory rooms that filled the top floor of the clinic, and supplies, he could call on the laboratory assistants available to help out with serological or biochemical tests, or to handle animals that might be used experimentally.[75]

These circumstances constrained Krebs to involve himself in a research problem of interest to Wittgenstein. Although untrained as an experimentalist, she was particularly concerned with problems involved in the diagnosis of syphilis, and he directed his attention to one of the prominent laboratory tests then in use, the gold sol reaction.[76]

By the 1920s laboratory tests had become central to the practice of internal medicine. Clinical research laboratories in Germany devoted great attention to extending and refining the diagnostic methods available, and an enormous amount of their effort was expended on the problem of identifying syphilis. The large outflow of research publications on this subject was a measure not only of the devastating personal and social consequences of syphilis, but of the complexity of dealing with a disease that appeared in manifold forms; that evolved over a period of many years, manifesting several stages with markedly different symptoms; and that could become latent in an individual for long periods and then reappear with severely debilitating effects. The presence of the powerful new therapeutic weapon salvarsan made it more urgent than ever to recognize promptly a disease that in its early stages could often escape detection or be mistaken for other diseases. Treatment with salvarsan was most effective in the primary or secondary stage, before irreversible deterioration had taken place. It was also notorious that energetic treatments with salvarsan repeated over several months could cause all the symptoms of syphilis to disappear without eradicating the minute spirochaete discovered in 1905 by Fritz Schaudinn to be the infective cause of the disease. Physicians had a saying that a syphilitic (luetic) infection in the central nervous system can "well sleep, but has not died."[77] In the late or "quaternary" stages of syphilis the sensory and motor disturbances due to degeneration of the spinal cord (*tabes dorsalis*) and the abnormal mental states (paresis) often mimicked other forms of neural and mental disease. It became critical, therefore, to seek better methods to discriminate cases in which these symptoms were manifestations of syphilitic lesions of the central nervous system from other cases in which they reflected different underlying pathological processes.[78]

The most commonly used diagnostic test was the Wassermann reaction. August Wassermann and several collaborators had first published the method in 1906. Applying current immunological concepts, they reacted patient serum with serum from monkeys pretreated with syphilitic material and tested whether or not it could afterward hemolyze red blood corpuscles. Wassermann took the reaction at first to be an indication of whether or not the patient blood contained a syphilitic antibody. The test was complex and required considerable judgment. At first it was relatively unreliable, but after gradual modification of the procedures it attained, by the 1920s, over 90 percent accuracy in identifying positive cases. There remained, however, disagreement over the nature of the reaction, and it was regarded as insufficiently sensitive to rely on a negative result as proof of the absence of syphilis. During the two decades following Wassermann's initial publication more than a thousand papers appeared on the reaction in the German literature alone.[79] Meanwhile investigators sought with nearly as much intensity other methods to supplement the Wassermann reaction. Of these the most important was the gold sol reaction.

If the main sources of the Wassermann reaction were concepts taken from the immunology and serology of the beginning of the century, that of the gold sol reaction was the growing field of colloid chemistry. Richard Zsigmondy, one of the leading proponents of that field, the inventor of the ultramicroscope that could make large colloidal particles visible, had chosen to study suspensions of colloidal gold as the paradigmatic example of a metallic colloidal sol; that is, of a system in which colloidal aggregates of metallic atoms are dispersed within an aqueous medium containing also electrolytes such as sodium or potassium chloride. Zsigmondy prepared gold sols by reducing the charged gold ions in a gold chloride solution to metallic gold by means of formaldehyde.[80]

A gold sol prepared according to Zsigmondy's directions was a perfectly transparent deep red when viewed by transmitted light. The sol was, however, extremely sensitive to minute quantities of other substances and could, under various conditions, appear violet or bluish and acquire an opalescence. Zsigmondy attributed these changes to variations in the size and degree of dispersal of the colloidal particles. The red sols contained small, finely dispersed particles. Progressive increases in the size of the particles, or lessening the distance between them, produced the spectrum of shades from reddish violet to blue. The gold sol could be readily flocculated and separated out of the medium by the addition of salts or other colloids. On the other hand, certain colloids, such as those of some proteins, added to a gold sol could "protect" it to some degree from flocculation by a salt. The properties of pure gold sols and of gold sols combined with other colloids were also very sensitive to factors such as hydrogen ion concentration and temperature.[81]

Although the reactions of the gold sol were, according to Zsigmondy, superficially similar to chemical reactions, they did not take place following chemical affinities but the special laws of colloid chemical reactions. A second colloid, for example, could flocculate a gold sol only when the two were mixed in certain proportions and within certain concentration ranges. The properties of such colloidal systems, and their changes, he attributed to the sizes of the particles, the positive or negative charges on their surfaces, the interactions of oppositely charged particles when mixed together, the adsorption of one type of colloidal particle on the surface of another, and the influence of their relative sizes and concentrations on the distribution of such particles. When colloidal proteins were involved, the effects of the hydrogen ion concentration could be explained in terms of the amphoteric nature of proteins. Colloidal protein particles were positively charged in acidic solutions, negatively charged in alkaline solutions, and at a hydrogen ion concentration characteristic for each type of protein — its isoelectric point — there was no net charge.[82]

The color changes of the gold sol made it a very sensitive indicator for the presence of minute quantities of other substances. This property prompted Carl Lange, an assistant physician at the Rudolf Virchow Hospital in Berlin, to devise, in 1913, a new diagnostic test for syphilis. Cerebrospinal fluid was obtained from syphilitic patients by means of a lumbar puncture, sometimes done to relieve pain caused by abnormal increases in its pressure. Because of the intimate connection of the fluid with brain and spinal cord tissue, however, it appeared likely that alterations of the cerebrospinal cord could afford indications of pathological changes within the central nervous system. The "cardinal question" that clinicians hoped that tests on cerebrospinal fluid could answer was whether a given disease of the central nervous system was luetic or nonluetic; that is, due to syphilitic infection or some other cause. The Wassermann reaction proved less effective with cerebrospinal fluid than with blood serum, so there was a search for other tests. Lange viewed the gold sol as particularly promising, because its reactivity with minute quantities of other substances might enable diagnostic tests to be carried out on such small amounts of cerebrospinal fluid that a test could be repeated frequently to follow the effects of therapy.[83]

Following Zsigmondy's procedure, Lange established a clear deep red gold sol by adding 1 percent gold chloride, 2 percent potash, and 1 percent formol to doubly distilled water. Then he prepared 12 successive dilutions of 1:10, 1:20, 1:40, until 1:20,000 of the primary solution and placed them in tubes lined up in a rack. When he added equal quantities of normal cerebrospinal fluid to each of the tubes there was no change in the sol. Syphilitic fluid, on the other hand, produced color changes within one or several of the tubes representing a restricted range of concentrations, leaving those of greater or lesser concentration unchanged. Moreover, both the degree of color change and the concentrations at which it occurred appeared to differ in keeping with the nature and severity of the syphilitic symptoms. Representing his results graphically with the concentrations of the gold sol on the horizontal axis and successive color changes — red, reddish blue, bluish red, light blue, whitish blue, and colorless (the last two stages representing, respectively, incipient flocculation and complete precipitation of the sol leaving a colorless solution) — on the vertical axis, Lange obtained characteristic patterns that he believed were not only specific to syphilis but capable of differentiating its various stages. Nonluetic diseases of the central nervous system also produced changes, but the curves were typically displaced to the right and, therefore, differentiable from syphilitic forms. Shown here (see next page) are two examples of Lange's graphical representations.[84]

Lange's method caused great excitement in clinical circles when his paper appeared, because it raised hopes that it could not only determine whether diseases of the central nervous system were luetic or nonluetic, but also differentiate, through characteristic variations in the reaction curve, further types within both groups.[85] It was, moreover, far more sensitive than any other

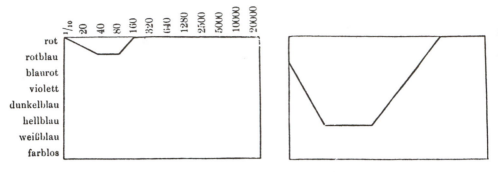

Figure 4.3 Left, Lues with headache. Right, Tabes.

diagnostic test for syphilis, affording positive indications of early stages of nervous system involvement when the Wassermann reaction was negative. The very properties of the gold sol that made it so sensitive, however, made it difficult to apply widely in clinical practice. It was necessary to prepare the gold sol with the greatest care, using special Jena glassware and the purest possible reagents to attain the desired clear red solution rather than one with a bluish tint. Few clinical laboratories were fully equipped for the delicate procedures required, and the clinical assistants who employed the method were seldom trained in colloid chemistry. Following Lange's directions, clinicians in some laboratories found that the test did not work (*nicht geht*) or that the preparation of a usable sol was too capricious to count on. Some clinics, therefore, avoided adopting the method altogether. In others investigators sought to "improve" the method, and a steady flow of papers reported variations on Lange's original procedure. To one observer it appeared in 1922 that "the number of different methods is almost as large as the number of authors who have occupied themselves with the G.-R." Even those who used the test successfully found that each gold sol they prepared differed slightly from every other one in its sensitivity, or the "hardness" or "softness" of its reactivity, so that they commonly talked of the "individuality" of the gold sols.[86]

More controversial even than questions concerning the practical clinical application of the gold sol were those concerning the theoretical explanation of its reactions. The effects of syphilitic cerebrospinal fluid on it were attributed to causes as diverse as a "luetic antibody," an enzyme, and a thrombin-antithrombin reaction. The view that gained most support was that it was a flocculation reaction between the colloidal gold particles and a colloidal constituent of the cerebrospinal fluid. To identify the latter substance Heinrich Fischer fractionated the protein components of cerebrospinal fluid in 1921, tested them separately with gold sols, and concluded that the globulin fractions were the principal cause of the flocculations. The albumin fractions, on the other hand, inhibited the reaction; that is, they acted as "protective colloids."[87] During the next 3 years papers continued to appear offering further refinements of the method or the theory of the reaction. The explanations of the many variations in the degree of the reaction or the range of dilutions over which it occurred invoked in particular the effect of the hydrogen ion concentration on the original state of dispersal of the gold sol and on the charge of the amphoteric albumin and globulin. The efficacy of the gold sol reaction in identifying syphilitic cerebrospinal fluid was generally ascribed to increases in the concentration of protein in that fluid derived from the metabolic breakdown of central nervous system tissue. When Hans Krebs took up the problem in 1924 the gold sol reaction was gradually proving its clinical worth despite its complications, but there was still no comprehensive theory able to reduce its many complexities to a common explanatory framework.[88]

The majority of the papers on the gold sol reaction were published by physicians or assistants working in the various university clinics in Germany. Some of these authors admonished their colleagues about the need to keep in mind "fundamental facts of colloid chemistry," such as the critical dependence of colloidal solutions on the hydrogen ion concentration, and the effects of the masses and the charges of the particles on flocculation reactions.[89] Hans Krebs was probably attracted to the problem in part because he thought he knew quite a bit about colloid and physical chemistry. The physicalist approach to histological staining that he had acquired in Möllendorff's laboratory had induced him to study the major textbooks of colloid chemistry by Zsigmondy and by Herbert Freundlich. He may also have read by this time Leonor Michaelis's *The Hydrogen Ion Concentration: Its Meaning for Biology and the Methods for Measuring it*. This little book by one of the leading physical chemists of the time greatly stimulated Krebs. By comparison with the textbooks to which he was accustomed he not only found Michaelis's writing to be exceptionally lucid, but it went more deeply into the fundamental principles of the subject. Michaelis derived the theoretical relationships mathematically and then applied them to phenomena such as adsorption potentials, membrane effects, and isoelectric points that were pertinent to colloid chemistry. Krebs went over the text again and again until he felt he had a secure grasp on the subject.[90]

Much as he had learned about colloid chemistry from books, Krebs had little practical experience with its laboratory methods. Nor was there anyone present in the clinical laboratory who could instruct him in such methods. He must have taught himself by trial and error, following directions set forth in handbooks of clinical serology or in Zsigmondy's textbook, until he had acquired the skill to prepare a perfectly transparent ruby red sol. He reviewed the numerous modifications of the method published in the journal literature, and must have tried out many of them, seeking the method that would work best for him.[91] Krebs thus plunged into a research problem on which many other physicians with backgrounds and positions similar to his own were already engaged in clinics throughout Germany. He did so without any special advantages other than his keenness to be involved in research, his disciplined energy, and his capacity to concentrate intently on whatever problem he took up.

Like those who had preceded him, Krebs encountered pitfalls in his way. His early results were irregular and he found, as many others had, that the successive gold sols that he prepared varied in their properties. Although a well-prepared gold sol was supposed to be stable for several months, he found that his became altered and that he had to make up fresh ones quite often.[92] It was through "an accident in the preparation of the gold reaction" that he made the first observation he considered noteworthy. A small addition of potash to a gold sol previously suitable for diagnostic tests made it, he found "completely unusable." Although to all appearances identical to a normal one, such a sol had lost its capacity to change color or to flocculate with pathological cerebrospinal fluid. Following up this unexpected result, he tested gold sols with potash added in graduated, precisely measured quantities and ascertained that the gold sol reaction gradually weakened as the alkalinity increased. Other alkalis acted similarly. The obvious next question was whether gradually increasing the acidity might have the inverse effect. The gold sol turned out to become increasingly sensitive with additions of successively larger quantities of acid, until it became unusable for diagnoses because it gave with normal cerebrospinal fluid curves resembling the reactions of "proper" gold sols with syphilitic liquor. Pursuing these phenomena further, he discovered that by varying the hydrogen ion concentration he could imitate, with normal liquor, curves considered characteristic for tabes, lues, and paralysis. Like some of his predecessors in the field, he concluded that results that had been identified as specific to these pathological states were instead consequences of differences in the hydrogen ion concentration at which the gold sol reaction occurred. A practical compensation of his finding was that he learned that he could salvage for diagnostic use gold sols that when first tested with cerebrospinal fluid appeared unusable. If a gold sol was oversensitive he could correct it by adding alkali, if it was too insensitive he added acid, until it passed the "biological test" of reacting properly with normal and pathological samples of cerebrospinal fluid. From these experiences Krebs drew the not entirely original inference that "the H-ion concentration is of decisive significance for the outcome of the gold sol reaction."[93]

    Through a "second accident," Krebs stumbled onto a method that enabled him to prepare a gold sol that did not require as strict control of the hydrogen ion concentration as did the current methods that he had tried out. In all the methods he had studied in the literature, one first heated gold chloride with the reducing agent (formaldehyde or glucose) or with the potash, and then added the other of these reagents. Whether by chance or design, Krebs at some point heated the reducing agent first with the potash and only then added the gold chloride. He noticed, in contrast to the gold sols he had previously prepared, that those resulting from this seemingly minor change in the order of operations were unaltered by relatively small variations in the quantity of potash added. Although he could not explain why this technique had such an outcome, he exploited it to devise a procedure with which he believed he could establish a gold sol "with a certainty that I have not seen with any of the other methods that I have tested."[94]

    Thus, Krebs joined a growing number of clinical investigators who thought that they had been able to make significant improvements in the procedures for preparing diagnostic gold sol solutions. Like others before him, he too hoped that with his refined method he could elucidate the nature of the gold sol reaction. Following the precedent of Fischer and others, he embarked on a research program to test the gold sol reaction with the various proteins found in blood serum and cerebrospinal fluid. He also set up the procedures for introducing the reaction into the routine service of the clinical laboratory, which had apparently until then not performed it diagnostically.[95]

IV

At the III Medical Clinic Krebs met David Nachmansohn, who had passed his *Ärtzliche Prüfung* at the same time as Krebs, and was also serving his mandatory year of hospital practice. A few years earlier Nachmansohn had been a reluctant medical student more interested in philosophy, literature, and history, but his parents and friends had insisted that under the bleak conditions of postwar Germany he would need the economic security that medicine could afford. By the time he finished his medical education he had become enthused about biomedical research, in part by reading about the great scientists of the past. Lacking practical laboratory experience, he was working on a thesis on sleep that was mainly a theoretical analysis based on the existing literature.[96]

Krebs found Nachmansohn to be an engaging, warm-hearted person, and they quickly became friends. Among their shared cultural interests was an enthusiasm for Goethe's *Faust*, which they had each read by now many times, and the ending of which both probably now viewed as a call to them to devote themselves to creative research. Nachmansohn had become an active supporter of the Zionist movement. Inspired by one of the German leaders of that movement, Kurt Blumenfeld, Nachmansohn believed that Jews would best be able to exert their creative energy in the new homeland that appeared realizable in Palestine after the liberation of that land from Turkish rule and the Balfour declaration of 1917 promising a Jewish national state there. Nachmansohn thought for awhile that he might become a physician in Palestine. He tried to interest Krebs in Zionism, but when he recognized that Krebs perceived himself as a deeply rooted German, Nachmansohn did not press him.[97]

Another strong friendship that Krebs established at the III Medical Clinic was with Bruno Mendel, a physician 3 years older than himself. Mendel had already built up a large private practice around a new treatment for arthritis that he had developed using a drug introduced earlier to treat gout. He had been able to get the nearly insoluble compound into a concentrated solution and had arranged with a small pharmaceutical firm to produce it in the form of ampules. Injection of the drug gave immediate relief from crippling pain, but the treatment had to be repeated at short intervals. Mendel was on the staff of the clinic and worked there regularly, although he received no salary.[98]

At about or shortly before the time Krebs became acquainted with him, Mendel read several papers recently published by Otto Warburg on the metabolism of cancer cells. As noted previously, this work created a stir because it appeared to provide the first clues about the abnormal metabolism of cancer that might lead ultimately to a means to treat that dreaded disease. At the

Kaiser-Wilhelm Gesellschaft in Dahlem, in the western suburbs of Berlin, Warburg had devised innovative methods to measure the rate of formation of lactic acid in tissue slices surviving in a fluid medium in flasks attached to manometers (for further details, see Chapter 5). The striking discovery that Warburg had made was that apparently cancer tissue, unlike normal tissues, produced lactic acid through glycolysis aerobically as well as anaerobically. Warburg's publications on this subject in 1923 and 1924 also further stimulated interest in the metabolic role of lactic acid that the work of Otto Meyerhof had impressed on the medical world, especially after Meyerhof shared the Nobel Prize in 1922 for his work on muscle metabolism (see Chapter 1, pp. 14–15).[99]

To Bruno Mendel it was surprising that despite this and other evidence for the broad significance of lactic acid in the vital processes connected with intermediary metabolism there had been little systematic investigation of the lactic acid content of human blood under physiological and pathological conditions. Reviewing the literature on the subject, he concluded that the reason for this gap was that the methods available to determine lactic acid quantitatively required such large amounts of blood (more than 100 cm^3) that they were impractical for clinical use. He set out, therefore, to devise a micromethod.[100]

Although Mendel had little experimental experience or systematic training in chemistry, he proved to be a resourceful self-taught investigator. He sought advice from those with the expertise he lacked and turned it to good account. From the literature on lactic acid he learned that if that compound is converted to acetaldehyde and the latter is reacted with veratrol, a phenol compound, it gives a distinctive color. He decided to try to convert these reactions into a quantitative colorimetric test for lactic acid. Simple though the basic procedure was, he encountered many practical obstacles. By patiently examining and varying the conditions and the concentrations of the reagents, Mendel arrived, during the time that Krebs saw him daily in the clinical laboratory, at a very satisfactory method, requiring only 1 cm^3 of blood, that could be performed in 1¼ hours.[101]

It is evident that Krebs quickly came to admire the skill and determination with which Mendel overcame the limitations in his scientific background, the thoroughness and patience with which he pursued the problem he had chosen for himself, his openness to advice, and his remarkable success in identifying and solving a strategic problem that others with superior credentials had overlooked. As a young physician himself attempting to launch an investigative career on his own with limited experimental training, Krebs undoubtedly identified with Mendel's position and probably to some degree hoped to emulate his approach to research. Moreover, Krebs found Mendel to be an attractive personality. A handsome fair-haired man with an athletic physique, Mendel was also poised, well-mannered and articulate.[102] Son of a well-known physician and naturally aristocratic in his bearing, Mendel probably became for Krebs a significant role model as well as a valued friend.

Such models may have been particularly important to Krebs just then because he was beginning to experience some disillusionment with the research world he was seeking to enter. The image of research that he had formed derived from lectures by distinguished senior professors recounting major contributions they had made to scientific and medical knowledge. Much of the experimentation he now observed around him in the laboratories of the III Medical Clinic bore little resemblance to his ideal. Some of the clinicians he saw at work at the benches knew less than he did about the scientific principles underlying their research problems. Some of them appeared to him to be engaged in research mainly for the prestige that it could bring them or for the luster it could lend to their future private practices. He began to realize too that scientific publication was not necessarily meaningful. The major scientific journals accepted papers from recognized research institutions without critical scrutiny, seldom rejected submissions, and encouraged excessive length because the editors were compensated according to the number of pages they published. Much of what he read in these journals seemed to be relatively worthless.[103] To identify within this milieu exceptional individuals such as Bruno Mendel probably helped him to sustain his respect for the activity in which he was beginning to participate, and encouraged him to believe that he too could make a mark on a current problem in medical research.

By the time Krebs entered the III Medical Clinic economic stability was returning to Germany. The replacement of the worthless mark by the *Rentenmark* and the strict regulations that accompanied this change quickly stilled the inflationary whirlwind.[104] It was undoubtedly easier for his father to provide Hans with the financial support on which he continued to depend than it had been during the previous years. Although Georg Krebs's savings had been wiped out along with those of many other middle class Germans, his strong current income enabled him to see his two sons through to the completion of their educations without undue hardship.

The busy clinician and investigator at the III Clinic was not too preoccupied to appreciate and to take some part in the intense cultural life that attracted so many young people to Berlin during the 1920s. Working in the immediate vicinity of world famous operas, theaters, and museums, he frequented them as often as he could. He probably heard musical performances by such eminent conductors as Otto Klemperer and Wilhelm Furtwangler. In the theater his taste probably did not run to the more daring Expressionist movement, but he saw many plays by George Bernard Shaw, who became one of his favorite dramatists.[105]

The liberated attitudes among the young men and women of Berlin were quite visible to Krebs. There, for the first time he met couples who replied to his question about whether they were married by saying "We are living together." Although he was too shy and perhaps too conservative to enter into the new norms, he did begin to enjoy a more active social life than he had known as a student. He met a woman named Fernanda Steingötter, who worked as a technician in the cardiology department doing electrocardiograms, and began to see her regularly. Fernanda had a married friend named Ursula Bucky, who worked in radiology, with whom Hans also became good friends. Hans, Fernanda, Ursula, and her husband often went together or with other friends to parties and outings, or got together to play phonograph records. Hans was still

Figure 4.4 Hans Krebs in 1924.

reticent and timid about starting a conversation in a group, but his female friends found that he was quite sociable and had a lively sense of humor. After listening quietly to a conversation for awhile he was apt to add a funny comment that made them giggle and laugh. He was, they thought, a lovely person to have at a nice party.[106]

While Hans was in Berlin Wolf continued his studies in electrical engineering in Brunswick, making the short trip to Hildesheim weekly to be with his father. Every Sunday morning they sight-read together a piano arrangement of a Hayden symphony, the senior Krebs playing the left hand and his younger son supplying the right hand. They called it their *Morgenandacht*. His enjoyment of his son's regular visits did not alleviate Georg Krebs's loneliness for female companionship, however. Sometime in 1924 he sought his children's advice concerning the widow of a wealthy Hildesheim banker whom he had taken out a few times and wanted to marry. To win the family over this woman invited Wolf to a lavish party at which she played the piano, not very well in his opinion. Wolf, Hans, and Lise all thought her rather ostentatious and unintelligent, and talked their father out of his plan.[107]

V

Although Hans may have come home from Berlin for short visits during 1924, that year was probably the first one in his life in which he did not live at home for any extended holiday periods. Through most of the year that he spent at the III Clinic he must have continued the experiments facilitated by his new procedure for setting up a gold sol. An additional benefit of his new method he soon found was that he could produce gold sols of unusually high concentration by repeating the sequence of operations — they were purplish red rather than ruby. His first priority was to "pursue *systematically* the significance of the H-ion concentration" whose critical importance his early efforts to produce gold sols had driven home to him. He decided to test the effects of different degrees of acidity on gold sol flocculation reactions with blood serum. Here he encountered one of the technical limitations of working in a clinical laboratory. Hydrogen gas electrometers to measure the pH quantitatively had been in use for several years, but were not yet manufactured commercially, and the laboratory of the III Medical Clinic did not possess one. Titrations with indicators were too inaccurate for his purpose. He was able, therefore, only to prepare six gold sols with successive increments of added potash, thus providing a series of decreasing acidity, but the exact hydrogen ion concentrations of which he did not know. Devising a clever permutation of the standard diagnostic gold sol reaction, he tested each of these gold sols with 24 successive dilutions of the blood serum.[108]

A single such experiment required 288 individual tests (following the customary diagnostic procedure he repeated each test 1 minute after drawing the serum from a patient and 24 hours later). From his later publication on the subject it is not evident how many experiments of this type Krebs performed, but he must have spent at least several months on preliminary experiments leading to the single set of results he afterward reported. The most significant observation he made during that time was that with the gold sols of "higher acidity" there were two flocculation zones. One zone lay in the "region of the highest serum concentration," the second zone was at "very low" serum concentrations. Moreover, he noticed that the appearance of the process in the two zones was so different that he suspected there were two different reactions involved. In "zone 1" there was no color change in the sol, and a precipitate formed that was similar in color to the sol itself. In "zone 2" the sol underwent the characteristic changes from red to bluish. (He later wrote that "for one who has *seen* this experiment the different appearances were more self-evident than might appear from" his description.) Examining the differences further, he found that the zone 1 flocculation could be reversed by adding either more acid or more alkali, whereas the zone 2 flocculation was irreversible. With less acidic gold sols the two zones tended to move together until they merged in a flocculation that displayed mixed characteristics.[109]

Drawing on commonly described phenomena of colloid chemistry, Krebs inferred that the zone 1 flocculation was due to the precipitation of a component of the serum, probably globulin, that was insoluble at its isoelectric point and carried the gold sol particles down with it. The zone 2 reaction was an instance of the flocculation of two oppositely charged colloids — the negative gold sol and the positive protein — that takes place within a narrow range of proportions of the two components. An acidic gold sol was necessary for both processes: in the first case because the isoelectric point of globulin is acidic, in the second because amphoteric proteins become positively charged only in acidic solution.[110] Krebs must have arrived at his interpretation gradually over the course of his investigation, carrying out the experiments on the reversibility of the flocculations to test his first ideas about the processes involved and in turn inducing him to develop further his explanatory scheme.

After Krebs had been preparing gold sols for half a year both for diagnostic tests and for his research, his new method "one day suddenly failed," although he had made no conscious changes in the technique. He spent weeks trying "to find the solution to the mystery" of what had gone wrong. Belatedly he recalled that at just the time his method stopped working he had replaced the rubber stopper connecting the distillation flask to the condenser in the apparatus he used to distil the water for the gold sol with a cork. He inferred that the rubber stopper must have imparted to the distilled water some impurities that were essential to the success of his method. When he put a rubber stopper back into the apparatus he once again produced beautiful gold sols. Although he could not say what the impurities were that seemed to make the difference, he continued to rely on them. Krebs had benefited from a good measure of beginner's luck. Had he been more attentive to the warning given in Lange's original directions for preparing gold sols, that "a rubber stopper used in the distillation apparatus in place of a cork introduced impurities that interfered with the process,"[111] Krebs would probably not have discovered the advantageous variation on Lange's procedure that propelled him to his further analysis of the gold sol reaction.

While Krebs was working alone on the gold sol reaction with the support of Annelise Wittgenstein she suggested that they might undertake concurrently a joint investigation of another problem related to syphilis and the cerebrospinal fluid. As a clinician Wittgenstein had been particularly concerned with the well-known resistance of tertiary syphilis to drugs, such as salvarsan, that were highly effective in treating the earlier stages of the disease. Because the symptoms of the late stages — tabes and paresis — characteristically involved the central nervous system, and because substances injected into the blood were known to enter only with difficulty into the brain and spinal cord, it was widely assumed that the therapeutic problem was how to get antisyphilitic drugs across the "blood-brain barrier" so that they could attack the spirochaete harbored within the tissue of the central nervous system. Adopting a maneuver that other clinicians had already tried, Wittgenstein treated tertiary syphilis by injecting salvarsan directly into the cerebrospinal fluid. She removed about 30 ml of the fluid by lumbar puncture, added a small amount of the drug to it, and put the fluid back in. Krebs himself performed this procedure many times in the clinic under her supervision.[112]

Wittgenstein proposed to Krebs, probably during the summer of 1924, that they carry out together an experimental study of how substances introduced into the blood pass into the cerebrospinal fluid and what factors influence the degree to which different substances can do so. Eager though she was to do such an investigation, Krebs quickly realized that she had no idea how to go about it. Wittgenstein was an effective clinician in his view mainly because she managed patients very well and took a personal interest in them; but she had no laboratory training and seemed to know little about physical chemistry. It fell entirely to him, therefore, to study the existing literature on the cerebrospinal fluid and to devise a research plan.[113]

The most general result of chemical analyses that various investigators had carried out on cerebrospinal fluid was that its composition differed far more from blood serum than did the composition of the lymphatic fluids of the body. Whereas the latter contained most of the same substances as serum, only with lower concentrations of protein, normal cerebrospinal fluid included only traces of the characteristic serum proteins. The inorganic ions differed both quantitatively and qualitatively. In contrast to the serum, for example, the concentration of potassium ions was higher than that of sodium ions. These differences led some to conclude that cerebrospinal fluid, unlike lymph, was formed only in small part by the physical process of diffusion across the meningeal membranes that separate the fluid anatomically from the blood; that it was mainly "a specific product of the brain."[114]

During the preceding three decades there had been numerous attempts to elucidate the question of how cerebrospinal fluid is formed by examining whether foreign substances injected into the blood of animals or human patients appeared in the fluid. The most recent and most comprehensive of such experiments had been completed in 1921 by Lina Stern and R. Gautier at the physiology laboratory of the University of Geneva. Noting the discordant results that previous investigators had reported, Stern and Gautier sought to attain more favorable conditions for the passage of substances into the cerebrospinal fluid by injecting them subcutaneously or intravenously into anesthetized rabbits, dogs, and cats whose kidneys had been excised so that the substances would not be excreted before they had time to reach the fluid. They injected various salts that could be identified in the fluid through distinctive reactions; a series of alkaloids that could be identified by their physiological effects if the cerebrospinal fluid contained them; and several dyes that could be identified by the fact that they would color the clear fluid if they entered it. With respect to most of the individual substances tested Stern and Gautier obtained consistent results, but they could discern no correlation between the properties of the substances and whether or not they were able to penetrate into the cerebrospinal fluid.[115]

Their results showed, they concluded,

> That certain foreign substances injected into the blood find their way
> into the CR fluid, whereas others, very similar from a chemical and
> physical point of view are never detected there. No physical or
> chemical law can explain that difference. Matters take place as if
> there exists between the blood on the one hand and the CR fluid on the
> other, an apparatus in which a special mechanism can carry out a kind
> of selection among the substances contained normally or accidentally
> in the blood, allowing some to pass and holding back or stopping
> others.
>
> It is this mechanism...to which we have given the name *blood-
> brain barrier*.[116]

Stern and Gautier interpreted this process "from a teleological point of view" as
the means by which the organism maintains "a constant liquid milieu surrounding the nervous elements." At the end of their paper they asked whether the
intimate mechanism of this barrier was "a biological or vital phenomenon, or
rather a physical or physical-chemical phenomenon?"[117]

When Krebs reviewed Stern and Gautier's paper along with the previous
literature on the subject it seemed to him that all that had been established was
that certain substances could penetrate from the blood to the cerebrospinal fluid
and that others could not, and that in certain diseases the permeability of the
meningeal membranes separating these fluids was increased. These were merely
descriptive results. As far as he could see no one had found any general
regularities governing the exchange of materials. Stern and Gautier were, in his
opinion, invoking a *vital* explanation that did not lead to a closer analysis of the
function of the meningeal membranes.[118]

It was probably while Krebs was already engaged in his study of the
literature on this problem — perhaps in August or September 1924 — that a
timely paper appeared in *Pflüger's Archiv* by Günther Lehmann and A.
Meesmann on "The Existence of a Donnan Equilibrium between Blood and the
Aqueous Humor and the Cerebrospinal Liquor Respectively." The aqueous
humor of the eye was the only other fluid in the body that appeared to have the
same chemical and anatomical relationships to the blood that the cerebrospinal
fluid had. Lehmann and Meeson argued that it was probable a priori that there
was a free exchange of water and salts but not of proteins between these fluids
and the blood. If so, then the relation between them should conform to certain
"purely physical theories," including particularly what had become known as the
Donnan equilibrium. If two solutions, one containing a colloidal ion, are
separated by a membrane impermeable to the colloid, then after the diffusion of
the ions that can cross the membrane has reached an equilibrium, the ions will
not be equally divided on both sides of the membrane. The concentration of the
crystalloid ions of charge opposite to that of the colloidal ion will be greater on
the side containing the colloid, whereas the concentration of crystalloid ions
having a charge in the same direction as that of the colloid will be greater in the

colloid-free solution. The Donnan equilibrium predicted also that the unequal distribution of positively and negatively charged ions would create a potential across the membrane. Lehmann and Meesman confirmed the existence of a Donnan equilibrium between the aqueous humor and the blood by showing that the relative concentrations of chloride ions and the relative pH of the two fluids conformed to its prediction, and by measuring a potential difference of the expected direction and magnitude between the two fluids in rabbits and frogs.[119]

As soon as Krebs read Lehmann and Meese's paper he saw that the Donnan equilibrium was a promising starting point to approach the problem of the penetration of substances into the cerebrospinal fluid from a "definite physical–chemical point of view." Although he was already roughly familiar with the Donnan equilibrium from the textbooks of physical and colloid chemistry that he had studied, he knew that he needed to understand it more thoroughly if he were to apply it to his investigation. He went back to the original paper on "The Theory of Membrane Equilibrium in the Presence of a Non-dialyzable Electrolyte," published by Frederick Donnan in 1911 in *Zeitschrift für Elektrochemie*. The paper appeared to Krebs a model of clarity. As he took in the meaning of the theory that Donnan had presented, he recognized that the quantitative statement of the distribution of ions across a membrane (e.g., $[Na^+_1] \times [Cl^-_1] = [Na^+_2] \times [Cl^-_2]$), where the brackets represent the concentrations of sodium and chloride as exemplary ions and the subscripts 1 and 2 indicate, respectively, the colloid-containing and colloid-free solutions) could apply only to equilibrium conditions, because it was derived from thermodynamic considerations.[120] Donnan had written, however,

> If on one side of a membrane an electrolytically dissociated substance
> is present in sufficiently large quantities relative to an undialyzable
> anion, it will strongly "attract" the cation of a second completely
> different (and otherwise completely dialyzable) electrolyte and will in
> the same way "repel" the anion.[121]

This dynamic view of the processes involved induced Krebs to think that the principle of the Donnan equilibrium could also be applied qualitatively to nonequilibrium situations such as the penetration of substances from the blood through the meningeal membrane to the cerebrospinal fluid. Because of the proteins in serum, the blood corresponded to a solution containing colloidal anions, whereas the near absence of proteins in the spinal fluid made it approximate a colloid-free solution. Anions might, therefore, be "propelled" across the blood-brain barrier. Through this reasoning he formulated the organizing question for his investigation: "Do anions penetrate more easily than cations from the blood into the liquor?"[122]

When he had come to understand the situation, Krebs tried to explain it to Wittgenstein. From the difficulty he had getting her to grasp his reasoning he concluded that she had no knowledge of physical or chemical principles. She was, nevertheless, enthusiastic about participating in the experiments that he suggested could be built on this point of view.[123]

Drawing on his earlier experience with histological staining in Möllendorff's laboratory, Krebs decided to use basic and acidic dyes as the anions and cations to be tested. The experiments, therefore, became an application of Möllendorff's techniques of vital staining. Krebs and Wittgenstein planned to inject the dyes into the veins of the experimental animals, to remove samples of cerebrospinal fluid and blood, and to determine colorimetrically how much of each dye each fluid contained. Believing that many of the inconsistent results of previous investigators were due to their not testing different substances under comparable conditions, Krebs decided to standardize the procedures. Instead of seeking an optimal concentration and conditions for each individual substance, he would inject the same molar quantities of all the dyes used and withdraw the samples after the same time interval. In preparation for the experiments Krebs collected dyes from a local chemical firm, while Wittgenstein arranged for the necessary animals and assistants to handle them.[124]

Before he actually started the new investigation, Krebs took three weeks off to attend his first major scientific meeting, the 88th Assembly of German Scientists and Physicians (*Versammlung Deutscher Naturforscher und Ärzte*). He was undoubtedly attracted to the meeting, in part, because it was to take place in Innsbruck, so that he could revisit some of his favorite places in the Alps. Leaving Berlin on September 18, he arrived in Austria the day before the *Versammlung* opened on September 21, and stayed through the entire week of meetings. It was an unusually large meeting of the venerable *Gesellschaft*: over 7,000 scientists and physicians attended. At the ceremonial plenary session the president of the society, Dr. Wilhelm His, gave the opening address, speaking with passion about the responsibility of the *Gesellschaft* as a "bearer of national unity," in defense of the traditional values of *akademische Lehrfreiheit*, and about the need to make it possible for the middle classes to dedicate themselves to *akademische Bildung*.[125] These were values in which the young Hans Krebs had been reared, and to which he could give his full assent.

The many disciplinary sub-sections (*Abtheilungen*) of the *Gesellschaft* met through the next six days. There is no record of what sessions Krebs attended, but he is very likely to have heard papers delivered in the sessions of the internal medicine sections and the section for physiology and physiological chemistry. The most prominent discussion in the latter section was "the present state of insulin research," a topic that undoubtedly reinforced Krebs's sense of the momentous importance of the discovery of insulin for medical science as well as for practice. A major highlight of the week for him was the opportunity to meet Wolfgang Pauli, one of the pioneers of colloid chemistry. Krebs's interest in Pauli is further evidence of the priority that colloid chemistry then held in his own investigative aspirations.[126]

Krebs lingered in Austria for two days after the close of the *Versammlung*, then crossed into Italy, where he enjoyed a holiday week. On October 11 he returned through Austria to Berlin.[127] A few days later he and Annelise Wittgenstein began their preliminary experiments on the passage of substances into the cerebrospinal fluid. They attempted to use guinea pigs, rabbits, and cats, but found that they could withdraw only a few drops of cerebrospinal fluid from these small animals, not enough for a reliable determination of its color; therefore, they turned to large dogs. They withdrew spinal fluid by inserting a syringe through the occipital protuberance into the cisterna magna (a reservoir of fluid between the corpus callosum and the cerebellum). Although the procedure was simple, it required two assistants, one to hold down the hind quarters and legs of the dog, the other to hold its forebody and head. To establish a standard dose for the dyes they began with uranin, an acidic dye well known to penetrate into the spinal fluid.[128]

By the end of November Krebs and Wittgenstein had performed 12 experiments and had probably established the procedures that they would use to begin testing systematically the dyes that Krebs had obtained. Between November 29 and December 8 they performed five experiments on three different acidic dyes: uranin, patent blue V, and asculin, all of which colored the cerebrospinal fluid as expected. On December 9 they injected pyronin 6, an amphoteric dye that they chose because it was not "entirely basic.., but possessed also acidic properties." It did not color the fluid. After repeating two of the tests of acidic dyes they turned on about December 18 to another amphoteric dye, rhodamine B. Somewhat to their surprise this dye penetrated in "substantial quantity" into the liquor, and they repeated the experiment on December 17 with the same outcome.[129]

By this time Krebs had nearly completed his required year of hospital service. By January 1925, he would need only to go through the formality of obtaining his MD degree to be qualified to enter medical practice. That was, however, not his immediate priority. It is evident that his first experimental efforts as an independent investigator had whetted his appetite to go further, and that he was more concerned to prepare himself for a future in research than to make arrangements for the professional base that he assumed he would eventually need in internal medicine. His experiments on the cerebrospinal fluid reinforced the conviction he had earlier acquired that his most urgent need was for more systematic training in basic chemistry. It was easy enough for him to detect that a dye had entered the spinal fluid by observing its color, but if he wished to broaden his attack on this or other problems, he would have to learn how to carry out the ordinary methods of qualitative and quantitative analysis. He felt that he knew something about colloid and physical chemistry but little about the other branches of chemistry.[130]

Krebs knew about medically trained scientists, such as Siegfried Thannhauser, who had gone on to obtain PhDs to attain strong biochemical foundations for research. He was, however, at 26 too impatient to get on with things to entertain such a course, especially since it would prolong for several more years his financial dependence on his father. It happened that there existed in Berlin a course expressly designed for MDs who wished to acquire laboratory training in chemistry without undertaking a lengthy degree program. It was taught in the Department of Chemistry at the Pathological Institute of the Charité Hospital by Peter Rona, a collaborator of Leonor Michaelis. An added benefit for Krebs was that the *Charité* was located within a 10-minute walk of the III Medical Clinic, so that he could anticipate the possibility of returning in his spare time to continue the experiments on cerebrospinal fluid. David Nachmansohn had already enrolled in Rona's course, and he urged Krebs to do the same.[131]

The main obstacle involved in this plan was that Krebs had to ask his father for support for at least another year. Despite his doubt that his son could earn a reasonable livelihood in research even if it were related to clinical needs, Georg Krebs reluctantly agreed to finance Hans through Rona's course.[132]

The Research Apprentice

At the beginning of January, 1925, Hans Krebs walked through the entrance to the Pathological Institute of the Charité Hospital and into the Division of Chemistry, to begin his practical training in the methods of the science taught there. In one large laboratory room with many benches new students like himself worked side-by-side with more advanced students, with research assistants to the director, and with a few independent investigators. David Nachmansohn, who had already been working enthusiastically in the laboratory for several months, probably told Krebs that he could expect to learn a lot there.[1]

Peter Rona, born in Budapest 54 years before, had been director of the Division of Chemistry since 1922. Although he had a long list of publications, many of them in association with Leonor Michaelis, Rona was not regarded as an outstanding original investigator. His reputation was based mainly on his wide knowledge of chemistry, his efforts to introduce more physical chemistry into medical chemistry, and his ability to recognize and encourage talented students. The course he offered was unique in Berlin, and it attracted premedical as well as postmedical students. At the time Krebs entered Rona's course there were probably 20 students in the laboratory, along with Rona's staff assistants and collaborators.[2]

The students were expected to work their way through several laboratory manuals. They began with Riesenfeld's elementary qualitative inorganic analysis, then moved on to a textbook of quantitative analysis. Next they were required to make several organic preparations and finally to do the exercises in Michaelis's *Praktikum der physikalischen Chemie*. Many of the students worked in the laboratory 10 to 12 hours per day, and some of them came in even on Sunday. Working at their own individual paces, it took them from 1 to 2 years to complete the course.[3]

Rona spent only the mornings in the laboratory. In the afternoon he left for an office where he edited the review journal *Berichten über die gesamte Physiologie und experimentelle Pharmakologie*. Once a week he gave a chemistry lecture. He was generally well regarded as a lecturer. At the beginning of each lecture he spoke slowly and softly, but he became more emphatic as he went along. He explained physical–chemical problems clearly, and his demonstration experiments always worked.[4]

No teacher makes the same kind of impression on all students. To Nachmansohn Rona was inspiring. Nachmansohn learned from him not only basic principles, but all about the latest work of such leaders in biochemistry as Warburg, Neuberg, and Meyerhof. Krebs was, on the other hand, unmoved and little influenced by Rona. Although he thought the lectures were of interest, he perceived Rona as a timid speaker who showed no enthusiasm for his subject. Part of the difference probably derived from the wide reading in chemistry that Krebs had done. Much of what was new to Nachmansohn was already familiar to Krebs. Moreover, it seemed to Krebs that Rona was not around much in the laboratory, and that he had been lured into editing because it was lucrative. Most of the practical instruction in the laboratory fell to Rona's assistant Robert Ammon, whom Krebs found helpful.[5]

Despite his reservations about Rona, the atmosphere in the laboratory was very stimulating to Krebs, mainly because of some of the younger researchers that Rona had brought together there. Particularly impressive to him was Hans H. Weber, a member of the staff, who was carrying on a significant investigation of the muscle proteins myosin and myogen. Weber was not only an able experimentalist, but an articulate, enthusiastic conversationalist. Through Weber Krebs heard much about what was going on at the forefront in biochemistry. Another young biochemist in the laboratory who impressed Krebs favorably was Karl Meyer. In addition to his research Meyer had the unusual job of writing a book for Rona.[6]

The students were expected to spend every day in the laboratory, but were left to work on their own schedules. Krebs was quickly able to organize his time so that he could get on with his experiments at the III Clinic without impeding his progress in the course. Having established earlier the routines for injecting the dyes, collecting samples of serum and cerebrospinal fluid, and comparing their color to standard concentrations of the dye, he could make the short walk to the clinic, carry out each of the operations, and return immediately to the Charité to proceed with his analytical exercises. Presumably the technicians at the Clinic laboratory managed the necessary preparations and handled the animals in his absence.[7]

On January 10, less than 2 weeks after beginning the course, Krebs and Wittgenstein resumed the experiments. Thereafter, they performed several each week. The first experiment was a repeat of one done in December with an acidic dye, and it confirmed that in general acidic dyes pass readily into the cerebrospinal fluid. Now they turned to a series of basic dyes, expecting no doubt from the prediction of the Donnan equilibrium that these would less easily do so. The first of them, methyl green, killed the dog. The next day they tried another basic dye, toluene blue, which also proved fatal to the animal. They then tried "neutral red" (a basic dye), which they had employed earlier. It was not lethal, but was toxic, and did not reach the cerebrospinal fluid. Between January 17 and February 4 they performed eight more experiments using four different basic dyes. All were toxic, and none appeared in the cerebrospinal

Figure 5.1 Entrance to the Pathological Institute of The Charité in Berlin. Photograph was taken in 1959. The exterior appearance is little changed from 1920s.

Figure 5.2 Peter Rona with students and associates, November 1924. Rona is in black suit. David Nachmansohn is just behind the man and woman to Rona's left. Robert Ammon is the light-haired person, third from the right in the second row. Karl Meyer is eighth from the right in the second row. (From *Arzneimittelforschung*, 10 (1960): 321–322.)

fluid. Four more acidic dyes interspersed in experiments during the same period all colored the fluid and none were toxic.[8]

As described in Chapter 4, Krebs had begun the investigation dominated by the idea of testing whether the Donnan equilibrium could account for the passage of dyes from the blood into the cerebrospinal fluid; that is, whether the meningeal membranes separating these fluids in vivo was analogous to a simple semipermeable membrane separating two such fluids in vitro. In keeping with this view he had chosen exclusively crystalloidal dyes, assuming that they alone could penetrate a semipermeable membrane. Gradually he came to view the Donnan equilibrium as only one of the physicochemical factors governing the process. Returning again to the viewpoint he had assimilated in Möllendorff's laboratory, he now examined the effect of the dispersibility of dyes on their ability to penetrate to the cerebrospinal fluid. His experiments up until then having confirmed that among crystalloidal dyes only the acidic ones entered the fluid, he now began to compare the behavior of colloidal acidic dyes with the crystalloidal ones previously tried. On February 10 he tested congo red. It was somewhat toxic and did not appear in the liquor. On February 17 he tried "water blue." It did not color the liquor. It remained so long in the blood that he began to draw samples of the blood on succeeding days, and found that the concentration decreased only slightly from day to day. He tried one more congo red experiment, but the dog died. Thereafter, except for continuing to check the blood of the dog with "water blue" in its veins, he conducted no further experiments for about 3 weeks. He had already sufficient evidence to conclude that the dispersibility was a significant factor.[9]

While he divided his day between these experiments at the III Clinic and his analytical exercises in chemistry at the Charité, Krebs probably spent much of his evenings and weekends writing up the results of the experiments he had previously carried out on the gold sol reaction. Convinced that he had arrived at important conclusions, he was now anxious to publish them. Having no one to turn to for advice, he had to rely on his own judgment about how to formulate and present his work.[10] His opinion that too many papers were published too uncritically in journals representing medical research did not deter him from emulating the common practice of extracting several publications from the same investigation.

Krebs wrote three papers on the gold sol reaction. The first, intended for rapid publication in the *Klinische Wochenschrift* he limited to a description of the modified procedure he had devised to prepare the gold sol, to examples of curves obtained with it using normal and *Tabes* cerebrospinal fluid, and to a discussion of the effects of pH and other factors on the reaction. In the second paper, planned for the *Biochemische Zeitschrift*, he described a broader group of flocculation reactions of the gold sol that he had conducted using serum albumin, casein, and gelatin, and developed the theory that there were two flocculation zones induced (1) by precipitation of the protein at its isoelectric point, bringing down the gold sol particles with it, and (2) a mutual precipitation of gold sol and protein particles caused by the mutual aggregation of colloidal particles of opposite charge present within certain relative proportions. In the third article he elaborated for the *Zeitschrift für Immunitäts Forschung* a fuller "theory of the colloidal reaction in the cerebrospinal liquor," in which he offered explanations of the "general physicochemical foundations" of these reactions.[11] He must have worked a long time drafting these papers and searching in the literature of the field for the information he needed to interpret his work within a larger context.

Following the style of his first scientific paper on vital staining, Krebs attached to his report of his own results discussions of their significance and their relation to the existing state of the problem that substantially exceeded in length the experimental portions of the papers. Like some of his predecessors in this field he repeatedly invoked "simple considerations of colloid chemistry" as the "key" to understanding the phenomenon.[12] He derived these considerations largely from the textbook discussions of Szigmondy, Freundlich, and Michaelis, and even referred his readers at one point for further explanation "to the textbooks of colloidal chemistry."[13] His own discussions were, however, very full, and revealed a strong drive to reach a single physicochemical explanation not only for the basic reactions involved, but for each of the manifold variations encountered in his experiments and in the clinical use of the gold sol and other colloidal diagnostic reactions. In his explanations he stressed the combined effects of the hydrogen ion concentrations, the amphoteric nature of proteins and their differing isoelectric points, and such basic principles of current colloid chemistry as that the properties of a mixed colloid are the additive sums of the properties of their component colloidal particles, and that the properties that predominate depend on the relative numbers of the particles of the components present rather than their relative masses. After applying his general theoretical framework to the characteristic curves obtained for each of the pathological types of cerebrospinal fluid with the gold sol, he dealt with the more complicated "double maximum" curves obtained with benzoin, another colloidal suspension sometimes used diagnostically. He could, he thought, explain all of the variations in the shapes of these curves entirely in terms of variations in the physical factors involved. He summarized his scheme in graphical form.

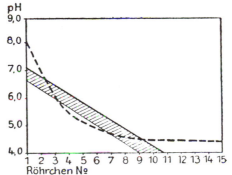

The dotted line represented the change in the hydrogen ion concentration in the medium within the series of tubes of graded dilutions of the gold sol. The shaded area represented the isoelectric zone of the globulin–colloid complex.

Wherever the two curves overlapped flocculation must take place. The relation between the two curves under different circumstances determined whether there would be one, two, or no zones of flocculation.[14]

Pleased with the way in which he had been able to integrate his results as well as those of other clinical investigators into this comprehensive theoretical framework, Krebs wrote proudly in the conclusion of his third paper:

> In the foregoing I believe that all of the essential appearances of the colloidal reactions are reduced to a simple plausible physical chemical explanation. We have obtained a picture of the mechanism of the process that underlies the production of the individual types of curves.

On the basis of the physical structure of the colloids, the quantities and types of proteins, and the hydrogen ion concentration of the medium, he claimed,

> We believe we have by and large derived the entire multiplicity of the appearances of the colloid reactions solely from quantitative variations of these few elements. This outcome seems to us to approach very nearly the fundamental general ideal of an exact scientific-physical theory.[15]

In April and May Krebs sent his papers off to the three journals in which he hoped to have them published. All three were accepted without criticism or correction.[16]

The detailed manner in which his three papers discussed the application of textbook principles of colloid chemistry to the observations he had made can be seen as a mark of Krebs's inexperience in the art of investigative reporting. Much of what he explained might have been taken for granted on the research forefront. Nor was he reluctant to claim the broadest significance for his relatively modest experimental venture. Statements such as "The observations that I have made during this investigation seem to me to be of important, perhaps fundamental meaning for the understanding of the gold sol reaction"[17] suggest a degree of youthful self-assertion. (When shown the longer passage quoted, in 1978, Krebs was somewhat embarrassed by its "boastful" sound. "I wouldn't say this sort of thing today," he commented, "but I overstated the case then.... Blowing one's own trumpet, this is something which has become strange to me.")[18]

Nevertheless, for papers he had written without help, presenting an investigation he had defined and carried through by himself and supported with background knowledge he had acquired mainly through independent reading, these were not unimpressive publications. They reveal more than an independent-minded investigator with strong initiative. The papers are lucid, carefully argued, penetrating and convincing. The young physician pursuing his first opportunity to carry out research on his own was displaying already a probing curiosity to reach beyond the result of a limited experimental outcome, to connect his results with broader considerations, and to devise an intellectually satisfying explanation for what he observed; a desire to get, as he often put it, "into the depth of things."

After a lapse of about 2½ months, Krebs and Wittgenstein resumed in mid-July their experiments on the permeability of the cerebrospinal fluid to substances injected into the blood. For the first time they chose a nondye, the organic ion salicylic acid (injected in the form of its sodium salt). Krebs detected its presence in the cerebrospinal fluid by means of ferric chloride, with which it gave a violet color reaction. After several additional experiments with acidic dyes during the rest of July, they tested in August two other organic non-dyes, ferrocyanide and thiocyanide, each requiring a color reaction to reveal its presence. It is tempting to infer that Krebs extended the investigation to these substances during the summer because he had by then made enough progress in his exercises in Rona's laboratory to perform simple qualitative analyses with confidence. During September they returned to three of the basic dyes that had had toxic or fatal effects in January and February. Safron O was again fatal. With brilliant cresyl blue they followed up their earlier observation that a fluorescent violet blue substance, which appeared afterward in the urine, was probably a breakdown product of the dye. In October they tested another basic dye, fuchsin. After a few more tests they ended the investigation, having performed in all about 90 experiments.[19]

Eager for additional research experience, Krebs said to Rona sometime during the year that he would like to do some experiments in his laboratory if that would be possible. Rona generally encouraged students to take on projects so that publications from his laboratory would maintain his own reputation as an active experimentalist. Having read a new book by L. Latles on *The Individuality of the Blood*, Rona suggested that Krebs might find in it a subject for further research, but gave little help on how to go about it. Not particularly inspired by this idea, but thinking now that he had better please Rona by complying, Krebs read the book and decided that he could study the process of "isohemagglutination," in which human serum from one individual agglutinates the red blood corpuscles of blood from another individual of different blood group. Tracing the literature further back, he found that Bordet at the Pasteur Institute had found, in 1899, that electrolytes play a major role in agglutination processes in general, and he decided to test the effects on isohemagglutination by varying the concentration of the medium and by changing the ions present in it. In carrying out a series of such experiments he gained experience with the methods of electrodialysis, and now had access to an electrometer to measure the pH quantitatively. He probably also familiarized himself in general with the importance of the ionic composition of the media within which biological phenomena occur; but he discovered no clear-cut effects on isohemagglutination, and when he completed his investigation he felt that it had been insignificant.[20]

David Nachmansohn was also eager to carry out a piece of research in Rona's laboratory, and discussed his interest with Krebs. Drawing again on his earlier experience in Möllendorff's laboratory, Krebs proposed that they study together the relationship between vital staining and the physical adsorption of dyes. He worked out a plan to compare the rates of adsorption of several dyes in the white clay, kaolin, with the rates at which they were taken up by live microorganisms. As they began the work Nachmansohn formed a great admiration for his friend's capacity to define and approach a research problem and to organize experiments. Krebs was, he felt, teaching him how to go about scientific research.[21]

As he neared the end of his first year in Rona's laboratory Krebs had, despite his driving energy, not finished the chemical course, and he had not yet given much thought to what he might do afterward. Then an unexpected opportunity suddenly changed his direction. During the previous year, his friend Bruno Mendel, whose family were friends of Albert Einstein, met Otto Warburg at a dinner party at the Einstein's. Learning of Mendel's interest in his work on cancer, Warburg discussed his current experimental results with him, and they soon began to communicate with each other regularly by telephone. Eventually Warburg remarked that he did not have enough collaborators to carry out all of his experimental ideas. Mendel suggested that his friend Hans Krebs might be a very suitable assistant. When Warburg replied that he had no funds available for such an assistant, Mendel, who was as well connected as he was persuasive, was able to raise enough money to provide Warburg with support for a modest salary for 1 year for Krebs.[22]

Not knowing the details of how this lucky turn of events had been arranged, Krebs learned in early December that he might be offered a position in Warburg's laboratory, and went immediately to the Kaiser-Wilhelm Institute for Biology in Dahlem, in the western outskirts of Berlin, for an interview with Warburg. As he entered the building he met his old medical student friend from Freiburg, Hermann Blaschko, who had recently become an unpaid research assistant in the laboratory of Otto Meyerhof, on the floor below Warburg's laboratory. Krebs appeared to Blaschko to be quite convinced that he would get the job. At the interview Warburg had in hand a record of Krebs's scientific publications, and raised no questions about his past training or work. He asked Krebs why he was interested in the position, to which Krebs replied that he wanted to learn biochemistry and to gain research experience. Warburg inquired about Krebs's long-term plans, and Krebs said that he would return to clinical medicine and prepare himself for academic medicine. Warburg then warned Krebs bluntly that he could not help him toward an academic career, because he was an outsider with no connections to a university, and was disliked in the university. He could teach him something, but at the end of the 1-year appointment Krebs would be on his own. If he wanted to make an academic career he had better attach himself "to some old ass of a professor." Krebs, who had never worried greatly about how to manage his long-term future, knew very well that he had at hand a rare chance to work under the direction of one of the greatest biochemists of the time. He accepted the position without qualms.[23]

Writing his father to inform him of the good news, Hans added, "If you are ever in need of cash, I shall do my best to help you."[24] The gesture was clearly light-hearted. Hans's salary of 300 marks per year would just be adequate to meet his own needs,[25] but there lay beneath it symbolic meanings of which he may have been only partly conscious. It was in part an expression of his relief at being finally, at the age of 25, no longer a financial burden to his father, but he appears to have been, also in a less tangible sense declaring his independence from the dominating figure in his early life who had questioned his talents, and who still doubted his ability to succeed on the course he had chosen for himself.

I

With his new job scheduled to begin on January 1, 1926, Krebs left Rona's laboratory soon after his interview with Warburg, so that he could spend the rest of December completing the articles that he planned to publish on the investigation he and Wittgenstein had carried out at the III Medical Clinic. Well aware that his future in research would depend on his publication record, he complied with what he took to be the prevailing attitude that scientific productivity is measured by the number of one's publications. Wittgenstein, who wanted to obtain as many publications as possible from the work, encouraged him to turn it into multiple titles spread among several journals.[26] Out of the relatively simple series of experiments they had conducted he managed to compose eight different "communications." He wrote in addition a paper on his minor study of isohemagglutination, for which Peter Rona appeared as the senior author. Despite whatever misgivings he may have had about current publication norms, Krebs was obviously willing to conform with them to find a place within the medical research system. If he did not strive for brevity under these conditions, he did work hard to make his writing as logical and precise as he could.[27]

Treating the investigation from two general points of view, Krebs incorporated many of the same experiments into one set of papers on "Studies of the Diffusion of Substances out of the Blood Plasma," and into a second set on "Studies of the Permeability of the Meninges Under the Consideration of Physical Chemical Points of View." For each topic he wrote a compact "preliminary" paper, one of them intended for the *Deutsche Medizinischen Wochenschrift*, the other for the *Klinische Wochenschrift*. These papers summarized the results succinctly and located them concisely within the context of previous work. The longer papers broke the investigation down into several components, presenting in separate communications the discussion of the general problems, the experiments on anionic crystalloid dyes, cationic crystalloid dyes, and anionic colloidal dyes. They included full protocols for the majority of the 88 experiments performed. Wittgenstein expanded his drafts even further, on the grounds that the extra details would be useful for clinicians.[28]

The general conclusions that Krebs drew were that cationic dyes diffuse more rapidly than anionic dyes out of the blood plasma, because they are more easily adsorbed by tissue proteins; that crystalloidal anionic dyes pass easily into the cerebrospinal fluid, in contrast to crystalloidal cationic dyes; and that the meninges are impermeable to colloidal anionic dyes. A large part of the phenomena could be ascribed to three physicochemical "laws": the Donnan equilibrium, adsorption, and dispersibility, but there were also deviations from the regularities accountable by these principles that depended on "secondary phenomena."[29]

Krebs framed the experimental investigation with an incisive discussion of the physicochemical point of view that he brought to the problem, taking a clear position on the perennial issue of the relation between physicochemical and vital processes. The "protective function" that some attributed to the choroid plexus or the other meninges he characterized as a "*vital* function not [amenable] to closer analysis," and the mark of a "teleological way of thinking." His goal was, on the other hand, "to discover the contributing physicochemical factors, to test whether, in addition to the 'physiological permeability' following from the selective regulatory activity of living cells there is also involved a 'physical permeability' derived from the physicochemical conditions."[30] The principle "on which our problem is posed," he wrote:

> ...is the analogy between the meninges and a semipermeable membrane which separates a protein-rich fluid (the blood) from a protein-poor one (the liquor). The permeability of the dead membrane is determined by the laws formulated above. Do these also prevail in vivo? Is the permeability of the meninges for electrolytes *to a large extent independent* of the active activity of plexus cells, and consequently *dependent* upon the given physico-chemical conditions?[31]

In the end he concluded cautiously that the "physicochemical processes play an essential role in the transport of substances from the blood to the liquor," without claiming that they account fully for it.

> When we maintain that dialysis has a marked significance for the formation of the liquor, that in no way excludes the involvement of purely vital secretory processes. Even if the formation of the liquor may in general be submitted to vital regulation, that does not prevent many partial processes from taking place according to purely inorganic forces.[32]

The careful manner in which Krebs formulated these larger implications may reflect the attention he had given to the general mechanism–vitalism question as a medical student when he had read the writings of Hans Driesch and presented a talk on the subject to the *Freie Wissenschaftliche Vereinigung*. As we may recall (Chapter 4, p. 96), he had decided then, despite his initial mechanistic inclination, that it was a subjective matter whether one believed or not in the possibility of a completely mechanistic explanation for biological phenomena. As a young investigator he now espoused a cautious, pragmatic position consistent with that view. Leaving room for "vital" processes whose fundamental nature he did not discuss, he adopted the physicochemical point of view as the appropriate means to submit biological phenomena to "closer analysis." He aimed to explain as much of a given process as he could in terms of the available physical laws. Philosophically his statements on the subject were unexceptional expressions of moderate mainstream thought, but his desire to link the limited investigative venture he had pursued to these larger issues was not an insignificant feature of his incipient scientific style.

Six of the eight papers resulting from the investigation appeared under the authorship of Annelise Wittgenstein and Hans Adolf Krebs. The other two were by Hans Adolf Krebs and Annelise Wittgenstein. The alternation was intended to convey that they were equal collaborators. Krebs felt, however, that the partnership had been unequal. He had defined the investigation, established its viewpoint, and written the basic papers. Wittgenstein had participated in the experiments, done some background reading and extended his manuscripts, but in his opinion she had relied on him for all the important aspects of the work. Although considerably older, she had grown personally rather attached to him and had given him an elegant Swiss watch to show her appreciation. Nevertheless he thought that he had been exploited. It particularly annoyed him that she talked to others about the investigation as hers. When his father and Wolf visited him in Berlin he complained that she was taking too much credit for what he had done. His father advised him that, since she was the senior person and he the junior one, he could do little about it, but that in the future he might find ways better to protect his intellectual property.[33]

II

The Kaiser-Wilhelm Gesellschaft occupied several comfortable buildings grouped in a campuslike setting in the spacious Berlin suburb of Dahlem. As Hans Krebs approached the top floor of the Institute for Biology on the day after New Year 1926, to begin work in Otto Warburg's laboratory, he was in an elated mood. He not only had his first paid job, but it was, he thought "The best job I could have dreamed of." Although he knew about Warburg's outstanding reputation, and had read some of his recent papers, he knew little about his personality beyond the strong impression he had received during the brief interview in December. Bruno Mendel had told him that Warburg could be extremely stimulating and interesting in conversation about the day-to-day aspects of scientific work.[34]

Warburg's laboratory was small but very well equipped. He and his assistants all worked in a single large room. There were three parallel chemical benches, each with a reagent shelf along the center and workers on both sides. An adjoining room housed the water baths and manometers that were so central to Warburg's current work, and there were two other small rooms, one containing centrifuges and other equipment, the second an animal room.[35]

At the time Krebs joined Warburg's group it consisted of five research assistants and a *Diener* to do odd jobs. Two of the assistants, Hans Gaffron and Robert Emerson were, like himself, physicians who were there to obtain research training. Unlike him, they were unpaid and subsisted on income from their families. The other three, Erwin Negelein, Franz Wind, and Fritz Kubowitz, were permanent assistants. They were not generally trained as scientists, but had formerly been mechanics in the Siemen's factory in Berlin, where they had maintained and operated instruments. Warburg taught them the chemistry they

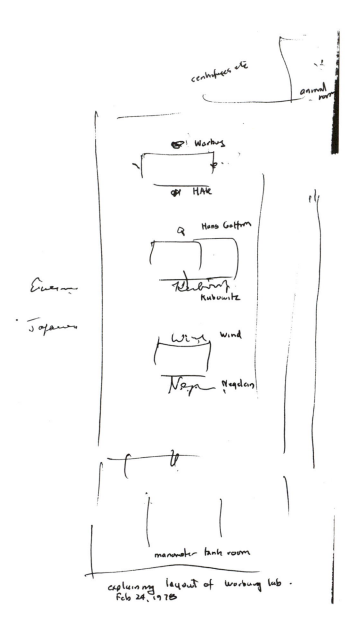

Figure 5.3 Sketch drawn by Hans Krebs, February 24, 1978, while describing the layout of Warburg's laboratory. Some of the captions are added by the author following their conversation.

needed to know to carry out experiments in his laboratory. There were no other technicians or secretaries. Warburg handled all administrative matters by himself, even typing his own letters.[36]

Krebs learned immediately that the Chief, as everyone in the laboratory called Warburg, was authoritarian, and a demanding person to work for. Warburg was in the laboratory promptly at 8 AM every morning, 6 days a week, and left at 6 PM. He expected everyone else to be present, without fail, whenever he was. They were to work at experiments throughout the day, with the exception of a 30-minute break for lunch, and to use their evenings and Sundays to enter results into their notebooks, reduce data, plan for the following day, and catch up on the literature. Accustomed as he was to punctual reliability and hard work, Krebs had no difficulty conforming to these expectations.[37]

Warburg assigned Krebs to the opposite side of the same bench at which he himself worked. For the first few days he had Krebs just watch him perform the routine operations on which the investigations in the laboratory depended. Then Krebs began to learn to do them himself. He found Warburg, as a teacher, friendly and helpful. The assistants were also very willing to answer his questions about the many technical details of the methods employed in the laboratory.[38]

The first method Krebs had to learn was the manometric technique that Warburg had developed for measuring biological oxidations. Warburg had begun to investigate such processes almost as early as Battelli and Stern or Thunberg (see Chapter 1, pp. 7–9), but his interest derived from a different set of problems. Influenced by the views of Jacques Loeb concerning changes in the rate of respiration of eggs associated with their fertilization, and then becoming more generally interested in theories of cellular oxidation, Warburg devised his method originally to measure the respiration of nucleated red blood cells. For this purpose he adopted, in 1910, a micromanometer that Joseph Barcroft and John Scott Haldane had used to measure the oxygen and carbon dioxide contents of very small samples of blood. The manometer was in the form of a "U" made from fine capillary tubing, graduated with millimeter scales. The upper end of one arm was connected to a closed flask within which the oxidation took place. The other arm was open. A key feature of the Haldane-Barcroft manometer was that the bottom of the U-tube communicated to a short rubber reservoir, to which a thumbscrew was attached. By turning the thumbscrew one could contract or expand the rubber tube, raising or lowering the levels of the fluid with which one partially filled the manometer. During the course of an experiment, one adjusted the thumbscrew at regular intervals to return the level in the closed side to its initial point; that is, to maintain a constant volume in the closed space within which gas was absorbed or released. In doing so one caused the level in the open side to rise, if the process was releasing gas, or to fall if gas was being absorbed. The changes in the difference between the levels in the two sides then measured changes in the pressure within the closed side. Using Boyle's law, one could calculate the corresponding changes in volume. Since the calculation depended on there being no change in temperature, the manometers were mounted in such a way that the

Figure 5.4 Otto Warburg. From Hans Krebs, *Otto Warburg: Cell Physiologist, Biochemist, and Eccentric* (Oxford: Clarendon Press, 1981).

flasks were immersed in a constant temperature water bath. Besides the precision that Warburg's method afforded, its central advantage was that, as it allowed one to read the changes in the level of the manometer fluid at short time intervals, one could measure not only the total consumption or absorption produced by a given process, but also the changing rates of such a process over the course of an experiment.[39]

For a process that absorbed or released a single gas, the volume change was a direct measure of the quantity of that gas. After determining the total volume of the flask, excluding the volume of the fluid contained in it, and of the portion of the closed manometer arm above the level of its fluid, one could establish a "vessel constant" that enabled one to convert the manometer readings to the gas volumes. Biological oxidations, however, simultaneously absorb oxygen and release carbon dioxide. To measure the former, therefore, Warburg did what investigators of respiration had done ever since Lavoisier. He absorbed the carbon dioxide in alkali contained in a well within the manometer flask.

Having devised his basic method, Warburg improved it and applied it during the next 15 years to an expanding range of problems. He could use it to measure not only processes that themselves consumed oxygen or produced carbon dioxide, but also for those that formed other products that could be made, through secondary reactions, to yield a gas. Since the oxidations he studied took place in a liquid medium, it was crucial that the gases produced or absorbed in the liquid come to rapid equilibrium with the gaseous phase. To ensure this condition, Warburg devised a mechanical system that continuously oscillated the manometer mounted on the side of the water bath, "shaking" the flasks so as to increase the rate of exchange of the gases between the fluid and the space above it.

The Warburg manometer was an elegant instrument, simple in design, precise and reliable when properly used. To use it in Warburg's laboratory, Krebs had to master numerous craft skills. In preparing for a set of experiments one had to measure the volume of the enclosed side of each manometer, a space that included both the interior of the vessel and the capillary manometer tube down to the zero point on its millimeter scale; to fill the manometer with the special "Brodie" fluid whose density conveniently provided a standard atmospheric pressure of 10,000 mm; to prepare the gas mixture needed for each experiment by transferring to a mixing cylinder the proper amounts of each of the component gases to be included; to fill the closed side of the manometer with this mixture, and to saturate the fluid in the vessel, without introducing bubbles into the manometer fluid; to adjust the initial level of the manometer fluid high or low, depending on whether one expected gas to be produced or absorbed during the experiment; and to apply grease to the joint between the manometer and its flask so as to ensure that it was airtight. In addition one had to prepare for the particular experiment to be performed, the tissue or chemical system to be tested, the solution in which it was to be placed, and whatever reagents were to be employed.[40]

The water tanks on which the manometers were mounted so as to immerse the vessels in a constant temperature bath were less elegant, but effective pieces of equipment. The temperature was maintained by Bunsen burners controlled by a thermoregulator. Six manometers could be mounted on each side, so that for a given experiment one could prepare up to ten experimental manometers, the remaining two being "thermobarometers" that recorded changes in the ambient temperature and pressure. The shaking device to which they were attached was driven by an electric motor through a rather noisy system of belts and pulleys that could be shifted so as to vary the amplitude or frequency of the movements they imparted to the manometers. The purpose of the shaking was

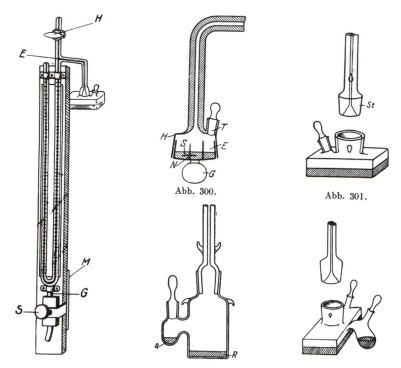

Abb. 300.

Abb. 301.

Figure 5.5 Left: Warburg manometer; S thumbscrew to adjust height of fluid; E, open end of manometer; H, stopcock opened during filling of manometer, closed during operation. Other figures are various sizes and shapes of manometer vessels for different types of experiments.

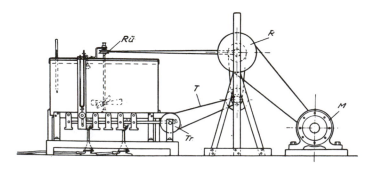

Figure 5.6 Water bath in which manometers are maintained at constant temperature, both heated by Bunsen burners shown underneath. Shown with six mounts for manometers, one manometer in place. On *right,* motor and belt drives for shaking the manometers. (From H.A. Krebs, "Stoffwechsel der Zellen und Gewebe," *Methoden der wissenschaftlichen Biologie*, Vol. 2 (1929), pp. 1049–1059.)

to increase the rate of diffusion of gases between the liquid and the gas space of the manometer vessel. For the manometer readings to be accurate measures of the change in volume of the gases, equilibrium between the two phases had to be maintained. The rate of shaking was adjusted by trial and error until increasing it caused no further effect on the manometer readings. Although each of these operations was in itself relatively simple, they had to be closely coordinated and carried out in rapid succession to attain a successful set of experiments. No great manual dexterity was required, but one had nevertheless to handle things with care and skill to avoid breaking the delicate manometers.[41]

To take the readings accurately also demanded a special skill. One first turned off the shaking mechanism and adjusted the fluid in the closed side of each manometer to the zero point with the thumbscrew. Then, because one had to make six manometer readings "simultaneously," it was important to be very quick. Krebs learned to scan all six manometers and memorize the last digit of each reading at once, write them down, and then record the remaining digits, which did not change rapidly. All the while he had to keep his eye on the thermobarometer, because sudden small changes in the outside temperature or pressure could disturb the readings of the experimental manometers. If he were using two sets of manometers, one on each side of the tank, he would read the second set 2 minutes after the first set.[42]

One took a set of readings, therefore, all in "a few seconds." What did Krebs do in the 10-minute intervals between such readings? Given both Warburg's and his own attitudes about wasting time, he undoubtedly kept himself busy carrying out preparations or calculations, washing apparatus, or doing other tasks related to the experiments. He needed, therefore, to be constantly alert during the 2- or 3-hour duration of a set of experiments, to interrupt himself at the proper moment to take each set of readings, and to return immediately to whatever else he was doing. It was a procedure that exploited very well the reliability, punctuality, and powers of concentration that Krebs possessed in abundance.[43]

While Krebs assimilated from Warburg and his other assistants the performance of these manual operations in the laboratory, Warburg also showed him how to reduce the data acquired, and how to enter the record of each day's results in a laboratory notebook. Several routine calculations had to be made for each manometer used. The "vessel constant" was a coefficient that enabled one to convert the observed pressure changes into changes in the volume of the gas. Such a constant had to be calculated for each combination of manometer and vessel at the temperature at which the experiment was conducted and for the particular gas mixture and volume of fluid placed in the vessel. If there was only a single gas absorbed or released, one could then use this coefficient to convert manometer readings directly to gas volumes. If, however, two gases were exchanged at once, for example, if one measured both the oxygen consumed and the carbonic acid produced by respiring tissue, then the situation was more complex. Warburg had devised a method, taking advantage of the different solubilities of such pairs of gases in the fluid medium. One performed two parallel sets of experiments, duplicating each condition in two manometers whose vessels contained different volumes of the fluid medium. One could then obtain six equations for the six unknowns involved (that is, the partial pressure changes of the two gases in each manometer and the volume changes of the two gases, assumed to be the same in the duplicate runs), and solve for the volume changes of the two gases.[44]

Like the others in the laboratory, Krebs recorded his readings first on a loose piece of scrap paper. At home in the evening he transferred the essential data onto a page of his laboratory notebooks laid out in vertical columns. He did not, however, preserve all of the raw data. From each reading of the experimental manometers he first subtracted the changes in the readings of the thermobarometer. Sometimes further corrections had to be made for other controls. Then he changed the "corrected" readings, which indicated accumulated pressure changes over time, to incremental changes during each time interval by subtracting the previous reading. Sometimes he further converted the pressure readings to gas volume changes before entering only the final number into the permanent notebook record. Tedious though the repetition of these procedures appears, Krebs found that when he had reduced them to habitual routines he could carry them out for the experiments of a day in about half an hour.[45]

It is not certain just how long it took Krebs to master these skills sufficiently to begin an experimental project. Krebs recalled, in 1976, that Warburg showed him how to use the manometers and that after he had watched Warburg carry out operations for "two or three days," "I started to make experiments myself." This seems a very short time to reach a level of competence necessary to begin a research project. The earliest preserved laboratory notebook that Krebs kept begins with the date May 7, 1926, but Krebs believed in 1978 that there might have been an earlier one, and his recollection is supported by the fact that the surviving notebook does not contain the early phases of the experimental work that Krebs completed during his first half year in Dahlem. At first, he undoubtedly had to carry out some experiments that were mainly exercises, but Warburg evidently gave him very soon a research problem to work on.[46]

The investigations in progress in the laboratory when Krebs joined it were oriented around two general problems that composed Warburg's long-time research agenda. One of them, mentioned in Chapter 4, (p. 101), concerned cancer tissue. Warburg had posed the question whether the growth of tumors can be explained by differences between the kinds and the rates of the chemical reactions in cancer tissue and in that of normal organs. For this purpose he had devised in 1923 the manometric tissue slice method to measure the rates of aerobic respiration and anaerobic glycolysis.[47] The other, more basic problem, already discussed briefly in Chapter 1 (p. 4), concerned the catalytic mechanism through which cellular oxidations take place. Because the initial research project that Warburg assigned Krebs was subsumed within the second of these two larger problems, it will be convenient to summarize only its background at this point, keeping in mind that Warburg actually pursued both problems concurrently. In 1924, Warburg integrated a decade of work on cellular oxidations with

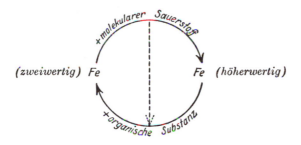

the claim that "there exists in respiring cells a cycle." Molecular oxygen, Warburg maintained, reacts in the cells with bivalent (ferrous) iron, raising it to a higher oxidation state. The iron in this state reacts in turn with organic substances, returning thereby to its lower bivalent state. The organic substances of the cell are, therefore, no more "autoxidizable" inside the cell than they are outside of it. Only the iron has the property of reacting directly with molecular oxygen, just as it does in a test tube. Iron cannot perform this role, however, in any form; to act catalytically it must be combined with certain classes of organic substances. The iron existing in this combination in cells Warburg designated "the oxygen-carrying component of the respiratory enzyme [*Atmungsferment*]," or for convenience simply the *Atmungsferment*.[48]

Early in his career Warburg had produced some evidence for this view from studies of sea urchin eggs. The fluid contents of centrifuged eggs continued for a time to absorb oxygen as rapidly as did intact eggs, and if he added additional iron to the few hundreds of a milligram of iron per gram of cell substance naturally present, the rate increased in proportion to the iron added. When he returned to this problem during the 1920s he did not seek to verify this result with other organisms. Instead he resorted to what he called model investigations, in which he could, under conditions that were simpler than those of living cells, establish oxidations whose characteristics so closely imitated cellular oxidations in his view that he could assert that the "process of oxygen-transport in the test tube...is identical with that in the cells."[49]

Pure crystalline hemin, heated to glowing red and extracted in hot hydrochloric acid formed an iron–nitrogen "chemical" that acted, according to Warburg, as an "oxidation catalyst." Placed in solution with amino acids at body temperature in the presence of oxygen or atmospheric air, it caused the amino acid to be rapidly oxidized. (Leucine was converted to ammonia, carbon dioxide, and valeric aldehyde; cystine to ammonia, carbon dioxide, and sulfuric acid.) It, therefore, catalyzed the oxidation of one of the three main classes of substances normally oxidized in cells. Other compounds of iron-containing nitrogen acted similarly. To support his view that the iron compounds in his "model" experiments acted just as iron does in living cells, Warburg set out to show that the substances that inhibit cellular respiration also inhibit these catalytic oxidations. The most successful example he could bring to bear in 1924 was the action of hydrocyanic acid (HCN), a specific inhibitor of cellular respiration.   At a concentration of $^N/10,000$, HCN noticeably reduced the rate of oxidation, and at $^N/1,000$ it "causes the catalytic activity virtually to disappear."[50]

The iron–heme charcoals that acted so strongly on amino acids did not act on the other two classes of foodstuffs consumed by respiring cells, sugars and fatty acids. To overcome this apparent contradiction of his theory, Warburg identified a "reactive form" of sugar — fructose — that absorbed oxygen rapidly when placed in a neutral solution of sodium phosphate.   That this was not an "autoxidation," but one mediated by iron, Warburg sought to show by demonstrating that this reaction too is inhibited by HCN.[51]

Warburg left open the question whether other heavy metals, particularly copper and manganese, might act in the same way that iron does. Only for the latter was there sufficient evidence that it is an essential constituent of cells. A potential objection to his theory that he believed he had to answer in advance was that there was one amino acid, cystein, that was regarded as autoxidizable, and that its apparently direct oxidation by molecular oxygen could also be inhibited with HCN. To uphold his criterion that inhibition by HCN is sufficient evidence for an iron-catalyzed oxidation, he had to show that this so-called autoxidation was in fact a deceptive effect produced by traces of metal in the cystein preparations used. In 1923, one of his co-workers was able to show with experiments carried out on carefully purified cystein, using quartz glass vessels rather than ordinary glass, that the elimination of the potential sources of metallic impurities sharply reduced the rate of oxidation.[52]

In 1925 Warburg's assistants completed several investigations designed to extend the reach of his concept of cellular oxidations.   Muneo Yabusoe determined the iron content of various normal and tumor tissues.[53] Franz Wind furthered the "model" approach by searching for other carbohydrates that might, like fructose, be oxidized by molecular oxygen in neutral phosphate solution. He found that dihydroxyacetone and glyceraldehyde — two compounds regarded as possible intermediates in anaerobic carbohydrate metabolism — were not only oxidized 20 to 30 times as rapidly as fructose, but that these oxidations were accelerated by the heavy metals iron and copper. The oxidations were inhibited by potassium cyanide, and also by pyrophosphate, further supportive evidence for the view that the oxidations were catalyzed by the metals, because both substances were known to form complexes with metals. Their actions could, therefore, be explained as removing the metals from the sites of their catalytic action.[54]

Erwin Negelein examined the action of another known respiratory poison, hydrogen sulfide. To test its action "on the chemical processes in cells," he measured its effects on the rates of respiration and of fermentation of yeast cell suspensions placed in the usual way in manometer flasks. He found that hydrogen sulfide (H_2S) inhibited both processes, but that the concentration required to stop fermentation was much greater than that which inhibited aerobic respiration. "It is therefore possible," he concluded, "with the help of hydrogen sulfide to separate the respiration of yeast completely from its fermentation."[55]

The two effective inhibitors of cellular oxidations that Warburg had now identified, HCN and H_2S, were both prominent "general cell poisons." Carbon monoxide was also a powerful respiratory poison, but was regarded, in 1925, as a "special blood poison" that acted "only on organisms with circulating blood."[56] That was because carbon monoxide (CO) displaced oxygen from the hemoglobin in the blood, thereby blocking its oxygen-transport function. Cellular oxidations were, therefore, not inhibited directly, but by preventing the oxygen from reaching the cells. This property of CO meant, however, that it combined with a particular class of iron-containing compounds, as hemoglobin is an iron porphyrin. It was, therefore, for Warburg, who hoped to identify more closely the iron compounds constituting the "oxygen carrying component of the *Atmungsferment*" a particularly interesting question "whether carbon monoxide inhibits cellular respiration." To find out, he filled the gas space of manometer flasks containing yeast suspensions with mixtures of CO and O_2. Gaseous mixtures containing 75 to 80 percent CO inhibited the respiration by 35 to 72 percent, depending on the quantity of oxygen present in the mixture. "It follows from these experiments," Warburg concluded, "that the *Atmungsferment* combines with carbon monoxide and [that this complex] occupies in the ferment molecule the place that normally reacts with oxygen. In this way the oxygen-carrying activity of the ferment is blocked."[57]

With this discovery Warburg not only added a third substance to his list of the inhibitors of cellular respiration, but gave a decisive new turn to his investigative strategy.[58] HCN and H_2S appeared to act as general "complex builders" with metals, so that their effects provided little insight into the nature of the iron compounds involved in the *Atmungsferment* in cells. The fact that CO was known to react particularly with a certain class of iron–porphyrin compounds suggested that its action on cellular respiration was due to the existence of such a compound within the *Atmungsferment*. Instead of relying entirely on his model experiments to elucidate the nature of that compound, Warburg now had a favorable prospect to study its properties in living cells.

When Warburg discovered that carbon monoxide inhibited respiration in living cells, Hans Krebs was in the laboratory. It must have been soon after he arrived. Shortly afterward the distinguished British physiologist A.V. Hill visited Dahlem, and Warburg explained to him the experiments that had just been done. Hill asked, "Is this carbon monoxide inhibition affected by light?" Through an association with John Scott Haldane, Hill was aware of investigations carried out 30 years earlier in Cambridge that had shown that light diminishes the affinity between carbon monoxide and hemoglobin. Warburg replied to Hill's question "We do not know, but we can do the experiment at once." He had on hand, for other photochemical experiments, a lamp covered by a water-tight jacket, that he could immerse in the water bath to illuminate the manometer vessels. Within 24 hours Warburg found that the respiration of yeast partially inhibited by CO immediately increased when he switched on the light. Krebs, who was present at the discussion between Hill and Warburg, and at the subsequent experiment, felt that he had witnessed a dramatic scientific event.[59]

III

The first experimental problem that Warburg gave Krebs to solve was whether the oxidation of sugars in ammoniacal solutions was an "oxygen transfer through metals" rather than a "true autoxidation." Warburg had himself already observed that sugars are oxidized in such solutions, and had done some preliminary experiments showing that the oxidation is inhibited by HCN. Assuming that what the ammonia provided was a mildly alkaline milieu for the reaction, he expected Krebs to explore further the role of mild alkalis in the model reactions he had earlier studied.[60]

When Warburg had studied the oxidation of fructose with Muneo Yabusoe in 1924, he had thought that this reaction occurred "only in phosphate solutions, but not in the solutions of other salts," and regarded it as "a specific reaction between phosphate, fructose and molecular oxygen" catalyzed by metals.[61] His subsequent observation concerning the reaction in ammoniacal solution thus required a modification of this view, but, by 1926, he was less interested in these model experiments than in the new opportunities that carbon monoxide offered him to explore respiration in living cells. A question left over from an earlier stage in his investigation was a convenient means to introduce a new assistant to his methods. Warburg knew in advance that the experiments would work. All of the procedures, except for the preparation of the solutions, were the same as those used in the experiments of 1924. Krebs had little to work out for himself. He could follow closely what had already been done, and if he worked competently he would obtain useful results.[62]

The first step that Krebs probably took was to confirm the primary observation that fructose is oxidized in an ammoniacal solution. He composed the solution by mixing ammonium chloride and ammonia solutions in proportions calculated to produce a mildly alkaline buffered solution. Then he added fructose and placed the solution in a manometric vessel containing caustic alkali in an inner cup to absorb the carbon dioxide that would form. Attaching the vessel to the manometer, he filled the closed side with oxygen gas and shook the manometer in the water both at 37.5°C. Within an hour large pressure changes in the manometer confirmed that the fructose was being oxidized rapidly. The rate was of the same order of magnitude that Warburg and Yabusoe had found 2 years earlier for fructose in phosphate solution.[63]

In subsequent experiments Krebs established that the oxidation he had observed in ammoniacal solution was distinct from the oxidation of carbohydrates that occurs in other alkaline solutions such as sodium carbonate. The rate was up to 100 times larger than those he measured at comparable hydroxyl ion concentrations in other alkalis. Emulating the design of Warburg and Yabusoe's investigation, Krebs then followed the "time course" of the oxidation by setting it up in a large solution and measuring the rate in 10-cm^3 samples withdrawn at first every hour, then at longer intervals, up to 72 hours, and examined the dependence of the rate on the concentration of the ammoniacal buffer solution, the oxygen pressure, and the hydrogen ion concentration.[64]

Having established the basic parameters of the oxidation, Krebs turned to the effects on it of metals and of the inhibitors that Warburg had previously used. The addition of heavy metals accelerated the oxidation, but only "relatively little." For example, 10^{-3} ferrous sulfate increased the rate by about 65 percent. HCN, H_2S, and pyrophosphate each inhibited the reaction.[65]

Krebs probably performed these experiments between January and late April 1926. He had completed his initial assignment expeditiously, and the results supported Warburg's general concept that carbohydrates "do not react directly with oxygen but through the mediation of a heavy metal."[66] The action of the metal on the reaction was, however, much less impressive than in the other carbohydrate oxidations that Warburg and his assistants had examined. Perhaps in part to seek an improvement in that situation, and in part simply to expand the scope of his project, Krebs began in early May to explore the effects of other solutions on the reaction.

Working immediately across from Warburg at the laboratory bench, Krebs could easily discuss with him the problems that arose during the course of his experiments. He found Warburg as a supervisor approachable, informed, and kind. Having discussed with Krebs the nature of the problem he wished him to investigate, Warburg allowed him room to pursue it day-by-day on his own, expecting him to find and read the pertinent literature and to devise the individual experiments for himself. If Krebs had nothing to report for several weeks, Warburg — who could undoubtedly observe that his new assistant was well-organized and working hard — did not press him, but he was immediately available when Krebs needed to talk something over with him. Knowing that Krebs was not well-trained in chemistry, Warburg taught him what he needed to know to pursue his experiments. He was critical when Krebs made mistakes, but he corrected them tactfully and politely. When Krebs had obtained his first positive results, Warburg said encouragingly, "Now you have discovered something."[67]

Considerate though he was of his assistants in the day-to-day work of the laboratory, Warburg exerted absolute control over its operation. Those who worked with him could take initiatives only within the bounds of the problems that he gave them. He did not tolerate questions about his judgments or remarks that he thought impertinent. Neither Krebs nor the other research assistants challenged his authority. His scientific achievements, his penetrating intelligence, his singleness of purpose, and his personal skill in experimentation commanded their respect and their allegiance. They felt that he dealt with them fairly, that he demanded from them no more than from himself, and that he set the high standards they hoped to emulate.[68]

By precept and example Warburg imparted to Krebs and others who came to his laboratory for research experience his personal scientific values. He stressed how important it was to pursue a narrowly defined problem persistently and to devote a large amount of time to it. This appealed very much to Krebs, who believed he had already started off in that direction before he came to Dahlem; but Warburg also stretched Krebs's mental horizons by insisting that in doing so one should also take on the large central questions of the time in one's field, that one should invent precise new methods, and that one should carry out with them many experiments without thinking too long about whether each one was worthwhile. Warburg's prolonged study of cellular oxidations must have seemed to Krebs a prime examplar of what Warburg meant by a problem that was both large and narrow; and his manometric and tissue slice methods admirably suited for his manner of pursuing it. Whenever possible, Warburg asserted, one should strive for quantitative measurements, but it was also important that the measurements lead to generalizable results, not to mere data. Here too, the practices that Krebs observed in his laboratory seemed perfectly suited to Warburg's doctrines.[69]

Well-trained in mathematics, Warburg tended even in casual conversation to express ideas in mathematical terms. Instead of saying "the rate is constant," for example, he customarily said "dx/dt is constant." As Krebs became familiar with Warburg's methods, he recognized the importance of the mathematical derivations that underlay the interpretation of much of the data. The calculation of the vessel constants, of the changes in volume of two gases simultaneously in the method using two volumes of fluid in duplicate vessels, or of the "retention" of carbonic acid in alkaline solutions and complex fluids such as blood serum were easy to carry out in practice, but they rested on Warburg's strong grasp both of theoretical physical chemistry and mathematical reasoning. Warburg was, Krebs learned, still doing lessons in mathematics. Warburg's proficiency in devising methods based on mathematical derivations made Krebs aware of the deficiency in his own mathematical education. He had studied algebra and trigonometry in the Gymnasium, but the premature completion of his schooling to prepare for his induction into the army had caused him to miss taking calculus. Now he tried to make up for that loss by studying textbooks of differential and integral calculus in his spare time. He acquired a general understanding of these subjects, but not a practical facility for manipulating and solving differential equations.[70]

If Warburg seemed to Krebs considerate with those who worked in his laboratory, he did not accord similar treatment to outsiders. At the time Krebs entered the laboratory Warburg's work on cancer was attracting enough public attention so that reporters sometimes tried to interview him. He dismissed such intruders curtly, once going so far as to reply to one who entered the laboratory unannounced to find him, "I am sorry. That person is dead."[71]

Warburg was no more sparing of his scientific colleagues. He admired his own teachers Ludwig Krehl and Emil Fischer, his father the physicist Emil Warburg, and the biochemist Carl Neubauer, and he respected a few other scientists, including Fischer's son Hans and his own one-time student Otto Meyerhof. Of most of his contemporaries, however, he had a low opinion. He expressed his views about them freely in conversations in the laboratory. Very sure of his intellectual superiority, he thought his own approach to scientific problems was the only sound one, and that people who were different from him could not be much good. Although his young assistants recognized that he exaggerated, they imbibed some of his attitude that the scientific standards outside their own environment tended to be lower.[72]

Warburg engaged in forceful public polemics over scientific questions on which he differed with his colleagues. At the time Krebs came into his laboratory he was still maintaining his long-standing controversy with Heinrich Wieland over the question of whether in biological oxidations hydrogen or oxygen is activated (see Chapter 1, p. 4). Grossly exaggerating the opposition to his views, Warburg perceived himself as surrounded by scientific adversaries whom he must defeat to make his ideas prevail. In the laboratory his comments on views he opposed were more drastic even than in print. He spoke often as though he needed to rally the young against the entrenched stands of the old. The young assistants in his laboratory were certain that Warburg was right in these disputes; they accepted his positions "as gospel."[73]

Particularly disdainful of the medical-research establishment in Germany, Warburg thought that the lucrative private practices available to those in academic medicine had corrupted them, and that pseudoscience and nepotism were rampant. He often told those around him that August Wassermann — the discoverer of the famous Wassermann test for syphilis — was not interested in science, but only in making money.[74] An incident that took place at about this time in the III Medical Clinic where Krebs had spent his hospital year seemed to justify Warburg's attitude toward academic medicine. A position had become available on the teaching staff, for which Annalise Wittgenstein and Bruno Mendel were both candidates. To Krebs it appeared obvious that Mendel was better qualified, but Wittgenstein was appointed. Word leaked out that the director of the clinic, Professor Goldscheider, had made an agreement with a member of the Faculty Board to support Wittgenstein in return for support for his own candidate for another position. The affair became enough of a scandal so that Albert Einstein wrote a letter of protest to Goldscheider. Although apologetic, Goldscheider professed not to be able to do anything about it. Mendel angrily left the clinic and used his own means to set up an independent laboratory.[75]

Even though he was no longer connected with the III Medical Clinic, these events touched Krebs personally. Mendel was then his closest friend — they telephoned one another almost every evening to discuss the work of the day — and Wittgenstein's case for appointment rested entirely on the experimental investigation Krebs had conducted jointly with her and to which he believed she had made no significant contribution. Even though the young Krebs may have clung to a more "idealistic view of the world"[76] than did the skeptical Warburg, this example of the conduct Warburg deplored undoubtedly increased Krebs's susceptibility to the belief that the standards in large pockets of the world around him were deteriorating.

For their 30-minute lunch break Warburg's younger assistants assembled in a common room in the building, where the wife of the superintendent had prepared a spartan meal consisting almost every day of milk, rolls, and a boiled egg. They paid her each a small sum for her expense. There they mingled with workers from other laboratories in the building, especially the four or five from Meyerhof's laboratory. The talk ranged widely, from exchanging news about what had happened that morning in their respective groups, to world events.

Warburg was not present, since he normally walked to his nearby home for lunch. In his absence conversation often revolved around the "Chief." His strong opinions and his eccentricities provided lively topics for discussion, but there were also frequent expressions of admiration. Meyerhof was undoubtedly discussed as well, but even though his scientific stature was nearly as great as that of Warburg, he was a more retiring person. The dominant presence for the group was clearly the head of the laboratory on the top floor.[77]

* * *

The foregoing portrait of Warburg at the time Krebs worked in his laboratory is based largely on Krebs's later testimony. It fits well with views of others who encountered his vivid personality then and later, but Krebs's experience was, of course, subjective. Others present at the same time undoubtedly perceived and responded differently to the Chief. For our purposes, however, Krebs's experience of Warburg is the most pertinent one.

Krebs's recollections of Warburg's attitudes and scientific outlook in the 1920s may have been "clarified" by his later understanding of Warburg and by the fact that Warburg's eccentricities became more pronounced as he grew older.[78] This picture is, I believe, nevertheless on the whole realistic.

* * *

Beyond the immediate domain of Warburg's laboratory Krebs quickly sensed the stimulating scientific environment that pervaded the Kaiser-Wilhelm Institutes in Dahlem. Much of Germany's scientific leadership either resided there or visited there. In the same building with Warburg and Meyerhof were eminent figures in other fields of biology, including Carl Correns, Richard Goldschmidt, Max Hartmann, and Otto Mangold. In a nearby building was the Biochemical Institute of Carl Neuberg, whose theory of fermentation then held sway in the field (see Chapter 1, pp. 11–12). Outside the biological sciences the liveliest center in Dahlem was Fritz Haber's Institute for Physical Chemistry. Krebs began to attend regularly the famous Haber Colloquia, held every Monday at 5 PM, where guest scientists came from all over Europe to present papers. Haber presided, introducing topics and providing penetrating commentary. Covering all sciences, the Colloquia formed a common meeting ground for directors and workers in the various specialized institutes. To Krebs it did not matter that much of what he heard in physics or chemistry seemed over his head. It was exciting just to see the outstanding scientists of the time in action, to witness the searching discussions, and to be aware of the dramatic developments occurring in these fields.[79]

While absorbing the broader scientific culture of Dahlem in the niches of time allocated to it, Krebs spent his active working days pursuing his allotted problem, the oxidation of fructose in ammoniacal solutions. Following up his initial confirmation of the reaction, he tested variations in the salt content of the solutions. Substituting ammonium sulfate or nitrate for the ammonium chloride,

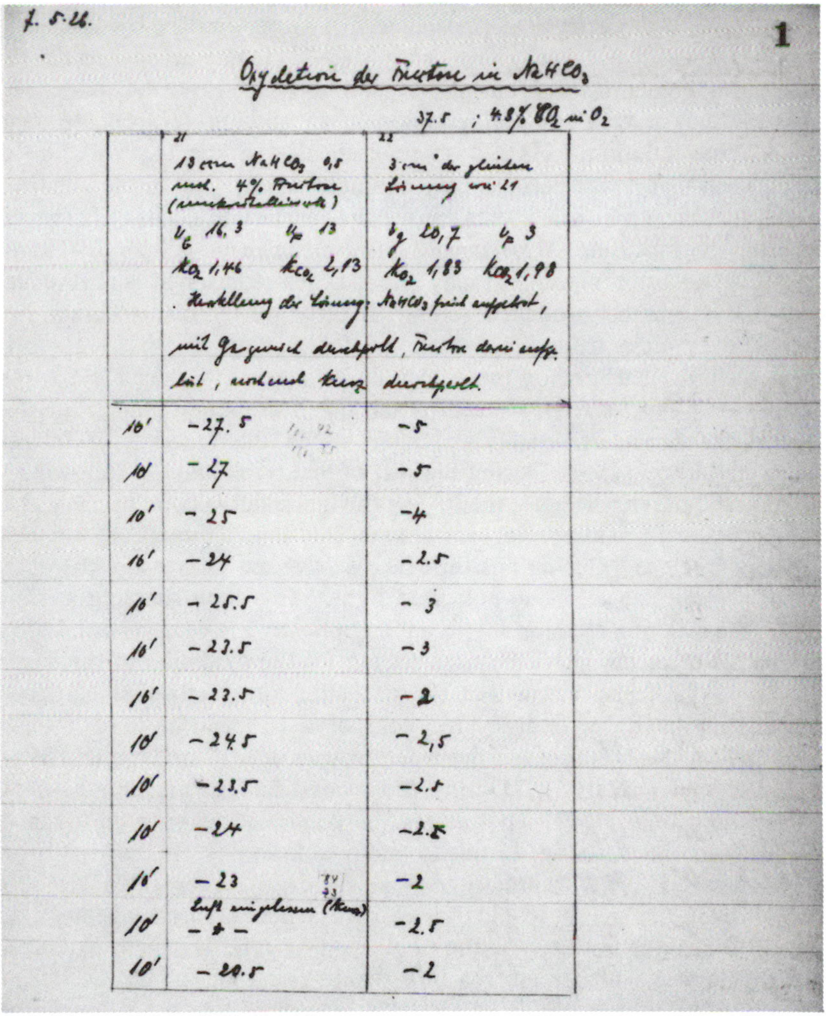

7. 5. 26. **1**

Oxydation der Fructose in $NaHCO_3$

37.5 ; 4.8% CO_2 in O_2

	21	22
	13 ccm $NaHCO_3$ 0,5 mol. 4% Fructose ([illegible])	3 ccm der gleichen Lösung wie 21
	v_G 16,3 v_F 13	v_G 20,7 v_F 3
	k_{O_2} 1,46 k_{CO_2} 2,13	k_{O_2} 1,83 k_{CO_2} 1,98
	Herstellung der Lösung: $NaHCO_3$ frisch aufgelöst, mit Gasgemisch durchperlt, Fructose darin aufgelöst, nochmal kurz durchperlt.	
10'	−27.5	−5
10'	−27	−5
10'	−25	−4
10'	−24	−2.5
10'	−25.5	−3
10'	−23.5	−3
10'	−23.5	−2
10'	−24.5	−2,5
10'	−23.5	−2.5
10'	−24	−2.5
10'	−23	−2
10'	Luft eingelassen (kurz) − [illegible] −	−2.5
10'	−20.5	−2

Figure 5.7 First page of Hans Krebs's earliest surviving laboratory notebook, used in the laboratory of Otto Warburg. The experiment employs Warburg's method for measuring simultaneously the absorption of oxygen and the release of carbon dioxide, by means of duplicate runs with different volumes of fluid in the manometer vessel: on left, fluid volume 13 cm^3, on right 3 cm^3.

he found, did not alter the situation. With ammonium phosphate, however, the rate was double that in the other ammonium salts, suggesting that the effects of the ammonia and the effects of phosphate discovered earlier by Warburg and Yabusoe were additive. Next, perhaps on May 7, the day he opened the first of his laboratory notebooks that has survived, Krebs tried out the oxidation in a solution without an ammoniacal component in sodium bicarbonate, another mildly alkaline solution. He did so undoubtedly in keeping with the initial presupposition that it was because they maintained a pH just to the alkaline side of neutral that the ammoniacal salts caused the reaction to occur. He employed, perhaps for the first time, Warburg's duplicate run method with different fluid volumes, to measure simultaneously the oxygen consumed and the carbon dioxide that might be produced (either directly or by displacement in case another acid resulted from the oxidation), looking up in Warburg's original article describing that method the equations he needed to calculate the results. The outcome, "Fructose is oxidized by the O_2 of the air in $NaHCO_3$", further broadened the range of conditions under which the reaction of interest to Warburg could take place. During the rest of that week and the following week Krebs repeated the experiment, modifying the quantitative conditions, and found that glucose too is oxidized in bicarbonate solution, although 15 times more slowly than fructose. During this time he also learned to measure the changing ability of the solution to rotate polarized light. This long-standing method for following the rate of a reaction involving an optically active compound provided an alternative means to chart the time-course for the oxidation of the sugars.[80]

On May 14, Krebs found that the oxidation of fructose in $NaHCO_3$ "is completely inhibited by hydrocyanic acid at a concentration of 10^{-3}," thus assuring that in this solution too the reaction was one of the type that Warburg attributed to metal catalysis. During the second half of the month, in which Krebs recorded only a few experiments, he continued to vary the quantitative conditions for the reaction in bicarbonate solution. He carried out one experiment in NH_4HCO_3 solution, probably to see if here also the separate effects of two salts on it would be additive when present together; but he observed no striking result. At the beginning of June he again expanded the enquiry by testing whether the reaction would occur in sodium acetate, or in sodium chloride, with a "trace of NaOH", but found "no oxidation" in either solution, even though the latter was "at a pH in which in NH_4Cl there is a strong oxidative *Stoffwechsel*." The latter phrase implies that Krebs viewed himself, in Warburg fashion, as studying not a mere catalytic chemical reaction, but a model system for reproducing metabolic processes.[81]

During the next 10 days Krebs again recorded only one experiment. Then, on June 12, he tested further qualitative changes of the solution in which the fructose oxidation took place. He entitled the experiment "Oxidation in concentrated salt solutions: $CaCl_2$, NaCl." To each of three vessels containing, respectively, sodium chloride, calcium chloride, and water, he added fructose and a 3:1 ratio of $NH_4Cl: NH_3$. In the first of these the rate of oxidation was about double that of the control, whereas that including $CaCl_2$ was 10 times as high. What did this outcome mean? Krebs wrote down:

NH$_4$Cl served as a buffer to stabilize [H].

NH$_3$

Result.   In CaCl$_2$ relatively strong oxidation,
in NaCl at the same molarity — about 8 X
less than in CaCl$_2$.

He then commented on the gradual sinking of the rates of oxidation, explaining them as due to the weakness of the buffering against acidity.[82] Comparing this experiment with Krebs's first experiments employing ammoniacal salts alone, we can see that the observed effect of CaCl$_2$ might have been regarded as an enhancement of a particular phenomenon identified as the oxidation of fructose in ammoniacal salts. The initial presupposition of the investigation, however, had been that the ammoniacal salts acted simply as a mild alkali. Accordingly he construed the primary action as due to CaCl$_2$ and relegated the ammoniacal salts to the background role of maintaining the pH. The distinction may appear superficial, but such small differences in the perspective from which the results of an experiment are viewed often influence the direction of an investigation.

In the next experiment, headed "Fructose in CaCl$_2$", Krebs leaned further in the direction suggested by his interpretation of the previous one. This time the result he recorded was "Strong oxidation in CaCl$_2$, is constant [instead of sinking, as in the preceding experiment], because the NH$_3$ concentration is relatively high." Thus, he again attributed to the ammoniacal component not a direct effect on the oxidation, but a more effective buffering action. Apparently now perceiving in the effect of CaCl$_2$ a possible opening toward an expanded class of solutions in which the fructose oxidation might occur, he again sought, on June 16, to enlarge his new opening by testing "Fructose in neutral salts," including CaCl$_2$, MgCl$_2$, NaCl, KCl, Ca(NO$_3$)$_2$, Na$_2$SO$_4$, and LiNO$_3$. The two calcium salts stood out clearly as more effective than any of the others. Two days later, however, when he included CaCl$_2$, SrCl$_2$, MgCl$_2$, and BaCl$_2$ in a similar experiment, the strontium and barium exerted major effects. He drew a carefully plotted graph showing linear rates of oxidation caused by the various salts he had tested, their slopes ranging from the three most active of them, CaCl$_2$, SrCl$_2$, and BaCl$_2$, down to KI and KSCN, whose rates were lower than in the NH$_4$Cl–NH$_3$ buffer alone.[83]

By now the investigation was expanding in more directions than Krebs could follow. Rather than to spread his effort in a search for further salts that might activate the reaction, he chose to fix on the condition "Fructose in CaCl$_2$" and subjected it to the crucial test of whether there was "hydrocyanic acid poisoning." In addition to a vessel to which he added HCN and a control without it, he added a second control with caustic alkali placed in the inner cup. The fact that the measured O$_2$ consumption was the same in both controls told him that "CO$_2$ is apparently not formed" in the oxidation. Meanwhile, the HCN inhibited the reaction almost completely (95 percent) during the first 30 minutes, after which the rate of oxidation returned gradually to that of the control. Krebs construed this result to indicate that "The inhibition is reversible (cyanhydrin formation)." That is, he assumed that the HCN had reacted with fructose in a well-known reaction that produces the cyanhydrin of fructose, thereby removing the poison from the solution.[84]

In a second experiment, on June 18, Krebs examined the "temperature coefficient of fructose in $CaCl_2$-NH_3." His notation suggests that the meaning of the experiments he had begun with $CaCl_2$ 6 days earlier was shifting. Where he had before seen a $CaCl_2$ solution whose pH was stabilized by an ammoniacal buffer, he now saw a "$CaCl_2$-NH_3" system in action. This reorientation regrouped the new reactions within the class of oxidations in ammoniacal solutions that had been his initial topic for study, relegating the calcium salts (along with the barium and strontium salts) to the status of a "great influence" on such oxidations. The subtle inversion of perspective again influenced the direction of his immediately succeeding experimental steps. Although he did carry out one more experiment on the action of other neutral salts, he concentrated for the last 10 days of June mainly on the $CaCl_2$-NH_3 system, varying the concentrations of each of the constituents in the fructose reaction. From time to time he compared the oxidation of glucose with that of fructose, finding invariably the rate of the former much lower than that of the latter.[85]

At the beginning of July, Krebs deviated from the main line of his investigation — the question whether the oxidations he was studying were catalyzed by oxygen-carrying metals — to ask himself about the products of the fructose oxidation. Specifically he asked "Does formic acid arise?" His choice is not immediately obvious if he regarded his system as a model for a metabolic oxidation, as formic acid was an unlikely metabolic intermediate; but Warburg had not contended in general that the oxidations in his models followed the same pathway of reactions as those of cellular oxidations, and the intermediate steps of metabolism did not particularly interest him. At any rate, Krebs looked up methods for determining formic acid, tried several of them, and selected one that appeared usable to him under the experimental conditions. On July 1, he began an experiment aimed at the question of whether formic acid was produced in the oxidation of fructose in the $CaCl_2$-NH_3 solution. Somehow his plans were altered, however, for after measuring the change in the rotation of polarized light and the oxygen consumed, he did not complete the formic acid determination. He pursued the question of the oxidative products no further. It would be interesting to know whether he dropped his brief foray in that direction because it appeared unpromising, or whether Warburg wanted him to pursue the central goal of the project, which was at this point to test the effect of metals on what Krebs was now calling the "NH_3-$CaCl_2$ Model."[86]

If the model system were to be helpful to Warburg's view of cellular oxidations, the rate of the oxidation catalyzed by metals ought to reach an order of magnitude near to that occurring in cells. Warburg expressed these rates in terms of the quotient:

$$Q_{metal} = \frac{cmm\ [mm^3]\ O_2\ consumed}{mg\ metal\ X\ hours}$$

For the comparison to be meaningful it was necessary to determine the quantity of the metal in the tissues whose oxygen consumption was measured. Warburg had done so for iron and obtained Q values between 10,000 and 100,000. In this context the value that Krebs had found in his early experiments with fructose in ammoniacal solutions was a disappointingly small $Q_{Fe} = 91$. It now became urgent, therefore, to find if the NH_3–$CaCl_2$ model could produce rates more like those in living cells.[87]

In his first try, on July 3, Krebs added fructose in a $CaCl_2$–NH_3 solution at three different concentrations of $FeSO_4$. The highest of the three accelerated the oxidation by about three times, but the rate was inconstant. The lower two concentrations had no effect, and Krebs added during the course of the experiment more $FeSO_4$ in one, and $FeCl_3$ in the other. The intended comparison was between the effect of ferrous iron (Fe^{++}) in the sulfate and ferric iron (Fe^{+++}) in the chloride. The latter produced a constant rate, but he could not calculate the quotient, because the total quantity of iron was not known. Repeating the comparison in a second experiment that day, with equal quantities of iron in the ferrous form and the ferric form, he found that the effect of the metal was greater when added to the solution before the NH_3, and that with ferrous iron the effect diminished with time, whereas with the ferric iron the rate was again constant. He now calculated initial Q values of 4,850 for ferrous iron and 3,470 for ferric iron. These rates, reaching to more than one third of the lowest rates for living cells, were obviously encouraging.[88]

On July 5, Krebs tested "Fe^{III}, Mn^{II}, [and] Cu^{II} at a pH of 7.4," and obtained the values $Q_{Fe} = 1,283$, $Q_{Mn} = 340$, and $Q_{Cu} = 4,050$. He commented "Cu acceleration at pH 7.4, 3.15 X as much as Fe^{III}. Mn is not very active." In an effort to improve on these results he repeated the experiment on July 8 at pH 8.5 with auspicious success:[89]

$$Q_{Fe} = 2,710, \quad Q_{Mn} = 22,250, \quad Q_{Cu} = 29,708.$$

All of these values were high enough to convince Krebs (and probably also Warburg) that the "NH_3–$CaCl_2$ model" supported Warburg's picture of cellular oxidations. In conducting these four experiments, Krebs must have felt that he was reaching the climax of his research project, and by the end of the series must have been confident that he had achieved a success in his first assignment. There were, however, a number of directions in which he still needed to extend the results thus far attained.

Even while carrying on this group of experiments at the heart of his agenda, Krebs again branched out, applying the system he had established to another question. On July 6 he performed an experiment on "Glucose 'anaerobic' in $CaCl_2$–NH_3." The title indicated that although he was not working under true anaerobic conditions, he wished to ascertain whether the solution in which he had found sugars so effectively oxidized might also activate the anaerobic glycolytic reactions of carbohydrate metabolism. He used three vessels, one containing only glucose and the $CaCl_2$–NH_3 solution, the others including respectively ferric iron and copper sulfate. Allowing the solutions to stand for

6 days, he measured the disappearance of the glucose polarimetrically each day. On the second day in the three vessels 64, 58.4 and 60 percent of the glucose, respectively, had disappeared. On the first of the solutions he made a determination of lactic acid, the expected product of glycolysis and calculated that it accounted for 15.7 percent of the glucose consumed; but he distrusted the result because he suspected that a side reaction had consumed some of the reagent with which he titrated the acid. On the same day he undertook a true anaerobic experiment, measuring the gas produced from glucose in the usual $CaCl_2$-NH_3 solution in the presence of nitrogen gas. There was, however, "No gas formation anaerobically!"[90] After these two unfavorable results Krebs again returned from his short digression to occupy himself with the core investigation of oxidations in the $CaCl_2$-NH_3 system.

For his further exploration of conditions pertinent to these oxidations Krebs employed only copper as the metal. Clearly that was because of the three metals he had tested copper attained the highest rates of oxidation, but to give copper priority on those grounds indicates also that Warburg, who had earlier built his model of cellular oxidation around iron, was open to the idea that iron was only one example of the oxygen-carrying properties of a generic class of "heavy metals." Warburg was, in fact, well aware that in some organisms copper might replace iron in this role. Between the 8th and the 19th of July Krebs used the combination of the $CaCl_2$-NH_3 system and copper to test the dependence of the fructose reaction on the concentration of $CaCl_2$, and of the combined salts in the solution, of the quantity of the metal, and of the oxygen pressure. He retested the inhibition by HCN and included in addition H_2S and citrate. H_2S acted similarly to HCN, while citrate stopped the reaction altogether. All three acted, he assumed, by forming complexes with the copper. He extended the system to the oxidation of glucose, mannose, galactose, saccharose, and maltose and found that all of these sugars except saccharose were oxidized, but at different rates, all lower than fructose. He asked also whether "amino acids are oxidized in $CaCl_2$-NH_3," but found for leucine, the only one he tried, no evidence of a reaction.[91]

Probably satisfied by now that he had gathered sufficient data concerning oxidations in $CaCl_2$-NH_3 to fulfill the primary goals of his investigation, Krebs took up again on the 19th the question of the anaerobic reactions of fructose and glucose in this solution. Besides measuring their disappearance polarimetrically, he tried various methods to detect possible products of the reaction such as keto hexoses or lactic acid, without reaching any definite results.[92]

In the early phases of the investigation, as we have seen, Krebs had treated the ammoniacal component of the solution as a means to maintain mildly alkaline conditions. The fact that the oxidation was so much stronger than when other bases replaced the ammonia in solutions of the same degree of alkalinity had changed his point of view sufficiently so that he now wondered whether ammonia might form a complex with the sugars, placing them in an active, more readily oxidizable form. Accordingly he carried out an experiment in which he measured the percentage of glucose that disappeared by the reduction in the polarization of light and titrated the solution afterward to find how much base had been consumed. He estimated that "per 1 mole glucose 0.532 mole HN_3 disappears."[93] He did not, however, follow up this lead. On the 26th he tested whether iron in the form of a trisodium ferropentacyanamine compound [$Na_3Fe(CN)_5NH_3$] prepared by Warburg can operate as an oxygen-carrying catalyst. In a first experiment it activated the oxidation of alanine, fructose, glucose, and acetate in an ammonia solution, but 2 days later he found that in his "$CaCl_2$–NH_3 model it is completely ineffective as a catalyst." At the very end of the month he asked a question around which much of his prior investigation had implicitly hinged: "In the $CaCl_2$-model is NH_3 or OH necessary?"[94]; but he did not have time to attempt an answer, because the laboratory closed for the annual two-month summer vacation.

The long hours spent in the laboratory, and the need to reduce data, plan experiments, and keep up on the pertinent scientific literature in the evenings did not preclude Krebs from an active engagement in outside life. His capacity to organize himself effectively left him some time in the evenings and most of the weekend (that is, Sunday, since the laboratory worked a 6-day week) free to do other things that he deemed worthwhile. He continued to read widely in history, literature, and philosophy. Unable to afford a piano, he could not carry on his favorite personal cultural activity, but he took full advantage of the cultural richness of Berlin. He attended musical concerts, theater, opera, and cabaret. Through his medical contacts he was able to obtain free tickets to concerts and plays as *Theaterarzt*, enabling him to sit in the front row. It meant that he had to bring his kit with him and to be prepared to administer aid if someone suffered a heart attack or other emergency, but that never happened, and he was able to see many outstanding performances.[95]

Having missed out, because of the war, on the dancing lessons that German middle class youth normally took as teenagers, Krebs decided to make up for his loss by enrolling, in 1926, in a group dance class. He came to enjoy the activity greatly. Meanwhile he continued to see Fernanda, the woman he had met at the III Medical Clinic 2 years before, and their friendship grew closer.[96]

IV

Each year Warburg spent August and September in his country home on Rügen, the large island just off the coast of Germany, 200 kilometers north of Berlin. He took his laboratory notebooks along and did much of the writing of his scientific papers there.[97] For Krebs a 2-month enforced holiday was a challenge to use his time as effectively as possible while taking advantage of the opportunity to be free of direct responsibilities for an unusually extended period of time. Having been frugal enough to save, even on his small salary, enough money for some recreation, Krebs decided to travel to a place in which he could improve his knowledge of one of the foreign languages he had studied in school — that is, French or English — and where he could live cheaply. He chose the French Alps. On July 29 he obtained at the French consulate in Berlin a visa to spend 1 month in France, and probably left on his trip a few days later. He spent most of his time in the Alps at Argentieres and Talloires, then stopped off for some time in Paris, where he received, on August 27, permission to cross Belgium by train without stopping, on his way back to Berlin.[98]

For the second month of his holiday Krebs probably occupied himself with scientific pursuits. Besides catching up on the literature, he had a special writing assignment. Warburg had been invited to write, for a handbook of methods in general biology, a summary of the manometric and tissue slice methods that had previously been described only in scattered form in the research papers in which he had originally presented the various stages in their development. Not wishing to distract himself with a review of what he had already done, he asked Krebs to write the article. Krebs composed it mainly by extracting, almost word-for-word, the relevant portions of Warburg's descriptions. He managed, however, to insert additional useful details of operative techniques and calculations that would not have occurred to Warburg as necessary to state. As a relative beginner, Krebs could see more readily than Warburg what would not be self-evident to someone learning to use the methods.[99]

During September, or as soon as the laboratory reopened in the first week of October, Krebs read an article just published by Heinrich Wieland and F.G. Fischer on the oxidizing and inhibiting activity of iodic acid. They asserted that the anticatalytic activity of such acids was due to the same mechanism as the reactions through which the acids were removed from solution: a conclusion at odds with Warburg's view that such substances form complexes with the metals that catalyze oxidations. If Wieland and Fischer's concept applied to the action of hydrocyanic acid in his experiments, Krebs reasoned, then, since the acid disappeared by means of a well-defined stoichiometric reaction, there ought also be a stoichiometric relation between the number of molecules of HCN placed in the solution and the number of oxygen molecules not absorbed by the sugar because of the action of HCN.[100]

To test this hypothesis, Krebs began, on his return to the laboratory, a series of experiments designed to answer the question "How many molecules of O_2 does one molecule of HCN prevent from being absorbed?" On October 5 he measured the oxidation of fructose in an ammoniacal solution in the presence and in the absence of 10^{-4} M HCN. He calculated that "10^{-6} moles of HCN prevented the uptake of at least 4.45 X 10^{-6} moles of O_2." The next day he repeated the experiment with copper added to the solution and obtained a ratio of 0.27 X 10^{-6} moles of O_2 per 10^{-6} moles of HCN. He noted that "With a high metal content the HCN inhibits less than by a low one!! The fact does not decide either in the sense of Wieland or of Warburg," On the same day he tested the

"Influence of pH on the relation $\dfrac{\text{Number of HCN molecules}}{\text{Number of } O_2 \text{ molecules not taken up}}$"

by changing the ratio of NH_4Cl to NH_3 so as to maintain a more alkaline medium than in the previous experiment. Under these conditions 10^{-6} moles of HCN prevented the absorption of 20.8 X 10^{-6} moles of O_2.[101] In his notebook he provided an explanation for these differences:

With increase in the pH the inhibiting action of HCN becomes greater. The cause is perhaps a stronger binding of HCN to the metal. The equilibrium of xCu + yHCN $\rightleftarrows$ (Cu)x (HCN)y lies strongly in favor of the right side. The concentration of free HCN would then be relatively small (as soon as the excess is bound to the sugar) and the complex combination would thereby gradually be decomposed.

He explained the fact that the HCN did not totally inhibit the reaction on the grounds that at this pH (9.8), "a part of the O_2 uptake is an *alkali* oxidation"[102] rather than one catalyzed by metal. In one further experiment on the subject he again examined the influence of pH on the ratio and also determined analytically that no HCN remained in the solution after its inhibiting effect had disappeared.[103]

Although it is possible that Warburg put Krebs onto these experiments to test Wieland's view, I think it more likely that Krebs came upon the question himself, probably in his reading during the time that Warburg was away from Dahlem. He may have sensed an opportunity to exert an investigative initiative and his own scientific judgment about an issue arising between Warburg and one of his adversaries. To identify in the literature questions that he might be able to decide through well-chosen experiments was, as we have seen, a distinct characteristic of the research initiatives that he had taken on his own before coming to Warburg's laboratory.

By this time — if not before — Krebs must also have begun to draft portions of the manuscript for the paper that he expected to submit eventually reporting the investigation he had pursued in Warburg's laboratory. Warburg may well have advised him to start before he completed the investigation itself, because the writing might reveal gaps in his evidence that he would need to repair through further experiments. Just as he had used some of Warburg's previous papers as guides to his experimental approach, Krebs probably used them now as models for the form in which to write up his results. Warburg's scientific papers were notable for the concise, lucid manner in which he introduced a problem and the succinct, forceful way in which he presented his methods, results, and conclusions. His style contrasted with the common practice Krebs had followed in the papers he had written on his own, when he had sometimes included full protocols of the majority of the experiments he had performed and lengthy discussions of their meaning and relation to the work of others. To emulate and satisfy Warburg Krebs must have made a major effort to overcome his prior habits. It was not only necessary to be clear, as he had striven to be even then, but to be rigorously selective, to sort out carefully the most salient problems, results, and conclusions from the secondary ones, to define economically the *main* points of the investigation and omit much of what might previously have appeared to him worthwhile to discuss. From all the data he had accumulated he must pick out just those experiments, or parts of more extended experiments, that best supported or illustrated the arguments he would make. Warburg believed also that one should not vacillate over a question, but take a strong, unequivocal stand, even though one might have to revise it later.

One should not report on the detours one might have taken along the way. After constructing the "edifice" one should remove the "scaffolding" and present only the experimental results and reasoning essential to justify the conclusions one had reached. Warburg, therefore, expected from Krebs a carefully considered, finely honed manuscript.[104]

Fragments of an early typewritten draft of the paper Krebs was writing have survived. They include the following introductory paragraph:

On the Autoxydation of Carbohydrates in Salt Solutions Containing Ammonia and Bicarbonate.

by Hans Adolf Krebs.

In this work it is shown that a series of carbohydrates (fructose, glucose, galactose, mannose, maltose), dissolved in neutral and very weak alkaline concentrated aqueous ammonium chloride-ammonia mixtures or in concentrated aqueous bicarbonate are oxidized at body temperature by the oxygen of the air. Just as in the oxidation of fructose in concentrated phosphate solutions discovered by O. Warburg and M. Yabusoe, here also the oxygen is transported by heavy metals: the addition of heavy metals accelerates the oxidations, complex-builders (hydrocyanic acid, pyrophosphate) and hydrogen sulfide inhibit them. The oxydations show, therefore, analogies to respiration, to the combustion of organic substances in living cells; they are "respiratory models" in the sense of the theory of O. Warburg.[105]

Even though this paragraph seems to be a clear, concise summary of the most salient results of his own experiments and of their relationship to Warburg's broader theoretical program, Krebs's handiwork apparently did not please his chief. Warburg lined out the final sentence with a blue pencil and changed the word "autoxidation" in the title to "oxidation." Subsequently Krebs eliminated the paragraph entirely and began his paper from a different direction.

Another preserved fragment read:

It follows from the investigation that the formation of a labile reactive form of fructose in ammonium chloride – ammonium mixtures is favored to a high degree by the salts of the alkaline earths.

Below this typewritten statement Krebs added with his pen:

End products of the oxidation.

End products of the oxidation could not be identified. Carbonic acid does not form, formic acid — if at all — only in small amounts.[106]

Neither of these statements escaped Warburg's blue pencil. We can surmise that Warburg told Krebs that he did not have sufficient evidence to speculate about a labile form of the carbohydrate or about possible end products. As we have seen, Krebs had, in fact conducted only a few preliminary experiments on these questions, and by Warburg's standards it would have been premature to discuss them in print.

On October 16 and 17 Krebs drew 11 graphs representing the results of experiments that he planned to incorporate into his paper. Warburg wished wherever possible to display quantitative results in graphical form, a mode well suited to the data derived from the manometrical methods. For some of the experiments involved, Krebs had already drawn graphs in his notebook at the time he performed them, but he now simplified the originals, reducing the time axes from the actual duration of the experiments to the periods crucial for the conclusions to be drawn from the results, and omitted from them curves that were less pertinent to the results he wished to use. These selections of data to be included in the final graphs corresponded to similar selections he must have been making as he decided what data to include in his discussions in the text of his paper.[107]

After finishing the above experiments on the ratios of HCN molecules to O_2 molecules, Krebs wrote up a portion of his intended manuscript in which he discussed Wieland and Fischer's view, drew the inference that, if they were correct, the number of HCN molecules added to the solution "must stand in a definite stoichiometric relation to the number of oxygen molecules that are, as a consequence of the effect of hydrocyanic acid, *not* taken up," and reported "We have tested the consequences of this theory and found that they do *not* hold true." (He then lined out the words "this theory," and changed "We" to "I.") Adducing examples of the data just gathered, he summarized the overall result that "According to the experimental conditions the ratio varies between 0.5 and 20." After enumerating the conditions that he had varied, he concluded "It follows from these facts, that the disappearance of the effect of hydrocyanic acid is conditioned by a process that is different from the reaction that causes the anticatalytic action of the hydrocyanic acid."[108]

Krebs must have been pleased with a result and an argument that appeared to disarm a challenge to the views of his chief. Nevertheless, Warburg crossed out these passages in his manuscript.[109] He probably wanted his research assistant to limit himself to the immediate results of his investigative assignment, not to engage himself in the broader theoretical issues surrounding Warburg's own position.

Beginning again another introduction for his paper, Krebs wrote it out this time in longhand, on the left side of the page, as he had learned to do long ago in his school essays, so that Warburg could make corrections in the wide right-hand margin. He did not make another attempt to frame the general outcome of the investigation and its meaning, but simply described how it had begun and what he had found:

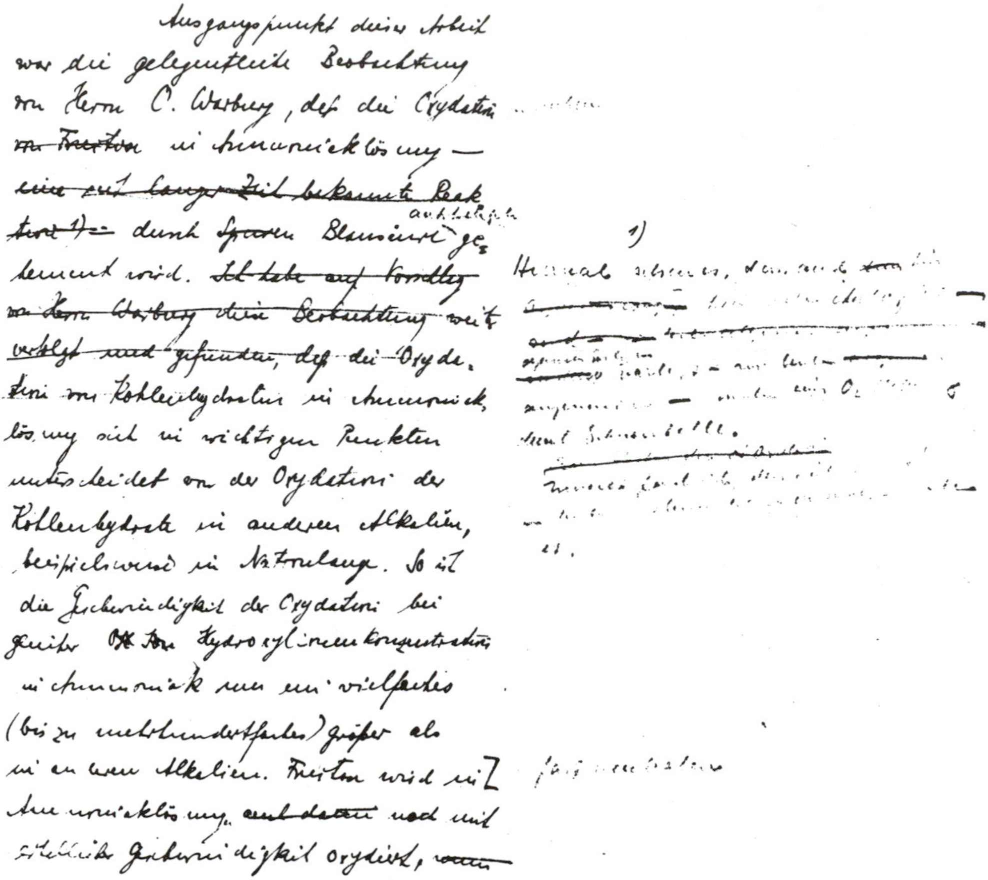

Ausgangspunkt dieser Arbeit
war die gelegentliche Beobachtung
von Herrn O. Warburg, daß die Oxydation
~~von Fructose~~ in Ammoniaklösung —
~~eine seit langer Zeit bekannte Reak-~~
~~tion 1) —~~ durch Spuren Blausäure ge-
hemmt wird. ~~Ich habe auf Vorschlag~~
~~von Herrn Warburg diese Beobachtung~~ weiter
~~verfolgt und~~ gefunden, daß die Oxydation von Kohlehydraten in Ammoniaklösung sich in wichtigen Punkten
unterscheidet von der Oxydation der
Kohlenhydrate in anderen Alkalien,
beispielsweise in Natronlauge. So ist
die Geschwindigkeit der Oxydation bei
gleicher ~~OH Ion~~ Hydroxylionenkonzentration
in Ammoniak um ein vielfaches
(bis zu mehrhundertfaches) größer als
in anderen Alkalien. Fructose wird in
Ammoniaklösung ~~erst daran~~ und mit
erheblicher Geschwindigkeit oxydiert, ~~wenn~~

Figure 5.8 First page of Hans Krebs's handwritten draft of introduction to his first paper from Warburg's laboratory, with corrections by Warburg.

The point of departure for this work was the casual observation by Herr
O. Warburg, that the oxidation of fructose in an ammoniacal solution —
a reaction known for a long time — is inhibited by traces of hydrocyanic
acid.   At the suggestion of Herr Warburg I have followed up the
observation and have found that the oxidation of carbohydrate in
ammoniacal solution is different in important respects from the oxidation
of carbohydrates in other alkalis, for example in caustic soda solution.

Summarizing briefly the nature of the differences, including the fact that the rate
of the former was "up to several hundred times larger," and that hydrocyanic
acid inhibits only the former, he stated in the next paragraph:

The addition of heavy metals accelerates the rate of oxidation in ammoniacal solution only a little.   But if one adds much calcium chloride to it, the
catalytic effect of the added heavy metals [he specified in the margin
("copper, manganese, iron")] is powerfully increased.   The reactive
capacity of the metals is here of the same order of magnitude as in living
cells.

Krebs next mentioned that other sugars also underwent the reaction and
enumerated the substances that inhibited it.   "The oxidation of carbohydrates in
ammoniacal solutions," he wrote, "is therefore a heavy metal catalysis — just
as the oxidation of fructose discovered by Warburg and Yabusoe in phosphate
solution."   "In testing the question whether carbohydrates are also oxidized in
other solutions by oxygen," he went on, "I found that the carbohydrate is
oxidizable in bicarbonate."   In the last introductory paragraph he said that he
would occupy himself in the paper only with the oxidations in ammoniac and
bicarbonate solutions, not those in other alkalis. "I have," he ended the section,
"not investigated the question, which substances are the end products of the
oxidation.   Carbon dioxide arises in these oxidations at most in traces."[110]
With this more limited account of his work, Krebs undoubtedly satisfied
Warburg's desire that he not generalize beyond the immediate results, or discuss
aspects of the investigation barely begun.   Nevertheless, Warburg rewrote more
than half of it on the margin provided.   He eliminated unessential or redundant
phrases, added some specific details, including numerical values, where Krebs
had been too general, and rephrased much of the prose to focus it more sharply
on what Warburg considered the salient points.[111]
In both of the drafts that he had composed Krebs indicated (in the title in the
first version, in the text in the second), that he intended to describe in the
subsequent sections of his paper the oxidations carried out in ammoniacal and
in bicarbonate solutions.   This decision, reached probably in the writing itself
as well as in consultation with Warburg, led him to recognize that the relatively
few experiments in bicarbonate solution that he had carried out during the
previous May did not furnish adequate data for his purpose.   Accordingly, on
October 20, after a gap of nearly 2 weeks in which he may have been concentrating on the paper, he resumed experiments on "fructose in bicarbonate."

Because in this solution, unlike in ammoniacal solution, some carbonic acid *was* produced, he had to measure it as well as the oxygen consumed, and had to deploy Warburg's rather complex formula to calculate whether under the conditions of his experiments there was sufficient "retention" of carbonic acid in the solution to require a correction factor.   He went on to recapitulate in bicarbonate solution the series of experiments on the influence of the three metals and three inhibitors on the oxidation of fructose and several other sugars that he had already done in the "$CaCl_2-NH_3$ system."[112]   All of the experiments confirmed the picture he had already drawn up, and he incorporated most of the data obtained into a short final section of his manuscript that he appended to a longer section he had probably already completed treating the experiments on ammoniacal solutions.   On November 16 he submitted his manuscript, bearing now the title "On the Role of Heavy Metals in the Autoxidation of Sugar Solutions" to the *Biochemische Zeitschrift*.   To do so he needed only to carry it over to a nearby building and hand it to the editor of that journal, Carl Neuberg.[113]

V

The work that Krebs produced during his first 9 months in Warburg's laboratory typified the complementary relation between training and research in a well-organized experimental laboratory.   Warburg had essentially delegated to him a "gap" left over from his own prior research, one whose closure would be useful to his ongoing investigative program even as it enabled the research apprentice to master the methods used in the laboratory.   In the sense that Warburg had already solved similar problems and that the strategies to attack this one were all in place, the problem was routine.   A competent beginner could hardly fail to achieve some success with it.   The investigative goal was, nevertheless, open enough to challenge both Krebs's operative skill and his judgment.   There were subproblems not entirely foreseen, results sufficiently unanticipated so that he had to modify his initial point of view to assimilate them, judgments to be made about how far to pursue each facet of the problem. There were also opportunities to identify further investigative questions along the way, although Warburg clearly allowed Krebs only limited scope to depart from his initial assignment.

   One of Warburg's more generous traits was to permit his assistants to publish under their own names the results of investigations for which he had provided the organizing ideas as well as the experimental methods.   Krebs was able to get out of the work, therefore a publication that identified him as a productive researcher in a well-known laboratory.   In form and content his paper was typical of the secondary papers that Warburg's assistants regularly published in the wake of their leader's more germinal ones.   Krebs's paper slightly modified some of the subsidiary conditions affecting the model Warburg used to support his conception of the oxygen-carrying role of metal catalysts in cellular respiration, and provided some incremental support for that model.   It did not substantially alter the standing of Warburg's views on the subject.   The work was already behind the times in the sense that Warburg was moving beyond the model approach within which the problem he asked Krebs to take up was embedded. The investigation that Krebs completed was thus a minor contribution to the field, but it was a decisive contribution to its author's scientific education. In pursuing it he not only learned to use manometric methods that were at the forefront of the field, but learned something about the power and precision with which they could be applied to suitable problems, the efficiency and versatility with which they could be deployed, the way in which they lent themselves to investigations requiring many experiments carried out under closely controlled, systematically varied conditions. He acquired also familiarity with a small but strategic repertoire of chemical analytical methods. Beyond that, he absorbed from Warburg a scientific style, a manner in which to approach and define problems, and to set priorities. From Warburg he learned the importance of total concentration on work that he considered to be of the utmost importance.

Inspiring though Warburg was to Krebs from the day that the young physician walked into the laboratory of the formidable biochemist, he was also intimidating. Krebs found no trouble adapting to Warburg's demands for hard work and to his autocratic leadership. He had for much of his life conformed to the expectations of figures of authority. He admired Warburg greatly and aspired to emulate him, but he also measured himself against Warburg's standards and his achievements, and he found the comparison humbling. Before he entered Warburg's laboratory Krebs had already published on his own or with co-authors 10 scientific papers. He had resourcefully picked research problems suitable to his local circumstances, searched out the relevant literature, designed his own investigations, written his papers without assistance, and had them all accepted in leading journals. Now what he had accomplished then appeared to him superficial and dilettante. The problems he had pursued were narrow, the experiments simplistic.[114]

Sometime after Krebs's publications on the passage of dye stuffs into the cerebrospinal fluid appeared, Lina Stern, the senior author of the most comprehensive study of the subject preceding his own, visited Berlin. She made contact with Krebs, came to see him, and discussed his earlier work in a very friendly, encouraging way. Pleased though he was at her appreciation for what he had done before he came to Warburg,[115] Krebs was not convinced that the work was really important. He made no effort to find out whether it was being followed up elsewhere. He did not want to look back.

At the III Medical Clinic Hans Krebs had set off energetically, with little guidance from others, to enter the field of medical research. He formed his own opinions of the work of others, did not hesitate to express his judgments in print or to assert rather aggressively the significance of his contributions to the problems he had pursued. In Warburg's laboratory he suppressed his own originality and worked contentedly as a loyal lieutenant to an imperious mentor.

6

Initiative and Dependence

While Hans Krebs completed his medical training in Berlin, his year in Rona's laboratory, and his first year in Warburg's laboratory, Germany enjoyed greater outward stability than anything he had known since the outbreak of the war when he was a young teenager. After the end of the inflation German industrial production revived resiliently, and economic conditions for many people approached prewar levels. Although the republican government remained weak and divided by party factionalism, the forceful leadership of Gustav Stresemann in the Foreign Ministry gradually restored Germany to a respected place in the international community. His most significant achievement, the Locarno pact of 1925, guaranteed the western frontiers of Germany and introduced some order into its relations with France and Great Britain. Krebs was among the many who admired Stresemann and whose confidence in the future of his nation was strengthened by the Foreign Minister's presence.[1]

During these years Krebs's father continued his busy medical practice. Having survived the inflation better than many middle-class Germans, because his income remained high and because he had made shrewd investments, such as land purchases, that weathered the economic storm, Georg Krebs was again financially prosperous. On the orchard he had bought in the outskirts of Hildesheim after the war he built a small summer house where he could retreat for rest and refreshment from his demanding professional life.[2]

Although Hans himself subsisted on a small income, he did not turn to his father for further help. He did not view his financial stringency as a hardship. Among the young research assistants at Dahlem and elsewhere in Germany who aspired to scientific careers, he felt fortunate to have a paid position at all. His personal future remained uncertain in the sense that he did not know whether he would prove able enough for a research career, or whether he could eventually find an academic niche to sustain such a career; but he was keen to go on as long as he could, and comforted by the knowledge that if things did not work out in that direction he could fall back on medical practice and expect to make a good income. Moreover, he was conscious that many of the prominent cultural figures in Berlin were financially poor. For artists, intellectuals, and young scientists in that metropolis, poverty was not an indication that one was unimportant.[3]

During 1926 a young follower of Adolf Hitler named Joseph Goebbels became the *Gauleiter* for the National Socialist party in Berlin. He began putting out a party newspaper, the *Angriff*, that was filled with violent attacks, often directed at Jews. Krebs recognized these papers as the voice of an enemy. To know what such an enemy was about, he occasionally looked at the *Angriff*. He found it too repugnant to read very much in it, but he was not unduly worried. The voice seemed to him that of a small extremist group that could not cause serious harm. He shared the view that in a democracy even such groups had to be allowed.[4]

I

During the same week, in November 1926, that Krebs finished his paper on the role of heavy metals in the oxidation of sugars, Warburg gave him a new project on the metabolism of human cancer tissue. This work followed up some questions left by the other main line of Warburg's research during the previous 3 years. Ambitious ever since his student days to contribute to the cure of cancer, Warburg did not take up the subject experimentally until 1923. Because the most salient characteristic of tumor tissues was their rapid growth, Warburg approached the problem of cancer by examining the "energy-yielding reactions" at the expense of which the growth must take place. Since "one knows," as he thought, "that the energy-yielding reactions are bound to the structure" of the tissues, he sought a method that would avoid their mechanical destruction, or the use of antiseptic substances that would inhibit the reactions. His solution was to measure in his manometric system the gaseous exchanges in thin slices of the tissues suspended in a solution in which they could survive for the duration of the experiments. By means of a theoretical calculation and the measured rate of diffusion of oxygen through tissues, he established the "tissue thickness limit" that would permit sufficient oxygen pressure throughout the tissue slice so that the rate of respiration would be independent of the oxygen concentration. This limit — about 0.2 mm in ordinary air, 0.5 mm in pure oxygen — turned out conveniently close to the thinnest slices one could make by cutting the tissues free-hand with a razor blade. Since the blade cut through only one out of every 20 to 50 layers of cells, most of the cellular structure of the tissues remained intact.[5]

According to the current view (see Chapter 1, p. 14–15), cells derived their energy primarily from the decomposition of carbohydrates. The anaerobic decomposition of sugars, called glycolysis, yielded lactic acid, whereas aerobic respiration fully oxidized them. Warburg used his tissue slice method to measure both glycolysis and respiration. The measure of the latter was the rate of oxygen consumption. To measure the glycolysis he sometimes determined analytically the quantity of lactic acid produced in large-scale experiments employing multiple slices, but he was able to show that under suitable experimental conditions the carbon dioxide produced was equivalent to the lactic acid formed, because the latter displaced an equal molar quantity of carbonic acid from the medium. It became, therefore, more convenient to measure also glycolysis manometrically.[6]

In 1923, one of Warburg's assistants, Seigo Minami, measured these quantities in slices of a standardized experimental tumor tissue, Flexner rat carcinoma. He obtained the material by implanting pieces of the tissue under the skin of rats, allowing them to grow to a certain size there, and then removing them for the experiments. To compare the tumor with normal tissue, Minami ran similar experiments on rat liver, pancreas, and submaxillary gland and epithelial tissue. The rate of respiration in the tumor tissue, Minami found, was within the same range as the normal tissues. The rate of glycolysis, on the other hand, was much larger: the ratio between the average rate in carcinoma and that in liver tissue was 30:1.[7]

This striking quantitative difference induced Warburg to believe that he had uncovered the crucial clue that might lead eventually to the cause of the uncontrolled growth of malignant cancers. During the following years he pursued the question intensely. In 1924, he devised the "improved method for measuring respiration and glycolysis," mentioned in Chapter 5 (pp. 137–138), that relied on duplicate runs with two different fluid volumes to enable the simultaneous measurement of the oxygen consumed and the carbon dioxide emitted.[8] With two other assistants, Karl Posener and Erwin Negelein, Warburg extended the measurements to other cancerous and normal tissues. In the first experiments Minami had measured glycolysis both in air and nitrogen, and found that although in cancer tissue the process occurred both anaerobically and aerobically, the rate was higher in the absence of oxygen. Examining this difference more closely, Warburg and his associates now found that the presence of oxygen reduced the rate of glycolysis. In most normal tissues the aerobic rate was diminished so far that it usually vanished, but in tumor tissue the anaerobic rate was so high that even with the aerobic reduction it remained large enough to account for a major portion of the carbohydrate consumed.[9]

Warburg interpreted these results in accordance with Otto Meyerhof's theory of the lactic acid cycle in muscle tissues (see Chapter 1, pp. 15). Meyerhof had found that respiration causes a portion of the lactic acid formed anaerobically in muscle to disappear, and had inferred that this was due to the resynthesis of carbohydrate from the missing lactic acid with energy supplied by the further oxidation of the remainder of the lactic acid. Representing Meyerhof's cycle as follows,

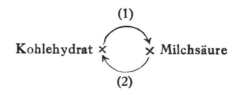

Warburg suggested that his own results made it probable that Meyerhof's explanation of the effects of respiration in muscle was more generally applicable to other tissues. Warburg defined the *Meyerhof quotient* as the ratio of the "lactic acid caused to disappear" by respiration, to the respiration itself: that is, as the difference between the lactic acid formed anaerobically and that formed aerobically, divided by the respiratory oxygen consumed. In normal as well as cancerous tissue, he found that this ratio was usually between 1 and 2, the same range that Meyerhof had found in muscle. The ratio of aerobic glycolysis to respiration was, however, much higher in tumor tissue than in normal tissue.[10]

If the property that distinguished malignant cancer tissue from normal tissue was rapid, uncontrolled growth, Warburg reasoned, then in the growing tissues of young organisms the rates of the energy-yielding reactions ought to be intermediate between that of tumor tissues and the stable tissues of mature animals. Just as he expected, in embryonic epithelial chicken tissue the aerobic rate of glycolysis was larger than in older tissue, but not as large as in tumor tissue, and the rate declined with the age of the embryo from which the tissue was taken.[11]

Warburg and his associates confirmed that other cancer tissues, including human cancer tissue obtained from the surgical clinic at the *Charité*, behaved similarly to Flexner rat carcinoma, and that other normal growth tissue had larger rates of aerobic glycolysis than did stable tissue. In 1924, Warburg proposed the hypothesis that tumors originate from the effects of insufficient oxygen in a normal tissue of the body. Those cells in an affected area that lack the ability to cover their energy requirements from glycolysis are destroyed, whereas the cells that "are glycolytically effective survive." If the lack of oxygen becomes chronic, these cells, growing like embryonic tissue, become tumor tissue.[12]

Although he believed he had answered the fundamental question of how tumors originate, Warburg acknowledged that "a second question, why [tumor tissue] grows in a more disordered, limitless manner the greater the disproportion between glycolysis and respiration" remained for the present unanswered.[13]

Among the normal tissues that Warburg, Posener, and Negelein tested in 1924, rat retina tissue stood out with a rate of aerobic glycolysis four times as high as that of the embryonic tissues. Because frog retina tissue displayed no aerobic glycolysis, however, Warburg suspected that that measured in the more delicate retina tissues of "warm-blooded animals might be the result of damage to the tissues."[14]

Noting that Louis Pasteur had been the first to observe, in 1861, that respiration "inhibits" fermentation: that is, that the fermentations produced anaerobically by organisms such as yeast diminish or disappear in the presence of oxygen, Warburg wrote, in 1926, that "Respiration and fermentation are therefore connected through a chemical reaction that I call the 'Pasteur reaction' after its discoverer."[15] The chemical nature of this "Pasteur reaction" had, of course, still to be discovered.

At the time Krebs joined the laboratory in Dahlem, Warburg had sufficiently consolidated his investigation of cancer tissue so that he was collecting the papers he had published on the topic since 1923 into a volume entitled *On the Metabolism of Tumors*. Although he believed that he had made the case for his theory of the origin of tumors, Warburg received some criticisms from other investigators. One of these was that spontaneous human tumors might behave differently from transplanted experimental animal tumors. Even though Warburg believed that unlikely, and had in fact already conducted some experiments on human tumors surgically removed, he thought it necessary to respond to the claim by investigating human cancer tissue more extensively. It was that task that he gave Krebs in November 1926.[16]

In preparation for this project Krebs had to learn, in addition to the manometric techniques he had already mastered, the craft of preparing the tissue slices. After killing the animal from which one wished to obtain the tissue, one removed the appropriate organs, placed them on moistened filter paper, and cut them into a series of thin slices with a razor blade first dipped into Ringer's solution. After making many more slices than one would use, one immersed them in a suitable solution in a shallow disk and cut them with a scissors into regular squares. Placing them in a second glass dish with a flat bottom, one viewed them in transmitted light to pick out those that appeared to be thinnest and most uniform. In the case of tumor slices, which often contained necrotic tissue, one had to pick slices from the nonnecrotic portions of the tumor. With a little practice one could do so by observing the color differences by naked eye. Then one placed the slices chosen into the manometric vessels already containing the solutions in which the experiments were to be run. Krebs found it easy to carry out these operations, but he had to be quick about them. Otherwise the tissues were likely to have died by the time he was ready to measure their metabolic activity.[17]

Before actually beginning experiments on human cancer tissue Krebs performed, between November 18 and December 8, a series of measurements of the respiration and glycolysis of an experimental animal tumor, Jensen rat sarcoma, in different media. These included pigeon blood serum, horse blood plasma, goose serum, the Ringer's with bicarbonate solution that Warburg customarily employed with tissue slices, and salt solutions differing from it by being richer in potassium chloride, in differing potassium concentrations, and sodium free. He measured regularly the anaerobic and aerobic glycolysis and sometimes calculated the Meyerhof quotient, noting with exclamation points in his notebook those values of the latter that exceeded the usual limiting ratio of 2. In part these may have been preliminary experiments intended mainly to familiarize Krebs with the procedures involved; but the effects of varied media, including the serum of normal animals, were also of interest to Warburg, because some earlier investigations had claimed that normal blood serum dissolves carcinoma cells. Krebs observed no such action.[18]

By the time that he had completed these experiments Krebs was approaching the end of the year for which the money raised by Bruno Mendel had provided his salary. Although Warburg had at the beginning committed himself to employ Krebs only for that year, he now appeared appreciative enough of the quality of Krebs's work to offer to continue him in his position with funds drawn from his own budgetary resources, raising his salary from 300 to 400 marks per month. The main reason Warburg gave for his decision was that he wanted Krebs to follow through with the study of human cancer tissue. Krebs accepted the extension also, however, as a more general encouragement to believe that Warburg thought he was a useful member of the laboratory. That meant that he could complete capably the research projects that Warburg assigned to him, not necessarily that Warburg regarded him as a promising potential independent investigator.[19]

To perform the experiments on human cancer tissue, Krebs had to transport a set of manometers and supporting equipment to the *Charité*, where arrangements had been made with the professors of surgery in three clinics to supply him with tumor tissue excised in operations. It would have taken so long to bring the tissue back to Dahlem that the material would not have survived for the experiments. On the day preceding each suitable case, Krebs was informed about when the operation would take place so that he could be on hand to receive the tissue immediately afterward and begin the experiments at once.[20]

The first material Krebs obtained in this way, on December 14, was lymphatic tissue taken from the armpit of a patient with breast cancer. The excised tissue contained only about 30 percent cancer cells, the rest being connective tissue. Krebs measured its aerobic and anaerobic glycolysis in Ringer solution and in his own blood serum. In his serum the anaerobic glycolysis was smaller than in Ringer's solution, and decreased during the experiment, but "because of the small glucose concentration" the reason for the effect could "not be judged." On the same day he tested also a nasal polyp tissue and a gastric carcinoma and in both cases the glycolysis in serum sank over the course of the experiment. Three days later he measured the glycolysis of lymphatic tissue from another stomach cancer in Ringer's solution, normal serum, and the serum of a cancer patient. In the first medium the anaerobic glycolysis remained constant. In "cancer serum" it sank somewhat, although he was not certain that the decline was real. In normal serum there was "a gradual decrease to nothing."[21] Although each of these early results might appear to have lent some support to the views of those who asserted that normal serum causes cancer cells to disappear, there is no indication of whether or not Krebs, or Warburg, ever entertained such a conclusion.

Although his primary obligation during this period was to the human cancer study, Krebs worked at Dahlem on days in which no cancer material became available. He did not have another project there, however, and aside from preparations he might have made for the experiments at the *Charité*, he must have spent his spare time helping out others in the laboratory. He recorded no experiments between December 17 and January 7, 1927, but there is no record of whether or not he left Berlin during this time.

During the last 3 weeks of January, all of February, and the first week of March, Krebs continued experiments on the various forms of cancer tissue with which the surgeons furnished him at the *Charité*. He obtained enough to keep him busy 3 or 4 days each week. In most cases he compared the rates of anaerobic glycolysis in Ringer's solution with that in normal serum and in cancerous serum. Although there were differences in the rates in individual experiments, they were not systematic. The overall results indicated to him that normal serum does not contain substances that either destroy cancer cells or inhibit their metabolism. At the same time his measurements of anaerobic and aerobic glycolysis confirmed, with a single exception, Warburg's view that human cancer tissues behave similarly to transplanted animal tissues.[22] The investigation yielded no surprises or novel insights; it served mainly to protect conclusions Warburg had earlier reached from some actual and potential objections.

II

While Hans Krebs was studying the metabolism of cancer cells in Dahlem, his brother Wolf was completing his studies in electrical engineering in Brunswick. Even though the Technische Hochschule was much smaller than the one he had left in Munich, Wolf had found it in some ways more advantageous. Smaller classes and laboratories enabled him to enjoy more personal interaction with the professors than had been possible in the large lecture halls in Munich. The faculty were less eminent, but younger and in some ways more modern than their counterparts in Munich. In this environment Wolf flourished. He excelled in his studies to such an extent that he was sometimes called "*eine Kanone*" (the heavy artillery). In the electrical engineering course one had to choose either the specialty of power engineering, which dealt with electric motors and power stations, or transmission engineering, which dealt mainly with high voltage lines and their insulation. Wolf chose the former, which connected with the interest in electrical machines and devices that he had had since his childhood. He was particularly influenced by Professor Unger, who thought so highly of his talents that he urged him to enter academic engineering and offered him a fellowship. Wolf demurred, however, preferring to apply himself to practical problems in electrical industry.[23]

When Unger recommended Wolf for a position at Siemens, the leading German electrical engineering company, he was turned down on grounds that were obviously based on his Jewish background. Indignant, Unger next recommended him to the *Allgemeine Elektricitätsgesellschaft* (AEG) in Berlin, a firm founded by Jews. There he was quickly hired for a position in the department responsible for the design of synchronous machines.[24]

During the month between the time that Wolf obtained his diploma, at the end of the winter term of 1926-1927, and the time he was to begin at AEG, at the beginning of March, his father rewarded him for his fine academic performance by taking him on an extended skiing holiday in Switzerland. Georg Krebs himself did not ski, and found the mountains in winter little to his liking, but Wolf, who had not been skiing since the joint expeditions he had taken with Hans from Munich, took group lessons with a ski instructor and reached a level of proficiency well beyond what either brother had previously attained. He then went on a 3 day skiing tour from one mountain valley to another.[25]

In Berlin Wolf followed the advice of his sister Lise, now living with her husband in the suburb of Charlottenberg, to find a room in central Berlin close to the urban and suburban railroad line on which he could easily make the daily trip to the AEG factory on the north side of the city. He made sure to take a room in a house with a piano, so that he could continue his favorite leisure activity. This was a luxury that Hans could not at that time afford. Wolf regularly visited Lise, who still took a strong interest in the welfare of her "little" brother, but he saw little of Hans, who appeared to him to be very busy and preoccupied with his own work.[26]

During the second week in March Hans probably transferred that work back to Dahlem, having gathered sufficient evidence at the *Charité* that the metabolism of human cancer tissue behaves in accordance with what Warburg had established for experimental tumors. Between March 7 and March 14 he conducted the same type of experiments on Jensen rat sarcoma tissue. In contrast to his initial results in December, he now found no significant difference between the rates of aerobic or anaerobic glycolysis in cancerous and normal blood sera.[27] By this time he must have satisfied the main objectives of the project that Warburg had given him; but he did not immediately write up his results. He began instead to carry out similar experiments with rat retina tissue.

As noted earlier, Warburg had already discovered, in 1924, that mammalian retina tissue, like tumor tissue, maintains an unusually high rate of anaerobic glycolysis, and that even aerobically its rate of glycolysis was one and a half times as large as its rate of respiration. It was, therefore, a natural extension of the work Krebs had done up until then to test also on this tissue the effects of different blood sera.

Beginning on March 15, Krebs examined the effects on the anaerobic and aerobic glycolysis of rat retina tissue of normal human, horse, pigeon and rat serum, of cancerous serum and of dialyzed serum. On the 23rd and 24th he compared the rates of anaerobic glycolysis in undiluted rat serum with that in serum diluted by one-eighth, one-fourth, and one-half with Ringer's solution. The result was that "Dilution of the serum with 1/8 volume Ringer accelerates the glycolysis by about 21%, with 1/4 volume by about 40% (with 1/2 volume about 44%)." The outcome led him to think that blood serum contains a substance that inhibits the glycolysis, and he asked himself on the 28th "whether the inhibitory substance in rat serum is dialyzable?" He found no appreciable difference, however, between the rate in dialyzed and undialyzed serum.[28]

Continuing to examine different blood sera, and sera prepared under different conditions, for a clue to the source of the inhibition, he tried on April 2 "The effect of copper on rat retina in serum." The reason for his choice was probably that Warburg had just discovered that blood serum contains very small quantities of copper. In several experiments that Krebs performed during the next week copper did somewhat lower the rate, but so did iron and zinc. On April 7 and 8 he tested rat retina in the blood sera of other species (human and rat sera), to which he referred as "immune serum." He apparently expected a possible immunological reaction to affect the glycolysis.[29] By then he had performed

22 sets of experiments on rat retina tissue in as many days. Apparently he had not uncovered any decisive leads.

* * *

Discussing in 1976 the experiments with copper mentioned in the preceding paragraph, Krebs responded to my question "Do you think that maybe what you had in mind was the new observation of the presence of copper suggested that there may be some catalytic effect?" with the following general comment:

> Well, some effect, yes. The basic philosophy behind this is that if a substance is there in a living system — I have expressed this many times and other people have many times — it isn't there just for the entertainment of the biochemist, but it must have a function. Life has evolved in such a way that there are very few, if any, things that are useless to the body. And we now know, for instance, that copper is a constituent of some important cell components and it is necessary. But if you first make the observation that there is a substance — and what is also decisive there was that the substance was present in a constant concentration in the biological sense, that is, within a narrow range. That means its presence was regulated, and then if one wants to know what role it might play one could do hundreds of experiments, of different kinds; but as we had some techniques ready to test this and that, such tests were carried out.[30]

Engaging though this view is, in that it places a small subset of experiments into a much broader context of meaning, it is impossible to sort out the extent to which the "basic philosophy" Krebs discussed was actually present in his mind in 1927, and the extent to which he was in 1976 retrospectively assimilating these experiments into a philosophy that he worked out self-consciously only during the intervening years. The next experiment Krebs performed, however, manifests an orientation — if not a philosophy — toward biological functions that he must already have absorbed at the time, because the viewpoint was embedded in the experimental design itself.

* * *

On April 11, 1927, Krebs measured the glycolysis of pigeon retina tissue. The experiment was not a mere extension to another species of the investigative line he had been pursuing with rat retina. He headed the experiment in his notebook "Pigeon retina (illuminated)." Underneath that he described the tissue (it was, he noted "very easy to prepare"), and drew a sketch showing how "the greater part is colored yellow, an outer part is red."

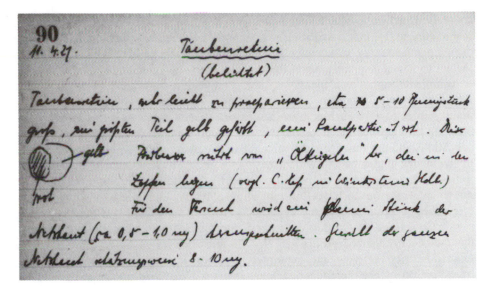

The red color, he remarked, derived from oil droplets in the dish. He cut out small sections from both portions of the retina for the experiments and measured the anaerobic glycolysis of red and yellow retina pieces in Ringer's solution, a red piece in pigeon blood serum, and the aerobic exchanges of a yellow piece in Ringer's solution. He alternately illuminated the manometer flasks for 10- and 15 minute intervals with a 70-watt lamp placed 20 cm away, and left them in relative darkness for equal periods. The rates he recorded for anaerobic glycolysis on the first three of these experiments were, respectively:

		1	2	3
$Q_M^{N_2}$	Dark	161	155	168
	Light	94	96	148
	Dark	148	138	174

The results, as he summarized them, were: "Enormous metabolism of the retina. Red and yellow retina the same. With illumination smaller glycolysis in Ringer (not in serum). Aerobic, no pressure changes with illumination."[31]

There is good reason to believe that the motivation for this experiment was not a suggestion from Warburg,[32] but an idea that occurred independently to Krebs. What he probably had in mind was that because birds have exceptional visual acuity, their retinal tissue might be exceptionally active and, therefore, require levels of energy-yielding reactions significantly higher than those in the rat retinas with which he had been working.

The experimental design with alternating "light" and "dark" intervals was obviously borrowed from Warburg's recent studies on the effects of carbon monoxide on respiration; but the idea behind it, as Krebs expressed it, in 1976, was that, because, "it is the function of the retina to absorb light and transmit some information to the brain, it was just feasible that if one gives the retina some work to do, that it might influence quantitatively the metabolism." He was drawing an analogy to investigations of muscle, whose metabolism had been shown to increase greatly when the muscles perform mechanical work.[33]

Simple though these ideas were, they reveal a biological orientation that Krebs brought to biochemical investigations, even as an apprentice following mainly direction given him by his mentor. He wanted to make connections between the chemical phenomena he could observe and measure under laboratory conditions and the functional significance of the phenomena within the conditions of life of the organisms to which they belonged. In the event, as these results indicate, the experiment supported only part of his idea. Illumination appeared not to increase, but to lower the rate of glycolysis. Unexpected also, given the large energy requirements that he assumed for pigeon retina, was the absence of aerobic reactions.[34] On the other hand, the generally "enormous metabolism" that he observed sustained his idea that the metabolism of a bird retina must be extraordinarily active, and prompted him to pursue this new subline of investigation. Once the effect had been observed, Warburg, too, was undoubtedly interested to see Krebs follow up on it.

Before moving further in this direction, however, Krebs branched out another way, on the same day, to an experiment on "rat kidney in rabbit serum." He was probably extending to other tissues the question that had come up in the preceding studies with rat retina: how serum from different animal species might affect the metabolism. Using the two volume method, he measured one set in the blood serum, and another set in Ringer's solution, the Q_{O_2} and Q_{CO_2} of the kidney slices, and calculated their ratio, a coefficient designated γ by Warburg. Both rates in the foreign serum were about double that in Ringer's solution.[35]

Although this experiment lay fully within the boundaries of exploration arising from Warburg's prior work on the metabolism of cancer tissue in comparison with normal tissues, Krebs was probably also influenced at the time he performed it by a paper that had recently emanated from the laboratory downstairs. In 1926, Otto Meyerhof, in collaboration with his highly talented assistant Karl Lohmann, had adopted Warburg's tissue slice methods to support the application to other tissues of the interpretation of glycolysis and respiration that he had worked out primarily for the metabolism of muscles:

> That during respiration in the presence of sugar lactic acid undergoes a cycle, and that the rates of the two phases of metabolism [glycolysis and respiration], which can be influenced independently of one another, determine whether cleavage or synthesis dominates, so that lactic acid either arises or disappears.[36]

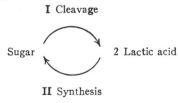

I Cleavage

Sugar   2 Lactic acid

II Synthesis

Meyerhof and Lohmann sought also to reconcile Meyerhof's conclusion based on muscle studies, that lactic acid forms only anaerobically, with Warburg's finding that in cancer and in growing normal tissues there is also an aerobic glycolysis. In their experiments they relied mainly on Warburg's indirect methods for determining the appearance of lactic acid by means of the carbon dioxide displaced by it from the medium. In experiments employing blood serum as the medium there was an additional complication. Some of the acid that entered the medium — in particular the carbonic acid produced by respiration and the lactic acid produced by glycolysis — was "retained" in the serum by combining with serum proteins or other bases. Moreover, although the degree of "retention" varied with the pressure in the gas phase, it was not directly proportional to the pressure. From equilibrium considerations, including especially the dissociation constants for the acids, Warburg had derived methods to calculate an approximate relationship between the change in the retention (Δu) and the change in pressure (Δp). The expressions $\left(\dfrac{\Delta u}{\Delta p}\right)C$ and $\left(\dfrac{\Delta u}{\Delta p}\right)M$ represented the change in retention respectively of carbonic and of lactic acid as functions of the changes in pressure. Experimentally they were determined by displacing bicarbonate from the medium with another acid at two different pressures and regarding the ratio between changes in quantities of acid displaced at those points and the pressure difference as approximately constant over the interval between them.[37]

Using rat liver, kidney, and brain slices, Meyerhof and Lohmann measured Q_{O_2}, Q_{CO_2}, the ratio γ, which they called the *Apparent respiratory quotient*, and $Q\dfrac{B}{(M)}$ which was a measurement of the change in bicarbonate that they employed as an alternative means to measure the change in lactic acid. They regarded an increase in bicarbonate as a direct indication of a decrease in lactic acid, just as Warburg had treated a decrease in bicarbonate as a means to measure, under appropriate circumstances, the formation of lactic acid. They also believed that the expression for the retention of carbonic acid $\left(\dfrac{\Delta u}{\Delta p}\right)C$ could be used directly in the calculation of the change in lactic acid retention. Testing the effects of prior starvation or nutrition, of the presence or absence of glucose, and of lactic acid on each of the tissues, they showed that the measured rates varied in accordance with Meyerhof's conception of the lactic acid cycle.[38]

In the experiments on rat kidney tissue that Krebs undertook he was apparently not testing the conclusions that Meyerhof and Lohmann had drawn from their experiments on that tissue among others; but he had read their paper and was aware of their approach. He also encountered in his next experiment questions concerning the application of Warburg's retention formulas and other assumptions that had some bearing on Meyerhof and Lohmann's methods as

well. On April 13, he compared the aerobic metabolism of rat kidney tissue in
rat serum and human serum. He expressed his results as follows:[39]

Human serum (first 20')   Rat serum

Q_{O_2} -37.8 Q_{O_2} -22.7

Q_s + 7.5 Q_s -28.0

$Q_M^{O_2}$ -30.3 $Q_M^{O_2}$ -50.7   !!

γ - 0.2 γ + 1.27 M.Q. [Meyerhof Quotient] 2.2

To obtain these figures he had used the two volume method to determine both
the oxygen absorbed and the carbon dioxide evolved. Q_{O_2} represented the
former. Q_s (for "$Q_{säure}$" or Q_{acid}) represented the latter, on the assumption that
the carbon dioxide expelled into the gaseous phase was equivalent to the total of
the carbonic acid produced from the respiration and of the bicarbonate displaced

by lactic acid produced from glycolysis. $Q_M^{O_2}$ was a measure of the lactic acid

[*Milchsäure*] produced from aerobic glycolysis. Krebs obtained it by adding
together the two figures above it, following "the arbitrary and often incorrect
assumption" Warburg had made that $X_M = X_s + X_{O_2}$.[40] As the exclamation
marks that Krebs put beside that figure in the second column indicate, the
resulting large negative rate for the aerobic glycolysis of rat kidney in rat serum
appeared improbable enough to him to raise doubts about the correctness of the
assumption in this case. "It is questionable," he wrote underneath, "whether the
negative pressure is dependent only upon the uptake of O_2 and 'lactic acid
resynthesis.' Ammonia formation also causes a negative pressure."[41] On the
facing page he wrote:

> Compare to this experiment: Meyerhof and Lohmann, B.Z. 171.. p. 281
> [the article summarized above]. p. 284. Contrary to Meyerhof and
>
> Lohmann $\left(\dfrac{\Delta u}{\Delta p}\right)$M should be used, if (as in the preceding experiment)
> the lactic acid disappearance is greater than the respiratory formation of
> CO_2.[42]

That is, his result prompted Krebs to disagree with a simplifying assumption
Meyerhof and Lohmann had made, that one could equate the retention formula
for lactic acid with that for carbonic acid. In a broader sense, however, he
construed his experimental results within the framework of their work: that is,

he viewed the large negative values for $Q_M^{O_2}$ as indications that under his aerobic conditions lactic acid had disappeared in the resynthesis of carbohydrate. In a second remark in his notebook he found supporting evidence for this interpretation in a recent paper from his own laboratory:

> According to Warburg, Wind and Negelein (Kl. Wo. 5, 829, 1926) the kidneys also resynthesize [carbohydrate from] lactic acid in the body. They found, for example, in the aorta 28 mg % lactic acid, and in the renal vein 13 mg %.[43]

That is, Warburg, Wind, and Negelein had, by removing blood samples from the arteries and veins of living, anesthetized animals, found evidence that normal organs, such as the kidneys, consumed more lactic acid than they produced,[44] a result that Krebs also interpreted in accord with Meyerhof's lactic acid cycle.

Regarding the objective of his own experiment Krebs concluded only that "In foreign serum the respiration of the kidneys is not damaged." In a second experiment performed the same day on rat kidney and testicle slices anaerobically in human serum he found similarly "no difference in foreign serum."[45] That ended both his working week, and this investigative subline. Its principal significance lay not in its negative outcome, but as part of the continuing education of Hans Krebs as an experimental investigator. One could learn quickly to perform the experimental operations for manometric tissue slice investigations and to carry out the routine calculations necessary to reduce the data gathered. Only by confronting problems such as those that arose during this subsidiary series of experiments, however, could he grow to appreciate the limits of the methods he was using and of the assumptions underlying them.

In the next week Krebs resumed the investigation he had begun on pigeon retina metabolism. In the next experiment, on Wednesday, April 20, he attempted to measure the respiration and the aerobic and anaerobic glycolysis of the tissue. The results were uncertain, probably, he thought, because he had made an error in the retention measurement, and because the slices, which had disintegrated during the shaking, were difficult to weigh. Something in the measurements, which is not immediately obvious because he did not record any reduced data, made him ask if there was "no respiration?", and whether there was "another gas besides O_2 and CO_2 [present]?" Trying again on the same day, he now began runs in serum and Ringer's solution aerobically and changed the conditions to anaerobic during the experiment by sweeping out the initial atmosphere of 5 percent CO_2 in O_2 with an atmosphere of 4.8 percent CO_2 in N_2. The results he obtained in serum:

$$Q_S^{O_2} \quad +162 \quad +165 \quad +212$$

$$Q_{O_2} \quad -5.2 \quad -6.4 \quad -45$$

$$Q_M^{O_2} \quad +157 \quad +159 \quad +167$$

confirmed his initial observation that the rates of glycolysis were very high, and the very small consumptions of oxygen in two of the three cases must have reinforced his doubts about whether any respiration was taking place.[46]

On the 23rd Krebs concentrated his attention on the aerobic and anaerobic glycolysis of the retina tissue in pigeon serum and Ringer's solution. In each medium he began one run aerobically and ended it anaerobically, and in the other run reversed the order. Continuing his interest in the effects of light on the metabolism in spite of his first negative result, he again alternated a dark and an illuminated period, but the light was "without influence." The high, similar rates of anaerobic and aerobic glycolysis (with N_2, $Q_M = +124$; with O_2, $Q_M = +145$), together with the fact that the overall manometer readings under aerobic and anaerobic conditions differed little from one another, must have served as a further indication that there was little or no respiration in this tissue. Still persisting in his belief that light ought to have an effect, he tested it again in a similar experiment 2 days later, but again found "light without influence." Once again, on the 27th he compared the anaerobic and aerobic rates of glycolysis. The results (with O_2, $Q_M = +150$ and $+130$; with N_2, $Q_M = +137$ and $+112$), indicated to him that there was "no aerobic and anaerobic difference."[47]

By this time Krebs had consolidated his first findings on pigeon retina tissue sufficiently to be confident that its rates of aerobic and anaerobic glycolysis were higher than that of any other tissue that had been measured in Warburg's laboratory, and that there was a very low rate of respiration, if any at all. These quantitatively dramatic results must have compensated him for whatever disappointment he may have felt in not being able to demonstrate an effect of the work that a retina ought to do in bright light. He now sought to generalize his positive results by trying the retina of a different kind of bird.

On April 28, Krebs immediately confirmed for chicken retina in chicken blood serum what he had already found for pigeon retina. The anaerobic and aerobic rates of glycolysis ranged between $Q = +113$ and $+137$, and there was "no respiration." During the first 10 days of May he repeated variations on the same experiments, with both chicken and pigeon retinas. He examined some special conditions, such as the influence of HCN and CO, with negative results, and the decline in the rates of glycolysis when he used the slices 16 to 18 hours after removing them from the animal. By this time, he was mainly gathering supporting data to prepare a paper reporting his discovery of the special properties of bird retinas.[48]

On May 12 and 13 Krebs measured the respiration and glycolysis of embryonic chicken tissues. On the 16th he combined two distinct subareas of Warburg's ongoing investigation of the metabolism of various types of normal tissues, by examining the metabolism of embryonic chicken retina tissue. In this and two similar subsequent experiments, the situation proved to be different from that of mature retina tissue. There was "a respiration present," and "the Pasteur reaction is intact." That is, in distinction to mature bird retina tissue in which aerobic and anaerobic glycolysis were essentially equal, and the respiration was nearly null, the Q_{O_2} rates in embryonic retina tissue were in the range of -10 to

-15, and the aerobic rates of glycolysis were lower enough than the anaerobic rates to yield Meyerhof quotients of 2 or a little higher.[49]

In the course of these experiments Krebs continued to show a developing awareness of the degree of uncertainty and the assumptions embedded in Warburg's outwardly precise manometric methods for measuring respiration and glycolysis. In an experiment on May 14 on "pigeon retina aerobic and anaerobic," he noted that the glycolysis values "in O_2 and N_2 [were in] agreement within 3.8%." He asked himself, "How large can the respiration be in the maximum possibility, if the measurements are subject to an error of 3%?" After summarizing why he thought the error could not be larger than that, he went on to reason:

> If it be assumed that the Pasteur reaction is completely suspended, and that therefore the respiration produces negative pressure exclusively by consuming O_2, and further that the 3% errors in $Q_M^{O_2}$ and $Q_M^{N_2}$ are mutually reinforcing,
>
> Result: Q_{O_2} = -20 (this is an unfavorable example, unfavorable because $Q_N^{O_2}$ is more likely to be 3.8% smaller than $Q_M^{N_2}$).[50]

Despite this last disclaimer, the thrust of Krebs's reflections is clear. The overall trend of his experiments was leading him to believe that there was little or no respiration taking place in bird retina tissue. He was realizing that the experimental results themselves were partially indeterminate. There could be, after all, a significant respiration. Beyond what the measurements themselves directly proved, one had to make judgments that involved some guesswork about what was actually going on within those tiny slices placed only under his indirect scrutiny.

After his final experiment of this series, on May 21, with pigeon retina slices in chicken serum, Krebs calculated the now expected result of a rate of respiration so small (Q_{O_2} = -3.9) as to be virtually nonexistent compared to rates of anaerobic and aerobic glycolysis, respectively, of +209 and +118. He then engaged himself again in an extended discussion of the question "How large can the respiration be?" To explore the possibilities he assumed a rate of Q_{O_2} = -10 and calculated how much error would be necessary in his measured values for the rates of glycolysis to accommodate such a rate. Next he calculated what the true $Q_M^{O_2}$ and $Q_M^{N_2}$ values would have been if the measurement of each contained an error of 5% and they were in opposite directions:

$$Q_M^{O_2} = 194 \ -10 = 184$$
$$Q_M^{N_2} = 207 \ +10 = 217.$$

The difference between these two -33, divided by the constant K_M, he wrote, "would be the pressure produced by the respiration." He made three different calculations of what the rate of respiration would then be in accord with three different assumptions about the Pasteur reaction:[51]

Q_{O_2} = -21.4, if the Pasteur reaction is completely suspended.
Q_{O_2} = -13.0, if the Meyerhof quotient = 1
Q_{O_2} = -9.3, if the Meyerhof quotient = 2.

With these further considerations on the interplay between suppositions and measurements in the construction of data, Krebs broke off not only his experiments on bird retina tissue, but the entire investigative project that Warburg had given him on the metabolism of human cancer tissue that had led him to it. The probable reason was that Warburg now needed Krebs's assistance to extend the scope of his discovery that the blood contains copper.

During the 7 months in which he had been engaged in the study of the metabolism of cancerous and normal tissues, Krebs came to appreciate and admire the power of the methods Warburg had devised for this purpose. They enabled one to examine the processes in cells that were intact but subject to more direct experimental control than was possible in experiments with living animals or perfused whole organs. He was learning from experience how quickly and easily one could test a variety of ideas or examine the effects of diverse conditions on a given process. Warburg's investigation of tissue metabolism was focused narrowly on the quantitative rates of respiration and glycolysis, their relation to the differences between cancer tissue, stable and growing normal tissue, and the implications for establishing conditions under which cancer cells would not grow. The versatility of his methods, however, led Krebs to imagine that they might be applicable to many processes beyond those with which Warburg was presently concerned, and he thought that he would like to explore such possibilities.[52]

Krebs did not pick out a particular process to study, or develop a detailed plan of action. His sensitivity to the broad potential scope of such an endeavor was rooted in the influences of his earlier medical training. Most prominent of these was the impact on him of the lectures of Franz Knoop during his second preclinical year at Freiburg (see Chapter 3, pp. 76–78). More than anyone else in the field Knoop had espoused the importance of uncovering each of the many chemical steps connecting foodstuffs with final end products and with the synthesis of the constituent substances of the organism. It was largely the message he had absorbed from Knoop that enabled Krebs to envision the general significance of applying new methods to the problems of intermediary metabolism. During the intervening years certain events, such as Thannhauser's lectures on metabolic diseases, had reinforced his sense of the importance of the subject. The recent visit by Lina Stern may have stimulated him to look up in Oppenheimer's *Handbuch* the outlines of her earlier pioneering work with Battelli on the metabolism of isolated tissues (see Chapter 1, pp. 7-9);[53] but during the 6 years since he had heard Knoop's lectures he had never studied the literature of intermediary metabolism in depth as he had the literature of physical and colloid chemistry. He had, therefore, not fixed his attention on any concrete set of problems within the field when it occurred to him to take it up himself.

One day, which might well have been during the spring of 1927 while he was pursuing his experiments on retina tissue (he recalled in 1976 only that it was "early" during his time in Warburg's laboratory), Krebs was bold enough to say to Warburg that in his opinion the tissue slice method "is a useful tool for studying intermediary metabolism," and that he would like to study metabolic processes with the techniques that Warburg had developed. Warburg told him, however, that such experiments would be of no interest to him. Because his laboratory was small, he said, he required all of the people in it to work on his problems. There was no room for individuals to follow up their own ideas.[54]

Before meeting this rebuff Krebs might well have expected Warburg to be open to his suggestion, because of the close connections between the questions Warburg was asking about glycolysis and respiration and the questions others were asking about intermediate steps in these processes. The Meyerhof cycle which, as we have seen, became involved in Warburg's study, was itself about an intermediary process if viewed in the context of the overall decomposition of carbohydrates. Meyerhof was just then beginning to test in Warburg's experimental system claims about the intermediate steps within glycolysis, such as Neuberg's methylglyoxal theory and Embden's alternative triose candidates, dihydroxyacetone and glyceraldehyde. From the paper of Meyerhof and Lohmann mentioned earlier Krebs would have seen an exemplar of how to apply the manometric tissue slice methods to such questions. They added each of the proposed intermediates to the medium of various tissue slices and determined whether or not lactic acid formed at a rate higher than it did when they added glucose to the medium.[55]

Warburg was, however, remarkably resistant to considerations about the intermediate steps in the metabolic processes he was studying. He expressed his attitude succinctly in one of his papers on the metabolism of carcinoma cells in 1924. "When we speak of a glycolytic *metabolism*," he wrote in a footnote, "we have in our sight only the end products that actually appear, and avoid those *phases* of glycolysis that might perhaps arise in some internal cycle and again disappear."[56] Moreover, he was disdainful of the methods that the Thunberg school used to attempt to connect together reaction sequences of the oxidative stages of metabolism (see Chapter 1, pp. 18–22). Reactions that can be produced in tissue extracts, he believed, have little to do with what takes place in living cells.[57]

Having no choice in the matter, Krebs conformed to Warburg's requirement. The vista that had opened up to him seemed compelling enough, however, so that he clung to the idea that when he was in an independent position he would do something about it.

III

Whenever possible Warburg substituted manometric for conventional analytical methods, in order to take advantage of the rapidity and precision of the manometric techniques. After he had found copper in blood serum he worked out a way to determine the "loosely bound" copper — that is, copper that could be detected in the serum without combustion — by means of the catalytic effects he had previously discovered of minute quantities of metals on the oxidation of cysteine (see Chapter 5, p. 140). After separating the serum from the whole blood and mixing it with a hydrochloric acid solution to drive out the bicarbonate, he mixed it with a pyrophosphate solution and measured the initial rate at which cysteine was oxidized in this solution. He was able to show that this rate is proportional to the concentration of copper in the solution. He developed a similar method, using borate in place of pyrophosphate, to measure the loosely bound iron in serum. Having done this he wanted to survey the iron and copper content of the serum of many different types of blood, under varying physiological conditions, to establish the range of variation that occurs and the physiological factors that influence the content.[58]

During the last week in May Warburg turned these analyses over to Krebs. Krebs first measured the copper content of rat blood serum, then began performing the analyses of blood obtained from pregnant and nonpregnant women in samples supplied by a university female clinic. He continued to do such analyses, some on human patient blood, some on animal blood, through June and up until the laboratory closed at the end of July for the long summer holiday. Although he tested a few variations on the methods during this time, the analyses quickly became routine, and Krebs felt that he was now serving in the capacity of a technician for Warburg.[59]

While he carried on with this task, Krebs was also writing up his paper on the metabolism of retina tissue. By now he was familiar enough with his chief's standards so that by the time he submitted a draft to Warburg he received it back with small corrections but with its basic organization intact. The introduction is so exemplary of the compressed style that Warburg imposed on Krebs that it can readily be quoted in full (here in its final version):

> According to earlier experiments in this Institute, retina tissue stands out for its especially large glycolytic metabolism. Surviving rat retina forms anaerobically 30 to 35% of its dry weight per hour in lactic acid, aerobically 12 to 16%. I have occupied myself with the metabolism of bird retina and found that the retina of the chicken produces up to 55% of its dry weight per hour in lactic acid, the bird retina even up to 84%. The glycolytic metabolism of the bird retina is thus far greater [Warburg had here strengthened this phrase: in Krebs's draft it had read "yet significantly greater"] than the glycolytic metabolism of the rat retina.
>
> Furthermore it turns out that the surviving bird retina either does not respire, or respires so little that its oxidative metabolism vanishes in comparison to the glycolytic metabolism. If one does not assume that the

oxidative metabolism of the bird retina is destroyed [Warburg substituted the last two words here for Krebs's "disappears"] during its removal from the body — which is improbable[2] — it follows from my investigation that the bird retina lives at the expense of its glycolytic metabolism.

Footnote 2 was added by Warburg, who started to write "according to the experiments of Dr. Krebs," crossed it out, and put down "Contrary to suspicions expressed earlier by me (this journal *152*, 133, 1924), this appears now improbable also for rat retina. *Warburg.*"[60]

The succinct language of these paragraphs expresses clearly that Krebs had carried out an investigation similar to prior investigations in the laboratory, but that he had identified special circumstances that enabled him to draw an original conclusion about the metabolism of the bird retina, and that his findings had induced his chief to modify an earlier opinion. By this time Krebs must have learned to avoid inserting into his paper discussions of aspects of his investigation, such as the attempt to show an effect of light on the metabolism of the retina, that had not succeeded. Nor did he indulge in mention of the adaptive biological considerations that had probably influenced him to take up the metabolism of bird retinas. A scientific paper, Warburg had made clear, should not bear traces of the scaffolding that had been necessary temporarily to construct the investigative edifice.

After a short description of the methods he had used, Krebs presented in a table selected data from 5 of the 15 or so experiments he had performed on pigeon and chicken retinas, along with fuller protocols of two exemplary experiments. Only in writing his conclusions did he fall into a discussion that Warburg thought inappropriate. Clearly reflecting the thought he had given to the various assumptions inherent in the methods and the degree of error possible, Krebs wrote:

The pressure changes in oxygen and in nitrogen (per milligram tissue) are, within the limits of accuracy of the measurements, in all experiments the same. If one calculates the errors in the methods, it follows that the respiration (Q_{O_2}), in the maximum possible case, was 1/15 of the glycolysis ($Q_M^{O_2}$).

This means that in oxygen, for every 45 glucose molecules that the retina decomposes, it oxidizes at most one of them to carbonic acid and water, and ferments the others to lactic acid. The metabolism of the bird retina in oxygen is therefore an almost pure fermentation metabolism.

For this involved reasoning Warburg substituted simply

$Q_M^{O_2}$ and $Q_M^{N_2}$ are, within the limits of accuracy of the measurements, in all experiments the same. The respiration is therefore null or very small.[61]

Krebs's thoughts about the effects of the maximum possible error in the experimental system were clearly, in Warburg's view, not pertinent. The efforts of his assistant to educate himself about the limits of his methods did not belong in a published paper.

Krebs delivered his manuscript next door to the *Biochemische Zeitschrift* office on July 22. Eleven days later, as the summer holiday was about to begin, he submitted another paper, this one reporting his work on the metabolism of carcinoma cells. Because Warburg's assistant Fritz Kubowitz had helped with some of the experiments, he was listed as second author. This paper was a spare summary of the methods and results obtained. Contrary to predictions by other authors that the serum of normal blood dissolves carcinoma cells, Krebs began, the experiments showed, within the limits of experimental error, no difference when the metabolism in cancerous and normal serum was compared. Nor was there a sensible difference in Ringer's solution. "Finally," he wrote in the introduction, "this work is a contribution to the question, whether spontaneous human cancer behaves differently from transplanted rat and chicken tumors." Of the 18 human tumors they had tried, only one differed from the animal tumors, in the sense that its respiration was large in comparison to its glycolysis. In the section on results he pointed out that the large individual variations in the measured rates were because cancer and connective tissue are so irregularly mingled in human tissues that it was difficult to obtain multiple slices containing the same proportion of cancerous cells. He drew no broader conclusions. In this research Krebs had mainly discharged Warburg's obligation to answer criticisms of earlier work, even though Warburg was quite certain in advance that the criticisms were not valid. Both Warburg and Krebs understood, however, that if Warburg was aiming at an eventual capacity to control human cancer, it was essential to remove all doubt that conclusions reached primarily through the study of experimental material were fully applicable to clinical material.[62]

Deciding again to use his holiday to improve his knowledge of a foreign language, Krebs chose this year to travel to French-speaking Belgium. He departed on August 3. There is no record of when he returned to Berlin. On October 3 he resumed his work in the laboratory.[63]

By the time that Hans Krebs returned from his holiday, Wolf Krebs was making auspicious progress in his work at AEG on the other side of Berlin. Given the task of improving and simplifying the design of electric machines through mathematical analysis, he found that he had to compute certain functional relationships over and over for each particular situation — for example, for each of the loads to which a machine would be subjected — and that the tedious repetition became terribly boring. Aware that there existed nomographic methods through which one could construct a set of calibrated lines representing families of solutions, so that one could afterward obtain the solution for any specific set of parameters merely by placing a straightedge across the calibrated lines, Wolf set out to learn how he might use such methods. After studying books on the subject and taking a course in it, he was able to apply the technique successfully to solve his problem. Not only did the nomograph greatly simplify his own work, but it was passed on to other engineers in the section, and he received a bonus for his contribution. During the same period his supervisor devised a modified pattern for the windings in an electric machine intended to minimize the losses in the windings. Wolf quickly worked out mathematically a general solution to the winding problem and obtained a patent for it.[64]

During this time Hans and Wolf met occasionally, sometimes to go to a concert together. On one occasion Wolf briefly met Hans's girlfriend Fernanda. Their father was coming to visit Berlin, and Hans wrote him to say that he wanted to introduce Fernanda to him. He made it clear to his father that he realized that he was not yet in a financial position to marry, but he wanted his opinion nevertheless on whether she would be good for him. Georg Krebs declined even to meet her, however, referring Hans instead to a verse in Beethoven's opera *Fidelio*. When Hans looked it up, he read "When nothing combines with nothing the sum remains small. If at table you find only love, you will be hungry after dinner."[65]

Wolf thought that Fernanda was a nice person, but not a particularly attractive woman, and that Hans was insecure enough about his own attractions and his personality so that he was glad to have someone who seemed attached to him.[66] Although this was the subjective opinion of a younger brother, there is some corroborating evidence that Hans did have in these years a low opinion of his own personality. The photographs taken of him then show him typically with his head slightly lowered in a diffident expression, as though unaware that he was a good-looking man. A passage in a small notebook in which Krebs began in 1973 to put down notes for an autobiography reveals the recollection of a bleak early assessment of himself: "As a boy, and later as an adult, I always thought I was horrible — ugly in appearance, rather stupid and unpleasant socially.... This feeling was fed by what I considered lack of warmth and lack of friendliness towards me on the part of people at large."[67] Hans undoubtedly wasted little time brooding about himself. The way in which he filled his life, both inside and outside his work, with systematic, purposeful activity can plausibly be viewed as driven in some part by a need to compensate for feelings of social inferiority.

In his autobiography Krebs wrote simply that he took to heart his father's admonition not to marry without money, and he treated the manner in which his father conveyed the message as appropriately clever.[68] It was also, however, a cavalier, if not cruel way to dismiss his son's feelings, and must have hurt at the time. It is not clear how long afterward Hans continued to see Fernanda. Even if his father had not dissuaded him, their relationship was unlikely to become permanent, because Fernanda's mother strongly opposed her marrying a Jew.[69] Nor is it clear whether Hans himself ever learned about that second obstacle to his intentions.

In Berlin Wolf soon formed his own associations with several fellow engineers at AEG, who traveled to and from work together, and with some of whom he joined a rowing club for weekend sport. Nevertheless, he may have been disappointed to have so little contact with Hans. The brotherly links that had been so visible earlier when he, as the gentle "nestling" of the family readily followed the willful older brother's lead, seemed now somehow missing. Hans appeared not even to realize how little interest he showed in Wolf's professional activity, and he kept Wolf in the dark about his own.[70]

It would, I believe, not have been in character for Hans to have been truly indifferent about his brother's development. His sense of family was strong. Perhaps the problem was that, besides being busy, Hans was typically uncommunicative about his feelings; but it is possible that he had also during these years some need to keep a distance from his talented younger brother. For all the initiative he had shown in his educational pathway, for all the discipline and energy with which he pursued his life, Hans Krebs was, at the age of 27, hardly well established. He was a medical doctor who had not begun to practice, and an aspiring scientist limited to the role of compliant assistant to an authoritarian chief. He was paid, but not well; he was hopeful about his future, but could not yet see its shape. Meanwhile the younger brother who had already outshown him academically, who overshadowed him in his father's affections, and who excelled him even in their common recreational interests — Wolf had attained a more advanced level at the piano, and had now become a much better skier than either had been when they last skied together in Munich — had got off to a fast start in his chosen career. On the surface Hans thought of his brother as somewhat lazy. Underneath, it may have meant that for Wolf achievement seemed to come effortlessly, whereas for Hans it required unremitting diligence.

Among the childhood activities that Hans kept up diligently as an adult was widespread reading. He felt that he never had enough time for general reading, but in fact he maintained an ambitious agenda. He read as a matter of course books such as Erich Marie Remarque's *Im Westen Nichts Neues* and Oswald Spengler's *Der Untergang des Abendlandes* that attracted the general attention of German intellectuals. His favorite modern writer became Thomas Mann. Although Krebs found *Buddenbrooks* tedious, he enjoyed greatly the humor in *Bekenntnisse des Hochstaplers Felix Krull*. He read *Der Zauberberg* in 1927. As a physician he was impressed by the accuracy of Mann's description of the medical aspects of tuberculosis. As one who kept himself fully occupied with meaningful activities he was struck by the portrayal of people who have nothing to do but talk, because all their needs are provided by the institution in which they are patients. As one who appreciated good language, he admired Mann's ability to write long complex sentences that were nevertheless perfectly clear.[71]

IV

During the summer vacation Warburg wrote a paper "On Loosely Bound Copper and Iron in Blood Serum," based on the experiments that Krebs had performed on that topic during the preceding 3 months, and submitted it in September to the *Biochemische Zeitschrift* with Krebs as co-author. When the laboratory reopened in October Krebs, nevertheless, had to continue the uninspiring task of carrying out day-after-day further such analyses on blood samples drawn from healthy, sick, and pregnant persons. He must, therefore, have been greatly relieved when his chief finally gave him in the first week of December, a more challenging project.[72]

Among the several major questions to which Warburg directed the work of his laboratory in 1927, his own interest centered on pursuit of the observation made the previous year on the action of light on the inhibition of cellular respiration by carbon monoxide. These effects could be used, he believed, to elucidate the chemical nature of the *Atmungsferment*. The question of the chemical constitution of the respiratory catalysts of cells had taken a new turn when David Keilin discovered, in 1925, what he called cytochromes, or respiratory pigments, widespread in the tissues of plants and animals. Through spectroscopic means he identified three variations on a substance that was alternatively oxidized and reduced in living tissues and that was recognizable through the characteristic absorption spectrum of the reduced form. Keilin was unable to extract any of these substances from the tissues in an unaltered state. Nevertheless, from the spectroscopic properties of pigments that he did extract he obtained "ample evidence" that the cytochromes belonged to a family of pigments known as "hemochromogens." These were compounds of hematin (the iron pyrrhole compound combined in hemoglobin with the protein globin) with nitrogenous substances different from globin.[73]

In 1927, Warburg followed up his observation of the effect of ordinary light upon the respiration of yeast cells poisoned with carbon monoxide by examining the effects of light of different wavelengths and the same intensity. He found that blue light exerted the strongest action, green and yellow light acted weakly, and red light had no effect. He inferred that these differences represented the degrees to which light of various wavelengths was absorbed by the *Atmungsferment*, and that the latter was, therefore, probably a red pigment. The "immediate assumption" that he drew from this result was that the pigment he had identified in this way must be "identical with Keilin's cytochrome." In that case carbon monoxide ought to alter the spectrum of cytochrome, because it combines with the *Atmungsferment*. When Warburg passed a mixture of carbon monoxide and oxygen gas through a yeast suspension, however, the reduced spectrum of cytochrome was not altered. Warburg concluded that

We must consequently distinguish in living cells at least two pigments resembling hemoglobin, the pigment whose presence is proved by carbon monoxide and Keilin's cytochrome. Both pigments are respiratory enzymes, but have different functions. The first pigment absorbs molecular oxygen and activates it. Keilin's cytochrome — itself not autoxidizable — transports the activated oxygen to the organic molecules.[74]

To characterize more closely the first of these substances Warburg asked Krebs, in December 1927, to find a model system that would react to carbon monoxide in the same manner that living yeast cells did; that is, one that would catalyze the oxidation of a substrate, and that would be inhibited from doing so by carbon monoxide, but that the inhibition would be removed by light.[75]

Warburg had by then concluded, from "The accumulation of identical and very special properties...that the *Atmungsferment* is an iron pyrrol compound in which the iron is bound to nitrogen as in hemoglobin."[76]   Therefore, he suggested to Krebs that he begin with a system in which the iron pyrrol compound heme would be used as a catalyst for the oxidation of cysteine, a substrate Warburg had used during his studies of the iron charcoal model in 1924.[77]

In a "preliminary experiment" on December 7, Krebs compared the oxidation of cysteine in a borate solution containing 10^{-4} Fe and 10^{-4} HCN with the same solution plus heme. In the presence of heme the oxidation was more rapid, and the amount of oxygen consumed indicated that the cysteine had been fully converted to cystine. He proceeded on the same day to test the effect of CO on the reaction, comparing the rate of oxidation in 20 percent O_2 and 80 percent CO with the rate in air. The result, however, was that "CO is without influence," an outcome he undoubtedly treated merely as an indication that his experimental conditions needed to be modified.   In another preliminary experiment, on December 13, he tested whether "The effect of heme remains constant." He did not examine the influence of CO this time, but incorporated into the experiment a comparison of the reaction in light and darkness, employing two lenses and a mirror to project the light of an ordinary bulb through the water bath into the manometer vessel.[78] The rates in light and darkness were approximately equal, as he would expect for an experiment in ordinary air, and there was "a slight increase with time."   The effect was steady enough, however, to make the system appear a suitable one for further investigation.   After repeating the experiment with a "small O_2 pressure" (4.9 percent O_2 in N_2), Krebs was ready to make the first full experimental test of his system: a comparison of the rate of oxidation of cysteine in alternate periods of light and dark with a mixture of 2.5 percent O_2 in CO, using as a control 2.5 percent O_2 in N_2.[79]

Warburg had interpreted the inhibition of cellular respiration by CO as due to the displacement of O_2 by CO in combination with the iron contained in the *Atmungsferment*. From the ordinary principles of chemical equilibrium he had derived a "distribution equation" [*Verteilungsgleichung*]:

$$\frac{FeO_2}{FeCO} \cdot \frac{CO}{O_2} = K$$

Since the respiration remaining in the presence of CO was proportional to the ratio of $FeO_2/FeCO$, that ratio in the equation could be replaced by $\frac{n}{1-n}$, where n = the measured rate of oxidation in a mixture of CO and O_2 divided by the rate in the absence of CO. All of the quantities on the left side of the equation being measurable, one could, therefore, calculate from experimental results the constant for the equation. In his experiments on yeast cells Warburg had found K_{light} to be much larger than K_{dark}, and interpreted that to mean that light shifted

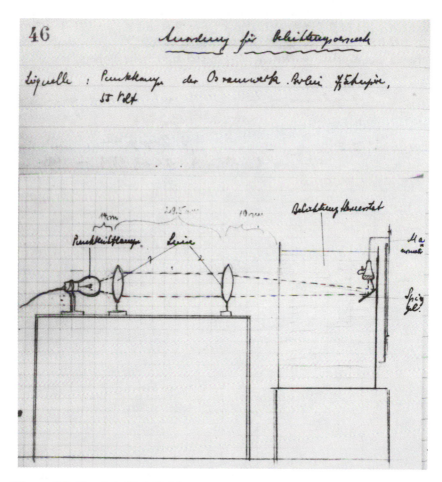

Figure 6.1 Sketch in Krebs's laboratory notebook of arrangement for illumination experiment.

the relative affinities of CO and O_2 for the *Atmungsferment* strongly in favor of the latter combination.[80]

From the result of his first full experiment, Krebs calculated that $K_{dark} = 34.5$, and $K_{light} = 56$. Although this was a sensible difference in the expected direction, it was much smaller than the differences that Warburg had observed in living yeast. Krebs concluded, "the light effect is very slight." The "CO action" itself was also "relatively slight," the rates of oxidation in CO being more than half those of the control.[81] His first test of a model system must, thus, have left Krebs feeling that he had in hand only a faint version of what Warburg sought.

Searching for conditions that might enhance the weak effects he had observed, Krebs tried using larger quantities of heme and a stronger light source, but did not obtain more distinct results. On December 15, testing the system in darkness and light at a pH of 9.5, he calculated $K_{dark} = 8.0$ and $K_{light} = 21.4$. The next day, at pH 9.6, he got $K_{dark} = 14.9$ and $K_{light} = 60$. These stronger effects encouraged him to draw graphs showing the change in the slope of the oxidation curve with illumination:

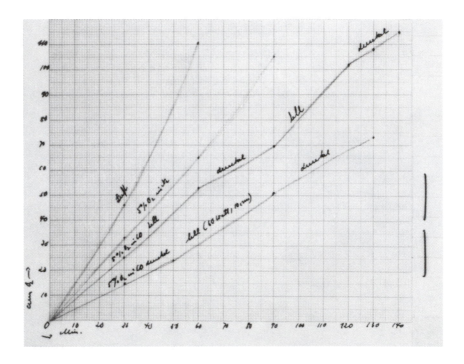

On the following day he obtained three different constants for the distribution equation in the dark and with two light intensities ($K_{dark} = 14.3$, $K_{light\ (75\ watt)} = 26$, $K_{bright\ light} = 40$). Although this was an improving trend, his results were still not good enough to suffice for the quantitative experiments for which Warburg wanted him to provide a model system. Hoping to do better, Krebs tried the effects of different media on the reaction. On the 18th, however, he encountered a new complication when he tested two concentrations of O_2 (21.4 and 6.0 percent), on CO. The results were for the higher concentration $K = 5.3$ and for the lower $K = 9.6$. According to the distribution equation, however, the constant should not vary with the concentration of the two gases. That it did so in this case prompted Krebs to comment "Dependent upon O_2 pressure ! This proves that there is non-heme-Fe present. Since this is not inhibited by CO, the measured value for K in the higher O_2 pressure is too large!"[82]

To try to rid his system of the interference of oxidations caused by the presence of non-heme-Fe, Krebs repeated the experiment at the beginning of the next week with an addition of pyrophosphate to see if it might inhibit the iron by forming a complex with it. At 37.4°C the K values for the two concentrations of O_2 agreed, but at 10°C in CO, K came out too small. There was also "A decrease in the CO effect with temperature." On the same day he repeated the experiment at 27°C with pyrophosphate and a new heme solution, and obtained again K values that "agreed" for 11.6 percent O_2 and 2.45 percent O_2 in CO. The oxidation was, he wrote down, "Almost independent of O_2 pressure!", implying that he seemed to have found a way around the problem of non-heme-iron.[83]

During the remaining days before Christmas Krebs explored further the effects of varying the oxygen pressure and the quantity of cysteine on the reaction. Concurrently a clinician named Dr. Berger carried out, under his supervision, several experiments concerning the catalytic effect of copper on the oxidation of cysteine; but it is not clear that these were connected with his own immediate project. Hoping to settle the question "Is the observed transport of O_2 a heme effect or an Fe effect?", he compared the rates of oxidation of cysteine in a solution containing heme with that in a solution containing a quantity of inorganic iron equivalent to that in the heme, in both cases with pyrophosphate added. Both at 37.5°C and 20°C the oxidation was reduced to a very low level in the solution without heme. Krebs concluded that "under these experimental conditions pyrophosphate inhibits [the action of] iron. Certain heme effect."[84]

Although this result persuaded Krebs that he was dealing with a genuine action of the heme, the effect was still not sufficiently pronounced for his needs, and he continued to explore ways in which he might be able to enhance the effect. He recorded also an experiment by Werner Cremer, a younger man who had recently come to work with Warburg after completing a doctorate with Heinrich Wieland. Cremer tested the action of "CO haemochromogen." That was the term used to designate a combination of *reduced* heme with a nitrogenous substance, but Krebs apparently thought at the time that it applied to free reduced heme. Shortly afterward he looked up an article by Mortimer Anson and Alfred Mirsky "On haemochromogen and the relation of protein to the properties of the haemoglobin molecule," and learned from it that "the pigment component of hemoglobin is named 'heme.' 'Reduced heme' is different from 'hemochromogen.' 'Hemochromogen' [applies] only in the presence of N-combinations."[85]

During the first 2 weeks of January 1928, Krebs continued varying the pH, the concentration of cysteine, the temperature, and other parameters in his quest for conditions that would render the catalytic effect, and the actions of CO and light on it more pronounced, and that would minimize the dependence of the process on the pressure of O_2; that is, that would reduce the possibility that complicating factors were involved. He tested mesoheme (hydrated heme), without obtaining significantly better results than with heme itself. Cremer examined whether hematoporphyrin — that is, heme without iron — would catalyze the oxidation.[86]

The article by Anson and Mirsky that Krebs had read just after Christmas included a discussion of the chemical equilibria of hemochromogen. In the system

heme + nitrogen compound $\rightleftarrows$ hemochromogen

they wrote, "an excess of nitrogen compound is needed to shift the equilibrium to the right." The quantity needed varies according to the nature of the nitrogen compound, a trace of globin producing more of its particular hemochromogen (that is, of hemoglobin) than high concentrations of most other nitrogen compounds did. "Only pyridine and nicotine (of the substances we have tried) even compare in intensity of activity with globin." It was probably this passage that stimulated Krebs to try out, on January 18, the effect of "nicotine–heme" on the oxidation of cysteine. Comparing the rates in heme solutions with and without nicotine, he obtained the dramatic result that there was a "tenfold increase in the effectiveness through nicotine!"[87]

This result (which Krebs recalled in 1978 as a "tremendous" increase in the catalytic activity) was not directly predictable from Anson and Mirsky's description of the intense activity of nicotine on heme. Krebs must have realized immediately that he had had a major break and that nicotine–heme might provide a more effective model system than free heme. He moved quickly, on the same day, to the crucial test of the actions of CO and of light on the reaction. In his first effort he obtained the sharp effects that had eluded him in his previous experiments. Carbon monoxide strongly inhibited the action of nicotine–heme in the dark, whereas light largely restored the uninhibited rate of oxidation. K_{dark} was 6, K_{light} 64, and the graph he now drew (see next page) displayed the sharp kinks he required for a successful model. Three more experiments on January 20 and 21 consolidated this auspicious initial result with nicotine–heme. Because he had found the rate dependent on the O_2 pressure he inferred that there must be inorganic iron present in the solution, part of which combined with CO in the presence of that gas. Nevertheless, in experiments using 5.3 and 21 percent O_2, he calculated from the distribution equation that "K is, within the limits of error, constant," and concluded hesitantly "The theory is therefore correct?" A repetition of the experiment the same day left him still not quite certain whether there was a "satisfying agreement in K with 5% and 21% O_2?" On the 23rd he found, by testing the system at 6°C and 20°C that there was "a very large temperature coefficient." On the next day he found that nicotine added to reduced heme doubled the rate of oxidation attained with unreduced heme. The same day he tested the action of 10^{-3} HCN on the nicotine–heme system and obtained a complete inhibition.[88]

Having attained such hopeful results with nicotine–heme, Krebs tried several other combinations — including casein–heme, proline–heme, and histamine–heme — during the last week of January to see if there might be something still better. These three proved not to be, but when he used, on the 28th, the other compound that Anson and Mirsky had mentioned as acting powerfully on the equilibrium of hemochromogen, he again obtained a striking result. With

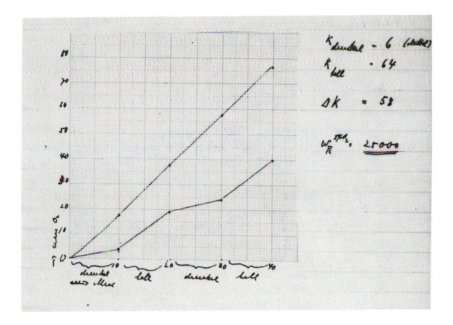

pyridine–heme CO inhibited the oxidation of cysteine more strongly, and light more nearly removed the inhibition than with nicotine–heme.[89]

During the first week of February Krebs conducted further experiments with both nicotine– and pyridine–heme, and tried out three more possible combinations of nitrogenous substances with heme.[90] By this time he had already reached his goal, and was probably already writing his paper "On the effect of carbon monoxide and light on heme catalysis." He began the paper:

> I have, at the suggestion of Herr Warburg investigated the effect of carbon monoxide and light on heme catalysis and found that a heme catalysis — the transfer of molecular oxygen through heme to cysteine — behaves toward carbon monoxide and light similarly to the respiration of living substance.

On February 5 he performed another experiment on nicotine–heme, attaining a catalytic action 15 times as large as with free heme, and 60 percent inhibition with CO. Illumination with a 75-W lamp at 6 cm distance caused the inhibition largely to disappear. Inserting these results into his paper as the representative experiment of its type, he completed the manuscript and carried it the next day to the office of Carl Neuberg for publication.[91]

Warburg must have been pleased with the outcome. Two weeks after Krebs finished this paper, Warburg delivered at the Kaiser-Wilhelm Gesellschaft a lecture "On the Chemical Constitution of the *Atmungsferment*," in which Krebs's results played a prominent part. "The enzyme about which I shall speak," Warburg stated, "is the *Atmungsferment*, about which one can say that it rules the organic world; because for everything that occurs in living matter respiration delivers the driving force." After describing the properties of hemoglobin, Keilin's cytochrome and the effects of carbon monoxide on hemoglobin, Warburg compared the properties of the *Atmungsferment* with those of hemoglobin and described his experiments showing the effects of carbon monoxide and of light on living yeast cells. Then he went on,

> We can approach the properties of the *Atmungsferment* more closely if we separate from hemoglobin its protein component, the globin: Free heme acts catalytically and is able, for example, as D.C. Harrison (Cambridge, England) found to oxidize cysteine catalytically in aqueous solution. According to experiments by H.A. Krebs this catalysis is inhibited by carbon monoxide at approximately the same gas pressure as respiration is. The light sensitivity of the carbon monoxide combination of free heme is small, however, in fact it is perhaps 10,000 times smaller than the light sensitivity of the carbon monoxide combination of the *Atmungsferment*.
>
> This deficiency also can be avoided. If one couples heme with pyridine or nicotine, one obtains a strongly active catalytic combination, whose iron atom transfers 2,000 molecules of oxygen per hour to cysteine. The carbon monoxide compound of these hemes is, according to experiments by H.A. Krebs, decomposed by light of 1/10,000 the intensity of the sun, it is therefore just as light sensitive as the carbon monoxide compound of the *Atmungsferment*.
>
> We can therefore repeat the experiments previously described for living cells in simple solutions *without* living cells.[92]

Warburg presented two of the graphs Krebs had drawn of the effects of alternate dark and light periods on the inhibition of pyridine and nicotine heme by carbon monoxide and drew attention to the similarity between them and the curves he had obtained with living yeast cells.

The usefulness of these model systems extended beyond replicating actions of the *Atmungsferment* outside of living cells. In the short time since Krebs had provided him with this system Warburg had already determined the effect of different wavelengths of light on its carbon monoxide inhibition of the nicotine–heme model. The resulting "action spectrum," he showed, coincided with an ordinary absorption spectrum for carbon. Because the model system was "a clear aqueous solution in which nothing but the catalyst — the nicotine–heme — absorbs light," Warburg could be confident that the different effects of different wavelengths on the activity of the system were due entirely to the differences in their absorption. Then he was in a position to determine the action spectrum also for living yeast cells and to infer that it too represented the absorption spectrum of the *Atmungsferment*.[93]

At the close of his lecture Warburg pointed out "that for the results about which I have spoken I owe thanks in great part to the work of my co-workers, Herr Negelein and Krebs."[94] Krebs was not present at Warburg's lecture, but he must have seen the text soon afterward. It appeared in *Die Naturwissenscha-*

ften on May 18. He was obviously proud of the success he had attained with the model system and the contribution he had thereby made to Warburg's broader attack on the properties of the *Atmungsferment*. He felt also, however, that Warburg's public references to his experiments were overly generous. It was clear to him that Warburg had only delegated to him a portion of his own investigation and had formulated for him the problem to solve. Krebs realized also that his success in solving the problem had involved some very good luck. The luck was, as he put it much later, "that it worked at all."[95]

V

The rapidity with which Krebs published his paper on heme catalysis after relatively few experiments on pyridin- and nicotine-heme, and the alacrity with which Warburg incorporated the results into his work on the *Atmungsferment* indicate the confidence that Warburg placed in the suitability of the new model system; but there was still much to do to establish the conditions under which the system would function optimally, and to explore further properties that might resemble those of the *Atmungsferment*. For the rest of the spring and summer of 1928 Krebs's main task was to consolidate his initial results and to gather further supporting data for them. After trying two further heme compounds, colloidin- and picolin-heme, neither of which was "as good as the pyridine [heme] experiments," Krebs moved to test whether his model system was inhibited, as Warburg had earlier found cell respiration to be, by hydrosulfuric acid (H_2S) and alkali sulfides. The result was the opposite from that expected. On February 17 Krebs observed that an addition of Na_2S increased the rate of oxidation in a nicotine-heme system by ten times. Following up this observation through the rest of February and all of March, he decided that it was due to the autoxidation of H_2S rather than to an action on the heme catalysis. That led him into a useful investigation of the effects of heavy metals on the autoxidation of hydrosulfuric acid and alkali sulfides, but it also prevented him from showing that his model system behaved in the presence of these substances like the respiration of living cells.[96]

The first 2 weeks of April Krebs spent on an Easter holiday trip in Italy. No details of his itinerary are known, except that he obtained his visa in Berlin on March 23, went as far as Sicily, and was in Como on April 13. He was back in the laboratory in Dahlem on April 18.[97] During 1928 he also took up a new weekend recreational activity, sculling on the extensive system of lakes and rivers that surrounded Berlin. He did so in the company of a young woman whose parents belonged to a rowing club. Often Hans and Violet rowed together all day Sunday; on occasion he packed clothes in the storage compartment of his scull and embarked on a water trip of several days duration. Violet had to go home at night, but Hans stayed at hotels along the way. Although they found they had much in common and were attracted to one another, neither of them ever brought up the subject of possible marriage. Violet's parents were English, and she spoke that language fluently. Hans took advantage of the situation to practice English conversation. To his brother Wolf it appeared, in fact, that his principal motivation in spending time with Violet was to improve his English.[98]

In May Krebs applied for a position as director of the laboratory of the Municipal Hospital in Mannheim.[99] Warburg wrote a recommendation for him and may have suggested that he should try for the job. Krebs did not get it, and there is no indication that he was strongly interested in it. He appears to have been quite satisfied to be working as Warburg's assistant, and had apparently given little further thought to what he would do afterward.

As Krebs pursued the catalytic action of the heme–cysteine system during May and June he encountered increasing complexities. He realized, for example, that the activity of pyridine–heme was dependent on the presence of ferrocysteine, and proportional to the concentration of ferrous ions added. Ferrocysteine, he concluded, reduced the iron in the heme to ferrous iron. Cyanide, on the other hand, formed a combination with heme containing iron in the ferric form, thereby inhibiting its catalytic form. These phenomena forced him to be more attentive to the various chemical combinations into which heme can enter, and to use more carefully the nomenclature applying to these forms. Heme dissolved in alkalies he now called hematin, reserving the term heme for the compound reduced by cysteine. To follow the dissociation of the cyanide compound of hematin he made spectrophotometric measurements of the changes in absorption of different wave lengths of light. These and additional experiments on the parameters affecting the reaction of the model system to carbon monoxide and light occupied him until the start of the summer holiday in mid-July.[100]

Having saved his money carefully, Krebs was in a position by the summer of 1928 to travel more extensively than he had in previous years. Perhaps influenced by his friendship with Violet to choose a place in which he could speak English, he booked a room in a boarding house on the Isle of Wight. He took a steamer from Hamburg to Southhampton, where he disembarked on July 21. After staying there overnight, he reached his destination late the next morning. As he finished his lunch in the dining hall, a man sitting with his wife and daughter at a nearby table opened a conversation with him. When Krebs told them that he was a German and hoped to improve his English, the family immediately began to help, correcting his mistakes tactfully. They invited him to go with them on excursions, taught him to play beach cricket, and invited him to visit them at their home in Wembley at the end of his holiday. It was a kind of warmth extended to a stranger that Krebs had never experienced in Germany, and it made a deep impression on him.[101]

When he returned to work on September 22, Krebs wound up his investigation of hematin catalysis with several experiments on the effects of cyanide.[102] While he was in the midst of them, on September 24, he read an article that had just appeared in the *Biochemical Journal* by Malcolm Dixon, on "The Action of Carbon Monoxide on the Autoxidation of Sulphydryl Compounds." Taking issue with Warburg's view that cell respiration is due "primarily to catalytic systems which are poisoned by small amounts of cyanide" and that "the cell respiration as a whole was poisoned by carbon monoxide," Dixon contended that

Warburg's data "do not exclude the possibility that a part of the oxygen absorbed may be utilized by systems on which CO has no action." Dixon presented experiments on the effects of CO on the catalysis by hematin "of the autoxidation of cysteine and reduced glutathione." Both of these substances were sulfhydryl (SH-) compounds oxidizable to disulfide (-S-S-) compounds. The former served as the principal substrate in Warburg and Krebs's experiments, the latter had been shown by Frederick Gowland Hopkins to be oxidized in tissues. In Dixon's hands CO had little effect on either catalytic process. In discussing his results Dixon directly contested those that Krebs had recently presented:

> These experiments make it quite clear that carbon monoxide produces no inhibition of the oxidation induced by haematin. They therefore stand in direct opposition to the recent results of Krebs [1928], who, using similar methods, found that CO produced a 70% inhibition of the catalysis of the autoxidation of cysteine by haematin.

Dixon explained "the discrepancy between my results and those of Krebs" in terms of the tendency of hematin in solution to break down into less complex iron compounds whose catalytic action, in contrast to that of fresh hematin, is inhibited by CO:

> It seems possible that Krebs may have used a stock solution of haematin, or haemin which had become partially decomposed, and that this may have been responsible for the inhibition he observed. At any rate, whether this is correct or not, I have never been able to detect any inhibition by CO when the haematin has been freshly made up, and have always found a marked inhibition after it has been allowed to stand for a few days before use; and this effect would seem to provide an adequate explanation of the discrepancy.[103]

In his laboratory notebook Krebs summarized Dixon's argument with the query "CO acts only on old hemin solutions?" and indicated his rejection of such an explanation by adding his own: "Perhaps D. shook [the manometers] too slowly." This was Krebs's first experience with a public criticism of his own published results, and he must have turned immediately to Warburg for advice on what to do. Warburg left no doubt; it was essential to clarify the situation in print, otherwise readers would be left confused about whose claims to accept.[104] Warburg was characteristically aggressive in responding to criticisms of experimental work done in his laboratory, and Krebs apparently needed so little urging to react similarly, that he submitted on the very same day the following note to the *Biochemische Zeitschrift*:

On the Effects of Carbon Monoxide on
Hematin Catalysis according to M. Dixon
H.A. Krebs

Dixon has investigated the inhibition of hematin catalysis through carbon monoxide described by me and expresses the suspicion that the inhibition only appears if the hematin solution is old.   This very improbable supposition is incorrect.

We used hemin recrystallized from pyridin-chloroform-glacial acetic acid whose purity was proven through the determination of its carbon monoxide capacity. The catalytic activity of freshly prepared solutions of this hemin was inhibited by carbon monoxide in the manner described by me.

As was clearly shown in his paper, Dixon worked with impure cysteine containing metal, with impure solvents containing metal, and probably also with impure hemin. Because of the impurity of his reagents, the reactions in his solutions were too large. Under such conditions the gas and fluid volumes are not in equilibrium, and what one measures manometrically are not chemical rates of reaction, but rates of accidental convection, which are naturally not influenced by carbon monoxide.[105]

Not until the day after he had given this note to Carl Neuberg for publication did Krebs check experimentally whether "old" hemin would be affected differently from "new" hemin by carbon monoxide in his experimental system. There was no significant difference.[106]

* * *

In 1976 I commented to Krebs that the "last paragraph where you explained Dixon's results is somewhat ironic in tone." When he agreed, I asked if "you were a little bit indignant about this situation." He replied, "No, this was essentially, may even have been formulated by Warburg. He liked to ridicule his opponents. Well, opponent is not the right term. From the other person's point of view it was a difference of opinion merely."[107]

Since the note was written in a style for which Warburg was well known, it is quite plausible that he either wrote it for Krebs or told Krebs what to write. On the other hand, Krebs's recollection was influenced by the fact that he later became close friends with Malcolm Dixon at Cambridge, learned to appreciate Dixon's relaxed attitude toward controversies, and was eventually embarrassed by Warburg's stubborn polemics.[108] There is ample evidence from later incidents that Krebs himself reacted impatiently to criticisms that seemed to him unwarranted. The attitude expressed in his note could well have been his own, or one that he fully shared with Warburg. In view of the scrupulous care with which Warburg rid his reagents of impurities, Dixon's guess that Krebs had used old or impure hematin would have appeared to Krebs to merit the curt rebuff that it drew from him.

* * *

On September 28 Krebs shifted abruptly from the investigation of the respiratory model system he had been studying for the previous 10 months to an unrelated problem. Ten days later he submitted to the *Biochemische Zeitschrift* two papers reporting the outcome of the preceding work: one "On the Effect of Carbon Monoxide and Cyanide on Hematincatalysis," the other "On the Effect of Heavy Metals on the Autoxidation of Alkali Sulfides and Hydrosulfuric acid."[109] The new project was to examine the effects of thyroxin on rat tissue slices. The suddenness and completeness with which Krebs ended the one investigation and took up the other reflected the fact that Warburg characteristically did not linger over a problem when he had solved it as far as he could at a given stage, but moved on to something else. That does not mean that Krebs one day entered the laboratory and was told to begin a new project at once. Warburg probably had discussed with him for several weeks the subject that he wanted him to take up next, giving Krebs ample time to explore the problem, read up on the pertinent literature, and organize his approach.[110]

Thyroxine, the active hormone of the thyroid gland, had been isolated in 1915 by Edward Kendall, and had since become the subject of numerous experiments and clinical trials. Among the multiple physiological ways in which the hormone was found to counteract the symptoms of thyroid deficiency was that it dramatically accelerated the rate of metabolism. Thyroxin also raised the overall rate of metabolism in experimental animals. The effects were, however, complicated, and the question of how thyroxin acted on the metabolism remained open. In 1922 Joseph Aub and his co-workers at the Harvard Medical School showed, by administering thyroxine to anesthetized and denervated cats and cats whose adrenal glands had been removed, that the effect could not be due to increased muscular activity or tonus. They concluded, rather metaphorically, that "the thyroid secretion acts as a draught, stimulating the resting body cells to an increased rate of combustion."[111] During the same year Masaji Tomita, working in Dahlem at the Kaiser-Wilhelm Institute for Experimental Therapy, demonstrated that thyroxin can increase the rate of alcoholic fermentation in yeast. In 1927, Felix Haffner at Tübingen concluded from studies of the effect of thyroxin on the metabolism of mice that although the hormone accelerates the oxidative processes, it does so indirectly. It acts directly on the *anaerobic* phase of metabolism, the increase in respiration being a protective response of the organism to remove the excess lactic acid formed. Other investigators had already shown, however, that thyroxine can increase the metabolism even of animals whose glycogen reserves have been exhausted by treatment with phlorizin; therefore in addition to carbohydrate metabolism it must be able to stimulate a higher protein and fat metabolism.[112]

Because of the complexity of the actions of thyroxin on the whole organism, Warburg's tissue slice method provided an obviously attractive opportunity to try to localize its action on the metabolism of isolated tissues. During 1927 a worker in Warburg's laboratory named Dresel examined the action of thyroxin on testicle slices and observed an increase in the rate of metabolism. This result was of considerable potential interest, because of current views that the various endocrine glands of the body interacted on one another. Dresel's work did not, however, lead to a publication.[113]   If, as seems likely from the lack of other information about Dresel, he worked only for a short time in Warburg's laboratory, Warburg may well have asked Krebs to follow up what Dresel had begun.

Krebs started the new project by measuring in liver slices from a well-nourished rat the aerobic consumption of oxygen and formation of carbon dioxide, and the anaerobic formation of lactic acid, in the same manner that he had measured these quantities 2 years earlier in tumor tissue. As before, he compared the rates when the slices were immersed in Ringer's solution with the rates in blood serum, finding the latter higher. After performing two such experiments he proceeded on October 1 to make the same measurements on liver slices from rats that had been injected 2 days earlier with preparations of synthetic thyroxin, recently made available in Germany from the Sichering firm. The metabolic rates were substantially higher, both in Ringer's solution and in serum, than the comparable rates for normally nourished rats. During the next 2 weeks Krebs carried out ten more such experiments on liver slices from nourished and thyroxin-injected rats, including one from starved rats, with similar results. It had been relatively easy to confirm the generally known effect of thyroxin in accelerating metabolism.[114]

On October 17 Krebs turned from manometric experiments on liver slices to more conventional *Gesammtstoffwechsel* experiments; that is, to measurements of the respiration of intact rats, again comparing the rates for thyroxin-injected animals with that for normally nourished ones. He carried on such experiments for 3 days, interrupted them for two experiments on the metabolism of choroid plexus tissue from rabbits, which yielded exceptionally high rates, then continued the overall metabolism experiments through the first week of November. With that he dropped the project and did not return to it.[115]

We can only guess that the reason Krebs pursued no further a problem of considerable potential significance was that the experiments he had performed until then offered no leads to anything beyond the verification that in tissue slices thyroxin also increases the metabolism. We may recall that when Warburg first applied tissue slice methods to the metabolism of cancer cells in 1923 he quickly discovered the anomalously high rate of glycolysis that gave direction to all of his subsequent research on the subject. In this case nothing striking turned up. All three measurements increased in roughly similar proportions. Consequently the numbers pointed to no particular aspect of metabolism on which thyroxin might act. Warburg and Krebs must have agreed that it would be best not to become mired in an investigation that did not seem to be getting anywhere. Moreover, Warburg had another problem in mind for Krebs to take up.

Some critics of Warburg's theory that cancer metabolism is characterized by abnormally high rates of glycolysis had asserted that this may not be a specific phenomenon but a concomitant of a general increased breakdown of cellular constituents. One must determine whether proteins and fats were also broken down more rapidly. Realizing that he would have to investigate such possibilities even if he considered them unlikely, Warburg asked Krebs to devise a method to measure proteolysis manometrically. Although other convenient methods already existed, Warburg said to Krebs that one should develop a manometric method whenever possible, not only because they are precise and rapid, but because they enable one to follow the time course of the change in question. Perhaps he discussed with Krebs at the start the idea that one could in this case take advantage of the fact that peptides are stronger acids than free amino acids are. When peptides are cleaved, therefore, the solution becomes more alkaline and carbonic acid is absorbed. Consequently it ought to be possible to measure the rate of cleavage of peptides by measuring the decrease of the pressure due to carbon dioxide in the manometer in which such a reaction is taking place.[116]

Although the measurement itself was simple, it was not so simple to calculate, from the measured change in pressure the corresponding change in the quantity of the peptide. To develop a method for that, Krebs went back to the book on *The Hydrogen Ion Concentration* by Leonor Michaelis that he had so admired when he first read it, to find formulas for the dissociation constants of amphoteric substances and of carbonic acid. Starting with these he derived equations from which he could calculate a vessel constant he could then use to convert a measured pressure change into a quantity of peptide dissociated into amino acids. Because one needed to specify the initial conditions, the method was applicable only to relatively simple situations, such as when one began with a known quantity of a well-defined dipeptide. To test the method he performed experiments mainly with the dipeptide alanyl-glycine, using rat intestinal mucous membrane to bring about the cleavage (through the action of its digestive enzymes). Joseph F. Donegan, a professor of physiology who had come from Ireland to work in Warburg's laboratory, assisted Krebs with the experiments after Krebs had taught him the necessary manometric techniques. The method proved to be precise under the specified conditions. When he compared some of his results with those he obtained by the standard Van Slyke method of measuring the change in amino nitrogen, they coincided closely.[117]

By January Krebs had written a paper on the method, much of it comprised of the derivation of the equations employed in it. Warburg went step-by-step over the mathematics Krebs had used and corrected several of the assumptions he had made. Krebs handed the paper "Manometric Measurement of Peptide Cleavage," with Donegan as co-author, over to the *Biochemische Zeitschrift* on January 21. Krebs and Donovan got along very well, and their short collaboration led to a lasting friendship.[118]

VI

Krebs conducted so few experiments during January and February 1929, that it seems possible that he was occupied with other matters for some of this time. Perhaps it was during this period that he interviewed for another job for which Warburg had recommended him. The position was in a clinical laboratory. When he learned that the project would be to identify the active principle in the liver extract that cured pernicious anemia, he did not like the idea. To him the problem appeared unmanageable. When he reported his reaction to Warburg, his chief fully understood. He had once been interviewed for a job by an immunologist who thought he could isolate the chemical substance in bacteria responsible for the agglutination of serum. Warburg agreed that the job was not suitable for Krebs and advised him to send a wire stating "I am not free."[119]

It was typical of Warburg to believe that most clinicians knew so little chemistry as to think that there must be an isolatable chemical substance behind every physiological or pathological process. Warburg expressed his attitudes toward other people in science and medicine so forcefully and so colorfully that Krebs occasionally wrote down pieces of the daily laboratory conversation. On the first working day of the new year, for example, Warburg related:

> During the holiday Runnstrom from Stockholm was here. He began to talk the usual nonsense about methylene blue. That man does not dare to speak too much about iron, because he would like to get a position in Sweden. I asked him whether he was aware that people were once willing to be burned for the truth. Today any Professor will betray the truth for 100 marks. It would be something unusual if he were only willing to do it for 1000 marks.[120]

Warburg managed to convey in this pithy comment his scorn for the methylene blue reduction methods developed in Sweden by Thorsten Thunberg to study cellular reactions (and indirectly for the hydrogen activation theories of his adversary Wieland that were incorporated into the interpretation of methylene blue experiments), the implication that resistance to his own concept of the *Atmungsferment* was based on political considerations, and his view of academic scientists as both mercenary and corrupt.

Even while disparaging other scientists, Warburg expressed to those around him his beliefs about what science was and what it was not. On February 26, 1929, Krebs recorded an exchange between himself and Warburg:

> I mentioned that after the colloquium yesterday, in a conversation with Gaffron and me, Hartmann said, "The increase in metabolism during fertilization is not a fertilization problem but a reproduction problem."
>
> Warburg grinned and said, "And he is one of the best, how must the others be then? Such opinions occur because people do not know what natural science is. They think that natural science is the logical comprehension of nature. That is what the elementary school teacher imagines natural science to be: to sit at the writing table, to comb one's hair back, and to solve a problem. Thereby they know neither what it means to "solve" nor what in general they want to do. These opinions belong to esthetics and have nothing to do with science. Science, such as the laws of electricity etc., aims to discover something useful for the general welfare. One can naturally not come to an understanding with these people who regard science as esthetics and do not know that science is only a craft, a very modest craft.[121]

On May 29 Warburg told Krebs

> It is not enough that one should perform quantitative experiments in general. If one finds, for example, that a mouse consumes 5 g of bread in one day, this quantitative experiment is uninteresting. What matters is to do quantitative experiments that one can always repeat. If one finds that 1 g of sodium combines with a definite quantity of chlorine, one will find the same quantity every time, and one can justifiably generalize that sodium *always* reacts with this same quantity of chlorine. From the quantitative mouse experiment, however, one can conclude nothing general at all. The trick is precisely to do experiments whose results permit one to generalize.[122]

Powerful teachers instruct even in casual conversation, and the opinions Warburg voiced from day to day made a strong impact on those around him. They knew that he exaggerated, that he was often unfair to others, that some of his views were idiosyncratic; but his towering presence (despite his short physical stature) dominated their lives, and they did not question his scientific judgments.[123] They admired the disciplined way he pursued science, and they took to heart the ways in which he said it should be done. For Krebs, trenchant comments such as those quoted became maxims that helped to shape his aspirations.

For the most part Warburg reserved his harsh treatment for those outside his own laboratory. Krebs witnessed, however, the swiftness with which the chief could turn on a member of his own group when challenged. A bright, good-looking, but rather eccentric man named Walter Kempner had recently entered the laboratory. Krebs was assigned to teach Kempner the experimental techniques employed in the laboratory, which Kempner learned readily; but Krebs also found him rather rude at times. One day at lunch Krebs attempted to introduce him to his friend David Nachmansohn, who was now working in Meyerhof's laboratory. Kempner retorted, "I do not consider myself introduced. I know enough people already." After about a year Kempner said something in the laboratory that Warburg considered so arrogant that he dismissed him on the spot.[124]

There seemed little risk that such a fate would befall Krebs. Still shy and reserved, Krebs remained in awe of his chief. He continued to work diligently and to conform to what was expected of him.

Krebs continued also to enjoy the cultural advantages of Berlin. Among the theatrical productions he took in was one of the original performances of Berthold Brecht and Kurt Weill's latest hit, *The Three Penny Opera*. Both the striking music and the theme of the underground life of prostitutes and beggars made a great impact on him.[125] Meanwhile, Lotte Rittmann, the young woman to whom he had been attracted as a student in Munich, visited a cousin in Berlin and Krebs began seeing her regularly. One day he invited Wolf to join them at the opera. Unaware that Hans was still seriously interested in Lotte, Wolf telephoned her the next day and was mistaken for Hans. Soon, however, Lotte began to go out with Wolf instead of Hans, a switch that may have raised another barrier between the brothers.[126]

Late in February Krebs returned to the hematin catalysis model to re-examine his earlier inability to inhibit the oxidation of cysteine by means of H_2S, one of the inhibitors of cellular respiration. After several unsuccessful attempts, he began looking for other hematin-catalyzed oxidations upon which H_2S might act. On the 27th he began investigating the oxidation of linoleic acid. On March 3 he performed an experiment in which linoleic acid was oxidized only in the presence of hematin, and the catalytic oxidation was inhibited by Na_2S. Two days later he submitted to the *Biochemische Zeitschrift* a note announcing that "I have filled the gap" in the previous work.[127] The fact that the model could not imitate all of the pertinent properties of the *Atmungsferment* with a single substrate was apparently of little concern, perhaps because in Warburg's conception of cellular respiration the identification of substrate pathways was unimportant.

Through the rest of March Krebs pursued mainly the cleavage of dipeptides, working particularly with leucyl–glycine. When he returned from the Easter holiday at the end of the first week in April, Warburg gave him another methodological problem: to determine manometrically the carbon dioxide content of a gas mixture. Krebs solved the problem readily, placing in the manometer vessel, in contact with the gas to be analyzed, a weakly acidic solution of permanganate, which he then mixed inside the vessel with iodide. The reaction made the solution alkaline, absorbing the carbon dioxide from the gas. To obtain a scale that would accommodate mixtures containing up to 10 vol % CO_2, he used in the manometer arms a fluid whose density was just double that of the standard Brodie solution. He published a paper on the method in mid-July. Meanwhile he went on with the study of dipeptide cleavage up until the summer holiday began on August 1.[128]

Krebs approached the summer holiday of 1929 with high expectations, because arrangements had been made for him to travel to the United States for the Nineteenth International Congress of Physiology in Boston. There were no equivalent congresses in biochemistry, and biochemists customarily attended the physiological congresses, which were regarded as major events in their field. Warburg had been at the previous Congress in Stockholm, and encouraged Krebs to go. To enable him to do so, Warburg made a few telephone calls and obtained for Krebs a small grant from the German Physiological Society. Further financial aid came from Joseph Aub, who had earlier visited the laboratory in Dahlem and was eager to have the people working in his own laboratory at Harvard learn Warburg's manometric methods. Robert Emmerson, who had been one of Warburg's assistants when Krebs entered the laboratory and had subsequently returned to Boston, arranged with Aub for Krebs to be paid a sum of about $200 to teach the manometric techniques in Aub's laboratory.[129]

On or about August 1, Krebs boarded the *Bremen*, the newest and fastest German ocean liner, for its maiden voyage. Like other Europeans, Krebs visual-

Figure 6.2 Physiologists and biochemists on board the *Bremen*, 1929. Krebs is leaning on railing at right.

ized America as the land of endless opportunity. Even though the five-day voyage was uneventful, it must have given him a sense of high adventure. Upon arriving in Boston he spent the 2 weeks prior to the Congress instructing in Aub's laboratory at the Harvard Medical School, where the international meeting itself began on August 19.[130]

More than 1,000 scientists from 35 countries gathered for the meeting, over which William H. Howell, of Johns Hopkins, presided. The famous Pavlov, now elderly but still active, was present, and the renowned Harvard physiologist Walter Cannon served as local arrangements chairman.[131]

After opening speeches by the Lieutenant-Governor of Massachusetts and President Lowell of Harvard University, the distinguished Danish physiologist August Krogh gave a plenary lecture on "The Progress of Physiology,"[132] to which Krebs listened attentively. During his talk Krogh said that

> For a large number of problems there will be some animal of choice, or a few such animals on which it can be most conveniently studied. Many years ago when my teacher, Christian Bohr, was interested in the respiratory mechanisms of the lung and devised a method of studying the exchange through each lung separately, he found that a certain kind of

tortoise possesses a trachea dividing into the main bronchi high up in the neck and we used to say as a laboratory joke that this animal had been created expressly for the study of respiration physiology. I have no doubt that there is quite a number of animals which are similarly 'created' for special physiology purposes, but I am afraid that most of them are unknown to the men for whom they are 'created' and we must apply to the zoologists to find them.[133]

This idea struck a strong chord in Krebs. Warburg, too, had often stressed the importance of choosing an organism suitable to a given problem; but the way in which Krogh stated this view inspired Krebs to elevate it to a general principle of biological research.

During the scientific sessions, which lasted from Monday until Friday, Krebs probably heard a number of interesting papers, but, as in most international meetings, the contacts he made with other biochemists were more stimulating to him. He was treated with a friendly respect that he appreciated he owed more to his position as an assistant to the esteemed Warburg than to his own achievements. Among the other young biochemists he met were Carl and Gerty Cori, who had left Austria for St. Louis, and the buoyant, charming Hungarian Albert Szent-Györgyi. Szent-Györgyi told Krebs that he was fortunate to be in the laboratory of a great scientist. He claimed that he himself had had no mentors, and was therefore a self-taught amateur.[134]

While Krebs was in Boston he received an invitation from Hedwig Michaelis, the wife of Leonor Michaelis, to join them and some friends at their summer home in Woods Hole. He was also contacted by Detlev Bronk about a possible position in a new research institution Bronk had established in Philadelphia, the Johnson Foundation. Bronk had asked Warburg to suggest candidates for the fellowships that he would have available. Concerned that growing anti-Semitism would make it difficult for Krebs to obtain a position in Germany, Warburg thought that his opportunities might be better in America, and recommended him to Bronk.[135]

After the Congress closed Krebs joined an excursion to New York that had been organized for the participants. While he was there he developed a small abscess on his leg and was confined to a bed at the Presbyterian Hospital for several days to avoid the risk of infection. When one of the resident physicians, Robert Loeb, learned that an assistant to Warburg was a patient there, he came to see him. Loeb's father, the late Jacques Loeb, had been a friend and admirer of Warburg, and the son saw to it that Krebs received the best treatment available. Mortimer Anson, whom Krebs had met at Dahlem, and whose work on hematin compounds had been crucial to his own recent studies, also looked him up at the hospital, visited him several times while he was there, and brought him books to read. Anson had already invited Krebs to lecture at Princeton on catalysis.[136]

One hot day while he was still in New York, Krebs decided to go to a movie, mainly because the theater was air conditioned. As a result he saw his first "talking" film, starring Al Jolson in *Sonny Boy*.[137]

Figure 6.3 Hans Krebs at the Physiological Congress in Boston, 1929.

Traveling to Philadelphia for an interview with Detlev Bronk, Krebs learned that the fellowship would last only 1 or 2 years and that Bronk wanted him to work on biophysical rather than biochemical problems. The prospects appeared too risky to Krebs, and he declined the offer.[138]

Krebs was as much impressed with the warm reception he received repeatedly in the United States as he had been during his holiday in England. He concluded that Anglo-Saxons were generally more friendly than Europeans. At Woods Hole, however, he learned that expatriated Germans could be equally gracious and outgoing. Leonor and Hedwig Michaelis made him feel completely at home during the week he stayed with them. It must have been particularly heartening to him to find that the man whose scientific writings he so admired was also modest, understanding, and marked by exceptionally broad intellectual interests.[139]

On the return voyage Krebs found himself on the same boat with a group of a dozen German physiologists and biochemists on the way home from the Congress. Among them was Franz Knoop, whose lectures at Freiburg had first aroused his interest in intermediary metabolism. Krebs found Knoop approachable and interesting. During the 5 days at sea Krebs was stimulated by a great deal of shop talk about the current research interests of his scientific fellow passengers.[140]

When Krebs returned to Dahlem after these heady 2 months abroad, at the beginning of October, he received a major setback. Warburg seemed disappointed and impatient that he had not accepted the job with Bronk, and told him very firmly "You must be gone from here by April 1." Moreover, he made it rather clear that he would write no more letters of recommendation for Krebs.[141]

This sudden development seems to have been as unexpected as it was shocking to Krebs. Despite the fact that Warburg had warned him at the beginning that he could remain only for a limited time in the laboratory because there was no room in it for independent investigators, and reminded him occasionally in 1929 that he could not stay indefinitely, the successive extensions beyond his first year appear to have induced Krebs to believe that he could stay as long as he remained useful to Warburg's research interests. He had felt no urgency about finding a job elsewhere, and had not suspected that there was a deadline on his time in Dahlem. The peremptory manner in which Warburg now informed him that there was such a limit led Krebs to infer that Warburg wanted to get rid of him because he did not consider him good enough to become an original scientist.[142]

VII

Sometime during 1929 Krebs went to hear Gustav Stresemann speak, and noticed that the great foreign minister appeared very ill. Three days after Krebs returned to Dahlem on October 3, Stresemann died, and Germans were reminded again of the fragility of their national condition. By the end of that month news of the stock market crash was plunging the whole world into uncertainty.[143] Faced simultaneously with his imminent departure from Dahlem, Krebs could hardly have avoided a sense of insecurity enveloping both his personal life and the life of his country. The blow that Warburg had delivered to him must have come all the harder in the wake of a journey in which he had repeatedly experienced the pride of identification as Warburg's assistant. Given his reticence about recalling unpleasant memories, the strength of Krebs's feelings about the matter are conveyed with unmistakable force in his statement almost 50 years later that "Warburg handled me rather fiercely in dismissing me."[144]

Despite his sense that he had been summarily dismissed, Krebs did not allow himself to become depressed during the final 6 months that he had been permitted in Warburg's laboratory. Carrying on dutifully with the work on proteolysis, he found that the manometric method he had devised was suitable to study the cleavage of proteins as well as that of simple dipeptides. Under such circumstances it was not possible to calculate the vessel constant, so he calibrated the relation between the pressure changes and the quantity of amino acids formed in his method by means of the Van Slyke amino-nitrogen method, which had itself recently been adapted to manometric measurements. With these adjustments in his procedure, Krebs studied through the winter of 1929–1930 the enzymatic cleavage of several proteins, including particularly casein and gelatin.

He then focused his attention on the proteolytic enzyme papain obtained from the juice of the papaya plant, and was able to explain the "activation" of that substance by means of cyanide, hydrosulfuric acid, and cysteine as the result of the formation of complexes with metallic ions that otherwise inhibited the process. On February 24 he submitted his last two papers from Warburg's laboratory, one on "Manometric Measurement of Protein Cleavage," the other on "Experiments on the Proteolytic Action of Papain." He kept on doing similar experiments through the middle of March, turning his attention to another proteolytic enzyme, cathepsin, which he obtained by grinding rabbit spleen. On Monday, March 24, he performed one more experiment, on yeast proteinase, and then simply wrote down in his laboratory notebook "End in Dahlem."[145]

* * *

In his autobiography Krebs wrote that "during my last few months in Warburg's laboratory, I did a great deal of heart-searching about the kind of career I should aim at." Warburg advised him against looking for a post in biochemistry on the grounds that very few existed and that anti-Semitism would probably block his attempts to obtain a suitable one. Biochemistry was, in Warburg's opinion, not yet a profession, whereas medicine was a profession at which he could earn a good living. Believing Warburg also regarded him as mediocre, yet still keen to involve himself somehow in research, Krebs resolved to fall back on the plan he had had in mind before becoming Warburg's assistant: to look for a position in academic medicine in which he could combine clinical and laboratory work.[146]

His restrained account of his "heart-searching" probably does not reveal the intensity of the questions and doubts that Krebs must have confronted during this wrenching period. If, as he recalled long afterward, he had no grounds to think that he was competent to pursue a successful scientific career, why would he choose a course in which he could expect either failure or at best a mediocre career? We may plausibly surmise that he was in fact unsure both of what Warburg actually thought of him and of how reliable Warburg's assessment might be. If Warburg never gave him "any inkling" that he thought highly of him as a student,[147] neither apparently did he ever tell Krebs that he did not have the potential to become a scientist. Krebs must never have asked Warburg directly for an opinion of his ability. If Warburg never praised his performance, that may have reflected the common trait in German society to expect good work as a matter of course. Few of the authoritative figures in his life, from his father to his Gymnasium teachers, to Warburg, had ever let him know that his efforts were good enough, and the entire German educational system provided little means for students to evaluate their overall standing. Warburg's counsel not to try to become a biochemist might be taken either as discouragement based on Krebs's shortcomings or as an effort to protect him from unfavorable outward circumstances.

In assessing Warburg's apparently unfavorable opinion of him, Krebs might also have reflected on the fact that Warburg had given him no chance to demonstrate that he could do original work, that his prejudices against academic medicine may have led him to assume that Krebs was badly trained, and that Warburg could be a poor judge of people whose abilities differed from his own. There were some grounds, then, for resisting what he perceived to be Warburg's assessment of him.

The most surprising aspect of Krebs's situation was not that he was caught by surprise to be told that he could not remain longer in Dahlem, but that he seemed content to be there as long as he was. Intending to spend a year in Warburg's laboratory to gain research experience, he had stayed on for four, and had no plans to move on until Warburg forced the issue. For an individual who had previously displayed exceptional drive and self-motivation, he had become strangely passive. During his last 2 years in Dahlem the projects that Warburg gave him were, if anything, narrower and more routine than the earlier ones. He had already learned the powerful methods in use in Warburg's laboratory and absorbed as much as he could of Warburg's scientific style. We might have expected Krebs to be impatient to begin the independent research that Warburg would not permit him to do in Dahlem. There is no certain solution to this puzzle, but perhaps the explanation lies in part in the powerful ambivalence of Warburg's effect on him. Inspired on the one hand to emulate him, Krebs felt himself on the other hand dwarfed in comparison to him. In a note to himself that he made in preparation for his autobiography, Krebs once wrote:

> Importance of humility. Warburg experience was very useful because it was humbling.
> Diffidence at all levels is a stimulus to effort. The opposite — excess of self-confidence (not self-confidence but excess!) is liable to induce inadequate effort.[148]

These are the views of a senior scientist who had amply proven himself and could look back on such an experience as the stimulus to successful efforts. During the winter of 1929–1930 he could probably not have given so optimistic an interpretation of the humbling experience that he was still undergoing. Perhaps he did see by then that prior to entering Warburg's laboratory, in the III Medical Clinic and in Rona's laboratory, where he compared himself to lesser investigators, he had displayed excessive self-confidence. Now he had found humility and diffidence, but he could not yet know that it would lead to greater effort.

In Krebs's temperament there were elements both of strong, willful determination and of timid diffidence. The comfort he took in his role as obedient research assistant to Warburg may reflect the same side of his character that had induced him as an adolescent to pick the safe goal of preparing himself to join his father's medical practice. He had afterward struck out on a more independent route, but in Warburg's laboratory Krebs seemed to fall again into a state of dependence. The shock of his abrupt "dismissal" may, therefore, have had the salutary effect of driving him toward self-reliance.

7

Moves Toward Autonomy

In his quest for a clinical position with research opportunities Hans Krebs faced multiple obstacles in early 1930. Not only would his Jewish background count against him, but he was seeking to launch his career in the midst of a deepening economic crisis that was causing widespread unemployment in Germany and threatening to bankrupt the government.[1] The clinics to which he applied for assistantships had many applications for few positions. Moreover, although his 4 years with Warburg had given him an exceptional scientific experience, it had left him in an unfavorable position to compete for medical posts. As the director of a clinic in Wurzburg put it in replying to his inquiry, "Since you are already 30 years old and have worked very little in internal medicine," and "most especially since, as I suspect, you intend to devote yourself to an academic career," he could give Krebs no hope of a position within the foreseeable future.[2] On the other hand, the very fact that Krebs had worked in the laboratory of the renowned Otto Warburg, and had published 16 papers from there, provided reason to regard him with respect. The director of the University clinic of the Charité Hospital in Berlin regretted that he had nothing to offer Krebs, but wrote that "in view of your achievements and what else I know about you, I can only wish that it were possible for you to be a member of the clinic."[3]

Such sentiments provided scant compensation for the fact that, having been rejected, as he thought, by his mentor for research, Krebs now had to bear the unpleasant additional rejection of his efforts to return to the clinical path. In this disheartening situation he found only one source of encouragement. At the Physiological Congress in Boston the previous fall he had met Dr. Klothilde Gollwitzer-Meier, a cardiovascular physiologist and physician 6 years older than him. They got on quite well, and back in Berlin met frequently to discuss mutual scientific interests. Dr. Gollwitzer-Meier formed a high regard for his ability, and drew on him for criticisms of various articles she was preparing for physiological textbooks. A personal friendship quickly grew between them, and she took a strong interest in his future career. As a well-respected scientist and clinician, recently appointed directing physician of the Internal Medicine Department of the St. Hildegard Hospital, she was in a position to exert some influence on his behalf. While Krebs was spending his last weeks in Dalhem, his friend "Thilde" recommended him to two of the leading investigators of metabolic diseases in Germany. One of them was the same Siegfried Thannhauser whose lectures Krebs had attended in Munich 8 years before. Thannhauser, now in Düsseldorf, wrote him at the end of February that "the conditions in my clinic do not at present permit me to give any promises for the immediate future," but he invited Krebs to discuss the matter further with him at the Annual Congress of Internal Medicine in Wiesbaden in April. The second person Gollwitzer-Meier contacted for him was Dr. Leo Lichtwitz at the Municipal Hospital in Altona, near Hamburg.[4]

In Wiesbaden Thannhauser probably explained that, although he had nothing available in Düsseldorf, he was expecting to receive a call to Freiburg, where he might be able to invite Krebs to come at a later time. Lichtwitz, who was also at the meeting, offered him an immediate post as an assistant in the Department of Medicine at Altona. He would have mainly clinical responsibilities. Little research was normally carried on at the municipal hospital, but Lichtwitz understood Krebs's desire to do some, and agreed to find money to provide him with a technician. Krebs was to begin on May 1, just 1 month after his departure from Dahlem.[5]

With his immediate future finally secured, Krebs went off with his father for a holiday at a health resort near Trieste. The elder Krebs being by this time uninterested in vigorous exercise, they spent what was for the son an exceptionally lazy time. The father was pleased and relieved that his son had decided to go into clinical medicine, where he could expect to earn a good living. While relaxing together, they met an older man, accompanied by a young woman, who took them for several rides in their automobile. At the end of the stay, Hans Krebs and the young woman parted as close friends.[6]

Near the end of April Krebs returned briefly to Dahlem. If he were to carry out research at Altona, he would need to have apparatus required for the kinds of experiments he had learned to do in Warburg's laboratory. The laboratory of the Altona Municipal Hospital already contained a few Warburg manometers, but not enough for his purposes. He decided, therefore, to apply to the *Notgemeinschaft der Deutschen Wissenschaft* for a grant to purchase 18 more manometers and other supporting equipment. To obtain such a grant he would have to have Warburg's support, but Warburg would agree to recommend him only on condition that Krebs work on a problem of interest to him. The project he wished Krebs to carry out was an investigation of whether proteins are hydrolyzed in tumor cells in the same way as in normal tissues. Krebs had no choice but to agree to these terms, even though he regarded the question as uninteresting, because the answer could be predicted in advance. Preparing his application in Dahlem on April 28, two days before he was to report at Altona, he dutifully requested the equipment grant "in order to carry out a work 'on the proteolysis of human cancer cells.'" Proteolysis in normal cells and cancer cells would be measured, he wrote, "with new methods worked out by me during the last year." Five days later he received a stiff note from Warburg. "In the tone of the enclosed application, there is still something that displeases me. For pedagogical reasons, I ask you to write [in place of 'new methods worked out...by me'] ...new methods devised by Professor Warburg and elaborated by me.'" Thus, even after requiring Krebs to leave his laboratory, Warburg attempted to limit his former assistant's research to secondary experiments subordinate to his own interests, and gratuitously humiliated him besides. We can only wonder whether Warburg dictated these terms out of self-centered insensitivity, or because he thought Krebs incapable of highly original work.[7]

In Altona, Krebs quickly found that clinical duties claimed all his attention. He was attached to a department in which patients were received, and had to be ready at all times to examine them. Not only was he busy throughout the day, but was on call during weekends, and on duty all night once every week. Having been out of touch with medicine for several years, he had to read extensively to refresh his knowledge and deepen his background. Moreover, he found clinical experience not only arduous, but absorbing and compelling. Three weeks after his arrival, he did perform two experiments, each lasting several days, on cobalt treatment of anemia in rats. The subject was remote from his previous scientific goals, he obtained no clear-cut results, and he pursued the matter no further. Otherwise, he carried out no research during his first four months there. Even if he had been able to spare the time, he would have been hindered from experimentation by his lack of the necessary apparatus. On May 15 he received word that the *Notgemeinschaft* had turned down his grant application, on the grounds that he was receiving free room and board at the Municipal Hospital![8] Some of his scientific friends apparently worried that his circumstances might force Krebs out of research altogether. Joseph Donegan, who had returned to Ireland after working with Krebs in 1929 in Warburg's laboratory, paid a visit to Dahlem in July 1930. Surprised and disappointed to find that Krebs was no longer there, Donegan learned from Hans Gaffron that in Altona Krebs would have time and laboratory space to carry on his work, "if only" he "had his manometers." While still in Berlin, Donegan wrote to Krebs expressing his concern:

I do hope you will have soon suitable conditions to continue your work, as it would be a shame if a "manometric" expert of your standing were cut off from research work. Doubtless you realize how unjust it would be and how dangerous for your future contentment if you allowed yourself to drift away from the laboratory life. Above all, be sure wherever you settle down to see that you will have ample opportunity to continue your special line and I shall look forward with pleasure to your next publication.[9]

In October Donegan wrote again asking Krebs if he had yet received his apparatus, and added "I understand how miserable it is to have the time and will to work and to be lacking the necessary materials. Especially so in your case as you have gone so far and with such success in research work that it would be a catastrophe for you if you had to leave it."[10]

These admonitions undoubtedly arose from Donegan's high regard for his young colleague's scientific promise, rather than from detailed knowledge of his current situation. Yet the impression that something might be amiss — "it is really difficult to understand the business" he wrote of Krebs's departure — must have been influenced by what Gaffron, one of Krebs's close scientific friends in Dahlem, told Donegan about that recent event. Gaffron may have imparted a sense of anxiety about Krebs shared by the colleagues who had known and admired him there. Hindsight should not distract us from the real uncertainty of Krebs's scientific prospects in 1930. Keen interest in continued involvement with research he undoubtedly had, but, given his own testimony that he had at the time no reason to suppose that he had outstanding talent as an investigator, he must have realized that he could not give unlimited priority to that goal. As he concentrated his effort on clinical work he found it quite rewarding. He proved to be a caring physician who spent as much time as he could with his patients, and became sensitive to their emotional needs as well as their physical problems.[11] Brought up in the tradition of medical service, trained primarily in medicine, seeking to remain financially independent of his family in a world that recognized the need for physicians far more widely than the need for biochemists, responding vigorously to the world of the hospital to which he had returned, Krebs might very well have appeared in 1930 to be headed toward a clinical life rather than a laboratory life. Perhaps he needed the encouragement of younger colleagues such as Donegan who, unlike his mentor, openly praised his scientific ability, to sustain his determination.

What Gaffron and Donegan may not have known, however, was that even while he had to postpone research in Altona, Krebs was busy making plans for a further move that would afford him more favorable opportunities for independent work. On July 2, Dr. S. Lauter, an assistant to Thannhauser, wrote Krebs to inform him that Thannhauser would be going to Freiburg on October 1, and to ask if Krebs would be interested in taking a position there as an assistant, to begin on the same date. Krebs had misgivings about leaving Lichtwitz so soon after he had been hired, but Thilde Gollwitzer-Meier encouraged him to go ahead. On July 5 she wrote him that he should "not let the matter with Thannhauser slip by, even if you offend Lichtwitz. You must think of yourself." Krebs may have found himself in a dilemma, for in addition to the gratitude he must have felt toward Lichtwitz for giving him a job when he most needed one, he quickly came to admire his new chief and to enjoy the intellectually stimulating environment that Lichtwitz maintained in his department. Seeking a compromise, he inquired whether it would be possible to come the following April 1, instead of October 1. Thannhauser agreed, although he insisted that Krebs make it clear to Lichtwitz that he had sought the new position and had not been lured away.[12] Lichtwitz must have been more understanding than his new assistant feared. Krebs's remaining time at Altona was a happy one, even though he had given notice, less than 3 months after his arrival, that he intended to leave.

In September, perhaps because he had received his apparatus, or because the technician he had been promised became available to him, but probably mainly because he had been placed in charge of a ward, instead of examining inpatients, and found it afterward easier to organize his time, Krebs resumed regular laboratory research. From then until he left Altona, he managed to carry out experiments, on an average, during more than 2 of every 3 days. Although he was frequently interrupted for clinical emergencies, his able full-time technician, a young woman who had been one of the first diabetic patients treated with insulin, carried on whatever operations were underway until he could return to the laboratory.[13]

Some historians of science have recently emphasized that the research programs that scientists carry out are "shaped" by local institutional circumstances.[14] Although these assertions tend to be one-sided, such factors do influence the research opportunities available to and the limits imposed on individual scientific investigations. The circumstances under which Krebs assumed his post in Altona sharply circumscribed the nature and the scope of the experiments he could pursue. What he did, however, cannot be explained by reference to his local position alone; his research path was the result of an interplay of forces, directed by his prior aspirations and experiences, by the long shadow of his former chief, and by contemporary developments elsewhere within the field of intermediary metabolism, as much as by the contingent restrictions and opportunities provided by his current institutional setting.

I

The investigation of proteolysis in tumor tissue imposed on Krebs at Altona was an extension of the experiments on enzymatic proteolysis that he had already performed in Dahlem, using the method he had devised in 1928 for measuring manometrically the cleavage of peptides.[15] Five weeks before leaving Warburg's laboratory, Krebs had completed an investigation of the proteolytic plant enzyme papain, in which he established that various heavy metals inhibit the enzymatic activity.[16] When, in Altona, he finally was able at the beginning of September to take up his laboratory activity again, he applied the same methods he had previously developed, to "cathepsin," the supposed intracellular proteolytic enzyme of animal tissue. After doing a few further experiments involving cathepsin and papain, he was interrupted for nearly a month, presumably by clinical duties. On October 4 he took up the action of heavy metals on cathepsin. Thus, he appeared to be moving systematically from his earlier studies toward the study of proteolysis in cells, in preparation to follow Warburg's direction to compare the process in normal and tumor tissue. On the same day that he resumed this task, however, he wrote down in his laboratory notebook some notations about a different problem, which he labeled "methylene blue respiration."[17]

Probably by scanning the latest issues of the few leading biochemical journals of the time, as he regularly did, Krebs had come across two articles that treated, in different ways, the same recently discovered phenomenon. For both papers the starting point was the observation made 2 years before, by George Harrop and Guzman Barron, that in a glucose solution containing methylene blue, mammalian red blood cells respire, absorbing molecular oxygen and evolving carbonic acid. This was a striking result, not only because mammalian erythrocytes normally are metabolically inert, but because this action might be related to the reduction of methylene blue in the presence of tissue extracts in the Thunberg system. One of the papers related to this finding that Krebs listed in his notebook was a short report in the June issue of the *Journal of Biological Chemistry* of a paper that W.B. Wendel and Philip A. Shaffer had presented at the March meeting of the American Society of Biological Chemists. In the experiments of Harrop and Barron methylene blue had appeared to inhibit the formation of lactic acid, even while stimulating the red cells to respire. Wendel and Shaffer thought it possible that the "decreased production" of lactic acid actually derived from the oxidation of the lactic acid formed. Their published abstract then asserted "Further study shows that the lactic acid which disappears from blood or erythrocyte suspensions in the presence of methylene blue is oxidized only to pyruvic acid, and, further, that this oxidation is quantitatively coupled with the oxidation of hemoglobin (to methemoglobin) and also of other known substances." The evidence they gave for the second claim was that the ratio of lactic acid oxidized to hemoglobin destroyed was constant, and that the total oxygen consumed was more than twice the quantity required to oxidize both of these substances.[18]

The second paper that caught Krebs's attention was by his own former chief. The May issue of the *Biochemische Zeitschrift* carried an article by Warburg, Fritz Kubowitz, and Walter Christian bearing the title "The Oxidation of Carbohydrate by Means of Methemoglobin (on the mechanism of a methylene blue catalysis)."[19] For Warburg even to discuss methylene blue as a respiratory catalyst was a stunning reversal of the attitude toward that subject that he had recently maintained. As the memo quoted in the previous chapter, of a conversation that Krebs typed out in January 1929, makes vividly clear, Warburg had been disdainful of the methylene blue method that the Thunberg school and others employed to investigate cellular respiration.[20] In October of that year, however, while he was visiting the Johns Hopkins Medical School, Barron demonstrated for him some of his experiments on red blood cells with methylene blue. This experience convinced Warburg that the reduction of methylene blue really was caused by an enzymatic action, rather than the action of unstable "transformation and decomposition products," as he was still claiming in the Herter Lecture, which he delivered during that very visit.[21] The reason that Barron's work impressed him so much more than that of Thunberg was "because here we have large, constant effects, not in some undefined sort of cell extracts or precipitates, but in living cells, and furthermore in a type of cells in which the normal respiration is too small to complicate the investigation." When he returned to Berlin, Warburg and his two assistants measured the respiratory quotient of rabbit erythrocytes undergoing "methylene blue respiration." Finding the $CO_2:O_2$ ratio to be less than one, they concluded that the oxidation was incomplete, and identified the product of the partial oxidation of glucose as pyruvic acid, by isolating the phenylhydrazone of that compound from the phosphate solution in which the red cells were suspended. Like Wendel and

Shaffer, they demonstrated that methylene blue in the presence of red blood cells oxidizes hemoglobin to methemoglobin. Since this conversion involves the oxidation of the ferrous iron in hemoglobin to ferric iron, Warburg was able to incorporate the phenomenon of methylene blue respiration into his own respiratory mechanism by asserting that here too the oxidation of sugar is a "combustion by means of iron heme."[22]

When Krebs compared the article of Wendel and Shaffer with that of Warburg, a hypothesis neither of them had proposed occurred to him:

> Following 1. [the article of Wendel and Shaffer] it is to be assumed that in 2. [the article of Warburg] it is the lactic acid which is oxidized, that therefore 2 partial processes can be distinguished.
> 1. Glycolysis by means of living cells
> 2. Oxidation of the lactic acid (perhaps without living cells??)

On the same day Krebs tested his idea experimentally. Using human erythrocytes suspended in phosphate solution, he measured the respective oxygen consumptions under four conditions:

With glucose added to the solution
With lactate added
With glucose plus methylene blue
With lactate plus methylene blue.

As could be predicted from the experiments of the previous investigators, the combination of glucose and methylene blue caused a large increase in the respiration; but lactate and methylene blue had little effect, contrary to his own idea that it is lactic acid that is being oxidized. Wondering if "perhaps the lactate does not penetrate" into the cells, he planned to "test an acidic solution." Instead he tried the next day to get around the difficulty by adding lactate and methylene blue to hemolyzed red cells, assuming, in accordance with his hypothesis, that lactic acid might be oxidized without living cells. From his results, however, he had to conclude "There is no oxidation of lactate. Only formation of methemoglobin."[23] (It is not immediately evident how he made this inference from the single set of manometer readings that he recorded. Perhaps they only led him to the conclusion that lactic acid is not oxidized, and that he accepted from the results of Wendel and Shaffer and Warburg that methemoglobin is formed.)

After obtaining these two negative results, Krebs abandoned his brief digression and returned to his mandated investigation of proteolysis. Although his hypothesis seemed to lead nowhere at the time, we can see in it a germinal significance far out of proportion to the two days time that he invested in it. The testing of his simple idea appears not only to have been his first small step toward an independent line of research, but also his first attempt to implement the idea he had not been permitted to carry out in Warburg's laboratory, the application of Warburg's methods to study intermediary metabolism.

Although Krebs was here in part following up an investigation by Warburg himself, he was viewing Warburg's results from a very different perspective.

For Warburg the more significant effect of methylene blue respiration was the transformation of hemoglobin to methemoglobin, and the main point was a new way to confirm the essential role he attributed to iron heme compounds in respiratory oxidations. Krebs paid only peripheral attention to the hemoglobin-methemoglobin reactions discussed both in Warburg's paper and Wendel and Shaffer's paper. He seized instead on the connections between glucose, lactic acid, and pyruvic acid that one could infer from the juxtaposed papers. For him, that is, the combined observations evoked a potential opportunity to separate the overall respiratory process into its two component stages, the glycolytic conversion of glucose to lactic acid, and the subsequent oxidation of the lactic acid. He may even have had in mind, although his fragmentary note does not explicitly say so, that he might be able to isolate the single oxidative step leading from lactic to pyruvic acid. Unlike his mentor, who was still preoccupied with the uniform general mechanism of respiratory oxidations,[24] Krebs approached the phenomenon of methylene blue respiration from the direction of those biochemists who sought to break the chains of metabolic processes down into their separate links.

Tacitly Krebs assumed the standard interpretation of the time, that the cellular respiration of carbohydrates is divisible into an anaerobic and an aerobic phase, and that the latter begins with the oxidation of lactate to pyruvate. His speculation that glycolysis requires living cells and that the oxidation of lactate might not was, however, a curious inversion of the current view. As we have seen in Chapter 1 (p. 15.), Meyerhof had recently been able to reproduce glycolysis in cell-free muscle extracts,[25] whereas respiratory oxidations had been demonstrated in isolated tissues only under conditions in which the cells were presumed to be largely intact. The most likely explanation for this idiosyncracy is that Krebs consciously or unconsciously associated two connections that were made separately in the two papers. Warburg had converted hemoglobin to methemoglobin in the presence of methylene blue both with intact red cells and with hemoglobin in solution. Wendel and Shaffer had asserted that the oxidation of methemoglobin and of lactate were "quantitatively coupled reactions." Krebs may, therefore, have surmised that if one of these two coupled reactions can take place "without living cells" then perhaps the other one also can.

The foregoing episode reveals an incipient feature of Hans Krebs's scientific style that proved to be characteristic. He was able to make a   connection between two articles in the current literature that led him to a simple but imaginative insight. Without pausing to explore deeper theoretical implications of the idea that he had had, he moved at once to test it experimentally in its rudimentary form. After two preliminary experiments turned out negative, he put his idea aside as readily as he had picked it up, and returned to his primary line of research. The wider aim behind the idea, however, did not vanish. He remained alert for similar opportunities to enter into the territory of intermediary metabolism that had long interested him.

II

As he went on with his mandated study, Krebs decided after a few more days that his manometric method for measuring proteolysis was too variable, and that it would be better to stick with the proven van Slyke method for determining the rate at which amino–nitrogen appears.[26] From tests of various experimental conditions on the activity of papain and cathepsin he progressed during October, November, and December to comparisons of the rates of proteolysis obtained from extracts of different tissue types.[27] Still inclined, however, to branch out from his assigned task, he went back on October 27 to Warburg's paper on methylene blue respiration, focusing this time on the other reaction involved, the formation of methemoglobin. Repeating Warburg's experiments with red blood cells, he then tried to reproduce the phenomenon with liver extract substituted for the methylene blue. His first effort failed, and he returned again to his main line. Late in November, however, he worked out a successful method for measuring the formation of methemoglobin manometrically. With it he was able, in early December, to convert hemoglobin to methemoglobin, both within red blood cells and in solution, by means of liver extracts. Pushing onward, he tested the effects of temperature, pH, and other conditions on the rate of the reaction. Through December and early January 1931, he alternated between proteolysis experiments and the line of investigation that appeared to be opening up for him; but the increasing frequency of the methemoglobin experiments and the declining frequency of the proteolysis ones leave little doubt that he found the prospects for his own new initiative more promising than for his supposed central problem.[28] By January 13 he had reached the conclusion that there was "No distinction [between the rates of formation of methemoglobin] from dissolved and undissolved hemoglobin. It follows from that that the active principle [in the liver extract] penetrates into the cells."[29] After 2 more days of experiments in this direction, Krebs switched abruptly, on January 15, to a problem that appears on the surface to have had no connection with the research he had been pursuing up until then.   The subject of his experiment that day was "yeast and monobromoacetic acid."

Whatever may have prompted Krebs to take this new turn just then, the inspiration was a recent set of investigations by the young Danish physiologist Einar Lundsgaard. In 1926 Lundsgaard had found unexpectedly that monoiodoacetate injected into a rabbit caused it to die about 20 minutes later in a state of extreme rigor mortis. Following up this observation with a brilliant sequence of experiments on intact animals and isolated muscles designed to close in step-by-step on the source of this effect, Lundsgaard reached the conclusion, by 1929, that the iodoacetate blocks the glycolytic formation of lactic acid in muscle tissue. In itself such a result was not extraordinary. It had been known for 15 years, for example, that fluoride inhibits glycolysis in muscles as well as fermentation in yeast. Iodoacetate might be seen as simply one more such agent, if Lundsgaard had left it at that, but he noticed that a muscle poisoned with iodoacetate could still contract for a time. He established, in fact, that such a muscle can perform as much work as a normal muscle, until it stiffens up. As

Lundsgaard quickly foresaw, this observation constituted a direct threat to the theory built up by Meyerhof over the past decade, that the formation of lactic acid is connected immediately to muscular contraction. The poisoned muscles obviously could contract under circumstances in which lactic acid could not form.[30]

The fact that muscles poisoned with iodoacetate did not enter rigor mortis until they had undergone contractions for a time led Lundsgaard to suspect that there must be some other substance in them, essential to their activity, which becomes eventually exhausted. A likely candidate was a phosphate compound discovered in muscle extracts in 1927, known as phosphagen, and already suspected to play some role in contraction. Lundsgaard was able to show that the phosphagen of poisoned muscles disappears when they contract, whereas in normal muscles the phosphagen content decreases only slightly. As a "working hypothesis," he proposed that "Phosphagen is the direct energy-forming material of muscle contraction. During contractions a steady resynthesis of phosphagen takes place. The energy required for this synthesis is derived from the formation of lactic acid." Therefore, when lactic acid cannot form, the phosphagen consumed cannot be replaced, and when it is gone the muscle can no longer contract.[31] Lundsgaard submitted a paper detailing his experiments and his interpretation to the *Biochemische Zeitschrift*, in October 1929. Beforehand, however, he wrote a letter to Meyerhof describing his findings. The news caused turmoil.[32] There was much discussion of it, both in Meyerhof's laboratory and in Warburg's laboratory, and Hans Krebs heard a good deal of this talk.[33]

Shortly afterward, Meyerhof and his group left Dahlem for Heidelberg, where he had been appointed head of the Kaiser Wilhelm Institute for Medical Research. Although understandably resistant to Lundsgaard's view at first, when he had studied the typescript of Lundsgaard's paper Meyerhof had to acknowledge that "this man may be right." Lundsgaard also wrote in his letter to Meyerhof that he would like to work in his laboratory to learn the modern methods of investigation of muscle metabolism, and to apply them to his discovery. Lundsgaard arrived in Heidelberg early in 1930, where he and Meyerhof collaborated for about 6 months, working out further implications of what soon appeared as a "revolution" in muscle physiology. In May Krebs's friend Hermann Blaschko joined in the work, came to know Lundsgaard well, and to regard him as an extremely intelligent scientist who thought problems through to their deepest levels.[34]

Although the most dramatic impact of Lundsgaard's discovery was on the question that Meyerhof had made central to the special field of muscle metabolism — how do the chemical processes in muscles achieve mechanical work? — Lundsgaard had already extended his investigation to take in the more general metabolic problem of how iodoacetate acts on the enzymatic decomposition of carbohydrate. In February 1930, he published two papers examining this question for the case of alcoholic fermentation. In the first paper he showed that monoiodoacetate, in a concentration of 1:5,000, completely inhibits fermentation in both living and dried brewer's yeast.[35] In the second he reported that yeast subjected to a range of concentrations of iodoacetate that inhibit fermentation nevertheless respire at near normal rates. Monoiodoacetate, therefore, provides, he asserted, "a method which makes possible the separation of the cleavage [or glycolytic metabolism] and the oxidative metabolism, in that it is able to eliminate the first of these without significantly affecting the second."[36]

For Lundsgaard these results entailed more than a promising new investigative method. Just as he had already challenged Meyerhof's special theory of muscle contraction, now he called into question the more general assumption that the oxidative metabolism of carbohydrates begins with the products of glycolysis; that is, the view commonly accepted during the 1920s that the oxidation is composed of successive anaerobic and aerobic phases. The fact that the yeast could continue to respire when their fermentation had been halted suggested to him that there may be "A decomposition of carbohydrate that is oxidative from the beginning, independent of the cleavage metabolism and of the products arising from the latter." He implied that this inference would also exclude the Meyerhof cycle, since that theory presumes that the lactic acid formed in glycolysis "covers completely the oxidative metabolism."[37]

One current view that Lundsgaard did *not* challenge was the scheme of alcoholic fermentation itself. He referred to Carl Neuberg's work as having "given, during the last ten years, an extraordinarily great extension to knowledge of the paths of the anaerobic decomposition of carbohydrates." Along with nearly everyone in 1930, Lundsgaard accepted that the key step was "the cleavage into a C_3-chain, probably methylglyoxal." He was less sanguine about knowledge of the oxidative path. Most physiologists, he wrote, "justifiably refrain from expressing themselves with certainty concerning the oxidative steps of carbohydrate metabolism."[38] This was the common perception of the relative state of knowledge about these two aspects of carbohydrate metabolism at the time, as we have seen in Chapter 1, despite Lundsgaard's disagreement with the common perception of their relation to one another. As we have also seen, there was no lack of hypothetical reaction schemes covering the oxidative steps, and there was nearly as much hypothetical about the Neuberg fermentation scheme as about the Thunberg–Wieland–Knoop oxidation scheme, but as Lundsgaard's typical commentary indicates, contemporaries did not perceive the situation that way. There may have been also a growing interest among Lundsgaard's generation of younger biochemists in tackling the problem of oxidative intermediary metabolism. Symbolic of the shift perhaps is a discussion that had taken place a year or so earlier in a colloquium in Meyerhof's small office in the laboratory at Dalhem. One of his young assistants asked him what happens in carbohydrate metabolism during the stages in which pyruvic acid is broken down. Meyerhof looked uneasy for a moment, and then replied, "it becomes CO_2 and water, doesn't it?" For Meyerhof, who had concentrated on fermentation and glycolysis, that was good enough. The oxidative stages lay only on the horizon of the intellectual domain on which he had fixed his attention. Those whom Meyerhof was training to become the next generation, however, was less satisfied, and began to set their sights on the territory beyond that horizon.[39]

An agent, such as monoiodoacetate, that could separate the oxidative from the glycolytic metabolism, might obviously play a role in the future elucidation of the oxidations. Already the other agent known to inhibit glycolysis had been utilized to help define the relation between the two processes. In Meyerhof's laboratory Fritz Lipmann showed, in 1928, that sodium fluoride at a concentration of 10^{-2} M completely inhibited the formation of lactic acid in chopped muscle tissue and reduced the respiration by 50 percent. By adding lactic acid to the poisoned muscle tissue he could restore the normal respiratory rate.[40] In 1930 in Cambridge, Eric Holmes extended similar methods to the metabolism of brain tissue. Holmes measured the respiration of minced tissue in Barcroft differential manometers, which operated similarly to Warburg manometers except that both sides contained reaction flasks. In one side one placed a control, so that the change in pressure measured the difference between the quantity of a gas absorbed or released in the test flask and in the control flask. Fluoride, Holmes showed, reduced the oxygen consumption of brain tissue both with and without added glucose. When he added lactic acid to the same tissue, however, it consumed oxygen at the normal rate, whether or not fluoride was present.[41] Unlike Lundsgaard's findings with yeast and iodoacetate, these experiments with fluoride fit readily into the standard view that glycolysis is the anaerobic stage preceding the aerobic stage of carbohydrate decomposition. Glucose must be converted to lactic acid before it can be oxidized. If, therefore, the first of these processes is blocked by fluoride, one would expect that glucose added to the medium cannot be oxidized, whereas lactic acid, the product of glycolysis, can directly enter the oxidative stage.

Holmes did not question the orthodox view of the connection between glycolysis and oxidative decomposition, but he did find reason, later in the same year, to doubt the elaboration of this relationship represented by the Meyerhof cycle. Continuing his studies of brain metabolism, he measured, with Charles Ashford, the changes in the carbohydrate content, the oxygen uptake, and the lactic acid consumption of chopped tissue to which they added lactic acid in the medium. From these relationships they could calculate a defined Meyerhof quotient, that is, a ratio between the total quantity of lactic acid that disappears and the quantity that is oxidized, a calculation that in Meyerhof's theory assumed that the lactic acid not oxidized is resynthesized to carbohydrate. Since they had *added* lactic acid from outside, they believed that according to the Meyerhof cycle there should be a net increase in the quantity of carbohydrate present in the tissue. Observing no such increase, they concluded "The fact that this is possible surely demands a suspension of judgment in the cases of those tissues where the existence of a 'Meyerhof cycle' is claimed, but in which no actual synthesis has been demonstrated by chemical means."[42]

III

Two of Hans Krebs's close friends, Blaschko and Nachmansohn, worked in Meyerhof's laboratory and participated in research related to questions that Lundsgaard's work raised for Meyerhof's theory of muscle metabolism. Krebs was himself attentive enough to Meyerhof's views to buy and read his integrative monograph *The Chemical Processes in Muscles* when it appeared in 1930 (just too soon to include Lundsgaard). Undoubtedly Krebs followed with interest the unsettling effects of Lundsgaard's discovery on the view he had often heard Meyerhof express, that the formation of lactic acid is more closely connected to the process of contraction than anything else.[43] It was not this aspect of Lundsgaard's investigation, however, that most attracted him. Rather, it was the two papers on yeast fermentation that stimulated him to carry out similar experiments.

Reading Lundsgaard's assertion that iodoacetate can block fermentation in yeast without inhibiting its respiration, Krebs must have perceived that there was a way to test this conclusion further by applying to yeast poisoned with iodoacetate the same approach that Lipmann had applied to muscle tissue poisoned with fluoride. If adding lactic acid to the muscle could restore its respiration, then perhaps adding alcohol to yeast could restore its respiration. That is, if the product of glycolysis can enter the oxidative stage of muscle metabolism, then the product of fermentation might similarly be able to enter the oxidative stage of yeast metabolism. Such reasoning implies that he questioned from the start Lundsgaard's inference that iodoacetate separates fermentation entirely from respiration and demonstrates that the two processes may proceed independently from the first step. By finding suitable conditions, Krebs must have expected, one might show that iodoacetate also inhibits the respiration. We cannot be certain just how he formulated the problem to himself, or of the order in which he reasoned it out, since his viewpoint at the beginning of his investigation can be inferred only from the design of the first experiment itself.

In his initial experiment of January 15, Krebs measured the oxygen consumption of suspensions of baker's yeast. In each of four manometer cups he placed 1 cm^3 of suspension. The medium consisted of a phosphate solution containing 0.5 percent glucose. A NaOH solution in the auxiliary compartment of each cup was used to absorb the CO_2 produced. The first flask served as the control. To the second and third he added monobromoacetic acid in concentrations of 1/100 N and 1/1,000 N. Into the last cup he put 1/100 N bromoacetic acid plus 10 percent alcohol. Undoubtedly Krebs used monobromoacetate in place of monoiodoacetate because he had none of the latter available, and Lundsgaard had mentioned in his first paper that the two substances had virtually identical effects.[44]

Recording the pressure changes at 10-minute intervals, Krebs could see very quickly that N/100 monobromoacetate reduced the respiration to about half the rate of the control, whereas in the flask containing N/100 monobromoacetate and alcohol the rate was nearly the same as in the control flask. Within the first 30 minutes of the experiment, therefore, he had reason to suspect that he was on the right track. In the next 30 minutes the respiration in the flask containing N/1,000 bromoacetate also began to fall noticeably below that in the control, which remained steady. At the end of 50 minutes, respiration had nearly ceased in the flask containing N/100 bromoacetate. He added 5 percent alcohol to it, but attained only a slight and temporary return of the respiration.

After an hour and a half the respiration had declined also to a very low level in the flask containing N/1,000 bromoacetate. Adding 1 percent alcohol to it, he was able to restore the rate nearly to the control rate, although it began to decline again after 20 more minutes.

The outcome was clear to Krebs;

1.   M/100 monobromoacetic acid inhibits respiration in sugar and in alcohol (in alcohol not as rapidly as in sugar.

2.   M/1000 monobromoacetic acid increasingly inhibits the respiration, almost completely in glucose, almost none in alcohol. Monobromoacetic acid-poisoned yeast therefore behaves as muscle tissue does, in that the respiration is increased by the addition of the product of the fermentative cleavage.

He drew a graph of his results, depicting elegantly the manner in which the addition of alcohol restored the respiration of yeast poisoned with M/1,000 monobromoacetic acid to a level approximating that of the unpoisoned yeast.[45]

Certain features of Krebs's new experimental venture clearly resembled those of his brief excursion into methylene blue respiration 3 months earlier. Both times he was exploring relationships between the anaerobic and oxidative stages of carbohydrate decomposition. The several investigators on whose work he drew were themselves interested in a range of problems to which methylene blue or iodoacetate, respectively, could be applied. Out of this range he fixed his attention in both cases on a particular zone within which the papers he had read overlapped. That zone embraced the use first of methylene blue and then of iodoacetate as agents to separate the two components of the overall metabolic pathway. His strategy in both cases was to compare the respiratory rate of a particular tissue in the presence of glucose, the starting point for the entire path, with that in the presence of the substance that served as the end point of the anaerobic portion and the starting point for the oxidative stage. This pattern suggests that Krebs was not merely reacting to any chance opportunity to apply Warburg's methods to intermediary metabolism, but that he had formed an active interest in carbohydrate metabolism.

In neither of these situations did Krebs bring to a current problem a novel theoretical conception or an innovative general experimental approach. His originality was limited to his capacity to connect ideas or conclusions presented separately by different authors, and to apply a method previously utilized on one problem to an analogous problem where it had not yet been done. He appeared not as a deeply meditative scientist thinking a problem through from its fundamentals, but as one rapidly absorbing current information and strategies, perceptive at bringing together ends left apart in the latest literature, alert to exploit gaps in existing arguments or experiments. These characteristics are hardly surprising. He was taking his first steps on his own, in a field replete with able scientists who had more experience than he had in the problems he hoped to investigate. He had still as much to assimilate as to contribute.

The most obvious difference between his first and his second attempts to enter this field was that his negative initial results in October dissuaded him from going further, whereas in January the appearance of a distinct effect on his first try encouraged him to pursue the new line. He must have felt heartened that in the midst of the mainstream of current work in intermediary carbohydrate metabolism he had located an unoccupied spot from which he might be able to launch himself on a course of independent investigation.

Satisfying as this initial outcome must have been, it was still only a preliminary indication that called for further development. "Next time," he wrote down, "wash the yeast to remove the alcohol!" By overlooking this step, he realized, he had not entirely eliminated the interfering effects that residual alcohol present in the yeast might exert on the experiments that were intended to test the action of iodoacetate on respiration in the presence of glucose. Also, he added, "investigate the influence [of iodoacetate] on fermentation and on respiration in parallel [experiments]."[46] Thus far he had measured only the respiration of the yeast, assuming from Lundsgaard's experiments that the iodoacetate completely inhibited the fermentation.

After performing a few proteolysis experiments, Krebs returned on January 20 to his yeast investigation. In place of the monobromoacetic acid he was now able to utilize monoidoacetic acid that he had obtained by mail from Lundsgaard himself. In his second experiment he incorporated exactly those refinements that he had set out for himself at the end of the first one. He washed the yeast in water, and he set up parallel fermentation and respiration experiments. The procedure required five simultaneous manometer set-ups: two controls for fermentation and respiration, one fermentation with iodoacetate, and two respiration experiments with iodoacetate. In all except the second of the iodoacetate respiration experiments he included glucose in the medium. In the latter he substituted for the glucose an equivalent concentration of alcohol. He used iodoacetate in a concentration of N/1,000. For the fermentation experiments he made the flasks anaerobic by filling them with argon, and measured the rate by the carbon dioxide formed. The results were unilluminating. The iodoacetate completely inhibited the fermentation and the respiration in glucose, and inhibited even the respiration in alcohol in increasing degree, reaching an 89 percent fall during the last 30 minutes of the 60-minute experiment.[47]

The next day Krebs repeated the experiment, using "less iodoacetate." The concentration this time was N/10,000, or one-tenth that of the preceding one. The results this time were that the iodoacetate "inhibits fermentation up to 90%. Inhibits respiration little, in alcohol more than in glucose??"[48] This equivocal outcome hardly supported the anticipation that alcohol should be able to restore respiration otherwise suppressed because an inhibited fermentation could not supply the alcohol required to sustain it. Having improved the rigor of his experiments he now found the situation less clear than before.

Perhaps reasoning that iodoacetate and bromoacetate may not, after all, act in exactly the same manner, and that he had better stick to the one that had initially worked for him, Krebs repeated the experiments once again on the same day, with a concentration of N/2,000 bromoacetate. This time the results were more satisfactory. Fermentation and respiration in glucose were both completely inhibited. Respiration in alcohol was only partially inhibited, 30 percent during the first 30 minutes, 60 percent during the third 30 minutes. This pattern fit his general viewpoint rather well. The next day, perhaps seeking conditions that would enable the respiration in alcohol to attain its normal rate, he carried out the same procedures with N/10,000 bromoacetate. The outcome only introduced a new complexity. The lower concentration still inhibited fermentation fully, but respiration only a little, and about the same amount in glucose as in alcohol, contrary to his view that when one blocked the fermentation one needed to add alcohol to sustain the respiration. The result led him to comment, "The inhibition of respiration and of fermentation therefore do not run parallel here, perhaps because at first alcohol is formed through fermentation?" Thus, to preserve his theoretical position in the face of this discordant experiment he had to entertain a secondary hypothesis, that in the initial period before the fermentation had ceased (the iodoacetate yeast fermented a little bit at first, declining to near zero during the first 20 minutes of the experiment) it had been able to generate enough alcohol to sustain the respiration during the remainder of the experiment. Obviously the situation called for continued investigation.[49]

Two days later, performing the same experiment yet again, with a concentration of bromoacetate intermediate between those of the two preceding trials (N/4,000), Krebs attained results approaching closer to the situation he sought. Fermentation and respiration in glucose were now fully inhibited. Respiration in alcohol was reduced only by 40 percent, and remained steady. Still, he was most likely unsatisfied with anything less than full restoration of the normal rate of oxygen consumption. Searching for more favorable conditions, he did the experiment again using a bicarbonate solution to provide an alkaline medium. All in this same day he carried out the procedures three more times with three different concentrations of bromoacetate. Two of them, N/4,000 and N/400, had no effect. With N/100 bromoacetate the fermentation was inhibited, but only gradually. He noted that in alkaline solution the rate of fermentation of yeast was smaller, in proportion to that of its respiration, than in phosphate solution.[50]

During the next week Krebs had little time for any experiments. After 6 days, on January 29, he was able to return to this investigation long enough to repeat the last portion of the preceding experiment, substituting iodoacetate for the bromoacetate. The fermentation of the yeast was slightly inhibited, its respiration was "not noticeably influenced."[51] After this, he abandoned the yeast investigation. The results he had attained were suggestive enough to sustain his interest in the general propositions he had in mind, but not clear-cut enough to provide the definitive demonstration he would need to prove his point.[52] Somehow he made the judgment at this point that it would not be worthwhile to continue to adjust the conditions to try to improve the results. From this distance, however, we cannot be certain whether he felt that there were no obvious further steps to take, whether he thought that the effort would be too tedious to undertake with his limited time, or whether he already had in mind to pursue the same problem eventually with other biological material.

For about a week after giving up the study of yeast metabolism Krebs stuck to his ongoing proteolysis investigation, which had by now reached a stage in which he was routinely measuring the rates at which extracts of various human tumor tissues hydrolyze proteins. The timing of his work during this period depended largely on when tumor material became available to him through surgical operations at the hospital or from autopsies performed at the associated Pathological Institute.[53]

On February 11 Krebs performed an experiment unrelated to anything he had been doing at Altona until then, but which harked back to two chronological layers of his past. The title he gave the experiment was "The metabolism of the choroid plexus." In it he measured the oxygen consumption of the tissue, and the anaerobic and aerobic formation of lactic acid. The experiment was a straightforward extension of the type of measurements Warburg had carried out on numerous tissues during the 1920s, and that Krebs himself had performed on human cancer tissues as one of his first assignments in Warburg's laboratory. One of Krebs's motivations for applying the measurements now to the choroid plexus was simply that this was one of the few tissues Warburg had "forgotten." He had, however, a deeper personal reason as well. Before he even encountered Warburg, his studies of the passage of dyes into the cerebrospinal fluid had interested him in the long-debated question of whether that fluid is formed by passive diffusion of solutes and water through the choroid plexus, or whether it is a product of active secretions. Now it occurred to him that one could shed some light on the issue by determining whether or not the choroid plexus maintained a high rate of metabolism characteristic of secretory cells. If there was any current outside stimulus involved in his taking up this problem, at this particular time, beyond his general desire to branch out into areas of his own choice, it may well have been the recent papers of Eric Holmes treating the relative rates of metabolism of different types of nervous tissue. Krebs emulated Holmes's approach in that he began by comparing the metabolic activity of the choroid plexus to that of another portion of the brain, the cerebral cortex. The fact that the choroid plexus consumed oxygen twice as rapidly as the cortex tissue must have given Krebs immediate encouragement that his study could bear decisively on the question at issue.[54]

As he began this investigation, one of his fellow assistants in the Department of Medicine, Hans Rosenhagen, asked to join in. Rosenhagen, a neurologist, was interested in the experiments because they involved the brain, and he wished also to learn the experimental techniques used in such studies.[55]

On the same day that he performed these first experiments on the choroid plexus, Krebs was using Jenson sarcoma, a standardized transplantable rat tumor, in his proteolysis studies. Two days later, on February 13, he tested the effects of iodoacetate on the formation of lactic acid in this tissue. The results were clear cut. The normal Q value was 28.2. With an iodoacetate concentration of 3×10^{-5} M, the rate fell to 6.6; with 3×10^{-4} to 1.9; and with 3×10^{-3} to 2.1.[56] Whether he had made the choice in advance, or decided on the spot to test material he happened to have on hand with iodoacetate, from this juncture onward he pursued the general problem he had formulated around the effects of iodoacetate exclusively with animal tissue. Lactic acid, the product of animal glycolysis, therefore, replaced the role alcohol had up until then played in his experimental system.

His attention now directed simultaneously on three lines of investigation, Krebs rotated rapidly between experiments on proteolysis, the choroid plexus, and the iodoacetate effect. On February 17 he compared the metabolic rate of choroid plexus tissue with that of the gray matter of the brain, and again found the first of these far more active. At the same time Dr. Rosenhagen measured the rate of the metabolism of the thalamus tissue of the brain, which turned out close to that of gray matter. Again using the same material for two purposes, Krebs tested on the 19th the action of iodoacetate on cerebral gray matter. He tested four conditions: glucose added with and without iodoacetate, and lactate added with and without iodoacetate. He used 5×10^{-4} iodoacetate and carried out the experiments in phosphate solution. On the first try he achieved the definitive outcome that had repeatedly eluded him with yeast. With glucose the iodoacetate totally blocked the respiration. With lactate the respiration was almost exactly equal to the normal respiration for the first 30 minutes, declining somewhat in the second half hour.[57]

In the wake of this auspicious success Krebs again shifted suddenly to what appears an unrelated experiment, although one clearly within the bounds of intermediary carbohydrate metabolism. On the next day he measured the effects of pyruvic acid on the oxygen consumption, carbon dioxide production, lactic acid formation, and respiratory quotient of rat kidney slices. To measure all of these quantities he used Warburg's technique requiring double runs with differing volumes of fluid in the two manometer flasks. One double run with only glucose added to the Ringer's solution represented the control; to the other he added 18 mg/100 ml pyruvic acid. To measure the anaerobic formation of lactic acid, he replaced the oxygen in two of the vessels with argon halfway through the experiment. The pyruvic acid nearly doubled both the respiration and the anaerobic glycolysis, while the respiratory quotient changed only slightly.[58]

While the choice of rat kidney may perhaps be explained by the fact that he was utilizing that same tissue in his proteolysis work just then, it is difficult to connect the experiment itself in any close way to his ongoing special metabolic investigations. Perhaps we need not expect a tight connection, or a specific motivation. Pyruvic acid had become so central to the whole field of intermediary metabolism that anyone entering this area would sooner or later test its activity within his particular experimental system. In that sense he merely confirmed that it is a highly active metabolite. More intriguing is why he should have tested the effects of pyruvate on glycolysis, as current theory associated the substance with the oxidative stage of carbohydrate metabolism. The fact that Krebs did not include an anaerobic run at the beginning, but only converted two of the flasks to that condition during the course of the experiment, after he had made measurements for long enough to calculate the aerobic values, tempts us to the possibility that he tried this as an afterthought, perhaps with no preconceptions about what would happen. That the pyruvic acid raised the Q value for the anaerobic formation of lactic acid from 4.7 to 11.7 ought to have been a striking effect. Krebs made no comment in his notebook about it, but it obviously engaged his interest, for he performed, on the following day, an experiment designed to explore more fully this effect. Simplifying the aerobic part of the experiment by measuring only the oxygen consumption, and using argon in two of the four runs from the start, he verified that pyruvic acid substantially accelerates both the respiration and glycolysis of kidney tissue.[59]

On the same day Krebs pursued a step further his study of the action of iodoacetate on brain tissue, by testing its effects on the respiratory quotient. He again applied the double run method to measure simultaneously the oxygen consumption and carbon dioxide production. To both the normal tissue and that poisoned with N/5,000 monoiodoacetate he added 0.2 percent Na-lactate; therefore, he clearly intended to establish conditions in which he anticipated that the respiration would be uninhibited by the iodoacetate. The overall rates were somewhat lower than he expected, leading him to suspect that some white matter had been incorporated into the slices of gray matter. "At any rate," he noted, there was "no inhibition by the monoiodoacetate." So far, so good; but the respiratory quotient for the normal tissue was 0.39, whereas for the poisoned tissue it was 0.5; the iodoacetate must have altered the oxidative process in some manner. Calculating that the combustion of lactate theoretically should produce a respiratory quotient of 0.660, which was closer to that of the poisoned than the unpoisoned tissue, he surmised that perhaps in the normal tissue there was a "resynthesis" — that is, that some of the lactate was converted back to carbohydrate in the sense of the Meyerhof cycle — whereas in the poisoned tissue the synthesis might have been inhibited by the iodoacetate, therefore, nearly all of the lactate was burned. He posed these interpretations only as shorthand queries. Clearly the experiment raised more questions than it answered.[60]

Returning once more, on February 24, to the metabolism of the choroid plexus, Krebs measured the respiration, aerobic and anaerobic glycolysis of four types of nervous tissue — choroid tissue from the surface of the lateral ventricle, white matter, cortex, and medullary stem tissue — all taken from the brain of a rabbit. Again the choroid tissue was by far the most active. Its Q_{O_2} value was -17.5, compared with -10.4, -9.9, and -4.6, respectively, for the other three tissues. Probably quite satisfied now that he had established the extraordinary metabolic activity of the choroid plexus, he closed out this investigation and moved quickly on to the several other lines that remained unfinished. The next day he performed simultaneously a set of experiments on the effect of pyruvic acid on the respiration of rat kidney slices, and an identical set on liver slices. In each case he compared the oxygen consumption of the tissue (in phosphate Ringer's solution) with glucose alone, to that with glucose plus lactate, glucose plus pyruvate, and glucose plus pyruvate and lactate. In both tissues lactate increased the respiration somewhat more than pyruvate did, although both had substantial effects, and the two together raised it higher than either alone, although not enough to suggest that the effects were additive. At the bottom of the record of the liver tissue experiment, he noted that pyruvate added to glucose alone increased the respiration by 11 percent, whereas added to glucose plus lactate it raised the rate by a further 17 percent.[61] There is no other clue in his laboratory notebook to indicate what particular idea Krebs may have been testing. It is perhaps significant, however, that instead of exploring further the surprising anaerobic effect he had found in his previous experiments with pyruvate, he fixed his attention on the expected aerobic effects. At first glance this course appears almost as though he was missing the road that was more likely to lead to something novel. Perhaps he simply did not have any explanation for the anaerobic effect that would give him a direction to follow. Or perhaps he returned to the aerobic effects because in his efforts to separate glycolysis and oxidative carbohydrate metabolism he was aiming all along at strategies to investigate the latter. If so, it would seem a prerequisite to test in his system of Warburg manometers and tissue slices the behavior of the two substances, lactate and pyruvate, most commonly invoked as the principal members of the chemical reaction supposed to initiate the aerobic phase.

After 2 days dutifully spent measuring proteolysis in various avian and human tissues, Krebs pressed forward on the iodoacetate investigation, which he clearly saw now as a most promising means to advance his interest in carbohydrate metabolism. On February 27 he performed an elaborate set of measurements using slices of testicle tissue. For each of the three crucial conditions — anaerobic glycolysis, respiration with glucose, and respiration with lactate — he set up a set of five runs, using four concentrations of monoiodoacetate in a series of orders of magnitude, plus a control. The results were highly satisfying. The lowest two concentrations had no effect, but the highest two bracketed nicely the ideal demonstration he was seeking. He expressed the result in his notebook as follows:[62]

[Iodoacetate concentration]	N/300	N/3000	N/30000
Fermentation — inhibition	100%	83%	0
Respiration — inhibition			
(a) in glucose	100%	52%	0
(b) in lactate	11%	0	0

Such figures would encourage the belief that with some further adjustments he could attain a result in which fermentation and glucose respiration were totally suppressed while lactate respiration remained completely normal.

Krebs found time that same day to carry out five measurements of proteolysis on human tissues obtained from a postmortem examination, and to test the proteolytic action of washed and centrifuged human cells (of unspecified type) on various types of protein.[63] On March 3 also he was both able to add two more measurements of the proteolytic action of cathepsin and to perform a more intensive set of experiments on iodoacetate. The latter, using Jensen sarcoma tissue, was very similar to the preceding set on testicle tissue. The results were also similar, but less clean. The lower of the two concentrations of iodoacetate he used inhibited glycolysis by only 25 percent, and glucose respiration not at all. The higher concentration inhibited the glycolysis by 84 percent and the glucose respiration by 68 percent, but also lowered the lactate respiration by about one third. On the same day he compared the effects of iodoacetate on glucose and lactate respiration only, using rat kidney slices. These results too were equivocal, although in the right general direction. The glucose respiration dropped by two thirds, the lactate respiration by one fifth. On March 9 he carried out the same procedures with rat testicle tissue, and with kidney cortex tissue. The results followed the same general pattern as in the previous experiment.[64]

On the same day, March 9, Krebs added a new dimension to this investigation. In an experiment headed "Monoiodoacetate: various hydroxyacids, etc.," he measured the respiration of rat testicle slices placed in phosphate Ringer's solution containing glucose and monoiodoacetate. In each of six manometer vessels he placed a different additional substance. These included the neutral salts of tartaric, citric, pyruvic, β-hydroxybutyric, and lactic acid, and the amino acid glycine. Two additional flasks containing only the slices and phosphate Ringer's solution served as controls. The values for the oxygen consumption that he obtained for four of the trials were:

Control	Q_{O_2}	=	-14.9
Tartrate		=	-4.7
Citrate		=	-4.9
Pyruvate		=	-10.9

The second set he carried out using a different type of manometer vessel and a separate control.

Control	Q_{O_2}	=	-10.3
Glycine		=	-3.5
β-Hydroxybutryic acid		=	-5.8
Lactate		=	-12.9

In the earlier experiments of the same day on testicle tissue with the same concentration of iodoacetate, he had found that respiration with glucose alone gave $Q_{O_2} = 3.8$. It appeared, therefore, that of all the substances he tried, in addition to lactate, only pyruvate acted in a similar way to restore the aerobic respiration in tissues whose glycolysis had been blocked. That outcome was apparently so uninteresting to Krebs that on the next page, where he had placed the usual heading "Results," he did not bother to write anything down.[65]

We can readily see why these results would have appeared negative to him. He knew already that lactate increased the respiration of iodoacetate-poisoned tissues. That pyruvate acted similarly was a new finding, but an entirely expected one, as it was commonly accepted that the first step in the oxidation of lactate gave rise to pyruvate. The significance of this experiment lies less in what Krebs found than in what he tried; for his strategy seems transparent. With a system in which he could block the anaerobic phase of carbohydrate metabolism and restore the oxidative phase by adding the substance assumed to initiate that phase, he could also hope to restore oxidative activity by supplying substances that occupy subsequent steps in the oxidative pathway. It is possible that such a maneuver only occurred to him on the spot, but more likely that something like this had been all along the general goal of his efforts to separate carbohydrate metabolism into its partial processes. This experiment, more than any other, reinforces our view that in seeking to isolate these two phases it was the oxidative portion that he wished to study. By now, if not before, he had probably framed the idea he has recently described as his starting point: that, "if it was possible to establish the pathway of glycolysis, then it ought to be possible to establish the pathway of oxidative metabolism."[66]

By this time, as we have seen, the nature of the oxidative path of carbohydrate metabolism was widely perceived as one of the central unsolved problems of intermediary metabolism. That is no doubt exactly why Krebs was attracted to the problem. Otto Warburg wrote, much later, "A scientist must have the courage to attack the great unsolved problems of his time. Solutions usually have to be found by carrying out innumerable experiments without much critical hesitation."[67] All along Warburg had instilled the attitude encapsulated in these sentences into those who worked in his laboratory. Hans Krebs took the lesson to heart. In these experiments on iodoacetate we can follow his first attempts to live up to his mentor's precept.

The phrase "without much critical hesitation" in Warburg's motto is as important as the rest of the statement to understand Krebs's scientific approach. There is no evidence, from contemporary documents or from his later recollections, that Krebs undertook a deep study of the theoretical and experimental foundations of intermediary metabolism before he began his own experiments. He kept up with the current literature, and he gradually expanded his knowledge of the earlier background as well; but he did not pause to construct a detailed conceptual structure to attack the problem.[68] Equipped by Warburg with simple but powerful methods that enabled him to carry out, if not "innumerable" experiments, at least several sets of multiple experiments on any given day that he could spend in the laboratory, Krebs preferred to try out whatever occurred to him, as soon as possible, knowing that whenever an idea did not work out, he would have invested relatively little time and energy in vain, and could move on just as quickly to another idea.

The experiment on "various hydroxyacids, etc." of March 9 displays these characteristics particularly well. The six substances Krebs chose to test do not suggest that he was examining any specific theoretical metabolic pathway. Lactate and pyruvate represented the two substances that almost everyone expected to play central roles in oxidative metabolism. He probably chose citrate because it was one of the small group of organic acids known since the work of Battelli and Stern to activate respiration in isolated tissues. The fact that he selected citrate rather than succinate, fumarate, or malate probably indicates no more than that, at the time, he was not concerned about the hypothetical schemes into which the latter substances had been incorporated. Tartrate was an active hydrogen donor in the Thunberg methylene blue system. β-Hydroxybutyric acid was one of the ketone bodies that had a long accepted place in the β-oxidation scheme of fatty acid metabolism. Glycine represented amino acid metabolism. This was a scattered approach to the problem. Krebs was just scanning the horizon of oxidative intermediary metabolism, looking for a lead to pursue. He was not so much testing metabolic theories as testing the capacity of his experimental system to provide him with a foothold on the current research front.

IV

When Krebs undertook this first step toward an enlargement of his metabolic investigation, on March 9, his time at Altona had nearly run out. Only 3 weeks remained until he was due in Freiburg. Perhaps he was already beginning to prepare his apparatus for the move, as he carried out only one more set of experiments, on the proteolytic action of tissue slices,[69] during the remainder of March. Determined, however, to wrap up the results of the work he had already accomplished before he packed up his bags, he began on the day after the last iodoacetate experiments to assemble the information necessary to publish papers on each of the three problems on which he had done substantial work. First he reviewed the literature relevant to the iodoacetate investigation. Since he had begun in January, Hans von Euler, Ragnar Nilsson, and Karl Zeile in Stockholm had published an article that also followed up on Lundsgaard's experiments on yeast, but they had focused on the effort to identify the glycolytic reaction that iodoacetate blocks.[70] Krebs made a reference to the four pioneering papers of Lundsgaard, placing two exclamation points after the articles on yeast that had been his own starting point. He took note also of Eric Holmes's recent articles on brain metabolism, summarizing Holmes and Ashford's opinion as, "Meyerhof cycle is not proven, is held to be questionable." From Holmes's earlier article he picked out the conclusion "Fluoride inhibits in pyruvate and glucose, but not in pyruvate and lactate." This result undoubtedly suggested to Krebs interesting comparisons with the results he himself had obtained with iodoacetate.[71]

As we have seen, although Krebs had been able to inhibit anaerobic glycolysis and glucose respiration strongly with iodoacetate in animal tissues while reducing lactate respiration only slightly, he had never been able to block the first two totally while leaving the latter entirely unaffected. In his notebook he now wrote a probing reflection on the meaning of this situation, and on how he might examine it further when he resumed his work:

On monoiodoacetic acid

Cause of the inhibition even in the presence of lactate
1) Because the cells are deprived of glycolysis: In that case the decrease in the respiration must be independent of the monoiodoacetic acid.
2) Perhaps because there exist 2 effects of the monoiodoacetic acid
   a) On the glycolysis, and as a consequence of that on the respiration.

b) Directly on the respiration, developing gradually. (with
   higher concentrations it must develop rapidly).

Whether 1 or 2, or both, actually happen, is not yet determined. If 1 is correct, then the respiration must also decrease in lactate without glucose and without monoiodoacetic acid, if the cells contain no glucose. It appears that in fact the respiration does < ... > decrease in lactate, but not as much as in glucose. It remains to test (by measurements of glycolysis without glucose), how much of carbohydrate capable of undergoing cleavage the cells contain, and by simultaneous measurements of the respiration in lactate, whether and for how long the respiration is sustained after the exhaustion of this carbohydrate.[72]

This valuable glimpse of the young scientist reasoning his way through an unresolved experimental difficulty captures the intimate interplay between daily thought and laboratory operation that Krebs all too seldom recorded in his notebook, but that lies at the heart of creative scientific activity. It suggests also one of the early signs of his research productivity: that an unexpected complexity posed not merely an obstacle, but an opportunity to define further experimental questions.

On March 21, Krebs wrote in his notebook a note on "The Lactic Acid Cycle in the Brain," which indicates his continuing concern over the doubts Holmes and Ashford had raised about the existence of the Meyerhof cycle in such tissues:

Holmes found, to be sure, an inhibition of respiration with fluoride, that can be overcome with lactate (Biochem. J 24, 914, 930).
Yet Holmes and Ashford (Biochem. J. 24, 1119) found no increase in carbohydrate, when lactate disappears, and therefore doubt the existence of the cycle.
Yet they worked with phosphate Ringer, where it is *certain* that the Pasteur reaction is suppressed, since even in serum a partial interruption occurs.[73]

To expand slightly on this abbreviated expression of his thoughts, Krebs reasoned in the first statement that Holmes's result with fluoride actually supports the Meyerhof cycle insofar as the oxidation of lactate was in Meyerhof's theory essential to respiration. The remainder of the note attempts to disarm the experimental objection Holmes and Ashford had raised to the Meyerhof cycle by assuming that the suppression of the Pasteur reaction under their experimental conditions would permit the carbohydrate resynthesized to break down again, through aerobic glycolysis, instead of accumulating.

Despite this argument, another note that he wrote in the back of his notebook implies that Krebs took seriously the assertion by Holmes and Ashford that the existence of the lactic acid cycle in tissues other than muscle remained to be proven, and that he contemplated making such an effort himself. The investigation would be an extension of the experiments he had already carried out. One would "inhibit the respiration, by inhibiting the fermentation, and then abolish the inhibition of respiration by supplying a product of glycolysis." As a glycolysis product he pondered trying not the usual lactate, but glyceraldehyde, a three-carbon breakdown product of carbohydrate that had often been suggested as an alternative to the methylglyoxal of Neuberg's glycolytic scheme. One of the obstacles to the investigation he foresaw was that one "lacks a specific inhibitor of glycolysis!!" His recent experiments had left him unsatisfied that monoiodoacetate and monobromoacetate were specific enough, and fluoride had the disadvantage that it "does not penetrate into most cells."[74]

Even as he mused in private over unresolved questions surrounding his iodoacetate investigation, and projected ways he might deal with them in the future, Krebs was finishing a paper intended to present his results as a completed piece of work. In doing so he was conforming to normal practice; a scientist is constrained by the customary mode of formal journal communication to divide his ongoing research activity into segments that can be treated publicly as bounded, coherent investigations. In this case the impending break in his activity dictated by his move superimposed a more arbitrary incentive to regard the point at which he had arrived as the termination of what he had begun.

The paper that Krebs submitted to the *Biochemische Zeitschrift* on March 22 was a model of succinct argument. Noting Lundsgaard's finding that monoiodoacetate blocks lactic fermentation in animal cells without affecting their respiration, he asserted:

> A closer investigation of the effect of monoiodoacetate on cellular metabolism, about which I am reporting in this article, leads to new results that are of general significance for the question of the connections between respiration and glycolysis. In particular, it turns out that cells poisoned with iodoacetate and no longer capable of glycolysis can respire only in the presence of lactic acid.... If one suspends gray matter of the brain, testicle tissue, or rat sarcoma in Ringer solution containing glucose and adds N/3,000 monoiodoacetate to it, glycolysis and respiration stop. If one adds lactate to the solution, however, the respiration appears.
>
> These facts become understandable, if one accepts that the same lactic acid cycle that Meyerhof found in muscle also takes place in brain or testicle cells. In a first, anaerobic phase of metabolism carbohydrate is cleaved to lactic acid, in a second, aerobic phase the lactic acid disappears, mainly through resynthesis [of carbohydrate]. If one inhibits the first phase, the anaerobic lactic acid formation, one breaks the cycle and brings the metabolism to a halt. The second phase, the respiration, stops. If one substitutes for the first phase of anaerobic lactic acid formation an artificial supply of lactate, the respiration reappears.[75]

His experimental results, Krebs claimed, fully support this theory. The same concentration of iodoacetic acid necessary to inhibit glycolysis also inhibits respiration in the presence of glucose.

Following a description of his methods, Krebs presented his data in tabular form. He reported the results of one experiment for each of the three types of tissue, grouping those for glycolysis together in one table, and those for respiration in three separate tables. This format emphasized the aggregate results rather than the full set of data for any given experiment. He also included one complete protocol, taken from the experiment of February 24 on rat testicle tissue, which had most nearly approximated the ideal conditions he had sought.[76]

A close look at Krebs's published data shows, as does his laboratory notebook record, that the lactate did not in every case fully restore the normal rate of respiration at the same concentration of iodoacetate that fully inhibited the glycolysis and glucose respiration. The only public concession he made to such departures from his unqualified general statement of the results, was to comment that "the abolition of the inhibition is complete over short experimental times. During longer experimental times the respiration with monoiodoacetate sinks even in solutions containing lactate, perhaps because as a consequence of the inhibition of the glycolysis the cells are gradually being destroyed.[77] He gave no hint in his paper that he was uncertain whether these lowered respiration rates were an indirect effect of the inhibition of the glycolysis, or a separate inhibitory action of iodoacetate exerted directly on the respiration.

Perhaps Krebs was not entirely candid in omitting public discussion of an imperfection in his results about which he had some private concern. Yet he was making a type of judgment that a scientist must often make. He was in all likelihood not suppressing real doubts about the validity of his statements, but had the self-confidence to decide that these were secondary problems that would eventually be resolved without damage to his conclusions.

We may also notice in Krebs's paper a logical hiatus in his introductory discussion of the significance of his results. In the literature that formed the immediate background to his work, two separate issues relevant to the validity of the Meyerhof cycle had been raised. Lundsgaard's assertion that the aerobic decomposition of carbohydrate may proceed independently of glycolysis from the first steps onward challenged the premise, shared by the Meyerhof theory and most other current views of carbohydrate metabolism, that the oxidative steps begin with the product of glycolysis. Holmes and Ashford's finding that there is no increase in the quantity of carbohydrate present in brain tissue, even when the added lactate has disappeared, challenged the applicability to that tissue of the most distinctive feature of the Meyerhof cycle itself, the claim that a portion of the lactate is not oxidized, but resynthesized to carbohydrate. Krebs's experimental result constituted an effective reply to Lundsgaard's more general challenge, but did not bear on the more specific challenge to the Meyerhof cycle brought up by Holmes and Ashford. As we have seen, Krebs privately found reason to discount Holmes and Ashford's experimental result as due to a suppression of the Pasteur reaction. Privately, he also shared the opinion that the existence of the Meyerhof cycle in these tissues had yet to be proven. Nevertheless he concluded publicly, "These investigations support the interpretation expressed earlier, that the same lactic acid cycle that exists in muscle is also present in other tissues."[78] The interpretation to which he referred was one that Otto Warburg had expressed in his monograph "The Metabolism of Tumors," in 1926. It is not unlikely that Krebs's interpretation of his own results was somewhat swayed by loyalty to his former chief.

Warburg's influence perhaps worked to Krebs's disadvantage in this situation. Warburg's insistence on brevity in scientific writing probably served in general as a salutary curb on the tendency Krebs had displayed in the papers he had written on his own in 1925 and 1926, to include elaborate discussions of the relationship between his work and previous work in the field. Here, however, he compressed his discussion so far that he did not even define the issue clearly. He barely alluded to Lundsgaard's argument, and did not mention Holmes and Ashford's argument at all. Thus, by emulating too strictly his mentor's succinct style, he failed to situate his work as effectively as he might have within the contemporary stream of investigation.

Despite such minor flaws, this little paper was still a solid scientific achievement for an investigator striving to emerge from the shadow of his autocratic mentor and to generate his own line of research even while still obligated to do Warburg's work, all in the midst of a busy life as a clinician. The magnitude of the contribution cannot be compared with that of the other young scientist on whose discovery it depended. It added only a secondary increment to Lundsgaard's impressive discoveries. It served notice, however, that a determined and competitive newcomer was entering a demanding field. For someone who had still to convince himself and others that he was capable of first-rate, original work, these were no small gains. When asked 45 years later about this paper, Krebs described it as "an important step in my independent thinking." It was "limited in scope," but it was "a beginning, by way of publication, my first indication that I was interested in the intermediary stages of the oxidation of carbohydrates."[79] Although this judgment draws on insight derived from the unfolding of later events, it is an eminently sound historical evaluation. The paper on the effects of iodoacetate was the 28th scientific paper that Krebs had published, but in a deeper sense it was the first publication of his own research career.

The second paper Krebs wrote, co-authored with Rosenhagen, was "On the Metabolism of the Choroid Plexus." Compared to the iodoacetate investigation, both the paper and the research on which it was based were entirely uncomplicated. A direct application of Warburg's procedures, the project had required only three separate sets of experiments, none of which raised problems. From the striking result that the metabolism of the choroid membrane was of the order of magnitude of the tissues of secretory organs such as the liver or kidneys, he drew a conclusion whose broad implications contrasted with the simplicity of the investigation. "This means, that the formation of the cerebrospinal fluid occurs in cells, in which prerequisite conditions for active work are present. The proof of a large energy-metabolism in the choroid plexus supplies the foundation for accepting that the formation of the fluid and its passage through 'the blood-fluid barrier' is determined not only by physical forces (dialysis) but also by the secretory work of the plexus cells (dilution, concentration)."[80] So convincing was this compact argument, that the seemingly minor publication setting it forth has often been cited in support of the secretory theory of the cerebrospinal fluid.

Krebs sent his paper on the choroid plexus off for publication on the eve of his departure. There was one further paper that he was expected to complete, the report on his investigation of proteolysis that he owed to Warburg. The investigation had shown just what Warburg wanted it to show, that there were no significant differences between proteolysis in tumor cells and in normal tissue cells. It is revealing of Krebs's attitude toward this work, that this highly organized man, who truly lived by the motto "never put off until tomorrow what can be done today," did not get around to submitting his paper on the "Proteolysis of Tumors,"[81] until 2 months after he had ended the experiments and left Altona.

V

Early in 1931 Georg Krebs remarried. Maria Werth, a teacher who had earlier been his patient, was more than 30 years younger than the elder Krebs, now 64. She was also a Roman Catholic with strong religious beliefs. In 1930 Georg Krebs had come to Berlin to see Wolf, who was recovering from an operation for appendicitis, and mentioned his plan to marry. Knowing how lonely his father had been, Wolf encouraged him. Hans and Lise, to whom their father wrote for their advice, had reservations about him marrying someone so much younger — Maria was exactly 2 years younger than Hans — but did not oppose him taking the step. None of the children was able to attend the wedding. Despite the differences in their ages and their religious outlooks, Georg and Maria Krebs appeared to be very happy together.[82]

For most of the year that Hans Krebs spent in the Municipal Hospital of Altona, he had been looking forward to the move to Freiburg, where he anticipated that more ample facilities and the university setting would afford him expanded scope for his research ambitions. The intervening months had been for him, however, far more than an interlude. He had taken his first crucial steps along the road toward independence as a scientific investigator. Moreover, his research experiences were not the only ones that really mattered to him. His clinical work also became deeply meaningful to him. The intellectual atmosphere in the hospital was stimulating, and he felt that he received fine training there. His friend David Nachmansohn was also on the clinical staff, and he formed strong friendships with two other colleagues, Georg Tidow and Walter Auerbach. He took pleasure in working closely with people whom he respected and appreciated.[83] Looking back on this period from the distance of nearly half a century, Krebs remembered it as "a time when the work itself gave the greatest satisfaction, because we knew that everything was organized in an excellent, a fair way, and that we really did good medical work as a team, as good as was done anywhere in Germany."[84]

There were also unforgettable moments of dramatic tension in Krebs's medical life. He experienced the tragedy of watching several young children under his charge in the ward die of diphtheria even though they were treated with diphtheria antitoxin. The serum that had been so effective when it was introduced in the late nineteenth century appeared somehow ineffectual, and it was suspected that the reason was that more virulent forms of diphtheria bacteria had appeared.[85]

Once Krebs worked, together with a young nursing sister named Katherina Holsten, throughout the night struggling to save a child desperately ill with diphtheria. Although they administered antitoxin, they saw the child die shortly afterward. Krebs soon began to stop by Katrina's station in the hospital for coffee and to converse with her and the other nurses. As they became better acquainted, Hans and Katrina frequently went out together, for long walks along the Elbe, or dancing in the evening.[86]

However optimistic Krebs may have felt about the prospects before him when he departed for Freiburg, he must also have felt regret for the place and the people that he left in Altona. Of those he left behind, none felt the loss of his departure more acutely than did Katrina.[87]

8

Freiburg: The Foundation of a Career

At Altona, Hans Krebs recalled much later, his research time had been too
limited to undertake an ambitious project. Only when he came to Freiburg was
he "completely free, for the first time, to follow my own ideas on research and
to choose my own subject."[1] His clinical duties in his new post were, however,
as demanding as they had been in his previous one. Here too, he had "full
clinical responsibility for a ward of twenty-two patients." Here too he had to
leave his laboratory for emergency calls, as well as for the normal ward rounds;
and here too he was given extra responsibilities to catch up on the medical
experience he had missed during his years with Warburg. In addition, he
sometimes had to take on time-consuming responsibilities as the teaching
assistant for Thannhauser's lecture course.[2] The change in the pace of his
experimental activity when he moved from one institution to the other was, in
fact, probably less sharp than it afterward appeared to him when he looked back
in the light of his comparative achievements at these two places.

Krebs was able to bring to Freiburg the manometers and associated apparatus
he had acquired in Altona. A second small grant from the Ella Sachs Plotz
Foundation of Boston, probably obtained through his contacts with Dr. Joseph
Aub, permitted him to purchase additional equipment, and to hire a technician.
Thannhauser also defrayed some of Krebs's laboratory expenses with funds
from his own Rockefeller Foundation grant. Krebs was given ample laboratory
facilities, with the prospect for further improvement when the new hospital
buildings under construction would be completed.[3]

From the beginning, Thannhauser proved to be a helpful, supportive chief.
A cheerful, jovial man, he was not authoritarian. Although he was too busy to
have much time for talk, he was tolerant and easy to get along with. Since his
own specialty was metabolic diseases, he appreciated fully the significance of
the research areas Krebs intended to pursue. Krebs regularly discussed his work
with his chief, but the two never worked in collaboration, and there is no
indication that Thannhauser influenced the direction of Krebs's investigations.[4]

Although Krebs arrived in Freiburg still uncertain of his own capacity to
make significant scientific contributions, he was viewed there as an important

Figure 8.1 Siegfried Thannhauser

acquisition for the research activity at that institution. Identified mainly as a product of the famous laboratory of Otto Warburg, he was seen as the person who would introduce Warburg's powerful manometric methods into the local scientific setting. Undoubtedly the reception he received helped to sustain his confidence in himself.[5]

In contrast to Altona, where it took him 4 months to get his research under way, at Freiburg Krebs began recording experiments in his notebook less than 2 weeks after his arrival. The difference may have been in part because he had brought his apparatus with him, in part because he had already established a line of investigation he could continue, in part, perhaps, just because he had already been through the process of organizing himself under similar circumstances to carry on research. On the other hand, during his first 2 months he proceeded at the unusually slow pace of about one experiment per week,[6] suggesting that his new clinical duties must, for a while, have claimed most of his time and energy.

I

The first group of experiments that Krebs performed in Freiburg was an extension of the investigation of the effects of iodoacetate on animal tissue that he had been carrying out during his last months at Altona. The new experiments were focused, however, on an additional effect, the action of methylglyoxal on tissues poisoned with iodoacetate. They represent both a logical next step in the progression of his personal research pathway, and a response to new investigations by others in the field of intermediary carbohydrate metabolism. As seen in Chapter 1 (pp. 11–12), Carl Neuberg's theory of alcoholic fermentation, and its application to muscle glycolysis, proposed in 1913, was still very prominent in 1931. Methylglyoxal was still regarded by many investigators as the nodal intermediary compound in the breakdown of hexoses in animal tissues to form lactic acid, as well as in the fermentation of sugar in yeast. The strategy that Krebs pursued in his new experiments follows immediately from this prevailing theory. If one could overcome the iodoacetate inhibition of glycolysis by adding methylglyoxal to the medium of tissue slices, then one might infer that iodoacetate blocks one of the steps in glycolysis in which the hexoses are converted to methylglyoxal. Supplying the methylglyoxal from outside could then restore the subsequent stage, its conversion to lactic acid. Krebs *might* have reasoned out this approach from the position that he himself had reached in his study of the action of iodoacetate. It appears more likely, however, that he obtained the idea from reports of contemporary research in the current journal literature, and merely adapted what others were doing to his own experimental system.

Biochemists were interested in methylglyoxal in the years leading to 1931, not only because the reaction schemes built around it were chemically plausible, but also because they recognized that the role of this three-carbon compound was not yet firmly established. The situation remained much as Richard Kuhn and Rudolf Heckscher had put it in 1926: "The occurrence of methylglyoxal as an intermediary product of sugar metabolism, which appears possible on the basis [of the findings of Neuberg and of Dakin and Dudley], and which is capable of making many of the facts of metabolic physiology understandable, nevertheless requires more extensive support." They noted the competing viewpoint of Gustav Embden and his associates, whose organ-perfusion experiments had provided evidence that two other three-carbon compounds, glyceraldehyde and dihydroxyacetone, were "powerful lactate builders." Kuhn and Heckscher offered a segment of that broader support for methylglyoxal that they deemed essential. With extracts of liver tissue to which they added methylglyoxal, they found the latter converted to lactic acid in amounts consistently greater than that of the lactic acid formed in the controls. They regarded their results as the demonstration that an enzymatic, intramolecular dismutation, or Cannizzaro reaction, of the type incorporated into the Neuberg scheme, took place in the extracts.[7]

Neuberg himself devoted special efforts, during the late 1920s, to solidify the evidence for the role of methylglyoxal in glycolysis. With Maria Kobel, he was able to convert hexose diphosphate to methylglyoxal in a yeast extract. By this time the phosphate esters of hexose sugars were finally coming to be recognized as important intermediates in carbohydrate metabolism, therefore Neuberg could regard this conversion as representing a stage in the glycolytic breakdown of carbohydrates. In 1929 Neuberg and Kobel were able to produce lactic acid from methylglyoxal in ether extracts derived from lactic acid bacteria, in sufficient quantity to isolate the lactate and to show that it accounted for 80 to 100 percent of the methylglyoxal consumed.[8] Shortly afterward Marthe Vogt demonstrated the same process in extracts obtained from rabbit and pig kidney and liver tissue.[9] At the end of the decade, those who supported the methylglyoxal theory of glycolysis thus had reason to feel that they were gaining ground, even though decisive evidence for that scheme was still not at hand.

After Lundsgaard showed that iodoacetate inhibits glycolysis, some investigators inferred that, if this effect were due to blocking the conversion of methylglyoxal to lactate, then in tissue extracts treated with this poison, methylglyoxal ought to accumulate. At the University of Vienna, Hermann Barrenscheen, Karl Braun, and Miklos Dreguss reported, in December 1930, that they had been able to detect such a result. In minced liver, kidney, and muscle tissue, they obtained large yields of methylglyoxal in the presence of hexose phosphate and iodoacetate, whereas controls gave negative results.[10] Shortly afterward, Harold Dudley concluded, from experiments on extracts of chicken muscle, that iodoacetate inhibits the enzyme "which converts methylglyoxal into lactic acid." He had actually examined not the conversion of methylglyoxal to lactic acid, but of phenylglyoxal to l-mandelic acid. Since he believed that the same enzyme, glyoxalase, catalyzed both of these homologous reactions, Dudley inferred that his results applied to the physiologically more important one as well. "The available evidence," he wrote in February 1931, "supports the view that sodium iodoacetate owes its power of interfering with normal glycolysis" to the fact that it inhibits this enzyme. "The probability that methylglyoxal is the immediate precursor of lactic acid in the glycolytic chain of reactions," Dudley thought, "is strengthened by this observation."[11]

The topic of methylglyoxal was prominent enough in intermediary carbohydrate metabolism in 1931 that no special explanation for Krebs's interest in it is necessary. He had already displayed, in his first independent research initiatives, the tendency to pick up ideas for experiments from the most recent articles contained in the biochemical journals that he looked through at every opportunity. His attitude toward the problem of methylglyoxal was no doubt conditioned, however, by the fact that Neuberg and Kobel had been engaged in the investigations designed to strengthen the case for the role of methylglyoxal during the same years that Krebs spent in Warburg's laboratory, adjacent to the building in which Neuberg himself worked. As noted in Chapter 3, Krebs and the other younger scientists at Dalhem thought that Neuberg overdramatized his theory when he asserted that "the formation of methylglyoxal is the essence of glycolysis."[12] There is no evidence, however, that Krebs questioned the prevailing theory. It would be consistent with his general approach that when he took up the investigation of methylglyoxal in 1931, he probably had no carefully worked out theoretical position regarding its role in metabolism. Rather, he was most likely reacting to the recent findings by simply examining how the results he could obtain with his tissue slice and manometer techniques would compare with results that others had obtained through the more common methods. Either just before or shortly after taking up the problem, he reviewed the articles summarized in the preceding paragraphs.[13] His view of its recent history was, therefore, probably very much as herein described.

On May 12, Krebs measured the respiration, and the aerobic and anaerobic formation of lactic acid in liver slices from starved rats, comparing the rates with 0.2 percent methylglyoxal added to the medium to the rates without methylglyoxal. The medium he used was Ringer's solution with 0.2 percent glucose added. To measure simultaneously the oxygen consumption and carbon dioxide production in the aerobic tests, he used the usual Warburg method of a double run with different fluid volumes in the respective reaction vessels. Comparison of the methylglyoxal results with the controls showed that the respiration was about the same in the two cases, but that both aerobically and anaerobically the methylglyoxal substantially increased the rate of formation of lactic acid. (In the control, Q_{O_2} = - 15.4, Q_{CO_2} +13.7, that is, about the expected respiratory quotient for the respiratory consumption of carbohydrate. With methylglyoxal, Q_{O_2} during the first 10 minutes was -16.7, but Q_{CO_2} was 37.5. The excess carbon dioxide Krebs attributed to the aerobic formation of lactic acid. In the anaerobic control, $Q_M^{N_2} = \approx 0.9$, indicating very little lactate formed, whereas for the first 10 minutes with methylglyoxal $Q_M^{N_2} = +28.8$.)

These results were quite compatible with the dominant view that methylglyoxal is the direct precursor of lactic acid in glycolysis. They were not reliable results, however, because, as Krebs commented, the rates of formation of lactic acid diminished rapidly over the course of the experiment.

"It remains to be investigated," Krebs wrote down,

1) whether lactic acid formation goes in parallel with the consumption of methylglyoxal.
2) to add less methylglyoxal, and only during the experiment, from the side arm.
3) to test in the presence of lactate (so that the lactic acid formed does not cause new effects that increase with time).[14]

These remarks offer an intimate glimpse of an astute investigator analyzing an experiment he has just carried out, responding both to what the experiment has taught him in a positive sense, and to inadequacies in his experimental design that he could not foresee in advance, to improve on it in the future. The outcome itself, and Krebs's comments on it, suggest that he viewed his result as supportive of the accepted role of methylglyoxal in glycolysis. It also suggests that he recognized that more was needed to attain a definitive test of the validity of the theory.

Instead of repeating the experiment as he had planned to, according to these notes, Krebs went on directly to the central effect he had probably intended to probe from the start of his work at Freiburg, that of iodoacetate on the anaerobic formation of lactic acid in the presence of methylglyoxal. Fifteen days elapsed before he could carry out the next experiment, and his very limited time may well have made him a little impatient to move to the heart of the matter. He did incorporate into this experiment, however, one of the refinements that he had suggested to himself for the previous one, by halving the concentration of methylglyoxal. He utilized rat liver and testicle slices, in each case comparing the quantity of lactic acid formed with iodoacetate and methylglyoxal to that formed without the iodoacetate. In the liver tissue iodoacetate reduced the anaerobic Q_M from 27.9 to 17.0, and in testicle tissue from 21.2 to 15.0. Krebs regarded these values as conspicuously low, but noted that at least they remained constant over time. The inhibitions, he wrote down, were 22.5 percent for liver, and 29.1 percent for testicle; he regarded these inhibitions as "small."[15] There is no indication of how, in a more general sense, he may have interpreted the experiment and its result. The experimental design does not suggest that he was testing whether methylglyoxal can restore glycolysis inhibited by iodoacetate, for it did not include a measurement of the rate with iodoacetate alone. The experiment appears instead to assume that methylglyoxal normally gives rise to lactate, and the test may have been to see whether iodoacetate blocks glycolysis before or after the step in which methylglyoxal is formed. If so, the fact that there was an inhibition, but that it was "small," would have rendered the outcome indecisive.

Krebs may have suspected that the low inhibition in this experiment was related to the concentration $(0.6 \times 10^{-4}$ M$)$, of the iodoacetate he had used. At any rate, when he next had an opportunity to perform a set of experiments, on June 11, he measured the rates of respiration and glycolysis in nourished rat liver slices in the presence of three different concentrations of iodoacetate $(3 \times 10^{-3}$ M, 3×10^{-4} M, and 3×10^{-5} M$)$, the largest of which was 50 times the concentration used in the preceding experiment. At this highest concentration, the respiration fell gradually to one fourth of the control rate, whereas the anaerobic glycolysis was reduced to one tenth of the normal rate.[16] Although the conditions in this experiment were not strictly comparable to those of the previous one, the general result might have suggested that in the earlier one methylglyoxal had sustained a large portion of the respiration and glycolysis that otherwise would have been inhibited by the iodoacetate.

Research workers in Thannhauser's department customarily presented their latest results at the regular meetings of the Freiburg Medical Society. On June 2, Krebs made his initial appearance before this group. He was the last of several speakers, the first of whom was Thannhauser discussing endogenous hypoglycemic crises. By comparison with his senior colleagues Krebs spoke quite briefly, on the topic "Investigation of Carbohydrate Decomposition in Living Cells." His talk summarized essentially the contents of the paper on the effects of iodoacetate on glycolysis and respiration that he had written at the end of his stay in Altona. The main point he made was that his experiments made the existence of the Meyerhof lactic acid cycle in tissues other than muscle "very probable." Apparently Krebs did not mention the extension of the investigation to methylglyoxal that he had undertaken since his arrival in Freiburg.[17]

Nearly a month went by before Krebs could perform any more experiments, and when he did get back to the laboratory it was to take up a project unrelated to his previous work. Between July 3 and July 11, he carried out a number of experiments on the oxidation of squalene, a hydrocarbon contained in the liver oil of certain sharks, but otherwise believed to be metabolically unimportant. He did this, apparently, because Thannhauser happened to have some squalene on hand, and was interested in its properties.[18] Meanwhile, on July 8 he returned to his investigation of the action of methylglyoxal in the presence of iodoacetate. Using rat liver and testicle slices, he compared the rates of glycolysis with three different substrates — glucose, hexose diphosphate, and methylglyoxal — before and after adding iodoacetate. His strategy appears self-evident. These were the three substances most frequently identified as precursors of lactic acid according to current views on glycolysis. Both with and without iodoacetate lactic acid formed much more rapidly in the vessels containing methylglyoxal than in the others. For the case of the testicle tissue, the rate with glucose, already only about one third of that with methylglyoxal before the iodoacetate was added, fell afterward to less than one half of its initial rate. With hexose diphosphate, the rate was minimal from the beginning. (With liver slices the rates with both of these substrates were so low that Krebs did not bother to complete the runs.) With methylglyoxal the iodoacetate did not substantially reduce the initially high rate. On the face of it, this experiment would appear to have supported the theory that methylglyoxal is a direct precursor of lactic acid in glycolysis, and to have suggested in addition that iodoacetate inhibits glycolysis at a stage prior to that at which methylglyoxal forms. Under the heading "results," Krebs wrote down only "small inhibitions," so that we cannot tell whether he regarded the outcome as significant enough to draw such inferences from it.[19] He must have felt at least that he was on a fruitful line of investigation, however, for he continued in the same direction in another experiment 2 days later.

At about this time some change in Krebs's circumstances must have either made more time available to him for research or have provided him with the assistance necessary to keep his research going during his absences from the laboratory. He began to carry out experiments almost every working day.

In the next experiment, Krebs compared, in testicle slices, anaerobic glycolysis in the presence of glucose with that in the presence of methylglyoxal. For each substrate he used three different concentrations of iodoacetate and a fourth control without iodoacetate. With glucose the iodoacetate (in its highest concentration, 3×10^{-3} M), reduced the glycolysis from $Q_M = 6.8$ to $Q_M = 0.8$. With methylglyoxal the rates were abnormally high, higher even with iodoacetate than without it ($Q_M = 47.5$ in control, $Q_M = 82.2$ with 3×10^{-3} iodoacetate). Nevertheless, Krebs inferred from this result, "Lactic acid formation from glucose is inhibited, from methylglyoxal not!"[20] No doubt he regarded this as a provisional indication to be pursued, rather than a general conclusion.

In spite of deficiencies that marred each of the preceding experiments, collectively they appeared consistently favorable to the view of methylglyoxal as a key intermediate in glycolysis, and they pointed toward the inference that iodoacetate interferes with the formation of methylglyoxal, rather than with its conversion to lactate. Probably as a preliminary step toward further exploration of the steps in glycolysis preceding methylglyoxal, Krebs tested the action of iodoacetate on the oxidation of fructose, and found there was no inhibition. (He recorded few details concerning this experiment in his notebook.)[21] The next day, however, he turned to an experiment that, on the surface, appears unrelated to the preceding series. It was on the oxidation of "ketol" in rat liver slices. The connection with what he had been doing up until then is contained in an article in an issue of the *Zeitschrift für physiologische Chemie* that had just appeared, which inspired his new experimental tack. Published early in 1931 by Martin Henze and R. Müller, the article was entitled "The Transformation of Acetoacetic Acid by Methylglyoxal." It is not difficult to imagine how this title would have caught his eye at a time in which he was himself studying methylglyoxal. What he found, when he read the article, however, led him to consider a possible role for methylglyoxal different from the one he had been testing. Henze and Müller had discovered that in an aqueous solution of methylglyoxal and acetoacetic acid a spontaneous reaction occurred, producing an unknown dihydroxyacetone, or "ketol," for which they gave the formula $CH_3COCH(OH)$-CH_2COCH_3. With sodium hypobromite they were able to convert this compound to malic acid, by removing the two methyl groups at the ends of the chain. In their discussion, Henze and Müller speculated about the possible biological significance of these reactions. Perhaps they could explain the still uncertain metabolic fate of acetoacetate, and clarify the last stages in the β-oxidation series of fatty acid degradations. These reactions could link acetoacetate with the sequence malic acid → oxaloacetic acid → pyruvic acid, whose prominent position in theories of oxidative metabolism we have followed in Chapter 1. Moreover, Henze and Müller thought, the reactions they had found might explain the antiketogenic effects of carbohydrate, "and especially to bring a closer understanding of the methylglyoxal which stands at the center of the transformations of sugar."[22] To someone like Krebs, nurtured in the view that the goal of biochemistry is to "put together...in an unbroken series of equations"[23] the reactions by which foodstuffs are broken down in the organism, or used to synthesize body constituents, the possibility of linking up two of the few fragments of those series that were known would be enticing. Krebs procured some of the new "ketol", prepared by a colleague named Dr. Löw, according to the directions of Henze and Müller, and tested its effects on the respiration and anaerobic glycolysis of rat liver slices. In the first experiment, carried out on July 14, he obtained small increases over the control in both processes. In a second experiment the next day on several tissues, however, Krebs observed no significant differences,[24] and he dropped the problem for the time being. The preliminary tests had offered nothing striking enough to command further immediate attention, though he kept the idea in mind for some other time. On July 22 he turned to the effects of insulin on the consumption of sugar in rat liver slices. He found no consumption either in the controls or in the vessels that contained insulin. After one more experiment on insulin in blood, he dropped that question too.[25] Although it is unclear what stimulated him to test insulin at just this time, that he should do so at some point during his study of intermediary carbohydrate metabolism was almost inevitable. Ever since the discovery of insulin, whose absence in the animal rendered it unable to metabolize sugar, investigators had been seeking to identify the stage in the metabolic pathway for which they assumed insulin is required. After this rather desultory try at the problem, Krebs interrupted the entire series of experiments on carbohydrate metabolism to take up a new research endeavor that he had probably had in mind for several weeks.

If we compare the research on iodoacetate and carbohydrate metabolism that Krebs carried out during his first weeks at Freiburg, with those he had done at Altona, we can see that the experiments themselves looked very similar. In both cases he used this agent to inhibit the metabolism of tissue slices, then tested the capacity of various known or suspected substrates to restore the normal rate. The *problem* he was investigating at Freiburg, however, was not the same as the one he had been pursuing before his move. Then he had sought mainly to separate the oxidative from the anaerobic phase of carbohydrate metabolism in order to study the latter. Now he sought principally to elucidate the anaerobic phase itself, in particular, to examine the role of one of its putative intermediates. The continuity of a scientific investigation is sometimes maintained by its steady focus on a particular problem, while the investigator changes the methods by which he attacks the problem; or, as in this instance, by the retention of a particular experimental procedure, while he changes the questions to which it is applied.

We may also note several points at which Krebs considered future experimental moves that appeared to be natural extensions of the investigative course he had been following, but actually moved in another direction less predictable from what had come before. When he ended his work in Altona, he had in mind that he should examine next the possibility, raised by the results he had so far attained, that iodoacetate exerts separate effects on glycolysis and on respiration. When he resumed his research, however, he did not follow this intention, for he had in the meantime become interested in the role of methylglyoxal in glycolysis. Similarly, after performing the first experiment in Freiburg, he outlined, as the next logical steps for him, to investigate whether the consumption of methylglyoxal parallels the formation of lactic acid, and to perform these tests in the presence of lactate; but he did not take either step. He skipped instead to another general phase of the investigation. Shortly afterward he performed a preliminary experiment on fructose and iodoacetate; but instead of following it up, he turned to the experiments on ketol suggested by the work of Henze and Müller.

Such small discrepancies between work planned and work carried out are typical, not only of Krebs, but of any creative scientific investigator who has more ideas than he has time to execute them, and who must continually adjust his expectations to the fluidity of daily experience. Krebs's research style made him especially prone to such short-term switches, however, because he was never a long-range planner. New ideas for experiments often occurred to him, and when they did he liked to try them out as soon as possible, even if they took precedence over what he had previously been doing or had in mind to do. He did not devise extended research prospectives or plans. Rather, he "would make a decision every day,"[26] about what to do next. This routine, combined with his habit of using whatever spare time he had in the laboratory to look over the latest issues of the biochemical journals in the nearby library, and to pick up ideas to test from whatever articles attracted his interest, generated a research pathway that was, on a local scale, malleable, opportunistic, and subject to frequent changes of course. Yet Krebs always had the sense that his "general trend"[27] was fixed. His path was, in fact, guided within a broad but well-bounded channel, by the powerful but specialized techniques he had learned from Warburg, by his commitment to the general idea of applying these techniques to the study of intermediary metabolism, and by the limitations, as well as the strengths, of the particular scientific skills that he had to offer to this field of investigation.

* * *

After I had begun to examine in detail Hans Krebs's laboratory notebooks for the years 1931–1932, I remarked to him, in April 1977, that there seemed to be some kind of rotation among the several lines of investigation recorded in them. He responded that there was a general trend that was fixed;

But then this general trend was quite often interrupted when I had an idea and thought it worthwhile exploring whether it would lead anywhere.... I wasn't very systematic.... And I think in this respect I am different, at least from some people.... I tried out a lot of things, and some people...stick to a specific line, and sometimes I have asked myself whether I am not too easily diverted. But when I survey the whole story I am satisfied that such diversions were warranted.[28]

II

Although the contrast that Krebs drew in his autobiography between the limitations on his research at Altona and his freedom to follow his own ideas in Freiburg seems too marked, it was based on a real change in the nature of his research, which took place about 4 months after he arrived in Freiburg. He began then a new line of investigation that he chose deliberately as a strong test of the effectiveness of the tissue slice method in intermediary metabolism. The outcome of this investigation so overshadowed what he had been able to achieve up until then, that it appears eventually to have displaced from his memory the efforts he had already begun in Altona to chart his own course (although not beyond recall when reminded of them, as we have seen in Chapter 3).

If not free for the first time, Krebs did become in Freiburg freer than he had been, to undertake ambitious research projects. The reason probably was not that he had more time available, as his clinical duties were still very heavy, but that several factors concurred to enhance the use he made of the time he had. With funds available to hire a full-time technician, he could expect to keep his experiments going even when he was called away to the clinic. He had in addition the prospect of attracting medical students to carry out research projects under his direction for their MD theses. He knew that when the new buildings were finished he would have three rooms to use for his research. At least as important as these tangible gains, however, may have been the influence his new environment had on his own outlook. He felt that he was entering a distinguished academic center, one that encouraged him to work on fundamental scientific problems.[29] Whereas he had regarded Altona as a temporary post almost as soon as he arrived there, he must have aspired to remain in Freiburg for a long time. He could, therefore, more easily contemplate undertaking investigations of large scope and long duration. Not the least of his new freedoms was that he had disposed of his lingering obligation to Warburg. When he had completed his article on proteolysis, in July 1932, he was no longer within the shadow of his former chief's wishes; and all of the apparatus he had acquired through his earlier bargain with Warburg he could now use for his purposes alone.

The phenomenon that Krebs chose to study was the formation of urea in the liver. Retrospectively, he has given several very logical reasons for selecting this particular problem as his starting point. He wished to study a synthetic process, because the particular advantage that the tissue slice method held — that intact cells could be expected to carry out integrated metabolic processes that no longer occur in ground tissue or extracts — might best be displayed in such a situation. The synthesis of urea appeared exceptionally simple, and most of the other known syntheses, such as those of proteins or fats, were impossible to study in this way because of the lack of adequate analytical methods. Moreover, urea was synthesized in the organism at such a high rate that it would be easily measurable.[30]

When he summarized these reasons for his "choice of the problem," in a history of the investigation written in 1973, Krebs included information on the comparative rates of urea synthesis and other biosyntheses that could not have been available to him in 1932.[31] Such ahistorical elements in his description naturally lead us to question whether the reasons themselves are strictly historical, or whether they may represent in part a logical reconstruction that Krebs worked out after he had been asked to explain the success of the investigation. Krebs himself I found to be acutely aware of the difficulties involved in reconstructing one's own past mental states. In 1978 I showed him my first attempt to write a history of his study of the synthesis of urea. I had elaborated these reasons, and added some conjectures of my own concerning the grounds for his choice. He penciled in the margin, "pebbles on the beach"[32] — by which he meant that there are very many problems lying around to be tackled with a new method such as he had, and that the investigator just has to pick one of them up. The pebble picked must be suitable to the method; but rather than to worry too much over whether it is worth doing, it is better just to try it. That was his style. "I think," he told me, when we discussed the point, that "without searching very deeply, I thought this was a suitable system to study."[33] Historians are prone to overexplain why a scientist has taken certain steps that prove afterward to have been crucial.

It is possible that in this case, as in others, Krebs was induced to take up the problem by noticing an article in the current literature.   In early 1931 two papers appeared in the *Biochemische Zeitschrift*, by Kyoji Kase, purporting to demonstrate the enzymatic formation of urea in liver extracts.[34] The data were suggestive, but less convincing than their author took them to be. If Krebs did come across this article, through his habitual practice of browsing through the journal, both the claim and the deficiencies in the results could well have stimulated him to think that the tissue slice method was better adapted to the study of the problem than the methods Kase had employed. It is not necessary, however, to identify such a specific and immediate source for Krebs's choice, because the synthesis of urea was one of the oldest and best-known unsolved problems in the field of metabolic biochemistry.

III

By the middle of the nineteenth century, physiological chemists assumed that the urea animals excrete in their urine is the nitrogenous end product of the breakdown of tissue proteins. The first significant effort to establish experimentally "the steps preceding the formation of urea in the animal organism" was made in 1869 by Otto Schultzen and Marceli Nencki. They showed that, when either glycine or leucine was added to the diet of an animal that produced a stable output of urea, the daily quantity of urea increased. These two amino acids had been identified as partial decomposition products of protein, and Schultzen and Nencki concluded that they were "the previously unknown transition links between protein and urea." Because these acids contain only a single nitrogen atom, whereas urea has two, they inferred that "the formation of urea is in part...a synthetic process." They expressed the reaction (for the case of glycine) as:

$$2 \ C_2H_5NO_2 + 6O = N_2COH_4 + 3 \ CO_2 + 3 \ H_2O$$
$$\text{glycine} \qquad\qquad \text{urea}$$

Schultzen and Nencki believed that there must be further transition links, and that their equations left unexplained the "last phase" of the synthetic process. They speculated that the amino acids gave rise to cyanate groups, which might combine with ammonia separated simultaneously from protein, to produce the urea.[35] This conjecture stimulated Woldemar von Knieriem, in 1873, to test whether an ammonium salt (ammonium chloride) added to the diet would cause more urea to form. Using methods similar to those of Schultzen and Nencki, on a dog and on himself, von Knieriem observed a definite increase in the urea output, with no rise in the NH_3 content of the urine. His result could be explained by their theory that NH_3 combines with cyanate, he thought, but it was just as plausible that the urea arises from ammonium carbonate by the elimination of water and CO_2. Von Knieriem also added aspartic acid and asparagine to the list of amino acids, derived from proteins, that produce urea in the organism.[36]

Using more elaborate methods to eliminate the possibility that ammonium chloride merely stimulates a general increase in the protein metabolism, Ernst Salkowski confirmed von Knieriem's results in 1877. To settle the question whether the urea derives from a combination of ammonium with cyanate or from the dehydration of ammonium carbonate, Salkowski fed rabbits the substituted ammonium compounds methylamine and ethylamine. If the first theory were correct, a monosubstituted urea should result. If, on the other hand, the dehydration process was what took place, a disubstituted urea should be produced. Finding traces of monoethylurea in the rabbit's urine, Salkowski believed that he had shown the first alternative to be "highly probable."[37] His evidence was not accepted as conclusive, however, and both theories continued to attract adherents during the following decades. In 1880 Edmund Drechsel proposed a third alternative, that ammonia combines with carbamic acid (NH_2COOH) to form urea.[38]

Feeding experiments of the type that Schultzen and Nencki, von Knieriem, and Salkowski had carried out were able neither to provide decisive evidence for any of these hypotheses, nor to locate where within the animal the urea is formed. It marked a crucial advance, therefore, in 1882, when Waldemar von Schröder was able to duplicate, on an isolated perfused dog liver, the effects of ammonium salts on urea formation that von Knieriem and Salkowski had obtained with intact animals.[39] Over the next decades many other investigators took up von Schröder's approach. In 1898, at the suggestion of Nencki, Sergei Salaskin completed the replication of the results of the early feeding experiments by organ perfusion experiments, when he found that leucine, tyrosine, or aspartic acid added to the blood passing through an isolated liver yielded an increase in the percentage of urea in the fluid emerging from the perfused organ.[40] For the next 15 years it was generally accepted that the liver can produce urea both from ammonia and from amino acids.

In 1913, Cyrus Fiske and Howard Karsner questioned Salaskin's conclusion that amino acids can form urea. Repeating his experiments with a new method for determining urea nitrogen devised by their teacher, Otto Folin, they could detect no "suggestion of urea formation" from perfused cat and dog livers.[41] In 1915 Barend Jansen repeated the liver perfusion experiments, with results that supported Salaskin. Jansen suggested that Fiske and Karsner had used an inefficient perfusion system, in which the blood may not have been fully arterialized. Jansen also made an important technical advance by using a method that Eli Marshall had developed 2 years before to determine urea by means of the enzyme urease. The urease hydrolyzed urea to ammonia and carbon dioxide, and the ammonia could then be measured. The urease method was simpler than the previous methods used, yet very exact and highly specific for urea.[42]

These efforts to understand the formation of urea by direct investigations of the process were reinforced during the early twentieth century by concurrent advances in protein chemistry. Emil Fischer and Franz Hofmeister proposed that proteins are probably composed entirely of amino acids linked in peptide chains.[43] Feeding experiments with amino acids and studies of the action of digestive enzymes provided evidence that ingested proteins are hydrolyzed into their individual amino acids before they are absorbed into the circulation.[44] These developments led biochemists away from the nineteenth-century idea that proteins as a whole undergo a degradative oxidation, and focused their attention on the metabolic reactions of the individual amino acids.[45] The hypothesis, supported by Knoop and others, that the further degradation of amino acids begins with an oxidative deamination, provided a clearly delineated set of chemical reactions by which to comprehend some of the steps in this process. Such considerations guided Wilhelm Löffler, in 1916, when he joined the growing list of those who investigated the production of urea by perfusing isolated livers. Löffler tested a "series of amino acids" to find whether their ability to form urea involved "a reaction common to all of these substances." Glycine, alanine, leucine, aspartic acid, and serine all increased the urea content of the perfusing fluid by the same order of magnitude. From this result he concluded that all must act in the same way, splitting off NH_3 in an oxidative deamination of the type postulated by Knoop. Whatever the final steps in the conversion of amino acids to urea may be, Löffler inferred, the process must "proceed by way of the intermediate stage of ammonia."[46] He thus affirmed the role of ammonia as an obligatory intermediate, which Fiske had recently denied.

Continuing his research, Löffler sought to establish more rigorous criteria to identify a substance as a source of urea nitrogen in perfusion experiments. He saw two ways to do this. The first was to determine the quantitative relation between the nitrogen in the urea formed and that in the source compound that disappeared. Only in this way, he believed, could one answer such questions as whether both NH_2 groups of the urea were derived from amino acids, or whether one came from another nitrogenous compound. The second means was to identify in the perfusion fluid the nonnitrogenous product left by the removal of the nitrogen from its source substance. For the case of ammonium salts he was able to show that the decrease in ammonia nitrogen corresponded to the increase in urea nitrogen. This result proved, according to Löffler, that urea nitrogen is derived entirely from ammonium salts. The outcome argued against the old theory of Salkowski that ammonia combines with cyanic acid to form urea, favoring instead the theory that ammonium carbonate is transformed to urea by the elimination of water. For amino acids he could not directly meet either of his criteria, because the available analytical methods were not adequate to determine the very small amounts present and the even smaller quantitative changes on which the interpretation of the results would depend. He was able, however, to demonstrate the deamination of several amines that corresponded to decarboxylated amino acids. The products of these reactions were readily identifiable in the perfusion fluid. Because these compounds contain the same carbon skeleton and amino groups as do the protein *Bausteine*, Löffler argued that their reactions must be analogous.[47]

After Eduard Buchner discovered cell-free alcoholic fermentation in 1897, biochemists became very interested in the question of what other metabolic reactions might occur in vitro, and which ones required intact cells or even intact organisms. During the preceding investigation Löffler noticed that the amines were deaminated when he used Ringer's solution as the perfusing fluid, whereas urea formed only if the fluid included blood. Consequently, he thought, the latter, a synthetic reaction, requires the oxidative capacity of the intact organ.[48] In 1920 he pursued further the question of "whether a specific cellular function is essential for the appearance of a reaction, that is, [whether] a biochemical reaction in the true sense is present." He tested the effects of various poisons, including phosphorus, alcohol, chloroform, nicotine, and potassium cyanide, on the ability of the isolated liver to produce urea. The agents that stopped the formation of urea coincided with those that he considered to damage severely the cell structure of liver tissue, from which Löffler concluded that "urea formation in the surviving liver is bound up with the integrity of the cell structure."[49]

Over a 40-year period beginning with the "classical" experiments of von Schröder,[50] the investigation of the formation of urea by the method of perfusing isolated livers had acquired considerable momentum. Numerous individuals had contributed to what appeared to be a progressively clearer delineation of the nature of the processes involved. After 1920, however, there were no further decisive advances. The perfusion techniques seemed to have reached a limit. Ten years later those who were working with them were still trying to ascertain the optimal conditions for studying the phenomena, but had attained no deeper insights into the chemistry of the reactions themselves.[51] Not everyone shared Löffler's belief that this synthetic process required intact cells and must, therefore, be studied in surviving whole organs. During the 1920s several people used minced liver tissue, hoping to demonstrate the action of an extractable enzyme. Harold Goldthorp, St. J. Przylecki, S. Kawahara, and Emil Abderhalden were among those who reported that ammonium salts added to minced liver produced urea. In 1931, as we have seen, Kase believed he had proven that under carefully controlled pH conditions liver pulp can form urea from amino acids added to the preparations.[52] These results were so equivocal, however, that they have since been regarded as instances of the failure of efforts to demonstrate urea synthesis in the absence of intact cells.[53]

The inability of the biochemical methods to penetrate further into the chemical processes of urea synthesis during this decade left room for Emil Werner to revive on chemical grounds alone the theory that cyanate is an intermediary compound, although, it had never been found in the body tissues or perfusion fluids.[54] Starting from studies of the reactions of urea that convinced him that it has a cyclic, rather than the usually accepted carbamide structure, and deriving on this basis a reaction mechanism explaining how cyanic acid is converted to urea, Werner then argued "It has been abundantly proved that in all syntheses, without exception, of *free* urea, the final change is direct union of ammonia with cyanic acid in the keto form O:C:NH. Is there any reason to suppose that *free* urea is produced otherwise in the living cell?"[55] That this argument, based as Werner himself said, on "a purely chemical point of view" should have received "respectful attention from some biochemists"[56] in the absence of any compelling support from experiments on biological material, is an indication of the impasse that had been reached. Reviewing the subject of the formation of urea in 1929, Harold H. Mitchell and T.S. Hamilton wrote:

> The ability of the liver to form urea from amino acids has been investigated by many different methods with such contradictory results that it seems impossible to reconcile the recorded experiments or, in most cases, to explain their divergent results. Much of the confusion is probably due to the use of inadequate chemical methods, to the selection of unfavorable experimental conditions, or to the inadequate control of experimental procedures.[57]

In 1930 Robert A. McCance wrote in *Physiological Reviews*:

> ...All are agreed that mammals excrete 80 to 90 percent of the protein they metabolize as urea and ammonia, and that the latter forms normally only a small percentage of the total nitrogen. The details of this process, however, form some of the most baffling problems in biochemistry.[58]

Although the situation at the time Krebs entered this field was perceived to be quite unsatisfactory with respect to the processes that served as the general source of urea in animals, a more specialized source had been distinctly characterized for many years. During the 1880s Drechsel isolated from casein a substance that produced urea by hydrolysis. A little later Ernst Schulze identified this substance as the amino acid arginine, which he had isolated from plants. In 1898 he showed that the process yielded, besides the urea, a second amino acid, ornithine.[59] Albrecht Kossel and Henry Dakin were able to extract from animal tissues an enzyme that catalyzed this transformation. The reaction was representable by the equation:

$$NH_2C(NH)(CH_2)_3CH(NH_2)COOH + H_2O \rightarrow NH_2CONH_2 + NH_2(CH_2)_3CH(NH_2)COOH$$
$$\text{arginine} \qquad\qquad\qquad\qquad \text{urea} \qquad \text{ornithine}$$

The liver was especially rich in this enzyme, which they named *arginase*. Kossel was particularly interested in protamines, simple proteins that contain large amounts of arginine, and he believed that arginine was a major constituent of proteins in general. He hoped, therefore, that further study of this reaction might lead to a general understanding of the formation of urea in the animal organism.[60] As it became clear, however, that arginine was only one of more than 20 amino acids comprising proteins, the significance of the "arginase" reaction seemed to diminish. As Löffler put it in 1917, "out of the great mass of urea originating in the organism, only the small part which originates from the decomposition of arginine can be formed according to this reaction."[61]

When Krebs took up the question of urea synthesis, he had only a superficial knowledge of the history just summarized. What he knew about the subject probably came mostly from standard handbooks such as that of Oppenheimer. In Freiburg he bought Mitchell and Hamilton's *The Biochemistry of the Amino Acids*, the source for the first of the two evaluations of the unsatisfactory state of the problem quoted earlier, and he may have obtained also from that book some general orientation about the subject. The first original research articles that he read on urea synthesis were the current two by Kyoji Kase, and those of Löffler. Löffler's investigation was the dominant recent contribution, and it still defined the state of the question in 1931. Gradually, during the course of his own investigation, Krebs deepened his familiarity with the earlier primary literature, until he had worked back to the original paper by von Knieriem. It was, Krebs felt, with von Knieriem that his "problem essentially started," because von Knieriem "showed that ammonia is a precursor" of urea.[62]

IV

The first problem Krebs faced in his intended study of urea synthesis was the necessity to work out a special analytical method. Until now, although in his research on intermediary metabolism he had defined his problems independently, he had been able to operate entirely with the methodological tools that Warburg had given him; that is, he had measured rates of respiration and glycolysis in tissues subjected to varied circumstances, due mainly to the addition of substrates or inhibitors to the medium. Now it became essential to identify quantitatively the specific product of the metabolic process he wished to examine. The difficulty in doing such analyses in general had, through the preceding decades, posed a central obstacle to progress in intermediary metabolism. Biochemists had to rely on the classical methods of organic chemistry. To isolate the product of a biological reaction they attempted to separate it from the tissue material or extract in which it had formed by the techniques of solution, precipitation, crystallization, and the formation of derivatives that had characteristic, easily detectable properties. If possible, they sought to isolate the product or its derivative in sufficient quantity to determine its melting point and its elementary composition, the two traditional means to make a reliable identification. The conditions under which metabolic experiments were carried out, however, pressed such methods to, or beyond, their furthest limits. In the first place, biochemists often had to distinguish compounds so similar in their properties, and likely to be present together, that they lacked the analytical means to tell them apart. Second, the products they wished to identify frequently appeared in such small quantities as to elude these classical methods, especially when it was important to determine how much of the compound had formed. Third, these methods were long and involved, ill-suited for investigations that required numerous comparative determinations.

Fortunately for Krebs, urea was an exception to these limitations, because of the urease test that Marshall had devised in 1913. The first analytical test based on an enzyme action, the urease method offered what was, for the time, an unusual combination of precision and specificity. Even more helpful for Krebs's purpose was that, in 1927, Donald Van Slyke had developed a manometric modification of the urease method. Urease converts urea to ammonium carbonate, according to the reaction $CO(NH_2)_2 + 2 H_2O = (NH_4)_2CO_3$. Normally the quantity of urea was then estimated by measuring the quantity of ammonia formed. Van Slyke measured instead the volume of CO_2 released by the reaction (displaced from the carbonate by acidification). This method was not more accurate than the other, but it was far more rapid. The Van Slyke method enabled one to perform one determination every 4 minutes. Performed on 0.2 ml. samples of blood or urine, the method could measure the urea content to tenths of a milligram.[63]

For Krebs the main task was simply to adapt Van Slyke's method to the special experimental conditions under which he needed to work. Van Slyke carried out the urease reaction in a stoppered volumetric flask, then transferred the CO_2 to a standard Van Slyke blood gas apparatus to measure the pressure change from which he calculated the quantity of CO_2 formed. Krebs wished to carry out these operations within the Warburg manometric apparatus. On July 26, 1931, he took up the question. Before attempting to establish experimental conditions suitable for carrying out a urea determination, he wrote down the reactions he expected to measure manometrically:

1. $O:C(NH_2)_2 + 3 H_2O + CO_2 = 2 NH_4 + 2 HCO_3^-$. With an alkaline reaction 1 molecule of CO_2 disappears for each molecule of urea. At pH 7.3 the reaction goes, for practical purposes, completely from right to left (according to the dissociation constant for CO_2).
2. With an acidic reaction CO_2 evolves.
   $2 H_2O + O:C(NH_2)_2 + 2 H^+ = 2 NH_4^+ + CO_2$

From 1. it follows that in the formation of urea CO_2 is liberated!! Try with metabolism!

From these remarks it appears that Krebs entertained the idea of utilizing the urease reaction under alkaline conditions, in which urea would be formed instead of decomposed. He next tested the action of commercial urease under three conditions: (1) In Warburg-Ringer's solution, made alkaline with bicarbonate, and with no urea present, apparently to test whether the reverse reaction would take place; (2) the same solution together with 1 percent urea; (3) the same as (2), but with 0.2 ml of 0.1N HCN added. (1) gave no readings, (2) gave low readings, and (3) gave large readings. Krebs commented simply "Method therefore works: acceleration with HCN."[64]

What had apparently not worked, was the idea of carrying out the reversed reaction under alkaline conditions. Whether one utilized alkaline or acidic conditions, it was necessary to decompose urea, forming CO_2 and ammonia. If this were so, Krebs inferred, then it would be preferable to operate with an acid reaction, "because here retention plays no role." Under neutral or alkaline conditions, some of the CO_2 remains in solution as bicarbonate, so that the manometric readings do not give a direct, quantitative measure of the quantity of CO_2 formed. Warburg had worked out a method to calculate the retention, but it was complicated. The experiments would be simplified if the urease determinations could be carried out at pH 5.0, where no appreciable quantity of CO_2 is retained. The difficulty was that the activity of urease, according to Van Slyke, required a neutral solution. In Van Slyke's procedure one acidified the solution only after the reaction was complete, to expel the CO_2 from solution. Nevertheless, Krebs tried the urease reaction in his system with an acetate buffer to maintain the pH at 5.0. The readings were satisfactory. "The method therefore works," he wrote down. "Little retention." With that fortunate outcome, he was ready 2 days later to test the method quantitatively. Making up a solution containing 0.376 mg of urea in acetate buffer, he obtained from the manometer readings a measured result of 0.370 mg urea. A parallel run in which he replaced the Ringer's solution with blood serum gave 0.362 mg. This was, he felt, "A good result, considering the fact that the measured urea quantity is not very exact (0.02 ccm.[cm³]!)."[65] In 2 days work Krebs had arrived at a method in which he had sufficient confidence to begin applying it to measurements of the urea formed in tissues.

In his historical summary of 1973, Krebs wrote that at the beginning of his investigation of urea synthesis "questions which suggested themselves...included the following:"

1. Is ammonia an obligatory intermediate in the conversion of amino nitrogen to urea nitrogen? If it is, ammonia must yield urea at least as rapidly as amino acids. If it is not, the rate of urea formation from amino acids might be more rapid than the rates from ammonia. (...).
2. How do the rates of urea formation from various amino acids compare?
3. Do substances which had been suspected to be intermediates, e.g., cyanate, behave like intermediates in that they can be converted to urea?
4. Do pyrimidines yield urea directly, or via ammonia?[66]

Just as in the matter of his choice of the general problem itself, we may ask whether historically these are the questions that Krebs had really formulated to himself at the beginning, or whether they too are in part the product of a subsequent rational reconstruction. There is no surviving record of his having put such questions down before doing the research. In this case, however, it appears very plausible that he did have questions like these in mind, because they are similar to the questions that other investigators of urea synthesis had already been examining. As we have already seen, it was characteristic of his style to glean experimental questions from the recent scientific literature, rather than to develop a deep rationale of his own before beginning a new line of research. Moreover, the questions fit very well with the approach that we shall see he followed in the early stages of the investigation, and imply no foreknowledge of its later course. Although he may not have delineated precisely these four questions in this neat format, Krebs's own later reconstruction of his initial orientation rings true as a good approximation to what he would most likely have asked himself in July 1931.

Krebs performed his first experiment on the formation of urea in liver tissues on the same day (July 8) that he had completed the first quantitative test of his urease method. Clearly he did not wish to waste any time putting his new analytical tool into action. In this initial attempt he compared the rate at which urea formed in a liver slice from a nourished rat by itself (in slightly alkaline Warburg–Ringer's solution) with the rate at which it formed when alanine was present, and when phenylalanine was present. He measured the respiration of the tissues for 8 minutes. Then he removed the tissues, mixed 2 cm^3 of the solution from each vessel with a buffer to bring the pH to 5.0, tipped the urease into the solution from a side arm of the vessel, and allowed the reaction to proceed for 1 hour and 45 minutes. The Q value for the formation of urea without addition was 0.23. Phenylalanine raised it only slightly, to 0.30. Alanine increased it to 1.20. Krebs considered all these rates "very small," but treated the increase caused by alanine as significant. He made the following calculations:

$$\text{Ratio} \quad \frac{\text{alanine oxidized}}{\text{NH}_3 - \text{urea}}$$

$$C_3H_7O_2N + 3\ O_2 + 2\ H_2O = 3\ CO_2 + 3\ H_2O + NH_4OH$$

Therefore 6 O_2 that are consumed $\rightarrow$ 2 NH_4OH
$\rightarrow$ 1 urea

In the experiment there appears, for $\frac{11.8}{1.2} = 10\ O_2$ [only] 1 urea[67]

That is, if one assumed that the alanine is completely oxidized, then one ought to obtain two molecules of ammonia, or one molecule of urea, for every six molecules of oxygen gas consumed. Krebs found instead, that the ratio of the oxygen absorbed during the experiment (Q_{O_2} = 11.8 with alanine) to that of the urea formed (Q_{urea} = 1.2 with alanine), was 10 to 1. Considerably less than the expected amount of urea had appeared, therefore, the obvious inference would be that the oxidation of alanine had not been complete. From his equation, however, we can see that Krebs began his investigation with the commonly accepted view that urea nitrogen is derived from the decomposition of amino acids, with ammonia as an intermediary product. Whether he himself *assumed* that view at the time, or was already testing it, cannot be ascertained from his compressed notations. At any rate, that view at least provided the framework within which he thought about the problem. Similarly, we cannot be certain, from the design of the experiment, whether he had incorporated into it the spe-

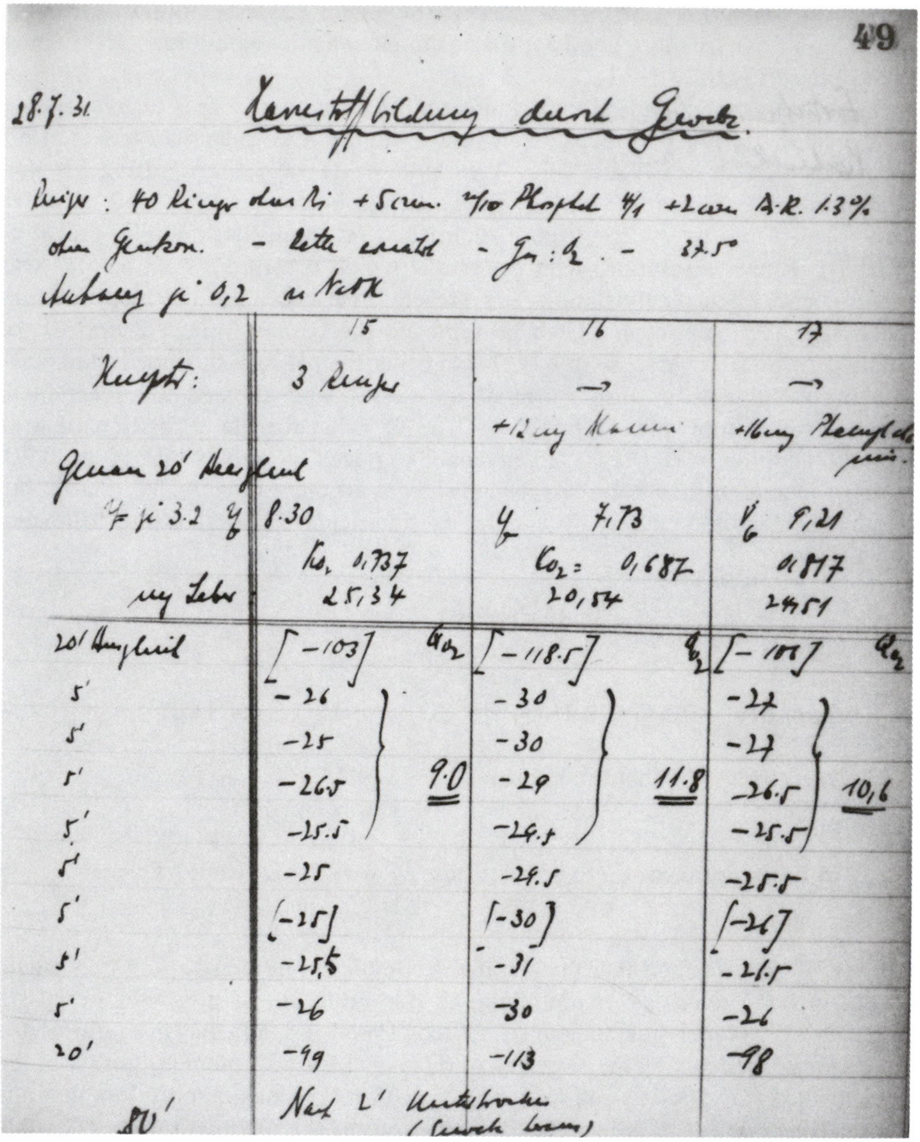

Figure 8.2 First experiment on the formation of urea in liver tissue slices, July 28, 1931.

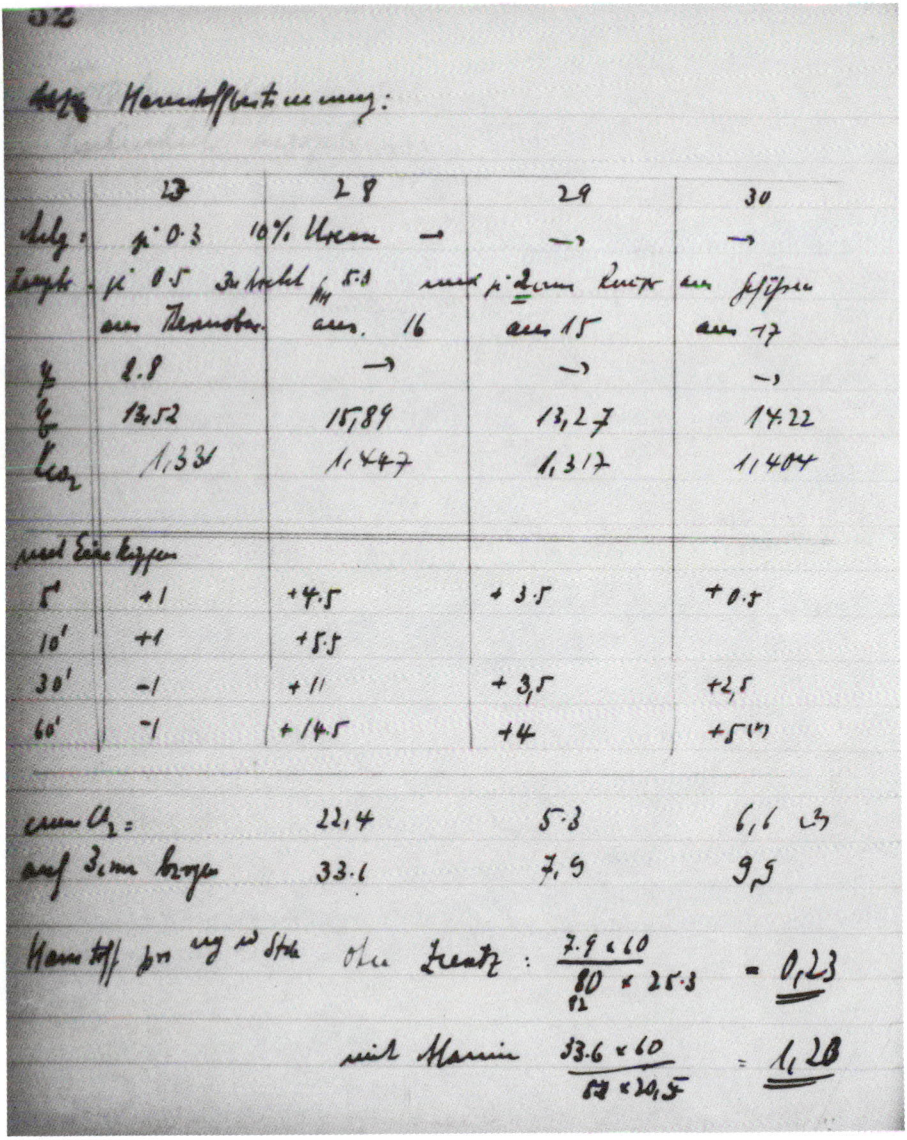
Harnstoffbestimmung:
27
28
29
30
10% Urea
8.8
13,52
15,89
13,27
14.22
1,331
1,447
1,317
1,404
5'
10'
30'
60'
+1
+4.5
+3.5
+0.5
+1
+5.5
-1
+11
+3,5
+2,5
-1
+14.5
+4
22,4
5.3
6,6
33.1
7,9
9,9
Harnstoff
0,23
1,28

mit Phenylalanin $\qquad \dfrac{2.9 \times 10}{80 \times 245} = 0{,}3 \, 0$

Ergebnis. Sehr kleine $\overset{+}{\text{N}}$-Wirkung

Im Kleinen $\underline{1.23}$ segen $\overset{+}{\text{N}}$-Kohlensäure

pro mg und Stunde. Oben durch
wenig.

Kleine freie CO_2 !

verhältni $\dfrac{\text{Volumetr. Kleinen}}{\text{NH}_3\text{-Kohlenstoff}}$

$C_3H_7\,O_2\,N + 3\,O_2 + 2\,H_2O = 3\,CO_2 + 3\,H_2O + 1\,NH_4\,OH$

Also $6\,O_2$, die verbrennt wird $\longrightarrow$ $2\,NH_4\,OH$

$\longrightarrow$ $\frac{1}{2}$ Kohlenstoff

Im Versuch verdient für $\dfrac{11.8}{1.2} = 10\,O_2 \quad - \quad 1$ Kohlenstoff cific question "How do the rates of urea formation from various amino acids compare?" or whether he was merely utilizing two common amino acids to test the more general view that any amino acid should raise the rate.

On the next day Krebs tested the effects of the two amino acids alanine and glycine, and of ammonium chloride, on the rate at which urea formed in nourished rat liver slices. He added these three substances in the relatively large concentration of 200 mg/100 ml, roughly twice the normal concentration of glucose in the blood. Unlike the preceding experiment, he also added glucose to the Warburg-Ringer's medium used for all of the vessels. Employing the method of duplicate measurements with different fluid volumes, he determined this time both the oxygen consumed and the carbon dioxide produced, to calculate the respiratory quotients for each condition. His objective in so doing was probably to obtain an indication of whether or not the added substrate was being metabolized.[68] In this case, for example, one would expect a lower respiratory quotient when more nitrogenous substances were being oxidized than when the metabolism of the tissue was being maintained primarily on the carbohydrate in the medium. The quotients, however, did not vary in a systematic manner. (In later years it was realized that respiratory quotients are less reliable as a guide to the types of substrates being consumed in isolated tissues than they are to the foodstuffs consumed in intact organisms, because partial decomposition products may accumulate in indeterminate ways in the medium.)[69]

The comparative results of the urea measurements were more striking. Alanine and glycine produced no more than the control tissue. Ammonium chloride produced more — just about as much, Krebs noticed, as alanine had produced in the experiment of the day before. This comparison led him to write down what appears as a simple summary statement of the "results," but which in fact included an inference that he reached by relating the results to broader considerations:

Today, in the presence of sugar, no formation of urea from alanine, only from NH_3
From NH_3 just as much as previously from alanine.
See in that regard, O. Warburg, Bioch. Z. [vol.] 152.
Metabolism of Tumors, p. 140.
Sugar inhibits the formation of NH_3.[70]

The fact that alanine had produced urea when there was no glucose present, but did not do so when glucose was there, whereas in the latter situation NH_3 produced what alanine did in the former, thus appeared significant enough to him so that, with the aid of some older results of Warburg that he remembered, he proposed the theoretical explanation that "sugar inhibits the formation of NH_3." While carrying out experiments on carcinoma cells Warburg had observed that, in the absence of sugar, these tissues produced ammonia in quantities, proportional to the oxygen consumed, that one would expect if the cells were oxidizing protein. When he added sugar to the medium, much less ammonia, or none at all, was produced. Although he could not establish a direct connection between glycolysis and the formation of ammonia, Warburg had concluded, in a paper published in 1924, that sugar "protects protein from oxidation."[71] This effect seemed to echo, at the level of tissue metabolism, a concept of the protective role of nonnitrogenous foodstuffs that had been passed down in studies of nutrition since the time of Liebig.[72] Warburg's results now provided for Krebs an explanation of his own results; or, put the other way, his own result suggested a more specific explanation for the effect Warburg had observed. The situation was analogous to those Krebs had been studying in his experiments with iodoacetate. Iodoacetate blocked the first stage in glycolysis, and one could restore the last stage by supplying the methylglyoxal whose formation was blocked, or could restore the aerobic phase of carbohydrate decomposition with lactate. In the same way, according to Krebs's view, glucose blocked the first stage in the formation of urea from amino acids, and one could restore the final stage by supplying that intermediate — in this case ammonia — whose formation had been blocked. Embedded in Krebs's reasoning here, as in his response to the preceding experiment, was the standard view that ammonia is an obligatory intermediate in the formation of urea from amino acids.

The explicit conclusion that sugar inhibits the formation of NH_3 and the implicit ideas surrounding it formed a very provisional hypothesis. It was based on two preliminary results of the initial experiments Krebs had carried out in the first days of a new line of investigation. His evidence was incomplete not only in the sense that the immediate results themselves needed repetition to test whether they were artifacts, but they encompassed only a fraction of the observations that ought to be made if the hypothesis were to be consolidated. The same results ought to apply to other amino acids, yet the only other amino acid he had tried, phenylalanine, had failed to produce urea even without glucose. At the very least, it would be necessary to verify that ammonium chloride produced urea at the same rate, without glucose, that it did with glucose present. The interest of Krebs's simple conclusion lies in the very fact that it was not a well-supported hypothesis; it was his immediate response to an unanticipated pattern that he perceived in the results of these two successive experiments, and that he was able to connect with some experiments of Warburg with which he had been familiar from several years back. His idea is typical of the many flashes of insight that occur to an imaginative investigator immersed in his daily work.

The following day (July 30) Krebs returned to his investigation based on the action of iodoacetate on carbohydrate metabolism. This time he added a new factor, by utilizing liver and testicle tissue from rats that had been treated with phlorizin before they were killed. Phlorizin, a plant glucoside, had been well known since the late nineteenth century as an agent that can render an animal diabetic: that is, it can cause the animal to which it is administered to excrete sugar in its urine. During the first three decades of the twentieth century there were numerous investigations of the action of this drug, but the question of how it acted remained a center of controversy. The glycosuria itself appeared to result, in part at least, from a specific action on the kidneys. Studies of the respiratory quotient and of other effects indicated also, however, that in "phlorizinized" animals carbohydrates are not metabolized normally. Some investigators maintained, after the discovery of insulin, that phlorizin simply prevents the pancreas from secreting insulin; but other research showed that it exerted effects distinguishable from the effects of the absence of insulin. There was also great interest in, and divergent opinions about, where in the course of carbohydrate metabolism phlorizin blocked the process. Gustav Embden and some others suggested that it prevented lactic acid from forming. Since phlorizin also inhibited the consumption of intermediates regarded as steps in the aerobic phase of carbohydrate decomposition, however, other investigators argued "that the oxidative pathway is blocked by phlorizin at some late stage." For the same reasons that phlorizin diabetes was a major object of research, phlorizin itself was frequently utilized as a means to study intermediary metabolism, along with other agents that appeared to inhibit some particular stage in the metabolic pathways.[73] Phlorizin was, therefore, another obvious agent for Krebs to incorporate into his research on carbohydrate metabolism in tissue slices. Characteristically, it was probably a current article, in the *Biochemical Journal*, that drew his attention at a strategic time to the possible usefulness of phlorizin for his experiments, and that led him back to the more general reviews of the subject in the recent literature.[74]

In his experiment, Krebs compared the effects of glucose and lactate on phlorinized rat liver and testicle slices, each one with and without iodoacetate present. Under both conditions lactate initially stimulated a higher respiration than glucose did in the liver tissue, but with both glucose and lactate the rates sank to very low levels over the course of the experiment. He remarked especially on the fact that this decline took place when glucose was present. For the testicle tissue, he considered the Q values too small, and noted that there was "a large inhibition without lactate." There is no indication of how Krebs interpreted the experiments as a whole, or what his reason was for including in the tests the simultaneous actions of two inhibitors, phlorizin and iodoacetate. Since there were no controls run without phlorizin, he appears to have treated the effects of that agent as the background condition, the glucose and the lactate as potential modifiers of that condition, and the iodoacetate as a secondary effect that might in turn modify or explain the actions of the primary modifiers.[75]

Appearing now to give equal priority to his two main lines of investigation, Krebs alternated experiments on carbohydrate metabolism with further experiments on urea synthesis. On August 3 he tested the rate at which ammonium chloride could cause urea to form in liver tissue under three sets of conditions: (1) In bicarbonate Warburg–Ringer's solution and an atmosphere of 5 percent CO_2 in O_2; (2) in the same fluid medium and 5 percent CO_2 in argon, that is, anaerobically; and (3) in phosphate Ringer's solution and pure oxygen gas, that is in a medium containing no CO_2. Under the first of these Q equaled 2.67, in the other two the rate was insignificant. Krebs concluded that urea is formed only aerobically and with CO_2 present in advance, and he calculated that the urea that had appeared under those circumstances represented

63 percent of the theoretical yield from the NH_4Cl present in the medium. On August 4 he compared the formation of urea from ammonium chloride in four tissues, liver, spleen, kidney, and diaphragm muscle, using for each one the same conditions that had proven effective in the preceding experiment. Only liver tissue produced a significant quantity, a result that mainly confirmed the long accepted view that urea is manufactured in the liver. Krebs calculated that the tissue had converted 0.87 percent of its own weight into urea in one hour, a figure that probably encouraged him to believe that the tissue slices can synthesize urea at rates comparable to its production in the intact body.[76]

The next day the first medical student to do research in Krebs's laboratory began work. Kurt Henseleit had come to Thannhauser looking for a subject for his MD thesis, and Thannhauser had sent him to Krebs. Born in Berlin in 1907, Henseleit studied medicine at the University of Berlin, where he passed his predoctoral examination in 1929. During the winter semester of 1930 he came to Freiburg to complete his medical studies. Henseleit had no laboratory experience. Krebs decided to try him out anyway on the methods he had just developed for his investigation of urea synthesis. On the first day, he had Henseleit do a simple manometric determination of the urea content of a known sample. Making his first entry in a new laboratory notebook, Henseleit recorded every detail of the experimental method, and of the procedures for calculating the results. The latter he copied out from the methodological article on metabolism in tissue slices that Krebs had written for a biological manual while in Warburg's laboratory. Henseleit obtained a result of 0.968 mg urea compared with the 0.987 mg that had been measured into the solution. In spite of this close agreement, Krebs, who entered a more summary version of the experiment into his own notebook, remarked "The urea was not measured very accurately." Nevertheless, it must have been an impressive first effort for the laboratory novice. Krebs judged him to be a potentially skillful experimentalist who learned quickly. Either then, or soon afterward, he decided to entrust to Henseleit the practical bench work for the main line of experiments on the formation of urea.[77]

On Henseleit's second day Krebs put him right to work at the current forefront of his urea investigation. Using the same conditions that Krebs had utilized in his own most recent experiment on the rate at which urea formed in liver slices with ammonium chloride added, Henseleit compared the rates with and without glucose in the medium. The Q values he obtained were, respectively, 3.503 with glucose and 4.455 without it. Henseleit wrote down as the result, "Glucose inhibits the formation of urea in the rat liver." Krebs independently calculated the rates from Henseleit's measurements, and arrived at slightly different values (3.65 and 4.66). He also expressed the outcome more cautiously: "In glucose, less than *without* glucose."[78] Whereas Henseleit's statement was in the form of a general conclusion, Krebs's appeared only to summarize a single result. Yet Henseleit's statement must also have reflected his director's view, for the student could hardly have made the judgment entirely on his own in his second day in the laboratory. These small differences in the way the two handled the same results, as well as Krebs's practice of making his own record of Henseleit's experiments, suggest a certain delicacy in the way Krebs handled his new research assistant, the first person he had directed in the laboratory who was not a mere technician. Should Henseleit simply follow instructions, or should he be learning to work with some independence? At the beginning Krebs was probably uncertain about just how closely to supervise; about whether Henseleit could only perform manual operations, or could draw the immediate conclusions to be gained from individual experiments.

The design of this experiment suggests that it may have been an effort by Krebs to explore the idea he had had 8 days before, that glucose inhibits the formation of ammonia from amino acids. From that hypothesis one could deduce that ammonia should produce as much urea, in the presence of glucose, as in its absence. (In his notebook Krebs had entitled the experiment "Urea formation — With and Without Glucose.") If we scan the results ourselves we might see them simply as indecisive. The comparison between 3.65 and 4.66 might be read either as evidence that ammonia produces urea at a substantial rate with and without glucose, or that glucose lowers the rate somewhat. In the case of alanine, the inhibition with glucose had been essentially complete. It is clear, however, even if one does not attribute Henseleit's stronger conclusion to him, that Krebs himself took the result as meaning that glucose decreased the output of urea from ammonia. It was, therefore, unfavorable to his view that glucose inhibits only the *formation* of ammonia conceived of as a step in the synthesis of urea. There is no indication that he pursued the idea further; and it did not surface again in his investigation.

* * *

In April 1977, I asked Hans Krebs if he could remember any instances during his research when he had had a sudden flash of insight. He answered, "No, I can't. And one reason is the majority of flashes turn out to be flops." He added, "And one has to follow up so many ideas, and it would be very difficult for one to find out how really such developments start." After further discussion between us about some of the circumstances in which ideas may occur, Krebs said, "At the first moment, many flashes may look large or may look small, but whether they are really large or small only the follow-up can show."[79]

The insight that glucose inhibits the formation of NH_3 in liver tissue was one of that majority of flashes that turn out to be small. After a brief follow-up, it faded from view.

V

The next experiments that Krebs instructed Henseleit to perform on urea synthesis were not guided by specific theoretical questions, but were standard systematic explorations of the effects of varying the conditions on the rate at which ammonia gives rise to urea in liver slices. On August 7 Henseleit tested the influence of the concentration of NH_3, obtaining a maximum $Q = 3.64$ at 12 mg/100 ml. The following day he tested the influence of the hydrogen ion concentration, finding the maximum activity at pH 7.5. Krebs now copied Henseleit's final reduced data directly into his own notebook, but still drew for himself curves representing the results in graphical form.[80]

On August 10 Henseleit compared the production of urea when the tissue slices were immersed in human blood serum, with its formation in bicarbonate Ringer's solution. Neither with nor without NH_4Cl did the liver tissue form urea in the serum. Henseleit stated the result as "rat liver forms no urea in human serum." This time Krebs expressed the result in slightly broader terms: "Serum (human) inhibits the formation of urea." Henseleit tested at the same time the ability of rat kidney tissue to produce urea from NH_4Cl. When he had calculated how much urea one of the slices had produced, and compared it to the quantity that one should have been able to wash out of the tissue at the beginning, he inferred that there was a deficit. The result, Henseleit decided, was that "The kidney consumes urea," although he considered also that some urea might actually have been washed out during the preparation of the slices. Henseleit must have gone through this reasoning on his own, for Krebs did not consider such a conclusion in his own record of the experiment. Krebs merely commented, "Therefore, no sensible urea formation in the kidneys."[81]

While he worked in Krebs's laboratory, Henseleit still had to attend medical lectures every day. The experiments he performed, however, could normally be completed within a morning or afternoon, or even separated into two parts if need be. From the start, Henseleit was able to carry out at least one set of experiments on almost every working day.[82]

On August 11, Henseleit tested the influence of a number of factors on the formation of urea. He measured "the influence of time" on the rate with NH_4Cl, and found the rate nearly constant over 4 hours. Once again he tested the effects of glucose on the formation of urea from NH_4Cl, and observed, in contrast to the previous try, that "Glucose favors the formation of urea." (It raised the Q value from 2.39 to 4.48.) The amino acid glycine by itself, however, gave less urea than NH_4Cl did. In blood serum the rate was very small.[83] The diverse effects tested in this one set of experiments suggest that Krebs was not pursuing a single dominant line of questions, but just looking around for a lead to follow. That was characteristic of him. In 1976 he said to me, "I always had the habit of trying out many things and exploring just whether there was a possibility."[84] The Warburg tissue slice–manometric method itself favored such an approach, because it permitted multiple simultaneous experiments, and because a set of experiments could be carried out so quickly.

On the 12th, Henseleit tested whether guinea pig kidney cortex or kidney medulla tissue can produce urea. He concluded that "The medulla substance does not form, but rather consumes urea." Krebs treated the same result, on the other hand, as a likely experimental artifact. "Therefore disappearance of urea (perhaps in the preparation they were not uniformly washed out)." From a similar experiment carried out the next day, in which some urea was added to the medium before the experiment began, Henseleit concluded that "Urea formation takes place also in the kidneys." He had calculated that the quantity measured afterward somewhat exceeded that present at the beginning; but Krebs regarded the values Henseleit had found as too small to be significant, and wrote down the results as "1. No urea formation in the kidney cortex, 2. Questionable urea formation in the medulla." He considered that the washing had still not been thorough enough.[85]

Henseleit again tested a heterogenous group of factors simultaneously on August 14. A comparison between the formation of urea from NH_4Cl in blood serum and in the usual Warburg–Ringer's solution showed a small increase with serum; Krebs considered the results using serum as inaccurate, because it was a "differential determination [because serum itself contains urea]." This time glucose exerted "no definite influence." The only novel element in the experiments of the day was a test of "urea formation from thymine." Thus Krebs was taking up at this point the last of the four questions that he much later listed as those that "suggested themselves" in the investigation. "Do pyrimidines yield urea directly, or via ammonia?" Because these constituents of nucleic acids contain the skeleton of the urea molecule (N-C-N), it seemed plausible that the pyrimidines might split off this group and give rise directly to urea. In that case nucleic acids would provide a source for urea independent of the main source in the decomposition of amino acids. In the experiment, thymine yielded a Q value of 2.7, compared with 2.08 for NH_4Cl. Henseleit concluded, "Urea formation from thymine is possible." His chief summarized the situation in much stronger language: "Thymine forms urea!!" Krebs stated emphatically, "as much as NH_3."[86] Krebs thus saw in the result a very promising lead to follow.

These repeated small differences between the way Henseleit and Krebs viewed the results of the same experiments do not mean that Henseleit was developing truly independent opinions. Because Krebs and Henseleit undoubtedly discussed such matters during the day, even Henseleit's own statements must have reflected what he had been told; but the nuances are at least enough to indicate that the new assistant was attempting to make his own interpretations of his day-to-day results, and the subtle distinctions between these interpretations and those of his director are suggestive of the difference between one who is merely responding to his immediate results, and one who is attempting to fit the individual experiments into a broader picture. Krebs's experience, and his sense of the purpose of the investigation, enabled him to pick out from a set of effects that Henseleit could evaluate only in terms of the magnitude of the measured differences, those that were most likely to reflect some significant underlying phenomena. Krebs's judgments were not invariably better than Henseleit's, however, for his sense of what might turn out to be significant could also lead him to read more into a given result than was there. In the case of the measurement with thymine, it was clearly his theoretical expectation that fixed his attention on this very preliminary positive reading.

After this date, Krebs stopped copying all of Henseleit's results into his own notebook. Evidently he had come to trust Henseleit's records, and his ability to calculate the experimental data himself, sufficiently to make that unnecessary. Henseleit kept, in fact, a more meticulous notebook than Krebs did, writing in a more legible hand, and recording the conditions and data of the experiments in more extended form. In part Henseleit had to do it that way also because he did not have the experience necessary to eliminate what was not essential to keep. If he was also neater, that was in part because Krebs kept a record only for "his own eyes," whereas Henseleit had to keep a record easily accessible to his chief.

VI

During the first 2 weeks that Henseleit performed all the experiments for the urea investigation, Krebs himself pursued several strands of the research on carbohydrate metabolism that he had previously taken up. On August 6 he repeated the experiment on phlorinized rat liver that he had carried out a week earlier, following exactly the same procedures, except that he substituted monobromoacetate for monoiodoacetate. That was a tactic he had tried before when iodoacetate had not brought the results he sought. In this case the results were exactly the same.[87] Whatever he was looking for he apparently did not find, and he turned to another of the lines he had recently begun. This was the action of the "ketol" that Henze and Müller had thought might arise from the action of methylglyoxal on acetoacetate, and play a role in several key aspects of intermediary metabolism. Krebs tested, on August 7, the action of ketol on glycolysis in rat liver tissue, and for comparison, he also tested pyruvate. Neither substance much effected the anaerobic rate of formation of lactate. "Little keto effect," he wrote down, "but also little pyruvate effect!!".[88] The latter result contrasted with an experiment he had carried out in Altona, in which pyruvate doubled the rate of glycolysis in kidney slices.[89]

Moving again to a different line of attack on carbohydrate metabolism, Krebs tested the effects of glucose and fructose, as well as the combined effects of glucose and pyruvate on anaerobic metabolism in rat brain tissue. In each case the rate was higher with glucose than with fructose, whereas glucose together with pyruvate gave a much higher rate than either of the sugars alone. Krebs probably had no explanation for these differences, but they seemed at least to offer an opening for further exploration. On August 12 he followed up with measurements of respiration as well as glycolysis in brain tissue, comparing the effects of the combination of pyruvate with glucose to that of its combination with fructose. The result was that "with pyruvate there is full respiration with fructose:" that is, the combination produced a Q value nearly equal to the combination with glucose. Fructose and pyruvate produced very little glycolysis, however, in contrast to glucose and pyruvate. The next day he tested the effects of glucose and fructose alone on the respiration of guinea pig brain tissue, and found that glucose raised the rate somewhat, but fructose did not.[90]

On the 14th, the same day that Henseleit found thymine to produce urea, Krebs returned once again to ketol. He tested its effects on the aerobic and anaerobic metabolism of rat liver slices. In neither situation did ketol raise the rate sensibly — anaerobically, in fact, the rate declined. Interesting though a possible metabolic role for ketol must have appeared to Krebs to draw him to it several times, in none of his tests had he found experimental justification for such a role. When he summed up the results of his efforts, they were all negative.[91]

Three days later, Krebs tested the actions of glucose, fructose, and lactate on the respiration of brain tissue treated with bromoacetate. With fructose and glucose there was inhibition, but "no, or little, inhibition" with lactate. This result merely confirmed what Krebs had already published in his paper on iodoacetate. On August 20, he carried out a similar experiment, using glucose and lactate, on diaphragm muscle poisoned with iodoacetate. All the readings were low and undifferentiated. "Poor pressures," he remarked, "perhaps because slices too thick (unsliced diaphragm)."[92] In his ongoing study of carbohydrate metabolism, even more than in his new investigation of urea synthesis, Krebs now seemed to be casting around for an interesting lead, but finding little to take him beyond what he and others had already learned. In the last 10 days in August, he made no further entries in his laboratory notebook. Perhaps he took a short vacation.

Henseleit meanwhile went on with the urea experiments, day after day, sometimes 6 days a week. After the experiments of August 14, Krebs placed highest priority on the pursuit of the initial evidence Henseleit had obtained that thymine, perhaps pyrimidines in general, give rise to urea. The next day Henseleit tested three different concentrations of thymine. In contrast to the first trial, however, thymine now gave much less urea than NH_4Cl did. (The largest Q for thymine was 0.705, against 2.89 for NH_4Cl.) On August 17 he tried again, this time with three pyrimidines. Thymine, thymosine, and uridine all yielded some urea, but none of them at rates close to that for NH_4Cl.[93] What had looked just 3 days before like the beginning of a hopeful new branch of Krebs's investigative trail was already petering out.

After this setback, Henseleit's experiments shifted from such specific investigative questions that Krebs had in mind, to a long series of efforts to improve the basic procedures to determine the rate of formation of urea. In most cases he examined the effects of the conditions he tested on the formation of urea from NH_4Cl. Several of the experiments checked the effects of the thickness of the tissue slices on the rates. He explored hydrogen ion concentrations different from the standard pH of 5.0 maintained by the acetate buffer, but uncovered no advantage in shifting to another concentration. He examined again the effects of the concentration of NH_3 on the rate, but only confirmed that the 0.12 mg/100 ml originally found to provide the maximum yield was the best concentration to use for most experiments. He checked several times the effects of anaerobic conditions, and reaffirmed that the liver produces urea only aerobically. Several further runs on other tissues reinforced the original conclusion that only liver tissue produces urea. From time to time he tested again the effects of glucose on the formation of urea from ammonia. In most cases the glucose appeared to have little or no effect. In early September, however, Krebs and Henseleit noticed that when the liver tissue came from nourished rats, the rates were higher than if the rats had been starved before death, and they found that this effect also took place if they nourished a starved rat with glucose alone. Then finally, late in September, they were able to attain a "clear influence of glucose in the sense of an increase in the urea formation" from NH_4Cl by adding the glucose to the tissue medium.[94]

Henseleit also tested the effects of using phosphate Ringer's solution in place of the usual bicarbonate Ringer's solution. Often he simply carried out multiple repetitions of the now standard measurement of the rates at which NH_4Cl formed urea in liver tissue.[95] The motive for much of what he was asked to do was probably to improve the reliability of the results, and to find conditions under which the rates would reach a maximum. The results recorded in Henseleit's notebook for this period suggest that there was need for such refinement. Although parallel experiments carried out simultaneously usually gave consistent figures, the rates attainable from NH_4Cl in separate experiments, even with standardized concentrations of the substrate, and standardized media, varied widely, from $Q < 1$ to $Q > 4$. Since the additional effects due to the other substances tested were usually less than this range of variation, it was evident that uncertainty would surround the interpretation of such experiments. The fact that thymine formed urea at the same rate as ammonia did in one experiment, but at much lower rates in subsequent trials, or that glucose sometimes inhibited, sometimes increased, and sometimes had little influence on the formation of urea from ammonia, would suggest that Krebs could not have been fully satisfied with the consistency of his results, and more extensive experience with the procedures was the only way available to improve them. We may suspect also, however, that he did not always have compelling reasons for the particular experiments he instructed Henseleit to perform. In keeping with his manner of planning only from one day to the next, Krebs customarily discussed with Henseleit each morning what experimental protocol he wished him to follow that day.[96] There must have been some days, during these weeks in which no special new investigative directions seemed to emerge, in which he directed Henseleit to repeat the basic experiments mainly to keep him busy.

Krebs too was very busy in September, but not in the laboratory. The only entries he made in his notebook, up until the last day of that month, were summaries of several of Henseleit's experiments, a list of the results of the urea experiments up until then, and some references from the journal literature on subjects that particularly interested him. The most likely reason for his inability to do more himself was that about this time a second hospital ward was placed under his care. He had then greater clinical responsibilities than any of his colleagues, the reason given him being that he still had to catch up for the medical experience he had missed while in Warburg's laboratory. Under the circumstances, he must have been particularly appreciative of the fact that Henseleit was turning out to be a skillful, independent, and hard-working experimenter.[97] Work could go on at a steady pace in one line of investigation, even when Krebs had little time for research.

On September 28, Henseleit tested once again the formation of urea from pyrimidines, utilizing thymine, thymosine, and uracil. This time the rates were no more than one eighth of the rate from NH_4Cl.[98] In many situations when Krebs tried out an idea and got a negative result, he dropped the idea without further ado. In this case, however, he kept returning to try it. Probably this particular idea was attractive enough to him on conceptual grounds, so that he resisted, at least mildly, the repeated finding of evidence against it.

After this date, Henseleit carried out no further experiments for 3 weeks. At about the same time Krebs resumed his personal experimentation. On September 30, he returned to the line of investigation he had begun nearly 8 months before under the influence of Lundsgaard's work, the action of iodoacetate on fermentation.[99] His first objective now was to test whether the ethyl ester of monobromoacetate would act in the same manner on the fermentation and respiration of yeast that the sodium salt he had formerly used did. It did.[100]

Krebs was probably stimulated to return to this problem by the latest publications of others on the subject. In an issue of the *Biochemische Zeitschrift* that appeared in the summer of 1931, Peter Boysen Jensen described some new experiments on the effects of iodoacetate on yeast that supported Lundgaard's interpretation of its action on glycolysis. The September issue of the same journal carried an article by Fritz Zuckerkandl and Luise Messiner-Klebermass on the influence of tyrosine, and other substances containing amino groups, upon the decomposition of sugar in yeast. In their paper the authors discussed recent experiments using iodoacetate, and mentioned Krebs's own article on that topic. In his usual manner, Krebs skimmed these issues as quickly as they appeared in the library, and included these articles in the references he put down in his notebook.[101] This was clearly an active field of investigation, and it must have been evident to him that he too would have to remain active in it if he hoped to have anything further to contribute. He did only this one experiment, however, before he was diverted back to some problems raised by the work on proteolysis that he had carried out for Warburg in Altona.

The article on proteolysis in which Krebs summarized his work on that topic with the desultory conclusion that "The measurement of the proteolytic action of carcinoma cells reveals, altogether, no peculiarities in comparison to the proteolytic action of normal tissues," had just appeared in the *Biochemische Zeitschrift* in August. Already during the previous winter, however, he had engaged by correspondence in a debate over the effects on proteolysis of heavy metals and substances that form complexes, with Ernst Waldschmidt-Leitz, who had been doing similar research. In his article Krebs acknowledged that these questions needed further examination. It was to them that he devoted most of the 8 days between October 8 and October 22 in which he could find time for research. Among the conclusions he reached was that Waldschmidt-Leitz had been correct in one of his main criticisms of Krebs's previous position.[102]

VII

During his first 6 months in Freiburg, Krebs had carried on his research on intermediary metabolism independently, resourcefully, and as persistently as his time would allow; but he had yet to uncover anything really new about the processes he studied. His scattered experiments on carbohydrate metabolism left him about where he had been when he left Altona. His return to proteolysis, a subject that had never much interested him, was only to clear up some residual difficulties remaining from his earlier experiments. In his most important new venture, he had achieved a significant technical advance in the demonstration that isolated tissue slices can synthesize urea. Some biochemists, including Warburg, doubted that slices could carry out integrated synthetic metabolic processes that must be coupled as well to an intact source of energy, because the tissues were likely to be "damaged."[103] His initial success in disproving such skeptical views offered him major prospective advantages over those who had studied urea synthesis through the cumbersome methods of organ perfusion, or those who tried to preserve the process in an extract from the tissues. This methodological accomplishment could only pay off for him, however, if he could make it reveal more about the metabolic pathway itself than was already known. So far he had been able to do little more than confirm the long-established conclusion that amino acids and ammonia both give rise to urea in the liver.

* * *

While Hans Krebs was reviewing with me a preliminary attempt I had made in 1978 to write a history of his investigation of urea synthesis, he agreed that at the end of the period described in the present chapter, his attempts "were in a sense unsuccessful.... I really didn't get much further beyond what had already been done." I asked him whether there was any time at which he had the feeling that the investigation would wind up as just a fairly ordinary confirmation of the earlier ideas. He answered, "I think in general I was, then as today, an optimist, and...thought if you persist and keep at it something might turn up...I was confident that something would turn up if you try long enough, and do different kinds of experiments, not just doing the same."[104]

Expressed so long after the events, this view was probably not a direct memory of a feeling that Krebs had experienced sometime in September or October 1931, but his reconstruction of how he would probably have felt in such a situation. I believe that it nevertheless provides a reliable insight into how he did feel then. In most respects Krebs knew himself well. His comment expresses the optimism that, as a young scientist he repeatedly displayed in his actions, and that he often needed. That optimism sustained him when he failed to obtain encouragement from others, when his professional prospects were uncertain, and when, as happened often in his research, he was unable for periods of time to locate the route toward a novel contribution.

The vagueness of that expectation that "something might turn up" is also a perceptive reflection on the young investigator's scientific style. His approach was one of trial-and-error search, of trying many things because he did not spend a lot of time working out in advance which ones had the best chance for success. That approach was, in turn, more than personal style alone; for it was, in a sense, forced on him by the absence in his repertoire, of heuristic strategies powerful enough to guide him more directly toward solutions for his problems.[105]

* * *

To understand Krebs's position in the fall of 1931, it is useful to recall how general was the idea around which he oriented his investigative goals. He simply planned to apply Warburg's tissue slice methods to study the processes of intermediary metabolism. When he began on his own, he had no special training in the methods that had previously been applied in this subfield, and was not even steeped in its earlier literature. He merely saw that Warburg's method offered certain crucial advantages, such as the ability to do multiple experiments quickly and easily, and to measure accurately the *rates* of processes that directly or indirectly produce or absorb oxygen or carbon dioxide.

Despite these advantages, the application of Warburg's methods to the study of intermediary pathways was still encumbered with some of the same restrictions that had made it so difficult in the past to establish intermediate steps with certainty, including the fact that many intermediates disappeared as rapidly as they formed. The lack of specific analytical methods to identify substrates in very small quantities was also a severe problem for the tissue slice method. Like his predecessors, Krebs had to rely heavily on the postulate that to qualify as an intermediate a substance must be consumed in the tissue at least as rapidly as the overall process took place. As we have seen in Chapter 1, however, one could never depend entirely on that postulate, for a substrate that failed the test might not have penetrated into the cells, or one that appeared to pass it may merely have stimulated in some more general way a metabolic process of which it was not a step.

Such restrictions Krebs shared with anyone working in this field in those years. In the search for potential pathways, however, he bore an additional personal limitation. Having had less than a year of systematic training in chemistry, he did not possess the extensive knowledge of the properties and reactions of organic compounds necessary to reason deeply about the metabolic steps that would be most likely, on theoretical grounds, to take place. That was one reason why he was so dependent on the current literature for ideas about possible pathways that he could test.

The somewhat scattered approach that Krebs followed was thus perhaps the only one available to him. He could only follow up every plausible suggestion that he could come across, trying out candidates for metabolic roles in his system, until one of them turned out to yield manometer readings large enough to fix his attention on it. He became, therefore, an investigative scanner, gazing back and forth across his experimental horizon for an unusual effect, waiting patiently for something to appear sufficiently out of place to warrant focusing his effort.

These limitations themselves, however, also conferred on Krebs some real benefits. If his lack of expert knowledge of organic reactions made it difficult for him to choose the most promising theoretical possibilities in advance, it freed him at the same time from some of the biases built into the conceptual frameworks within which others operated, for example, the elegance of the sequence of dismutation reactions that made the methylglyoxal theory of glycolysis so enticing, or the resistance that biochemists with experience in organic chemistry often displayed toward biological reaction mechanisms that were not analogous to reactions carried out in the laboratory. Moreover, the tissue slice–manometer method was ideally suited to Krebs's horizon-scanning tactics, and not only because of the simplicity and rapidity of the experiments it permitted. Provided one could gain control over the experimental conditions, the precision with which the method enabled one to measure incremental processes made it especially easy to spot a reaction rate that was out of line with expectations, or to compare the quantitative effects of numerous possible intermediates. No other method available at the time offered so effective a means to exploit the fundamental postulate that an intermediate must be metabolized at no less than the rate of the overall reaction.

In October 1931, Krebs had yet to identify through these methods any stage of such a process that was not already known, and nothing guaranteed that he would find one. Nothing guaranteed, therefore, that he would emerge from the field of hopeful young biochemists whose futures were still insecure, in a world whose future, in 1931, was precarious.

* * *

This examination of Krebs's circumstances suggests that 45 years later he expressed a realistic recollection of a realistic attitude toward his prospects, when he said to me, "I wasn't at all sure whether I could really make significant contributions to research, so that it was in any case a matter of trying it out first." He was not greatly troubled over what his future would hold if he did not do well as a research scientist, because he was, in any case, "much attracted by clinical medicine," and he knew that he could rely on that as an alternative. "There was the relative security of a qualified doctor, to make a living somehow, that was never difficult in any country."

> Even if I were not successful in the academic career, one could always make a living as a practicing physician, and this practical aspect was of decisive importance. So I didn't waste much time on thinking what I would prefer to do, because that was the one thing I had to do in order to make a living.[106]

* * *

Whatever might come in the long run, Krebs was undoubtedly as happy at Freiburg as he had ever been. Here, too, he made good friends both among the hospital staff and the academic scientists. He enjoyed the stimulation of an environment that included such distinguished senior scientists as Ludwig Aschoff, Hans Spemann, and Hermann Staudinger, as well as the director of his first effort at laboratory research, Wilhelm von Möllendorff. He also came into contact with the brilliant younger biochemist Rudolf Schoenheimer, who formed a very high opinion of his scientific ability. Krebs developed a close friendship

Figure 8.3 Hans Krebs hiking in the Black Forest.

with another talented young scientist, Franz Bielschowsky. For an assistant at so early a stage in his career, he had excellent laboratory facilities.[107]

At Freiburg Krebs still had to live frugally on the small income he received. His life was, however, not entirely austere. He enjoyed free room and board, and even his cleaning was provided for him. With such freedom from most of the cares of everyday living, he could work 14 hours a day and still have time to pursue other activities that mattered to him.[108]

Familiar from his student days with the beautiful environs of the Black Forest, which descended almost to the eastern outskirts of Freiburg itself, Krebs hiked avidly on the many nearby walking trails. On a Saturday afternoon or a Sunday he could cycle up into the hills and then walk for hours along these beautiful paths. They led one through impeccably maintained forests and meadows, alongside farmhouses and cultivated fields that scarcely seemed to encroach on the natural beauty of the region, and over elevations that afforded splendid vistas across grand valleys toward distant peaks. There too he could pursue his long standing amateur interest in botany. (When winter came he also began skiing regularly on weekends on some of these same slopes.)

To those who did not know him well, Hans Krebs often seemed a man who lived for his science alone. Those who came closer to him, however, learned that the breadth of his interests in music, literature, and theater, his awareness of political and other world events, made him a versatile serious conversationalist. Not given to small talk, he nevertheless tempered the severity of his work habits with a playful enjoyment of the unusual little occurrences of the day, and he could be moved to great laughter by simple humor. He was willful, and he could be discouragingly incommunicative to those with whom he had little in common. With his patients, and with those whom he liked and trusted, however, he exhibited a warmth and a gentleness that won their loyalty as well as their admiration.

Nor were his friendships confined to his professional life. Long past his painfully shy youth, Krebs easily attracted the affectionate friendship of women he encountered during his daily activities, and when he took time for recreational pursuits, he often had female companionship. Some of these women came to care for him deeply.[109]

Reared in a society in which a man was expected to attain financial security before entering marriage, Krebs could not consider taking such a step.[110] That prospect remained as distant as his ultimate professional fate. In the meantime he lived a productive, disciplined life, devoted to his immediate medical responsibilities and his scientific aspirations, but far from destitute of other interests.

The Ornithine Effect

Kurt Henseleit resumed his experiments on October 19, 1931. His first moves were a continuation of the efforts to improve the basic methods employed in the urea research. In phosphate–Ringer's solution, he had found earlier, the action of urease on urea is partially inhibited. In an attempt to obviate this difficulty, so they could try using phosphate-Ringer's solution in the main experiments, Henseleit examined the influence of calcium chloride added to that solution, and discovered that the urease reaction then took place at the same rate as in bicarbonate Ringer's solution. On the same day, he tested a urease preparation, made in the laboratory from an extract of soya beans that he had ground up in a coffee grinder. Making the urease this way was less expensive than to buy it; but the new urease also worked three times as fast as the commercial urease they had been using.[1] They adopted the extract for their future experimental determinations.

On October 21 Henseleit's experiments took a new turn, as he began to test "urea formation in the rat liver from amino acids." Using a bicarbonate–Ringer's medium containing glucose, he compared the rates at which slices of this tissue formed urea in the presence of NH_4Cl, arginine, alanine, methylamine, glycine, and phenylalanine, carrying out duplicate runs for each. The subject of the experiment implies that Krebs was now satisfied that they had arrived at adequate basic procedures, and could, therefore, concentrate on the more specific questions at which the investigation was aimed. In this case he could have had in mind two questions: whether ammonia produces urea at at least the rate of the amino acids, as expected of an intermediate, and how the rates of different amino acids compare with one another. The presence of methylamine suggests that he wished in addition to check whether amino acids were the unique source of the amino groups that were suspected to take part in the synthesis, or whether amines in general could play the same role. The experiment thus appears as another instance of Krebs's tendency to try several things at once. The results were as follows:

	Q
NH_4Cl	3.42
Arginine	28.9 and 28.8
Alanine	1.38 and 1.28
Methylamine	0.45 and 0.28
Glycine	0.85 and 0.39
Phenylalanine	0.25 and 0.31

The enormous rate from arginine — Henseleit noted that it was "8 times as large as from NH_4Cl" — could be expected. As we have seen, arginine had long since been identified as a special source of urea by means of the enzymatic reaction: arginine $\rightarrow$ ornithine + urea. Nevertheless, Henseleit put down that it would be necessary to test whether urease itself cleaves arginine. If so, then the reading could be an artifact of the method of urea determination. The other result notable enough for Henseleit to record was that "From the other substances, with the exception of alanine, the urea formation is very small." That was not a predicted result, although it did conform to the outcome of the very first experiment on the formation of urea that Krebs had carried out in July with alanine and phenylalanine. The work of Wilhelm Löffler, the general view that urea was the product of the breakdown of all of the amino acids constituting the body proteins, and the common structure of all amino acids with respect to the α-amino group that was regarded as the source for the urea nitrogen, all would have led Krebs to anticipate that the amino acids should behave similarly. The relation between the rate at which alanine and NH_4Cl gave rise to urea in this experiment would fit the generally accepted view, but that view could provide no explanation for why the other two common amino acids, phenylalanine and glycine, produced negligible quantities. Finally, the fact that they did not produce urea rendered the fact that methylamine also produced none an indecisive test of whether amino acids were the sole source for the amino groups. Later the same day Henseleit tested and eliminated the possibility that the special effect of arginine was due to the urease.[2]

The next day Henseleit tested arginine under anaerobic and aerobic conditions, and in the presence of octyl alcohol. The absence of oxygen doubled the rate. Octyl alcohol (under aerobic conditions) multiplied it by five. Henseleit attributed both effects to the destruction of the cell structure, liberating the enzyme arginase. The same day he tested the action of potassium cyanate (KCNO), with and without NH_4Cl. The purpose of this experiment was evidently to test the possibility that cyanate may be an intermediate in the synthesis of urea. The outcome was negative. Potassium cyanate alone formed "no urea," and with NH_4Cl no more than the latter formed alone.[3] With this single result Krebs was satisfied that he could dispose of the theory that had been maintained, without much experimental support, ever since Schultzen and Nencki proposed it in 1869.

At about this time Krebs's attention was drawn back to the iodoacetate question, by the appearance in the latest issue of *Biochemische Zeitschrift* of an article on that subject by Albert Szent-Györgyi and his co-workers. The starting point of Szent-Györgyi's paper was Krebs's own recent publication. "Through the study of monoiodoacetate," Szent-Györgyi wrote, "Krebs has recently come to the conclusion that in rat brain, testicle, and sarcoma tissue, lactic acid forms an intermediate stage in respiration." Krebs's results, Szent-Györgyi indicated, needed to be tested for the system that he himself was investigating, "reduced heart muscle tissue." Szent-Györgyi had recently devised a method for investigating metabolism in isolated tissues that differed in detail from the tissue slice method Krebs utilized, but that afforded similar advantages. In place of slicing tissues, Szent-Györgyi minced them in a "Latapie-grinder," which produced a coarse suspension, the particles of which were large enough to allow many of the cells contained in them to remain intact. He, too, measured the metabolism of the tissues manometrically, using a Barcroft differential manometer. The procedure differed from that of the Warburg method only in that one always compared the difference between two rates, usually between that produced by the conditions being tested and a control placed in the vessel connected to the other arm of the manometer.[4]

What Szent-Györgyi reported was that lactate did increase the respiration of heart muscle tissue inhibited by iodoacetate. Lactate also increased the respiration of the same tissue, in the same proportion, however, when there was no iodoacetate present. Szent-Györgyi concluded that the influence of iodoacetate on respiration does not rest on the suppression of the formation of lactate, as Krebs had contended. Krebs had observed only an "apparent," not a real restoration of the respiration in his experiments. Szent-Györgyi argued that his results favored the original interpretation of Lundsgaard, which he himself had also supported on other grounds, that "the paths of oxidative and fermentative decomposition are, for the most part, separate."[5]

Krebs could hardly avoid reacting to such a challenge to his interpretation of his results in the paper that represented his only published contribution to the field of intermediary metabolism. He turned to another paper that Meyerhof and an associate had published shortly after his own, in which Meyerhof had independently reached the same conclusions that he had. Meyerhof and Eric Boyland had worked with frog muscle tissue, and had, in fact, provided experimentally more convincing evidence than Krebs had, that iodoacetate inhibits simultaneously respiration and the formation of lactate, whereas lactate added from the medium can restore the suppressed respiration. Meyerhof, who noted that Krebs's article had appeared after their own work had been completed, naturally interpreted the results in the same manner that Krebs did. Krebs had, after all, viewed his results as support for Meyerhof's conception of the lactic acid cycle.[6]

Glancing over one of the tables in the Meyerhof–Boyland article, Krebs saw that, like Szent-Györgyi, they had found that lactate added to unpoisoned muscle tissue increased its respiration. When he calculated the percentage increases from Meyerhof's table, however, Krebs found that in normal muscle the increase amounted to 79 and 81 percent (in two runs respectively), whereas in the iodoacetate poisoned muscle it was much larger, 165 and 215 percent.

Szent-Györgyi's interpretation could, therefore, not explain Meyerhof's results. "Probably," Krebs wrote at the bottom of the page on which he had summarized these considerations, in Szent-Györgyi's experiments "the muscles contained lactic acid!!"[7]   Having satisfied himself that Szent-Györgyi's work was technically flawed, and did not threaten his own, Krebs did nothing further about the issue, but returned to his proteolysis experiments. He must have taken some satisfaction from the fact that his first independent scientific publication since leaving Warburg was receiving regular attention from the major investigators in the field.

Meanwhile, Henseleit went on testing various substances that might be involved in forming urea in the liver. Using tissue from a starved rat, he carried out another experiment with mixed objectives, on October 24. The substances chosen this time were NH_4Cl, thymine, thymosine, alanine, and glycine, all repeats from previous trials. Once again the pyrimidines and glycine formed "little urea." In contrast to the situation when the tissue had come from a nourished rat, "The urea formation from alanine was just as large as that from NH_4Cl." On the same day Henseleit tested the influence of insulin on the formation of urea from NH_4Cl, and found that it increased the rate, but "only in the presence of glucose."[8]

On the 26th of October Henseleit performed a set of experiments entitled "Urea formation in the rat liver from NH_4Cl and amino acids," but that again included more diverse objectives. Half of the experiment was a comparison of the urea formed by the tissue alone, with NH_4Cl, with alanine, and with alanine and NH_4Cl together. The reason for testing the two substances together was, as Krebs recalled in 1976, that he "had some guess" that one of the nitrogens in urea "comes from ammonia and the other comes directly from amino acids."[9] Although time may have allowed some further details of this idea to slip from his mind, it is not necessary to assume that he had worked out any more specific a hypothetical mechanism than he remembered, as he so often did test simple ideas without extended thought. If the guess was correct, then adding the two substances together ought to increase the rate more than would either substance alone. The outcome, in fact, favored his idea:

	Q
No addition	0.52
With NH_4Cl	1.13
With alanine	1.59
With NH_4Cl + alanine	3.98[10]

The remainder of this experiment was less focused. It included a miscellaneous group of substances that might possibly donate nitrogen to form urea. Two of them were the amino acids cystein and cystine. These substances might merely have represented an exploration of whether any amino acids in addition to alanine would form significant quantities of urea; although it would appear an unusual coincidence that Krebs should choose for that purpose the two amino acids that contain sulfur. A third substance was asparagine

[$NH_2COCH_2CH(NH_2)COOH$], the β-amide of the natural amino acid aspartic acid.[11] A possible motivation for this test was that asparagine might donate the β-amide group to form urea. The fourth substance tested was ammonium carbamate (NH_2COOH). It probably was included as a test of the theory Edmund Drechsel had proposed, in 1880, that this salt may combine with ammonia to give urea.[12] Finally, Henseleit tested choline, a compound containing a quaternary ammonium ion, that was an important constituent of plant and animal tissues. Krebs probably had in this case no strong theoretical reason for implicating choline in urea synthesis, and probably tried it mainly because he could obtain it easily from colleagues in Freiburg.[13] He was evidently again casting his net widely, fishing for an effect to which he could fasten his investigation. According to his later recollection, the decisive determinant of the order in which he tested substances was not advance expectations of how they might react, but "the availability of the substances.... As they came along, they were tested."[14]

In this set, the only substance that had any notable effect was asparagine. Its Q value of 3.35 was the highest of any single substance tested that day, whereas the rest of the newcomers yielded little or nothing.[15] Because asparagine can readily be hydrolyzed to ammonia and aspartic acid, however, even the effect that Henseleit observed with it might have been due more to ammonia than to the asparagine itself.

After an uncharacteristic 4-day break, Henseleit came back on the last day of October to carry out a massive set of experiments, consisting of 18 simultaneous runs. Each of them used rat liver tissue previously nourished with carbohydrate. Two of the tests were combinations of lactate and pyruvate with NH_4Cl. Since neither of these substances were potential donors of urea nitrogen, Krebs must have had in mind the possibility of a more general effect, probably related to the action of glucose that they had noticed earlier. By testing these two intermediates of carbohydrate metabolism, he might be able to discriminate between the possibility that the influence of glucose was specific to that compound, and that it was more generally related to an increase in the carbohydrate metabolism. For the remainder of the substances tested — thymine, thymosine, asparagine, glycine, uridine, and aspartic acid, all except the last one being substances previously employed — Henseleit in each case compared the rate with that substance alone, to the rate for the same substance together with NH_4Cl. It appears evident that Krebs was examining whether the summation effect they had observed with alanine and NH_4Cl could be extended to any other nitrogenous substances; that is to say, he may have been building on the initial support that this prior result had seemed to offer for his idea that ammonia might provide one of the nitrogen atoms of urea, while other metabolites supply the second atom. None of them, not even alanine this time, exhibited the effect. In every case the rate with NH_4Cl together with the other substance was less than the rate with NH_4Cl alone. (The latter was Q = 4.11, however, itself higher than in most of the preceding experiments.) Lactate and pyruvate with NH_4Cl also did not match the rate of NH_4Cl by itself.[16] The outcome of this entire set of experiments was, therefore, wholly negative.

Henseleit carried out a similar set of comparisons on November 2, substituting liver tissue from a starved rat for the nourished tissue used in the previous set. He employed lactate and pyruvate just as before, but cut the list of nitrogenous substances down to alanine, asparagine, and glycine. The change in the nutritive condition of the tissue appeared to bring about a striking change in the results. NH_4Cl itself yielded a Q of only 1.50, compared with 4.11 before. Lactate and pyruvate both raised the rate from NH_4Cl alone substantially, to 2.68 and 3.14, respectively. Alanine alone gave about the same rate as NH_4Cl alone, with NH_4Cl it increased the rate about the same amount as did the nonnitrogenous metabolites. Asparagine produced urea at about the same rate, with or without NH_4Cl, a finding that probably only strengthened the suspicion that it was merely hydrolyzed and supplied ammonia to the tissue. Glycine again failed to deliver much in the presence or the absence of NH_4Cl.[17]

These results left Krebs about where he had been with respect to the direct steps in the synthesis of urea. If anything, they may have weakened support for the idea that alanine could yield one of the urea nitrogens. Its effects were so like those of lactate and pyruvate that all three might plausibly be attributed to their general stimulating influence on the metabolism of a tissue impoverished of nutrient matter. The alanine might even have been converted to pyruvate in the tissue. The only promising lead the experiment did open up, in fact, was this connection it suggested between the rate of general metabolic activity in the tissue and the rate at which the tissue produced urea. It was in that direction that Krebs now moved.

Again using liver tissue from a starved rat, Henseleit tested on November 7 the effects on urea formation from NH_4Cl of eight substances that were all implicated in glycolysis or aerobic respiration. These included glucose, fructose, pyruvic acid, succinic acid, malic acid, lactic acid, glycerol, and sodium citrate. Glucose and pyruvate raised the rate somewhat above that for NH_4Cl alone. Malic acid decreased it, whereas the others had only slight effects. Because there was some doubt about whether the rat from which the tissue was taken had actually been starved, he repeated the experiment on November 9, but obtained similarly inconclusive results. Choosing now only those substances that had seemed to exert some positive influence (glycerol, lactic acid, pyruvic acid, fructose, and glucose), he tried once more, on November 11, doing duplicate runs for each substance. This time glycerol with NH_4Cl gave less urea than NH_4Cl, whereas NH_4Cl with the remaining four substances, regarded as intermediates in carbohydrate metabolism, continued to cause modest increases over the rate with NH_4Cl alone.[18]

Perhaps because the effects of these four substances were too small to appear conclusive, yet seemed to suggest a consistent pattern, Krebs pursued the situation persistently. The next day Henseleit tested the same substances, using liver tissue from nourished rats. The results were similar, except that all of the increases were somewhat larger: NH_4Cl, Q = 1.97; NH_4Cl + lactate, Q = 3.09 and 2.98; NH_4Cl + pyruvate, Q = 3.51 and 3.02; NH_4Cl + fructose, Q = 3.91; NH_4 + glucose, Q = 3.57 and 3.21. Glycerol, which was also tested, again decreased the rate. Despite the consistency of the new results, this outcome did not make the nature of the effect clearer, because if it were due to a general metabolic stimulus one would not expect the effect to be more pronounced in a tissue that was already well-nourished than in a nutritively deprived tissue. In still another such experiment, carried out on nourished rat liver tissue on November 13, Henseleit again obtained similar increases with fructose, pyruvate, and glucose, although all of the rates, including that for NH_4Cl, were lower than in the previous trial. Three new substances added in this experiment, glycogen, sodium butyrate, and sodium formate, all depressed the level below that with NH_4Cl alone. Thus, the usual four intermediates of carbohydrate metabolism seemed to stand out distinctly from other substances.[19]

While Henseleit worked on this problem, Krebs's time must again have been preempted mainly by his medical duties. During the first half of November Krebs managed to carry out personally only three experiments, all on proteolysis.[20]

On the 15th of November Henseleit carried out yet another experiment, most of which was very similar to those he had been performing for the past 8 days. To the standard four substrates of carbohydrate metabolism he added the sugar sorbose. The animal from which he took the liver tissue had been nourished solely with carbohydrate before it was killed. The effects of the substances tested were much less distinct than in the preceding experiments. The levels with NH_4Cl by itself were relatively high (3.06 and 2.76). Only that of glucose together with NH_4Cl exceeded this rate (3.98 and 4.46), whereas those of fructose, sorbose, and lactate with NH_4Cl fell below the level for NH_2Cl alone.[21] Perhaps Krebs would have expected such an outcome, as the substrates of carbohydrate metabolism would be least likely to stimulate an increase when added to the medium of tissues that had already been well nourished with carbohydrates in the intact animal.

This experiment differed from the preceding experiments in one significant way. In addition to the substances mentioned in the previous paragraph Henseleit tested one that bore no obvious relation to them, and that he had never tested before. Even the way in which he wrote down the title of the experiment suggests that it was somehow tacked on to the rest of the procedure:

Influence of Sugar and Acids on the Formation of Urea from NH_4Cl
       Influence of Ornithine

The ornithine, which came from the chemical supply firm of Hoffmann-LaRoche, was tested by itself, and together with NH_4Cl, each in duplicate. Alone it did little. Together with NH_4Cl, however, it yielded urea at the rates of Q = 6.74 and 8.04.[22] These were higher by a wide margin than any that Krebs or Henseleit had been able to obtain previously under any conditions. According to Krebs's subsequent testimony, the result was entirely unexpected.[23] At last, it appeared, he had found a dramatic "effect"; one that could bring his investigation to a sharp focus.

* * *

If he had no reason to expect in advance that ornithine would exert an unusual effect, why did Krebs insert it into the series of substances that he was testing? Why, in particular, did he try it just at a time when he had turned away from tests of more ordinary amino acids, and appeared to be fixing his attention on the influence of intermediates in carbohydrate metabolism on the formation of urea? In his published account Krebs gave no specific reason for trying it, indicating only that he included ornithine among a large number of substances he tested as possible precursors of urea nitrogen.[24] While discussing the matter with me, he said "it was just, without any too specific ideas, that we tested the effect of all sorts of substances. That was part of the general philosophy — just to investigate systematically which substances influence the rate either as inhibitors or activators."[25] If, as he also stated to me, "availability" of substances was the decisive factor, then we should infer that he tested ornithine in this experiment because it happened to become available to him at just that time.

There is an important flaw in this explanation. Of all of the amino acids that he could have tested, ornithine was not only among the less prominent, but it was among the least likely to have been casually available to Krebs, because it was one of the most expensive amino acids one could buy. Hoffmann-LaRoche, from whom he procured it, charged 6.0 Swiss francs per gram of ornithine, ten times the cost of a gram of alanine. Of the other amino acids he had tested, glycine cost 0.30 Fr, phenylalanine 1.0 Fr, aspartic acid 0.55 Fr, cysteine 1.25 Fr, and cystine 0.65 Fr per gram. Among those amino acids he had *not* yet tested at this time, he could have purchased glutamic acid (0.50 Fr), histidine (2.0 Fr), isoleucine (3.60 Fr), proline (3.5 Fr), serine (4.0 Fr), and tyrosine (1.25 Fr) considerably more cheaply than ornithine. Of all the amino acids available from Hoffmann-LaRoche, only lysine (7.50 Fr) and tryptophane (11.00 Fr), exceeded the price of ornithine. Krebs's budget was tightly restricted, and he had to be very careful about what he spent on chemical supplies.[26] We would expect him, therefore, to have had some strong motivation to buy ornithine.

One such motivation could have been the intention to test systematically every amino acid; that is, to compare *exhaustively* the rates at which the different amino acids form urea. Even if that had been his plan, however, there would seem to be no need to move to the most expensive of them when there were still so many of the cheaper ones left to try. It is hard to believe that he would have felt it necessary to test every single amino acid, unless the testing of some of them began to reveal some systematic distinctions to pursue further. Moreover, the experiments that Henseleit had carried out until then reveal no such pattern of systematic exploration. He had repeatedly used the same few common amino acids — alanine, phenylalanine, and glycine — that the laboratory probably kept in stock.[27] He tried only three other moderately priced amino acids, cystine, cysteine, and aspartic acid once each. In the one case in which he did employ a relatively expensive amino acid, arginine (4.0 francs per gram), there was an obvious special motivation, as it was a known special source of urea.

We may ask, therefore, whether Krebs could have had any other reason, which he himself might afterward have forgot about, that would have made ornithine a *logical* choice to test. There are several plausible possibilities. In an earlier short historical account of this investigation I made the conjecture that the choice might have been connected with his "guess" that one of the urea nitrogens comes immediately from an amino acid. Such an idea could, in principle, have directed his attention to the two diamino acids, ornithine and lysine, that contain, in addition to the α-amino group common to all amino acids, a second amino group at the other end of its carbon chain. Perhaps those extra amino groups would provide the nitrogen that goes directly to urea, while the ordinary α-amino group passes through the stage of ammonia.

Another possibility is that Krebs initially became interested in ornithine because it is the other product of the arginase reaction through which urea is formed in the liver. We have seen that he had included arginine among the substances he tested in October, and was well aware that the exceptionally high rate at which it yielded urea was due to this special reaction. Ornithine was not a natural constituent of proteins, and most of the limited attention that biochemists had previously given to it was centered around its place in the arginase reaction. A number of attempts had been made to find out what becomes of the ornithine that is produced in this way in the liver. Early feeding experiments suggested that animals can degrade the substance, but when Kurt Felix and H. Röthler perfused an isolated cat liver with ornithine, in 1924, they could find no evidence that the ornithine disappeared. In their experiments it appeared to yield neither ammonia nor urea. The metabolic fate of ornithine remained an unsolved problem. The compound might be decomposed in another organ, or it might be decarboxylated to form putrescine, a diamine derivative of ornithine. Intestinal bacteria were already known to be able to carry out this reaction. Putrescine, too, could be degraded by animals, but was also not decomposed in Felix and Röthler's perfusion experiments.[28] Thus, Krebs might well have been attracted to try his hand at the puzzle of how the ornithine that arises in the arginase reaction is further decomposed, and since Felix and Röthler's evidence against its forming urea was not conclusive, the situation would have invited a more rigorous test of whether or not it did, by means of the tissue slice method. In some respects this hypothesis is more plausible than my earlier conjecture, because it provides a motive specific to ornithine, whereas with the other interpretation one still has to explain why he chose ornithine over the natural protein constituent lysine.

It is attractive to think that there must have been an explanation such as one of these behind Krebs's move, because it helps to "make sense" of his research pathway. Believing, as we do, that all observations are "theory-laden," we try to find some degree of theoretical intention underlying each operational step the scientist takes. Associating random search with unimaginative science, and skeptical of anecdotal accounts of purely "chance" discoveries, we would prefer to find some anticipatory reason for Krebs's choice than to accept that he merely stumbled onto ornithine.

As historians of science we regularly construct explanations such as these, from circumstantial evidence, and present them with confidence. Normally, however, we do not submit our interpretations to the scrutiny of our historical subjects. In this case I had the opportunity to do just that, because Krebs himself read the draft of the manuscript in which I offered the first of these conjectures. I hoped that when he saw the logic of my case he would recognize that some such reasoning must have occurred, even though it had since vanished from his mind, or even that he would be stimulated to recall some further details about what had happened. Instead, he reaffirmed the view he had previously expressed. "I took ornithine really because it was there." Later in our discussion he amplified his position: "I tested, I think, all the amino acids I could get.... I would not subscribe to [your account], but I think it was really just a blind, or an unprejudiced collection of facts." To my argument about the cost of ornithine Krebs had a ready reply. He did not need very much of it. He did not object to my "exposition," because I had made it clear that it was my own reconstruction, but he could not agree with it.[29]

Since Krebs did not object, I published my interpretation as it stood, acknowledging that he had not accepted it. Since then, however, I have become less certain that one can determine whether this, or any alternative interpretation, is valid. The situation confronts the historian with the central issue concerning the writing of history based in part on the oral testimony of surviving participants. How should the historian weigh the memory of the participant in such an event against the historian's own sense of the logic of the historical situation as he can reconstitute it from contemporary documents? Here the participant's memory seems to be contradicted in two respects by the evidence. First, if availability were the foremost criterion for choosing a substance, ornithine should have been among the least available choices. Second, Henseleit's laboratory record shows that up until at least this stage of the investigation, Krebs was not "testing all the amino acids I could get."

The standard wisdom among historians is to be skeptical of the accuracy of the aging scientist's memory, even to regard it as desirable to expose fallacies in the retrospective account the scientist gives of his own past activities. My experience with Hans Krebs suggests, however, that we ought to be very cautious about overturning the accounts our subjects give of themselves. In numerous cases in which I could check Krebs's memory against contemporary evidence, I found it, not infallible, but remarkably firm and reliable. It is hazardous to insist that he remembered an important situation such as this one wrongly, unless the historian has very strong evidence for such a conclusion. One can think of any number of fortuitous reasons for which Krebs might have had some ornithine at hand to test. He might have ordered it for some reason other than the one he used it for. One of his colleagues at Freiburg might have purchased it and given him a little of it. If in any such way he had access to the substance, it would have been characteristic of Krebs to try it out as a possible precursor of urea, without giving extended thought to whether that was worth doing. Only the outcome of this particular test would set it apart from numerous other cases in which he tested some substance that came into his hands, or tested some passing idea, as a brief digression from the main thrust of an investigation.

The sources of information available to reconstruct Krebs's experiment on ornithine are exceptionally full. In addition to his original scientific publications on the subject, there are written historical accounts by Krebs, and a complete laboratory record of the investigation that included that experiment. Beyond that, it was possible for the historian to go over all these records with the investigator himself, to question him repeatedly over a 5-year period concerning the circumstances of the experiment. Even with all these advantages, it is necessary to admit in the end that we cannot conclusively establish either of two fundamentally divergent accounts of the genesis of the experiment. There is a lesson in this experience, to be taken to heart when historians interpret other events for which the sources of information are less complete. Our confidence in such interpretations might suffer beneficial checks, if our historical subjects could regularly read what we have written about them, and reject those that they know to be incompatible with their own memories.

I

In his later discussions, Krebs referred to the exceptionally high rates at which mixtures of ornithine and ammonium ions synthesized urea as "the ornithine effect."[30] We may ask when was this effect discovered? The answer depends on what is meant by an effect. Ian Hacking has described an "effect" as an "instructive phenomenon" — or regularity — revealed through experimentation.[31] If so, then the readings that ornithine together with ammonia yielded in Henseleit's experiment did not constitute an effect until those who observed it had drawn some instructive inferences from it. That did not happen all at once. "When you first make an observation," Krebs commented in discussing this situation in 1976, "which may turn out to be a discovery, you are not sure at the first occasion whether it is a discovery."[32] At the very first, he was skeptical that it was even a valid observation. The ornithine, he thought, might be contaminated with arginine or urea, either of which could have accounted for the readings. Such possibilities were very easy to check. By adding urease to a sample of the ornithine, and to a sample of ornithine together with an extract of liver containing arginase, he quickly eliminated these potential sources of error and satisfied himself that the phenomenon was real.[33] It was still not evident, however, that there was a specific "ornithine effect." Ornithine might only have been the first substance they happened to come upon that exhibited a more general effect.

The day after observing the action of ornithine, Henseleit performed a set of experiments that included two additional tests of that compound, carried out identically to the first trial. The results confirmed the initial finding. (In this experiment NH_4Cl alone gave Q = 1.87 and 2.44; NH_4Cl + ornithine gave Q = 6.37 and 5.99.) In the other half of the experiment he tested two new substances, valeric acid and formamide.

The use of valeric acid represented a standard biochemical research strategy of the time. If a particular compound is found to have some physiological action, check to see whether similar compounds whose molecules differ in specific ways from the compound in question exert similar effects. Valeric acid has the same carbon skeleton as ornithine, but without its amino groups:

$$COOH-CH(NH_2)-CH_2-CH_2-CH_2(NH_2)$$
ornithine

$$COOH-CH_2-CH_2-CH_2-CH_3$$
valeric acid

If valeric acid were to cause the tissue to form urea at a rate comparable to that with ornithine, then one could infer that it was the carbon skeleton, rather than the amino groups, that was responsible for the action. It was in keeping with this interpretation that valeric acid was tested only in combination with NH_4Cl, as it could not provide urea nitrogen. The rates, however, were lower than with NH_4Cl alone.[34]

Formamide ($HCONH_2$) represented a different approach, a continuation of the earlier strategy involving the pyrimidines, to see whether compounds that contained portions of the central structure of urea might give rise directly to that substance. Formamide alone, in fact yielded urea at the same rate as ammonia. Together with ammonia, however, it did not increase the rate over that of ammonia alone. The result probably raised the suspicion that the formamide had merely decomposed, releasing ammonia into the tissue. Henseleit noted at the end of the experiment that the formamide was old, and the test should be repeated with a purified preparation.[35]

Inherent in these first experiments involving ornithine is an indication of an ambiguity in Krebs's earliest conceptions of how ornithine might be connected with the synthesis of urea. As he later described the situation, he had tested ornithine in the first place as a potential nitrogen donor,[36] and therefore, used it in relatively high concentration, expecting it to be degraded. The notebook record supports his recollection that Henseleit initially employed relatively large quantities — 100 mg/100 ml, approximately equivalent to the quantities of alanine that he utilized. On the other hand, he also used concentrations in the same range when he employed the intermediates of carbohydrate metabolism, substances that he could not have regarded as possible nitrogen donors. The large quantities of ornithine used are, therefore, not conclusive evidence that he considered ornithine exclusively in the perspective of such a role. The titles of the first two experiments that Henseleit performed on ornithine imply, in fact, a different view. The second of these (for the first, see earlier discussion) was "Influence of ornithine on the formation of urea from NH_4Cl. Influence of valeric acid."[37] These titles suggest that Krebs entertained the idea that ornithine, like other substances he had been testing on the previous days, only influenced a process in which ammonia supplied the nitrogen. That was, in fact, the rationale behind the experiment of November 16; if it were the carbon skeleton that was essential, the action of ornithine could not be due to the nitrogen it contained.

Krebs and Henseleit had to break off their research on November 17, to begin dismantling the laboratory equipment to move into new quarters. The imposing new Medical Clinic of the Albert Ludwig University of Freiburg had been completed, and Krebs could begin to occupy the three rooms that had been allotted to him in the laboratories of the Department of Medicine. It took more than 3 weeks to reassemble the apparatus in the new space and prepare it for use. Meanwhile, on December 1st, the Clinic was officially opened with a festive celebration that included speeches by the Minister of Culture, the Burgomeister of Freiburg, and the Rector of the University; tours of the new buildings with short lectures by Thannhauser and others; and in the evening a performance of Richard Strauss's opera *Der Rosenkavalier*.[38]

The buildings were arranged in a series of wings connected at right angles to one another and framing spacious formal courtyards. Krebs acquired, in addition to his enlarged research facilities, a comfortable, well-furnished apartment at the corner of a residential wing of the building just a few minutes walk from his laboratory.[39]

When Henseleit resumed working, on December 10, he tested four different substances clearly chosen as possible nitrogen donors. Two of them, formamide and methylamine, were repeats of previous tests. The others, putrescine and cadaverine, were the diamines derived, respectively, from ornithine and lysine. The strategy underlying these choices appears evident. Bacteria could convert ornithine to putrescine. Putrescine could be degraded by animals and was suspected of being a decomposition product of ornithine in animals. If it were, then putrescine was a potential intermediate in the pathway through which ornithine gives rise to urea, and since putrescine has both of the amino groups of ornithine, it too should then be able to supply the nitrogen for urea.

$$COOH-CH(NH_2)-CH_2-CH_2-CH_2(NH_2)$$
ornithine

$$CH_2(NH_2)-CH_2-CH_2-CH_2(NH_2)$$
putrescine

The selection of cadaverine implies that Krebs was applying another standard strategy. Lysine, the amino acid from which cadaverine is derived, is the next homologue of ornithine:

$$COOH-CH(NH_2)-CH_2-CH_2-CH_2(NH_2)$$
ornithine

$$COOH-CH(NH_2)-CH_2-CH_2-CH_2-CH_2(NH_2)$$
lysine

Figure 9.1 The "New Clinic" in Freiburg, opened in November, 1931.

Figure 9.2 Hans Krebs' apartment in the New Clinic.

When a biochemist discovered a metabolic property of some particular molecule, he almost invariably checked to see whether homologous compounds possessed the same property. The surprising feature of this choice is that Krebs tested a derivative of lysine, but he did not test lysine itself at this time. At 7.5 Swiss francs per gram from Hoffmann- LaRoche, lysine was even more expensive than ornithine. Its costliness might have deterred Krebs from procuring it immediately. So strong was the chemical presumption that the effect of any given organic compound was most likely to be shared by a homologous compound, however, that it appears a curious lapse that he did not give priority, as one of his first steps after observing the action of ornithine, to obtaining some lysine to test.[40]

The title of this experiment — "Urea Formation From Formamide, Cadaverine, Putrescine, Methylamine, and its Influence on the Formation of Urea Formation From NH_4Cl" — suggests that Krebs was entertaining the idea that these substances might *either* donate nitrogen to urea, *or* influence the rate of a process by which ammonia donates the nitrogen. The first possibility was manifested in the tests of each substance alone, the second in the tests of each together with NH_4Cl. None of the substances alone yielded as much urea as NH_4Cl alone, and none together with NH_4Cl yielded more than the latter alone. For three of the substances, these results seemed to settle the matter. Henseleit wrote "No urea formation from cadaverine, putrescine, methylamine," and he tested them no further. For formamide the situation was less clear. Although it gave by itself Q values of only 1.36 and 1.52 (compared with NH_4Cl, 3.14 and 2.19; and putrescine, 1.00 and 0.83), Henseleit interpreted this result as "little formation of urea from formamide." None of these substances, however, in his view exerted any influence on the formation of urea from NH_4Cl.[41]

Something about formamide was interesting enough to Krebs to induce him not to give up on it as readily as he abandoned putrescine and cadaverine. Perhaps it was the one run in which "old" formamide had given as much urea as NH_4Cl; or maybe there was a theoretical attraction. At any rate, when Krebs carried out the first experiment he had personally performed in nearly a month, it was on the subject of "urea formation from formamide, in bicarbonate and phosphate Ringer." First he measured, in each medium, the respiration of liver tissue (from a rat previously nourished with carbohydrate) alone, in the presence of formamide, and of alanine. The rates with formamide were significantly lower than in the other two cases, and falling, and Krebs noted with emphasis "Inhibition of respiration by formamide!!" In bicarbonate Ringer, formamide produced somewhat more urea (Q = 1.69) than did alanine (1.10) or the tissue alone (0.50), although all of the rates were low. In this experiment Krebs measured for the first time the ammonia evolved during the process, utilizing the Parnas–Heller steam distillation method. It is likely that he introduced such determinations at this time mainly because he received a Parnas–Heller apparatus that he had had on order. The results, however, were uncertain, due to a number of interfering factors.[42]

Inconclusive though these results were, Krebs was not deterred from pursuing formamide further. The next day Henseleit submitted the formamide to fractional distillation to obtain a purer preparation for future trials.[43]

On December 14, Henseleit brought together in one set of experiments the three substances that had shown some promise, either as possible donators of urea nitrogen or by influencing the formation of urea from ammonia. These were formamide, ornithine, and asparagine. His conclusions were:

No formation of urea from ornithine or asparagine.
From formamide, just as much urea formation as from NH_4Cl.
It remains to investigate whether formamide is decomposed to NH_3.
No increase through formamide in the presence of NH_3.
Enormous increase of urea formation from NH_3 through ornithine.[44]

The situation thus remained basically unchanged. Formamide was still of some potential interest, but so far the only striking result reached was the action of ornithine together with NH_4Cl. Implicit in the formulation of these conclusions is a view that ornithine acts in some manner other than to provide urea nitrogen. There is no way to be certain that Henseleit was reflecting a general view that Krebs was now beginning to favor, rather than drawing conclusions merely applicable to the conditions of this single experiment. Moreover, Henseleit habitually identified the experiments in which any substance was added alone as about urea formation *from* that substance, and those in which it was added with NH_4Cl as about the influence of that substance on the formation *from* NH_4Cl. His notation need not have been a shorthand representation for an underlying theory, and we have no direct record of what Krebs was thinking. Nevertheless, there is reason to believe that Henseleit's conclusions, as well as the titles of the experiments, do give clues about Krebs's position at the time. Since this experiment was, with respect to ornithine, entirely consistent with the previous ones, these "results" would also sum up the outcome of the whole investigation of ornithine until then. Henseleit's statements may, in fact, reveal as much as Krebs could have said at this point about the possible mechanism; that is, the statements summarized the only two general modes of action that Krebs could conceive of for ornithine. The third alternative, which we have seen that he had entertained earlier, was that an amino acid may supply one of the urea nitrogens directly, while ammonia provides the other one. When I questioned him in 1978 about the possibility that it was at *this* stage in the investigation that the idea came in (before I had constructed my own little hypothesis that the idea might have stimulated him in the first place to try ornithine), he could not be sure, but he thought that that concept did "not gel." He added, "When we showed that it is so much more rapid from ammonium chloride, I think I came to the conclusion that it goes through the stage of ammonia."[45] The failure of his own idea to "take shape," in the face of the activity of ammonia, thus led Krebs back to the standard view that ammonia is a necessary intermediate. Either of the modes of action with which Henseleit labeled his experiments — formation *from* ornithine, or influence on the formation *from* NH_4Cl — was compatible with ammonia as an intermediate stage. It was the fact that ornithine, *by itself*, yielded little or no urea, that was leading Krebs toward the second of these alternatives. To the question of *how* ornithine exerts that "influence," however, Krebs could, at the end of December, probably not have given any answer. His tests with valeric acid, putrescine, and cadaverine represent efforts to give some direction to the search for that answer, but these avenues were quickly closed off by the inactivity of those substances.

Krebs also returned once more, on December 18, to the question of the pyrimidines. Performing the experiment himself, he tested whether thymine, in phosphate Ringer's solution, would form urea by itself in liver tissue. The rate at which urea formed was low, and not significantly above the control tissue.[46] Unlike with some substances that he had dropped after one or two trials, because he believed that one "completely negative" experiment was enough to settle the matter,[47] Krebs had, ever since the beginning of the urea investigation in July, come back again and again to the pyrimidines in spite of repeatedly unpromising results. Evidently in this case the theoretical expectation that nucleic acid metabolism should provide an independent source of urea induced him to persist in the face of mainly negative results. It was also typical of him, however, not to allow himself to be bogged down in such a quest. Putting his main effort on paths that seemed to be opening up more easily, he intermittently interrupted himself to take further looks at the pyrimidines.

After this experiment, neither Krebs nor Henseleit carried out further research until after the beginning of the new year. Henseleit probably was gone for the Christmas holidays. Krebs was undoubtedly not off duty for this whole period, but he apparently did close his laboratory for the holiday. If he took stock of the state of his investigation of urea synthesis during this break, he must have felt by then that he had indeed made a real discovery, but that he could still not fully fathom its significance. The action of ornithine on the formation of urea from ammonia stood out in striking contrast to the rest of the substances he had so far tested. The steps he had taken since observing this action had been designed mainly to elucidate it by searching for other substances that might have a similar action. If he could find other such effects, Krebs might be led either toward a conclusion that a certain class of compounds exhibited the effect in common, or toward a mechanism for the specific action of ornithine. At this stage in the investigation he may not even have distinguished clearly between these two possibilities. Only the nature of whatever substances might prove to have such actions could illuminate the issue. We cannot tell either whether or not, when he interrupted his investigation for the holidays, Krebs had exhausted the ideas he had for testing related compounds whose structures might tell something about the manner in which ornithine acted, were they themselves to prove active.

* * *

In his succinct history of the investigation of urea synthesis, Krebs wasted little space describing these first efforts to elucidate the observed action of ornithine. "The interpretation of this finding was not at once obvious,"[48] was all he wrote about it. In August 1978, when he examined Henseleit's laboratory notebook page by page with me, he recognized at once the objectives of testing valeric acid, putrescine, cadaverine, and formamide, although he had obviously long forgotten about them. Now these attempts did not much impress him. "Those are just vague possibilities which we tested," he commented, and he quickly dismissed them by pointing out that all the results were negative.[49] To Krebs the scientist, not only had the negative results ended the matter at the time, but there was little historical interest in such short and false trails. What mattered to him was how he eventually arrived at the "correct interpretation."[50] His realization, when we looked at the experiments on putrescine and cadaverine, that he had "looked [to see] whether the breakdown product of ornithine would have an effect," led him to remark, "Well, retrospectively one must blame oneself for being really blind to the obvious. But fortunately it took only a few months." I replied, "But it is only obvious afterward, isn't it?", to which he agreed "Yes, that things become obvious once you know all about it, but to arrive at the obvious is not always...a straight row."[51] For the scientist, it was slightly embarrassing to be reminded, so many years after he had reduced the investigation in his own mind to its "essential" stages, that he had not been quicker to pick out the "straight row." For the historian, on the other hand, to uncover the blind alleys into which the scientist had first turned greatly enhanced the interest of the story.

II

The course that the urea investigation took immediately afterward suggests that, while reflecting on the state of the problem during the holiday interruption, Krebs had decided to shift his priorities. After his return he looked no further at derivatives of ornithine, but concentrated on a fuller investigation of the action of ornithine itself. As a prelude to this phase he devised a significant and novel way to improve the conditions, not only for the immediate experiments he intended to carry out, but for his entire research program in intermediary metabolism.

For most of the tissue slice experiments he had performed until now Krebs had, as we have seen, employed Warburg–Ringer's solution as the medium. In addition to the Na^+, K^+, Ca^{++}, and Cl^- ions of ordinary Ringer's solution, Warburg's solution contained bicarbonate and carbonate ions in concentrations close to that in the normal physiological medium. This modification was directly related to the conditions of tissue respiration that Warburg was studying, and it improved the metabolic performance of the tissues.[52] During the early stages of his urea investigation Krebs had made sporadic efforts to improve the conditions further, sometimes by using blood serum, sometimes by substituting phosphate for bicarbonate in the Ringer's solution. Both of these moves, however, entailed disadvantages. In phosphate Ringer's solution the absence of bicarbonate inhibited the urease reaction. Serum contained so much urea that the measurement of the urea produced in the experiment became unreliable.

These intermittent efforts during the summer and fall of 1931 suggest that, even though he was proceeding with the main course of his investigation, Krebs was not fully satisfied that he had attained the optimal conditions for performing the experiments. One indication that there was still something to be desired was the irregularity of the results, for example, the wide range of rates of formation of urea from NH_4Cl (Q values from 1.5 to 4.5) from one experiment to another. There was, however, a more profound reason for seeking to improve the conditions under which the tissues functioned in these experiments. It was important to establish not only that, to be regarded as an intermediate, a substance must yield urea at a rate no less than does a substance considered to be its precursor, but that these rates be of the same order of magnitude as the physiological formation of urea in the intact animal. "The point was," as Krebs put it in a conversation in 1978, "to have the whole phenomenon,...not merely a fragment of it."[53] What he meant was that, unless the rate at which urea formed in the tissue slices when he tested potential intermediates in the process approached the rate in the whole animal, one could not be certain that one was studying the main pathway of urea formation. One might have in hand only one of several metabolic routes, or even an insignificant side reaction.

Krebs did not record, either in his notebooks or his early publications on the subject, what Q value for his rat liver tissue slices would correspond to the rate at which the living rat produces urea. From a comment in his paper on the subject, it appears that it would have been around 15.[54] Therefore, the values for NH_4Cl that he had thus far obtained would have accounted for a little less than one third of the total process, and the maximum value he had so far recorded for ornithine and NH_4Cl together would barely have exceeded half of that rate. Such rates were sufficient to suggest that he was dealing at least with a major component of the whole process of urea formation; but if he could find ways to raise these levels, he could provide a more convincing case that he was studying the principal pathway.

At the beginning of January 1932, it occurred to Krebs that a better way to provide the medium most suitable for isolated tissues than the trial and error methods through which the varieties of Ringer's solutions had been developed, would be to imitate as closely as possible the actual physiological situation in which tissues normally exist. The inorganic ions present in the plasma, he thought, are not there by chance, but have been evolved because they are collectively optimal for the existence of the tissues they bathe. Once he had defined the problem in this way, he solved it in the simplest possible manner. He merely went to the library and looked up the concentrations of the various ions in mammalian plasma. He checked first the composition of human plasma, but he was also struck by the similarity of the plasma in all the vertebrates — except for frogs, in which the absolute concentrations were lower, but in the same proportions. This uniformity strengthened his conviction that one should duplicate the composition of plasma, insofar as possible, in experiments with surviving tissue. From the figures he found, he quickly devised a "physiological salt solution," with the following composition (compared here, as he did, with Warburg–Ringer's solution and mammalian serum):

	Animal and Human Serum (mg per 100 ml)	Warburg Solution (mg per 100 ml)	Physiological Salt Solution (mg per 100 ml)
Na^+	≈ 300	355	327
K^+	22	10.5	23.1
Ca^{++}	10	8.8	10.2
Mg^{++}	2	0	2.9
Cl^-	≈ 370	466	454
$PO_4^=$	10	0	11
$SO_4^=$	20	0	11.4
HCO_3^-	56 vol%	56 vol%	56 vol%
CO_2	2.5 vol%	2.5 vol%	2.5 vol%

The composition of his physiological salt solution differed from that of mammalian serum only in that it contained more Cl^-, to compensate for the absence of organic anions, such as proteins and lactate. On January 5, Krebs entered these compositions, together with the stock solutions one would mix together to produce it, in his laboratory notebook. The next day Henseleit began using the physiological salt solution in the urea investigation, and Krebs never found it necessary to modify his initial formulation. It was, as he recalled in 1977, "the briefest intellectual and experimental effort." It was also one of the most successful.[55]

During the next 3 days, while Henseleit began using the physiological salt solution for experiments on ornithine, Krebs himself followed up the equivocal evidence from Henseleit's earlier experiments that asparagine may give rise to urea. Although no urea had formed "from asparagine" in the last experiment carried out before Christmas, back in October it had yielded a rate as high as that for NH_4Cl. Like formamide, asparagine contained nitrogen in the form of an amide (in addition to its α-amino group), raising the possibility of a special mechanism by which the -CONH portion of urea could be formed from it. Asparagine might have been more interesting to Krebs in this regard than formamide, because it was a widespread constituent of tissues. As in the case of formamide, however, the effect of asparagine might only have been due to its having acted as a source of ammonia in the tissue, especially as the enzyme asparaginase, which catalyzed the release of the amide group, had been isolated from liver tissue.[56]

On January 6, Krebs used the Parnas–Heller method to measure the NH_3 given off by liver slices in physiological salt solution to which he had added asparagine. From the six runs he tried, he obtained only two readings, an indication that he may have been having difficulty adapting the Parnas–Heller method to his needs. The method depended on a colorimetric test for ammonia, and in two of the cases, he noted, the color in the medium itself made the results inexact. In the one result he obtained for an aerobic run, Q_{NH_3} equaled 3.14, whereas anaerobically it was ≈ 2.8. The result, as Krebs put it down was

"Enormous NH_3 — formation from asparagine. More aerobically than anaerobically. Speaks against the activity of living cells." It is not immediately evident why Krebs thought the NH_3 was not likely to have been formed by the cells — perhaps because the presence of such quantities of ammonia would have been toxic to them. At any rate, on the next day he carried out the reaction enzymatically in solution, using a glycerol extract of liver tissue. "Asparaginase in solution" produced in 2 hours enough ammonia to correspond to $Q_{NH_3} \approx 2.4$, which Krebs regarded as low. He attributed that result to the likelihood that the labile asparaginase might be "sensitive" to the conditions of the experiment. On January 9 he attempted to measure the asparaginase reaction manometrically, on the assumption that the ammonia formed at pH 8 must absorb CO_2 to form NH_4CO_3. For reasons that were not apparent to him, however, he obtained no readings.[57]

The observation that asparagine formed large amounts of NH_3 in the liver tissue, or its medium, must have led Krebs to conclude that in the earlier experiments it had not been a direct source of urea, but only of ammonia. He may now have been attracted, however, to the very possibility that the enzymatic conversion of asparagine to aspartic acid might be a physiological source for the ammonia assumed to form the intermediate step in the normal pathway to urea.[58] He did not follow up that possibility, however, but after working for 3 days on asparagine he turned to an unrelated problem.

Meanwhile, Henseleit was starting to repeat, with physiological salt solution, the experiments already performed on ornithine. In the first trial of the new solution, on January 6, the special action of ornithine with HN_4Cl appeared less impressive, however, than in the previous results. Liver tissue alone, and with ornithine alone, formed urea at higher rates than usual (Q = 0.71 and 0.82 for the tissue, 1.37 and 1.20 for ornithine), whereas ornithine together with NH_4Cl raised the rate less than usual (Q = 3.56 and 3.05, compared with 1.33 and 1.20 for NH_4Cl alone). Henseleit also repeated on this day the tests of other tissues, and found as usual that only liver tissue produces urea. In addition, he acquainted himself with Warburg's double run method for measuring simultaneously the consumption of oxygen and the formation of carbon dioxide. Krebs was interested in the rates of respiration for two reasons. He wanted to know whether they were steadier in the new medium than in previous solutions, as an indicator of whether the new medium was more favorable for the survival of the tissues. He also wished to see whether the respiration increased when urea formed, as he expected it should to supply the extra energy needed for the synthesis. In this case, however, there was no decisive difference (the oxygen consumption was 12.2 in the control, 10.5 with NH_4Cl, and 11.7 with ornithine and NH_4Cl). The respiratory quotients were all near 0.7, except for the tissue with ornithine, which gave the anomalously low figure of 0.37.[59] This set of experiments did not reveal any conspicuous advantages for Krebs's new physiological medium. Convinced of its superiority on principle, however, he went on using it.

The next day Henseleit extended the experiment to include again three of the substrates in carbohydrate metabolism — glucose, pyruvate, and lactate — that had become prominent objects of the urea investigation just before Krebs and Henseleit first observed the striking action of ornithine. Henseleit tested both for "urea formation from ornithine," and the "influence" of the substance on the formation from NH_4Cl, whereas for the other three substances he tested only for the latter influence; that is, he tested them only in combination with NH_4Cl, a distinction based on the obvious fact that the other substances could not be sources of urea nitrogen. Experimentally, however, it was appearing less and less likely that ornithine itself could be a source of urea nitrogen, as it yielded urea only in combination with ammonia. A new feature of this experiment was that Henseleit tested "the influence of the concentrations of pyruvate and of lactate." For both compounds he compared their action at 100 mg/100 ml and at 10 mg/100 ml, and observed influences on the formation of urea only at the larger concentrations. The most interesting aspect of this logical next step in exploring the nature of the "influences" involved, was that Krebs focused on the concentration effects of pyruvate and lactate before he thought of taking such a step for ornithine. In the experiment as a whole "the largest acceleration of the formation of urea from NH_4Cl," Henseleit noted, came again "through ornithine"; but that substance did not differ as strikingly from the other substances tested as it had before Christmas (NH_4Cl + ornithine, 96 mg/100 ml, Q = 5.12 and 5.22; the next highest, NH_4Cl + lactate, 100 mg/100 ml, Q = 4.10 and 3.65).[60]

On January 8 Henseleit again tested ornithine, lactate, and glucose, but he also added four amino acids that had not been tried before. All of the tests were of the substances together with NH_4Cl. The four new acids were histidine, hydroxyproline, tyrosine, and leucine. These substances, representative of several general types of the amino acids present in proteins, suggest that Krebs now felt that he should survey systematically whether there were any amino acids other than ornithine that might exhibit the same effect he had found it to exert. The temporal order of events was, as we can see, the inverse of what it should have been if Krebs's later recollection that he came across ornithine *through* the systematic testing of all types of amino acids had been correct. None of these other amino acids appeared to accelerate the formation of urea. (One of the readings for tyrosine, 4.86, equaled that for ornithine — the tyrosine duplicate being 2.96 — but Henseleit suspected that the vessels had been mixed up.) The most prominent, and perhaps most surprising, result of the experiment was that lactate and glucose accelerated the rate as much as, or more than ornithine.

NH_4 + ornithine (100 mg/100 ml)   Q = 4.72
NH_4 + lactate   (100 mg/100 ml)   Q = 5.52 and 5.68
NH_4 + glucose   (100 mg/100 ml)   Q = 4.42 and ____ [61]

There is no record of how Krebs viewed these particular results at the time, but their pattern is suggestive. Whatever the mechanism through which ornithine acted on the formation of urea, that action did not now appear to depend on properties that it shared specifically with other amino acids. The effect appeared to be similar enough to those exerted by lactate and glucose to imply that the effect might be general enough to be shared by dissimilar molecules. Because ornithine could not produce urea without ammonia, the fact that it contained nitrogen, whereas the other two substances did not, may not have seemed crucial. Moreover, ornithine had been found, along with glutamic acid, proline, and arginine, to give rise to glucose when fed to the phlorizin-poisoned dogs. On theoretical grounds it had been proposed that these four amino acids also undergo decarboxylation and deamination reactions converting them to succinic acid, which then leads through the decarboxylic acid sequence of the Thunberg-Knoop–Wieland scheme to pyruvic and lactic acid.[62] It may have appeared to Krebs at this point, therefore, that the ornithine effect could be explained through these reactions. In testing ornithine, glucose, and lactate, he might, therefore, be examining the same effect. That he did entertain such a possibility is supported by the fact that on the next day, January 9, Henseleit tested just these three substances. He used them only in combination with NH_4Cl; that is, focusing on them as "influences," rather than as sources of urea. (He carried out two parallel sets, one in physiological salt solution plus bicarbonate, one in the solution plus phosphate, an indication that Krebs may now have had some doubts that his biological solution had provided the optimal chemical medium for every circumstance.)

The outcome of the new experiment was very different from the preceding one.

	Salt solution + bicarbonate	Salt solution + phosphate
NH_4Cl	3.82 and 4.60	0.97 and 0.96
NH_4Cl + ornithine	5.52 and 6.47	3.47 and 3.10
NH_4Cl + glucose	3.32 and 3.59	0.79
NH_4Cl + lactate	0.87 and 1.03	1.04 and 1.03

The rates for lactate were so low that Henseleit commented "Its concentration is too high, and it therefore acts as an inhibitor." Glucose too lowered the rate.[63] This experiment must have quickly discouraged any further thought about an effect common to ornithine, glucose, and lactate. Ornithine again stood out conspicuously from the crowd, and Krebs now finally fixed his attention firmly on the need to study its specific action in greater detail. This brief episode within the longer investigation suggests that the experimental evidence did not always lead in a straight line toward one solution "area." It was not just a matter of filling in a vaguely perceived outline with more specific structural details. The results pointed sometimes in one direction, sometimes in another, toward possible solutions as diverse as they were vague.

III

As the accumulating experimental evidence that ornithine does not yield urea in liver tissues unless ammonia is added with it undermined Krebs's initial assumption that the ornithine acts as a source of urea nitrogen, he must have given much thought to the question of what other kind of effect it might have. He seems never to have entertained seriously the possibility that ornithine might donate the CO group of the urea molecule. In principle that may have been at an early stage of the investigation a viable alternative hypothesis; but the whole prior history of the problem, in which amino acids were treated as the likely source of the amino groups, would have predisposed Krebs to think of the "formation of urea from ornithine" as meaning that it was the nitrogenous portion of the urea that ornithine would contribute. The only alternative to that view expressed in Henseleit's laboratory notes was that ornithine increases the formation of urea from ammonia, in spite of the obvious fact that ammonia could not be the source of the entire urea molecule. We may question whether Henseleit's notes fully reflected Krebs's views, especially in light of the divergences between their respective conclusions that were visible in the parallel records they kept during the first weeks that Henseleit worked in the laboratory. By the time Henseleit had been with Krebs for 6 months, however, he would have acquired a closer feeling for how Krebs thought about problems. The notations in his notebook by this point were likely to be in line with, if not fully expressive of, Krebs's opinions. Consequently, Krebs was probably pondering mainly what kinds of "influence" ornithine might exert on the formation of urea from ammonia. As long as he was searching for other substances that might act similarly, he would not have been able to focus on the specific characteristics that influence might have, for the nature of the effect would not be clearly definable until the range of compounds that exerted it were known. After the four sets of experiments just described had been carried out, however, Krebs again narrowed his attention to the nature of the ornithine effect itself. He had far from exhausted other possibilities, especially since he had not yet tested the most plausible candidate, lysine. Nevertheless, failure of any of those substances he *had* tested to duplicate the effect was probably leading him by this time to favor the idea that the ornithine effect was specific. An effect that is specific with respect both to the agent and to the reaction influenced by it, but in which the agent does not contribute to the composition of the final products, suggests the possibility, in fact essentially *defines*, a form of catalytic action. There is reason to conjecture that it was at about this point in his investigation that Krebs began to think that, in some way he could not yet clearly define, ornithine may act as a catalyst promoting the formation of urea from ammonia and some other substance. If that were the case, one would expect that it should not require very much ornithine to produce the effect. In the experiments so far, he had utilized, not only for ornithine, but for all of the substances he tested, what he regarded as relatively high concentrations of them — much higher, in most cases, than the concentrations in which the substances would be present physiologically in the organism — because he anticipated that if there were any effects, they would be more likely to be visible at high concentrations. He also thought he could safely use such concentrations, because the substances in question were unlikely to be toxic. He had no rigorous way to determine what concentrations would be best, therefore, he just guessed that the normal concentration of glucose in the blood would be a reasonable standard. It was on that basis that he added most of the substances he tested to the manometer vessels in quantities that would give a concentration in the range of 100 mg/100 ml of the medium.[64]

When Krebs began to think of ornithine as a possible catalytic agent, the obvious next move was to find out whether it would work in lower concentrations, and whether, in general, the effect was independent of the concentration. On January 14 Henseleit took up these questions. Utilizing 18 manometers, he measured the respiratory exchanges and the formation of urea for three concentrations of ornithine in a geometrical progression differing by factors of four — 200, 50, and 12.5 mg/100 ml. The respiration measurements indicated that NH_4Cl alone increased the rate above the control, but ornithine together with NH_4Cl had no further "distinct effect." The result, therefore, did not support Krebs's hope that he could detect the increased energy required for the urea synthesis. The principal effect he was looking for was also less distinct than he might have expected, mainly because with NH_4Cl alone, urea formed at an "extraordinarily high" rate (5.84 and 6.12). At each of the three concentrations ornithine with NH_4Cl increased the rate further, but not by much (at 200 mg/100 ml, 6.73 and 7.05; at 50 mg/100 ml, 6.12 and 7.99; at 12.5 mg/100ml, 9.55 and 6.79). Henseleit noted, "ornithine increases at each concentration, but only slightly." The result was suggestive, but not decisive. (This was also the opinion Krebs expressed when we looked back over that experiment in 1978.)[65]

On the following day Henseleit employed the Parnas–Heller apparatus to determine how much NH_3 had disappeared from the solution in each vessel during this experiment. The outcome was very interesting. Henseleit listed the values for Q_{NH_3} and Q_{urea} in parallel columns. In five of the seven runs that included ornithine and NH_4Cl, the former values were close to two times the latter values. This pattern was consistent with the view that two nitrogen atoms from the ammonia were consumed for each molecule of urea formed, and therefore, that ammonia was the sole source for the urea nitrogen. That result would argue further against the possibility that ornithine serves as a donor of urea nitrogen, and consequently in favor of a catalytic role. Krebs must have been encouraged to think that he was on the right track, but still in need of better data.[66]

After the next attempt, Krebs may have been less certain where this track would lead. Henseleit carried out a second, very similar experiment, beginning on January 16. It differed from the first one in that he used just two concentrations of ornithine — 200 and 50 mg/100 ml. In this experiment he used tissue from a starved rat rather than one nourished with carbohydrate, and he also tested uridine, another pyrimidine, that Krebs had obtained from his friend Franz Bielschowsky. Uridine gave negative results. The rates for urea formation in the control tissue were unusually high. Unlike most previous experiments, ornithine alone produced urea at almost the same rate as NH_4Cl alone (NH_4Cl, 1.85; ornithine, at 200 mg/100 ml, 1.75, at 50 mg/100 ml, 1.78). Ornithine plus NH_4Cl raised the rate substantially this time, but in contrast to the previous experiment, the larger concentration had a larger effect:

| 50 mg/100 ml ornithine + NH$_4$Cl | 4.20 and 4.39 |
| 200 mg/100 ml ornithine + NH$_4$Cl | 7.26 and 7.69 |

Henseleit wrote down, "Increase through ornithine in the presence of NH$_4$Cl, but dependent upon the ornithine concentration." Nor did the ammonia measurements neatly fit the pattern that the earlier experiment had appeared to establish.

	Q_{NH_3}	Q_{urea}
NH$_4$Cl + 200 mg/100 ml ornithine	6.72	7.69
NH$_4$Cl + 50 mg/100 ml ornithine	8.69	4.37

For the lower concentration the ratio was as close as could be expected to the predicted 2:1, but for the higher concentration it was less than 1:1.

* * *

Looking back over 50 years, we cannot easily discern whether this experiment raised serious doubts for Krebs concerning either the idea that ornithine acts catalytically or the experimental approach he was taking to test that idea. In 1978, when we discussed this experiment, he could readily explain these anomalies. At the higher concentration some of the ornithine could be expected to decompose, yielding ammonia, which would "blur the stoichiometry" between the ammonia consumed and the urea produced. This extra ammonia could also cause the higher rate at which urea formed with the higher concentration of ornithine. Krebs constructed this explanation in immediate response to the notebook page as he examined it in August 1978. I had said that it looked to me as though he had been looking for support for a catalytic role, but that these results had not provided quite decisive support. He answered,

> Well,... it all makes sense...on the assumption that at low concentration it is merely catalytic. At high concentrations there is an additional formation of ammonia from ornithine. And that I think is correct. I just...would like to know. This is 50 milligrams percent.... That means roughly 3 millimolar. Yes. We now know that the catalytic effect in hepatocytes, where the rapid diffusion is permitted is already at .5 millimolar. But usually we add about one. So at the high concentration that would...suggest there is an additional reaction.[67]

Krebs thus analyzed the information in the notebook in front of him as he would confront any scientific problem, bringing to bear on it recent data that would clarify the old data. After he had expanded on this explanation somewhat, I interjected, "Now in retrospect it can be explained quite satisfactorily. At this stage, when you were just trying to make sense of it, would [this result] have made it more difficult to make sense of it?" Krebs replied:

One could — now we know definitely that this occurs, but at that time one could have guessed that at high concentrations amino acid was deaminated. It then would of course form urea, and the ornithine alone *did* produce urea, and ammonia. So that made it quite clear that one couldn't expect an ideal stoichiometry, such as would occur if it reacted catalytically.[68]

Krebs was generally aware of the danger of mixing his reconstructions of earlier thinking with remembering what he had actually had in mind at an earlier time. He expressed himself here cautiously — "at that time one could have guessed..." He made it very plausible that he could have explained the results this way in 1932, but stopped short of saying that he had done so. Can the historian decide the issue? No one understands how Krebs thought about such things better than he did, therefore, it would be rash to dismiss his own reconstruction. On the other hand, he was, in 1978, "making sense" of the experiment in terms of the eventual outcome of the investigation. At the time he first saw these results he could not have been quite so confident of his idea that the action of ornithine is catalytic. The only other evidence we have concerning his response to the experiment is what he did next. He did not, for some time, have Henseleit continue experimenting on the effects of lower concentrations of ornithine, but reverted to tests using that substance at a uniform high concentration. That does not mean that he had given up either on the catalytic idea, or on the means for examining that idea that he had just tried. More likely he merely put the question aside for the time being, hoping that some other aspect of the investigation would help to clarify matters.

There is an alternative way to view Krebs's position at the time of these experiments. When a substance had been found to exhibit some effect on the rate of a biochemical process, it was routine to examine the relation between the concentration of the substance and the magnitude of the effect. It is not necessary, therefore, to infer from the experiments that Henseleit carried out, that Krebs had already begun to consider the possibility of a catalytic action. In that case the ambiguous results would not have constituted a problem for Krebs at this point. The interpretation I have given is supported by Krebs's statement to me, in 1978, that "We tested the concentration because we had the idea that it is catalytic, *because* it is the nature of the catalyst that you don't need very much."[69] That recollection too must be treated with caution, however, especially since his published history of the investigation in 1973 can be read as implying that the idea came as a result of testing concentrations.[70] My reconstruction is, therefore, only a plausible, not an irrefutable one.

* * *

On January 20, Henseleit performed an experiment similar in most respects to the preceding one, except that he used ornithine only in the high concentration of 200 mg/100 ml. He also tested the anaerobic formation of urea from ornithine and NH_4Cl, with the usual negative results. The basic results in this experiment were very good. Perhaps because the liver tissue was taken from a starved rat, the control rate of respiration was low, and the addition of NH_4Cl raised the rate markedly, while NH_4Cl plus ornithine brought a further distinct increase. The "ornithine effect" on urea stood out especially clearly. Perhaps most encouraging was the new comparative measurements of NH_3 consumption and urea formation. In three of the four tests that included ornithine together with NH_4Cl, the ratio of Q_{NH_3} to Q_{urea} was reasonably close to 2:1. In another similar experiment, begun 3 days later, Henseleit again obtained very good ratios, so good, in fact, that he wrote down "In the presence of NH_3, approximately 2 molecules disappear for 1 molecule of urea formed." This satisfactory outcome was overshadowed, however, by a spectacular result Henseleit obtained from a kidney slice that he had included along with the usual runs on liver tissue. In contrast to the vessels containing liver slices, in which ammonia disappeared (the largest Q_{NH_3} being -10.0), when ornithine and NH_4Cl were present in the kidney medium, there was a large *increase* in the amount of ammonia present (largest $Q_{NH_3} = +18.7$. Henseleit commented, "Enormous formation of NH_3 by the kidneys." Krebs would have anticipated that ammonia would not disappear, as he knew already that kidney tissue did not produce urea, but he was not prepared to find that it formed in "enormous" quantities in that tissue. This was the second major surprise of the investigation, and it marks the initial event in the emergence of a new branch of the investigative trail Krebs had been following.[71]

IV

Throughout January 1932, Krebs remained heavily occupied with his hospital duties. After the experiments on asparagine that he performed from January 6 to 9, he was able to do little more at the laboratory bench himself, except to carry out a few tests on the oxidation of homogentisic acid,[72] a substance that is excreted in the metabolic disorder known as alcaptonuria. The circumstances that led him to take up that problem are unknown, but that he should do so in the midst of a very absorbing period in his main line of research, when his time was so limited, is perhaps an indication of the deep interest he had had from the beginning in the medical applications of intermediary metabolism.[73]

While Henseleit kept the urea synthesis investigation moving, Krebs pondered a great deal about what the ornithine effect might mean. It occurred to him, probably sometime during this month, that the effect must be connected to the arginase reaction of Kossel and Dakin, because the action of ornithine, like that of arginase, was concentrated in the liver.[74] It is not surprising that such a thought would come to him, because ornithine was, in fact, mostly known through its association with the arginase reaction. It was far less obvious *how* the two actions could be connected. At first they appeared, in fact, to be mutually contradictory. In the arginase reaction, ornithine was one of the two products, the other being urea itself. It was hard to see how *adding* ornithine to the tissue could give rise to this urea. It was even more puzzling that ornithine appeared not to be a source of urea nitrogen. If the arginase reaction produced ornithine at a high rate in the liver, then that ornithine must somehow be further decomposed, and, as previous workers had suggested, the decomposition of ornithine would be expected to yield nitrogen.[75]

In his search for a way out of these dilemmas, Krebs discussed his problem repeatedly with Thannhauser, and with many of the people in his surroundings. He talked about it with the clinicians with whom he made daily rounds of the wards, even though they were not biochemists. They all had a general feeling that the ornithine effect must be related to the high activity of arginase in the liver. None of them had a solution to offer him, but their opinions encouraged him to keep thinking in that direction.[76]

Krebs also pored through the earlier literature on arginase. Since Kossel and Dakin's discovery, in 1904, the activity of that enzyme had been studied extensively, but the papers he looked up did not hold the answer either. Although the immediate reaction — arginine → ornithine + urea — was well defined, little was known either about how the arginine itself arises, or what becomes of the ornithine. It appeared self-evident from the structure of the arginine molecule that the amidine group incorporated into it must be the source of the urea molecule:

$$COOH - CH(NH_2) - CH_2 - CH_2 - NH - C \overset{NH}{\underset{NH_2}{\lessgtr}} \qquad\qquad O = C \overset{NH_2}{\underset{NH_2}{\lessgtr}}$$

Arginine   Amidine group   Urea

Attempts had, therefore, been made to ascertain whether other molecules containing the amidine group might give rise to urea by analogous reactions, catalyzed either by arginase itself or by similar enzymes. In the notes on the literature that he took in January, Krebs wrote, for example, that Karl Thomas had shown in 1913 that γ-guanidinobutyric acid is converted in minced liver to urea and γ-aminobutyric acid. Later in the month Krebs noted similarly that Junji Karashima had found, in 1928, that γ-guanidinoacetic acid (glycocyamine) can also be cleaved in minced liver to yield urea and glycine.[77] Such information might provide potential clues about a mechanism common to these analogous reactions. It did not show Krebs the way out of his puzzle.

Probably believing that closer familiarity with the arginase reaction itself might help, in the last days of January Krebs had Henseleit repeat earlier studies of its distribution in various organs. Using organ extracts, as others had, Henseleit confirmed on January 26 that liver is the only tissue to contain large quantities of arginase. The Q rate for the formation of urea in liver extracts was about 100 times as large as for all the other organs (with the exception of intestinal lining, which was about one tenth of the liver value). On the 27th

Henseleit did the experiment again, leaving a longer time for the arginase to act, and got an even more striking result (liver extract, $Q = 259$; the next highest, $Q = 4.02$).[78] These results must have strengthened Krebs's conviction that the ornithine effect is connected with the arginase reaction. As January ended, however, he was still unable to visualize what that connection might be.

The Formation of Urea

When Henseleit first observed the enormous quantity of ammonia formed in kidney tissue to which he had added ornithine, it was an unexpected event that occurred within the context of the ongoing investigation of the ornithine effect. Three days later that event had already taken on the shape of a new investigative problem. The evolution of Krebs's point of view during these 3 days appears to be well captured in the respective titles in Henseleit's notebook of the experiment in which the initial observation was made, and of the first experiment designed to follow it up:

> January 23, 1932. Formation of urea and ammonia in rat liver and kidney, under the influence of ornithine.
> January 26, 1932. Deamination in the rat kidney.

It was thus immediately apparent to Krebs that the phenomenon was probably not due to some further special property of ornithine, but was a special property of the kidney tissue. In this experiment, therefore, Henseleit tested three substances on which the kidney might be expected to carry out a deamination reaction — ornithine, alanine, and thymine. The result was that "Only ornithine and alanine are deaminated." This result clearly pointed to the possibility that amino acids in general might be deaminated in the kidneys, and Krebs immediately pursued that line of thought. On January 27, Henseleit again tested "the deamination of alanine through rat kidney," and again obtained a very large effect (Q_{NH_3} without addition = 0.65 and 0.78; with alanine, 11.5 and 11.5). This experiment produced another surprise, however, in that there was an "enormous increase in the respiration through alanine. 1 mole NH_3 per 3 mole of O_2." That result must have raised for Krebs the question of whether the rise in respiration was connected to the rise in the formation of ammonia, or merely coincidental. On the 29th, Henseleit expanded the investigation to six amino acids. There was considerable variation in the results:

$$Q_{NH_3}$$

No addition	0.47	0.64
Leucine	1.97	1.58
Alanine	4.50	5.84
Ornithine	3.42	3.05
Lysine	2.04	2.09
Tyrosine	0.82	1.52

It would have been difficult for Krebs to interpret these results, as the phenomenon seemed neither to be specific to one type of amino acid, nor a uniform property of amino acids in general. What must have been clear to him now, however, was that another promising investigative lead had "turned up."[1]

From the beginning of February, Krebs spent much more time in the laboratory than he had been able to afford for any extended period in Freiburg before this. Previously he had been recording in his own notebook, on the average, less than one experiment a week; now he began to make an entry every second or third day. Another change in his medical duties must have occurred, this time freeing more time for research.

Despite the great interest that the new observations concerning deamination in the kidneys held for him, Krebs employed his expanded research time first to pursue the questions he had been pondering about the ornithine effect, especially its relation to the arginase reaction. On February 3 he carried out a "metabolism test" that measured the effects of four substances — lysine, ornithine, NH_4Cl, and guanidine — on the respiration, glycolysis, and formation of urea in liver tissue from a starved rat. The choices of lysine and guanidine indicate the questions he was pursuing. To test lysine, the amino acid closest in structure to ornithine, was clearly one more effort to see if there were any other substances that shared the ornithine effect. The only remarkable feature of the experiment was that Krebs had not tried lysine 2 months earlier, when he had first begun to explore the special action of ornithine. A probable reason was that before this he did not have any lysine available. Nevertheless, as discussed in Chapter 9, it is rather surprising that he was deterred for so long from making what should have appeared from the outset as a crucial test. The inclusion of guanidine indicates a more pointed examination of the connection between ornithine and the arginine reaction. Guanidine, $[NH=C(NH_2)_2]$, is the simplest molecule containing the amidine group that is also present in arginine, where it is the direct source of the urea molecule in the arginase reaction. If guanidine should give rise to urea in liver tissue, that would still not explain directly how ornithine enters the process, as ornithine does not contain an amidine group, but it would at least narrow the focus of the problem. To replicate the conditions of the ornithine effect, Krebs tested lysine and guanidine each by itself and in combination with NH_4Cl. The results were unilluminating. Guanidine and NH_4Cl gave rise to "enormous pressures" in the test for urea in the medium of the tissue slice; but when he tested the guanidine directly with urease, he found that his sample (from Hoffmann-LaRoche) already contained a large quantity of urea. Lysine with NH_4Cl yielded so little urea in the tissue that Krebs concluded only that the test "must be repeated."[2]

When he tested lysine again (the experiment is undated, and could have taken place anytime from later the same day until February 9), Krebs measured both the NH_3 consumed and the urea formed. He included duplicate tests of lysine plus NH_4Cl and of controls without the lysine. In all four runs done on starved rat liver tissue, "much more NH_3 disappeared than was consumed for urea." The quantities of NH_3 consumed in the two lysine vessels showed "great differences" in the decrease in the quantity of NH_3 (496 and 226 cm^3). "Consequently," Krebs wrote down, "lysine question uncertain." Although he made no comment on it, the quantity of urea formed with lysine and NH_4Cl was about the same as with NH_4Cl alone. One gains the impression that Krebs may have been looking for the opportunity to test lysine with some special hope that it might provide one of the critical clues to solve his puzzle. After this indecisive result he seemed, at least briefly, to cast around again very tentatively for some other lead to follow. After two experiments on the unrelated homogentisic acid question, on February 10 he tested the influence of insulin and glucose on the formation of urea. He found "no effect" from the former, and "slight effect" from the latter. Turning to his nascent study of deamination on the next day, he tested the effect of thyroxin on the formation of NH_3 from alanine, and here too he found no effect.[3] Meanwhile, Henseleit was fishing for new leads in other corners of the previously defined research area. On February 6 he went back to the pyrimidines, testing thymine and thymosine; but they were as inactive as ever. Krebs appeared to be as reluctant as ever to give up the idea, based on the structure of the pyrimidine molecules, that they must somehow yield urea. The more novel element in this set of experiments was that Henseleit tested the effect of lactate and ammonia on the formation of urea, not in *comparison* with the effect of ornithine and ammonia, but in *combination* with ornithine (NH_4Cl alone yielded Q = 1.64; NH_4Cl + ornithine, Q = 7.37; and NH_4Cl + ornithine + lactate, Q = 11.0). It is difficult to ascertain from the notebook record whether Krebs had a theoretical reason to see if these effects were additive, or whether he was just repeating the experimental strategy he had previously used when he combined amino acids with NH_4Cl. Henseleit's title, "Influence of lactate on the formation of urea from ornithine," only expresses the vagueness of the situation. This wording ought to suggest, as when he had previously used the same standardized phrase — with "ornithine" in place of "lactate," and "NH_4Cl" in place of "ornithine" — that Krebs was still entertaining the possibility that ornithine donates urea nitrogen, and that lactate may stimulate that process. That interpretation does not, however, fit with the general trend of his thought during the preceding weeks.[4]

* * *

I thought, in 1978, that Krebs himself might recall the original reasons for this experiment. When we came to these pages in Henseleit's notebook, I drew his attention to the title, suggesting "In a sense you were thinking of the lactate in a catalytic role and the ornithine as a sort of... " He interrupted, "Not necessarily. There was no ammonia added." After he had examined some of the data recorded, I pursued the point that in earlier experiments he had compared ammonia and lactate to ammonia and ornithine, and here for the first time combined them. I asked, "Is there any kind of rationale that might have led you to try this experiment?" He answered, "Well, nothing of the kind we can now make; but it was all a matter of hit-and-miss, trial and error." I fished a little further: "In other words, you just had two effects you knew were both accelerating effects?" Krebs replied, "Yes, yes. If they were independent, as they proved to be, then they should be additive. This occurs quite often that if two substances have an effect, it may be that they have a common denominator. Or it may be that they attack a process at a different stage and therefore become additive." Scanning the results, Krebs thought they might have appeared additive. The conversation ended at that point.[5]

Krebs was consciously attempting to reconstruct, from the logic of the situation, what he might have been thinking 36 years earlier, but there was no way that even he could regain direct access to what he actually had in mind. Perhaps the test was purely hit-and-miss. We cannot be certain, however, as Krebs naturally did not always remember ideas he had once entertained that turned out to be ephemeral. What is clear about his view of the situation in February 1932 is only that this first result appeared to him, for whatever reason, significant enough to pursue.

* * *

On February 11, Henseleit fixed again on the approach to which Krebs had returned so regularly, with so little to show for it: the search for a molecule, containing the urea molecule preformed, that might give rise to urea without the intermediate step of forming ammonia. Thymine was included as usual, but the focus this time was upon a new candidate, cyanamide ($H_2NC=N$). Cyanamide is converted to urea in the test tube by hydrolysis with alkali, so that it was plausible that it also yields urea physiologically. There had also been suggestions in the arginase literature with which Krebs was familiar, that cyanamide might be split off from arginine itself, and could then give rise to either creatine or urea. Henseleit tested cyanamide at 12 and 120 mg/100 ml. For comparison, he tested ornithine as well, all of the runs being with starved rat liver tissue, and without NH_4C. The rates for all the substances were low, ornithine giving the highest level ($Q = 1.85$). The largest rate due to cyanamide was only $Q = 0.80$. Once again, no new paths opened up.[6]

Krebs began making preparations, on February 12, to examine in another way the role of ornithine in the formation of urea. A strong test of whether ornithine donates nitrogen to the urea would be to determine whether or not the quantity of nitrogen contained in the ornithine added to the medium containing the tissue slices diminishes during the period in which the tissue is forming urea. This was not an entirely new strategy. Felix and Röthler had already attempted, in 1924, to ascertain whether ornithine is consumed in perfused livers, by measuring whether the quantity of nitrogen in the perfusion fluid afterward was equal to or less than that which the ornithine added to the fluid contained. They found that they could not recover the ornithine–nitrogen quantitatively, but attributed the apparent loss to the method rather than to an actual decomposition of ornithine. This indecisive earlier work thus invited a renewed investigation. Moreover, there existed a peculiar analytical situation regarding ornithine that facilitated the possibility of doing so. The standard method for measuring amino-nitrogen was that of Van Slyke. In this method one reacted a solution containing amino acids with nitrous acid, which evolved nitrogen gas according to the reaction: $RNH_2 + HNO_2 = ROH + 2 H_2O + N_2$. The specificity of the method for amino acids rested on the fact that the α-amino groups of amino acids "react quantitatively in 3 to 4 minutes at room temperature; while NH_2 groups in other types of substances react much more slowly." The nitrogen gas was measured manometrically. In principle, therefore, the Van Slyke method would be suitable only to determine whether the α-amino nitrogen of ornithine is used to form urea, and could reveal nothing about the fate of the second amino group on the other end of its carbon chain. In fact, however, Siegfried Edlbacher and H. Burchard had found, in 1930, that ornithine reacts anomalously. Eighty-eight percent of its total nitrogen reacts in the Van Slyke method within 5 minutes. The method, therefore, offered Krebs a convenient way to find out whether any of the nitrogen of ornithine is consumed to form urea. On February 12 he tried this method, with a known sample of ornithine. At the end of 5 minutes 91.5 percent of the total nitrogen content of the ornithine had reacted. Repeating the reaction 3 days later on a different sample of ornithine, he obtained 91 percent. The method was, therefore, practicable for his purpose.[7]

While Krebs tested the Van Slyke method for ornithine, Henseleit was repeating the experiment of combining lactate and ornithine with ammonia. In two successive experiments, carried out on February 13 and 15, he again found that the combination of lactate and ornithine yielded urea at a substantially higher rate than ornithine alone with ammonia. In these experiments, unlike the initial one, he included a test also of lactate and ammonia, probably so that it would be possible to ascertain whether the effects were additive. In the experiment of the 13th the effects proved almost additive (NH_4Cl + lactate, Q, average of two runs = 2.08; NH_4Cl + ornithine, Q, average of two runs = 3.24; NH_4Cl + lactate + ornithine, Q, average of two runs = 5.92). In the experiment of the 15th the effects were less than additive. In any event, Krebs did not treat these as two distinct effects operating on the formation of urea. Instead, he regarded the lactate effect as only a general stimulus to the metabolism of the tissue, which enhanced the ornithine effect. (Reviewing this situation in 1978, by which time a more specific mechanism for the action of lactate had been identified, Krebs commented, "I was satisfied with an easy explanation, that it is an easy source of energy.") Without seeking a more precise explanation for the role of lactate in the formation of urea, he simply decided to use the effect practically in subsequent experiments to maximize the ornithine effect. Perhaps he did take the easy way out on this question; but if so, that was an effective choice. It enabled him to keep his attention on his central problem.[8]

During the last of these two experiments Henseleit measured, in addition to the urea formed, the change in the quantity of NH_3, by the Parnas–Heller method, and the quantity of amino–nitrogen at the end of the experiment, by means of the Van Slyke method that Krebs had just finished testing on that same day. In three of the four runs in which ornithine was present (in the standard "high" concentration of 200 mg/100 ml), a very small proportion of the amino–nitrogen calculated to be present in the ornithine at the beginning disappeared: 23 of 590 mm^3 in one case; 26 of 590 in the second; 9 of 581 in the third. The fourth run was anomalous, in that 94 mm^3 of amino–nitrogen appeared to *form* during the experiment. (Each of these figures was per cubic centimeter of fluid. Henseleit expressed these quantities in the unusual form of the gaseous volumes measured in the manometric methods he used to determine them.) The quantities of urea formed were, however, of the same order of magnitude (43.9, 42.5, 30.2, and 34.4 mm^3/cm^3 of fluid), so that the nitrogen of the urea could, in fact, in two of the cases, have been accounted for by the decrease in amino–nitrogen. The test was, therefore, indecisive.[9] (In 1978, when Krebs discussed the experiment with me he agreed with my suggestion that from this result one could not tell whether or not ornithine was serving as a source of urea–nitrogen.) The solution to the central problem, therefore, continued to elude Krebs.

With none of the several experimental lines he had taken appearing to lead him out of his dilemma, Krebs apparently saw nothing else to do at this point but to go back to each approach once more, hoping that some further step might yield the clue he needed. On the 17th of February he had Henseleit test three more amidine compounds.

dicyanamide

$$H_2NC(NH)C \equiv N$$
$$\|$$
$$NH$$

dicyanamidine

$$H_2NC(NH)C(NH_2)$$
$$\| \qquad \|$$
$$NH \quad O$$

creatine

$$NH_2$$
$$|$$
$$H_2N^+ = C NCH_2COO^-$$
$$\|$$
$$CH_3$$

Krebs's rationale this time was clearly indicated in the title of the experiment, "Urea formation from homologs of arginine." Because arginine also contains an amidine group, the source for the urea molecule, he was seeking to understand the mechanism for this reaction by looking for homologous reactions that might share the same mechanism. Nothing turned up. Each compound yielded little urea by itself, and with ammonia no more than ammonia alone did.[10]

* * *

In retrospect, Krebs placed little importance on this experiment. Of the results, he said "I think they are all negative." When I asked if he had thought there might be other analogous reactions, he said "It was a matter of the specificity of the arginase." After a pause, he added, "So these are just very wild tests of what could be feasible. But as we knew so little about the — a lot of experiments were just analogy tests. Arginine reacts. The question was is there anything which has a faintly resembling structure, [which] might also react."[11]

The Krebs who had long since solved this problem appeared to have relatively little sympathy with the Krebs who was still struggling with it.

* * *

On February 17, Krebs himself returned to the lysine question. Using nourished rat liver tissue, he compared the effects on urea formation of NH_4Cl, lysine, and NH_4Cl plus lysine. (In addition he tested lactate with NH_4Cl.) The results were irregular, as he thought, because the tissue slices were too large. Nevertheless, the outcome was clear: "Lysine is without influence on the formation of urea."[12] Another avenue had closed.

I

Shortly after performing the experiment on lysine, Krebs made a decision to take over the investigation of the deamination of amino acids himself, while Henseleit carried on with the urea experiments. There are several plausible explanations for his choice. The new investigation was in a preliminary state, in which the procedures to be used were still unsettled, whereas the basic urea experiments had become relatively routine. Moreover, the deamination investigation was just opening up, at a time in which the urea investigation may have seemed to be bogged down. At this time, the deamination experiments may, in fact, have appeared more promising to Krebs. A simpler explanation would be that Krebs now foresaw that he would have time to work regularly in the laboratory himself, and considered it more efficient to establish a clearer division of labor.

During a week in which Henseleit was probably away, Krebs took up his investigation of deamination, on January 23, by measuring the formation of NH_3 from alanine, in five different rat tissues — testicle, liver, spleen, kidney, and brain cortex. He chose alanine obviously because it had produced the largest quantity of ammonia in the earlier experiment in which Henseleit had employed several amino acids. The most striking result of the earlier experiments, however, had been the high rate at which the process occurred in kidney tissue. Krebs's first priority was clearly to ascertain whether the kidneys really stood out in this regard, because that would contradict the prevailing opinion. The accumulated evidence from organ perfusion experiments supported the expectation, based on the view that the deamination of amino acids supplies the ammonia for urea, that the process is located principally in the liver. There were some indications that the liver was not the sole site for deamination, but the remainder of the process was assumed to be diffused generally through other tissues. The kidneys were believed to be the source for the large amounts of NH_3 excreted in the urine, but this ammonia was thought to be derived from urea, by a reversal of the reaction in which urea is formed from ammonia.[13]

In this experiment Krebs confirmed that the kidneys produced far more NH_3 than any other organ tested (kidneys, Q = 10.50; testicle, 0.50; liver, 1.35; spleen, 0.64; and brain cortex, 1.10). In the case of the liver tissue, Krebs also measured the urea produced, and calculated that the "total NH_3" that the liver yielded, in the forms of free ammonia and urea together, was only a little more than half of the ammonia produced by the kidney tissue.[14]

We can see in this experiment another of the steps by which Krebs's investigation of deamination was acquiring an identity distinct from the urea investigation that had spawned it. The intimate connection between them at the start is symbolized in a definition Otto Neubauer had given, in 1928, of the central problem of urea synthesis: *"How does urea originate from the ammonia split off from the amino acids?"*[15] What so quickly transformed deamination into a separate investigation for Krebs was the unexpected discovery that the organ in which amino acids were most actively deaminated was one in which little urea is produced. It was not merely a matter of an intermediate produced in one organ that is further transformed in another. Because the NH_3 produced in the kidneys was assumed to be excreted, this NH_3 was not likely to be involved in the formation of urea, and Krebs soon found himself studying a different physiological phenomenon. The problem a scientist is studying often shifts to another one in such unforeseen ways. In this case the result was a fork in Krebs's investigative pathway, at which he chose to follow both branches.

Having established to his satisfaction the exceptional activity of kidney tissue, on February 25 Krebs again tested the rates at which various amino acids produce NH_3 in that tissue. Doubling his standard "high" concentration, he employed 400 mg/100 ml of oxyproline, tyrosine, creatine, leucine, alanine, and phenylalanine. This time alanine did not come out on top. Its Q value was 22.9 compared with 27.2 for phenylalanine. The rest were much smaller (between 1 and 3.5). He also tested alanine anaerobically, and obtained the low value of Q = 2.0.[16] That simple comparison with the aerobic value of 22.9 for alanine probably led Krebs to adopt as his working hypothesis the predominant theory that α-amino groups of amino acids are removed through an oxidative process. Otto Neubauer had proposed such a mechanism in 1909 on the basis of feeding experiments with unnatural amino acids. Imitating the strategy through which Knoop had demonstrated β-oxidation of fatty acids, Neubauer had fed rabbits and dogs substances, such as phenylaminoacetic acid, and recovered corresponding keto acids from their urine. The reaction he had assumed to have taken place:

$$C_6H_5CH(NH_2)COOH + 0.5\ O_2\ =\ C_6H_5COCOOH + NH_3$$

was analogous to test tube reactions that required oxidizing agents such as permanganate. Although this was the favored interpretation for the normal deamination of natural amino acids in 1932, alternative interpretations also had some support. If the deamination took place by simple hydrolysis, the product would be the corresponding hydroxyacid; if by a reductive process, it would be the corresponding fatty acid:[17]

hydrolysis: $RCH(NH_2)COOH + H_2O = RCHOHCOOH + NH_3$
reductive: $RCH(NH_2)COOH + H_2 = RCH_2COOH + NH_3$

When Henseleit returned to work, on February 27, Krebs directed him to take up again the question he had dropped 6 weeks earlier, after two indecisive attempts — "The influence of the ornithine concentration." There are two plausible explanations for retrieving this aspect of the investigation at this time. The negative one is that all his efforts in the meantime to uncover clues about a specific mechanism for the ornithine effect had come to nothing, therefore, he may have had no ideas left except to press the general question of whether ornithine can act catalytically. A positive reason is that modifications he had since made in his basic experimental procedure — to utilize lactate to enhance the ornithine effect, and to work with concentrations of NH_4Cl higher than the 12 mg/100 ml that he had routinely employed since the preceding summer — may have given him reason to expect that it would be productive to repeat the experiments on lower concentrations of ornithine. It was. The results were:

		Q	
	40 mg/100 ml NH_4Cl	1.16	1.88
12.5 mg/100 ml ornithine +	40 mg/100 ml NH_4Cl	8.78	8.92
50 mg/100 ml ornithine +	40 mg/100 ml NH_4Cl	13.10	11.2
200 mg/100 ml ornithine +	40 mg/100 ml NH_4Cl	11.80	10.38[18]

This experiment must have given the investigation, for Krebs, a psychologically decisive turn. Not only were the rates the highest he had yet recorded for the ornithine effect, but they pointed strongly toward the independence of the effect from the concentration of ornithine. Clearly further explanation was still required, as the rate did fall off somewhat at the lowest concentration; but the fact that it was at least as high at 50 mg/100 ml as it was at the standard 200 mg/100 ml must have left in Krebs's mind little doubt about which way to proceed.

Fixing now on whether one could further amplify the ornithine effect at very low concentrations, Krebs next had Henseleit check the influence of pH, by adding bicarbonate in two different proportions to the usual physiological salt solution. The concentration of ornithine employed was now only 10 mg/100 ml. In the less alkaline of these two alkaline media, the Q values were a healthy 11.98 and 9.36, whereas in the more alkaline one they were 9.72 and 6.19.

Using the medium that had given the higher readings, Henseleit took the ornithine concentrations still lower on March 1. The results were:

		Q	
	60 mg/100 ml NH₄Cl	4.64	3.32
0.5 mg/100 ml ornithine +	60 mg/100 ml NH₄Cl	4.50	5.84
2.0 mg/100 ml ornithine +	60 mg/100 ml NH₄Cl	6.85	9.36
8.0 mg/100 ml ornithine +	60 mg/100 ml NH₄Cl	7.19	8.91
32 mg/100 ml ornithine +	60 mg/100 ml NH₄Cl	11.08	10.31

This result again seemed to indicate a dependence of the effect on the concentration; but the range of concentrations was so much lower than in the earlier experiments, that this outcome was probably not a setback to the catalytic view. Pressing the concentration effect even further the next day, Henseleit obtained the following results:

		Q	
	60 mg/100 ml NH₄Cl	0.63	1.71
0.1 mg/100 ml ornithine +	60 mg/100 ml NH₄Cl	1.13	1.25
1.0 mg/100 ml ornithine +	60 mg/100 ml NH₄Cl	4.22	5.22
10 mg/100 ml ornithine +	60 mg/100 ml NH₄Cl	7.63	9.42[19]

Although there was once again a correlation between the concentration and the magnitude of the effect, Krebs had now reached a level at which the absolute quantities of ornithine placed in the medium were so small that he could begin to adduce another argument for a catalytic role. The ornithine supplied was not sufficient to account for a major proportion of the nitrogen contained in the urea that formed. At this time, Krebs did not pursue the concentration effect further. He probably did not regard these results as definitive, but they were nevertheless persuasive enough to make him confident that the solution to the problem lay somehow in a catalytic action of ornithine. He was, however, probably still not able to visualize precisely what catalytic role ornithine played, or how it was connected to the arginase reaction.

II

Through the first 3 weeks of March, Henseleit's experiments on the formation of urea dealt with secondary issues. He performed a few more experiments on the production of urea in various tissues, including for the first time embryonic and aged tissue. The results were negative, except for embryonic liver and the inner membrane of the amnion. He tested the effects of heavy metals and other substances on the arginase reaction. He tested the effects of HCN, which, in accord with Warburg's earlier experiments, would suppress the respiration of the tissues, on the formation of urea. Henseleit examined again the influence of "easily combustible substances" — that is, of intermediates in carbohydrate metabolism — on the ornithine effect.[20] The only fundamentally novel experiment he carried out during this period was to test, on March 5, whether ground liver tissue could form urea in the presence of ornithine and NH$_4$Cl. Henseleit concluded, "No urea formation in liver *Brei*."[21] Krebs pursued the issue no further. This single experiment appeared sufficient to him to confirm the prevailing view that the synthesis of urea requires the intact structure of the cells. All in all, Henseleit seems to have been marking time during these weeks, probably because Krebs was biding his time on the ornithine question until he could reach some new understanding of the nature of its catalytic action. Meanwhile, Krebs was concentrating his own investigative energies on the problem of deamination in the kidneys.

On February 29, Krebs tested further the rate at which phenylalanine produced NH$_3$, confirming that the rate was much higher in kidney than in liver tissue. The rate in kidney was, however, less than alanine had generally yielded.[22] Although he continued to test phenylalanine, he shifted his emphasis back to alanine in subsequent experiments, not only because, of the amino acids he had tested it yielded the maximum rate, but because it was strategic for interpreting the nature of the deamination reaction. The next experiment he undertook, on March 1, was primarily an effort to identify that reaction. Using kidney cortex slices, he measured the rate at which 400 mg/100 ml alanine released NH$_3$ alone, and in the presence of 10^{-5}, 10^{-4}, and 10^{-3} M HCN. As in the case of Henseleit's urea experiments, Krebs used HCN to block the aerobic respiration of the tissues; in this case, however, his purpose was to prevent the substance resulting from the deamination from being further oxidized. Then he tested the solutions in which each of the slices had been placed, for pyruvic acid. In only one of the runs, that in which alanine was used with the highest of the HCN concentrations, did a significant quantity appear: 190 cm^3 of pyruvate in the total volume of fluid. Krebs wrote down as the result:

In HCN, large quantity of NH$_3$, large quantity of pyruvate, <u>both equal</u>

NH$_3$ <u>182</u>

pyruvate   190[23]

That result was clearly significant to him because the equal quantities of NH$_3$ and pyruvate were the stoichiometric proportions to be expected in accordance with the reaction

$$CH_3CH(NH_2)COOH + 0.5\ O_2 \rightarrow CH_3COCOOH + NH_3$$
alanine   pyruvic acid

Krebs's result was, however, not so much a demonstration of that reaction as an interpretation conforming to the view of Neubauer that this was the reaction in question. The interpretation of the result itself depended on some of the assumptions connected with Neubauer's view. Krebs did not record in his notebook what method he used to determine the pyruvate, but the fact that the quantity is given as a volume indicates that it was a manometric method. Most likely he used the carboxylase method of Carl Neuberg.[24] A yeast preparation containing the enzyme would decarboxylate pyruvic acid to acetaldehyde, and Krebs would have measured the quantity of pyruvate by means of the CO_2 released. This method was not, however, considered specific to pyruvic acid, but was a determination of the total quantity of α-keto acids present. The fact that Krebs identified this quantity simply as pyruvate implies that he not only accepted that the deamination was oxidative, but that he assumed with Neubauer that this oxidative deamination was the *first* step in the decomposition of amino acids.[25]

After these suggestive results, Krebs set out to gather further experimental evidence for the oxidative deamination reaction that his initial experiment appeared so nicely to support. On March 2, he measured the effect of 10^{-3} M HCN on the respiration and ammonia production of kidney slices from starved rats, with and without alanine. In the preceding experiment he had found that HCN appeared actually to increase the formation of NH_3 from alanine, but in this case it did not. The respiration, which was almost completely inhibited by HCN without alanine, was only reduced to about one quarter of the control rate when alanine was present. "Inhibition of respiration with alanine smaller than without alanine," Krebs noted.[26] This difference was not an anomaly for him, but a conveniently explainable effect. It fit his interpretation that HCN does not inhibit the oxidative deamination of alanine, but does block the further oxidation of pyruvate. Whether he set up the experiment to *look* for such a difference, or only observed it by happy accident, cannot be ascertained from the record.

The experiments Krebs had carried out so far invited confirmation of their interpretation by checking the effect of HCN on the metabolism of kidney tissue slices to which pyruvate itself is added. Two days later (March 4) he performed such an experiment, using four concentrations of HCN in the presence of 100 mg/100 ml of pyruvate. The result was not entirely satisfying. The highest concentration of HCN used (10^{-2} M) lowered the oxygen consumption only by half, suggesting that, in spite of the expected blocking of aerobic respiration, some of the pyruvate must have been oxidized. In a parallel set of experiments carried out with 200 mg/100 ml alanine in place of the pyruvate, Krebs encountered further complications. Measuring the ammonia formed by the slices, he now found, contrary to the preceding result, but in keeping with the one before it, that HCN increased the rate. This time, however, "The NH_3 increases enormously with the concentration of HCN (nearly improbable quotients)." (Q_{NH_3} in the control was 6.8; with 10^{-3} M HCN, 11.5; with 10^{-2} M HCN, 21.2). Moreover, the general influence of HCN seemed to disappear over time, as indicated by a gradual rise in the respiration. One result that fit expectations was that the quantities of pyruvate in the medium afterward were greater at the high concentrations of HCN, and there was none in the control. When Krebs went back to check the pyruvate present in the media of the slices to which he had added pyruvate rather than alanine, however, he met another unpleasant surprise. In the media to which HCN had been added, as well as in the controls, he found considerably less pyruvate than he had put in. "With HCN," he wrote down emphatically, "much pyruvate disappeared!!" That outcome was so unsatisfactory that he added underneath the query "Method??"

Since a substantial portion of the pyruvate had disappeared even from the thermobarometer control vessel, he suspected that the old pyruvate solution he had used was not good, and he decided to distill a new solution.[27] At this point he could probably not tell whether all of the anomalies he observed that day were due to methodological difficulties, or whether some of them pointed to metabolic complexities unforeseen from the interpretation of the deamination reaction that guided his investigation.

One of the conclusions that Krebs must have drawn from the confusing results of his latest efforts was that the carboxylase method was not adequate to demonstrate conclusively that the product of the reaction he was studying was pyruvic acid. Therefore, he carried out, on March 5, a large scale experiment to isolate that product in a form that would permit more specific identification. The standard method for α-keto acids was to purify them and react them with phenylhydrazine, converting them to phenylhydrazones that precipitated in crystalline forms with characteristic melting points. In 1930, however, Charles F.H. Allen, of McGill University in Montreal, had published a modification of this method, using 2-4 dinitrophenylhydrazine, which he claimed gave more satisfactory results with aliphatic carbonyl compounds. It was Allen's method that Krebs tried. Using 120 mg of kidney tissue, and allowing the experiment to proceed for 7 hours (3 hours before and 4 hours after the addition of 10^{-2} M HCN), he obtained crystals that melted at 215°C, close enough to the 213°C that Allen had given for the melting point of the 2-4 dinitrophenylhydrazone of pyruvic acid.[28] Whatever else may have been going on in his experiments, Krebs could now be confident at least that one of the phenomena involved *was* the conversion of alanine to pyruvic acid.

On March 7, Krebs used the HCN method to compare the formation of pyruvate from alanine in kidney and liver slices with its formation from glucose: that is, its production as a step in the main pathway of carbohydrate metabolism. (He used 10^{-3} M HCN and 10^{-2} M alanine and glucose.) No pyruvate formed from glucose in either tissue, or in liver from alanine. In kidney tissue alanine yielded pyruvate (measured by the carboxylase method) at a rate of Q = 14.4.[29] Krebs recorded no surprise at the fact that HCN did not make visible the assumed formation of pyruvate through carbohydrate metabolism. To judge from his later published view, Krebs may have inferred from this result that HCN did not block only the further oxidative decomposition of pyruvate, as he had probably thought up until then, but also the oxidative process necessary to convert glucose to pyruvate.[30] Instead of blocking only a specific later stage in oxidative metabolism, therefore, HCN perhaps blocked most oxidative metabolic processes, with the oxidative deamination of amino acids being an exception. On the other hand, Krebs might have drawn such conclusions only later, and have been, at this point, simply puzzled by the outcome.

On March 11, Krebs carried out a mixed experiment, half of which was devoted to the investigation of the synthesis of urea. Once again he tested whether lysine with NH_4Cl would produce urea in rat liver tissue. He measured both the urea formed and the ammonia consumed. The latter measurements were inexact, appearing in one of the two runs to show an increase in the ammonia. The result for urea was quite clear. Lysine plus NH_4Cl produced much less urea than did NH_4Cl alone. Krebs wrote down "Lysine *inhibits* urea formation and NH_3 consumption."[31] The "lysine question" seemed finally settled. This chemically most plausible candidate to share the ornithine effect had no part in it.

In the other half of the experiment, Krebs measured the change in the quantity of NH_3 in the medium of rat kidney slices to which he had added NH_4Cl. In one of them, which contained Ringer's solution but no other substrate, there was an increase in the quantity of ammonia in the medium, despite its presence at the beginning. In the other one, physiological salt solution with lactate in addition to the NH_4Cl, there was a decrease in the quantity of ammonia. Whatever may have been his expectation in trying the experiment, the result — "kidney + lactate, NH_3 consumption!!" — struck him as remarkable enough to follow up. Perhaps he guessed that lactate was somehow being converted to alanine, by combining with the ammonia. Alanine being among the nonessential amino acids, it must be made somewhere in the organism. On March 14 Krebs carried out an experiment that appears designed to test that possibility. This time he compared the consumption of NH_3 by kidney cortex slices in NH_4Cl Ringer's solution alone, with that of slices in solutions also containing respectively lactate and pyruvate. In the media containing pyruvate he found, through the carboxylase test, that the pyruvate disappeared rapidly. Moreover, with regard to the central point, "NH_3 disappears in the presence of lactate and pyruvate, more with the latter."[32] The result seemed in accord with the possibility that lactate and pyruvate can be converted to alanine in kidney tissue, the pyruvate being the more direct precursor. Krebs did not pursue the question further at this point. He returned instead to his main problem, strengthening his evidence for the oxidative deamination of alanine. Here was, however, a potential new fork in his investigative trail.

On March 17, Krebs repeated the experiment of March 4 that had produced so many anomalies. He examined the respiration of kidney slices in the presence respectively of 100 mg/100 ml of pyruvate and 200 mg/100 ml of alanine, measuring also the formation of ammonia and the change produced in the quantities of pyruvate. He used HCN in concentrations of 10^{-2} M and 10^{-3} M. All of the conditions were the same as in the previous experiment, except that he had prepared a new pyruvate solution. Nevertheless, the experiment employing this pyruvate turned out to be "not usable," because, as he thought, the pyruvate had been altered by "over alkalinization." The alanine experiment was usable, but puzzling. The respiration was "enormous," and little inhibited, even by the higher concentration of HCN. The Q values for the formation of pyruvate for the two alanine experiments (6.5 and 6.5) were approximately equal to those for the consumption of oxygen (7.1 and 6.5) and one half of that for the formation of ammonia (average 15.4). "Therefore," Krebs noted, "too little pyruvate, if [the reaction] were [*wäre*] 2 alanine + O_2 = 2 pyruvate + NH_3." The subjunctive verb *wäre*, together with the fact that the pyruvate that appeared was just about half what it should have been, suggests that Krebs might have entertained the possibility that the reaction taking place was actually different from the oxidative deamination he had assumed he was studying. He probably regarded it as more likely, however, that unresolved methodological difficulties were still preventing him from detecting all of the pyruvate that formed; and the most likely explanation for that failure was that the HCN was not fully preventing the disappearance of the pyruvate that formed. He noticed, in fact, that the respiratory inhibition caused by HCN again "disappears with time," a phenomenon he ascribed to binding of the substance by KOH.[33]

A week passed before Krebs found time to continue his investigation. On the 24th he repeated the pyruvate part of the preceding experiment, this time after neutralizing the pyruvic acid very slowly and carefully. He tested the action of the kidney slices on the pyruvate (the actual concentration of which was 32 mg/100 ml) both aerobically and anaerobically without HCN, and aerobically with 5×10^{-3} M HCN. In all cases, he noted, "Much pyruvate disappears!! — even anaerobically there are large quotients!!!" The HCN appeared to have done little to hinder the disappearance of the pyruvate. Krebs thought, however, that its apparent ineffectiveness might have been misleading. In the absence of HCN almost all of the pyruvate added had disappeared. Consequently, to establish whether the HCN had lessened its disappearance he should repeat the experiment over a shorter time period or with more pyruvate.[34] We may note that this was at least the second time that Krebs had encountered the phenomenon of pyruvate being consumed from a tissue slice medium under anaerobic conditions. Because pyruvic acid was generally considered to form a step in the oxidative phase of carbohydrate metabolism, its anaerobic disappearance should have caught his attention. His triple exclamation point suggests that it did — but not with sufficient force at this time to induce him to take it up as an independent research problem. (The pyruvate might also, of course, have disappeared from the medium by means of a spontaneous chemical reaction. The experiment apparently did not include a control without a tissue slice.) For him the main unsolved problem continued to be to find a way to prevent the pyruvate from disappearing under aerobic conditions.

If HCN could not solve Krebs's problem, maybe there was some other agent that could. On March 29 he tried fluoride, guanidine, and iodoacetate. Although the experiment was somewhat unsatisfactory, because the tissue slices were too large, it was clear that none of these substances prevented the pyruvate from disappearing. The next day he tried octyl alcohol, a general narcotic agent known to inhibit respiration, along with 10^{-2} M HCN, and an anaerobic run with no other inhibitor. The results were instructive. In the aerobic control with no inhibitors, "almost 1 mole of pyruvic acid disappears per mole of O_2," a proportion that perhaps suggested to Krebs the possibility of studying a stoichiometric reaction that removed pyruvate in the kidney slices. Under anaerobic conditions, and with the octylalcohol, only 10 percent as much pyruvate disappeared as did in the aerobic control. (In response to the experimental result of March 24, he was now using larger quantities of pyruvate than he had used then.) HCN again proved ineffective for his purpose, but this time he found in the result a clue to the cause of the problem. With that agent, he noted, there is an "enormous disappearance, even though the respiration is almost nil." The quantities of pyruvate that disappeared in the duplicate runs, he noticed, were proportional to the volumes of fluid in the vessels rather than to the weights of the tissue slices. What enabled him to perceive this relationship was that he had prepared the fluid volumes in the two vessels in the ratio of 4:1 to use the Warburg method to calculate both the oxygen consumption and the carbon dioxide produced.[35] He did not record an explanation for the correlation, but it clearly directed him toward the view that the pyruvate was disappearing through an outside chemical reaction rather than a metabolic process.

Alerted by this apparently chance observation, Krebs pursued the question of how pyruvate disappears in the presence of HCN, in his next experiment on March 31. Again adding pyruvate to kidney slices, with 10^{-2} M and 5×10^{-3} M HCN, and without HCN, he now added a crucial additional control, pyruvate with 10^{-2} M HCN but no tissue. Pyruvate disappeared under all conditions. For the question raised by the previous experiment, the most significant result was that "with 10^{-2} M HCN much *pyruvate* disappears even without tissue!!!"[36] That result caused him to begin searching for a purely chemical explanation of the effect.

Meanwhile, although he had not solved the problem of how to prevent the pyruvate from disappearing, he could now safely ascribe the problem to a side effect that did not call into question the nature of the metabolic reaction he was studying. He returned, therefore, on April 2, to the basic experiment of adding alanine to kidney slices in the presence of HCN. The results were not helpful. He found "little pyruvate," afterward, even in the presence of HCN. On April 5, he did an "analogous" experiment, using a phosphate buffer, and five concentrations of HCN ranging in geometric progression from M/60 to M/960. He did not measure the pyruvate, probably because the results of such measurements up until then had been so unrewarding, but concentrated on the effects of HCN on the respiration and the formation of ammonia. The new results clarified these aspects of the situation considerably. Without HCN the respiratory rate was Q = 46. With M/960 HCN it fell to 15.8; but with increasing concentrations the inhibitor decreased the respiration only a little bit further (to 9.4 at the highest concentration, M/60 HCN). Thus, the respiration appeared to be separable, under these conditions, into two portions. Krebs concluded, "In alanine a portion of the respiration is insensitive to HCN." HCN decreased the formation of NH_3 slightly, in contrast to some earlier experiments in which it had appeared to *increase* the formation so greatly that Krebs had doubted the validity of the results. Now he could conclude simply, "NH_3 — formation is not inhibited by HCN."[37]

On April 6, Krebs examined further the chemical action of HCN on pyruvate, and found, apparently to his surprise, that pyruvate "disappears independently of the pH!!" It is not clear whether or not he had yet in mind any specific hypothesis concerning the chemical reaction that might be taking place.[38]

During the same day, Krebs took another look at the phenomenon of the consumption of NH_3 in kidney slices that had raised the possibility 3 weeks earlier that pyruvate or lactate in the presence of NH_4Cl might give rise to an amino acid. Using only pyruvate and NH_4Cl this time, he tested whether HCN would inhibit the process. It did, but the results were irregular. The next day he compared the action of the three standard carbohydrate intermediates — glucose, lactate, and pyruvate — each with NH_4Cl, but without HCN. He found that without the additions, NH_3 was formed at a rate of Q = 0.60. With glucose the formation was smaller still: Q = 0.14. With both lactate and pyruvate there was a disappearance of NH_3, the Q value being -0.42. These results were mildly suggestive, but scarcely impressive. Krebs commented "But small consumption!!",[39] and he was apparently not tempted to follow this investigative side track any further.

Two days later Krebs examined whether thymosine, thymine, and leucine would yield ammonia in his kidney slice system. Each of them did, and HCN increased the quantity that each gave off, but only by small amounts.[40] At this point he interrupted his laboratory research for almost 2 weeks.

During the month of March 1932, Krebs had faced, in his two main lines of investigation, obstacles that were the converse of one another. Regarding deamination he was seeking to confirm a well-known, clearly defined hypothesis, that amino acids undergo physiologically an oxidative deamination to yield a determinate product, the corresponding α-keto acids. Choosing the representative case of alanine, Krebs had been able to verify the reaction qualitatively in kidney tissue. Unless he could do so quantitatively, however, he could show only that oxidative deamination takes place in this tissue, not prove that it is the sole, or even the principal, metabolic pathway. The obstacles in his way were, therefore, experimental. In the case of urea synthesis, he had attained a very clear-cut experimental result, for which he was still seeking a clearly formulated explanatory hypothesis. His obstacle was largely conceptual. The reason that he temporarily put aside his investigation of deamination on April 8 may have been that, with regard to urea synthesis he was finally reaching such a hypothesis.

III

There are no surviving contemporary documents to mark the steps by which Hans Krebs arrived at the conceptual solution of the problem posed for him by the observed ornithine effect. The attempt to reconstruct his mental pathway must, therefore, begin with retrospective statements made by Krebs himself many years after the event. After he had concluded that "ornithine acts like a catalyst," Krebs wrote in 1973,

When considering the mechanism of this catalytic action I was guided by the concept that a catalyst must take part in the reaction and form intermediates. The reactions of the intermediate must eventually regenerate ornithine and form urea. Once these postulates had been formulated it became obvious that arginine fulfilled the requirements of the expected intermediate. This meant that a formation of arginine from ornithine had to be postulated by the addition of one molecule of carbon dioxide and two molecules of ammonia, and the elimination of water from the ornithine molecule.[41]

(We shall return to the remainder of Krebs's account further on.) During my conversations with Krebs, we touched repeatedly on the topics compressed into this paragraph. His comments do not add up to a story that can be fully integrated with his investigative pathway, but they do provide a basis for some further interpretation of his written statement. The most obvious question is whether, when he likened the action of ornithine to a catalyst, he was comparing it to the action of any specific catalytic process or class of processes. It appears that he had no particular biochemical process in mind as a model, and he could in fact not have found one because there were no proven precedents closely enough resembling the phenomenon he had encountered to provide a detailed model. (If the Thunberg–Knoop–Wieland scheme had been confirmed it would have provided one, but there is no evidence that at this time Krebs connected his problem with that hypothesis.) He was, in fact, thinking in the most general terms, that *any* type of catalyst was considered to form some kind of intermediate union with its substrate. He had in mind that the general kinetics of enzyme actions, especially as formulated in the equation of Michaelis and Menten, assumed that enzymes enter into temporary combination with their substrates. In 1930 J.B.S. Haldane published a book on *Enzymes* that summarized the case for the theory that enzymes must combine with their substrates. Krebs read this influential book soon after it appeared, and it may have helped shape his view of the subject. He was also impressed that even in industrial processes using metallic catalysts, such as platinum and palladium, which had once been considered only to exert some sort of surface action, these catalysts were now thought to form transient intermediates with one or more of the substances whose reactions they accelerated.[42]

It is evident that Krebs was reasoning not from a highly structured comparison between two processes, but only from a very broad analogy. The analogical nature of his thought is retained in the careful statement "acts *like* a catalyst," which he used, not only in his historical account, but also in his first published paper on the synthesis of urea. Because the analogy was so general, the direct guidance that it could give to Krebs's thought was also limited to a very general approach. The analogy by itself suggested nothing about the nature of the intermediate combination that ornithine might form. If my interpretation that Krebs began in mid-February to consider that ornithine acts in a catalytic manner is valid, then he may have gone for a long time without getting much beyond this general orientation. For some of this time it might have appeared to him simply impossible to see how to fit that viewpoint together with his belief that the action of ornithine must be connected to its part in the arginase reaction; in that respect it was simply the *product* of a reaction catalyzed, in the usual way, by an enzyme.

The critical clue, of course, was that arginine itself is the intermediate. In his succinct statement Krebs made that identification the "obvious" conclusion derived from the "postulates" about catalytic action. In conversation in 1978 he mentioned a different version of this step:

> I know that after having discovered the ornithine effect and being satisfied with it, it took something like a month before it occurred to me that ornithine may give rise to arginine. And then we could do the critical experiments, namely measuring whether it disappeared. Because if that were the case, then it would be catalytic. If a small quantity would be effective and it would disappear. So before that I was just puzzled, and carried on doing experiments.[43]

This statement is difficult to interpret, or to reconcile with Krebs's published description. There is obviously a minor slip in that he meant that if ornithine did *not* disappear it would be catalytic. More significant is that this statement implies that the idea that ornithine might "give rise to arginine" was the *initial* explanatory insight, which then led to the idea that the action might be catalytic — the reverse of the order of the logic in the published statement. We are confronted here with a basic methodological question: whether to place more weight on a retrospective account that the subject of the earlier events has carefully formulated, or on his spontaneous, unrehearsed response to a question. Arguments can be given for either preference, but it is only when there are independent checks from other records that we can make such a choice with confidence. In this case there is only the general criterion of plausibility. I believe it less plausible that Krebs had in mind that ornithine may give rise to arginine before he began to think of its action as catalytic, than the other way around. On the other hand, the tone of the first part of the statement — that the idea *occurred* to him, as an insight rather than as an obvious conclusion deduced directly from the catalytic postulates — seems very plausible.

Even after he had thought of the possibility that ornithine gives rise to arginine, it may not have been immediately clear to Krebs how this could happen. He must have entertained at least briefly the idea that it does so through a reversal of the arginase reaction, because he pointed out to me, in 1978, that he eliminated that possibility on the grounds that the arginase reaction was known to be essentially irreversible. (Even had it not been, a reverse arginase reaction could not account for the formation of urea, because it would consume urea instead.) It became evident to him, therefore, that there must be some other route through which ornithine can be converted to arginine.[44] At this stage, if he behaved as he habitually did in later years, Krebs would have begun sketching formulas on paper to clarify what needed to be added to or removed from the ornithine molecule to produce a molecule of arginine. There was an important condition that gave the problem a tight structure: ornithine required ammonia to yield urea, and Krebs had shown the ammonia to be the likely source of its NH_2 groups. That meant that the ammonia must supply the NH and the NH_2 group of arginine that are not contained in ornithine. All that was left to do was account for the single carbon atom of arginine not supplied by ornithine, and to get rid of four extra hydrogen atoms. Krebs did so in the simplest manner possible, by assuming that CO_2 enters the reaction, its carbon atom being incorporated into the arginine, while its two oxygen atoms join with the leftover hydrogen atoms to form water. It should be stressed that, in contrast to the NH_3, which he included on experimental grounds, Krebs merely postulated the CO_2, to balance the equation. The resulting reaction was:[45]

$$
\begin{array}{c}
CH_2NH_2 \\
|\\
CH_2 \\
|\\
CH_2 \quad + 2\,NH_3 + CO_2 \\
|\\
CHNH_2 \\
|\\
COOH
\end{array}
=
\begin{array}{c}
HN=C\Big\langle {}^{NH_2} \\
CH_2NH \\
|\\
CH_2 \\
|\\
CH_2 \quad + 2\,H_2O \\
|\\
CHNH_2 \\
|\\
COOH
\end{array}
\qquad (1)
$$

Ornithin + 2 Ammo- + Kohlen- = Arginin + 2 Wasser
            niak   säure

In his historical account Krebs wrote that when he had postulated this equation, "It also became obvious at once that the synthesis of arginine from ornithine must involve more than one step since four molecules — one ornithine, one CO_2, two NH_3 — had to interact."[46] Here he condensed into a single deductive step a mental pathway that — like the metabolic pathway itself — may have been somewhat longer. It was not merely that too many molecules had to interact for the reaction to occur in one step, but that CO_2 was, in a sense a theoretical "stand-in" for a yet unknown source of the needed carbon atom. The formulation was not only incomplete, but in a sense it was a provisional conception of what the reaction might be like. This characteristic is implied in Krebs's first published presentation of the reaction. "A substance that possesses the properties required of the intermediate has long been known. It is arginine. Arginine can be *thought of (lässt sich denken)* [my italics] as originating from ornithine, ammonia, and carbon dioxide with the elimination of water."[47]

The compact description that Krebs gave of his formulation of the ornithine-arginine reaction in 1973 reads like a solution that came to him at some particular time. "It became obvious," and "it became obvious at once" seem to allude to sudden insights such as are popularly associated with moments of great scientific creativity. Even with the modifications in his account that I have suggested, it might still appear that some critical step in the train of reasoning that he described — most probably the idea that ornithine gives rise to arginine — must have occurred to him all at once. Yet Krebs also wrote "The solution of the problem developed gradually as the ornithine effect was studied in detail."[48] In our conversations about the solution he never associated it with any specific circumstance of time or place. He only reiterated that it "became gradually clear." Even when he had sufficient information to solve the problem, he said, it "took some time to work it out at the desk."[49]

It is, of course, possible that there was some sudden clarifying event that Krebs subsequently forgot so completely that even the stimulation of extended discussions about the details of the investigation could not bring it back to his mind 45 years later. It is also possible that when he remembered that the solution "developed gradually," the period in which he had a succession of ephemeral unproductive ideas had merged in his mind with the unfolding of the successful solution. If so, the time between the insight that ornithine may form arginine, and the full formulation of the above reaction (with the understanding that the familiar arginase reaction regenerates the ornithine) may have been comparatively short. I myself lean toward the view that it may well have been late in March, or even early in April, that he reached the critical stages in the mental progression outlined earlier and, as will be shown further on, if he did so this late, then he must have gone from the initial phase of this development to the fully worked out "provisional" solution within a period of 1 to 2 weeks. If we go so far in collapsing the "gradual development" into a compact period of time, can we not take one further step and infer from the compact nature of the solution — Krebs himself once referred to his mental process in our discussions of the solution as "pattern recognition"[50] — that the solution must have appeared to him in a single, or at most a few, clarifying insights? Perhaps so, but if it did, then such moments did not strike him with sufficient affective force to leave a permanent mark on his memory, in the manner of the dramatic "Eureka experiences" that are customarily invoked as the summits of creative activity.

The nature of the solution Krebs reached was one of a coherent pattern integrating several pieces into a whole. As soon as he had formulated it, Krebs found it compelling. "The evidence was so powerful, the coincidence of the occurrence of urea synthesis with arginine and the catalytic effect of ornithine, so that everything fitted in."[51] It was, in other words, just the *type* of solution that we might expect to become visible all-at-once. The apparent absence of a dramatic experience of sudden insight on Krebs's part is, therefore, relevant to the general question of the role of such experiences in creative activity. Howard Gruber, Vera John-Steiner, and others who have been concerned recently with the nature of creative thought emphasize that, although clarifying sudden insights are important, they are probably more frequent, individually less prominent, less abrupt, and constitute smaller "leaps" than in the popular image of the process. They are embedded in an ongoing matrix of dense thought that resembles growth more than it does a series of isolated acts.[52] It is important to recognize, however, that in this respect the thought patterns of creative individuals probably vary widely. Some people perceive solutions quickly and easily, whereas others have to work their way more slowly and painstakingly toward solutions of comparable complexity. Krebs has often described his mental activity in such a situation as "hovering over a subject," and in the context of the solution of the ornithine problem he commented "I don't know the details of the mental processes that make things gel, except that I do know it takes time."[53] (The metaphor of "gelling," which can be gradual, is a useful counterpoint to the more common metaphor of the instantaneous Gestalt switch.) Perhaps it took Krebs more time to reach his solution than it might have taken someone else in a comparable position. In a biographical memoir on Krebs, Sir Hans Kornberg and Derek Williamson, both of whom knew him well from long association with him in his laboratory, wrote "He usually required time to digest facts; often a colleague would make a specific point to him, only to find that it appeared not to have registered; however, the next day Hans would reopen the topic, having thought about the question overnight." Even if Krebs had to "hover" over the ornithine effect longer than someone else might have required, because he "was not a brilliant logician,"[54] when he did reach his solution it was no less brilliant than if he had grasped it in one great creative leap.

IV

Krebs habitually began writing up the paper in which he intended to report the outcome of a given investigation well before the investigation was completed. Because he did not save the drafts of his research papers, however, a rich potential record of the development of his scientific ideas has unfortunately vanished. If he followed his customary procedure in the case of his investigation of urea synthesis, we might expect him to have begun writing his first paper on "Investigations Concerning the Formation of Urea in the Animal Body" perhaps even before he had solved the ornithine problem. Krebs divided it into 10 sections, on the following topics:

1. "Method" (a description of the basic tissue slice method of Warburg)
2. "Units of Measurement for Urea Formation" (the calculation of values)
3. "Site of the Formation of Urea from Ammonia:" Krebs reported that it occurs only in the liver, and stated, in agreement with Löffler, that it takes place "in the living structure of the cell." If one destroys the cell structure, he reported, the process completely disappears.
4. "Formation of Urea from Arginine" (review of the nature and occurrence of the well-known arginase reaction)
5. "Influence of Non-Nitrogenous Compounds on the Formation of Urea from Ammonia:" Krebs reported comparisons of the rates at which urea formed in liver tissue from starved and nourished rats, and the influence of glucose, fructose, lactate, and pyruvate on the rate.
6. "Urea Formation from Nitrogenous Organic Compounds:" Krebs mentioned briefly that they had tested "many nitrogenous substances," including those previously proposed as intermediates, and found none of them formed urea at a faster rate than ammonia. Urea is formed from amino acids, he wrote, much more slowly than from ammonia, "as it must be if a direct formation of urea from amino acids does not occur, and ammonia is the intermediate in the conversion of amino–N to urea–N."

7 and 8. Dealt with the ornithine effect, and will be discussed below.

9. "Other Pathways of Urea Synthesis"
10. "Summary"[55]

It is possible that Krebs had some tactical reason for crafting his discussion so as to postpone the ornithine effect and its explanation to the last third of his paper, despite the fact that he regarded it as "the main result" of his work. The absence of any reference to ornithine in the title or earlier sections, and the independence of the topics treated there from knowledge of the action of ornithine suggest, however, that he could well have written much of the paper before he was in a position to write sections 7, 8, and 9.[56] While we were discussing this paper, in 1977, he remarked,

> At that time the papers were short. The writing up didn't take very much time. Especially as bits and pieces were written up all the time, it was a matter of putting together the final paper then. I spent a lot of time on writing, but usually while the work was still going on. And I find in general only when one tries to write it up, then do I find the gaps. I cannot complete a piece of work and then sit down and write the paper.[57]

Krebs did not specifically remember the stages in writing this particular paper; but its organization is consistent with the assumption that he constructed it in the same manner in which he portrayed here his general way of going about the process. We can only wonder if there might have been earlier versions of sections 7 and 8, the writing of which could have helped him to fill in some of the gaps necessary to solve the ornithine problem.

During the last week in March, Henseleit's experiments took on a character that suggests that Krebs had begun to sum up the urea investigation as a whole, and had decided that the most critical experimental shortcoming was the lack of a conclusive demonstration that ornithine acts in living cells "like a catalyst." Previously he had tried in three different ways to show that the action is catalytic in nature: to test whether the quantity of amino-nitrogen in the tissue slice medium remains constant; to determine if the ratio of ammonia consumed to urea formed is consistent with the view that the urea-nitrogen is derived entirely from the ammonia; and to see whether the magnitude of the ornithine effect is independent of the ornithine concentration. As related previously, each of these methods had provided suggestive, but not decisive results. Now Krebs focused his effort on a fourth approach, one that had probably begun to emerge during the set of experiments that Henseleit had carried out near the end of February on the effects of the concentration of ornithine. There the ornithine effect had still appeared not entirely independent of the concentration, for the effect diminished at the lowest concentrations. The *quantities* of ornithine employed at such concentrations, however, were so small that it became possible to argue that the ornithine would not have contained enough nitrogen to supply a significant portion of the nitrogen in the urea produced. The experiments that Henseleit performed during the 3 weeks beginning on March 21 are consistent with the view that Krebs had made it his highest priority to strengthen this argument.

To attain more definitive measurements of the formation of urea at low concentrations of ornithine, Henseleit repeated, with 10 mg/100 ml of ornithine most of the tests of the influences of other conditions that he had earlier tested at higher concentrations of ornithine. On March 22 he examined the influence of the ammonia concentration, on the 23rd the influence of changes in the pH. On the 24th he compared the rate in physiological salt solution with bicarbonate to that with phosphate. (He also included in this set of experiments one more test of the old suspected intermediate ammonium cyanate, and found once again that it produced no urea.) On the 26th he began the attempt to obtain the ornithine effect with a concentration of ornithine low enough — 1 mg/100 ml — to begin developing Krebs's catalytic argument. The result, however, was that there was "Little increase in the urea formation from NH_3 by means of 1 mg/100 ml ornithine."[58]

It was probably this disappointing outcome that led Henseleit to examine in his next experiment on March 29, "The effects of washing on the formation of urea." The fact that preformed ornithine in the tissue slices might affect the measurements had long been a source of concern to Krebs. When the concentration of added ornithine became very low that factor became increasingly critical. Perhaps Krebs would have attributed the failure of the 1 mg/100 ml ornithine in this experiment to increase the rate over that used by NH_4Cl alone to the presence of preformed ornithine in quantities sufficient to overshadow the small quantities added. For several weeks Krebs and Henseleit had already been washing tissue slices for 3 minutes three times in salt solution before placing them in the manometer vessels to obviate the problem both of preformed ornithine and preformed urea. Now, Henseleit investigated whether longer washings would affect the rates of urea formation from 10 and 1 mg/100 ml concentrations of ornithine (together with 60 mg/100 ml NH_4Cl, and 200 mg/100 ml lactate). Although the rates for the ornithine together with NH_4Cl did decrease with increased washing time, those for NH_4Cl alone, which presumably would act in conjunction with any preformed ornithine, remained nearly constant.[59] Krebs must have concluded that more washing was not necessary, for "3 X 3" remained the standard procedure. Continuing his systematic testing of other conditions on the effects of low ornithine concentrations, Henseleit found on April 1 that with 10 mg/100 ml of ornithine and 60 mg/100 ml NH_4Cl, 200 mg/100 ml lactate raised the rate of urea formation by 292 percent, and 100 mg/100 ml pyruvate raised it by 216 percent.[60]

Henseleit carried out only one experiment between April 1 and April 10, a test of the action of insulin on urea synthesis that proved negative. By then, if my interpretation that it was by this time that Krebs must have worked out his theoretical formulation is correct, the problem of completing the experimental demonstration of the catalytic action of ornithine would have become increasingly urgent. On April 11, Henseleit began to pursue that question intently. To make the argument that the ornithine could not supply a substantial portion of the urea nitrogen stand out most clearly, it was desirable to extend the duration of the experiment so as to increase as much as possible the total quantity of urea formed. If the ornithine were acting like a true catalyst, it ought to be able to go on producing urea indefinitely. Using 1 mg/100 ml ornithine, as in the experiment of March 26, Henseleit allowed the trial this time to go on for over 7 hours. There was, however, almost no ornithine effect (that is, the rates for ornithine + NH₄Cl were almost the same as for NH₄Cl alone). Henseleit ascribed the failure this time to the fact that the experiment had lasted so long that it exhausted the NH₃ available for the reaction. On the 13th he did the experiment once again, reducing the time to 4 hours to avoid that problem. This time he obtained just the result Krebs was looking for. The Q values were not outstanding (for NH₄Cl alone, 2.70 and 2.57; for 1 mg/100 ml ornithine + NH₄Cl, 4.40 and 5.21); but at the bottom of the page Henseleit calculated, "For each molecule of ornithine 24.5 additional molecules of urea are formed!"[61]

Henseleit did another experiment that day, testing the formation of urea from five more nitrogenous substances — hydroxyproline, succinamide, glycosamine, sarcosine, valine, and leucine. None of them yielded as much urea, with or without NH₄Cl, as NH₄Cl by itself did.[62] At this point Krebs would probably have been very surprised if any of them had. He was undoubtedly just gathering a little more information to bolster the assertion he was making in his paper, that they had tested "many" other nitrogenous organic compounds, with negative results.[63]

Henseleit went on with further experiments on small concentrations of ornithine, the effects of washing, and tests of other amino acids, but Krebs did not wait for them. Satisfied after the experiments of April 13 that he had his case, he must have finished his paper then or shortly after that date, and sent it off to the *Klinische Wochenschrift*, the standard place to submit preliminary research reports for rapid publication.

It is sections 7 and 8 of Krebs and Henseleit's first paper on the synthesis of urea that make that paper a "memorable" one in the history of biochemistry.[64] The 10 paragraphs making up these sections comprise one of the great classic, powerfully compressed announcements of major scientific discoveries. The writing is also a tribute to the lessons Krebs learned from Warburg about how to be succinct. If he wrote this paper in his customary manner, Krebs did not arrive at its final form with facile rapidity, but worked and reworked his sentences to achieve the extraordinary economy with which these sections summarize the conclusions he had reached. Because of its compactness, and because the article is, to my knowledge, not available in English, it is worth including here a complete translation of these two sections:

7. Effect of Ornithine on the Formation of Urea from Ammonia

We find with ornithine a special, unexpected effect on the formation of urea from ammonia. If to a test solution containing ammonia, lactate, and living tissue, one adds *d*-ornithine, the rate of the urea synthesis increases strongly through the addition of the ornithine. The increase in the rate of conversion reaches, under suitable conditions, 200–400%. We find, for example, (in the presence of 200 mg/100 ml d,l-lactate, 18 mg/100 ml ammonia).

Q_{urea} without ornithine   = 2.9
Q_{urea} with 10 mg/100 ml ornithine   = 11.2

The effect of ornithine is a specific one. We have investigated numerous substances, but have found none that can replace ornithine.

Closer investigation of the ornithine effect showed that the additional urea formed in the presence of ornithine does not derive from the ornithine. For the concentration of the ornithine, measured by the amino–nitrogen content of the solution, remains nearly constant during the formation of urea. Nearly the entire urea nitrogen comes from the ammonia added, whose concentration decreases in accord with the synthesis of urea.

Furthermore, it turned out that even traces of ornithine have large effects. Even 1/100 mg of ornithine per cubic centimeter of solution [or 1 mg/100 ml], increases the formation of urea by from two to three times. One molecule of the ornithine present in the test vessel thereby causes an additional formation of many times that number of urea molecules. For example, 3.89 mg of liver, suspended in one ccm [cm^2] of solution with 0.01 mg ornithine, forms 82.8 cmm [mm^3] of urea. In a control experiment the same quantity of liver without ornithine formed 41.1 cmm [mm^3] of urea. 0.01 mg of ornithine, equivalent to 1.7 cmm [mm^3], had therefore caused an additional formation of urea of 41.7 cmm [mm^3]. For each molecule of ornithine present in this experiment, 24.5 molecules of additional urea arise. If one chooses any desired duration of the experiment, one will obtain, for 1 molecule of ornithine, correspondingly additional urea.

According to these investigations, in the synthesis of urea in the living cell ornithine acts like a catalyst.

8. Ornithine Circuit [*Kreislauf des Ornithins*]

If one wishes to understand the effect of ornithine, one must accept that it takes part in the synthesis of urea as an intermediary product, that the synthesis does not proceed through the simple balance equation,

$$2\,NH_3 + CO_2 = C{=}\!O \Big\langle\begin{smallmatrix}NH_2\\[2pt]NH_2\end{smallmatrix} + H_2O \qquad\text{(a)}$$

2 Ammoniak + Kohlen-säure = Harnstoff + Wasser

but in several partial reactions, with the primary formation of an intermediary product, that must originate from ornithine, ammonia, and carbon dioxide. One must require of the intermediary substance to be sought that, in the living cell, it splits off urea and regenerates ornithine, at at least the same rate that the overall reaction a) takes place. For, as we find, in the balance ornithine is not consumed.

A substance has long been known that possesses the properties required for the intermediate substance: it is arginine. Arginine can be thought of as arising from ornithine, ammonia, and carbon dioxide, with the elimination of water. As required, arginine is cleaved into ornithine and urea with great rapidity in the liver.

We therefore draw the conclusion that arginine is the desired intermediate product of urea synthesis in the liver, and the primary reaction for the synthesis of urea from ammonia is then:

$$
\begin{array}{c}
CH_2NH_2 \\
| \\
CH_2 \\
| \\
CH_2 \quad + \ 2\ NH_3 \ + \ CO_2 \ = \\
| \\
CHNH_2 \\
| \\
COOH
\end{array}
\qquad
\begin{array}{c}
\quad\quad\quad HN\!=\!C\!\!\begin{array}{l}\nearrow NH_2 \\ \searrow \end{array} \\
CH_2NH \\
| \\
CH_2 \\
| \\
CH_2 \quad + \ 2\ H_2O \\
| \\
CHNH_2 \\
| \\
COOH
\end{array}
\qquad (1)
$$

Ornithin + 2 Ammoniak + Kohlensäure = Arginin + 2 Wasser

The second reaction of urea synthesis is the cleavage of arginine, known since Kossel and Dakin, under the action of arginase:

$$
\begin{array}{c}
HN\!=\!C\!\!\begin{array}{l}\nearrow NH_2 \\ \searrow\end{array} \\
CH_2NH \\
| \\
CH_2 \\
| \\
CH_2 \quad + \ H_2O \ = \\
| \\
CHNH_2 \\
| \\
COOH
\end{array}
\qquad
\begin{array}{c}
CH_2NH_2 \\
| \\
CH_2 \\
| \\
CH_2 \\
| \\
CHNH_2 \\
| \\
COOH
\end{array}
\ + \
\begin{array}{c}
\nearrow NH_2 \\ C\!=\!O \\ \searrow NH_2
\end{array}
\qquad (2)
$$

Arginin + Wasser = Ornithin + Harnstoff

In this way the abundance of arginase in the liver acquires its physiological meaning. The arginase action is a partial reaction in the synthesis of urea from ammonia. That is why one finds arginase in significant quantities only in those places where urea forms from ammonia and carbon dioxide: in the livers of mammals. It is clear why, in other organs, and in the livers of birds, which produce no urea, no arginase is found, or only 100 to 1000 times less than in mammalian livers.[65]

The preceding passage is a classic of scientific writing not only for the succinctness and clarity with which it forges its message, but for the manner in which it transforms an open-ended, ongoing research trail into a tightly circumscribed argument for a conclusion reached during the course of that investigative activity. Within it there are small traces of narrative form that allude to features of the investigative path Krebs and Henseleit had actually followed. The description of the ornithine effect as "unexpected" reflects the fact that Krebs himself had not been expecting to find it until he encountered it on November 15, 1931. The phrase "closer investigation showed" hints at a sequence of events that actually had led Krebs from the idea that ornithine may be a donor of urea nitrogen to the idea that it acts like a catalyst. The passage "we have investigated many substances" sums up a series of experiments that they had carried out at intervals during the course of the past 9 months until the substances tried had added up to "many." The phrase "It turned out that even traces of ornithine have large effects" makes reference to a denouement that Krebs had just reached when he wrote the passage. Yet the passage as a whole is not, and was never intended to be, a *description* of the investigation through which Krebs reached the conclusions he was presenting. As with almost all modern scientific papers, he was presenting not his investigation, but his *findings*. When we consider the total number of the experiments that he and Henseleit had carried out to arrive at that point, it is remarkable how little of it is directly incorporated into the presentation. Krebs excluded not only all of the experiments that had led nowhere, but most of those that had contributed to the successful solution. He reduced the great quantities of data he had accumulated to the bare minimum of information necessary to support his theory. The skill with which he did this was as important to the creation of his discovery as was the gathering of the information from which he made his selection. His conviction that what he presented was correct, however, rested not merely on the public case he made; it flowed from the totality of the investigative experience through which we have followed him.

The reduction of experimental evidence that Krebs attained in these sections was so extreme that he seemed very nearly to rest his case on a single experiment. After a cursory description of a single example of the basic ornithine effect, taken from the dozens of such experiments in the notebook record that he might have chosen, and dataless references to the experiments that had excluded other substances, as well as those that had provided weaker evidence for the catalytic nature of the action, Krebs described, in moderate detail, only the results of the experiment of April 13 that had finally provided the keystone he needed to hold his theory in place. It was almost as though all of the long investigation until then had merely served as preparation for carrying out that experiment. The rest of the case came from the compelling logic with which the "postulates" of catalytic action, the known nature of the arginase reaction, and the structural relations between ornithine and arginine that could be drawn on paper fitted together. As Krebs was now able to formulate the argument, it flowed so tightly and coherently, was so forceful in its simplicity, as to leave little trace of the lengthy struggle that had been required to put it together.

V

Although Krebs's compressed description of the *Kreislauf des Ornithins* might seem to imply that there were only two reactions involved, it was, as already mentioned, according to his account of 1973, "obvious at once that the synthesis of ornithine must involve more than one step." Krebs wrote next,

So I began to search for possible intermediates between ornithine and arginine. Paper chemistry suggested that citrulline COOH-CH(NH$_2$)CH$_2$-CH$_2$-CH(NH)-CO-NH$_2$ might play a role as an intermediate. This substance had just been identified independently by two biochemists in entirely different contexts. Wada isolated it from watermelons (*Citrulus*) and Ackermann isolated it as a product of the bacterial degradation of arginine.[66]

In discussing the situation in 1978 with me, Krebs put the matter in a more informal and personal form:

I never had any doubts that there were several intermediates.... This is no reconstruction retrospectively, but evidenced by the fact that I looked for them;...that I went immediately and I never stopped...I was looking for an intermediate with these criteria — that it must be formed, and it must readily give the same end product. I *immediately* looked for other intermediates, and then came to the citrulline.[67]

There are no details available about how Krebs set about on this search, whether he was able to think of any other possibilities at all, before he "came to" citrulline, or whether a significant interval of time passed between the time he began looking and the time he found citrulline. Paper chemistry could not suggest that citrulline played a role until one knew about the substance, and its composition had been established so recently that Krebs could not have looked it up in a textbook or handbook. Although he said to me at one point that he did not remember how he "ran across" citrulline, during another discussion he reconstructed that it must have been through his regular scanning of the current journal literature. The articles by Mitsunori Wada and Dankwart Ackermann had appeared in just those two journals — the *Biochemische Zeitschrift* and the *Zeitschrift für physiologische Chemie* respectively — that Krebs followed most closely. Moreover, Ackermann's article, entitled "Concerning the Biological Decomposition of Arginine to Citrulline," would certainly have caught his eye when it appeared near the end of 1931, because he had himself already by then included the decomposition of arginine in his own investigation. As he also pointed out in 1978, "a new amino acid in living matter was always a major event." Assuming that he had run across Ackermann's article, its description of the properties of citrulline, and perhaps in particular Ackermann's depiction of the reaction through which arginine gives rise to citrulline —

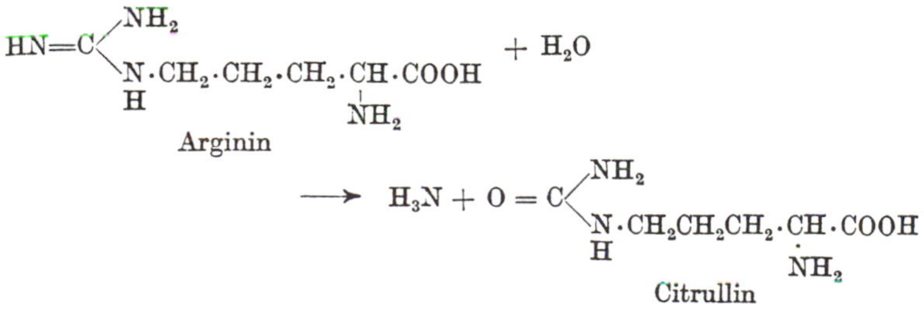

—would very likely have stuck in his retentive mind a few months later, sufficiently at least to cause him to look it up again after he had embarked on his search for intermediates.[68]

Once Krebs had thought of citrulline as a possibility, there is no mystery about why he should quickly have perceived it as the most plausible possibility imaginable. Part of the paper chemistry required only to view Ackermann's reaction running from right to left; and Wada had synthesized citrulline from ornithine. To fit citrulline into his existing scheme required only a simple extension of the same reasoning Krebs had applied to reach his initial solution. He could produce citrulline from ornithine on paper by adding *one* molecule of NH_3, one of CO_2, and eliminating one molecule of water:[69]

$$
\begin{array}{c}
\\
\\
CH_2NH_2 \\
| \\
CH_2 \\
| \\
CH_2 \\
| \\
CHNH_2 \\
| \\
COOH
\end{array}
\quad + NH_3 + CO_2 =
\begin{array}{c}
O=C{<}^{NH_2} \\
\quad\;\;{}^{CH_2NH} \\
| \\
CH_2 \\
| \\
CH_2 \\
| \\
CHNH_2 \\
| \\
COOH
\end{array}
\quad + H_2O \qquad (\mathrm{1a})
$$

Ornithin $+$ Ammoniak $+$ Kohlensäure $=$ Citrullin $+$ Wasser

Then he had only to add the second molecule of NH_3 from his initial scheme, and eliminate the second molecule of water, to convert citrulline to arginine (which amounts to the same thing as to reverse Ackermann's reaction):

$$
\begin{array}{c}
O=C{<}^{NH_2} \\
\quad\;\;{}^{CH_2NH} \\
| \\
CH_2 \\
| \\
CH_2 \\
| \\
CHNH_2 \\
| \\
COOH
\end{array}
\quad + NH_3 =
\begin{array}{c}
HN=C{<}^{NH_2} \\
\quad\;\;{}^{CH_2NH} \\
| \\
CH_2 \\
| \\
CH_2 \\
| \\
CHNH_2 \\
| \\
COOH
\end{array}
\quad + H_2O \qquad (\mathrm{1b})
$$

Citrullin $+$ Ammoniak $=$ Arginin $+$ Wasser

From the new scheme it is also "immediately obvious" why he knew that there had to be still at least one further unknown intermediate. The same argument, that four molecules cannot join together in a single step, applied to the three molecules that he incorporated into the ornithine–citrulline reaction.

Another question that cannot be fully resolved is, just *when* did Krebs first consider citrulline as a possible intermediate? There is, in his laboratory notebook, a very suggestive entry, dated April 21, 1932, with a reference to the article of Ackermann, under which Krebs copied the formula for citrulline:[70]

Below that are references to Wada's article, and to an earlier one by Koga and Odaka, containing the first, brief description of citrulline. (Krebs did not read this article, but obtained the citation from that of Wada.) It is tempting to think that it might have been on that day that Krebs perceived the connections earlier described. If he had already worked out the problem, and was merely making literature references to cite them later in his article, he would already have been familiar enough with the formula for citrulline; therefore, there would be little need to write it out at this time. (On the other hand, it should be noted that the configuration is that which appeared later in his own article, not that in which Ackermann depicted it.) If so, however, it is necessary to explain away the fact that just 4 days later, on April 25, Krebs tested citrulline for the first time, using a sample supplied to him by Ackermann. Ackermann was at Wurzburg, and it is barely possible that if Krebs wrote or telegraphed him on the 21st, the citrulline could have reached Freiburg by return mail by the 25th. An advantage of this interpretation would be that it would agree with the fact that Krebs made no mention of possible further intermediates in his first paper on urea synthesis. If, as I have assumed, he completed that paper shortly after April 13, he might have sent it off before he had been able to think of any plausible possibilities.

A further difficulty with this interpretation is that in a conversations in 1978 Krebs suggested that he may have "thought of the idea of citrulline" as long as several weeks before he "got the material to test it."[71] If that were so, then he must have already been planning to test citrulline at the time he wrote the first paper, but decided not to mention a question that had yet to be decided experimentally. Unless some other documentary evidence, such as the letters Krebs wrote to Wada or Ackermann, can be brought to light, the exact order of Krebs's reasoning about this question, and its temporal connections with the experimental investigation, must remain in doubt.

Once Krebs had formulated the citrulline hypothesis on paper, the critical experiment was obvious.   According to the basic axiom of intermediary metabolism, to be established as an intermediate, citrulline must not only yield urea in liver tissues as ornithine did, but yield it at least as rapidly as ornithine did. Krebs must have been somewhat impatient to receive enough citrulline to put it to the test.

A minor additional argument in favor of the view that Krebs may only have reached his citrulline hypothesis on April 21, is that on that same day he resumed the deamination investigation he had suspended since April 8. It is possible that, having concentrated solely on the solution of the urea synthesis question during that interval, he had now taken the problem as far as he could go until the citrulline arrived. In any case, it must have been with more than routine feelings that he prepared, on April 25, parallel measurements of the quantities of urea formed by ornithine, arginine, and citrulline, in the presence of NH_4Cl and lactate. He himself carried out the experiment. The concentrations of the three compounds were equimolar, each equivalent to 10 mg/100 ml of ornithine. The results did not immediately fulfill his hopes:

				Q_{urea}
		NH_4Cl + lactate	=	2.69
Ornithine	+	NH_4Cl + lactate	=	9.30
Arginine	+	NH_4Cl + lactate	=	12.6
Citrulline	+	NH_4Cl + lactate	=	6.44

Krebs's remarks about the result, fuller than usual, suggest both puzzlement and a commitment to the theory that did not allow him to accept this outcome with objective detachment:

Result: Citrulline accelerates, but less than ornithine, perhaps because it penetrates too slowly? No certain explanation!! It must yield urea more rapidly than ornithine (more slowly than arginine).[72]

In suspecting that the slowness of penetration of citrulline into the cells might explain the result, Krebs was constructing an auxiliary hypothesis to save his principal hypothesis. Under the circumstances that was the only reasonable response he could have made. Citrulline was the first substance he had found since ornithine to exert an effect of the same type and order of magnitude. It would have been irrational to abandon so beautiful a theory simply because, on the first try, it did not meet the stringent criterion for an intermediate.

If slow penetration was the obstacle, then one might try to overcome it by increasing the concentration of the citrulline, or by lengthening the time of the experiment. The next day Krebs combined both tactics, doubling the quantities of citrulline and ornithine (arginine was omitted this time, as the crucial question was the relation between the rates of these two), and running the experiment for 90 minutes instead of 60. The results:

			Q_{urea}
		NH_4Cl	3.71
ornithine	+	NH_4Cl	11.65
citrulline	+	NH_4Cl	8.90[73]

were an improvement, the two values being closer than before, but still not quite good enough. Probably confident now that it was merely a matter of refining the conditions, Krebs left the further testing of citrulline to Henseleit and returned to deamination.

On April 30, 1932, Krebs and Henseleit's first paper on the synthesis of urea appeared in the *Klinische Wochenschrift* — just 13 days after they had performed the experiment that formed the heart of its argument. On that same day Krebs received a telegram from his good friend in Berlin:

Congratulations on your very beautiful work.
Warm regards, Bruno Mendel.[74]

* * *

In contrast to the three long chapters over which Hans Krebs's investigation of the synthesis of urea has spread in this book, Krebs himself managed to describe, in 1973, his discovery of the ornithine cycle of urea synthesis in a space not much longer than the article in which he had originally reported his results. Like his presentation of the work itself in 1932, his later account of its history is stripped to what he regarded as the essential points: "The choice of the problem," "The adaptation of the urease method," "The design of a new saline medium," "The plan of the work," "The first crucial finding," "The analysis of the ornithine effect," and "The search for intermediates." No time is wasted on ideas or experiments that did not lead anywhere. The differences between his account and my account are not limited, however, to the degree of detail included. Krebs followed a logical order. The urease method and the saline solution being, in his view, essential prerequisites to the whole investigation, he described those first. He then mentioned having carried out a series of preliminary tests that showed that the tissue slices synthesize urea at physiological rates. "After this hopeful start," he wrote, "I decided to measure systematically the rate of urea synthesis in the presence of a variety of precursors hoping that the results may throw light on the chemical mechanism of urea synthesis."[75]

From the chronology preserved in the laboratory notebooks we can see that in relating this history Krebs did not follow strictly the order in which he and Henseleit had actually performed the experiments. He began testing amino acids as precursors at the very beginning of the investigation, and had to return at recurrent intervals to "preliminary" experiments intended to improve the basic procedures. He designed the saline medium not as a prelude to undertaking the investigation, but midway in its course. There are other discrepancies as well, some of which have already been discussed in the preceding chapters.

These discrepancies do not, I believe, result either from carelessness or lapses of memory on Krebs's part, but from systematic differences between the scientist and the historian concerning the objectives of a historical reconstruction of a scientific investigation. Krebs thought that he should explain the steps that were essential to making the discovery. He selected those steps and described them as skillfully as he had selected out the essential arguments in 1932 to present his discovery for the first time. His historical account was structured less by the sequence of activities and experiences preceding his solution of the problem than by the nature of the solution he eventually reached. He spent nearly as much time in his short article explaining the ornithine cycle and its later significance as he did on the steps of the research that had led to it. Some of the phrases in his historical account echo closely the language of the original scientific paper, as when he described the experiments at low ornithine concentrations that "established the fact that ornithine acts like a catalyst."

This is not to say that Krebs's history of the discovery was merely an updated version of the publications in which he had presented it. From his own perspective there was a major difference. As discussed earlier, the *Klinische Wochenschrift* article is essentially a compact argument for the conclusions he had reached, with only incidental traces of the events through which he had arrived at them. The historical paper is in narrative form. Krebs described, in first person, what he and Henseleit had done (although there are frequent lapses into the passive voice of the scientific style to which he had long been habituated). The narrative is based, however, on Krebs's reconstruction of what had been essential, rather than on the precise order of the events that had occurred between July 1931 and April 1932. He did not go back to his laboratory notebooks to remind himself of the way in which things had happened. He told the story as he remembered it; but by then the later significance of his discovery had affected the way in which he remembered it. In effect, he came to remember the story in the way he told it.

In my first effort to reconstruct the history of the discovery, in 1978, I commented on the discrepancy between Krebs's placement of the design of the saline solution at the beginning of the investigation and the actual time at which he had devised it. When he read my discussion, he wrote the problem off by calling the experiments preceding the new saline solution "preliminary."[76] Yet these "preliminary" experiments included the "first crucial finding," the discovery of the ornithine effect! To him it was not an important point. The reason that it was not, I believe, is because to a scientist the order in which experiments are done ceases to be significant after an investigation has been completed. Scientists are accustomed to rearrange the order in which they have performed their experiments, to provide the strongest arguments available for the conclusions they wish to present. When one of them is asked at some time long afterward, to recount "how he had made" a discovery for which he is known, he is not in the habit of regarding the historical sequence of his investigation as important. To the historian, on the other hand, that sequence may hold the key to the patterns of the scientist's creative activity. It is not a matter of one being wrong and the other right, but of priorities that differ in accordance with their respective purposes.

11

The Rewards of Success

The solution to the ornithine problem was the most important, but not the only scientific success that Hans Krebs enjoyed during April 1932. Within a few days of reaching that solution he also overcame the most prominent experimental obstacle he had been facing in his investigation of deamination.

When Krebs resumed his research on deamination, on April 21, he carried out one set of experiments using HCN, as usual. On April 23, however, he again began searching for other agents that might block more fully the disappearance of the pyruvate formed in the tissue slices from alanine. The first agent he tried, sodium hydrosulfide, was ineffective, because it was autoxidizable, and only small quantities of pyruvate formed. Two days later, however, he made a more auspicious choice.[1]

In 1911, Otto Warburg had found that arsenite (As_2O_3), in low concentrations, inhibits the respiration of cells. During the summer of 1926 he had Kurt Dresel look into the phenomenon further, in his laboratory. Dresel found that 10^{-3} M As_2O_3 strongly inhibited the respiration of various rat tissue slices, but acted only weakly on the glycolysis of these tissues. Dresel concluded that As_2O_3 can be used to separate respiration from fermentation in animal cells.[2] In 1930, Albert Szent-Györgyi pursued more deeply the question of how arsenite acts on cellular respiration. Working with suspensions of coarsely ground heart muscle and other tissues, Szent-Györgyi and his co-worker Ilona Banga found that with increasing concentrations of arsenite the inhibition increased rapidly up to a certain maximum, beyond which further increases caused no greater inhibition. Szent-Györgyi inferred that the arsenite "does not inhibit the entire respiration up to a certain point, but that it separates the total respiration *in a sharp manner into two parts, into an arsenite sensitive and an arsenite insensitive portion.*"[3] He then sought to identify what the arsenite sensitive oxidative processes might be. In early 1932 he reported that dehydrogenation reactions, especially that of lactate, appeared to be among the oxidative processes poisoned by arsenite.[4] This article, submitted to *Biochemische Zeitschrift* in February 1932, must have reached the library in Freiburg at just about the time Krebs returned to his deamination research in late April.

Coming across it could, therefore, have been the immediate stimulus that prompted him to employ arsenite at this point to his own problem. At the head of his first experiment with the substance, he in fact wrote down references to the articles of Szent-Györgyi and Banga, as well as to the basic article of Dresel. Since Dresel had carried out that earlier work shortly after Krebs came to Warburg's laboratory, Krebs must have known all along about the general effect of arsenite on cellular respiration. The timing suggests, however, that it may have taken Szent-Györgyi's most recent article to remind him of it as an agent potentially suitable to his purposes. Moreover, Szent-Györgyi's interpretation that arsenite divides respiration into portions sensitive to and insensitive to that poison fit very well with the conception Krebs had already formed that the oxidative deamination of alanine is insensitive to HCN, whereas HCN inhibits other oxidative processes.

On April 25 — the same day that he tested citrulline for the first time — Krebs carried out the first deamination experiments with arsenite, using otherwise his standard system of kidney tissue slices with alanine. He employed the arsenite in concentrations of 5×10^{-3} M, 5×10^{-4} M, and 5×10^{-6} M. The results were striking. With the middle of these concentrations, NH_3 formed at a rate of Q = 25.2, and pyruvate at a rate of Q = 22.6. Krebs wrote down, "With arsenite alanine gives much pyruvate and much NH_3 (best at around M/1000. $Q_{pyruvate}$ up to 22.6!!)." It must have been immediately apparent to him that he had found the agent he needed to meet his experimental objectives.[5]

Building on this encouraging outcome, Krebs extended the investigation in two major directions on April 27. The similar rates of formation for ammonia and pyruvate were suggestive evidence that all of the alanine deaminated is converted to pyruvate. To complete the demonstration it would be desirable to show that the quantity of alanine consumed corresponded also to the stoichiometric relationships of the oxidative deamination reaction. Accordingly Krebs now determined the amino–nitrogen before and after the experiment, using the Van Slyke method. The other extension of the investigation was to examine the effects of a different amino acid, leucine, in the system. In each run he utilized 10^{-3} M arsenite, the concentration he had estimated to be optimal from the preceding experiment. Leucine appeared to be inactive; it produced "little NH_3." The alanine result was, however, again highly encouraging. Q for NH_3 was 16.4; for pyruvate 28.0; and for the disappearance of amino–nitrogen, 27.1. The result, Krebs noted, was "with arsenite, 100% yield of pyruvate, calculated from the disappearance of alanine (probably more alanine disappeared, since amino-N was supplied). 57% yield of NH_3."[6] The low yield of NH_3 prevented Krebs from obtaining the full set of stoichiometric relations predicted from the oxidative deamination equation, but the correspondence between the alanine that disappeared and the pyruvate that appeared must have led him to think that he was well on his way toward attaining the quantitative demonstration he needed to show that that reaction formed the primary pathway of deamination.

Because he was studying a reaction presumed to comprise the first step in the degradation of amino acids in general in the organism, Krebs could not be content with a demonstration limited exclusively to alanine. On the same day,

therefore, he carried out a large-scale test on leucine, attempting to identify the
α-keto acid that should result from its deamination, by forming its dinitrophenylhydrazone. Employing 5×10^{-2} M arsenite, 300 mg of leucine, and 100 mg of
kidney tissue, he carried on the reaction for 10 hours. Nevertheless, he obtained
too little of the dinitrophenylhydrazone to analyze.[7]

In this experiment Krebs used the "natural" optical isomer, *l*-leucine,
obtained from Hoffmann-LaRoche. (The prefixes *l*- and *d*- as Krebs employed
them here indicated that the isomer in question rotated polarized light,
respectively, in a counterclockwise or a clockwise direction, under specified
experimental conditions. Only one of the two optical isomers of any amino acid
was found in proteins, and was, therefore, regarded at this time as the natural
isomer. Its opposite was often called then the nonnatural or unnatural isomer.
For some amino acids the *l*-isomer was the natural one, for others it was the
d-isomer.) In the preceding experiment he had not specified the isomer, and had
probably used a racemic mixture. Normally he had used such mixtures because
they were less expensive, and assumed that the unnatural isomer was inactive,
therefore, that he was in fact testing only the natural one. It is doubtful that he
had any special reason to switch to the isolated natural isomer, other than
possibly a routine check of that assumption.[8] Hoffmann-LaRoche in fact
supplied only *l*-leucine, and it was relatively inexpensive (1.25 Swiss francs per
g, compared to 0.6 Fr/g of racemic alanine, and 4.0 Fr/g of the natural isomer
d-alanine).[9] The fact that the natural isomer of leucine yielded so little of the
dinitrophenylhydrazone might not have struck him as peculiar, because in the
preceding experiment ordinary leucine had also yielded little NH_3. He might
well have interpreted both results as indicating merely that he had not found
conditions under which leucine acted effectively within his system. On the other
hand, the fact that from this point onward he began to record regularly which
optical isomers he employed, suggests that he had been alerted to the possibility
that there might be some unexpected effects involved.

Returning to racemic (*dl*) alanine, Krebs repeated, on April 29, the usual
tests for the deamination in the presence of arsenite with several tissues. As
before, only kidney slices produced large quantities of pyruvate. Again he
attained a 100 percent yield of pyruvate with respect to the alanine consumed,
and this time about 90 percent of the expected NH_3 as well. He seemed to be
approaching very nicely the desired quantitative demonstration of this prototyp-
ical oxidative deamination reaction. A large-scale test of *dl*-alanine also
produced expected quantities of the dinitrophenylhydrazone of pyruvic acid. On
May 3 he tested the natural isomer, *d*-alanine, on diaphragm muscle and brain
medulla slices. Neither tissue produced much pyruvate or NH_3. Becoming
interested by this time in the physiological significance of the large rate of the
deamination in kidney tissue, he wrote down references to several articles about
the acidification in the body that occurs during diseases of the kidneys. By this
time he must have begun to think of the deamination process he had discovered
in the kidneys as the source of the NH_3 that was known to help regulate the
acidity and alkalinity of the organism.[10]

In the meantime, nothing had taken place in the laboratory concerning urea synthesis since Krebs's first tests of citrulline on April 25 and 26. Henseleit had not carried out any experiments since April 21. Finally, on May 5, Henseleit performed another experiment comparing the rates at which urea formed in liver slices with citrulline, NH_4Cl, and lactate, to that formed with ornithine, NH_4Cl, and lactate. In accordance with Krebs's view that the slow penetration of citrulline into the cells may have prevented it from yielding as much urea as ornithine did in the first two experiments, Henseleit increased the concentrations again, employing now 200 mg/100 ml of citrulline and ornithine. This time he got just what Krebs needed. For ornithine the average Q for two runs was 9.82; for citrulline, 12.78. It was undoubtedly with considerable satisfaction that Henseleit entered in his notebook,

Citrulline...increases the formation of urea even more strongly than ornithine. That means that citrulline is the intermediary product between ornithine and arginine, and the rate is determined by the formation of citrulline.

Henseleit surmised that the increase might have been still larger, except for the fact that there was too little bicarbonate present.[11] After this single but critical experiment, Henseleit was again absent from the laboratory for a week, while Krebs continued his deamination experiments.

Krebs was now focusing his attention on the effects of the optical isomers of the amino acids on the deamination reaction. On May 6 he tested the natural d-alanine, again with several tissues, including this time kidney slices. In contrast to the result when he had used racemic alanine, the rate at which the kidneys produced NH_3 and pyruvate did not stand out distinctly above the rates for the other tissues.[12] By now he must have suspected that, far from being inactive, the nonnatural amino acids must contribute to the deamination in the kidneys, strange as it might seem that substances not normally present in the organism could play such a role. At this point he went back to an important paper that Gustav Embden had published in 1910, demonstrating just this point for a related process. Studying the conversion of leucine to acetoacetic acid in perfused livers, Embden had found that the liver formed very little acetate when perfused with leucine obtained from the protein casein, but the liver produced large quantities of acetoacetate when he used synthetic leucine. Since synthetic leucine was composed of a racemic mixture of the two optical isomers, whereas that derived from casein consisted only of the natural isomer, Embden had inferred that it was the "non-natural" d-leucine that had given rise to the acetoacetate. He conjectured that the natural isomer had not done so because it was consumed in synthetic processes for which the nonnatural isomer could not be utilized.[13] Either Krebs must have looked at Embden's article because he thought something analogous might be happening in his own deamination experiments, or he must have come to think so as a consequence of reading the article.

As his interest in the optical isomers of amino acids grew, Krebs needed to obtain pure isomers that were not readily available from commercial suppliers. Accordingly, he wrote to Felix Ehrlich in Breslau to ask for samples of isomers that Ehrlich had prepared several years before in his laboratory. Unfortunately, Ehrlich wrote back, on May 11, his supply was already severely depleted by frequent similar requests. He could send only the two "non-natural" isomers *l*-alanine and *d*-leucine.[14]

On May 12, Krebs moved to a direct test of the question of the effects of optical isomers, a "Comparison of *dl*– and of *d*-alanine" on deamination in kidney tissue. As usual he utilized arsenite to block the disappearance of pyruvate. The result was dramatic:

	$Q_{pyruvate}$	Q_{NH_3}
dl-alanine + arsenite	8.10	8.45
d-alanine + arsenite	1.42	1.30

The racemic amino acid had undergone the deamination reaction about seven times as rapidly as the natural isomer, a distinction that Krebs later described with understatement, as "unexpected."[15]

By the next day Krebs had received the nonnatural isomers of alanine and leucine from Ehrlich, and he quickly tested the latter against the natural *l*-leucine that Hoffmann-La Roche supplied. Measuring only the quantity of NH_3 formed and the decrease in amino–nitrogen, he obtained results that were the opposite of what he might have expected from the preceding experiment.

	Q_{NH_3}	$Q_{amino-nitrogen}$
d-leucine (nonnatural) + arsenite	1.93	3.2
l-leucine (natural) + arsenite	7.00	9.8[16]

At this point the situation could only have appeared confusing. (In light of later results we might almost suspect that Krebs had mixed up the two isomers in this experiment.)

On the same day, Henseleit returned once more to carry out another comparative test of the influence of citrulline and ornithine on the formation of urea from ammonia. In addition to measuring the urea formed, he now measured the ammonia that disappeared. The main result was again very satisfactory to Krebs's theory. Henseleit calculated that:

Increase through ornithine = 199%
        through citrulline = 245%.

The ratios between the NH_3 that disappeared and the urea that formed were, however, not strictly in accord with the theory. According to the equations for the reactions, with ornithine two molecules of NH_3 should be consumed for every molecule of urea formed (see Chapter 10, p. 332).   The measured proportion (144 NH_3/79.4 urea) was only 1.81:1, an outcome Henseleit explained away as due to the length of the experiment, there being insufficient preformed NH_3 to supply the quantity required. With citrulline one molecule of NH_3 should be used up for every molecule of urea formed (see Chapter 10, p. 335).   Here the proportion (134.4 NH_3/97.4 urea) was greater than the theoretical ratio, a discrepancy Henseleit attributed to the conversion of some of the citrulline to ornithine in the tissue medium.[17]

This experiment was the last that Henseleit carried out in Krebs's laboratory. Probably he discontinued his work on urea synthesis at this time because he had completed his medical education,[18] rather than because the investigation appeared complete in every detail. Nevertheless, Krebs was now satisfied that there was ample evidence to support his extended theory, and he carried out no further experiments on his own on the subject. Instead, sometime during the next few weeks he wrote up a second short article for the *Klinische Wochenschrift* to report the new findings concerning citrulline.

After summarizing succinctly the results presented in the first paper on urea synthesis, and showing that the formula of citrulline suggests immediately that it may be an intermediate step in the conversion of ornithine to arginine, Krebs invoked the basic axiom of intermediary metabolism as the crucial test of whether citrulline actually is an intermediate in the synthesis of urea in the animal body:

> If citrulline were to be regarded as an intermediate product in reaction (1)
> [See Chapter 6, p.], one would have to demand that in the presence of
> citrulline and ammonia in the liver, urea arises at least as rapidly as in the
> presence of ornithine, ammonia, and carbon dioxide. Experiment shows
> that this is the case.[19]

In support of the last assertion, Krebs summarized the data from the experiment that Henseleit had carried out on May 5, the first one in which this criterion had been met.

Concerning the proportions between the ammonia that disappeared and the urea that formed, Krebs stated the results only in very general terms that suggested they fit closely the theoretical predictions:

> If one measures the ammonia that disappears relative to the urea formed,
> one finds in the presence of ornithine...that about 2 molecules of ammonia
> disappear from the solution when 1 molecule of urea forms.   In the
> presence of citrulline, on the other hand, we find that only about 1
> molecule of ammonia disappears from the solution when 1 molecule of
> urea forms. In the presence of citrulline, therefore, half of the urea-N

originates — as is to be expected — from the ammonia of the solution, the other half from the citrulline.[20]

Perhaps it would have been more candid if Krebs had acknowledged that in the single measurement of this type carried out for citrulline, the ratio had been greater than 1:1, that it had been necessary to make an auxiliary assumption to save the approximation. Perhaps it would have been better if he had repeated the experiment until he had attained a closer agreement. That he did neither may probably be attributed to some combination of the facts that Henseleit was leaving, that he was himself very busy with clinical duties, that he might have used up the 20 mg of citrulline that Ackermann had sent him, and that he was extremely confident that his conclusions would not be overturned by further experimental evidence. There was, in fact, a self-confidence verging on brashness in the unqualified summary of his results with which Krebs concluded his paper:

A further step in the chemical mechanism of urea synthesis has been explained. The first step in urea synthesis is the joining of ornithine, ammonia, and carbon dioxide to form citrulline. The second step is the joining of citrulline and another molecule of ammonia to form arginine. The third step is the cleaving of arginine into ornithine and urea.[21]

The young investigator who had come to Freiburg 1 year earlier still unsure of his ability to make original contributions to science was now able to announce the solution of a major problem that had withstood the efforts of his predecessors for more than half a century.

* * *

Early in my conversations with Hans Krebs, in September 1976, I commented (with reference to his first, rather than his second paper on the synthesis of urea), that I was struck by "the self-confidence and authority" with which he discussed the subject. He replied,

Well this treatment I had learned from Warburg — not to hedge, and Warburg was very much of the opinion which was once expressed I think by Bacon first, that even if a statement is wrong, as long as it is clearly stated, it will add to the body of knowledge — rather than to be indulgent in over-careful statements; not to come down on either side of the fence and be diffuse.... The important thing is to be quite clear about what one thinks even if it turns out to be wrong, rather than to be woolly.[22]

Even though he was rapidly establishing his independence as an investigator, Krebs carried the imprint of Warburg in everything he did, from his laboratory methods to his style of scientific discourse. Warburg's impact on Krebs was, however, complex and sometimes self-contradictory. Here we see it bolstering

Krebs's self-assurance. Earlier we have seen how Warburg's apparent doubts about Krebs's scientific potential had been humbling to him.[23] Krebs had in himself tendencies toward both humility and overconfidence. Warburg probably stimulated both of these traits. Now that he had, for the first time in his scientific career, grounds for true self-confidence, Krebs faced the test of whether or not he would keep his confidence and his humility in balance.

I

On May 10, Krebs presented his recent experimental discoveries at a meeting of the Freiburg Medical Society. He was preceded by his friend Franz Bielschowsky, who described some new observations on the enzymatic decomposition of nucleic acids. Krebs entitled his talk "Investigations of Intermediary Protein Metabolism." Although his audience must have been most interested to hear about the new theory of urea synthesis, Krebs chose to begin with his "unexpected" finding that the rate of deamination of amino acids is "by far the greatest, not in the liver, but in the kidneys." "The discovery of this fact," he claimed, "explains a series of previously unexplained facts, for example, the concentrated appearance of ammonia in the urine and the renal veins (Nash and Benedict). The long sought-after precursor of ammonia in the kidneys would thus be found." Krebs went on to join this topic smoothly to his discoveries concerning urea formation with the transition sentence "The majority of the ammonia released in metabolism is synthesized to urea in the organism." With some understatement, he asserted that he had "succeeded in clarifying to a certain degree the chemical mechanism of urea synthesis in the liver."[24] His succinct account of that achievement was quite different in form from the discussion he had given in his two *Klinische Wochenschrift* papers:

> During the investigation of the conditions under which urea synthesis occurs, it first emerged that in starvation the capacity for urea formation diminishes.   Since the respiration of liver tissue does not decrease significantly in starvation, the decrease in the urea synthesis must have a *material* cause. The liver of a starved animal obviously lacks substances that are necessary for urea synthesis.   During the search for these substances it was first shown that carbohydrates could increase the urea formation, but even after the addition of carbohydrate there remained a difference in the quantity of urea formed between livers from nourished and starved animals. In the course of the investigation of the formation of urea from amino acids, a substance was finally found which causes a strong rise in the synthesis of urea in the liver, and which abolishes the distinction between a starved and a nourished animal. This substance is ornithine.[25]

After summarizing, in terms similar to those he used in his first *Klinische Wochenschrift* paper, the catalytic role of ornithine and the inference that arginine must be the intermediate, Krebs continued, "The formation of arginine from ornithine could, through experiments with citrulline that Prof. Ackermann, Würzburg, made available, be given a closer chemical clarification." He then finished his talk by summarizing the results of his experiments with citrulline and the three reactions constituting the chemical mechanism of urea synthesis.[26]

Although his discussion at the Freiburg Medical Society was compatible with the papers he had written, Krebs gave the topic here a very different emphasis. Whereas those papers consisted of arguments and evidence in support of a conclusion, with only incidental traces of the order of the investigation through which he had reached it, here he appeared to recapitulate the successive stages in which he had identified and resolved a problem. These stages correlate in a general way with chronological phases of the research Krebs and Henseleit had carried out. That is not to say, however, that Krebs led his audience through the course of the reasoning and experimentation that he had actually followed during the preceding 9 months. Although partly organized in narrative form, in contrast to the nearly pure analytical form of the *Klinische Wochenschrift* papers, Krebs's talk was a logical reconstruction of selective aspects of his investigation. He omitted many more of the steps he had taken, the subproblems he had faced and resolved, than he included — to say nothing of the retrospectively unnecessary detours he had made. Those many omissions made the question of the difference between urea formation in the tissue of a starved and a nourished animal appear far more prominent than it did in his other treatments of the subject, or in the overall course of the investigation as it can be elicited from his records. Nor does his reconstruction closely resemble the explicitly historical account he selectively reconstructed many years later, by which time different aspects of the investigation had come to appear more crucial. His little talk represented one way, among many, to *view* the investigation he had just completed; and it was an approach well suited to the particular occasion. Whereas his published papers were intended to assert his claim to have made a discovery, his talk was designed to interest a more general medical audience in what he had found. By setting up a problem defined simply, in terms familiar to medicine, then outlining with a minimum of technical detail the solution to the problem, he could quickly draw his audience in, and convey to them the essentials of his achievement.   Readily adapting the same results to varying circumstances of presentation, he showed himself to be an astute teacher, as well as discoverer.

In spite of the brevity of his talk, Krebs covered in it his recent observations on deamination as well as the mechanism of urea synthesis. In part that may have been because both seemed so fresh and important to him at the time that he preferred to divide his limited time between them even at the expense of developing either topic more fully. It may be, however, that he saw both problems then as parts of the same picture. I have described them as having separated out about 2 months earlier as branches of what had previously been a common investigation. Their juxtaposition here suggests that these two lines remained in Krebs's mind closely connected aspects of a broader investigation of "intermediary protein metabolism." In the priority he gave to his discovery of the high rate of deamination in the kidneys relative to his discussion of urea synthesis, Krebs expressed a feeling for the relative significance of these facets of his current work that did not accurately anticipate their eventual ranking as scientific contributions.

During the course of his talk Krebs remarked that the action of ornithine was the first known case of an amino acid constituent of protein that had an additional metabolic function as a catalyst. At this point the professor of physiological chemistry, Joseph Kapfhammer, stood up to object, "It is news to me that ornithine is a constituent of protein." Rudolf Schoenheimer, who was also present, was indignant enough at Kapfhammer's comment to interject that the objection amounted to hair-splitting, as it was well known that ornithine is formed enzymatically from arginine. Krebs regarded Kapfhammer as an unsuccessful, pedestrian scientist, who had tried to find fault because he could not appreciate the significance of what Krebs was talking about.[27] The incident — and especially the fact that he remembered it vividly 45 years later — reveals a glimpse of another side of the young investigator's personality. Although he was, in many respects, an extraordinarily patient person, he had very little patience with people who did not grasp what appeared to him obvious. Even though he had, in his early years, not considered himself outstanding, he tended to regard mediocrity in others with disdain.

After Henseleit ended his work in the laboratory on May 13, Krebs himself interrupted his research for 2 weeks. There is no record of what kept him from his laboratory between May 14 and May 28. Meanwhile, news of his discovery of the mechanism of urea synthesis was spreading rapidly through the German biochemical community. Thannhauser, who immediately understood the broad significance of the discovery, had extensive contacts with the biochemical leaders of Germany. It was through him that Franz Knoop and Otto Meyerhof first heard of Krebs's work. Krebs himself was not shy about publicizing his results by sending reprints of his articles to most of the well-known and lesser biochemists of Germany, and to strategic persons abroad as well. Very quickly he began to sense that his results were being received with enthusiasm. On May 18, Meyerhof wrote to thank him for the reprint "of your beautiful work, that has interested me very much," and to invite him to give a short talk on the contents of his *Klinische Wochenschrift* article at a colloquium on the metabolism of arginine to be held in Heidelberg on June 13. Krebs replied by return mail that he was "very pleased to be permitted to speak about my work in your colloquium." He would need only 10 to 12 minutes, and wondered whether it would be appropriate to present a formal lecture, or better just to speak in the form of discussion remarks.[28]

Krebs was invited also to give a second local presentation, to the Freiburg Chemical Society, on June 6. The distinguished polymer chemist Hermann Staudinger chaired the meeting, at which Krebs gave the first lecture, "The Formation of Urea in the Animal Body." Staudinger understood at once the significance of the reactions of urea synthesis that Krebs proposed, and suggested that organic chemistry could provide examples of analogous reaction sequences. Either then, or a few days later, Staudinger supplied an "analogy to the ornithine effect," and Krebs wrote out the structural formulas involved, on June 11, in his laboratory notebook. Diphenylketone reacts with methyl alcohol to form a methyl ester of diphenylacetic acid. The reaction is accelerated by quinoline, which forms an intermediate β-diketone that then reacts rapidly with the methyl alcohol, releasing the quinoline in a manner analogous to the release of ornithine from arginine.[29]   Although the reaction was neither physiologically nor chemically directly related to the ornithine reactions, Krebs must have welcomed the example, because of the strong presumption among biochemists that the reactions in living organisms proceed by means of the same types of mechanisms that occur in other reactions of organic compounds.

No one was more pleased with what Krebs had done than his own chief. Siegfried Thannhauser not only appreciated fully how pioneering this investigation of urea synthesis was, but was proudly aware that his young assistant had achieved it essentially on his own.   Unlike many heads of laboratories, Thannhauser made no attempt to claim a share of the credit for the important work that had just emerged from his. "I have," he wrote a year later, "merely made available the opportunities for carrying out this work; by far the greatest part of everything else is attributable to the merit of Herr Krebs." Recognizing the superior talent of the young investigator, Thannhauser immediately initiated steps to have him considered for appointment as a *Privatdozent*. He also urged Krebs to write up a full-length paper on the synthesis of urea as soon as possible. Krebs had already intended to do so, but had not been able to find the time. He told his chief, "I have so many clinical commitments, I need to sit down and take a few days off" to complete such a paper. Thannhauser readily granted the request. With his laboratory notebooks, drafts of what he had already written, and other data, Krebs set off on his bicycle, probably on the first or second weekend in June, for Todnauberg, a small village in the Black Forest. To reach his destination he had to board a cable car that lifted him majestically above towering evergreen trees, to a mountain top named *Schauinland*, or "look into the land," 600 meters above the village at the base of the lift. There he took a room in a hotel in what was, during the winter, a ski resort. Free from all interruptions, he finished the definitive version of his "Investigation of the Formation of Urea in the Animal Body" in 3 or 4 days of intensely concentrated work.[30]

Conceptually the full paper on the synthesis of urea was nearly identical to the preliminary papers. Section 5, entitled, "Ornithine Circuit (Theory of the Formation of Urea)" was taken almost word-for-word from the corresponding section in the first *Klinische Wochenschrift* article.   Now, however, Krebs embedded his theory into a highly detailed treatment of the methods, the experiments, and the results on which he based it. Where the preliminary papers had provided only the minimal amount of data essential to present the general argument, the full paper incorporated the results of multiple experiments in support of each aspect of the demonstration.   Where the first *Klinische Wochenschrift* article gave the impression of having been written in pieces, of which only the last third had directly to do with the ornithine theory, each section of the long article appeared to contribute toward that theory. Where the preliminary paper had been silent about ornithine until those later sections, the final paper began with a statement of the three reactions comprising the theory, so that the remainder of the paper appeared as a description of the evidence from which this theory had been derived.[31]

In the preliminary papers Krebs had indicated only briefly the experimental methods he had used. Now he described his methods — especially those for determining urea and for preparing physiological saline solution — thoroughly enough so that others could, if they wished, duplicate his procedures. Where he had previously given only a single result for the basic effect of ornithine on the formation of urea from ammonia, he now listed the results of 15 experiments using 100 mg/100 ml or 200 mg/100 ml of ornithine; of 13 using small concentrations of ornithine together with lactate; of six experiments each comparing the ornithine effect in tissue slices from starved and nourished animals; and of three experiments using very low ornithine concentrations that showed that the ratios of the molecules of urea formed to ornithine present ranged from 7.6:1 to 30.4:1.[32] In writing his definitive paper, Krebs transformed the brilliantly succinct, spare argument with which he had originally presented his proposal, into a nearly exhaustive treatment of the evidence that he could muster in support of his conclusion. We may ask, had all this evidence already been marshaled in his mind when he wrote out the argument in short form, so that it was merely a matter of explicating more fully what was implied in the first version? Or did Krebs fully clarify to himself the strength and limits of his evidence only during the process of writing the long version?

In his second *Klinische Wochenschrift* article, as we have seen, Krebs had written that "about two molecules" of ammonia, and "about one molecule" of ammonia disappear respectively in the formation of one molecule of urea from ornithine and from citrulline, even though from the laboratory record we can see that the experimental results differed significantly from these ratios. In the full paper he no longer skipped over these discrepancies. Utilizing explanations similar to those Henseleit had recorded in his notebook, Krebs suggested that the departure from the theoretical 2:1 ratio for ornithine was due to the availability of NH_3 from "unknown sources" other than that added to the solution; and the departure from the expected 1:1 ratio for citrulline was due to the conversion of some citrulline to ornithine.[33] In the first *Klinische Wochenschrift* article he had written, "The concentration of ornithine, measured by the amino–nitrogen content of the solution, remains almost constant during the formation of urea. Almost all of [*nahezu der gesamte*] urea nitrogen derives from the ammonia...." In the long paper he calculated that in a representative experiment the quantity of ornithine, measured by the amino–nitrogen, decreased by 30 cm³, that of ammonia by 287 cm³, so that "at least 90% of the urea-N must be derived from the ammonia."[34] Was he merely stating more precisely here, what he had meant by "almost all" in the first article, or was it in the course of working out his more detailed discussion of the question that he came to view these results in this more carefully qualified way? If we accept Krebs's own testimony that the only way in which he could find the gaps in his own reasoning, and the weak points in his evidence, was by writing the papers that described his results, then we may assume as most likely, that he refined his grasp of his own investigation in these ways, only as he worked in solitude at his writing desk on the mountaintop.

Krebs submitted the completed paper to *Hoppe-Seyler's Zeitschrift für physiologischen Chemie*, whose editor, Franz Knoop, received it on June 14. Three days later Knoop wrote back,

Dear Doctor Krebs!

I thank you very much for your beautiful paper. It is very convincing, how the way in which you come finally to the synthesis of urea by way of arginine and thereby to this significant role of ornithine, follows entirely by itself out of the sequence of your investigations. At first I was extraordinarily surprised when Thannhauser reported these facts to me; but after the event, one can almost imagine that he could already have arrived at such a conception at the writing table. The only question I have is, what does arginine do as such in large molecules, such as protamine?

Your paper arrived here on the 14th and will soon go into press. I am very anxious to see what else you will bring forth in this direction, and can only congratulate you heartily for your results up until now.

With friendly greetings, also to Professor Thannhauser.

Yours,
F. Knoop[35]

In view of the long effort it had taken him to formulate his theory, even after he had the basic experimental evidence in hand, Krebs considered Knoop's remark about deriving the conclusion at the writing table rather ironic. Nevertheless, this warm praise, from the very person whose lectures had introduced Krebs to the problems of biochemistry 10 years earlier, must have been particularly heartening to him. Knoop's special enthusiasm is also easy to understand, for Krebs's achievement was an elegant advance toward the goal Knoop had so long maintained, of filling in all of the steps in the intricate network of metabolic syntheses and degradations.

Scarcely less laudatory was the response Krebs received from another leading German biochemist. Three days after the second *Klinische Wochenschrift* article had appeared, Carl Neuberg wrote:

Berlin-Dahlem
5 July, 1932

Dear Herr Colleague Krebs!

Many thanks for your thoughtfulness in sending me a reprint of your article in the "*Klinische Wochenschrift.*" I have already read the article in question, as well as the second one, with the greatest interest, and I congratulate you sincerely on these wonderful successes. You have achieved a great thing [*Sie haben Großes vollgebracht*]!

With best wishes for further accomplishments.

Yours, as ever,
C. Neuberg[36]

Less prominent scientists in the field were also quick to appreciate the magnitude of Krebs's achievement. The director of the Pharmacological Institute in Frankfurt, Dr. Werner Lipschitz, invited him to speak there on his most recent investigations, taking the opportunity to "Congratulate you most heartily for your outstanding papers on the mechanism of urea formation."[37] Prof. Walter Schoeller, of the chemical firm of Schering-Kahlbaum, requesting reprints for the company library and for himself, wrote that "The research group at Schering has read with the greatest interest your beautiful investigations on the formation of urea in the animal body."[38] Krebs's old teacher, Peter Rona, added to a letter reminding him that he owed two referee reports on articles submitted to a journal Rona edited, a handwritten postscript: "Heartiest congratulations for the *wonderful* work on urea!"[39] Fortunately Rona probably did not suspect how little Krebs believed Rona had influenced him during the year Krebs had spent in his chemistry laboratory.

Amid the chorus of praises, Krebs received one critical comment. In his first *Klinische Wochenschrift* article, in the section headed "Site of the Formation of Urea From Ammonia," he had written:

> The formation of urea from ammonia takes place in the living structure of the cell (Löffler). If one destroys the cell structure by grinding the tissue, the formation of urea disappears completely. Tissue *Brei* is, therefore, an unsuitable material for the investigation.[40]

On June 13, Mortimer Anson wrote from Princeton:

> Dear Krebs —
>
> I don't know when I'll come to Freiburg. It probably will not be soon.
>
> My compliments (whatever they are worth) on your nice job.
>
> I do not like your dogmatic statement about the *necessary* connection between the $NH_3 \rightarrow$ urea ferment and the living structure of the cell. Your statement has time and again been made for your reasons about enzymes which now can be made to work without the "living structure" of the cell.[41]

Anson's seemingly faint praise for Krebs's overall achievement, coupled with his blunt complaint about this one point, probably did not offend Krebs as the same opinions coming from someone else might have done. Krebs and Anson had met at the International Congress in Boston in 1929, and became personal friends when Anson stopped in to see him every day in New York during the time that Krebs had to spend in the hospital. Afterward Krebs had visited Anson at Princeton.[42] Bright and articulate, Anson was also very outspoken, and his comments on the current biochemical scene were usually as acerbic as they were astute. Krebs would, therefore, have taken this criticism as intended in a friendly spirit. A more important question is whether or not he took it to heart as a cogent criticism.

Discussing this letter with me in 1976, Krebs indicated that Anson's comment did not influence his own thinking, although it might possibly have affected his "way of expressing matters."[43] In several other conversations referring to his own statements on the topic, Krebs insisted that he was only expressing the experimental situation. He had tried unsuccessfully to get the reaction into solution, and had concluded from his inability to do so that the cell structure was essential to the process.[44] The statement from his *Klinische Wochenschrift* article does appear to be a pragmatic summation of the circumstances under which this specific process had been found to occur. Moreover, the reference to Löffler suggests that Krebs regarded his experience as a confirmation of the same conclusion that Löffler had drawn in 1920 from his experiments on perfused livers. Löffler had, in fact, used very similar language (see Chapter 8, p. 252). In his longer article for *Hoppe-Seyler's Zeitschrift*, however, Krebs made a much broader statement, which suggests that there was more behind his view than the immediate experimental results. There he wrote that "since all essential metabolic phenomena are bound to the cell structure, the tissue *Brei*, used so often in the past — in which the structure is destroyed — is unsuitable for metabolic investigations."[45] In the same article he expressed the situation for the specific example of urea synthesis in a manner that seemed to imply a more fundamental position with respect to the relation between chemical processes and vital processes.

> The effect of arginine is not bound to the life of the cells, and takes place also in cell extracts. In this respect the formation of urea from arginine differs from the formation of urea from ammonia. One can see that, of the two partial reactions, it is the first [the conversion of ornithine to arginine] that is tied to life.[46]

Joseph Fruton has seen in this statement the reflection of a traditional attitude, traceable back to the influence of Claude Bernard, that the metabolic decomposition reactions of complex substances are purely chemical processes independent of life, but that syntheses require "vital" physiological processes.[47] The contrast that Krebs outlined here fits nicely within this dualistic framework, as the formation of urea from arginine is a decomposition reaction, whereas the first partial reaction is a synthetic one.

In 1978 Krebs read the preceding paragraph, which was included at that time in a preliminary account of his work on urea synthesis that I had written. He still maintained that his statement was "an empirical assertion," not a "philosophical viewpoint."[48] His emphatic denials of the latter possibility can be attributed in part to the hindsight knowledge that these reactions *were* later reproduced in preparations in which the cell structures had been destroyed, and perhaps to embarrassment at being portrayed as someone whose youthful position included overtones of a discredited vitalism. Nevertheless, I do not believe that these allusions to the "life" of the cells are telltale signs of an underlying vitalistic philosophy that Krebs may have held. As a medical student he had leaned toward a mechanistic view, and there is no evidence that he had developed since then any deeply reflective position on this issue. More plausible is that, whether fully aware of it or not, he had been strongly influenced by positions that Warburg had maintained during the years that Krebs worked in Dahlem.

Early in his career, Warburg had compared the respiration of intact cells with that of "killed cells and cell fragments." He had used avian red blood cells, bacteria, and sea urchin eggs. Pulverizing, heating, and treating the cells with acetone caused the rate of oxygen consumption to sink below that of the normal cells, sometimes only slightly, but often to a very small fraction of the previous rate. From such results Warburg came to believe that respiration, and in general the metabolic processes through which energy is made available for cellular functions, is dependent on the cell. He could not specify precisely how these reactions are "bound" to cell structure, but he thought that surface effects and the spatial separation of substances by means of semipermeable membranes must be involved.[49]

Formed through experiments that he had carried out before the World War, Warburg's view that the essential metabolic processes are bound to the structure of the cells hardened during the 1920s into a conviction that helped shape both his theory of cellular respiration and the methods he devised to investigate the theory. The single enzyme of respiration that he postulated — his *Atmungsferment* — was, he believed, present in such a low concentration that there was "not much hope of isolating the enzyme by the methods of analytical chemistry. Moreover, the enzyme is unstable and is quickly destroyed if separated from the cells." Imbued with the belief that it was useless to attempt to separate the enzyme from the cell, Warburg developed with great brilliance the methods for measuring absorption spectra that enabled him to study the characteristics of the enzyme without disrupting the cells. Moreover, the same conviction enabled him to dismiss, without further ado, the results of Thunberg and others who believed that they were examining specific enzymatic oxidations in tissue extracts by means of the methylene blue method. These supposed oxidases, Warburg asserted as late as 1930, "are not enzymes which were preformed in the living cell, but transformation and decomposition products of a substance uniform in life."[50]

The terms that Warburg applied in such discussions - "bound to cell structure," "living cells," and "life" — were, as we have seen, the same ones that Krebs applied to these questions as they related to the particular metabolic process *he* had taken up. Clearly Krebs approached the relation between the synthesis of urea and the presence of living cells with an orientation he had carried with him from Warburg's laboratory. He did not, of course, rule out in advance the possibility that urea synthesis could be separated from the cells, for he did carry out experiments using tissue *Brei*. He was, therefore, correct in his later opinion that the statement he had made in 1932 about urea synthesis being "bound" to cells was an "empirical assertion" that he could not carry out the process without intact cells. It is also true, however, that he showed very little persistence in his efforts to reproduce the phenomenon in extracts or *Brei*. One or two experiments were sufficient to persuade him that, at least under present conditions, it could not be achieved. It is difficult not to infer that the predisposition he had inherited from Warburg induced him to give up the quest more readily than he might otherwise have done.

II

During the early summer of 1932 Krebs moved steadily along with his deamination experiments. When he resumed the investigation on May 29, after a 2-week interruption, he already had the basic phenomena under control, and needed mainly to consolidate and extend the results attained so far. On that day he tested the effects of three concentrations of arsenite on the consumption of pyruvate added to rat kidney slices, and found that at 0.001 M that agent inhibited the disappearance of the pyruvate by 88.5 percent. Two days later he employed again three concentrations of arsenite to reexamine the conversion of alanine to pyruvate in the same tissue. The results were again best with 0.001 M As_2O_3. In this case he obtained

$$Q_{amino-nitrogen} = -11.7$$
$$Q_{NH_3} = 10.1$$
$$Q_{pyruvate} = 11.1$$

This appeared to be a convincing demonstration that alanine is converted quantitatively to pyruvate. Satisfied now that he had established that oxidative deamination is "practically the sole pathway" through which alanine is deaminated, Krebs turned during the following weeks to measurements of the rates of the reaction in other tissues and with other amino acids. Assuming that the basic mechanism was in all cases the same, that the product was, therefore, always the α-keto acid corresponding to each amino acid, Krebs no longer needed to identify or measure the keto acid formed in each experiment. Henceforth he usually measured only the decrease in amino–nitrogen and the increase in NH_3, which would be expected to occur at similar rates, if the oxidative deamination reaction was the principal phenomenon being measured.[51]

During the first 2 weeks in June, Krebs tested alanine with various tissues, in three different experiments, confirming repeatedly that the rate of deamination is much higher in kidney slices than in any other tissue tried. Sometimes for liver tissue he measured the rates at which both urea and ammonia formed, and compared the total to the rate of ammonia formation in kidney slices.[52]

On June 17, Krebs took up again the comparisons between the deamination of natural isomers and racemic mixtures of amino acids that had occupied his attention during the first 2 weeks of May. Now he tested alanine, leucine, and aspartic acid, and obtained in each case higher rates for the mixtures than for the pure natural isomers.

	Q_{NH_3}	$Q_{amino-nitrogen}$
l-aspartic acid	3.87	-7.13

	Q_{NH_3}	$Q_{amino-nitrogen}$
d,l-aspartic acid	5.96	-10.79
l-leucine	2.78	-3.35
d,l-leucine	4.57	-5.56
d-alanine	2.33	-2.04
d,l-alanine	7.90	-14.04

There were some problematic aspects of these data — in particular the anomaly that in all cases but the natural isomers of leucine and alanine, the amino-nitrogen disappeared at a faster rate than could be accounted for in the release of ammonia. Krebs, however, probably did not focus on this aspect of the experiment; the main conclusion he drew from it was that, for whatever reason, the nonnatural forms were "much more rapidly attacked" than the natural forms.[53]

Along with further tests of d,l-alanine with slices of various tissues, Krebs included in his experiments of June 19 one in which he used not an intact tissue slice, but an extract obtained from ground kidney tissue. The addition of alanine to this extract, he found, caused larger quantities of oxygen to be consumed, of NH_3 to be formed, and of pyruvate to be formed, than in a control without alanine. The increase in the pyruvate present at the end was, in fact, more than enough to account for the NH_3 formed in the deamination reaction, in spite of the fact that he had used no inhibitor to prevent pyruvate from disappearing.

	Without addition	With alanine	Difference
pyruvate (mm^3)	19.1	232	202 [sic]
ammonia (mm^3)	134	314	180
oxygen (mm^3)	-102.5	-162.5	-60[54]

It is not clear what Krebs's expectations in testing the kidney extract were. Perhaps he was merely checking routinely whether all or part of the oxidative processes that alanine undergo can take place in the absence of "cell structure." If so, then the figures were more interesting than predicted, because they suggested that the alanine was deaminated, but that the product of that reaction was not further decomposed as it was in the cells. If so, then Krebs had found a method, independent of the arsenite-inhibiting agent, to demonstrate the oxidative deamination reaction. It must have been evident to him also, however, that the experiment required improvement if it were to serve this purpose, for the quantities of additional oxygen consumed to ammonia and pyruvate formed were not in the 1:2:2 ratio expected for the reaction.

Krebs fixed his attention, on June 22, on the extension of the investigation to other amino acids. He tested glycine, dl-valine, d-glutamic acid, dl-phenylalanine, *d*-lysine, and *d*-ornithine, in each case comparing the results for kidney tissue with other tissues, especially liver. On June 24 he added serine, histidine, and tryptophane.[55]

During the last week of June, Krebs carried out only two more experiments. By early July, he must have felt near to the point at which he could publish his results. Probably he had already written portions of a paper, but there were a few gaps remaining to be filled. Having demonstrated with arsenite that alanine was deaminated quantitatively to pyruvate, he could now usefully utilize HCN as a second agent confirming the general reaction, even though some pyruvate was lost when it was used. It was now enough to show that with HCN too the quantity of NH_3 formed corresponded to the amino–nitrogen that disappeared. He performed two experiments comparing the actions of HCN and of As_2O_3. Then he surveyed the literature on the physiological regulation of the acid-base balance in the animal through the formation of NH_3 in the kidney.[56] By this time he must have been starting to formulate his interpretation that the exceptionally large deamination reaction he had located in kidney tissue is the source of the ammonia that serves this function. On July 7 he summarized his tests of nine amino acids with kidney and liver tissue, in a table undoubtedly intended for public presentation of his results. (With three more amino acids added, the table appeared in essentially the same form in his first paper on the subject.) If he was now writing up his investigation in earnest, one reason may have been that he was preparing to give a lecture on the subject on July 18, at one of the "Medical–Biological Evenings" held weekly at the University of Frankfurt.[57]

Krebs returned to the deamination of alanine in kidney extracts on July 13. Producing the extract in a different manner from the initial experiment of this kind — by mincing the tissue with a knife instead of grinding it, and by placing it in pH 7.4 phosphate buffer in place of physiological salt solution — he compared the oxygen consumption, the formation of NH_3, and the formation of pyruvate with no addition, with the natural isomer *d*-alanine, and with racemic *dl*-alanine. The control and the natural isomer yielded negligible quantities of ammonia and pyruvate, whereas the racemic mixture produced larger quantities of both. There is no indication in the record that Krebs saw any special significance in the inactivity of the natural isomer. He merely calculated the differences between the results for the control and the extract with *dl*-alanine, attaining the following measures of the "additional" reaction caused by the alanine:

O_2 consumption 114 mm^3
NH_3 formation 208 mm^3
Pyruvate formation 228 mm^3

These quantities, in the proportions of 1:1.82:2, were close enough to the expected 1:2:2 ratio for the oxidative deamination reaction, to satisfy Krebs with the result, and he included it in his paper. In its published form he made no mention of the isomers involved, heading the table in which he presented these figures simply as "Formation of Pyruvic Acid From Alanine in Kidney Extract." In his text he wrote, "From the kidney of the rat an enzyme (or enzyme system) can thus be extracted which deaminates amino acids oxidatively...and which one may therefore designate 'Amino acid oxydo-deaminase'."[58]

One loose end that Krebs tied up by means of the literature rather than through further experiments was the question of why HCN did not prevent all of the pyruvic acid formed by the deamination of alanine from disappearing. Back in March he had found reason to think that the pyruvate disappeared in the presence of HCN in the medium, rather than in the tissue slices (see Chapter 10, p. 321). Now, on July 24, he found in a paper by Ludwig Wolff, dating from 1899, that HCN can convert pyruvic acid to a dimeric form known as parapyruvic acid. Satisfied that that reaction explained his problem, Krebs incorporated into his manuscript the statement that "Cyanate possesses an undesirable secondary characteristic; it causes the pyruvate in the solution — even outside the cell — to be transformed into a dimer, into para-pyruvic acid."[59]

Through the end of July and the first half of August, Krebs continued to gather supporting data for his deamination investigations. Some of the experiments he carried out were refinements of the basic ones he had done earlier. Some of them extended the central demonstration of the oxidative deamination reactions to dog, cat, and human kidney and liver tissues.[60] In one set of experiments, performed on August 3, he added a new dimension to the investigation by testing, in addition to alanine, three dipeptides — glycylglycine, alanylglycine, and leucylglycine. He was probably stimulated to try these substances by the recent work of Max Bergmann in Dresden. Bergmann had been developing new methods to synthesize peptides and other related compounds. In a lecture that he gave at the Medical–Biological Evening in Frankfurt on July 11, Bergmann raised the question whether peptides might not be deaminated in the organism without first being completely decomposed into their constituent amino acids. It is possible that when Krebs spoke at the same forum 1 week later about the deamination of amino acids, someone in the audience who had heard both speakers might have drawn a connection between them. In Krebs's experiment, however, there was an "enormous increase" in the amino-nitrogen in the vessels containing the dipeptides, an effect that he attributed to their being split into the separate amino acids. The results were, therefore, "worthless."[61]

On August 5, Krebs once again tested urea, in comparison with alanine and β-hydroxybutyric acid, in kidney cortex slices, and was able to satisfy himself that "Urea → no NH_3 formation." The next day he tested the effects of various keto acids on the rate of the respiration of kidney and liver slices. After carrying out some further experiments on cat and human kidney tissue with amino acids during the following days, he returned finally, on August 16 and 17 to two more experiments on keto-acids. His purpose in testing these substances was probably to determine whether the increases in the respiration accompanying the deamination reactions were due directly to those reactions themselves, or to the further oxidative consumption of the products of those reactions. The results were not entirely clear-cut, but favored the second interpretation.[62]

By this time Krebs must have felt that he had acquired all of the data that were essential for him to complete his paper. It was also time to close down his laboratory for the summer holiday.[63]

III

Most likely, Krebs finished writing his first paper "On the Metabolism of Amino Acids in the Animal Body" during the first half of his vacation, before the end of August. He introduced it as a continuation of the same mode of investigation that he had applied to the synthesis of urea. After a brief description of the basic tissue slice method, he next discussed "The Site of the Deamination of Amino Acids in the Animal Body." Here he presented tables in which he compared the rates of the disappearance of amino–nitrogen, and of the formation of NH_3 when *dl*-alanine was added to 11 different tissues, and in which he compared the rates for 12 different amino acids in kidney and in liver tissue. "Almost all organs consume alanine," he wrote, "but the surprising result is that the greatest rate of conversion is reached, not in the liver — as one heretofore believed — but in the kidneys." The most essential conclusion from these results, he asserted, "is the proof that the deamination of amino acids takes place, for the most part, in the kidneys."[64]

In the next two sections — comprising about one quarter of the paper — Krebs discussed the physiological significance of this result. It had been known since 1921 that the ammonia excreted in the urine is formed in the kidneys themselves, not transported there through the blood, but the question of the chemical source of the ammonia had not been answered in a "satisfying" manner. Calculating that the rates of deamination in human kidney slices he had tested were high enough to account for the maximum rates at which ammonia is excreted in the urine, even during the extreme pathological condition of acidosis, Krebs asserted "we can therefore accept that the amino acids are the main source of urinary nitrogen." Summarizing the prevailing view that this excretion of ammonia plays a role in the regulation of the acid-base balance in the body, while conserving sodium, he concluded that this function enabled "us to understand why the kidneys are provided with the capacity to deaminate amino acids with such rapidity." He could now also supply the answer to the long unanswered question of why there is a lack of ammonia in the urine in diseases of kidney insufficiency. It is because "the kidneys have lost the capacity to deaminate amino acids with sufficient rapidity."[65]

The second half of the paper focused on the deamination reaction itself, "The Formation of Keto Acids From Amino Acids." Beginning with Otto Neubauer's conclusion from experiments on phenylamino acids, in 1909, that in metabolism amino acids are deaminated oxidatively to form keto acids, Krebs claimed that "The general validity of the Neubauer theory of oxidative deamination has up until now remained questionable, because it was not possible to transform the natural amino acids in general directly into keto acids in the animal body." He then presented his own experiments as the desired confirmation of the Neubauer theory. Beginning with the "fact" that pyruvic acid is rapidly decomposed in animal tissues, he summarized the three experimental procedures he had found — inhibition by arsenite and by cyanate, and carrying out the deamination in tissue extracts — to prevent the pyruvate from disappearing, and that had enabled him to demonstrate the reaction quantitatively.[66]

Until this point Krebs had described his results as though they applied directly to the metabolism of the natural amino acids in the organism. In his tables he indicated whether the pure isomer or a racemic mixture had been used in individual experiments, but he did not draw attention to the significance of that distinction. Only in the penultimate section of the body of his paper, entitled "The Metabolism of Optically Active Amino Acids," did he mention the "unexpected" difference he had found in "the behavior of the stereoisomers, the optical antipodes of the amino acids." In contrast to what Felix Ehrlich had found with amino acids in yeast, in 1906, the nonnatural form of alanine "is attacked much more rapidly than the natural form." Pure natural d-alanine is deaminated seven times slower than the racemic mixture. In the case of leucine and aspartic acid, the nonnatural forms are also attacked more rapidly, although the differences are not as great. The data he presented in support of these statements was mainly that of the experiment of June 17, described earlier, although he mentioned in passing other similar results. He rejected the possibility that the more rapid rate of the nonnatural amino acids was a deceptive appearance due to the natural forms being utilized for other amino compounds, because the difference showed up even in experiments with the kidney extracts, where no other reactions of amino acids occurred. He cited Embden's 1908 paper on the formation of "acetone" from nonnatural amino acids, and remarked that "The same facts underlie Embden's observation and our findings." Beyond that Krebs ventured no explanation for the remarkable phenomenon.[67]

After discussing the relationships he had found between the rates of the metabolism of the amino acids and the respiration of the tissues, Krebs summarized the two main "results" of his work as the "discovery of the fact" that the "deamination of amino acids occurs mainly in the kidneys," and "the proof that oxidative deamination is practically the only way in which the deamination of amino acids occurs in the animal body."[68]

Like his papers on urea synthesis, Krebs's preliminary article on amino acid metabolism was not an account of the investigation as such, but a discussion of his findings, organized in an order that bore only coincidental traces of the order in which he had carried out the research and made the "discoveries" that he reported in it. We can again find narrative "residues," in his reference to the "surprising result" of the rapidity with which deamination occurs in the kidney — a reflection of the actual surprise that had launched him on deamination as a separate line of investigation; in his statement that "we searched for conditions under which the consumption of the pyruvic acid would be blocked" — a bare allusion to an extended phase of the investigation in which he had confronted and solved the problem of the disappearing pyruvate; and in the reference to the "unexpected distinction" between the isomers, a distinction that he really had come upon unexpectedly. Overall, however, the paper arranged the investigation into a logical sequence of phases — moving from the more general question of where the amino acids are deaminated in the body, and the rates at which various amino acids are deaminated, to the more specific question of the reaction mechanism, and finally to the special question of the difference between the behavior of the isomers. In the investigation itself Krebs had, of course, not moved so systematically. He did not complete the solution of one problem before turning to the next. He had examined all except the last of these questions in preliminary form very early in the investigation, concentrated on demonstrating the specific nature of the reaction of alanine in the middle phase, and returned later to the more general questions to obtain fuller data. Most of the data he presented in his tables did not come from the experiments through which he had actually reached the conclusions he was here making public, but from later repetitions of these experiments carried out to confirm or improve upon those results. In all these respects the paper was typical of the scientific research literature in general.

Although Krebs presented his investigation of amino acid metabolism as similar in approach to his investigation of urea synthesis, this paper was quite different in character from the ones on urea that he had recently published. In biochemical terms it was far less original. Where he had proposed an entirely unprecedented sequence of reactions for the synthesis of urea, the deamination reaction he presented was only a confirmation of what had been proposed, on the basis of less direct evidence, more than 20 years before. The conclusion that Krebs regarded as new was that this process occurred mainly in the kidneys; but since other investigators too had found deamination in the kidneys, Krebs could really only claim that his result was more decisive, because it was quantitative.

The most novel aspect of Krebs's paper was not his immediate results, but the physiological significance he attributed to them. Connecting his unexpected finding that isolated kidney tissue deaminates amino acids at an exceptionally high rate, with existing views about the physiological functions of the kidneys in the whole animal, he came up with a new explanation for the source of the ammonia known to be excreted by the kidneys when they are in place in the organism.

His discussion of the meaning of his findings illustrates particularly well several general characteristics of Krebs's scientific style. More fully than the urea papers, it reveals the "biological" orientation that, in retrospect he has maintained was always central to his investigative outlook.[69] Not content with demonstrating that a particular chemical reaction takes place in living cells, or even with charting the distribution of the reaction within the cells of different tissues, he wished to understand the physiological function of that reaction within the more highly integrated level of processes that take place in the intact organism.

Second, this discussion illustrates what Krebs regarded as his most distinctive intellectual talent, the ability to perceive connections between phenomena that had previously been treated separately from one another.[70] It was by joining results he had attained at one level of investigation with those that investigators in a nearby scientific field had obtained while examining the organism at a higher biological level of organization, that he was able to construct his interpretation of the deamination reaction.

Third, this paper exhibits the same self-assurance that Krebs had shown when he announced a few weeks earlier that he had solved the problem of urea synthesis; but it suggests that he could feel such confidence even when the ground under him was less secure than it had been then. His interpretation of the physiological role of the deamination reaction in the kidneys was a deductive hypothesis, a bold extrapolation from what he had observed in isolated tissues to the more complex circumstances of the regulatory processes occurring in the living animal. He did not, however, present his views as hypothetical, but as a direct outcome of his investigation, as the definitive resolution of the question of the source of urinary ammonia as well as of the absence of that ammonia in kidney deficiency diseases. Perhaps the explanation appeared so plausible to him as to leave no room for doubt about its correctness, or perhaps he was once again following Warburg's advice not to hedge, even if he might turn out to be wrong.

The physiological inferences Krebs drew appear even more incautious when we take into account that in making them he seems to have ignored a gaping logical fissure within the discussion of his experimental results. As we have seen, his assertion that the deamination of amino acids occurs mainly within the kidneys rested heavily upon experiments in which he had used racemic mixtures of the natural and nonnatural isomers of the amino acids; yet he reported in this same paper that isolated natural isomers of amino acids are deaminated in the kidney slices at rates as low as one seventh of the rates of the racemic mixtures. In the paper he drew no connection between these two equally striking quantitative contrasts. Looking back now, this discrepancy appears to leap out from the data contained in the paper, and one is led immediately to wonder why he did not ask himself whether the high rates of deamination in the kidneys might represent principally the more rapid reaction of the nonnatural amino acids. If that were so, his physiological interpretation would be difficult to maintain, since the kidneys in the intact animal would be expected to have access only to natural amino acids. Similarly, in light of the fact that the oxidative deamination reaction he reported as having taken place in kidney extracts actually had occurred only with *dl*-alanine, it is difficult not to infer that he overlooked the same logical discrepancy when he concluded that he had extracted from the rat kidney a general "amino acid oxido-deaminase."

We may assume either that Krebs failed to notice these discrepancies, or that if he did notice them he left them unmentioned because he could not yet see how to resolve them. If the latter were the case, then was it not premature to publish on the subject? If the former were the case, then his failure to see these problems might still have been due to haste in getting a paper ready for publication. The timing of his paper suggests, in fact, that it might have been the advent of the summer holiday that induced him to publish what he had been able to complete until that point, rather than a sense that he had met all his investigative goals. Expecting to be away for a whole month, he may simply not have wanted to wait for further results that he might not be able to reach until late in the fall. As in the case of his urea investigation, he sent his manuscript to the *Klinische Wochenschrift* as a preliminary report that would appear quickly. He probably already had in mind that he would subsequently write a longer paper for Hoppe-Seyler's *Zeitschrift für Physiologischen Chemie*. There he could correct whatever might appear incomplete or unsatisfactory in the light of later experiments.

* * *

Commenting in 1970 on James Watson's *The Double Helix,* Krebs wrote that he did not believe that he himself had been motivated, as Watson acknowledged to have been, by a sense of competitive "racing."[71] By comparison with Watson, Krebs's competitive instincts undoubtedly were gentle. Yet his behavior in instances such as the present one suggests that he was certainly competitive enough to want to get his results into print at the earliest feasible moment. He too sought and obtained recognition. No doubt he felt that he was merely following normal practice, and the advice of his mentors. In fact, he was. Competition is so endemic to the operation of science as a social system[72] that if Krebs had had no such competitive drive, he could hardly have survived in his field.

If scientists cannot avoid competition, historians cannot evade hindsight. The logical defects in Krebs's first paper on amino acid metabolism appear to this historian obvious from an examination of the internal structure of the paper itself. There is, however, no way that I can tell whether I would have been able to notice them if I had not already known about the further course of the investigation of this problem by Krebs and others. Long before I could see the discrepancies, the author of the paper had himself become well aware of them. The lesson should be that the historian who can see in a scientific paper something that the scientist may not have seen when he wrote the paper, ought not to imagine himself to be more perceptive than his subject.

IV

By the time he began his vacation in mid-August, Hans Krebs must have been able to look back on the first half of 1932 as one of the most heartening periods of his life. He had answered, to his own satisfaction and that of the leaders in his field, the question of whether he could make first-rate contributions to the growth of scientific knowledge. He had, moreover, done so even while devoting the greater part of his time to his medical responsibilities. He was appreciated in Freiburg not only as a very promising young scientist, but as a capable, caring physician. He lived in an exciting intellectual atmosphere, stimulated by contacts with other scientists who were outstanding in their fields. His excellent research facilities not only permitted him to carry on his own investigations efficiently, but offered him the opportunity to attract younger investigators to work with him as his reputation began to grow. He lived in comfortable surroundings, close to a beautiful countryside in which he could conveniently pursue his favorite avocational activities. His circumstances were not only happy for the present, but gave promise of an auspicious future in Freiburg.

The only dark shadows crossing Krebs's bright pathway were the ominous developments in Germany at large. The dire economic conditions of the past 2 years were leading to ever deeper political and social instability. With the dismissal of Heinrich Brüning as chancellor of Germany, on May 29, the political situation became fragile. The revocation of a decree that had attempted to prohibit public appearances by the private military forces of the National Socialist Party — the SA and the SS — resulted in an escalation of violent encounters. Krebs must have taken particular notice of the news that a Nazi parade through Altona, the suburb of Hamburg in which he had recently worked, had brought about 17 deaths. In the elections of July 31, the Nazis increased the number of their seats in the Reichstag so dramatically that every thoughtful German had to confront the possibility that Adolf Hitler might come to power.[73]

Krebs was well aware of the threat. Although never politically active, he followed national events attentively. He had read as much of Hitler's *Mein Kampf* as he could stomach, and knew full well what might be in store for him, as a Jew, if the Nazis were to take over. The question of whether he would be safer leaving Germany had also occurred to him. Early in the summer Carl Cori, an Austrian biochemist 4 years his senior, who had already achieved eminence and had emigrated to the United States in 1928, offered Krebs a position in his laboratory at Washington University in St. Louis. Krebs took the offer seriously enough so that rumors spread that he would go. He was, however, reluctant to leave Freiburg at a time when things were going so well for him there. Moreover, much as he appreciated the dangers facing Germany, he was optimistic enough to believe that things might eventually "sort themselves out." Freiburg was relatively quiet. The violent disturbances that made headlines elsewhere did not occur there, so that the threatening events about which he read seemed still remote from his own life. Nor did he experience personally the effects of the increasingly blatant anti-Semitism in the nation at large. Throughout his life he had encountered "occasional" anti-Semitic remarks, but they were seldom directed at him, because most people did not take him to be a Jew. He was himself one of that large portion of German Jews who thought of themselves primarily as German.[74]

In keeping with his attitude toward life in general, Krebs spent his month-long holiday in a manner that was at once pleasurable and useful. The central activity he planned was to participate in the International Physiological Congress, held in Rome from August 29th to September 3rd. During the 10 days preceding the Congress he stayed at an Italian seaside resort west of Florence. Even there he was not idle, for he used the opportunity to take lessons in Italian from a private teacher.[75]

At the Congress itself Krebs delivered a paper on his "Investigation Concerning the Formation of Urea in the Animal Body." His presentation contained nothing that he had not already published in his two *Klinische Wochenschrift* articles, but he met quite a few people at the Congress who were interested in discussing the subject with him. Among these were Donald Van Slyke, whose analytical methods had been of such crucial importance to him. Van Slyke had already read and admired Krebs's papers on urea. Krebs found him especially kind and friendly, someone who took a personal interest in the welfare of younger scientists. Among others who attended the Congress, whom we might expect Krebs to have talked with either because of common interests or earlier acquaintance, were Meyerhof, Michaelis, Severo Ochoa, and Lina Stern. His old friend Hermann Blaschko was there too. It would be surprising if Krebs did not attend the lecture given by Albert Szent-Györgyi, whom he had known since the 1929 Congress. Szent-Györgyi discussed his memorable discovery of the chemical nature of vitamin C, "the first vitamin isolated in crystals." At the Congress Krebs also took the opportunity to meet Carl Cori, and to discuss with him Cori's offer to him to come to St. Louis. Afterward, however, both agreed that Krebs would not have available research facilities equal to what he already enjoyed in Freiburg, and Krebs decided to stay where he was.[76]

Still having vacation time left after the Congress, Krebs decided to spend another week in Italy, this time at Forte dei Marmi, near Pisa. When he boarded the train, he met Franz Knoop, who was also traveling north from the Congress. Knoop asked Krebs where he was heading, and when Krebs mentioned his plans Knoop asked if he could join him. Afterward Blaschko, too, joined them, along with another associate of Meyerhof, and a Swiss neurophysiologist. The five scientists lingered for a week on the Italian coast, happily discussing their various scientific interests, as well as many other topics. Krebs found that Knoop was, for a senior German professor, remarkably friendly and open with younger colleagues. While they were together Knoop reiterated that he had felt stupid never to have thought of the reactions of urea synthesis until he saw them in Krebs's paper.[77] If Krebs reacted to the activities in which he took part in Italy in the same way as he did in later years to similar events, he must have returned to Freiburg — not in a state of high excitement — but visibly animated by the stimulating discussions in which he had been involved.

V

When he resumed his research, on September 20, Krebs continued the deamination investigation from the point at which he had broken it off a month before. His *Klinische Wochenschrift* article was, by then, probably in press, but there was much more information to gather: extending the results to other amino acids and other tissues; varying the experimental conditions; and exploring further the unexpected rapidity with which non natural amino acids were deaminated, especially in kidney tissue. As he pursued these points of the investigation during the following weeks, much of the research settled into the routine application of procedures he had already established. During the course of the experiments, however, a few new problems arose.

On September 25 Krebs tested alanine, aspartic acid, and lysine in kidney slices, anaerobically and aerobically, using HCN as the inhibiting agent. In keeping with the view that the deamination was oxidative, he would have expected no reaction to occur under the anaerobic conditions. In the case of lysine, however, the readings, while inexact, nonetheless suggested the possibility that, despite the lack of oxygen some NH_3 might have formed. To check this possibility further, on October 3rd he tried anaerobically 17 different amino acids, and found that in nearly every case there was "a trace more NH_3 formed with the amino acids, especially with alanine and phenylanlanine." Not certain whether the quantities involved exceeded the expected experimental error, or whether the vessels were really oxygen-free, he decided that he would have to repeat the experiments. Before doing so, however, he turned his attention to other aspects of the investigation. On October 4 he carried out a large-scale experiment on valine with kidney slices, and identified the dinitro-phenylhydrazone of the expected product of the deamination reaction, α-keto-isovaleric acid. On October 8 he compared dl-alanine again with d-alanine in kidney and liver slices. As in the summer, he found that the racemic mixture was decomposed more rapidly than the natural isomer, especially in the kidney tissue. On October 10 he included alanylalanine along with several amino acids, and this time he concluded that the dipeptide "must be attacked." The next day he tried another dipeptide, alanylglycine, and found that it too appeared to be cleaved, releasing NH_3. Reexamining also the inconclusive earlier indications that amino acids might be deaminated under anaerobic conditions, he tested racemic phenylalanine and leucine, and now found that it was "certain" that NH_3 is formed anaerobically in both cases. On October 12 he similarly obtained NH_3 anaerobically from racemic alanine. In this instance, however, there was "more keto acid than NH_3!!", another surprising result, that led him to infer that "There must be a disappearance of the NH_3." From a second set of experiments that again yielded "too much keto acid" Krebs drew the same conclusion about the disappearance of NH_3. On October 15th 12 different amino acids all yielded small quantities of NH_3 in the absence of oxygen gas.[78]

During the rest of October Krebs went on with other deamination experiments, which did not substantially alter the situation. On November 2 he reached the end of the laboratory notebook that he had been using for nearly a year, and entered on the last pages a list of experiments to do in the future.[79] Most of these were further extensions of the work already carried out. During these 6 weeks he had consolidated some aspects of the earlier phase of the investigation and expanded its scope. He had also, however, turned up unexpected complications in the unexplained possibility that an oxidative deamination reaction could take place anaerobically, and that some NH_3 might disappear at the same time that it was forming. Both of these observations posed potential obstacles to his effort to demonstrate quantitatively that the exclusive pathway for the metabolic breakdown of amino acids was oxidative deamination.

As he expanded his investigation, Krebs found himself in need of substances that he could not readily obtain from chemical firms or make for himself. Following the normal custom, he wrote to other biochemists who had produced such substances for their own research purposes, asking if they could supply him with samples. In the course of making such requests he learned some lessons in scientific diplomacy.   Stimulated probably by the publication of Max Bergmann's lecture on dipeptides, in the *Klinische Wochenschrift* for September 17, 1932,[80] Krebs wrote Bergmann, on September 26, to ask for some of the dipeptides he had synthesized. To indicate how he intended to incorporate the dipeptides into his research on deamination, Krebs included a copy of the galley proofs of his own forthcoming *Klinische Wochenschrift* article. Away on a trip, Bergmann did not reply immediately.   While waiting, Krebs began the experiments on dipeptides mentioned earlier, on October 10, using two that he could purchase commercially. Finally, on October 19, Bergmann responded coldly,

> It would be difficult for me to hand over to you samples of the various dipeptides that we synthesize here in order for you to test their behavior in kidney tissue. In the first place, the preparation of these dipeptides is, in most cases, still very tedious; and, second, if you were to undertake the investigation, I would have to relinquish an essential part of my research program, which is, as is known to you, the role of the kidneys in amino acid metabolism. Our observation that the kidneys possess an enzyme that yields keto acids and ammonia from the decomposition products of proteins comes off so badly in the article whose proofs you have sent me, that I would give up very much if I were to turn over to you the further pursuit of these matters.[81]

Although he must have been taken aback by this rebuff, Krebs quickly replied in conciliatory terms:

Oct. 29, 1932

> Dear Herr Professor!
>   Allow me to thank you very much for your letter of 19.10.32. I shall henceforth, of course, not touch further on the questions on which you intend to work. I have, to be sure, already carried out a series of experiments on the question of the deamination of peptides, with a few simple peptides that can easily be prepared or are available from Hoffmann-Laroche. It has already been proven in this way, that amino acids bound in peptides can also be deaminated under specified conditions; the deamination appears, however, to concern only the free amino groups of the peptides. I shall, nevertheless, refrain for the present from publishing these experiments, if you wish it.[82]

Krebs had parried Bergmann's thrust deftly. As we have seen, he had carried out only a few preliminary experiments, mainly between the time he had written Bergmann and received Bergmann's answer. By implying that he had essentially completed a publishable investigation, he was disarming Bergmann's suggestion that Krebs wished to enter in the future an area that Bergmann already occupied, even while he offered generously to stand aside for Bergmann. He must have anticipated that he was putting Bergmann in an awkward spot. To request that a colleague not publish what he has already done, would appear unreasonable. Bergmann must have seen how his position had been turned against him, for in a second letter that he sent off immediately, he markedly shifted the grounds of his complaint:

> It is, of course, far from my intention to wish to hinder you in the publication of the results of your investigation. I did not protest against your experiments, but against the fact that in your papers and lectures you have not presented the historical background correctly.[83]

Assuming that the principal text to which Bergmann referred was the same as the published *Klinische Wochenschrift* article, the statement that probably aroused his ire was:

> "The most essential result of this section is the proof that the deamination of amino acids takes place for the most part in the kidneys.[26]"

In the literature cited at the end of the article, Krebs had put under footnote 26, "Compare in this regard Bergmann, *Klin. Wschr.* 1932, 1569."[84] The footnote was out of order, suggesting that Krebs added it hastily to his manuscript when Bergmann's article came out. Most of Bergmann's article concerned the methods by which he had synthesized artificial dipeptides; but he had ended with some broad questions about how these dipeptides might elucidate the part the kidneys play in protein metabolism. In a single sentence he ended on the topic of deamination: "We recognize here for the first time an enzyme that carries out the deamination of protein decomposition products, and that conveys upon the kidneys the ability to create ketoacids and ammonia."[85]

Krebs was far less receptive to Bergmann's new complaint than to the preceding one. He waited for nearly a month before writing back, on November 28, "This remark astonishes me. After the most careful examination, I can find nothing incorrect in my presentation...."

> Allow me to explain my view of the historical situation. The main point is, that your work is neither historically, nor in any other way, essentially connected with the work previously published by me.

Summarizing his prior results, Krebs emphasized that they concerned the oxidative deamination of free amino acids, a phenomenon discovered by Neubauer in 1909. His own investigation had begun from that of Neubauer, as he had acknowledged in his article. Bergmann had, on the other hand, "not worked at all with amino acids, but with artificial peptides." Since Bergmann had, in fact, stated that no enzyme was known that deaminates free amino acids, "I had no opportunity to cite your investigation in my work." While thus rejecting Bergmann's claim outright, Krebs offered to discuss the matter with him in person in December, when he expected to be in Berlin.[86]

There is no record of whether or not Krebs and Bergmann did meet to discuss their differences, but they must somehow have resolved the matter amicably, as Krebs went ahead with his plans to include dipeptides in his investigation. When he subsequently published the results, he discussed Bergmann's work on the dipeptides in detail, and attributed to it the inspiration for taking them up himself.[87]

On the face of it, Krebs would appear to have had more justification for his defense than Bergmann for his protests. Bergmann's statements about deamination in the kidneys were so general that we might judge Krebs to have been generous in making reference to his article at all. On the other hand, it is easy to understand why Bergmann viewed the situation differently. Because despite his second letter to the contrary, Krebs *had* cited him, Bergmann would have reason to suppose that Krebs did see then a connection between Bergmann's work and that "previously" published by himself. When he received Krebs's request for dipeptides, Bergmann had no way of knowing that Krebs had already initiated experiments with one or two peptides, and he could well have imagined that Krebs was asking him to allow him to begin work in an area that he had just learned about by reading Bergmann's article. Krebs was, in fact, not totally straight-forward in giving the impression that his first experimental trials constituted an investigation ready for publication.

The significance of this incident lies not in whether one or the other person was right or wrong; whether either one encroached on the prerogatives of the other; whether either was aggressive, oversensitive, or narrow-minded. Rather, the affair illuminates a difficulty that repeatedly confronts scientists who pursue closely related problems. Individuals within a research specialty area must maintain a delicate balance between cooperation and competition.[88] They are, at once, colleagues and potential rivals. Research pathways that run near to each other are apt to cross, and when they do, what appears to one investigator the natural extension of his own line of investigation, is liable to appear to the other as an intrusion onto a trail that he had previously staked out. When such conjunctures occur they may lead to a negotiation of the type that Krebs and Bergmann carried on, which can restore cooperation. As in other types of negotiation, however, if these exchanges are not handled with skill, tact, and a spirit of compromise, breakdowns may occur. Krebs was learning, among other things, to handle such negotiations skillfully.

During the same period, Krebs encountered a second complaint that impressed on him how easily the same senior colleagues who otherwise encouraged him, could be offended by perceived slights regarding their own contributions. On October 9 he wrote Carl Neuberg to ask for several keto acids. Unlike Bergmann, Neuberg wrote back that he would be pleased to comply with the request; but when he read Krebs's *Klinische Wochenschrift* article a few days later, Neuberg wrote again,

I have read your preliminary communication in the "*Klin. Wo.*" with great interest. You have written there that you utilized dinitrophenylhdrazine for the separation of the keto acids. Were you not satisfied with our method for the isolation of pyruvic acid, which was first described, "*Bio. Z.* 216, 496, 1929"? For you mention only the American work by Allen, which appeared 1 year after ours. Incidentally, the melting point given in the latter is incorrect, as our work has established. The derivative of pyruvate does not melt at 213, but at 216 on an ordinary thermometer, or 219° corrected.

Neuberg nevertheless promised to send the keto acids as soon as he could.[89] In this case Krebs evidently decided either that Neuberg's point was well taken, or that he could afford to mollify him on such a small matter. In his subsequent paper on the subject, he described Neuberg's method as the one he had used, and corrected the melting point in question to Neuberg's figure.[90] The two incidents with Neuberg and Bergmann, taken together, suggest that Krebs preferred to please the older scientists in his field whose good will was helpful to him, but that he would not cater indefinitely to their demands.

A happier scientific exchange took place between Krebs and a young British biochemist whose research pathway had passed close to the one he was now following. Barbara Holmes and two co-workers in the Biochemical Laboratory headed by her father, Frederick Gowland Hopkins, in Cambridge, had been investigating the production of ammonia in kidney tissue since 1929. Using suspensions of finely chopped rat kidney, Holmes and Antoinette Patey measured the formation of ammonia anaerobically and aerobically. When they added the amino acid glycine to the medium, they found that the quantities of ammonia formed aerobically increased, but not the anaerobic quantities. Patey and Holmes inferred, in 1929, that there are "three independent ammonia-forming systems, one operating anaerobically, and two aerobically. The extra ammonia formed aerobically with glycine, they were inclined to assume...represented an oxidative deamination of the glycine." They were unable, however, to identify the other product of the reaction. In 1930 they supported these conclusions with further experiments, showing in particular that the maximum rate for one of the aerobic deamination "systems" occurred at pH 5.2, but that a lesser peak occurred at pH 7.2. They inferred that the latter represented the portion derived from the deamination of glycine. They were not able to establish the precursors for the other two systems, although they suggested that the source of the anaerobically formed ammonia might be adenylic acid.[91]

A few weeks after beginning his own investigation of deamination, Krebs had, in April 1932, put down in his laboratory notebook several references from the "NH_3-literature." These included three articles by Holmes and her associates. Under the 1929 citation he had commented "Experiment with glycine, important!" Beneath the 1930 reference he had written, "Very important. Urea formation in the kidneys??"[92] The latter query alluded to the fact that during their study of the formation of ammonia in kidney tissue, Holmes and Patey had in some cases found an increase as well in the quantity of urea present. In his *Klinische Wochenschrift* article he mentioned Holmes and Patey among those who had thought of the possibility that amino acids are the source of urinary ammonia, and as one of three investigative teams that "had shown that the kidneys split off ammonia from glycine." He added, however, that "the lack of quantitative measurements had left the question of to what extent the amino acids are involved in ammonia formation in the kidneys undecided."[93]   Thus, in the manner of any scientist who must, in a few succinct statements, both recognize his predecessors and make room for his own originality, he had astutely placed them within the mainstream of the developments that had carried the problem up to the threshold from which his own investigation was now moving it forward. Krebs probably had not been directly influenced by Holmes and Patey, because, as we have seen, he had entered the problem of deamination from another direction. He had, however, appreciated the relevance of their work to his own.

> On October 26, 1932, Barbara Holmes wrote Krebs,
> Dear Sir
>   We have been following your very important work upon urea formation from ammonia in the liver and also upon ammonia formed by the kidney with the very greatest interest. I should be proud if you would allow me to discuss one or two points with you....

The first point was that she agreed fully with him that the kidney cannot form urea from ammonia, "Yet it undoubtedly does form urea from something." After summarizing the experiments that Patey had carried out on this subject, she went on,

> As regards the formation of urinary ammonia, Miss Patey and I came to the conclusion that it could not be a simple case of amino acid deamination, because ammonia is produced by the kidney when the urine is acid, whereas glycine anyhow is less readily deaminated at an acid pH. Also nephritic kidneys which have lost their power of producing ammonia...can usually deaminate glycine quite well. It is possible, as Miss Patey is inclined to believe, that the amino acids have first to be produced in the kidney by proteolysis, and then deaminated, and that the optimum pH of the two processes together may be definitely acid. We must try this if possible.

After a brief paragraph on her more recent studies of urea formation in tissue cultures, she ended diffidently "with apologies for troubling you ..."[94] Krebs responded warmly:

> Nov. 6, 1932
> Dear Mrs. Holmes,
>   I was delighted with your letter, and thank you very much for it. I have already followed the work of you and your associates for a long time with the greatest interest....It pleases me particularly to make personal

contact with you now through your letter, and to have to discuss a few questions with you.

Concerning Holmes's first question, Krebs gave his opinion that the source of the urea formed in the kidneys was arginine. He continued:

Now for the second point, the formation of urinary ammonia. You find that glycine is deaminated less readily under acidic conditions, and yet the kidneys excrete more ammonia under acidic conditions. In the first place, I can confirm your finding concerning the diminished deamination at higher hydrogen ion concentrations, and also, to be sure, for several other amino acids. Not all amino acids behave in the same way, however, so that an exact and systematic investigation of the influence of pH on deamination is required.

His agreement with their experimental findings did not lead Krebs to share Holmes and Patey's view "that it could not be a simple case of amino acid deamination." After a paragraph indicating his great interest in some experiments they had carried out on kidney tissue poisoned with uranium, he maintained his position regarding the central issue:

That the "aerobic system" really does yield ammonia from amino acids is made very probable from the following experiment. After poisoning with small quantities of As_2O_3 (through which the aerobic system is not significantly influenced) one finds equal quantities of ammonia and keto acids, if one adds alanine, valine, or leucine. Without amino acids, on the other hand, one finds no measurable quantities of keto acids, since not all keto acids can be measured manometrically. It follows, from the equivalence of the ammonia and keto acids, that in the presence of the amino acids, the formation of ammonia through the aerobic system is suppressed in the presence of the [added] amino acids. The simplest way to explain this would be to assume that the added amino acids displace another substrate from the deamination reaction. Since such displacements are assumed to take place only between similar substances, it is probable that the sources of the ammonia in the aerobic system [in the absence of added amino acids] are amino compounds.[95]

These other amino compounds, Krebs implied, might yield types of keto acids that are not measurable manometrically. He ended with a friendly apology for answering at such length, and an invitation to continue the discussion.

Krebs's explanation of the operation of Holmes and Patey's "aerobic system" was plausible; from a distance, however, it appears as a means to explain *away* certain complications, because he was not prepared to entertain the possibility that more was involved than "a simple case of amino acid deamination." He did not try to view the problem from the perspective of Barbara Holmes's investigation as a whole, but replied to her questions mainly from the standpoint of his own findings.   In doing so, he may have missed something; but few people can see any question from all sides.

The interest of these letters between Krebs and Holmes as an example of the informal intellectual exchanges that weld individuals of a scientific subfield into a community of inquiry, is matched by the interest of the sociological relationships that the correspondence both reflected and helped to shape.   There was an obvious potential for competition between the two scientists, and consequently for reactions protecting self interests, such as those that emerged in the contacts between Krebs and Bergmann.   Krebs and Holmes had been working on closely related problems.   Holmes had obtained suggestive evidence for oxidative deamination in the kidneys well before Krebs took up that question.   Subsequently Krebs had produced much more extensive evidence for the same phenomenon, overshadowing Holmes's limited results.   Furthermore, the two held significantly divergent opinions about the conclusions to be drawn regarding this process.   In spite of such potential sources of strain, there is no hint of anything other than a friendly exchange welcomed enthusiastically by both parties, a cooperative spirit, and mutual expressions of esteem for the contributions of the other person.   Perhaps that tone was set largely by the modesty with which Barbara Holmes opened the exchange, her open admiration for Krebs's work, and the diffidence with which she brought up her own conclusions.   Krebs, who genuinely admired her work as well, responded in the same tone.   He was undoubtedly pleased not only to make contact with Holmes herself, but through her to be in touch for the first time with the most important biochemical research laboratory in England.   They shared also the bonds between junior investigators in a field, neither of whom have influence over the career prospects of the other.   Because they worked in different countries, they were not even competing for recognition within the same national scientific communities.

Aside from such personal factors, the intrinsic relationship between their respective lines of inquiry were conducive to cooperation.   The research problem of each person included that of the other, but their highest priorities differed.   The main problem for Krebs was a subsidiary part of a broader problem for Holmes, and the converse also held true.   Studying the production of ammonia in the kidneys, Holmes found that the deamination of amino acids was probably one of several sources for that ammonia.   Examining deamination in various tissues, Krebs discovered that the kidneys were a principal location for that process.   Despite the similarity of their interests, they were not in direct competition.   Each obtained results that could illuminate the results of the other, without fully encompassing the investigative field the other was exploring.   Their research trails intersected, but did not converge, therefore, neither saw the other as threatening to preempt what he or she intended to pursue.   The relationships of harmony or disharmony between scientific colleagues are shaped by a subtle interplay of their personalities and of the patterns that link individual research trails into networks defining specialty areas.

VI

As he continued his deamination experiments through November, Krebs gave priority to the question of the optical isomers. On November 4 he tested three natural isomers, not against racemic mixtures as he had mostly done before, but directly against their nonnatural optical antipodes. In all three pairs the rate of ammonia formation and of decrease in amino nitrogen for the nonnatural isomer were higher than for the natural isomers — moderately so in one case, dramatically so in the other two.

	Q_{NH_3}	$Q_{amino-nitrogen}$
l-histidine (natural)	3.54	≈ 0
d-histidine	4.55	-3.70
d-valine (natural)	3.44	≈ 0
l-valine	23.0	-15.5
l-phenylalanine (natural)	5.96	≈ 0
d-phenylalanine	29.3	-19.1

The amino–nitrogen measurements he discounted as inexact.[96] The difference between the nonnatural and natural isomers with respect to ammonia alone, however, was striking. The rates for the natural isomers were, in fact, closer to the upper limit of the values for racemic mixtures that he had earlier obtained for some other tissues than to the rates of the nonnatural isomers in kidney tissue in two of these three cases — to such an extent, in fact, that it is surprising that he appears not to have reconsidered his conclusion that the kidneys are the principal site of deamination. This result would seem to pose the possibility that the exceptional rates in the kidney were attributable to the nonnatural isomers included in the racemic mixtures whose behavior had originally led him to this conclusion. To accept that possibility, of course, would be to abandon the very attractive interpretation of the physiological source of urinary ammonia that he had just published.

During the rest of November and on into December, Krebs pursued the same types of experiments on deamination that he had already carried out. He tested additional optical isomers, varied the pH, employed several dipeptides that contained optical isomers of one or both amino acids, and extended the tissues used to include Jensen sarcoma. Little occurred to change the overall picture. The nonnatural isomers continued, in general, to produce more ammonia than the natural ones, but the differences were not uniformly large. Sometimes, at optimal pH, even the natural isomers yielded ammonia in kidney tissue at rates substantially exceeding the largest rates attained in other tissues.[97] It is difficult to tell whether Krebs sensed during these weeks that he was moving toward a closure in this investigation, or if he just intended to go on gathering more information until something came along to turn his interest in a new direction.

If Krebs's research during the waning weeks of 1932 looks rather dull compared to that of 6 months earlier, the excitement generated by his achievements of the previous spring was still spreading. The most dramatic evidence yet of his new standing among his colleagues reached him on November 18, when he received a letter from the president of the Kaiser Wilhelm-Gesellschaft, the distinguished physicist Max Planck. It began,

> Dear Herr Doctor!
>   At the suggestion of Herr Professor Warburg, I am honored to invite you, on behalf of the Kaiser Wilhelm-Gesellschaft, to present a lecture on a theme from your area of research, at the next "Dahlem Medical Evening," the nature of which you know from your time in Berlin, in Harnack House. You will have available 45 minutes of speaking time....[98]

The rest of Planck's letter suggested the date of December 16, detailed the arrangements, and specified the travel costs that the Kaiser Wilhelm-Gesellschaft would pay. Krebs replied immediately, "I shall accept the invitation with the greatest pleasure." He suggested as his title, "Investigations of Protein Metabolism,"[99] a topic open enough to allow him to discuss whatever stage his recent investigation would have reached by then. Krebs must have been at least as pleased that the invitation had originated with Warburg as that it came from so prestigious an institution. Up until then Warburg had been conspicuously absent from the leaders of German biochemistry who had congratulated him on his urea work. Krebs must have wondered, during the months since its publication, whether the former chief who loomed so large in his own life was even aware of his success. Now he knew finally that Warburg had at least noticed it. (Later he learned that his friend Bruno Mendel had drawn Warburg's attention to it.)[100]

About 10 days after Krebs had received his invitation from the president of the Kaiser Wilhelm-Gesellschaft, he received, in his absence, another form of honor in another august institution. On November 30, Sir Frederick Gowland Hopkins delivered the anniversary address to the Royal Society of London, on the topic "Atomic Physics and Vital Activities." In his talk he moved from general speculations concerning the applicability of the data of atomic physics to the processes of life, through equally general views about the nature of enzymes, to arrive finally at illustrations of "current progress in animal biochemistry." From the research published during the past year he singled out, to typify new methods and successes, the work of Hans Krebs on urea — an investigation that had "approached on new lines a fundamental problem which for the past sixty years has been the subject of speculation." Most biochemists, according to Hopkins, had previously been content to believe "that urea arises by the direct removal of the elements of water from the molecule of ammonium carbonate."

> That urea does indeed arise in the liver by a synthesis from ammonia and carbon dioxide remains certain; but the research under reference, brilliantly carried out by Krebs, of Freiburg-im-Breisgau, has shown that its production is on no such simple lines as those mentioned. It calls for a mechanism involving a most interesting interplay among activated molecules. The facts as revealed have just that degree of unexpectedness — if I may use the phrase — which was to be expected in a biochemical phenomenon.

After summarizing the results of Krebs's research on urea, Hopkins commented further,

> In another respect this example illustrates the nature of current biochemical studies. The data were obtained by the methods of micro-analysis and only a few milligrams of hepatic tissue were employed in individual experiments. Yet the results were consistent and reproducible and experimental errors well under control. The high accuracy to be obtained in ordinary organic analysis by micro methods is now well recognized, but it is becoming clear that technique is so developing that kinetic studies can be made equally accurate on a similar scale. To studies of living systems this offers advantages which cannot be overestimated.[101]

Hopkins's address was printed in *Nature* on December 10. In Freiburg the notable physical chemist Györgyi Hevesy noticed it and showed it to Thannhauser, who showed it in turn to his assistant.[102] Hopkins's glowing words must have buoyed Krebs's spirits. To have his work selected by one of the most eminent biochemists in the world, especially by one noted for his broad vision of biochemistry, as the best example of promising new developments in the field, would be heady praise for any young investigator.

As his reputation grew abroad, Krebs was preparing at Freiburg for a major academic event. On December 9, in preparation for his habilitation as *Privatdozent*, he presented a public lecture on the subject "The Metabolism of Carcinoma Cells." Again he shared a stage with Franz Bielschowsky, who gave his habilitation lecture the same day, on "Forms of Disease Caused by Changes in Lipoid Metabolism."[103] Shortly afterward Krebs departed for Berlin to meet another lecture appointment.

Krebs traveled to Berlin by train, and was given a special room at Harnack House for the duration of his stay as guest of the Kaiser Wilhelm-Gesellschaft. His father traveled from Hildesheim to be present, along with his sister and her husband, who lived in Berlin. His former chief from Altona, Leo Lichtwitz, also came. The lecture began at 8:30 PM in Helmholtz Hall of Harnack House, and he delivered it to a large audience. After the lecture, invited guests joined Krebs for an informal reception and a "simple evening meal."[104]

Although Krebs's father may not have followed the technical details of the presentation, he was very pleased at the recognition his son was receiving, and he seemed finally convinced that Hans could make a successful career as a scientist. Most important of all to Krebs was the shift he sensed in Warburg's attitude. It seemed to him that Warburg had changed his mind fundamentally about him, and was now openly appreciative of his scientific ability. Whether Warburg had in fact been as skeptical about him before as Krebs imagined, or had only never expressed a positive opinion until then, to Krebs the event meant that he had proven to his mentor, at last, that he could do first-rate scientific work.[105]

During Krebs's stay in Berlin, Warburg invited him to a meal, at which he had the opportunity to discuss his work with Warburg at some length. Warburg acknowledged that he was particularly surprised and impressed by the discovery of the pathway of urea synthesis, because he had not believed that synthetic processes could be studied in isolated tissue slices.[106] Warburg must also have described for Krebs his own most recent achievement. Earlier in the year he had isolated from yeast an enzyme that was able, in the presence of a second enzyme and a co-enzyme, to catalyze the oxidation of the important metabolic substrate hexosemonophosphate. The new enzyme appeared yellowish red in solution in its oxidized form, and soon became known as the "yellow enzyme." The discovery was not only a landmark in the history of biochemistry, but marked the completion of a basic change in Warburg's outlook toward respiratory oxidation from what he had maintained so fiercely in the days when Krebs worked under his guidance. He had now abandoned both his belief in a single respiratory enzyme and his disbelief in the possibility that oxidative enzymes could be isolated from "living cells."[107]

Krebs went from Berlin to Hildesheim to visit his father, his stepmother Maria, and his 10-month old stepsister Gisela. He stayed at home only briefly. Aside from seeing the family, he had time to stroll through the town and enjoy the beauty of some of the streets that had meant so much to him as a child. On December 21 he was back in his laboratory in Freiburg.[108]

Warburg must have given Krebs a sample of the new yellow enzyme, because the first experiment Krebs carried out after he returned was to test the effect of the "Warburg enzyme" on the respiration of kidney tissue in the presence of alanine. There was, he noted, "with the enzyme *somewhat more O_2 consumed*!!!" The next day he repeated the experiment, using a kidney extract in place of tissue slices, and again observed a "sensible enzyme effect." The results were, however, too irregular in the extract, and he decided that he should return again to slices when he resumed the investigation. At the end of the day he closed down his operations for the Christmas holiday.[109]

VII

On December 14, the Dean of the Medical Faculty, Professor Eduard Rehn, addressed to the Ministry of Culture and Instruction of the state of Baden a letter, drafted by Thannhauser, in support of the recommendation that Krebs be

Figure 11.1 Hans Krebs in 1932.

appointed to the Faculty as a *Privatdozent*. Among the reasons cited in the letter were that:

> His recent scientific work, especially the paper on the synthesis of urea in the animal body, has established his international reputation. This paper is of fundamental importance, and will be regarded in the future as one of the classics of medical research. Dr. Krebs will therefore be a special asset to the teaching body of the Faculty.[110]

The Ministry approved "The habilitation of Dr. med. Hans Adolf Krebs into the Medical Faculty for the field of internal medicine" on December 22; and on the 28th the office of the Academic Rectorat informed "Herrn Privatdozent Dr. Hans Adolf Krebs" of his appointment.[111]

By the time that Krebs received this title, enabling him to teach within the Faculty of Medicine, he was no longer merely a promising young investigator, but a rising star in the international biochemical firmament. His theory of the synthesis of urea had, within a remarkably short period, won nearly universal acceptance as a discovery of the first magnitude. He had been invited to speak in the major research centers in the field in Germany, and his work had attracted admiring attention in the most important biochemistry school in Britain. Already his reputation had grown to the point where young biochemists were beginning to come to Freiburg to work with him. Very few aspiring investigators have had the good fortune to make the transition so swiftly from apprenticeship, through fledgling independent research, to established scientist.

* * *

It is easy to discern the characteristics of Krebs's theory of urea synthesis that made it appear immediately to his colleagues as a major discovery. Beforehand it was unexpected, yet afterward it appeared almost self-evident. It solved a problem that had frustrated many before Krebs, one that was generally recognized as a central problem in intermediary metabolism. Even though unanticipated, the solution fit all of the prevailing criteria for acceptable solutions to the general problem of filling in intermediary steps in metabolic pathways. The reactions involved were so convincing from a chemical standpoint, that a veteran in the field such as Franz Knoop could complain only that he had not thought of it long ago. The methods used to investigate the problem were well-proven ones, the novelty consisting mainly in the way Krebs had combined them to study the particular phenomenon in question. The test upon which Krebs had relied to demonstrate that the suspected intermediates were the actual ones was precisely the criterion that had become, over the preceding 20 years, a fundamental axiom in the field; that they must react at least as rapidly as the overall reaction of which they form a part. Thus, the theory of the "ornithine circuit" filled a well-recognized void in metabolic biochemistry, without challenging the established conceptions, procedures, or goals of the field. It solved a well-structured problem, with a solution that could be linked smoothly into the broader structure of that field. The discovery would seem to lie wholly within the bounds of a Kuhnian "normal science," challenging only Thomas Kuhn's own description of puzzle solving in normal science as "mopping up" operations. The discovery was in no sense revolutionary; yet to the science in which it occurred, it appeared as unprecedented, as surprising, and as freshly creative, as those discoveries that are sometimes thought to emerge only out of anomalies, crises, and breaks from paradigmatic patterns.[112]

It may appear less easy to explain why Hans Krebs was able to make such a discovery. A newcomer both to independent research and to the field of intermediary metabolism, Krebs seems to have brought to his chosen problem little more than two general methods that he had not originated, and a simple notion that he might apply them in an area that did not interest the person who had taught him to use them. His training in the methods of organic chemistry vital to success in this area was limited. He had not impressed his mentor with his capacity for original work, and was not certain of that capacity himself. His first efforts on his own were derivative, modest contributions. His only recourse seemed to be to test, in the tissue slice system he had inherited, all the ideas concerning intermediary pathways that he could unearth from the current literature. During his year at Altona, and his first months in Freiburg — even in the early stage of his work on urea synthesis — this approach seemed to yield little more than the confirmation or rejection of some reactions proposed by others. How then can we account for his stunning success?

In his autobiography, Krebs wrote, "On looking back I also feel that at the time I did not give due credit to the large slice of luck which contributed to the discovery."[113] There is little doubt that, during the course of his investigation Krebs had a very lucky break. No matter how we may account for the fact that he chose to test ornithine, it cannot be construed as an obvious thing to have tried during a systematic investigation of urea synthesis as the problem appeared when he took it up. The odds against including it by chance appear strong, and without the unexpected observation to which the choice of ornithine led, the investigation would most likely have terminated in a routine confirmation of the existing view.

Luck ended, however, with the observation. Krebs demonstrated his mettle in the way he exploited his break. It was not an immediate brilliant insight that led him on, for none occurred to him. The crucial factors were his conviction that the effect he had observed must be meaningful, and his persistence in searching until he found that meaning. Nor was this an isolated pattern in his research. As we have seen, each of the formative stages in his deamination investigation began also with an "unexpected" observation. It appears that Krebs was evolving a deliberate research strategy that involved pursuing obvious questions until something "turned up" to lift his investigation toward novel findings. The nature of this strategy was conducive to the kind of rhythm we have seen in his work at Freiburg. There were long stretches of routine, punctuated with relatively short — though not instantaneous — bursts of creative activity.

The strategy that Krebs followed was effective, in part because the methods that he had acquired from Warburg were particularly well suited to such an approach. The ease with which the tissue slice method permitted him to carry out many experiments multiplied the opportunities for the unexpected to occur. The precision of the manometric measurements made it relatively easy to detect the few anomalies that might arise during the course of numerous predictable readings.

This strategy was effective also, however, because Krebs himself possessed qualities of mind and of temperament that were well matched to it. He organized his life in general so as to keep moving onward at a steady pace in the midst of uncertainties he could not control. Despite the large and unpredictable demands of his medical duties on his time at Freiburg, he was able, with the aid of technicians, to maintain a regular schedule of experimentation. He preferred not to "haggle" with himself over whether any particular experiment was worth doing, but just to go ahead with it. Although he did not like to become bogged down in investigations that went nowhere, he could tolerate extended periods of relatively routine work. In part that may have been because he enjoyed routines. His daily habits were extraordinarily regular. His optimistic temperament allowed him to pursue a strategy based on confidence that unexpected leads really would turn up, and that they would guide him toward goals he could not foresee in advance. He could concentrate on one set of experiments after another, without planning in detail beyond the next day, because he always had hope that in so doing he would sooner or later come upon something important. During the periods in which nothing turned up, his approach might appear mundane, lacking in vision. It was in his response to the unexpected turns of events that, from the beginning of his independent career, Krebs displayed imagination of a high order. Creativity comes in diverse forms. Some of the most creative of scientists have been those whose minds range far ahead of their experiments, who spend much of their laboratory lives forcing from nature the data they require to validate what they have thought out in advance. Krebs illustrates a more reactive type of creativity: that of the investigator who bides his time while gathering data that he hopes will stimulate his mind and give direction to his thought. Both forms can be conducive to highly original achievements.

Krebs did not, however, achieve his success entirely by himself, for his accomplishments took place within a particular environment. Because he tended to find suggestive ideas in the formal literature, rather than in conversations with his associates, he was less dependent than many scientists are on local institutional frameworks to give specific direction to his work. When he went from one setting to another, as from Altona to Freiburg, his research program continued on the same general lines as before (and that continuity became still more pronounced in his later moves). Yet he clearly did draw benefits from his surroundings, and in particular from the qualities of his successive chiefs. Warburg provided him with methods, a style and standard of research, at the cost of overshadowing him and sometimes discouraging his ambitions. At Altona, Lichtwitz gave him the personal support that enabled him to launch his research enterprise even in an environment in which no one else was engaged in research. Thannhauser played a role that may have been more important than Krebs realized. Although an accomplished scientist, Thannhauser did not have the stature of Warburg, and did not exert a comparable intellectual influence on his assistant. Thannhauser gave Krebs, however, exactly what Warburg had withheld — his confidence, and the freedom to carry on research in directions of Krebs's own choice. Instead of exploiting Krebs's talents to advance his own position, Thannhauser nurtured and protected the young man's career; and when Krebs succeeded, Thannhauser made his success known to the scientists to whom it mattered. In a sense Thannhauser freed Krebs to make the best possible use of what Warburg had taught him.

What effect did his meteoric rise have upon Krebs himself? In his autobiography he wrote,

> The responses to my research efforts were very encouraging. I clearly recall thinking "If this is what the world of science considers good work, then let me have the tools and the time and I will produce more of it."[114]

In conversation Krebs had given, in 1976, a more spontaneous, and, in my opinion, more forceful expression of the same general recollection:

> I got plenty of recognition, and one thought which certainly was on my mind was that if this is the kind of work you want, please give me the tools and I'll try to do some more, and I think I also had the self-confidence that this had come so easily that I could produce more work of this quality.[115]

Despite the long time interval involved, these variations on the same theme most likely do recapture an approximation of thoughts that Krebs actually did have during those months of 1932 when recognition was showering down on him. We can also be certain, however, that his reactions were more complex than what is explicitly contained in these statements. The statements raise as many questions about his feelings as they answer. Although it is clear that he might have increased his research effort if he had more time released from his clinical responsibilities, it is less obvious why he felt himself lacking the "tools" he needed. Certainly his budget was tight, but that could hardly have been unusual in the straitened economic conditions of the time. For a scientist at his stage in his career, he enjoyed exceptional research facilities, support, and assistance.

There is also a suggestive ambiguity in Krebs's feeling that his discovery had come easily. Was he finding out that he was capable of doing very high level work with ease, or was he learning that science itself was apparently not as hard to do as he had imagined? Was the lesson that he was better than he had thought, or that the standards he had to meet were lower than he had thought? We can perceive here, as well, ambivalence about whether he strove to satisfy himself or to please others. Did he *know* that he had done good work, or did good work mean to him the kind of work that the arbiters of his field "wanted"? Since there is no way to penetrate further into the mind of the Hans Krebs of 1932, such questions must be left open. In any case, none of the answers, if we had access to them, would probably turn out to be simple. They suggest instead the subtlety of the interplay between autonomy and dependence on the approval of one's peers, with which any aspiring young scientist must contend.

Nothing in Krebs's outward behavior indicates that his sudden prominence markedly altered his personality, his activities, or his aims. Nevertheless, so rapid a transition from the period of self-doubt that had begun with his involuntary departure from Warburg's laboratory must have had deeper inward effects than he recalled four decades later. Quick early success carries risks as well as benefits. We have no evidence that Krebs worried much about either effect. Accustomed to concentrating on the present, he went on as he had before. It appears, however, that from this point onward he never seriously doubted his capacity to continue doing first-rate scientific work.

12

The Brief Life of a
School of Intermediary Metabolism

As his research flourished during 1932, Hans Krebs began to draw aspiring young investigators into his laboratory. One of the first to come was Theodor Benzinger. Born in Stuttgart in 1905, Benzinger studied science at the University of Tübingen, and obtained his PhD there in 1927, with a thesis in descriptive geology. Just as he was completing his degree, he had a change of heart, and under the influence of a friend who was studying medicine, he decided to become a physician. Beginning again at Tübingen, he finished his medical studies in Berlin, in 1931. On the advice of another friend, he sought and obtained a position as private assistant to Siegfried Thannhauser. Benzinger must have arrived at Freiburg not long before Krebs came there. One day, while he was looking through a window into the courtyard of the old building of the internal medicine clinic, Benzinger noticed a truck containing some boxes, and a slender young man in a white laboratory coat supervising their unloading. Benzinger went out and asked what was in the boxes. The man in the white coat answered that they contained Warburg apparatuses. Benzinger asked him if he knew Warburg, and received the reply, "Yes, I come from him." In response to further questioning, Hans Krebs explained that he was going to work in Thannhauser's clinic, and would use the Warburg apparatus there.[1]

A year later, Benzinger was again finding himself attracted to science. By then the scientist he had met in the old courtyard had made a major discovery, and his stature was rapidly rising within the internal medicine clinic. Benzinger went to Krebs to ask if he could accept him as a worker in his laboratory. The accommodating Thannhauser allowed Benzinger to give up the private ward for which he had been responsible, so that he would have the time. After pondering for a while about what Benzinger might do, Krebs asked him if he would like to work on the problem of uric acid synthesis in birds, the physiological equivalent of the synthesis of urea in mammals. Although it was recognized that the synthesis of uric acid must be a more complicated process, mainly because the structure of uric acid was itself more complicated than that of urea,

Figure 12.1 Theodor Benzinger

Krebs thought that the same methods that had worked so well in the study of urea synthesis might reveal something about the sources of uric acid.[2]

As in the case of urea, there was a widely accepted theory of uric acid synthesis in birds, the origin of which went back to the late nineteenth century. In 1886 Oskar Minkowski had carried out the fundamental experiment on which all subsequent theories were built. After extirpating the liver of a goose, Minkowski found that the uric acid excreted fell to 3.6 percent of the total nitrogen metabolized, whereas the quantity of ammonia excreted rose by 50 to 60 percent. The inference that he and others drew was that birds synthesize uric acid from ammonia in the liver. Minkowski, and most of those who came after him, thought that urea formed an intermediate step in the synthesis. They derived this idea from the structural formula of uric acid, which could be viewed as made up of two molecules of urea joined through a three-membered carbon chain.

Birds were assumed to form urea in the same way as mammals do, but then to carry out additional steps that mammals cannot perform. The question then arose, what was the source of the additional three-carbon atoms?   Initial suggestions were that it might be lactic acid, an obvious choice given the prominence of that substance in current theories of metabolism. In 1902, Hugo Wiener sought to identify the compound by injecting subcutaneously, into a chicken, urea simultaneously with various three-carbon compounds. He obtained the largest increases in the formation of uric acid when he employed the three-carbon dicarboxylic acids, malonic acid ($COOHCH_2COOH$), tartronic acid ($COOHCHOHCOOH$), and mesoxalic acid ($COOHCOCOOH$).   From these results, Wiener concluded that the most likely pathway for uric acid synthesis was:

(1)
$$
\begin{array}{ccccc}
NH_2 & & COOH & & NH-CO \\
| & & | & & |\qquad| \\
CO & + & CHOH & = & CO\quad CHOH \quad + \quad 2H_2O \\
| & & | & & |\qquad| \\
NH_2 & & COOH & & NH-CO \\
\end{array}
$$

Urea Tartronic acid Dialuric acid

(2)
$$
\begin{array}{c}
NH-CO \qquad H_2N \\
|\qquad| \qquad\qquad \searrow \\
CO\quad CHOH \;+ \qquad CO \; = \\
|\qquad| \qquad\qquad \nearrow \\
NH-CO \qquad H_2N \\
\end{array}
\qquad
\begin{array}{c}
NH-CO \\
|\qquad| \\
CO\quad C-HN \\
|\qquad| \qquad\quad CO \;+\; 2H_2O \\
NH-C-HN \\
\end{array}
$$

      Urea   Uric acid

Wiener's theory was generally accepted during the next three decades. In 1930, however, Antonino Clementi cast doubt on it by showing that when urea is injected into birds in such a manner that it cannot be decomposed by urease in the intestine, it does not cause an increase in the quantity of uric acid excreted.[3] That was the situation at the time that Krebs suggested the problem for Benzinger to investigate with the tissue slice method.

Although he had had some training in chemical analysis, Benzinger found himself a novice in the methods of a biochemical laboratory. Krebs had to teach him all the basic procedures he would use, starting from the proper way to wash glassware. Nonetheless, whether it was because of Benzinger's prior scientific experience, because he had completed his formal medical studies, or because of some other intuition about his personal abilities, Krebs gave Benzinger from the start more independence in carrying out the research than he had given Henseleit. Although Krebs "designed" the investigative strategy, he carried out no preliminary experiments of his own at formative phases of the work. He would suggest how to approach each major step, and then leave it to Benzinger to make his ideas work.

Benzinger started work sometime in early or mid-summer of 1932. It seems evident that Krebs intended for him to imitate closely the plan that had been successful for urea. As a first step, therefore, he instructed Benzinger to try to develop a manometric method for determining uric acid, utilizing an enzymatic reaction analogous to the reaction of urease on urea. To obtain the enzyme, Benzinger ground up swine kidney tissue. When he incubated the preparation with uric acid, the latter rapidly decomposed, absorbing oxygen. Oxygen continued to be consumed, however, even after the uric acid was gone. Thinking that he simply had to purify the enzyme further, Benzinger made many fruitless attempts to do so, feeling increasingly desperate about his inability to achieve the desired result. Finally, Krebs concluded there was no way to eliminate other enzymes that catalyze competing reactions, and Benzinger had to retreat to the standard colorimetric determination of uric acid of Folin, using phosphotungstic acid.[4]

The strategy that had succeeded for urea ran into further trouble at the next stage of the investigation. In the first place, Benzinger found it much harder to locate and remove the very small liver of a pigeon, and to make slices from it, than to do so with a rat liver. When he had managed that, he followed the procedure that Krebs had previously followed, placing the liver slices in physiological salt solution with ammonia and a carbohydrate added to the medium. At the end of the run, he could find no uric acid in the medium. Day after day he tried the experiment, without ever obtaining a trace of uric acid. So certain was he that the fault was his own, that Benzinger found it hard to admit these results to Krebs. Unperturbed, Krebs merely encouraged Benzinger to go on trying. "There must be something wrong with the analysis," he said, but "I don't know what it is." Feeling again that he just could not do anything right, and that Krebs was patient with him only out of kindness, Benzinger began to lose sleep at night. Finally he decided that, if the bird could make uric acid, but liver tissue could not, some other organ must do it. He started slicing up all of the tissues in the pigeon body, including even brain, muscle, and bone marrow. Nothing happened. Counting himself as lost, he now thought in desperation, if the bird can do it but no organ can do it, then it must take more than one organ to do it. Afraid even to tell Krebs what he was doing this time, Benzinger began testing all kinds of combinations of slices from different tissues. After many unsuccessful tries, he suddenly obtained an abundance of uric acid. The combination that did it was liver and kidney tissue.[5]

Benzinger achieved this first success in his investigation during the month of August, possibly after Krebs had left for the summer vacation described in the preceding chapter. Thannhauser was planning to lecture on "The Chemical Actions of the Normal Liver in the Processes of Intermediary Metabolism," at a meeting of scientists and physicians in Wiesbaden. Elated by his accomplishment, Benzinger told Thannhauser that it might be of interest for his lecture, that "we have done the *in vitro* synthesis of uric acid on pigeons, and that it is done in two steps. The first step is done in the liver, and the second step is done in the kidneys."[6] Thannhauser was very interested. In his lecture, he gave a lengthy description of Krebs's work on urea synthesis, then turned to deal with the possible objection that birds, whose liver does not contain arginase, nevertheless synthesize urea as a stage in the formation of uric acid.

> From a still incomplete investigation carried out by H.A. Krebs jointly with Benzinger, one can already say that the objection that birds would have to be capable of making urea without arginase, is not relevant. According to this investigation, the mechanism of uric acid formation in the bird liver is completely different. For the completion of the synthesis of uric acid in the bird it appears that not only the liver, but also the kidneys, have a role to play. Urea does not appear as an intermediate product.[7]

Thannhauser was thus rejecting the theory of uric acid formation, described earlier, that went back to Minkowski. By the time Thannhauser delivered this lecture, Benzinger must have tested whether the addition of urea to combined liver and kidney slices would increase the rate of formation of uric acid, with negative results.

When Krebs heard about Thannhauser's talk he was not pleased. To Benzinger he complained, "Why did you tell this to the chief? He understands nothing about it" ["*Warum erzählen Sie das den Chef? Der versteht doch nichts davon*"].[8] Whether or not his remark betrays a skepticism about his chief's powers of comprehension that he did not elsewhere acknowledge, Krebs was probably annoyed not because Thannhauser had got anything wrong in his brief summary, but because he thought it premature to disclose publicly such preliminary results.

During October Benzinger continued measurements of the uric acid formed by combined pigeon liver and kidney slices. The results were, however, irregular, ranging from $Q = 0$ to $Q = 4$. He attributed part of the problem to the fact that the relative quantities of liver and kidney tissue present were not constant. Early in November Krebs advised him to try another bird. Using tissue slices from a chicken, Benzinger encountered another surprise. The necessity for both kidney and liver tissue was apparently not general, but a special characteristic of the metabolism of pigeons. Chicken liver slices were capable of producing uric acid by themselves. From then on, he worked with chicken liver. On November 8 he compared the rates when the slices were in physiological salt solution to the rates when they were in water. From the fact that uric acid formed only in the former case, he concluded that its formation is a "vital process." On November 13 he began testing the effects of adding substances to the medium, especially NH_4Cl, and other substances in combination with NH_4Cl. Again repeating the pattern that Krebs had followed in the urea investigation, Benzinger started with amino acids — serine, aspartic acid, glutamic acid, lysine, phenylalanine, proline, and oxyproline — and found them all to be without effect. "A catalytic action of these amino acids," he concluded, "can be ruled out." During the next 2 weeks he found that ammonia added to liver slices from nourished chickens increased the formation of uric acid, but decreased the rate in the case of slices from starved chickens; that urea caused no increase; that lactate, glucose, and pyruvate plus ammonia substantially raised the rate; and that the three-carbon dicarboxylic acids, malonic, tartronic, and mesoxalic acid, thought to provide the carbon backbone holding the uric acid molecule together, either had no effect, or inhibited the formation. A few other substances he tried, such as glucosamine, guanidine, and α-ketoglutaric acid, had little or no action.[9]

By this time Benzinger was racing against time. Due to the economic depression, he was in a financially precarious situation, and he found that he could no longer continue without an income. Thannhauser was unwilling to give him a paid position, but arranged one for him in the *Medizinische Poliklinik* of the University of Koenigsberg. At the Christmas holiday Benzinger had to break off his experiments, pack up and leave for East Prussia. He did not even have time to write up his results, but took his data along with him to put in order, so that he could later send them to Krebs.[10]

During the 6 months that Benzinger worked under Krebs's supervision on uric acid synthesis, he had not had the good fortune to encounter an equivalent of the ornithine effect. Beyond confirming that birds can synthesize uric acid from ammonia, he had found no clues to the reactions involved. What he had accomplished was to refute a theory that had been around for 30 years, according to which urea and a three-carbon dicarboxylic acid combine to form the uric acid. Instead of solving a problem, he had made an old solution untenable, and thereby opened up the problem for a fresh attack.

For Benzinger himself, the experimental results he had obtained were less important than the experience of working under Hans Krebs. Impulsive, uncertain of himself, and easily disheartened, Benzinger was sustained by the calm, steady manner of his mentor. He felt that Krebs was warmly supportive, and infinitely patient with him. Even when Benzinger broke one of the precious Warburg manometers that Krebs had brought with him to Freiburg, Krebs did not seem to mind. Benzinger saw Krebs as a man possessing a very special serenity. Krebs had, in Benzinger's view, a "deep inside conviction that if the problem can be solved, and the methods are there, and the time is here for it, then he will succeed in doing it." He did not, therefore, have to worry about small setbacks, or periods in which the scientific problems in front of him appeared recalcitrant.[11]

Another assistant to Thannhauser who came into Krebs's orbit was Heinz Fuld. After completing an MD at Heidelberg, Fuld came to Freiburg in 1931 to fulfill his obligatory year of hospital training. At the end of that time, he applied successfully for a supernumerary clinical assistantship, and, like Benzinger, was put in charge of private patients of Thannhauser in the hospital wards. In this role Fuld attended the weekly meetings of the scientists and physicians of Thannhauser's internal medicine clinic at which members of the staff gave short talks in their respective areas of interest. It seemed to Fuld that the two obvious leaders within this group were Hans Krebs and Franz

Bielschowsky.   On scientific matters, Krebs appeared to Fuld to be the outstanding person in the group, and his opinions were taken as authoritative. Fuld and others regarded Krebs as intellectually more impressive than their chief.[12]

Fuld did not have aspirations for a scientific career, but he hoped to enter academic medicine, and was interested in gaining some research experience. Krebs, who was always keen to find clinical applications for his scientific investigations, saw that if his theories of urea synthesis and amino acid deamination were correct, it might be possible to detect an increase in the ammonia content of the blood of patients with liver diseases. This was because ammonia produced in the kidneys must be transported through the blood to the liver to be consumed there in the formation of urea. If the liver were failing, then some of the ammonia should accumulate in the blood. Because such a project would be particularly suitable for a person like Fuld, whose ultimate objectives were clinical, Krebs asked him if he would like to try it.[13]

Fuld probably began in Krebs's laboratory during the fall of 1932.   Krebs had to teach him all of the basic methods, including the use of the Warburg apparatus and the Parnas–Heller method for determining ammonia.   While learning to perform the latter, Fuld obtained some anomalous results. Krebs told him he had either calculated wrong, or there was ammonia contaminating the atmosphere. Fuld was surprised to learn how careful he had to be to avoid all possibilities for traces of ammonia to enter the room.[14] His experience was a common one for newcomers to this type of determination.

After modifying the Parnas–Heller procedures slightly for his purposes, Fuld measured the ammonia content of the blood of 13 healthy people, and found that it ranged from 0.02 to 0.06 mg/100 ml. He then began testing the blood of patients with kidney diseases, liver diseases, and various other illnesses. Often Krebs directed him to patients in his own ward who were suitable subjects, including severe alcoholics in liver coma. For his normal controls, Fuld drew his own blood. He was able to show that in cirrhosis of the liver and other diseases with liver involvement, the levels of blood ammonia were consistently above normal.   He concluded that the Parnas method to determine blood ammonia could   provide a useful supplementary clinical method for diagnosis and prognosis in liver disorders.[15]

When this work was completed, Krebs suggested another, more experimental project to Fuld. He should produce nephritis in rats by injecting cantharadine into the animals, and investigate the effects upon the deamination of amino acids in slices made from their kidneys. This research problem was a by-product of Krebs's theory that acidosis in kidney failure results from the inability of the diseased organ to carry out the deamination process. Fuld took up the plan.[16]

Like Benzinger, Fuld found Krebs inspiring to work for. Krebs seemed to him a remarkably independent person, who always knew where he was headed, had a wide grasp of biochemical problems, and was fertile in ideas for research. He explained carefully what needed to be done, was even-tempered and patient. With Fuld, too, Krebs suggested all the important steps in the investigation, then left him to work them out, checking each day to see what results he had obtained. He did not hesitate to point out Fuld's mistakes, even to call his results "nonsense" on occasion, but he did so in a tactful manner that caused no annoyance. A methodical man himself, Fuld particularly admired Krebs's discipline, the strict way in which he organized his time, the regularity of his habits. As a clinician, Fuld appreciated that Krebs looked after his patients with as much care as he looked after his laboratory work. As an avid skier and hiker, Fuld noticed with pleasure that Krebs too participated enthusiastically in these outdoor activities. To Fuld, Krebs was a natural leader, who attracted both the respect and the friendship of those around him.[17]

Near the end of 1932, the first person to come to Freiburg for the express purpose of working with Krebs arrived in his laboratory. Pawel Ostern, only 2 years younger than Krebs, had been born in Poland, and studied medicine at the University of Lwow. In 1927 he joined the staff of the distinguished Polish biochemist Jakob Parnas. Although he had had no previous chemical training, he proved himself extraordinarily gifted at carrying out difficult chemical investigations. While he was there he devised methods for obtaining inosinic and adenylic acid on a large scale from muscle tissue. Parnas, who had met Krebs in 1929 at the International Congress in Boston, and who was very impressed with his work in urea synthesis when it appeared, suggested that Ostern spend some time with Krebs. Ostern had received a Rockefeller Research grant that enabled him to move freely from one laboratory to another. Krebs quickly recognized that Ostern was a very able, hard-working scientist, and gave him a special analytical problem to solve.[18]

In his ongoing research on the deamination of amino acids, Krebs had found a growing need for better methods to determine the α-keto acids produced, in the very small quantities that arose during tissue slice experiments. For the case of aspartic acid, the deamination product was oxaloacetic acid. A method for oxaloacetic acid would also have broader usefulness in metabolic studies because of its place in the well known reaction sequence:

succinic acid $\rightarrow$ fumaric acid $\rightarrow$ malic acid $\rightarrow$ oxaloacetic acid.

For this purpose, Krebs followed his customary strategy to look for a reaction, specific to the substance in question, one of whose products could be measured manometrically in the Warburg apparatus. Looking up oxaloacetic acid ($HOOCCOCH_2COOH$) in the standard Beilstein reference work on organic reactions, he found that the compound reacts with aniline ($C_6H_5NH_2$), releasing CO_2. He then asked Ostern to see if a suitable method could be based on this reaction. Ostern worked out a very satisfactory one. The reaction was quantitative, although the spontaneous decomposition of oxaloacetic acid to pyruvic acid and carbon dioxide prevented one from obtaining 100 percent yields under physiological conditions. The determination was specific, because no other α-keto acid tested reacted with aniline, except for acetoacetic acid, which reacted much more slowly. With it Ostern could determine 0.1 to 2 mg of oxaloacetate with an accuracy of a few percent.[19] The development of such methods was vital to Krebs as he sought to expand the range of metabolic reactions that he could study quantitatively in tissue slice experiments.

Medical students continued to come to carry out research projects for their MD theses. Krebs was increasingly in a position to give these inexperienced investigators simple problems using methods that were now routine in his laboratory. One of them, Hildegard Manderscheid, examined whether the reactions of urea synthesis that Krebs had discovered in the mammalian liver also take place in other vertebrates. As the criterion for the occurrence of these reactions, she relied on the single test of whether ornithine added to the medium of liver tissue slices increased the rate of urea synthesis. For amphibians (a frog) and for reptiles (a turtle), she found that it did, whereas for a freshwater fish she could find no measurable synthesis of urea in the liver.[20]

In December 1932, Krebs's old friend Hermann Blaschko, who had fallen ill with tuberculosis, came, at Krebs's urging, to Freiburg to convalesce. Although Blaschko was placed in the ward of another physician, Krebs helped to care for him, and Blaschko stayed in Freiburg during the first months of 1933. While he was there he was greatly impressed with the working conditions that Krebs enjoyed. His laboratory was large and beautifully equipped, and the atmosphere in Thannhauser's clinic seemed very good.[21] Krebs's laboratory was then the scene of bustling activity, even when he was not personally present. While two or three junior investigators pursued projects he had suggested to them, his technicians were carrying out the manual operations for his own experiments. Every morning at 8 AM, Krebs did the rounds of his hospital wards and saw new patients. Then he came into the laboratory to give instructions to his technicians, and to discuss with the others the work they had done the day before. After lunch he returned to the laboratory whenever he was not on the wards, and after supper he was often in the laboratory again until 10 PM.[22]

At the beginning of 1933, therefore, Krebs was no longer a lone investigator, but the head of a small research group. He had the facilities necessary for several people to work with him, and promising young investigators were taking advantage of that opportunity. He possessed a distinctive experimental approach, and methods that other bright young scientists could best learn by spending time with him. His growing reputation gave promise that more would come in the future. His own investigative experience was now extensive enough so that he had a surplus of ideas for subsidiary investigations that he could suggest to the people who did. He was proving to be an able leader and mentor for those who wished to learn from him. Although his new academic status as a *Privatdozent* gave him no authority or resources of his own, leaving him still dependent on Thannhauser's support, he had clearly established his scientific autonomy in Freiburg through the force of his personality and his accomplishments. It appeared, in fact, that he was well on the way toward creating an incipient school of intermediary metabolism.[23]

I

The standing that Hans Krebs had attained within the biochemical community by the beginning of 1933 was reflected in a letter that Carl Neuberg wrote in January in response to a request that he recommend candidates for a chair in physiological chemistry at the University of Munster. After listing four people, each of whom had had "noteworthy successes," and suggesting that if a chemist was suitable Karl Lohmann should be considered, Neuberg continued:

> With the exception of Lohmann, I consider Privatdozent Dr. med. et phil. Krebs, of Freiburg, superior to all others. His brilliant and systematic work on the urea cycle has put him in the foremost ranks of our younger colleagues. Recently I heard him give a lecture that was outstanding for its clarity, precision, breadth of knowledge, and adroitness. He combines with his high qualities as an investigator the capacity also to be an outstanding teacher.[24]

Biochemists were not only greatly impressed with Krebs's work on urea, but accepted without serious question that the reactions he had discovered constituted the physiological metabolic pathway. A few individuals, whose backgrounds were medical or physiological, dissented from that judgment. One of them was a physician named Hach, in Thannhauser's own clinic. In a conversation with Krebs, Hach once said to him that he was reluctant to believe in these reactions, because the fact that tissue slices can carry them out does not mean that the whole animal does it that way. This criticism only irritated Krebs. He considered it a very silly view that one could cause a complex, synthetic process to occur within living tissues by slicing through them with a razor blade.[25]

Hach's criticism was merely an idle comment. It was not silly, however, to try to confirm the reactions of urea synthesis by experiments on intact animals. That is what Efim Semenovich London set out to do in Leningrad, at the beginning of 1933. A physiologist in the Section for General Pathological Metabolism of the Institute for Experimental Medicine, London had been involved in nutritional studies since the beginning of the century. He had been an assistant to Emil Abderhalden in some of the feeding experiments that had confirmed that fully hydrolyzed proteins can meet the nitrogenous nutritional requirements of animals. Later he spent years perfecting the method of "angiostomosis;" that is, of affixing cannulas permanently to various arteries and veins of a dog or rabbit in such a way that he could afterward withdraw samples of blood at frequent intervals from several points in the circulation. He used these techniques particularly to study the intermediary metabolism of proteins, fats, carbohydrates, and nucleic acids. By comparing the chemical composition of the blood, for example, obtained from an artery, from the portal vein, and from the hepatic vein, he hoped to detect the changes these substances undergo as they are absorbed through the intestinal wall and as they pass through the liver.[26] London's techniques can be viewed as a twentieth-century refinement of the approach Claude Bernard had advocated a half century before — to penetrate into the internal environments of living animals to follow the changes that nutritional substances undergo as they pass through the organism.[27]

London and his associates applied this method to the study of the changes amino acids undergo in the liver. They could not hope to detect the conversions that occurred to specific amino acids, because of the minuteness of the quantities present in their blood samples, but by comparing the total concentration of amino and imino nitrogen in the blood drawn from the portal vein with that from the hepatic vein, they inferred, during the late 1920s, that about one third of the free amino acids are converted to peptides. Finding the urea concentration higher in the hepatic vein, they concluded that another portion of the amino acids is deaminated, and that the resulting ammonia is the source of the urea. Their results fit into the general picture already provided by the perfusion experiments with isolated livers. London believed that limitations in the scope of their chemical analyses by comparison to those possible with the perfusion methods — they were limited to measuring concentrations rather than absolute quantities of substances entering or leaving an organ, and their blood samples represented only small fractions of the quantity that passed through — were compensated for by the advantages of examining metabolic processes within healthy, intact animals.[28]

With this background, London was naturally interested in Krebs's discoveries concerning the synthesis of urea in the liver. He had probably read the preliminary *Klinische Wochenschrift* articles when they appeared; but since the recent issues of *Hoppe-Seyler's Zeitschrift* were not available to him in Leningrad, he could not read the detailed description that Krebs published there until Krebs himself sent London a reprint, probably near the end of 1932 (whether in response to a request from London is not clear). On January 2, 1933, London wrote to thank Krebs, calling his investigation "beautiful and penetrating." He went on,

> It seems to me appropriate to test your discovery made with tissue slices on angiostomized dogs, in which the metabolism can be followed under entirely normal conditions. The situation is, however, that under present circumstances we are dependent upon chemicals sent to us from foreign countries.
>   Is it possible to receive some ornithine and citrulline in this way?[29]

There is no record of whether or not Krebs sent London any ornithine or citrulline. Given his attitude toward the question in general, however, he was probably not very sympathetic to the idea that his discovery should be tested under "normal conditions." At any rate, for some time he heard nothing further about what London was doing.

II

Krebs recommenced his personal research after the Christmas holidays with a group of experiments that appear unrelated to the line of investigation he had previously been following. On January 3 he measured the anaerobic formation of carbon dioxide and pyruvic acid in rat kidney and Jensen sarcoma slices, without addition and with three concentrations of acetaldehyde. No pyruvate appeared under any of these conditions, and at the higher concentrations acetaldehyde inhibited the glycolysis. The next day he again examined the anaerobic formation of pyruvic acid, this time in rat liver and sarcoma tissue. He compared the situation with no addition to that in the presence of α-ketoglutoric acid and of methylene blue. In the liver α-ketoglutarate increased the rate of glycolysis, probably, as he thought, because it was itself slowly fermented; and methylene blue also caused an increase. Still, no pyruvic acid formed in any of these anaerobic situations.[30]

The final experiment that Krebs carried out in this group was to measure the effects of acetate and succinate on the respiration of rat kidney and liver tissue. The results were:

		No addition	Succinate (200 mg/100 ml)	Acetate (200 mg/100 ml)
Liver Q	=	-12.7	-20.5	-18.8
Kidney	=	-21.9	-49.7	-21.1

Succinate, he noted, raised the respiration in both liver and kidney, whereas acetate did so only in liver.[31]

Krebs's motivations for carrying out this short series of experiments probably came from two directions. The focus on pyruvic acid may have reflected a growing interest in the special metabolic properties of that substance, long known, but that were impressing themselves on him more emphatically the more he encountered pyruvic acid in his own research. Benzinger, who had been working with Krebs during the preceding months, has recalled, "He became increasingly interested in pyruvate as a metabolite. I think he found at that time that it was extremely reactive — more so than glucose or lactic acid or the other things. And he had a feeling that it was somewhere in the middle, and all keto acids became of major interest to him."[32]

The other inducement to do these experiments was probably a routine writing task that Krebs had to carry out. He had been asked to prepare, for a new supplementary volume of Oppenheimer's *Handbuch der Biochemie*, an article on the "rates of respiration and of glycolysis in living cells." To do so, he must have had to undertake a massive review of the literature, as the bibliography he included in his article contained 321 references. Systematically he surveyed the measured values that numerous biochemists, mainly following the basic methods introduced by Warburg, had obtained for every type of tissue. In this portion of the article he provided 18 tables showing the aerobic and anaerobic rates of oxygen consumption, and anaerobic rate of carbon dioxide formation. Then he turned to the influence on such rates of various factors, such as temperature, medium, substrates, activators, and inhibitors. He included his own earlier experiments on the effects of amino acids, but drew most of the data from the contemporary work of others. Each of the experiments that he performed at the beginning of January can be seen to be inspired in part by the reading that he did in preparation for this article. Acetaldehyde, which he employed in the first experiment, had recently been shown by Otto Rosenthal to be an activator for glycolysis in rat liver slices. Methylene blue, Krebs described as a long-known activator of respiration. The experiment on acetate and succinate found its way into his article, following a description of those substrates — carbohydrates, lactate, ketoacids, and amino acids — that were recognized to cause the respiration to increase. In a paragraph on "Further Respiration-Raising Substrates," he pointed out:

> The substances which occur physiologically have not all been systematically investigated with respect to their effects on the rate of cell respiration. Many substances do not alter the rate of respiration of tissues, although they are oxidized in these cells, as in the case of some fatty acids (propionic and valeric acid), citric acid, glycerol, pyrimidine (l.c. 23 [a reference to his "own unpublished measurements"]). It is to be assumed, however, that with more exact investigations, many other substances will be found that increase the respiration. According to my own experiments (l.c. 23), acetate (1.5×10^{-2} M) increases the respiration of rat liver by about 60%, succinate (10^{-2} M) the respiration of rat liver and kidney by more than 100%.[33]

Perhaps at the time he performed the single experiment on acetate and succinate reported in this review article, Krebs already had in mind that he might himself carry out some of those "more exact experiments" to find other substances that increase the respiration. If so, however, he was not ready to begin. He returned instead to his long-standing deamination research.

From January 7 to the 27th, Krebs must have had more time than usual for his own research. He carried out experiments on 17 of those 20 days. Most of them were similar to those he had already done. His desire to include data for many amino acids provided a practically unlimited domain for systematic application of the procedures he had previously established. Among a few more novel experiments he carried out during this period, were two in which he added hemin and alanine to kidney slices, to test whether the amino acid could be deaminated in the absence of molecular oxygen if an alternative hydrogen acceptor were available. He obtained no definite effect. On January 16 he attempted to reverse the deamination reaction, adding pyruvate and lactate to liver and kidney slices, in the presence of ammonia, to see whether amino acids would be synthesized. The outcome was encouraging. "NH3 for the most part consumed!!," and "Much amino-N formed in kidneys + pyruvate + lactate," as well as in liver tissue, were the principal results he noted. This was a promising lead, but Krebs did not follow it. It remained an isolated observation in the midst of a series of experiments otherwise devoted to the deamination reaction itself.[34]

On January 24, Benzinger wrote from Koenigsberg, sending the experimental protocols he had finally been able to organize, together with a typewritten report of the results of his uric acid investigation. In straightforward style, he summarized the historical background leading to the current theory, then the experiments he had carried out that had proven that neither urea nor the dicarboxylic acids were intermediates. Then he went on to describe systematically examples of each of the types of experiment he had performed. His draft was 18 pages long, and included 15 tables. In his covering letter he asked Krebs to show the manuscript to Thannhauser as a way to account for his activities in the laboratory. He reported that he hoped to obtain a grant to continue his research; but that there was little interest in it in Koenigsberg, therefore, he had to be patient. When Krebs received the paper, he decided that the work already completed was publishable, but that the paper should be rewritten in tighter form. He intended to revise it himself, but apparently put the task off for some later time.[35]

During January 1933 Krebs also became interested in a theory of fatty acid decomposition that had been proposed during the previous year by the Dutch biochemist Pieter Verkade. With his associates at the Nederlandsche Handels-Hoogeschool in Rotterdam, Verkade had been testing earlier claims that the feeding of fats containing uneven-numbered fatty acids to diabetics could diminish acidosis, because, in accord with the β-oxidation theory, they could not give rise to the even-numbered carbon compounds leading to the ketone bodies. He and another member of his group put themselves on diets during which they substituted, for a portion of the normal fat component, a synthetic fat composed of the pure unsaturated C_{11}-fatty acid, undecanoic acid. Among the excretory products that they isolated from their urine was the corresponding dicarboxylic acid. This result proved "for the first time," in their view, that "the human organism is able to oxidize the end methyl group of undecanoic acid to a carboxyl group."

$$
\begin{array}{ccc}
CH_3 & & COOH \\
| & & | \\
(CH_2)_9 & \longrightarrow & (CH_2)_9 \\
| & & | \\
COOH & & COOH
\end{array}
$$

By analogy with the β-oxidation notation of Knoop, Verkade called this reaction "ω-oxidation." He assumed that the reaction was generalizable to other fatty acids, and that it provided a hitherto unknown pathway by which, during the first phase of their metabolic decomposition, the fatty acids are converted to dicarboxylic acids. He published this conclusion in preliminary form in the Proceedings of the Royal Dutch Academy of Sciences, indicating that his group was continuing the investigation and would put forth more details in a forthcoming article.[36]

Whether he saw Verkade's article, or learned about the work indirectly, Krebs was attracted to the theory, because it appeared to him that Verkade "was the first person to have found a new principle of fatty acid oxidation" since the original β-oxidation theory.[37] He wrote Verkade for a reprint and for further information on their results.   On January 26, Verkade responded to both requests.   In his letter he wrote out the reaction as a general, and extended scheme:

$$CH_3 \quad \xrightarrow{\text{``}\omega\text{-oxidation''}} \quad COOH \quad \xrightarrow[\beta\text{-oxidation}]{\text{Double-ended}} \quad \text{Lower dicarboxylic}$$
$$| \qquad\qquad\qquad\qquad | \qquad\qquad\qquad\qquad\qquad \text{acids}$$
$$(CH_2)_n \qquad\qquad\qquad (CH_2)_n$$
$$| \qquad\qquad\qquad\qquad |$$
$$COOH \qquad\qquad\qquad COOH$$

They had now isolated from the urine, after feeding the C_{11} fatty acid, both the C_{11} and the C_7 dicarboxylic acids.[38] Krebs wrote again on January 26 with a further question: "Is the double-ended β-oxidation deduced as a theoretical consequence of ω-oxidation (as, in fact, after the ω-oxidation has taken place both ends of the chain are identical), or have you also found direct proof for the double-sided β-oxidation, perhaps a dihydroxy — or diketo-acid?" He added that "The reading of your work has given me extraordinary pleasure."[39] The reasons for Krebs's special enthusiasm are clear. In ω-oxidation he perceived a "new pathway that can lead to the formation of succinic acid,"[40] and therefore, the possibility of establishing a new connection between two of the most important known partial sequences of oxidative metabolism.   The ω-oxidation theory was not only novel and potentially very significant; it also invited the more exacting tests of its validity that he could carry out with his tissue slice methods.

Through most of January Krebs and his colleagues went about their normal activities, relatively little affected by the critical German political situation. Like many others, Krebs hoped, after the election of November 6, 1932, in which the Nazis had for the first time sustained a loss in popular support, that the threat of their coming to power had passed its peak. During the winter it began to appear that the worst of the depression was over and that, despite the current political paralysis, conditions would begin to improve. All these calculations suddenly proved false, on January 30, when it was announced that Adolf Hitler had been appointed Chancellor of Germany.[41]

The first change that Krebs noticed after January 30 was that Nazi uniforms appeared everywhere in Freiburg. Even in the hospital, colleagues who had not been known to be Nazis suddenly came out in the open as members of local party organizations.   The Nazi press, political demonstrations, and radio broadcasts quickly came to dominate the public scene.[42]

In spite of this drastic change, Krebs and others in similar positions were at first not deeply disturbed.   Hitler had been made the head of a coalition government, and other members of his cabinet, as well as much of the public at large, believed that he could be controlled by the weight of the non-Nazis around him. Despite his strong awareness of the viciousness of Hitler's views, Krebs himself was, as he put down much later in a note for his autobiography, "one of those who thought, when the Nazis came to power, that they would not be so stupid as to carry out what they had set forth."[43]

III

While measuring rates of deamination in human placenta, lung, and liver tissue on January 27, Krebs carried out an additional set of measurements of the rates of respiration and glycolysis in the latter two tissues. His purpose was evidently to fill out gaps in the tables that he was preparing for his article for Oppenheimer's *Handbuch*. Within a day or two he had completed the article and sent it off to the publisher. On February 1, he continued his deamination investigation with an experiment that included 14 different peptides and amino acids.[44] On the same day he carried out another set of experiments, which has the appearance of the opening move in a major new line of investigation.

The title of the experiment was "Acetate + Rat Liver With pH Changes." In solutions of pH 7.4, 6.8, and 6.2, Krebs compared the rate of oxygen consumption with and without acetate added. The results were not satisfactory; there was a "rapid fall in the metabolism" in all the runs. Only at pH 7.4 did the acetate increase the rate of respiration somewhat. The experiment was clearly a follow-up of the experiment on acetate and succinate, with rat liver and kidney tissue, that he had carried out on January 4. The main difference was that, whereas then he had performed an isolated experiment, now he had clearly taken up a problem that he intended to pursue intensively. Two days later he repeated the experiment with different tissues, at pH 7.4, the reaction at which the previous readings had been highest. Liver and kidney slices from a mouse turned out to be a "poor object. No readings from acetic acid. Rapid fall in metabolism." Guinea pig liver and kidney were, however, "very good!". In both guinea pig tissues acetate more than doubled the respiration. Exploiting this favorable turn, Krebs employed the same tissues the next day at pH 7.2 and 6.4, and found "in the kidneys large increase in respiration through acetate, independent of pH" (at pH 7.2, without acetate, Q_{O_2} = -12.5, with acetate, -26.2; at pH 6.4, without acetate, Q_{O_2} = -11.4, with acetate, -30.2).[45]

Satisfied that the guinea pig kidney slices provided a suitable system for testing the ability of substrates to increase the respiration, Krebs expanded the investigation, on February 6, to include both acetate and the "succinate series," that is, succinate, fumarate, malate, oxaloacetate, and pyruvate. The results were very definite. Each of the three concentrations of acetate he used, and all five of the succinate series substances, raised the rate to nearly or more than double the control rates. To test whether the substrates were entirely consumed, he measured the bicarbonate concentration before and after the experiment. He reasoned that, if the acids were to disappear in the process, then free alkali remaining (the substrates actually added were the sodium salts of the acids) should convert some of the carbonate in solution to bicarbonate. In each of the vessels containing substrates there was an increase in the bicarbonate, but none in the controls.[46]

* * *

As will become clear, the sequence of experiments just described were the beginning of what Krebs intended from the start as an extended investigation. We may pause to ask what he initially had in mind as his objective. When we examined these pages of the notebook together, in May 1977, he recognized them as a distinct landmark in his research:

Holmes: Did you have in mind a clear new direction here, or is it just something...?

Krebs: Definitely, I wanted to know, this is the beginning of the work which led to the tricarboxylic acid cycle: the question being, what are the intermediates in the oxidation of foodstuffs?[47]

Krebs's response to my question juxtaposes two contrasting perspectives on the significance of these experiments. The first half of his statement is necessarily retrospective; it makes sense only in relation to later events. If, as historians of science, we seek the "roots" of major discoveries, then this identification, by the author of such a discovery himself, can be a satisfying confirmation that we have found the very tip of one. When we have reached the end of our story, we too may look backward and reflect on the sense in which his remark can be true. For now, however, to view the situation in that way would be out of place, because in 1933 Krebs could have had no prophetic vision that this work would lead to the tricarboxylic acid cycle. The second half of the statement can, on the other hand, be plausibly considered as a recollection of an idea that he had actually had as he began this work. He could very well have perceived himself, on February 1, 1933, as deliberately launching a new investigative pathway whose overarching problem was "what are the intermediates in the oxidation of foodstuffs?" That question is too broad, however, to explain the particular objectives of the experiments with which he began. As he himself suggested during a subsequent conversation on the same subject, it was only the very general idea that he had kept in mind since his time in Warburg's laboratory.[48]

The day after the discussion in which the exchange quoted took place, I suggested to Krebs a possible explanation for his having undertaken these experiments at just this time. He rightly rejected my superficial hypothesis, and then added, "The rapid oxidation of the C_4 dicarboxylic acids was known...mainly from the work of Battelli and Stern;...so...the first idea in these experiments was [merely] to expand the range of substances which behaved like the C_4 dicarboxylic acids."[49]

The likelihood that this is a valid recollection of the "first idea" that Krebs pursued is strengthened by the connection we can make between it and the research program Krebs had suggested in the *Oppenheimer Handbuch* review article that he finished just before he took up the experiments in question. That is, he may have been setting out to fulfill his own prediction that more exacting tests would show that many additional substances that are oxidized in cells also increase the rates of respiration of isolated tissues. The six substances he chose were all known to be oxidized in cells. They were, of course, *already* known to raise the respiration as well; but it would make sense to confirm those earlier findings in his own more exacting experimental system before moving on to substances that had not yet been shown to do so.

In pragmatic terms, therefore, Krebs's retrospective statement about his "first question" is very likely valid. If he had had nothing more in mind, however, his approach would seem to have been an extraordinarily narrow, empirical one. It is hard not to assume that he also harbored more specific ideas about how this systematic testing of substrates could lead him toward some partial answers along the way to the long range goal — "what are the intermediates in the oxidation of foodstuffs?" The design of his experiment on the "succinate series" suggests that one of his initial priorities was, in fact, to examine the Thunberg–Knoop–Wieland scheme of oxidative metabolism (described in Chapter 1, pp. 22-24). It can hardly be coincidental that the six acids he employed included all but one of the substances comprising the closed circuit of reactions that this scheme postulated. This procedure — to test a current hypothesis about metabolic pathways by means of his manometric tissue slice system — was, as we have seen, typical of the approach he had taken ever since he had been on his own. Persuaded of this argument at the time I discussed the matter with Krebs in 1977, I pressed the interpretation on him:

Holmes: You've pointed out that the scheme of reactions that Thunberg and Wieland suggested was only hypothetical.
Krebs: Yes.
Holmes: But would you have taken it seriously enough at this time for it to have guided your initial steps?
Krebs: Yes. Yes. Well, this scheme of Thunberg and Wieland postulated a reaction of acetate to condense to succinate; but there was not proof.[50]

Krebs thus acknowledged my view, but with some reluctance. In this conversation I clearly violated the norm of oral historians that one should not ask leading questions. This situation suggests, however, that it is sometimes useful to do so, for both the acknowledgment and the reluctance are revealing. The acknowledgment only confirms an interpretation that is strong enough to stand on its own from the contemporary evidence. The resistance of Krebs to emphasis on his interest in the Thunberg–Knoop–Wieland scheme can be readily explained in the light of subsequent events.

To the question what may have prompted Krebs to initiate at just *this time*, a general line of investigation that had been in the back of his mind for about 5 years, we can give no simple answer, but only suggest a variety of plausible contributing factors. The hypothesis of mine that Krebs rejected was that there was a methodological connection with some of the experiments he was then carrying out in the course of his deamination experiments. There was, he thought, not "any contact" between the two lines of investigation. His own retrospective suggestion was that it might have been a matter of having by then enough workers in his laboratory — including additional part-time technicians that he had been able to hire with financial support from Dromoto, a Hamburg firm that often gave such help to research workers in subjects of clinical interest — to enable him to take on another project.[51] I have suggested in addition that his reading for, and the writing of his review article on the respiration and glycolysis of tissues may have focused his interest on the questions that he took up experimentally. As we shall see further on, it is also possible that another article that he had been asked to write for Oppenheimer, on the decomposition of fatty acids, had by this time led him to review the literature on the Thunberg-Knoop–Wieland hypothesis itself. We might speculate, beyond these factors, that he was coming to feel that the deamination experiments on which he had been working for so long were not going to yield any further novelties, and that it was, therefore, time to move on to another problem. We should also recall that, even though Krebs afterward saw these experiments as the "beginning" of his work on intermediary oxidative metabolism, it was not the true beginning. Several times during his year in Altona he had briefly ventured into experiments in that realm; therefore, he was now essentially reviving an investigative ambition that he had not previously had the opportunity to pursue in a sustained way. Finally, although it may be sheer chance that he embarked on this course a few days after Hitler had come to power, it is not far-fetched to wonder if the new uncertainties about his future might have made Krebs feel that he should not delay implementing investigative ideas that he had envisioned for some time. To select any one primary explanation for his taking this important step would be to assume too deterministic a view of human behavior. Any or all of these factors may have influenced him, but Krebs need not have known, even at the time, what "caused" him to begin. At some point he simply decided to. As he commented to me with respect to the rationale behind another experiment we discussed,

> There must be some reason for doing it, yes, I think there must be some logic; but there is no proposition against which one cannot put up a counterargument, and it is this haggling about the validity of an argument which I think costs more time than to complete the experiment.[52]

* * *

On February 7, Krebs carried out further experiments on what he referred to this time as the *acetate-series*, comprising the same six acids he had previously called the *succinate-series*. All six acids again nearly doubled the control respiration level, and in each case the bicarbonate content in the vessel increased. In addition he calculated that, for acetate the oxygen consumed was sufficient to account for its complete oxidation, but that for the other acids it was not. The most significant addition to his procedure was that he determined manometrically for each vessel the "formation of keto acids," by the usual fermentation method. Only in the two that had contained oxaloacetate and pyruvate, did he obtain "pressure readings beyond the errors!!" The results, as he recorded them, were:

No certain formation of pyruvic acid from acetic acid (also not to be expected, since pyruvic acid is quickly decomposed).

It is certain that 1 COOH is decarboxylated.

In the second of these statements Krebs meant that, although the oxygen consumption in the cases of the dicarboxylic acids was not high enough to assume that they had been fully oxidized, the increase in the bicarbonate indicated that at least one of their two COOH groups had been released into the medium.[53]

The central result was the first statement. Since the only vessels that yielded a keto acid after the experiment were the two into which he had placed keto acids (oxaloacetic acid and pyruvic acid), there was no experimental sign that a keto acid had formed from any of the other acids. The fact that he interpreted this outcome as meaning that there was no "certain" evidence of "the formation of pyruvic acid from acetic acid," rather than more generally that there was no certain formation of any keto acids from any of the non-keto acids tested, shows that he was thinking in terms of the Thunberg–Knoop–Wieland framework. Acetic acid could not yield pyruvic acid by direct oxidative decomposition. If it had done so, therefore, it would have to have been through an intermediate synthesis, such as that predicted in the reaction sequence:

2 acetic acid → succinic acid → fumaric acid → malic acid
oxaloacetic acid → pyruvic acid

Krebs clearly did not regard his result as evidence contrary to that theory, because — as his parenthetical statement indicates — he would expect pyruvate to disappear, just as it had done in his deamination experiments with alanine before he had found out how to inhibit its decomposition.

If he wished to demonstrate that reaction, he would obviously think, by analogy to his deamination experiments, of employing a method to prevent the decomposition of the pyruvate. He chose, in fact, one of the same methods that had worked in that earlier investigation; he tested the oxidation of the series of acids in a guinea pig kidney extract. In this case "Some of the acids (*not* acetic acid) oxidize rapidly." There was "no certain formation of pyruvate," and a rapid fall in the oxidation.[54] Here, too, the test was only inconclusive. If acetate was not oxidized in this system, one could not answer the question asked.

After a 1-week absence from his laboratory, Krebs went back, on February 14, to an extensive deamination experiment, carried out also in kidney extracts. The next day he returned to the metabolism of acetate, but from a different perspective than that of his previous experiments. He compared the rates of respiration of guinea pig kidney slices with acetic acid, glyoxylic acid, and glycollic acid added to the medium. We may recall that Thunberg's original case for the synthesis of succinic acid from acetic acid had been the circumstantial one that acetic acid cannot be directly oxidized. His argument depended on Wieland's dehydrogenation theory (see Chapter 1, p. 20); but Otto Porges had previously reached the conclusion that acetic acid must undergo a synthetic reaction on the more pragmatic basis that none of the theoretical possible intermediates standing directly between it and the final end products of oxidation were metabolized by organisms. (Chapter 1, p. 7). It was clearly that question that Krebs wished to reopen, because glyoxylic and glycollic acid were the two chemically most plausible intermediates. In the experiment, both acids were oxidized more slowly than acetic acid, one of them more slowly even than the control, the other at about the same rate as the control.[55] This result seemed to rule out the alternative of a direct oxidation, and directed Krebs back toward further tests of the synthetic route. Meanwhile, however, he turned again to his deamination work, and made a discovery that enabled him to discount one of the complications he had encountered during the previous fall.

In his experiments of October 1932 (see Chapter 11, p. 369), Krebs had found that some NH_3 formed in his deamination experiments under conditions that he had had reason to believe were strictly anaerobic. As he reviewed that circumstance in February 1933, he must have decided that he ought either to confirm that result, in which case it would cast doubt on his view that oxidative deamination was the sole metabolic pathway, or to rule it out. The experiment of February 14 on kidney extracts, in which some amino acids were deaminated at high rates, may have provided him with a clue to the source of the anaerobic results. If the enzyme that catalyzed the reactions in the extract was as readily removed from the tissue as it seemed to be, then perhaps some of it could enter the solution from the tissue slices themselves, during the time that they were shaken in the manometers. That reasoning would explain why, on February 16, he carried out another set of experiments on anaerobic deamination in which he permitted the reactions to go on with the slices for 1 hour, removed the slices, and determined the NH_3 in the solutions immediately, then measured it again after 14 hours. He found that there had been "Enormous NH_3 — after-formation, after the removal of the tissues." He followed up immediately with a more rigorous test of this result. Using only *dl*-alanine, he again removed the tissue after 1 hour. He then replaced the argon he had used to give an anaerobic atmosphere with 5 percent CO_2 in O_2, and measured the oxygen consumption of the solution for 240 minutes. Afterward he measured the NH_3 and keto acid formed. The ratio O_2: NH_3: keto acid turned out to be very near the theoretical proportions (1:2:2) for the oxidative deamination reaction. That reaction, he could thus infer, had not occurred during the anaerobic phase when the tissue slice had been present, but during the aerobic phase when it was absent, because the "Slices give off the enzyme!!" Now he could explain away the earlier positive anaerobic results. He had inadvertently allowed the enzyme to catalyze the deamination reaction during the interval between the time at which he removed the slices and the time at which he made the NH_3 determinations. In future experiments he avoided this complication by adding HCl to the solution when he removed the slices, inhibiting the reaction. Afterward he found no anaerobic deamination.[56]

* * *

In 1977, we examined the pages of his notebook in which the preceding experiments are recorded, I asked Krebs why he returned to the deamination experiments soon after beginning a new line of investigation. He responded, "Well, I thought in different areas at the same time."[57] It is not unusual for an experimental scientist to keep more than one line of research going at once; but the ease with which Krebs diverted himself from one day to the next, from one problem to another that may or may not have been closely related, seems characteristic of his personal style. It is to display that style in action that I have in this book followed as closely as is practicable the chronological order of his research, even though one could describe some of the individual investigative pathways more coherently by reassembling the sequences of his experiments in a more analytical order. Moreover, by following close to the daily progression we can see, crossing the primary conceptual boundaries that separate the individual investigative lines, secondary links between them. When Krebs maintained that there was no "contact" between the two investigations he was pursuing during February 1933, he meant that mainly in the sense that the newer investigation did not arise out of some development within the older one. It is striking to see, however, how often the methods, the materials, and the strategies applied at a particular time in one line were paralleled by those used in another. Sometimes these junctures probably derived from the convenience of preparing slices, extracts, or reagents that could be employed in both investigations. At other times, perhaps, he tried a strategy in one investigation that was analogous to one he had followed in another. Another advantage in pursuing more than one "area" at the same time was that during periods in which one line might be bogged down, the other might be opening up, making the investigator less vulnerable to frustration when he appeared to be blocked in any single direction.

In reply to my query about his return to deamination Krebs also said, "Sometimes I felt, in writing up a paper — I don't know what the dates are in relation to writing up this paper — that I came across... gaps and therefore returned to the older problem."[58] Although he was reconstructing this possibility from his general experience rather than remembering the instance itself, it is plausible that his explanation does apply to the present situation. By February he might well have been working on the lengthy deamination paper he completed only in April (as we shall see, he fell behind in finishing his papers during this period). If so, he might have realized during that process the unsatisfactory state in which he had left the anaerobic deamination question several months before, and designed the experiments just described in order to clear up that problem.

* * *

Even as he kept both his deamination and his "succinate-series" experiments going, Krebs was planning to widen the scope of his investigation of the intermediates in oxidative metabolism. He was probably seeking an opportunity to test the "ω-oxidation" principle of Verkade. About the time he completed the experiments on anaerobic deamination just described, he wrote Benzinger that he intended to take up the metabolism of acetoacetic acid.[59] That plan too may have emerged from reading he did on the "decomposition of the ketone bodies" in preparation for his Oppenheimer *Handbuch* review of recent developments in the area of fatty acid decomposition.[60] Before setting out on either of these projects, however, he pursued a little further the problem of the "acetate–succinate series."

In the next experiment of this type Krebs added, to the six "natural" acids previously used, the three-carbon dicarboxylic acid malonate. Malonate was not regarded as a metabolite. Juda Quastel had, in fact, shown that malonate inhibits the oxidation of succinate. During the 1920s he had demonstrated this effect on bacterial metabolism, and in 1930 he found that the consumption of oxygen in minced muscle and brain tissue is less when malonate and succinate are added than when succinate alone is added. He ascribed this action to the competition of malonate with succinate for the enzyme that catalyzes the oxidation of the latter. Krebs was undoubtedly aware of Quastel's important work on malonate, but it is not evident that this factor influenced his use of it in this particular experiment. Here Krebs only compared the rate at which malonate itself may be oxidized to that of the other six acids. All of the "natural" acids were "rapidly decomposed," whereas malonate depressed the rate below that of the controls. Again only acetic acid appeared to be completely decomposed. Again also, he found no pyruvic acid afterward, even when the experiment was prolonged for 4 hours. This time he found reason to wonder whether that negative result was really due to the decomposition of pyruvate that had formed, because "*added* pyruvate reacts comparatively slowly." What he apparently meant was that the rate of oxygen consumption in the vessel to which he had added pyruvate was lower than in those to which he had added the other acids (Q for acetate = -30.0; for succinate, -33.8; for fumarate -29.6; for malate, -26.6; for oxaloacetate -34.7; for malonate, -10.5; for pyruvate, -20.6; for controls, -15.2 and -16.4). One would expect, therefore, that if the other acids *were* producing pyruvate, some of it ought to have accumulated. This result, therefore, would have appeared to Krebs more unfavorable than the preceding ones to the Thunberg–Knoop–Wieland scheme.[61]

Suspecting that the oxaloacetate in this experiment was decomposing spontaneously, Krebs placed some of it in bicarbonate salt solution, divided the solution into two parts, and kept one at room temperature, the other at a lower temperature. After 2 hours the bicarbonate content in the former had increased much more than in the latter, and he concluded that oxaloacetate decomposes rapidly at room temperature. Perhaps that result led him to seek ways in which he could block the decomposition of the oxaloacetate formed in tissues through the succinate series. On February 23, he narrowed his focus to the conversion of malate to oxaloacetate in guinea pig kidney slices. He tried in two ways to prevent the malic acid from being completely oxidized. One was to add arsenite to the solution. Just as he had earlier used arsenite in his deamination experiments to block the further decomposition of the keto acid pyruvate, now he hoped that that agent might block the decomposition of oxaloacetate, another keto acid. The second way was to carry out the reaction anaerobically. (When

I asked Krebs, in 1977, if he had any reason to expect malate to react anaerobically, he replied, "Well, nothing is impossible....This is all testing the possible and impossible things." He regarded it as another example of his style, of trying things without worrying too much in advance about whether or not they would work.) In the experiment he found, however that "Malic acid is *not* attacked anaerobically." The experiments with arsenite were more promising. The arsenite "inhibited the disappearance of acid more than the O_2 consumption." That is, it prevented the increase of bicarbonate that occurred in the control. Therefore it was possible that the arsenite had caused the malate to be only incompletely oxidized. After he had thrown away the solutions, Krebs regretted that he had not carried out further tests to identify the reaction that had occurred. "Unfortunately," he wrote down, "no pyruvate was tested. Oxaloacetate was to be expected!! No pyruvate."[62]

From a distance it would appear that the experiments that Krebs had carried out on the succinate series up until this time, especially this last one, were suggestive enough, yet incomplete enough, to invite further examination — that there was an opportunity to persevere until he had either confirmed or disproved the Thunberg–Wieland–Knoop theory. Yet he did not follow them up then. This was, perhaps, one of those occasions that illustrate Krebs's own view of himself as "easily diverted."

IV

While Krebs carried on his research and his medical responsibilities as usual, the political situation was growing more ominous. During February it became clear that the Nazi party was using its new power to intimidate, to take control of local and state police forces, and to press its campaign against its enemies. On February 27 the Reichstag building burned, and the next morning Hitler obtained from President Hindenberg an emergency decree suspending the basic rights of citizens.[63] By then Krebs must have lost his initial hope that the Nazis would not be able to carry out their program. His own future, both at Freiburg and in Germany, must have begun to appear deeply threatened. Nevertheless, he was not subjected to personal abuse, and he pressed on with his work with unabated intensity. On the day of the emergency decree he launched his new investigation of fatty acid decomposition.

The starting point for Krebs's test of Verkade's ω-oxidation principle was straightforward enough. The theory predicted that long chain fatty acids are converted by oxidation of their terminal CH_3 group to the dicarboxylic acids of corresponding length, and that the latter are progressively shortened at both ends by β-oxidation. There should, therefore, be dicarboxylic acids of intermediate length that are oxidizable in a tissue slice system. On February 28 Krebs tested seven such acids with guinea pig kidney tissue. The results were:

Control	Q = -15.1	C_8 (suberic acid)	Q = -21.1
C_5 (glutaric acid)	Q = -12.7	C_9 (azelaic acid)	Q = -17.7

| C_6 (adipic acid) | trace | C_{10} (sebacic acid) | $Q = -17.6$ |
| C_7 (pimelic acid) | $Q = -14.7$ | C_3 (malonic acid) | $Q = -11.1$ |

Krebs noted, "Relatively little increase in respiration, most with" C_8-dicarboxylic acid. "Everywhere increase in bicarbonate, most with C_8."[64] In spite of the fact that only the C_8 acid markedly increased the respiration, Krebs probably regarded these results as compatible with the ω-oxidation theory. The increase in bicarbonate was an indication that these acids had disappeared in the cells. As we have seen, he had drawn attention in his review article to the fact that relatively few of the substances oxidized in cells had yet been shown to increase the respiratory rate. Therefore, the failure of most of the dicarboxylic acids to do so did not rule them out as intermediates in fatty acid metabolism.

The next day, March 1, Krebs repeated the same experiment, but using liver slices in place of kidney slices. This time the results were uniformly negative. None of the seven dicarboxylic acids (C_3, C_5 to C_{10}) increased the respiration significantly, and in each case the bicarbonate *decreased*. Krebs noted the contrast between this finding and the increase in bicarbonate in kidney tissue. In liver, it appeared, the dicarboxylic acids were not decomposed.[65]

On March 2, Krebs tested the series of ordinary fatty acids, from C_3 to C_{13}, with guinea pig kidney tissue. He noted that "All acids are decomposed. Increase in respiration." (The control rate was $Q = -18.4$, the rates for the fatty acids ranged from -23 to -29.6.) He remarked also, "Nowhere decrease in bicarbonate (ω-oxidation?)."[66]

* * *

The form of this last notation suggests both that Krebs viewed this experiment on fatty acids as connected to his interest in the ω-oxidation theory and that he thought the result raised at least the possibility that the fatty acids did undergo such an oxidation. (It is not clear to me *how* he would have inferred the possibility from the result. If the fatty acids had been converted to dicarboxylic acids, one would have expected that the increase in the number of acidic groups *would* decrease the bicarbonate.) When I pointed out these statements to Krebs, in 1977, he misread "decrease" as "increase," and interpreted himself as having *ruled out* ω-oxidation: "I mention here that there was no increase in carbonate, which meant there could be no dicarboxylic acid formed." Several times during the course of our discussion of this and the previous experiments, when I asked if they had to do with Verkade's theory, he insisted that it was "really a general investigation of what substances are readily oxidizable." When I asked if he suspected a link between the oxidation of fatty acids and carbohydrate metabolism, he said "No, I didn't suspect that, but I was merely trying to collect data on which substances are oxidized."[67] Nevertheless, the query in the notebook indicates clearly that he *did* have in mind the question of ω-oxidation in these experiments, just as the design of the series of experiments preceding them reveals that he had in mind the Thunberg–Knoop–Wieland reaction scheme. Moreover, at other points in our discussion of these same experiments, Krebs spontaneously recognized the connections he here appeared to deny. It seems evident that, as he was drawn by our discussions back into an investigation that had taken place 34 years earlier, his attitude toward it was ambivalent, and that this ambivalence colored his recollections in tones that did not fully harmonize. Even while acknowledging that he had "tested" various theories, he resisted the implication he sensed in my questions, that he might have been deeply involved with any of them. Some of the reasons for that reaction depend on subsequent events, and will be best discussed later in our story. For now, however, we can point out that, in one sense his comments were correct. As we have seen, he had set out, in his Oppenheimer *Handbuch* article, a simple empirical program of examining oxidizable substances. He was, at the same time, interested in the current theories pertaining to these substances; therefore, he was, in these experiments, *both* "collecting data on which substances are oxidizable," *and* examining these theories. Undoubtedly the relative importance to him of the theoretical and the empirical objectives of his inquiry varied from time to time as he pursued it. In other words, he was not single-minded about what he was doing.

* * *

On March 3 and 4, Krebs repeated the tests of fatty acids, on other tissues and under varied conditions. He compared their effects on the respiration of rat liver and kidney, and on guinea pig liver and kidney from a starved and a nourished animal. He reduced the number of acids tested to three — caproic (C_6), enantic (C_7), and butyric (C_4). In these experiments one does feel that he was no longer as interested in the possibility of ω-oxidation occurring, as he was in simply finding out which substances would increase the respiration. The results were variable. In most cases the rates were higher for kidney than for liver.[68] In the experiment on rat tissues it appeared to him that there was "apparently increase only with butyric acid + liver." It may have been that observation that induced him to narrow his attention to butyric acid alone in the second set of experiments he carried out on March 4. There he found that butyric acid increased the respiration somewhat in guinea pig liver, much more strongly in kidney tissue.[69] At the same time, he carried out a larger scale experiment to attempt to isolate the products of the oxidation of butyric acid. The strategy he followed at this point indicates that it was not only because the respiratory action of butyric acid stood out in one of the experiments of March 3 that he singled it out for further attention, but because it fit into the plan he had already mentioned in his letter to Benzinger, to investigate the metabolism of acetoacetic acid.

As we have seen in Chapter 1, the problem of the place of acetoacetic acid in intermediary metabolism had been clearly defined since the first decade of the century. That substance was one of the three "ketone bodies" excreted in diabetic acidosis. The β-oxidation theory predicted that the progressive shortening of even–numbered fatty acid molecules should lead eventually to butyric acid, then either to β-hydroxybutyric acid or acetoacetic acid, or both, depending on the still uncertain details of the β-oxidation reaction mechanism. Embden's organ perfusion experiments had shown that fatty acids do give rise to acetoacetic acid in the liver.[70] Despite many investigations over the next two decades, however, there was still no definitive demonstration of the metabolic interconversions of these three closely related C_4 acids. Moreover, the relationship between acetoacetic acid and the supposed product of its own decomposition, acetic acid, also remained in doubt. In an overview of the subject Franz Knoop summarized the situation in 1931, and as it still held 2 years later: "The fatty acids are decomposed through β-hydroxy- or keto acids to the two-carbon-shorter acids, and this process goes on as far as the formation of the hydroxy derivative of butyric acid: how the latter is finally decomposed is still the object of discussion."[71] Krebs was about to enter this discussion.

Given the background of the problem, Krebs naturally assumed in advance that the products of the oxidation of butyric acid would probably be acetoacetic acid or β-hydroxybutyric acid, or both. The method he adopted to identify the products was one devised by Van Slyke, which permitted specific determinations of acetoacetate (plus acetone, if that compound were present), and β-hydroxybutyrate. With a reagent containing copper sulfate and calcium hydroxide one precipitated out the acetoacetate. From the filtrate one could then precipitate β-hydroxybutyrate with mercuric sulfate. After he had placed butyric acid (the concentration is not recorded) into 100 cm^3 of bicarbonate salt solution with 349 mg of liver tissue for 2 hours, he obtained 62 mg of acetoacetate and 32 mg of β-hydroxybutyrate, as compared to 0 of each in the control. This encouraging result (Krebs put exclamation marks after the figures) led him to repeat the experiment on March 7 on guinea pig liver and kidney tissue. He found in the liver, again, "large formation of acetone!!"; but in the kidneys "little formation of acetone!!" He used the generic word acetone because, as noted earlier, Van Slyke's method was not entirely specific. In this case, however, because there was no loss of acidity, he believed that the yield in question was exclusively acetoacetate. (There was, in addition, some β-hydroxybutyrate formed).[72]

At this point Krebs may well have thought that he had arrived quickly at a suitable method for studying the metabolism of butyrate, β-hydroxybutyrate, and acetoacetate. The situation looked less auspicious the next day, however, after he compared "ketone body formation" in guinea pig liver slices in the presence of butyric acid, glucose, lactic acid, and pyruvic acid, respectively. Operating again on a large scale, he obtained substantial yields of acetoacetate and β-hydroxybutyrate in all four cases, with pyruvate giving about three times as much as the others. That outcome apparently made him wonder if the results previously obtained with butyric acid were valid. To find out, he performed a control experiment by carrying out the Van Slyke method on four solutions containing, respectively, each of the four substances that had served as substrates in the preceding experiment. The pyruvate solution gave a precipitate with the reagent intended to separate out acetoacetate; and both the lactate and the pyruvate gave precipitates with the reagent intended to do so with β-hydroxybutyrate. Krebs commented wryly: "In the presence of lactate, β-hydroxybutyrate is inexact. In the presence of pyruvate, everything is inexact!"[73] Because lactate and pyruvate were likely to be present in the medium of respiring tissue slices, this was a rather dismaying observation.

During the following week Krebs carried out only two isolated experiments: one on urea formation in human fetal liver, the other on the formation of keto acids in brain tissue slices. On March 15 he performed another large scale determination of the acetoacetate and β-hydroxybutyrate formed from butyric acid in liver and kidney tissue, in spite of the uncertainties he had just encountered over the method, and obtained the paradoxical result: "Although in kidney larger decomposition [of the butyrate], much less ketone body!"[74] At the same time, undoubtedly seeking a way around the obstacle to the use of the Van Slyke method into which he had run, he explored another method to determine oxaloacetate by splitting off CO_2. Then, on March 18, he returned for 3 days to deamination experiments.[75]

On March 22 Krebs procured some human kidney tissue. He used the same material for two lines of investigation. With some of it he carried out further deamination experiments. With the rest he took up again the problem of the "succinate-series" that he had dropped just 1 month earlier. In the latter experiment all of the acids except for pyruvic increased the respiration slightly, and the oxygen consumption was sufficient to account for their complete combustion. Once having resumed this line, he continued on it the next day with the more usual guinea pig kidney slices. This time he compared the respiration with acetate, succinate, fumarate, and malate, each alone and in the presence of 0.001 M arsenite. Again he hoped to block the metabolic decomposition of oxaloacetate, so that if the other acids produced it through the Thunberg–Knoop–Wieland circuit of reactions, the oxaloacetate would accumulate. Using the new aniline method of Ostern, he could find no oxaloacetate. Again he assumed, not that it had not formed, but that it had spontaneously decomposed while he was making the usual bicarbonate determinations. Thus, the failure did not tell against the theory, but provided an obstacle to the one method he had devised that might otherwise be able to provide supporting evidence for the theory. The arsenite also exhibited an unexpected effect. It partially inhibited the consumption of all the acids, but it blocked completely the consumption of acetate.[76]

Although he could not explain this action of arsenite on the metabolism of acetate, the fact that it affected that acid differently from the others may have been what prompted him to examine more extensively the consumption of acetate in other tissues. The next day he tested it in four different rat tissues — liver, kidney, muscle, and intestine. In every tissue the acetate increased the rate of respiration and was fully consumed. "In the liver," he concluded, there was "apparently acetoacetic acid formed." Apparently he drew that inference from the change in the bicarbonate concentration. The condensation of two molecules of acetate to form acetoacetate in tissues had been observed before. On March 25 he tested acetate again, in guinea pig liver and muscle tissue. In this case there was little consumption in one, and almost none in the other; but again he found evidence of the formation of acetoacetate. After two experiments on deamination he tested acetate once more, on rabbit liver and kidney (again using the same material that he employed for one of the deamination experiments), and found "no particularly large decomposition of acetate in kidneys, none at all in liver!" At this point he seems to have lost interest in acetate for the time being, and reverted to an extended series of experiments on deamination.[77]

If we review the rhythms and patterns of Krebs's research during the 2 months after he initiated his general investigation of intermediates in the oxidation of foodstuffs, the most salient feature seems to be the frequency with which he changed course. Sometimes his experiments seemed to consist of a series of digressions, and of digressions within digressions. Not only did he alternate repeatedly between this general area and his more clearly delineated deamination experiments, he also bounced from one problem to another within the new investigative domain itself. From February 2 to the 23rd, when he was not carrying on deamination experiments, he was doing experiments related to the succinic series of acids and the theory linked with them. From February 28 to March 2 his experiments were directed toward Verkade's ω-oxidation theory. From March 4 to the 15th they had to do with the conversion of butyrate to the ketone bodies. Between March 22 and 25 he returned to the succinic series. Despite his own recollection that he was only surveying systematically all substances that might be oxidized in cells, the notebook record shows that most of his experiments of this period clustered around these problems. Nor does it seem, from that record, that he left each of these problems because the early results were unpromising, as his discussions in 1977 imply. We can see instead that in each case, when he took up a new problem, he obtained some suggestive results, but also encountered some obstacles. Whatever the ultimate outcome might have been, he left each problem at a time when his records suggest there were still promising leads to follow, or that further effort might overcome the obstacle. Rather than fitting his view that he "thought in several areas" at once, his moves might appear instead to confirm the worry he sometimes had that he was too easily diverted. The directions in which he moved at such times appear curiously unsystematic, in contrast with the tightness with which he organized other aspects of his life, such as his use of his time. Following him through his research path during these 2 months, we feel as though he were hopping from problem to problem, uncertain where to settle. The pattern visible here remained, in fact, characteristic of him throughout his scientific life — so much so, in fact, that members of his research group who were with him during the years in which I visited his laboratory sometimes talked about his "grasshopper approach" to science.

Such an approach would appear to entail risks. To scatter one's effort too much, to be too readily diverted, can prevent one from finishing what one has started, from pursuing a problem to the bottom, from surmounting the more recalcitrant obstacles that often stand in the way of the solution of a deep scientific problem. Appearances can also be misleading, however, even when we have the opportunity to view our subject from very close range — whether by working for many years beside him, or by examining the daily record of his work. Neither his long-standing associates nor I have had direct access to what Krebs had and held in mind during such times. My own belief is that there was more method in these patterns of digression than appears anywhere outside of

Hans Krebs's own vanished thoughts about what he was doing. In the months in question above, as in similar periods in his later career when he was exploring an area new to him, he may deliberately have pursued each particular problem just far enough to set up priorities for his future efforts. When he dropped a problem, it may have been either because he had lost interest in it, or only because he deferred it to take advantage of some special opportunity, or new idea, that led him temporarily in a different direction. As we shall see, Krebs seldom forgot about a problem or line of investigation when he put it aside. It remained in his remarkable memory, ready to guide his investigative steps once again, when and if some new development should redirect his attention to it. It may have been because he could keep many things in mind and return to them after short or long periods, that he was freed from the necessity to plod more systematically, step-by-step, through one problem at a time.

VI

Although Krebs carried out the research just described, through the month of March, without disturbance, he could not have remained unaffected by the worsening political situation. During that month the Nazis made it ever clearer that they would brook no opposition, or even independent action, either nationally or locally. Arbitrary arrests occurred more frequently, the legally constituted state governments were replaced by Reich Commissioners, and officials of local governments or other organizations who were not to the liking of the Nazis began to be dismissed. On March 23 Hitler obtained by legal means the powers of a dictator. At Freiberg, Krebs and those in similar positions began to see that sooner or later they would probably have to get out of Germany. His colleagues were confident, however, that of all of them, his professional future was most secure. Franz Bielschowsky, in particular, expressed that feeling to Heinz Fuld. Although no one knew what would happen to them under Hitler, Bielschowsky said, it was certain that Hans Krebs would be sought after all over the world. Krebs himself began to make some precautionary moves in that direction. Lowell Weicker, a member of the family that had founded the Squibb Pharmaceutical Company, had contacted him about the possibility of taking a research position in that firm in America. At Weicker's invitation, Krebs made a quick trip to Berlin late in March, to discuss the matter, and expressed interest in such work, although he made it clear that he would require a generous salary to make such a change in his career. He still did not think a forced departure was imminent, and he looked forward to giving his first course of lectures as a *Privatdozent*, from May 1st until the end of June. That same day, the Nazis opened an advertising campaign against the spread of "International Jewry," followed on April 1 by a nationwide 3-day boycott of all shops owned by Jews. On the first night of the boycott, Hermann Blaschko left the hospital in Freiburg, and took a train to Basel. On the train he sat down by chance next to David Nachmansohn, who was also fleeing Germany, along with many others. Despite this sudden escalation of the danger that he too shared with his friends and all German Jews, Krebs pursued his research vigorously during the first week of April.[78]

As he concentrated again on deamination at the end of March, Krebs fixed his attention particularly on the two dicarboxylic amino acids, aspartic and glutamic acid. Of the natural stereochemical isomers, these two were deaminated at the highest rates, but he had still not been able to isolate the keto acids that should be formed from them. To overcome this problem, he apparently applied two strategies at once: to do the experiments in kidney slices of animals other than rats, in the hope that the rates would be higher; and to block the disappearance of the keto acid by means of arsenite, as he had done with alanine. (For some of the other acids he had found this procedure unnecessary, because the keto acids formed from them did not decompose rapidly.) On March 25 (or possibly a day or two later), he tested aspartic acid in rabbit kidney slices, with or without arsenite. This was probably intended as a preliminary experiment, because he measured only the rates of NH_3 formation. He found that there was an "Increase through As_2O_3!!" Because he expected the arsenite merely to inhibit the disappearance of the keto acid, not to affect the rate of the deamination reaction itself, this was a surprising and unexplained result. Nevertheless, he went on, on March 29, with the main objective of the strategy he was employing, a large scale experiment with aspartic acid and arsenite. He isolated the dinitrophenylhydrazone of the keto acid produced, and found it to have the composition and melting point of the derivative from pyruvic acid. The product of the deamination reaction ought to have been oxaloacetic acid. By now, however, he was well aware, from his experiments on the succinate series, that the oxaloacetate had probably decomposed spontaneously to yield the pyruvate. As a check, he measured pyruvate manometrically, and oxaloacetate with the aniline method of Ostern, and found that small quantities of the oxaloacetate were still present.[79]

On April 1, Krebs applied the same procedures to glutamic acid. The dinitrophenylhydrazone of α-ketoglutaric acid, the expected product of the deamination of glutamic acid, had not been described in the literature. Krebs made the compound himself, using α-ketoglutaric acid that Hans Weil, a physician in Thannhauser's staff who had also been trained in organic chemistry, prepared for him. When arsenite was present, Krebs obtained a large enough yield from a large-scale deamination experiment to determine that the melting point and composition were the same as for the dinitrophenylhydrazone made from the α-ketoglutarate. As in the case of aspartic acid, he encountered an unexpected finding with respect to the ammonia produced in the experiment. When he compared the quantity formed in the presence of arsenite to that of the keto acid, he found that there was "more keto acid than NH_3!!" According to the stoichiometry of the reaction, the quantities should have been the same. In the smaller-scale manometric experiment that he carried out simultaneously, he observed, as he had with aspartic acid, that the reaction yielded more NH_3 with arsenite than without (Q_{NH_3} without arsenite = 1.18; with 0.05 M arsenite = 4.55).[80]

To see whether the increase in NH_3 with arsenite might be a more general effect that he had not noticed before, Krebs repeated the experiment on April 5, comparing glutamic acid with lysine. The effect occurred in both cases, but it was "with lysine little, with *d*-glutamic acid enormous!!" The crucial figures were:

		No arsenite	0.05 M Arsenite
Lysine	Q_{NH_3}	1.51	2.08
Glutamic acid	Q_{NH_3}	0.178	4.38

Continuing his examination of this puzzling phenomenon the next day, Krebs again obtained little NH_3 from glutamic acid without arsenite, and considerably more with it, though less than in the previous experiment. The rates were generally sinking over the course of the runs, and he commented that the problem "requires better experiments!" At the same time he added α-glutaric acid + NH_4Cl to another slice, and obtained a "large disappearance of NH_4Cl," evidence that he had been able to convert the keto acid to the amino acid. On the same day, he performed another large scale deamination experiment with glutamic acid, using dog kidney slices, and was again able to isolate the dinitrophenylhydrazone of α-ketoglutaric acid.[81]

On April 7, things went badly for Krebs in the laboratory. Having obtained some human placenta tissue, he utilized it for two sets of experiments on deamination, and on the oxidation of a variety of substrates, including lactate, pyruvate, glucose, butyrate, and acetate. In the first set the addition of amino acids caused no increase in the formation of NH_3; in the second set the respiration measurements failed, because he had forgot to put caustic alkali in the vessels to absorb the CO_2 formed.[82] These were trivial misfortunes, however, compared with the fateful event of that day. The Nazi minister of the interior issued a Law for the Restoration of the Career Civil Service, providing that certain civil servants were to be removed from their duties. Among the categories included were those of "non-Aryan" descent. Although an anti-Jewish campaign had gone on during the preceding week, this drastic law was generally unexpected,[83] and must have caught Krebs too by surprise.

Even in the face of this news, Krebs was optimistic enough to consider it uncertain whether he would actually be forced out of his position. On April 8 he carried on his research as usual, performing further experiments on the deamination of glutamic and aspartic acid, with arsenite and two other inhibitors. On the 10th he tested the effects of arsenite on the formation of NH_3 from glutamic acid, aspartic acid, and alanine, this time with rat kidney tissue. In contrast to the recent experiments in which he had used tissue from other animals, the arsenite here reduced the formation of NH_3 instead of raising it.[84] That same day he received a letter written on April 8 by a former colleague at Freiburg, Walter Herkel, who was now working with the physiologist Joseph Barcroft in Cambridge. Having read about the new law in the English newspapers, Herkel became concerned enough about Krebs's future to go to Frederick Gowland Hopkins and ask if there might be a position available for Krebs in Cambridge. Hopkins had answered, Herkel wrote, that the financial situation made it questionable, but that he "would be delighted" to have Krebs there, and would speak to the vice-chancellor about it. Herkel cautioned Krebs not to expect too much, and suggested there might be a better chance if he could at least begin in Cambridge with his own means.[85]

Krebs wrote back immediately, thanking Herkel, but still not quite believing that the worst would come to pass:

> I believe that your judgment of the situation from a distance appears darker than it actually is at the moment. Here in Freiburg, no one at the university has, so far as I know, been dismissed. To be sure, there is an imminent prospect of being put on leave (that means, for us, release from clinical duties, but continued salary and further possibility for scientific work). The leave is only a temporary measure. In most cases dismissal will follow.
>
> So long as I have not been dismissed, or otherwise lose the possibility for work, I should undertake no definite steps toward obtaining another position.

In case he must leave, Krebs added, he had already thought of trying Hopkins, because Hopkins's Royal Society lecture had indicated an interest in his work. He asked Herkel to inquire further about the possibility of a place with Hopkins. He could keep his head above water for several months without pay, he said, but not much longer than that.[86]

The possibility for continued work lasted for just one more day. On April 12, Krebs found in his mail a curt note:

> By order of the academic rectorate I inform you, in accordance with ministerial order A Nr. 7642, that you are on leave until further notice.
>
>   The Rector
>   Rehn.[87]

Along with Krebs, seven other *Privatdozents* of the Freiburg medical faculty were placed on leave, including Franz Bielschowsky and Rudolf Schoenheimer.[88]

VI

Krebs had also been too optimistic when he predicted that, even if he were forced to take leave, he would be able to do further scientific work. The administrative director of the hospitals, Eitel, sent him a note warning him to stop work in his laboratory at once.[89] Unable either to see his patients or do his experiments, and not knowing when the next blow would fall, Krebs decided to go off to the Black Forest, as he had done once before, to write up the scientific papers on which he had fallen behind.

Just before leaving Freiburg, Krebs sent off two articles he had already completed, for Oppenheimer's *Handbuch*. One of them, on "The Decomposition of Amino Acids" he had put together from parts of his earlier *Klinische Wochenschrift* article on deamination; a summary of his work on urea synthesis; and commentaries on Max Bergmann's study of the deamination of peptides and on contemporary studies of the special pathways of the decomposition of tryptophane and histidine.[90] The other article, on "The Decomposition of Fatty Acids," necessarily revolved less around his own, still incipient research on the subject. He began with Verkade's ω-oxidation principle, which he took as an observed process, but one whose significance was still in doubt. "To what extent ω-oxidation takes place in the animal body," he wrote, "cannot yet be foreseen." Under the subheading "Decomposition of Acetic Acid," he discussed mainly the reaction scheme of Thunberg, Knoop, and Wieland, which he depicted as follows:

$$
\begin{array}{cccccc}
\text{COOH} & \text{COOH} & \text{COOH} & \text{COOH} & \text{COOH} & \text{COOH} \\
| & | & | & | & | & | \\
\text{CH}_3 & \text{CH}_2 & \text{CH} & \text{CHOH} & \text{C=O} & \text{C=O} \\
& | & || & | & | & | \\
\text{CH}_3 & \text{CH}_2 & \text{CH} & \text{CH}_2 & \text{CH}_2 & \text{CH}_3 \\
| & | & | & | & | & + \\
\text{COOH} & \text{COOH} & \text{COOH} & \text{COOH} & \text{COOH} & \text{CO}_2
\end{array}
$$

$$
\xrightarrow{-2H} \quad \xrightarrow{-2H} \quad \xrightarrow{+H_2O} \quad \xrightarrow{-2H} \quad \longrightarrow
$$

2Essig-säure → Bernstein-säure → Fumar-säure → Aepfel-säure → Oxalessig-säure → Brenztrauben- + Kohlon-säure

Referring to an article by Thunberg in the previous edition of the *Handbuch* for the evidence in support of this theory until 1930, Krebs drew attention to the more recent work of Wieland and Sonderhoff on the crucial reaction, "The Conversion of Acetate Acid to Succinic Acid in Living Cells." They had been able to obtain a 5 percent yield of succinate from acetate added to the medium of yeast cells. In parentheses, Krebs inserted "(along with it, about 10% formed citric acid)." Thus, following the custom that had become an ingrained habit over the past two decades, Krebs took notice of the experimental observation that citric acid was connected with the phenomena under study, but did not allow that observation to impinge on a discussion centered on the role of the dicarboxylic acids. The results of Wieland and Sonderhoff still left it doubtful, according to Krebs, "whether succinic acid is an intermediate in the decomposition of acetic acid," because under their experimental conditions the rate of decomposition of succinate was only 30 percent of that of acetate; "whereas — if succinate were an intermediate in the decomposition — in view of the 5% yield, a much greater reaction of the succinate is required."[91] Krebs was, in effect, stating that the prerequisite for a strong demonstration would be to show either that the reaction itself occurs quantitatively, or that succinate meets the basic requirement for an intermediate — that it react at least as rapidly as the overall reaction of which it is a part — and that neither condition had been satisfied.

For animal cells, Krebs noted, "The occurrence of the formation of succinate from acetate has not yet been proven, whereas the other reaction steps have been proven in animal cells, especially through the work of A. Hahn." (See Chapter 1, pp. 27-29 for a summary of these investigations of Amandus Hahn and their bearing on this problem.) Krebs finished his discussion of the reaction scheme with a brief reference to the relevance of his own work to the question.

In contrast to yeast, succinate and its dehydrogenation products are, according to my investigations, decomposed in animal tissues more rapidly than acetate. Nevertheless, the Thunberg scheme of acetate decomposition, viewed as a whole, still remains a hypothesis.[92]

These passages are very revealing of Krebs's position concerning this central problem of oxidative intermediary metabolism during the period when he had just begun his own investigations in that area. They suggest that he took the Thunberg–Knoop–Wieland scheme seriously; that he treated it cautiously as "still a hypothesis," but one that he held to be promising. Moreover, it is evident that he saw his own early experiments on this subject as favorable to the hypothesis, strengthening the still insufficient evidence for the crucial synthetic reaction. His finding that succinate is decomposed more rapidly than acetate seemed to him to satisfy the axiomatic criterion for an intermediate that Wieland and Sonderhoff's experiments had failed to meet.

As he invoked this criterion, we may note, Krebs was thinking within a traditional framework, in which an intermediate is supposed to form and to decompose within a reaction chain that has a defined starting and end point. Like his contemporaries, he did not see a closed circuit of reactions as a distinct type of metabolic pathway, in which each step comprises an intermediate with respect to the others, because there are no fixed end points. His linear representation of the reactions lent itself to the traditional approach. There seems to be a beginning and an end, even though the end leads back to the beginning. In a closed circuit, would it not be as problematic if acetate were consumed more slowly than succinate, in his system, as the other way around? Krebs evidently did not ask himself such a question at this time.

Krebs was not alone at this time in giving the Thunberg–Knoop–Wieland scheme prominence. In another article submitted 2 months later for the same volume of Oppenheimer's *Handbuch*, Carl Neuberg and Ernst Simon presented the general problem of "the Endoxidation" of carbohydrates entirely from the point of view of "the well-known Wieland–Thunberg theory" — that is, the same reaction scheme that Krebs discussed in his section on fatty acids. As discussed in Chapter 1, the scheme, in fact, provided a potential common final pathway for carbohydrates, fatty acids, and amino acids. Neuberg and Simon summarized the evidence for each reaction in the sequence, acknowledging only faintly, with respect to "the formation of succinate out of acetate," that this step was problematic. "The outstanding experimental proof" for this reaction, they stated, has "up until now been carried out on plant cells." The absence of such proof for animal cells did not give them pause, probably due to their conviction that "The investigative results of recent years have produced support for the view that the terminal oxidative decomposition of carbohydrates, fatty acids, and amino acids takes place along similar paths in plant and animal cells."[93]

The articles that Krebs wrote for Oppenheimer's *Handbuch* were reviews of the current state of two subfields of intermediary metabolism, assigned presumably according to the editor's view of the structure of the specialty areas within the discipline. Their contents also overlapped extensively with Krebs's own current or recent lines of investigation. In the case of the amino acid article this near congruence can readily be explained; Krebs was probably asked to do that review because he was now a leading authority in the area, and his research defined a large segment of its leading edge. That was not true, however, for the fatty acids, on which he had published nothing. We may, therefore, raise the question, did Krebs project his own new research interests onto his treatment of that subfield, or did what he learned about the subfield, in preparation for his article, shape his nascent research interests? Undoubtedly the influences ran in both directions, as he simultaneously initiated a new investigative program and surveyed the current literature to carry out his assignment. The incident illustrates the subtlety of the interactions between scientific writing and scientific investigation, between the path of the individual scientist's private research and the collective movement of a subspecialty area.

On the day his Oppenheimer articles reached the editorial office of the publisher, Krebs was riding northeastward on his bicycle, his laboratory notebook in hand, ascending into the hills of the Black Forest toward the resort town of St. Peter. The trip was only about 15 kilometers, but it was not an easy ride, for St. Peter was about 500 meters above Freiburg. Once there, he booked a room in the Pension Schar and settled down to work, to hike, and to await developments that were largely beyond his control.[94]

A tiny village clustered on a knoll and dominated by an elegant baroque church, St. Peter was peaceful and beautiful. Toward the north one looked down on deep valleys and cultivated fields. The view to the south was of the massive Feldberg mountain range, and on the clearest days one could glimpse a few peaks of the Swiss Alps. A few hundred yards from the village a network of broad, well-kept hiking trails fanned out through forests and alongside farmyards, plunging into the valleys, or leading steeply upward toward the lesser summits in the region. In this tranquil setting, the drastic event that had overtaken Hans Krebs in his professional life must have seemed, for the moment, far away.[95]

During the first days at St. Peter Krebs probably spent most of his time on the "literary tasks" he had brought with him. Foremost among them was to finish the article that would sum up the results of his year-long investigation of the decomposition of amino acids. Within 2 or 3 days he had completed this work and mailed the manuscript off to Franz Knoop, editor of *Hoppe-Seyler's Zeitschrift*.

While writing his second paper on "Investigations of the Metabolism of the Amino Acids in the Animal Body," Krebs must have had scissors and paste with him, as he incorporated into it at least 90 percent of the text of his first *Klinische Wochenschrift* paper (see Chapter 11, pp. 362–366), only rearranging its sections in accord with subsequent shifts in his priorities. As in his definitive paper on urea, he added detailed descriptions of the methods that he had mentioned only briefly in the preliminary paper. The difference between the papers amounted to much more than an expansion of the discussion of procedures, however, because the same general conclusions were now based largely on data that he had not yet gathered when he drew those conclusions in the first paper. The tables that he included now contained measurements of the formation of ammonia and other relevant processes for more amino acids, and more measurements for each amino acid, than he had made when he wrote the first paper. Whereas he had then barely mentioned the isolation of the dinitrophenyl-hydrazone of the product of the deamination of alanine, he now described fully the isolation of those derivatives of the keto acids yielded by five different amino acids. From the new data he had amassed, he was able to draw some further empirical generalizations, such as a correlation between relative rates of deamination and the general types of natural amino acids. He added a long discussion of the experiments in which it had appeared that deamination occurred anaerobically, his recognition of the artifact responsible for that effect, and the procedures he had later followed to obviate it. He summarized Max Bergmann's hypothesis that dipeptides are directly deaminated in the kidneys, and pointed out that his own experiments with dipeptides could not decide the question. Peptides did yield ammonia in his system, but at a slower rate than the free amino acids composing them. It was likely, therefore, that the dipeptides had first been hydrolyzed, then deaminated.[96]

The most important change in the new paper, however, was that Krebs greatly strengthened his treatment of the deamination of optically active amino acids. Indicative of the importance he now attached to it was that he moved that topic from its almost parenthetical position near the end of the preliminary paper to a prominent place near the front of the larger paper. The original table comparing the rates of deamination of natural isomers of those amino acids with those of their racemic mixtures he replaced with one comparing directly the natural and nonnatural optical isomers of six amino acids (alanine, valine, leucine, phenylalanine, histidine, and aspartic acid). The contrasts were dramatic. Q values for the natural isomers ranged from 3 to 10; for the nonnatural isomers from 2.5 to 77.0, with three of them being greater than 30. Where in the first version he had remarked rather weakly that the nonnatural forms "are attacked more rapidly" than the natural forms, he now stated, that "From the behavior of the optically active compounds it is to be concluded that in the racemic mixtures it is predominantly the non-natural portion that yields ammonia."[97]

We have seen that, in his preliminary paper Krebs had based his "discovery" that "the deamination of amino acids occurs mainly in the kidneys" on those very experiments with racemic mixtures. It would seem, then, that his belated recognition that in those experiments he had been measuring predominantly reactions of the nonnatural form had cut the ground out from under his argument. Fortunately for his position, however, he now had sufficient evidence from the natural isomers to support a somewhat milder form of the same conclusion. The rates for the natural isomers in the kidney were not 10 to 20 times as high as the rates in other tissues, but they *were* two to four times as high as the rates in the liver, with all other tissues much lower still. Whether or not Krebs consciously recognized at some point the fallacy in his original reasoning, he did tacitly adjust his conclusion to the changed situation. In his conclusions he replaced the statement quoted above in this paragraph with the more qualified — and more realistic — assessment that "The kidneys are — beside the liver — one of the chief sites for the deamination of amino acids."[98]

In his preliminary paper Krebs's assertion that the absence of urinary ammonia in kidney diseases was due to the failure of those organs to deaminate amino acids was a speculative inference drawn from his results on normal tissue. Now he was able to back up his claim with more direct evidence. During the spring, he had carried out experiments on pathological human kidney tissue supplied to him from the clinic. With slices taken from patients who had died of tuberculosis, he could now show that those sections which presented pathological histological changes produced little or no ammonia in the presence of amino acids.[99]

The logical fissures that appear so gaping in the first paper had not been completely closed in the second; but Krebs had managed to reduce them to modest cracks. Having rather hastily drawn conclusions that were not fully supportable by the evidence he had available at the time he published them, he had subsequently been able to produce the evidence he needed to provide sound support for most of the same conclusions. That was not exactly a classical scientific method, but he had proven resourceful enough to take several questionable conceptual leaps and still land on his feet.

After he had finished his paper, Krebs was ready for some relaxation. In a cheerful mood he wrote to Hermann Blaschko on Easter Monday,

Dear Blaschko,

Do not be angry with me for my laziness about writing. During the last days and weeks I have had no time to rest.

I have now been sitting here in St. Peter for 4 days, in splendid summer weather, and I am spending my political leave here.

On Tuesday the blow struck us. All Jews in the Baden state service were sent home. The Chief and a few others are temporarily declared indispensable. Everyone counts as a Jew who is 25% "impure" (1 grandparent). We all had to submit geneologies, whereby some surprises came to light; for example, Post, 25%, Janssen (Pharmacology) 50%. Work in the laboratory was also forbidden within an hour's notice. It is likely that we shall be dismissed on June 1.[100]

One reason that Krebs could report these events almost light-heartedly was that "the Chief" was showing himself to be as supportive in time of need as he had been in times of triumph. Thannhauser, himself a Jew, had been spared from immediate action under the provision of the Civil Service Law that exempted those who had served in the World War. Now he acted swiftly to find places for Krebs and for Bielschowsky. By the time that Krebs wrote Blaschko he knew already that he would be able to obtain a temporary position in Zurich, in the laboratory of Wilhelm Löffler. As described in Chapter 8 (pp. 251–252), Löffler had carried out the most definitive experiments on urea synthesis before Krebs entered the field, and he was much interested to have the young scientist who had cracked the problem work with him. "Therefore," Krebs wrote Blaschko, "I have no need to be alarmed." Compared to many others who had received the same notice he had on April 12, Krebs did indeed have reason to feel fortunate. Thanks to Thannhauser he faced no prolonged period in which he did not know if he would find any place to continue his work.[101]

After recounting this situation to Blaschko, and answering some questions about which Blaschko had written him, Krebs ended buoyantly,

> I am keeping myself busy for the time being with literary matters, with resting up, and with sunbathing. For the first time since Forte [the holiday that they had spent together in Italy after the Physiological congress, in September 1932], I can expose myself to the sun in a bathing suit. I truly have good fortune with the weather.
>
> Let me hear from you again. I think that, from now on I shall have time to answer.
>
> With warm regards,
Yours,
Krebs[102]

On April 19 the anticipated second blow pierced the sunny calm of St. Peter. Eitel, the Director of the Freiburg Clinic, once again confronted him with a peremptory directive, mailed directly to his mountain retreat:

> By order of the Minister of Culture and Instruction, the State Commissioner, we hereby inform you that in preparation for the execution of the laws for the reconstruction of the professional service, you are relieved of your present employment, and you are given notice that your service will be terminated on July 1, 1933....We earnestly request that you certify your receipt of this notice by signing the enclosed form, and that you return this certification *immediately*.[103]

Even though he had fully expected such action to be taken, the harsh finality of this notification must have had a chilling effect on Krebs. He had known Eitel well, and had collaborated with his son on an investigation of the metabolism of the thyroid gland; yet Eitel dealt with his dismissal in totally impersonal terms.[104]

On April 22, Krebs cycled back down to Freiburg. Although barred even from entering his laboratory, he was permitted to live in his apartment for the duration of his enforced terminal leave. Now that his dismissal was official, it was time to take those "definite steps toward obtaining another position." Having decided to accept the position with Löffler, he planned to travel to Zurich on the 27th to settle the details, and to move shortly thereafter. On the eve of his departure, however, he received a letter that threw him into a quandary. A few weeks earlier he had written Albert Szent-Györgyi asking for some ascorbic acid. On April 22, Szent-Györgyi, who had been traveling, replied from the Hague, that he would forward a sample as soon as he reached home. He added,

> I very much regret that you have personal difficulties in Germany. During the last two days I have been in Cambridge, where they think that something can be done for you. I have naturally taken the opportunity to encourage people, and I hope that my opinion will also contribute toward the realization of the plan.

In a hand-scrawled postscript, Szent-Györgyi advised Krebs to write Hopkins if he wished to go to Cambridge, and to assure him that he would be satisfied with a very modest income. There were no "large" positions available, and Szent-Györgyi thought that Hopkins would be reluctant to offer a "small" position unless Krebs had taken the initiative on the matter.[105]

When he read this letter on the 25th, Krebs was at first in great doubt about what to do. In spite of the limitations on what could be offered him in Cambridge, he wrote Blaschko that day, he "had the greatest desire to go to England, if there was any possibility of getting started there. For who knows whether the swastika might soon be raised also over Zurich."[106] Blaschko had already decided to emigrate to England, and Krebs expressed enthusiasm about seeing him in London. As this letter suggests, however, it was not only his interest in Cambridge that induced him to pull back from his decision to go to Zurich, but also an apprehension about remaining where there was a possibility that he might be subjected a second time to Nazi authority.

Following Szent-Györgyi's advice almost to the letter, Krebs wrote Hopkins on the 26th, explained his position, and went on,

> I would regard it as very good fortune, if I could continue my work with you. It is self-evident, of course, that I would be satisfied with a modest income, if I could generally carry on my scientific activity.

He finished by offering to come to Cambridge in the near future to discuss the question in person.[107] On the next day he kept his appointment in Zurich, where Löffler offered him a position to last initially for 6 months, with the possibility of renewal, a salary of 350 to 400 Fr, and some research funds.[108]

In the meantime, Hopkins had written to Warburg enquiring about the "details" of Krebs's "present situation." Warburg wrote Krebs on the 26th, also offering him a laboratory room as a "guest scientist," a room, and a small salary; but advised him that England "seems to be safer and to provide richer prospects." Krebs wrote on the 29th to thank Warburg "from his heart, for the offer," but agreed that it would be better for him to seek a place in a foreign country.[109] On the same day, Hopkins was writing from Cambridge, in reply to the letter he had just received from Krebs,

> Dear Dr. Krebs
> I admire your work so much that I am very anxious to help you.

If it should prove possible to obtain the necessary financial assistance, I shall be glad to find a place in this laboratory for you. There is a movement in London to collect a fund for supplying maintenance in cases such as your own, and I have already sent your name, explaining that I should welcome you in this laboratory. It may take a little time, however, before I can let you know whether money has been allotted.

Unfortunately the Cambridge University itself is not able to find sufficient money to maintain the many applications that are being made.

I will let you know at the earliest opportunity what has happened with regard to the financial question.[110]

At the end of April, therefore, Krebs found himself in a dilemma. He could accept a definite offer in Zurich and resume work immediately, or he could hold out for an uncertain, but very attractive opportunity to begin again in Cambridge. Not knowing how long it would be before he would hear from Hopkins again, nor how real the prospects were for the "necessary financial assistance," he made up his mind to wait for as long as he could.

When Krebs was excluded from his laboratory, his little research group was also dispersed. Ostern left immediately for Basel, from where he wrote Krebs on April 24, "Most of all, I would like to thank you deeply for the care you have given me, and for all I have learned from you. I hope that I shall again have an opportunity to work together with you."[111] Heinz Fuld was not dismissed from his clinical post. He was Christian; but his ancestry was Jewish, and he knew that his time would come sooner or later. Krebs told him, "Heinz, get out soon. Don't hesitate." Anticipating the worst, the athletic Fuld practiced swimming across the Rhine, in case he should have to escape quickly. A few weeks later, however, he simply left the hospital for his parents' home in Mannheim, and from there made his way to London without trouble.[112]

From the time they gained power, the Nazis worked up public enthusiasm for the new order by organizing frequent mass demonstrations, beginning with a celebration of the electoral victory of March 12. On April 20 festivals were held in honor of Hitler's birthday. The climactic such event during the spring of 1933 was May day, designated "The Day of National Labor." In every city and town in Germany, huge parades were to take place, and every organization in the area was required to take part.[113] In Freiburg all members of the staff, except for its non-Aryan members, were expected to join the parade. Ludwig Aschoff, "the most distinguished member of the Freiburg medical faculty," opposed the anti-Semitic policies of the Nazis, and had sufficient prestige and courage to express his views openly. On the day of the parade he went to see a number of his Jewish colleagues to assure them of his disapproval of the Nazi policy. Aschoff's daughter Eva called Krebs by telephone on the night before the May day celebration, and asked him if he would like to go for a walk with her at 11 PM in the morning — the hour that the parade was to begin. Deeply touched by this gesture of support, Krebs accepted. The next day, as the demonstrations took place, they walked together toward *Jägerhäusle* and *Rosskopf*.[114]

Aschoff was not the only leading figure at the University to defy the Nazi anti-Semitic campaign. On the day after the May day parade, the pro-Nazi German Students Association put up posters all over Freiburg containing a proclamation "Against the Un-German Spirit." The 11-point manifesto described "the Jew" as a "dangerous adversary," who can think and write only as a Jew, not as a German. The Rector of the University at that time was Wilhelm von Möllendorff, the anatomist under whose guidance Krebs had carried out his first scientific experiments 10 years before. Möllendorff ordered the posters removed from the University. The cost of such resistance was high, however. Möllendorff was quickly removed from his office, replaced by the pro-Nazi philosopher Martin Heidigger.[115]

Less distinguished members of the Faculty were more easily intimidated than Aschoff or Möllendorff. Arnold Loeser, a pharmacologist who had participated with Krebs and Hermann Eitel on an investigation of the metabolism of the thyroid gland, was firmly anti-Nazi. When the members of the faculty were ordered to participate in weekly Wednesday evening drill sessions of local Nazi storm troopers, Loeser refused, asserting that he needed to carry on his research at that time. The director of the Pharmacological Institute, Dr. Sigurd Janssen, responded by telling Loeser that the Institute would be closed on Wednesday evenings. Janssen was not a Nazi; he was merely afraid to lend even oblique support to a show of independence.[116]

In the tense atmosphere that prevailed, Krebs was not himself treated rudely, but people who had been friendly with him before now tended to keep a safe distance. Those with whom he shared a similar fate met to talk over how they would get out,[117] but otherwise, he must have been largely cut off from social and professional contact. Under the circumstances, he concentrated on the only constructive thing he could do — write. Since he could not write all day, he also spent much of his time taking long walks.[118]

VII

The first "literary" business with which Krebs had to deal after May 1 was undoubtedly the revisions to his manuscript on the decomposition of amino acids. As editor of *Hoppe Seyler's Zeitschrift*, Knoop received his latest contribution with noticeably less enthusiasm than he had the urea synthesis paper the previous summer. "I can only congratulate you for your beautiful results," he wrote on April 30. "All that you have done strengthens and completes our previous views in the best way, and shows how valuable the Warburg method is for the direction of investigation that I have always pursued." With reason, Knoop saw Krebs's latest effort not as the strikingly original contribution he had made on urea synthesis, but as a useful extension and confirmation of what others, including himself, had already done. Knoop complained about the fact that much of the content had already been published word-for-word in the *Klinische Wochenschrift*, but let that pass. After asking for some minor changes of format, and making a cogent suggestion concerning the section on Bergmann's dipeptides, he came to a "personal" matter, of which he wrote "reluctantly."

He felt that Krebs had neglected to mention Knoop's own contribution to the
problem about which he was writing. For two pages Knoop went on with an
elaborate justification of the importance of his demonstration of the reversibility
of the deamination reaction — that amino acids are formed by the reduction of
keto acids — for the theory of oxidative deamination. It was, he said "unpleasant for me to make such claims....But when a young man, who in other respects
does good work, enters this field for the first time, and acts afterward as though
the results he has now obtained are preceded by those of only *one* person
(N[eubauer]),..this has a rather comical effect."[119]

Once again Krebs had received a lesson in the sensitivity of the senior
scientists in his field to their own positions and reputations. They were
supportive and encouraging, but they expected something in return. Failure to
recognize their contributions could easily make the rising young star appear in
their eyes as aggressively self-seeking. Krebs had no wish to create such an
impression. Whether or not he agreed with Knoop's assessment, he gave him
his due. The final version of his manuscript carefully acknowledged Knoop's
work in keeping with the way Knoop had represented it in his letter.[120]

Krebs omitted from his main article on amino acid metabolism a discussion
of the experiments on glutamic acid and aspartic acid that he had carried out
during the last week that he had been permitted to work in his laboratory.
Perhaps the paper had already been too near completion to fit them in, or
perhaps he viewed the investigation as incomplete. Now, however, undoubtedly
because he foresaw that he would not be able to continue it in the near future,
he decided to report these results in a short supplementary article entitled
"Further Investigations of the Decomposition of Amino Acids in the Animal
Body." Besides pointing out that he had now isolated the keto acid products for
two more oxidative deamination reactions, he stressed the novel result that he
had encountered with these two acids — that along with the quantity of keto
acids, the quantity of ammonia obtained increased when he added arsenite. He
interpreted this finding as meaning that "The poisoning prevents not only the
consumption of the keto acids in the cells, but also the consumption of
ammonia." The consumption of keto acids had been assumed to be their
decomposition; that of ammonia, however, he assumed to mean its entry into
another compound. He ended his discussion on a poignant note:

> The question, which nitrogen compounds arise from the ammonia... and
> from the amino acids, especially from glutamic acid in the unpoisoned
> kidney cell, I could not answer, since I had to break off the work.[121]

Unexpected observations such as this effect of arsenite on the observed quantity
of ammonia had, as we have seen, typically been for Krebs germinal points in
new lines or phases of his investigations. It must have been particularly
disheartening for him to have to stop just as he had uncovered so interesting a
lead.

From the early stages of his urea investigation Krebs had, as we saw in
Chapter 8, tested the pyrimidine compounds as possible precursors of urea.

Despite repeatedly negative results, he had been interested in them enough to return to them at intervals throughout the investigation. Now as he sat in his apartment looking for results in his laboratory notebooks that he could turn into scientific publications, he decided to pull together some of the experiments that he or Henseleit had performed over the last 2 years into a paper entitled "On the Decomposition of the Pyrimidines in the Animal Body." Since Franz Bielschowsky had made some of the pyrimidines and pyrimidine nucleosides for him, Krebs listed as authors of the paper Krebs, Henseleit, and Bielschowsky. Concerning the formation of urea he had only his negative results to give. On the positive side, the pyrimidines did yield ammonia, although at low rates. The rate was increased by adding HCN. The main conclusion he could draw was "to confirm with tissue slices the experience of earlier authors, that the pyrimidines can be decomposed only relatively slowly in the animal body."[122] This was, at best, a modest contribution, and it was perhaps for that reason that Krebs did not, in the end, publish the manuscript. It was a paper that he might not have written at all, if he had had other things to do.

During this period Krebs also did a little ghostwriting. Hildegard Manderschied's MD thesis "On the Formation of Urea in Vertebrates" appeared to contain results worth publishing. Krebs wrote the paper, and submitted it under her name. The text was a routine application to materials from amphibians, reptiles, and fish, of the methods that Krebs had worked out originally with mammalian tissue. The article contained, however, a striking visual novelty. At the end of a brief introductory paragraph describing the reactions of urea synthesis, he added "In urea synthesis ornithine therefore passes through a circuit corresponding to the following scheme:"[123]

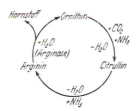

In his original papers, as we have seen, Krebs had not depicted the process this way, but in the form of conventional linear equations, in which ornithine appeared both as one of the initial reactants in the first reaction and of the final products in the last reaction (see Chapter 10, pp. 333, 336). The new way of representing the sequence provided a more emphatic, transparent way to visualize the "closed circuit" (*Kreislauf*), in which ornithine, citrulline, and arginine are continually regenerated, while CO_2 and NH_3 "enter" the circuit and urea is given off as the net product.

The new diagram appears to be both a dramatic departure and a striking anticipation of the now common mode of representing such processes. We are immediately led to ask whether Krebs devised this diagram purely out of his imagination, or whether he drew on some precedents. As we have seen, closed reaction circuits were not unprecedented. The Thunberg-Knoop-Wieland reaction scheme was a prominent example of such a scheme, and one that was very much on Krebs's mind at just this time. It was, however, not usually represented in such diagrammatic form, but, as Krebs himself portrayed it, as a linear sequence in which the reader must mentally identify the end of the chain with the beginning. One of the few people who *had* represented closed reaction circuits in maplike diagrams was Joachim Kühnau, who, as we saw in Chapter 1 (pp. 25-26), set out a series of interlocked reaction chains, including the Thunberg-Knoop-Wieland scheme, in a somewhat cumbersome network of interconnecting arrows. Krebs was also familiar with Kuhnau's article. There is no indication, however, that he connected his *Kreislauf des Ornithins* conceptually with any of these reaction schemes as examples of a general type of pathway.

Visually, Krebs's circular pathway resembles most closely two diagrams that had appeared in papers published by his own mentor, Otto Warburg. One of these depicted the cyclic oxidation and reduction of the *Atmungsferment*:[124]

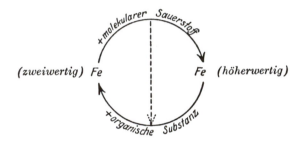

The other was a way of representing Meyerhof's view of the formation of lactic acid, and the resynthesis of carbohydrate from it, which Warburg introduced in 1924 as a form of *Kreislauf*.[125]

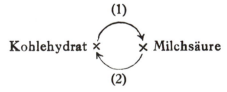

It is tempting to think that Krebs might have had these diagrams in the back of his mind when he drew his own, even though he did not conceive his *Kreislauf des Ornithins* as similar to either of these processes.

* * *

In September 1976, I drew Krebs's attention to the fact that the familiar diagram of urea synthesis appeared first in the Manderschied article rather than in his original papers on the subject. He did not regard the innovation as significant. "The original article," he said, "contains the corresponding equations. But this [circular diagram] is just one way of putting it, especially for the purpose of lecturing." When I responded, "So it doesn't represent so much a conceptual clarification as just a way of...?", he interrupted, "No. It is merely a didactic, visual help."[126]

Literally, Krebs was correct in his opinion, yet the "didactic visual help" may have been more than a trivial aid toward conceptual clarification. Visual imagery, it is increasingly recognized, is often intimately associated with creative scientific thought.[127] When I once asked Krebs what "mental images" he had "of...intermediary metabolic processes...distinct from the formal representations that one puts down on paper?", he answered "My image is essentially that which is on paper."[128]

* * *

On May 4 Krebs wrote Blaschko:

> I have nearly decided now to go to England if it is in any way possible. Hopkins wrote that he must still arrange the financial side. I hope it will happen! I stayed in Zurich only for a few hours. The situation there is not unfavorable, but in the long run even Switzerland is dangerous.[129]

As he kept himself busy with his writing, and awaited further word about his chances in England, Krebs learned from Thannhauser, on May 13, that the representative of the Rockefeller Foundation in Paris, Robert Lambert, had enquired about his situation. The Foundation had awarded Thannhauser a research grant in 1932 of 10,000 marks, of which Thannhauser allotted a substantial portion for Krebs's work. With Thannhauser's approval, Krebs wrote Lambert directly to describe his circumstances. He would rather go to Cambridge than to Zurich, he explained, but Hopkins had not yet been able to report on whether the financial means could be made available. Since he did have the assurance of laboratory space there, he decided to appeal to Lambert.

> As soon as the decision is made, I shall inform you about it. In the meantime, however, I would like to make the large request that you continue to give me the financial assistance that you have provided up until now. Out of the support that you have placed at Prof. Thannhauser's disposal, about 700 RM have been employed for my work. In the future, when I can work only as a guest of an institute, I shall naturally be more dependent than ever upon your support.[130]

Possibly Krebs was encouraged to make this request in part because it had been a personal Rockefeller research grant that had enabled Ostern to work as a guest in his own laboratory. Lambert replied promptly but briefly, to say that he planned to be in Cambridge later that week, and would talk to Hopkins about the matter.[131] Meanwhile, on May 15, Hopkins wrote,

Dear Dr. Krebs

>   I know you must be feeling impatient, but I feel I must ask you to
> wait a little before I can send any definite news of the situation.
>   The appeal for a large maintenance fund for workers from Germany
> has now been started, but the issue is not yet known.

After mentioning that a member of his staff had heard that there might be an
opening for a biochemist at Oxford, Hopkins closed with

>   I do not know whether you had any other offers of hospitality; if not, I
> would ask you to wait a little for further information from myself.[132]

Since he did have another offer of hospitality, Krebs had first to contact Löffler
to see if he *could* wait a little further. Löffler generously agreed to hold the
place open for him until Krebs received a more definite report from Hopkins;
but as Krebs put it in relaying this information to Hopkins, "Prof. Löffler wrote
me that he would be thankful to have an early decision." Krebs assured Hopkins
that he would "be happy to wait, if only your efforts can be successful." He
had "many reasons to prefer England," he added, "for the general working
conditions and the facilities of the laboratories in the Zurich institute are in no
way comparable to those of Cambridge."[133]
    On May 17, Krebs enjoyed a refreshing break from the combination of daily
monotony and anxiety that he must have been experiencing during these trying
times. He took the train to Basel that day to hear a lecture by Gustav Embden.
Three months earlier Embden had published in the *Klinische Wochenschrift* an
article "On the Intermediary Processes in Glycolysis in Muscle" that was
transforming the state of that field. Embden had long opposed Neuberg's
influential view that methylglyoxal is central to glycolysis, because, among other
reasons, in preparations from animal tissue the process produced pure d-lactic
acid, whereas methylglyoxal is transformed into a mixture of both optical
isomers. Now Embden was able to provide convincing evidence for a different
glycolytic pathway. According to Embden's view, fructose diphosphate is
decomposed into two triose phosphate molecules, dihydroxyacetone phosphate
and glyceraldehyde phosphate. These two compounds then undergo a Cannizzaro dismutation reaction yielding glycerol phosphate and phosphoglyceric acid.
The first of the latter two compounds is then transformed "with the splitting off
of the phosphate, into pyruvic acid." Finally, the pyruvic acid is reduced to
lactic acid "at the cost of an oxidative formation of triosphosphate [glyceralde-
hyde phosphate] out of the glycerolphosphate."[134]
    Embden's theory, the climax of developments to which he and others had
contributed over a long preceding period, was not a drastic departure from the
general pattern of the pathways of fermentation and glycolysis that Neuberg's
scheme had presented. In his incorporation of dismutation reactions, and of a
central step in which a six-carbon compound is split into two three-carbon
compounds, it was another in the family of theories with a similar overall
structure that had been proposed since the beginning of the century. For the
hexoses and trioses of the earlier schemes it substituted the phosphorylated

derivatives. It also overturned another long-standing assumption of intermediary carbohydrate metabolism, one that we have seen operative in Krebs's early efforts in the field in 1931: the belief that the anaerobic phase ends with the formation of lactic acid, and the probable first step in the oxidative phase is the conversion of lactic acid to pyruvic acid. Here, pyruvic acid appeared within the anaerobic phase, as the product of a balanced oxidation-reduction process, and lactic acid came *after* pyruvic acid in the sequence.

"As one can see," Embden wrote, "this picture of glycolysis omits the methylglyoxal that was accepted by Neuberg as an intermediary product in yeast fermentation as well as in glycolytic lactate formation."[135] The long reign of Neuberg's views was suddenly over. Krebs, who had, as we have seen, carried out experiments only 2 years earlier under the general influence of the methylglyoxal theory, and who had retained an interest in current publications concerning methylglyoxal even after he ceased to pursue the problem experimentally, must have been quite aware that a new era had opened in this subfield of intermediary metabolism. In Basel he heard Embden present an impressive lecture on the subject of his new pathway, and had the good fortune to travel back with him on the train to Freiburg.[136]

On May 22 Krebs heard further from Robert Lambert. He had had only 2 or 3 minutes to speak with Hopkins in England, and learned only what Krebs already knew — that Hopkins "would be delighted to have you in his laboratory, but that as yet no fund for salary was available." Lambert had told Hopkins "of our interest in seeing you established in a place where your research could be satisfactorily continued." He advised Krebs, however, to take the Zurich offer if it provided satisfactory conditions "and reasonable assurance respecting the future." Otherwise he should "reserve decision until Professor Hopkins can give you a definite statement. That might require a delay of several weeks." He added that he might be able to come to Freiburg to discuss the matter more fully on the 8th or 10th of June.[137]

Further delays could not have been welcome to Krebs, but he could only make the best of it if he wished to hold out for Cambridge. He replied quickly that the position in Zurich was temporary, and that he would rather go to Cambridge if it were at all possible. Löffler was keeping the place open for him, but needed a decision soon. "It would be difficult for me to make a decision," he wrote, "since I cannot judge how good my chances in Cambridge really are."[138]

Perhaps sensing Krebs's quandary, Lambert pressed the matter quickly. He returned to England, and reported back that Krebs's prospects in England looked so favorable that he ought to decline Löffler's offer. Even if Cambridge did not work out, there were other possibilities in Oxford or London. Undoubtedly one reason that Lambert judged the situation optimistically was that he was confident that the Rockefeller Foundation would be able to help meet the "necessary financial conditions." By the end of May Krebs could write Blaschko, who had by now reached London himself, that he "definitely believed that I will come to England." Still taking nothing for granted, he explored other leads. He wrote to his old chief, Leo Lichtwitz, who had since become director of the Ludwig

Virchow Hospital in Berlin, to see if there was anything available there, and he inquired of the *Zentralstelle für Judische Wirtschaftshilfe* whether that organization could assist him in finding a foreign position. He had already followed up Hopkins's suggestion about Oxford by writing the head of the biochemistry department there, R.A. Peters.[139]

Lambert visited Krebs in early June, as promised, and probably told him that he would recommend that the foundation fund his salary at Cambridge. It would probably be 2 or 3 weeks, however, before one would know whether the grant were approved.[140] Krebs waited until June 12 to write Zurich. When he had still no further news from Cambridge, he decided that he could not keep Löffler in uncertainty, and he wrote apologetically that "under the circumstances I can no longer ask you to keep a place open at your Institute."[141]

On May 31, Krebs had written Blaschko that Hopkins had written "I must still have patience. I have that in abundance."[142] Two weeks later, however, his patience had run out, and he decided to leave for England without waiting to know whether or not Hopkins had been able to manage the "financial side." He persuaded local hospital administrators who remained sympathetic to him to allow his technician, Georg Keller, to pack his Warburg apparatus, and other laboratory equipment that had been provided through grants, into 16 boxes. The local district police approved their shipment to England. On June 19 he said good-bye to Henseleit and a few other associates, walked to the railroad station, and caught the 11 AM train for Strasburg.[143]

* * *

Those with whom I was able to speak who had known Hans Krebs during the period leading to his departure from Germany uniformly remembered him as having passed through his ordeal in remarkably good spirits, with optimism. Contemporary letters support that assessment. His letters to Blaschko, in particular, convey a hopeful mood in the face of adversity. His letters to family and friends, to judge from their responses, were buoyant. They should not worry about him, he wrote, he had become an *internationaler Wertgegenstand* ["article of international value"] and would be assured of a place to continue his career in a foreign country.[144] Krebs did far more than to endure this trying period calmly, waiting to be saved by those who admired his achievements. He acted astutely and persistently in pursuit of his future prospects. "It was clear what we had to do," he said to me in 1976. "Try and make use of any reputation or connections to get out."[145] Krebs did just that. He followed up every lead he had or was offered. He handled the three-way negotiations with Hopkins, Lambert, and Löffler with diplomatic skill. Moreover, in his usual manner, even when barred from his normal professional activities he did not permit himself to waste time. Throwing himself into his writing, he had, by the end of May completed six papers, and was working on two more.[146] (Perhaps he realized afterward that by the end of this time he was writing papers mainly to keep busy, for the later papers seem to have left no trace.) He also kept up with the latest interesting developments in his field.

After recounting his departure from Germany in his autobiography, Krebs commented, "Optimism — in the sense of hoping for the best although preparing for the worst — has always been my keynote; instinctively I tend to fasten on to favourable aspects and play down adverse ones."[147] Optimism was essential to carry him through the events of 1933 that drove him out of his country; but his was not a simple, unbounded optimism. Various episodes during his life suggest that, under some circumstances he could feel profound pessimism.[148] If optimism was his keynote, I believe that it was an attitude he had to acquire, and to maintain, through strength of will. Despite the strong positive tone of his correspondence during the weeks of his forced leave and his dismissal, there are a few overtones suggesting that he endured some darker feelings as well. References to the likelihood of a swastika flying eventually over Zurich, and to Switzerland as still too dangerous, suggest not only a foreboding sense of future Nazi triumph, but some fear for his own future. So long as he was able to carry on his work in Freiburg, he was undeterred by the Nazi presence around him. Once that became impossible, he wanted to get farther away than Switzerland. In a letter to Hopkins upon his arrival in London he wrote, "It became almost too dangerous to stay in Freiburg any longer."[149] There are no indications that he was actually in imminent personal danger. It appears rather that the general atmosphere in Germany by then had made him increasingly apprehensive about what might possibly happen.

Krebs had, in fact, less to fear than many others who were dismissed at the same time that he was. Almost immediately he had a place where he could have gone to continue his work for a time, and he remained in Freiburg for as long as he did mainly because he hoped to go instead to a more attractive, permanent position. His friends, colleagues, and relatives often had the choice between trying to survive in Germany, or becoming refugees, with no certain employment in the lands to which they took flight. Though excluded from his former places of work in Freiburg, he was still protected by a chief who supported him strongly, in spite of his own special vulnerability as a Jew given an uncertain reprieve because of a distinguished wartime record. Nevertheless, we cannot be surprised if there were some inner cracks underneath Krebs's confident outer bearing. Even if not directly endangered — even though his long-term prospects might be auspicious — his immediate experiences were harrowing and humiliating. To be locked on an hour's notice out of a laboratory in which one had recently achieved distinction; to receive coldly impersonal notices of dismissal on no other grounds than one's racial background; to witness the rapid spread of violent words and brutal acts in one's surroundings, could leave only the most callow optimist unperturbed about what might happen next.

The ordeal of April and May 1933 confronted Krebs, I believe, with another deep problem, that of his own identity. Never in his life until then had he encountered anti-Semitism directed personally at him; nor had discrimination against Jews significantly hindered his professional advancement. Although Warburg had warned him that, as a Jew, he would have trouble finding an academic position, he in fact obtained a position ideally suited to his purposes. Raised in a household whose head believed that assimilation was the best

solution for Jews, never formally introduced into the Jewish religion, having as
a young adult relinquished his Jewish identity through an official declaration,
Krebs thought of himself as a German.   He later attributed the absence of
anti-Semitic remarks directed at him as due to people "not appreciating" that he
was a Jew.[150] Before April 1933 he may not have fully appreciated that fact
himself.   Suddenly he was treated not as a German, but as a Jew, and as an
enemy of the German people. Did he then come as suddenly to think of himself
as a Jew? There is some hint of his uncertainty over this question. In one letter
to Hopkins he wrote that "because I am a Jew" he had lost the opportunity to
work in Germany; but in several similar statements to others he attributed the
situation to his "Jewish descent."[151] Undoubtedly his immediate concerns did
not permit him to dwell on the problem, but his experience forced him for the
first time to view himself as a member of a group — whether defined sharply as
Jews, or vaguely as "non-Aryans" — that had been singled out in his own native
land for relentless persecution.

13

Reflections on the Formation
of a Scientific Life

Hans Krebs took 31 years to become a well-trained independent scientific investigator, and only 9 months more to make one of the most significant discoveries of his generation in his chosen field. Retrospectively it is easy to organize the varied episodes in his life until 1931 as the necessary preparation for his auspicious achievement. An early interest in nature, fostered by his father; the well-organized use of his time, even as a boy; the industrious student in his Gymnasium years, who absorbed information very well even if he did not shine; the disciplining effect of his short interlude of military service; the purposeful, determined student of medicine who absorbed from his teachers a keen interest in research; lectures by Franz Knoop that outlined the approach to intermediary metabolism he was later to pursue so successfully; the early opportunity to whet his appetite for research under the guidance of von Möllendorff; the resourceful exploitation of the local opportunities for clinical research during his hospital year; the year spent in Rona's laboratory to repair the deficiencies in his chemical education, were all climaxed by an apprenticeship in the laboratory of the great Otto Warburg that provided him with the methods, the standards, and much of the style that enabled him, as soon as he was on his own, to solve one of the large biochemical problems of his time.

Although all of these events did contribute to the accumulated personal resources that Krebs could bring to bear on his investigative enterprise, there was nothing inevitable, or even probable about the position he had reached by the summer of 1931 when he began his investigation of the formation of urea. As we have seen, his boyhood and youth were not marked by any driving theme, by an ambition to excel, by persistent concentration on a special interest that can be seen retrospectively as connected with the arena he later entered, or even by special talents marking him as a potential scientist. As a boy and as a young man, Hans did "everything reasonably well" but nothing with such distinctive success as to point his way toward some highly creative adult activity.

It would be misleading to invest the young Hans Krebs's sustained interest in collecting wildflowers with prescient meaning, in the manner in which biographies so often discern in such boyhood activities of future scientists evidence of deep, early involvement with nature. Krebs was equally interested in reading, music, bookbinding, and other hobbies that might augur future careers in very different directions. In school he was little exposed to science and satisfied with an education oriented instead around literature, the classics, and other humanistic subjects.

Krebs's pathway from childhood to adulthood did not manifest a persistent striving toward distant goals generated through some inner vision. It was determined largely by local circumstances and unforeseen vicissitudes. Anxious to do what was expected of him, he was heavily influenced by a succession of powerful older figures in his life. The proximity of a father whom he held in awe and admiration induced him to train for medical practice. A rigorous Gymnasium teacher, Johannes Gebauer, enhanced his interest in history, and a demanding but personable piano teacher, Richard Gerlt, inspired him to devote himself to intense practice despite his lack of special musical talent.

In medical school it was the contagious example of distinguished professors rather than a preset personal orientation that attracted Krebs toward research. Once he had acquired a taste for experimentation, he displayed a strong self-motivation to create opportunities for himself to pursue it; but the nature of the research was shaped by the environment in which he found himself rather than by deeply personal choices. In Möllendorff's laboratory his subject was histology, in the III Medical Clinic the topics of his research were those of interest to the clinicians who encouraged him. These early opportunities prompted him to see colloid chemistry as particularly pertinent to medical research, and he invested a great deal of energy in assimilating textbook knowledge of that field. Much of what he learned in that way proved to be irrelevant to what he later did.

Until 1926 Krebs assumed that the research he would do would lie somewhere within internal medicine and be closely connected with his clinical activities. The opportunity to enter Warburg's laboratory not only depended on unforeseeable circumstances, but completely reoriented his outlook toward research and toward the areas within which he might engage in it. Warburg stood apart from the medical establishment, and under his influence Krebs came to view himself as an aspiring biochemist rather than a physician with research interests. At the end, however, Warburg's attitude toward him, and his dampening counsel that biochemistry was not a viable profession for him, forced Krebs back to his earlier choice of combined clinical and experimental responsibilities. He now brought to that arrangement research experience and problems acquired outside the medical environment. Consequently, the related experimental topics he chose to study in Altona and in Freiburg were more independent of his responsibilities as a physician than he could have envisioned before his years in Dahlem.

Hans Krebs enjoyed a remarkable measure of good luck at critical junctures in his early career. His release from the army after a brief period of service accelerated his education instead of delaying it.   The helpfulness of von Möllendorff in giving him a project he could manage and encouraging him to publish on his own nurtured his conviction that research was a pathway open to him. His friend Bruno Mendel's contacts with Warburg brought him unexpectedly the training opportunity that shaped his investigative future. The special liking that Klothilde Gollwitzer-Meier took for him after meeting him in far-off America prompted her to help him obtain in Germany two clinical appointments favorably situated for his research interests, at a time when such positions were rare and no one else gave him encouragement. He seemed able to attract crucial interventions on his behalf just when he needed them most.

Krebs was fortunate also to pass personally unscathed through the turmoils of his age. He just missed active participation in a deadly war, and his father's professional security protected him from the ravages of one of the worst inflations in modern history. The rising waves of anti-Semitism in Germany did not directly touch him until he had had time to establish himself as so promising a young scientist that when he then fell victim to the policies of the Nazi regime there were admirers in his field ready to help him continue.

The large role that external conjunctures played in propelling and directing Krebs does not imply that he was himself a malleable, indecisive, or merely opportunistic individual. If he neither planned nor looked far into the future, he possessed in abundance the intelligence, the will, the discipline, and the capacity for relentless work to make the most of the opportunities that lay in his path. Nor was he merely ambitious. He treated his scientific work, as he treated his clinical activity, as serious responsibilities, and he sought to be as reliable as he was resourceful.

Self-perceptions can differ markedly from the perceptions of those around one. To his brother Wolf it appeared that every move Hans Krebs made was carefully calculated to advance his career, even down to the friendship he formed with an English-speaking woman to improve his knowledge of that language. To Hans himself it appeared that he had no grand design for his future, that the steps he took were often shaped by chance.

Deeply woven into the texture of Hans Krebs's early life was a tension between dependence and autonomy, between conformity to expectations and creative initiative.   Raised in a culture in which respect for authority was strongly instilled, Krebs subordinated himself readily to mentors whom he respected. Yet he was not slow to exercise his own judgment when he found himself in a position to do so.   There are striking parallels between his relationship as a son to his father and his relationship as a research apprentice to Warburg. In both cases he was at once inspired and intimidated. He admired both men greatly, but he had to struggle eventually to gain his independence from each of them. He escaped the domination of his father by leaving home, doing well at medical school, and abandoning his youthful plan to join his father's practice in favor of his new-found interest in research. He achieved his independence from Warburg by adapting Warburg's methods to an area of research that was not in direct competition with his former chief and attaining there an impressive success. By the time he had done this, the doubts that both of these men may have harbored about his capacity to become a creative scientist had evaporated, and they had acquired a pride in his accomplishment fully matching the esteem he felt for them.

NOTES

Introduction

1. Frederic Lawrence Holmes, *Claude Bernard and Animal Chemistry* (Cambridge, Mass.: Harvard University Press, 1974); Frederic Lawrence Holmes, *Lavoisier and the Chemistry of Life: an Exploration of Scientific Creativity* (Madison, Wisc.: The University of Wisconsin Press, 1985).
2. Howard E. Gruber, *Darwin on Man: A Psychological Study of Scientific Creativity*, 2d. ed. (Chicago, Ill.: The University of Chicago Press, 1981), pp. xx–xxii.
3. Gerald Holton, *The Scientific Imagination: Case Studies* (Cambridge: Cambridge University Press, 1978), pp. 3–6.
4. Robert J. Richards, *Darwin and the Emergence of Evolutionary Theories of Mind and Behavior* (Chicago: The University of Chicago Press, 1987), pp. 17–19.
5. Deepak Kulkarni and Herbert A. Simon, "The Processes of Scientific Discovery: The Strategy of Experimentation," *Cognitive Science*, 12 (1988): 139–175.

Chapter 1

1. I have described Lavoisier's investigation of respiration in detail in *Lavoisier and the Chemistry of Life* (Madison, Wisc.: University of Wisconsin Press, 1984).
2. F.L. Holmes, "Elementary analysis and the origins of physiological chemistry," *Isis*, 54 (1963): 70.
3. *Ibid.*, p. 75.
4. F.L. Holmes "Carl Voit and the Quantitative Tradition in Biology," in *Transformation and Tradition in the Sciences: Essays in Honor of I. Bernard Cohen*, ed. Everett Mendelsohn, (Cambridge: Cambridge University Press, 1984), pp. 455–470.
5. For strong statements of this position, see especially Jean-Baptiste Dumas, *Essai de statique chimique des êtres organisés*, 2d. ed. (Paris: Fortin, Masson, 1842), pp. 35, 43, 46; and Carl Gotthelf Lehmann, *Lehrbuch der physiologischen Chimie*, 2d. ed. (Leipzig: Englemann, 1853), 3: 202–204.
6. See Joseph S. Fruton, *Molecules and Life: Historical Essays in the Interplay of Chemistry and Biology* (New York: Wiley-Interscience, 1972), pp. 108–120.
7. F.L. Holmes, "Early Theories of Protein Metabolism," in *The Origins of Modern Biochemistry: A Retrospect of Proteins*, ed. P.R. Srinivasan, Joseph S. Fruton, John T. Edsall, Annals of the New York Academy of Sciences, vol. 325 (New York: N.Y. Academy of Sciences, 1979), pp. 171–187); F.G. Hopkins, "The Dynamic Side of Biochemistry," in *Hopkins and Biochemistry*, ed. J. Needham and E. Baldwin, (Cambridge: Heffer, 1947), p. 137.
8. See Robert E. Kohler, "The background to Eduard Buchner's discovery of cell-free fermentation," *Journal of the History of Biology* 4 (1971): 35–61; and "The Reception of Eduard Buchner's Discovery of Cell-Free Fermentation," *Ibid.*, 5 (1972): 327–353.
9. Olof Hammarsten, *Lehrbuch der physiologische Chemie*, 11th ed., (Munich: Bergmann, 1926), p. 701.
10. Robert E. Kohler, "The Enzyme Theory and the Origin of Biochemistry," *Isis*, 64 (1973): 181–196.
11. Fruton, *Molecules and Life*, pp. 314–322; Hammarsten, *Lehrbuch*, pp. 705–712; Thorsten Thunberg, "Der jetzige Stand der Lehre vom biologischen Oxydationsmechanismus," in *Handbuch*

der Biochemie des Menschen und der Tiere, ed. Carl Oppenheimer, 2d. ed., Suppl. Vol. (Jena: Gustav Fischer, 1930), pp. 245-273; Marcel Florkin, *A History of Biochemistry: Part III: History of the Identification of the Sources of Free Energy in Organisms*, Comprehensive Biochemistry, vol. 31 (Amsterdam, Elsevier, 1975), pp. 187-218.

12. Franz Knoop, *Der Abbau aromatischer Fettsäuren im Tierkörper* (Freiburg: Kuttruff, 1904); Knoop, "Der Abbau aromatischer Fettsäuren im Tierkörper," *Beitr. chem. Physiol.*, 6 (1905): 150-162; Fruton, *Molecules and Life*, pp. 450-456.

13. Franz Knoop, "Über den physiologischen Abbau der Säuren und die Synthese einer Aminosäure im Tierkörper," *Z. physiol. Chem.*, 67 (1910): 489-502.

14. Franz Knoop, *Oxydationen im Tierkörper* (Stuttgart: Ferdinand Enke, 1931), pp. 7, 10.

15. See, for example, Knoop, *Oxydationen im Tierkörper*, pp. 10-11, for an explicit discussion of this point. More often it was assumed implicitly.

16. Felix Hoppe-Seyler, *Physiologische Chemie* (Berlin: Hirschwald, 1881), pp. 987-993, 1000.

17. M.V. Pettenkofer and C. Voit, "Ueber den Stoffverbrauch bei der Zuckerharnruhr," *Z. Biol.*, 3 (1867): 380-444.

18. O. Minkowski, "Ueber das Vorkommen von Oxybuttersäure im Harn bei Diabetes mellitus," *Arch. Exper. Path.*, 18 (1884): 35-48; "Nachtrag über Oxybuttersäure im diabetischen Harne," *Ibid.*, p. 150.

19. Georg Rosenfeld, "Fett und Kohlenhydrate," *Klin. Woch.*, 43 (1906): 978-981.

20. Hans Christian Geelmuyden, "Über Acetongehalt der Organe an Coma diabeticum Verstorbener nebst Beiträgen zur Theorie des Acetonstoffwechsels," *Z. physiol. Chem.*, 41 (1904): 135-148.

21. Gustav Embden and F. Kalberlah, "Über Acetonbildung in der Leber: Erste Mitteilung" *Beitr. chem. Physiol.*, 8 (1906): 121-128; G. Embden, H. Salomon, and Fr. Schmidt, "Über Acetonbildung in der Leber: Zweite Mitteilung: Quellen des Acetons," *Ibid.*, pp. 129-155; G. Embden and Alfred Marx, "Über Acetonbildung in der Leber," *Ibid.*, 11 (1908): 318-319; G. Embden and Hans Engel, "Über Acetessigsäurebildung in der Leber," *Ibid.*, pp. 323-326.

22. G. Embden and Louis Michaud, "Über den Abbau der Acetessigsäure im Tierkörper," *Ibid.*, pp. 332-347.

23. Otto Porges, "Über den Abbau der Fettsäuren im Organismus," *Erg. Physiol.*, 10 (1910): 32-33, 45.

24. Knoop, *Oxydationen im Tierkörper*, p. 15.

25. See especially Philip A. Shaffer, "Antiketogenesis," *J. Biol. Chem.*, 47 (1921): 433-473; 49 (1921): 143-162; 54 (1922): 399-441; P.A. Shaffer and T.E. Friedemann, *Ibid.*, 61 (1924): 585-623; Knoop, *Oxydationen im Tierkörper*, p. 28.

26. Federico Battelli and Lina Stern, "Recherches sur la respiration élémentaire des tissus," *Jour. de physiol.* (1907), p. 1.

27. *Ibid.*, pp. 2-16.

28. Thorsten Thunberg, "Ein Mikrorespirometer: ein neuer Respirationsapparat, um den respiratorischen Gasaustausch kleinerer Organe und Organismen zu bestimmen," *Skand. Arch. Physiol.*, 15 (1905): 74-85.

29. Thunberg, "Studien über die Beeinflussung des Gasaustausches des überlebenden Froschmuskels durch verschiedene Stoffe," *Ibid.*, 22 (1909) 406-427, 430-436; 24 (1911): 22-61.

30. Battelli and Stern, "Oxydation de l'acide succinique par les tissus animaux," *C.r. Soc. Biol.*, 1910, pp. 301-303; "Oxydation der Bernsteinsäure durch Tiergewebe," *Biochem. Z.*, 30 (1911): 172-178; "Die Oxydation der Citronen-, Apfel- und Fumarsäure durch Tiergewebe," *Ibid.*, 30 (1911): 478-505.

31. Battelli and Stern "Citronen-, Apfel- und Fumarsäure," pp. 500-501.

32. Henry Dakin, *Oxidations and Reductions in the Animal Body*, (London: Longmans, Green, 1912), pp. 45-46.

33. Dorothy Moyle Needham, "A Quantitative Study of Succinic Acid in Muscle," *Biochem. J.*, 21 (1927): 739-750.

34. Knoop, *Oxydationen im Tierkörper*, p. 17.

35. Hans V. Euler, Karl Myrbäck and Ragnar Nilsson, "Neuere Forschungen über den enzymatische Kohlenhydratabbau (I)," *Erg. Physiol.*, 26 (1928): 533.

36. Knoop, *Oxydationen im Tierkörper*, p. 18.

37. Eduard Buchner and Jakob Meisenheimer, "Die chemischen Vorgänge bei der alkoholischen Gährung," *Ber. chem. Ges.*, 37 (1904): 417-418; A. Wohl, "Die neueren Ansichten über den chemischen Verlauf der Gährung," *Bioch. Zeit.*, 5 (1907): 52-55.

38. This approach began with the scheme proposed in 1870 by Adolf Baeyer, whose principal influence on this question occurred after 1900. A. Baeyer, "Ueber die Wasserentziehung und ihre Bedeutung für das Pflanzenleben und die Gährung," *Ber. chem. Ges.*, 3 (1870): 63-75.

39. Wohl, "Chemischen Verlauf der Gärung," pp. 52-55; see also Emil Erlenmeyer, "Über die Bildung von Lävulinsäure und von Alkohol aus Zucker," *Journ. prakt. Chem.*, 71 (1905): 382-384; A.V. Lebedew, "Über den Mechanismus der alkoholischen Gärung," *Biochem. Z.*, 46 (1912): 487-488.

40. Buchner and Meisenheimer, "Die chemischen Vorgänge," pp. 419-421, 426.

41. Arthur Slator, "Über Zwischenprodukte der alkoholischen Gärung," *Ber. chem. Ges.*, 40 (1907): 123.

42. Wohl, "Chemischen Verlauf der Gärung," pp. 58-64; Paul Mayer-Karlsbad, "Zur Frage der Vergärbarkeit von Methylglyoxal," *Biochem. Z.*, 2 (1907): 435-437.

43. Carl Neuberg, "Der Zuckerumsatz der Zelle," in *Handbuch der Biochemie des Menschen und der Tiere*, ed. Carl Oppenheimer, Suppl. Vol. (Jena: Gustav Fischer, 1913), pp. 581-582.

44. C. Neuberg and A. Hildescheimer, "Über zuckerfreie Hefegärung, I." *Biochem. Z.*, 31 (1911): 170-176; C. Neuberg and L. Tir, "Über zuckerfreie Hefegärungen, II." *Ibid.*, 32 (1911): 323-331.

45. C. Neuberg and L. Karczag, "Über zuckerfreie Hefegärungen, III," *Ibid.*, 36 (1911): 60-67; *Ibid.*, "IV," pp. 68-75.

46. F. Battelli and L. Stern, "Die Aldehydase in den Tiergeweben,"*Biochem. Z.*, 29 (1910): 130-151; Jakob Parnas, "Über fermentative Beschleunigung der Cannizaroschen Aldehydumlagerung durch Gewebesäfte," *Ibid.*, 28 (1910): 274-294.

47. Fritz Lipmann, F.F. Nord, and H. Waelsch, "C. Neuberg, Biochemist," *Science*, 124 (1956): 1244.

48. Theodor Schwann set the precedent for this approach when he offered the example of alcoholic fermentation as "the best known illustration" of that activity of cells for which he coined the term metabolic. Schwann, *Microscopical Researches into the Accordance in the Structure and Growth of Animals and Plants*, tr. Henry Smith (London: Sydenham Society, 1847; reprint, New York: Kraus, 1969), pp. 193, 197-198.

49. See especially, Justus Liebig, "Ueber die Bestandtheile der Flüssigkeiten des Fleisches," *Ann. Chem.*, 62 (1847): 257-369.

50. Claude Bernard, *Leçons de physiologie expérimentale*, I (Paris: J.B. Baillière, 1855), pp. 244-246; Ludimar Hermann, *Untersuchungen über den Stoffwechsel der Muskeln* (Berlin: August Hirschwald, 1867), pp. 67-69; F. Hoppe-Seyler, "Ueber die Processe der Gährungen und ihre Beziehung zum Leben der Organismen," *Arch. ges. Physiol.*, 12 (1876): 1-17.

51. P. Spiro, "Beiträge zur Physiologie der Milchsäure," *Z. physiol. Chem.*, 1 (1877-1878): 111-118; Georg Salomon, "Ueber die Verbreitung und Entstehung von Hypoxanthin und Milchsäure im thierischen Organismus," *Ibid.*, 2 (1878-1879): 65-95; Wilhelm Marcuse, "Ueber die Bildung von Milchsäure bei der Thätigkeit des Muskels und ihr weiteres Schicksal im Organismus," *Archiv. ges. Physiol.*, 39 (1886): 426-427.

52. Rudolf Boehm, "Ueber das Verhalten des Glycogens und der Milchsäure im Muskelfleisch," *Ibid.*, 23 (1880): 44-68; Pavel Petrovich Astaschewsky, "Ueber die Säurebildung und den Milchsäuregehalt der Muskeln," *Z. physiol. Chem.*, 4 (1880): 397-406; Joseph W. Warren, "Ueber den Einfluss des Tetanus der Muskeln auf die in ihm enthaltenen Säuren," *Archiv ges. Physiol.*, 24 (1881): 391-406.

53. Walter M. Fletcher and Frederick Gowland Hopkins, "Lactic Acid in Amphibian Muscle," *J. Physiol.*, 35 (1907): 247-309.

54. Gustav Embden and Friedrich Kraus, "Über Milchsäurebildung in der künstlich durchströmten Leber," *Biochem. Z.*, 45 (1912): 1-17.

55. P.A. Levene and G.M. Meyer, "The Action of Leucocytes on Glucose," *J. Biol. Chem.*, 11 (1912): 361-370; "On the Action of Tissues on Hexoses," *Ibid.*, 15 (1913): 65-68.

56. Embden and Kraus, "Über Milchsäurebildung," pp. 1-2.

57. Carl Neuberg, "Über die Zerstörung von Milchsäurealdehyd und Methylglyoxal durch tierische Organe," *Biochem. Z.*, 49 (1913): 502–506; M. Tschernorutzky, "Über die Zerlegung von Brenztraubensäure durch tierische Organe," *Ibid.*, 43 (1912): 486–499.

58. Neuberg and Karczag, "Zuckerfrei Hefegärungen, IV": 68–75.

59. Paul Mayer, "Beitrag zur Frage der Kohlensäurebildung durch Organe," *Biochem. Z.*, 62 (1914): 462–469.

60. Otto Meyerhof, "Die Energieumwandlungen im Muskel," *Arch. ges. Physiol.*, 182 (1920): 232–283: 312–315; *Ibid.*, 185 (1920): 11–32; Meyerhof, *Chemical Dynamics of Life Phenomena* (Philadelphia: J.B. Lippincott, 1925); Meyerhof, "Recent Investigations on the Aerobic and Anaerobic Metabolism of Carbohydrates," *J. Gen. Physiol.*, 8 (1926): 533; Meyerhof, *Die chemischen Vorgänge im Muskel* (Berlin: Springer, 1930), pp. 13, 46.

61. Meyerhof, *Die chemischen Vorgänge*, pp. 17, 110–124, 140–166; Fruton, *Molecules and Life*, p. 350.

62. Meyerhof, *Die chemischen Vorgänge*, pp. 166–168.

63. *Ibid.*, p. 1.

64. See Knoop, *Oxydationen im Tierkörper*, pp. 14–15.

65. For an important discussion of such questions by a prominent representative of this type of investigation, see Euler, Myrbäck and Nilsson, "Enzymatischen Kohlenhydratabbau," pp. 531–567.

66. Julius Pohl, "Ueber die Oxydation des Methyl- und Aethylalkohols im Thierkörper," *Archiv Pharm.*, 31 (1893): 281–302.

67. Beth and Hans Euler, "Versuche zum Nachweis von Gärungsenzymen im Tierkörper," *Z. physiol. Chem.*, 97 (1916): 311–313.

68. Thorsten Thunberg, "Zur Kenntnis einiger autoxydabler Thioverbindungen," *Skand. Arch. Physiol.*, 30 (1913): 289–290.

69. Hans Einbeck, "Über das Vorkommen der Fumarsäure im freschen Fleische," *Z. physiol. Chem.*, 90 (1914): 303–307.

70. T. Thunberg, "Über die vitale Dehydrierung der Bernsteinsäure bei Abwesenheit von Sauerstoff," *Zentralblatt für Physiologic*, 31 (1916): 91–93.

71. Thorsten Thunberg, "Zur Kenntnis der Einwirkung tierischer Gewebe auf Methylenblau," *Skand. Arch. Physiol.*, 35 (1918): 163–195; "Zur Kenntniss des intermediären Stoffwechsels und der dabei wirksamen Enzyme," *Ibid.*, 40 (1920): 8–29.

72. Thunberg, "Einwirkung tierischer Gewebe," pp. 194–195; Thunberg, "Intermediären Stoffwechsels," p. 6.

73. Thunberg, "Intermediären Stoffwechsels," pp. 62–63.

74. *Ibid.*, p. 31.

75. *Ibid.*, pp. 54–55.

76. *Ibid.*, pp. 31–34.

77. *Ibid.*, pp. 56–57.

78. *Ibid.*, pp. 3–11.

79. *Ibid.*, pp. 90–91.

80. Gunnar Ahlgren, "Sur le champ d'action des déhydrogénases musculaires," *Acta Medica Scandinavica*, 57 (1923): 508–510. The schematic presentation is slightly inconsistent with Ahlgren's discussion, because it does not include acetaldehyde. The text does not indicate whether he was uncertain on this point, or merely omitted the acetaldehyde step to simplify his diagram. In the original the arrows shown here were dashes. They were evidently intended to represent reaction steps.

81. *Ibid.*, p. 512.

82. Thunberg, "Der Gasaustausch einiger niederer Thiere in seiner Abhängigkeit vom Sauerstoffpartiardruck," *Skand. Arch. Physiol.* 15 (1905): 184–195.

83. F. Knoop, "Wie werden unsere Hauptnährstoffe im Organismus verbrannt und wechselseitig ineinander übergeführt?" *Klin. Woch.*, 2 (1923): 60–63.

84. Heinrich Wieland, "Über den Mechanismus der Oxydationsvorgänge," *Erg. Physiol.*, 20 (1922): 498–500.

85. Heinrich Wieland, "Mechanismus der Oxydation und Reduktion in der lebenden Substanz," in *Handbuch der Biochemie des Menschen und der Tiere*, ed. Carl Oppenheimer, II (Jena: G. Fischer, 1925), p. 264.

86. Joachim Kühnau, "Über den Abbau der β-Oxybuttersäure durch Fermente der Leber," *Biochem. Z.*, 200 (1928): 29–60.

87. *Ibid.*, pp. 33–42.

88. *Ibid.*, pp. 42, 58.

89. Aleksei Bach and David Mikhlin, "Über die sogenannte Succino-Dehydrase," *Ber. chem. Ges.* 60 (1927): 827–832.

90. Amandus Hahn and W. Haarmann, "Ueber die Dehydrierung der Bernsteinsäure," *Z. Biol.*, 87 (1927): 107.

91. *Ibid.*, pp. 107–114; Hahn and Haarmann, "Ueber die Dehydrierung der Aepfelsäure," *Ibid.*, pp. 465–471; *Ibid.*, 88 (1928): 91–92; 88 (1929): 587–593; "Ueber die Dehydrierung der Bernsteinsäure," *Ibid.*, 89 (1929): 159–166; "Ueber Dehydrierungsvorgänge im Muskel," 89 (1930): 563–572.

92. Amandus Hahn, E. Fischbach and W. Haarmann, "Ueber die Dehydrierung der Milchsäure," *Ibid.*, 88 (1929): 516–522; Hahn and Haarmann, "Ueber die Dehydrierung der Zitronensäure," *Ibid.*, 89 (1929): 332–334; Hahn and Haarmann, "Ueber den Abbau von Fruktosediphosphorsäure, Glyzerinphosphorsäure and Propionsäure im Muskel," *Ibid.*, 90 (1930): 231–236.

93. The most recent comprehensive account of these events is Michael Bliss, *The Discovery of Insulin* (Chicago: University of Chicago, 1982).

94. Erich Toenniessen, "Über die Bedeutung der Bauchspeicheldrüse für die Oxydation der Milchsäure," *Verhandlungen des 35. Deutschen Kongresses für innere Medizin* 35 (1923): 193–194; "Kohlenhydratstoffwechsel und Pankreas," *Klin. Woch.*, 3 (1924): 212–213; "An welcher Substanz des Kohlehydratabbaus greift das Pankreashormon an?" *Z. physiol. Chem.*, 133 (1924): 158–164.

95. E. Toenniessen, "Der Abbau der Brenztraubensäure im Säugetier-muskel and seine Beeinflussung durch Insulin," *Verhandlungen der deutschen Gesellschaft für innere Medizin*, 38 (1926): 454–456.

96. E. Toenniessen and W. Fischer, "Methylglyoxal als Abbauprodukt der Glykose," *Z. physiol. Chem.*, 161 (1926): 254–264.

97. E. Toenniessen, "Über die Zwischenstufen des oxydativen Kohlenhydratabbaus," *Verhandlungen der deutschen Gesellschaft für innere Medizin*, 39 (1927): 213–214.

98. E. Toenniessen, *Ibid.*, 40 (1928): 252.

99. E. Toenniessen and E. Brinkmann, "Über den oxydativen Abbau der Kohlehydrate im Säugetiermuskel, insbesondere über die Bildung von Bernsteinsäure aus Brenztraubensäure," *Z. physiol. Chem.*, 187 (1930): 137, 147–148.

100. *Ibid.*, pp. 139–150.

101. *Ibid.*, pp. 150–151.

102. See Siegfried J. Thannhauser, "Kann der Organismus aus Fett Kohlenhydrat bilden?" *Deutsche Medizinische Wochenschrift*, 53 (1927): 1676–1680.

103. Toenniessen and Brinkmann, "Oxydativen Abbau der Kohlehydrate," pp. 158–159.

104. Ahlgren, "Déshydrogénases musculaires," pp. 509, 512.

105. Thorsten Thunberg, "Der jetzige Stand der Lehre vom biologischen Oxydationsmechanismus," in *Handbuch der Biochemie des Menschen und der Tiere*, ed. Carl Oppenheimer, 2d. ed. Suppl. Vol. (Jena: Gustav Fischer, 1930), pp. 253–254.

106. Knoop, *Oxydationen im Tierkörper*, pp. 8, 22–23, 27–29.

107. Robert Kohler, "The History of Biochemistry: A Survey," *Journal of the History of Biology*, 8 (1975): 314.

108. T. Thunberg, "Beeinflussung des Gasaustausches des überlebenden Froschmuskels," p. 433.

109. For example, Knoop, *Oxydationen im Tierkörper*, pp. 18, 28.

110. For example, Thannhauser, "Kann der Organismus aus Fett Kohlenhydrat bilden?" pp. 1679–1680.

Chapter 2

1. Hans Krebs, with Anne Martin, *Reminiscences and Reflections* (Oxford: Clarendon Press, 1981), 6; HAK–FLH, Aug. 9, 1977 (Tape 80, p. 7), May 10, 1979 (Tape 89, p. 19).
2. HAK–FLH, May 10, 1979 (Tape 89, pp. 19, 22), Dec. 16, 1979 (Tape 105, p. 14).
3. HAK–FLH, Feb. 17, 1978 (Tape 54, pp. 5–6); May 10, 1979 (Tape 89, pp. 27–28); May 12, 1979 (Tape 92, pp. 15–16); Wolf Krebs-FLH, Aug. 3, 1977 (Tape 35, p. 24), Sept. 15, 1986 (Tape 153, p. 4).
4. Krebs, *Reminiscences*, p. 6.
5. HAK–FLH, May 10, 1979 (Tape 89, pp. 20–24), Dec. 16, 1979 (Tape 105, p. 15); Wolf Krebs–FLH, Aug. 3, 1977 (Tape 34, p. 7); May 4, 1988 (Tape 156, p. 28); Johannes Gebauer, *Geschichte der Stadt Hildesheim* vol. 1 (Hildesheim, A. Lax, 1922), p. 459; H.V. Jan, *Hildesheim zur Kaiserzeit* (Hildesheim: Gerstenberg, 1977), p. 43.
6. Krebs, *Reminiscences*, p. 9; HAK–FLH, May 12, 1979 (Tape 92, p. 1).
7. Wolf Krebs–FLH, Aug. 3, 1977 (Tape 34, p. 2); May 4, 1988 (Tape, 156, p. 28).
8. Krebs, *Reminiscences*, p. 7; HAK–FLH, Feb. 17, 1978 (Tape 54, p. 4). See Hansjoachim Henning, *Das Westdeutsche Bürgertum in der Epoche der Hochindustrialisierung.* Teil I (Wiesbaden: Franz Steiner, 1972), pp. 488–489.
9. Wolf Krebs–FLH, Aug. 3, 1977 (Tape 35, p. 23).
10. HAK–FLH, Feb. 17, 1978 (Tape 54, pp. 6–7), May 10, 1979 (Tape 89, p. 23), Dec. 16, 1979 (Tape 104, p. 3).
11. Krebs, *Reminiscences*, pp. 6-7; HAK–FLH, May 9, 1979 (Tape 88, p. 26), May 14, 1979 (Tape 94, p. 29).
12. Krebs, *Reminiscences*, p. 8; HAK–FLH, Aug. 30, 1976 (Tape 1, p. 3), Feb. 17, 1978 (Tape 43, p. 8), Dec. 16, 1979 (Tape 104, p. 7), Dec. 20, 1979 (Tape 110, p. 12). The description of the *Galgenberg* and *Steinberg* are based on my own visits to them in 1982.
13. Gebauer, *Hildesheim*, 1: 466–467.
14. HAK–FLH, May 12, 1979 (Tape 92, pp. 2, 14).
15. *Ibid.*, (Tape 92, p. 14).
16. *Ibid.*, May 14, 1979 (Tape 93, p. 5), May 15, 1979 (Tape 95, pp. 18–19).
17. *Evangelische Knabenmittelschule*, Zeugnisbuch für Hans Adolf Krebs, 1907, 1908, 1909, KC.
18. Krebs, *Reminiscences*, p. 5; HAK–FLH, Aug. 30, 1976 (Tape 1, p. 3), May 10, 1979 (Tape 90, pp. 33–36), Dec. 16, 1979 (Tape 104, p. 13; Tape 105, p. 12); Wolf Krebs–FLH, Aug. 3, 1977 (Tape 34, p. 1).
19. Krebs, *Reminiscences*, p. 8; HAK–FLH, May 10, 1979 (Tape 90, p. 36).
20. Krebs, *Reminiscences*, pp. 1–2. The description of Hildesheim in this and the following paragraphs is based on several guidebooks in Krebs's possession, photographs, and a personal visit in 1982 to the city and the few landmarks and streets that survived its destruction in World War II.
21. HAK–FLH, May 14, 1979 (Tape 93, p. 7), Dec. 16, 1979 (Tape 104, pp. 4–7), Dec. 20, 1979 (Tape 110, p. 12).
22. Gebauer, *Hildesheim*, 1: 468; HAK–FLH, May 14, 1979 (Tape 93, p. 9).
23. Gebauer, *Hildesheim*, 1: 469; HAK–FLH, May 14, 1979 (Tape 93, pp. 9–10), May 15, 1979 (Tape 94, p. 1), Dec. 16, 1979 (Tape 104, p. 13).
24. HAK–FLH, Feb. 17, 1978 (Tape 54, p. 8), Feb. 20, 1978 (Tape 56, p. 4); Wolf Krebs–FLH, Aug. 3, 1977 (Tape 34, p. 6).
25. Gebauer, *Hildesheim*, 1: 453–464.
26. HAK–FLH, May 14, 1979 (Tape 93, pp. 17–18).
27. Gebauer, *Hildesheim*, 1: 457.
28. HAK–FLH, Aug. 9, 1978 (Tape 81, p. 16), May 11, 1979 (Tape 90, pp. 8–10), May 14, 1979 (Tape 93, pp. 19–20), Aug. 6, 1981, (Tape 142, p. 8). Much later Krebs learned that a Hanoverian regiment in the reign of George I of England had participated in the conquest of Gibraltar. For the role of the army in German society, see G.A. Ritter and J. Kocka, eds., *Deutsche Sozialgeschichte 1870-1914: Dokumente und Skizzen*, 3d. ed., (Munich: C.H. Beck, 1982), pp. 221–240.
29. Gordon A. Craig, *Germany 1866-1945* (New York: Oxford University Press, 1980), pp. 63-69.

30. HAK–FLH, Aug. 9, 1978 (Tape 80, p. 6), May 11, 1979 (Tape 91, p. 31), May 14, 1979 (Tape 93, p. 4).

31. Uriel Tal, *Christians and Jews in Germany: Religion, Politics, and Ideology in the Second Reich, 1870-1914*, tr. N.J. Jacobs (Ithaca: Cornell University Press, 1975), entire, esp. pp. 290-301.

32. Krebs, *Reminiscences*, pp. 5-6; HAK–FLH, Aug. 9, 1978 (Tape 80, pp. 8-9), May 11, 1979 (Tape 91, pp. 21-24), Wolf Krebs–FLH, Sept. 15, 1986, (Tape 153, p. 6).

33. Krebs, *Reminiscences*, p. 5.

34. Wolf Krebs–FLH, Aug. 3, 1977 (Tape 34, pp. 1, 5), Sept. 15, 1986 (Tape 154, p. 25); HAK–FLH, May 11, 1979 (Tape 91, p. 17), Dec. 17, 1979 (Tape 106, p. 1).

35. Krebs, *Reminiscences*, pp. 8-10; HAK–FLH, Feb. 17, 1978 (Tape 54, pp. 8-9); Wolf Krebs–FLH, Sept. 15, 1986 (Tape 154, pp. 26-28).

36. Krebs, *Reminiscences*, p. 9; HAK–FLH, May 10, 1979 (Tape 90, p. 29), May 12, 1979 (Tape 92, p. 19), May 15, 1979 (Tape 95, p. 19), Dec. 20, 1979 (Tape 110, p. 16); Wolf Krebs–FLH, Sept. 15, 1986 (Tape 154, p. 26).

37. Krebs, *Reminiscences*, p. 12; HAK–FLH, May 11, 1979 (Tape 90, p. 5; Tape 91, pp. 14, 30), Dec. 20, 1979 (Tape 110, p. 15), Dec. 21, 1979 (Tape 111, pp. 1-2), Aug. 7, 1981 (Tape 150, p. 1).

38. Gebauer, *Hildesheim*, 1:464; Krebs, *Reminiscences*, pp. 9-10.

39. HAK–FLH, Feb. 17, 1978 (Tape 54, p. 10); Wolf Krebs to F.L. Holmes, August 16, 1988.

40. Gebauer, *Hildesheim*, 1:464.

41. Wolf Krebs to F.L. Holmes, August 16, 1988; HAK–FLH, May 12, 1979 (Tape 92, p. 2).

42. Königliches Gymnasium Andreanum in Hildesheim, *Zeugnisbuch für Hans Adolf Krebs*, A.400, KC.

43. HAK–FLH, May 11, 1979 (Tape 91, pp. 15-16); Wolf Krebs–FLH, Sept. 15, 1986 (Tape 154, p. 18); Wolf Krebs to F.L. Holmes, August 16, 1988.

44. HAK–FLH, Aug. 9, 1978 (Tape 80, p. 11), May 12, 1979 (Tape 92, pp. 3-11); Wolf Krebs–FLH, Sept. 15, 1986 (Tape 154, pp. 18, 26).

45. Wolf Krebs–FLH, May 4, 1988 (Tape 161, p. 27).

46. *Ibid.*, Sept. 15, 1986 (Tape 154, p. 28); HAK–FLH, May 11, 1979 (Tape 90, p. 3), Dec. 20, 1979 (Tape 110, p. 13).

47. HAK–FLH, Feb. 17, 1978 (Tape 54, p. 15); May 11, 1979 (Tape 92, p. 32); Craig, *Germany*, pp. 328-329.

48. Rudolf Zoder, "Johannes Heinrich Gebauer: 1868-1951," in *Niedersächsische Lebensbilder* (Hildesheim: August Lax, 1954): 2, 70-78; HAK–FLH, Aug. 4, 1977 (Tape 32, pp. 11-13); Feb. 20, 1978 (Tape 56, p. 4), May 14, 1979 (Tape 93, pp. 1-2).

49. HAK–FLH, Aug. 30, 1976 (Tape 1, p. 3), Feb. 17, 1978 (Tape 54, pp. 13-16), Aug. 9, 1978 (Tape 81, pp. 15-16), May 14, 1979 (Tape 93, pp. 1-2).

50. *Zeugnisbuch für Hans Adolf Krebs.*

51. Wolf Krebs–FLH, Sept. 15, 1986 (Tape 154, pp. 24-25); HAK–FLH, Aug. 12, 1977 (Tape 41, p. 5), Dec. 16, 1979 (Tape 104, p. 10).

52. Jan, *Hildesheim zur Kaiserzeit*, p. 8; HAK–FLH, Feb. 17, 1978 (Tape 54, p. 17), May 12, 1979 (Tape 92, p. 13); Craig, *Germany*, pp. 339-342.

53. Craig, *Germany*, pp. 342-344; HAK–FLH, Feb. 17, 1978 (Tape 54, p. 17).

54. G. Krebs, "Ohrbeschädungen im Felde," *Münchener medizinische Wochenschrift*, March 9, 1915, p. 348; Wolf Krebs–FLH, Aug. 3, 1977 (Tape 35, p. 25), Feb. 17, 1978 (Tape 54, pp. 15-16).

55. Krebs, *Reminiscences*, p. 14; HAK–FLH, Aug. 4, 1977 (Tape 32, p. 9); Wolf Krebs–FLH, Aug. 3, 1977 (Tape 35, p. 16).

56. Krebs, *Reminiscences*, pp. 12-13; HAK–FLH, May 10, 1979 (Tape 90, p. 31); G. Krebs, "Ueber Pharyngitis (Laryngitis, Tracheitis) sicca oder atrophica," *Monatschrift für Ohrenheilkunde*, 6 (1895), 1-17; G. Krebs, "Die Behandlung des chronischen Rachen- und Kehlkopfkatarrhs," *Therapeutische Monatshefte*, 10 (1896), 306-312, 379-384; G. Krebs, "Bemerkungen zur Probepunction der Kieferhöhle und zu deren 'seröser Erkrankung'," *Archiv für Laryngologie und Rhinologie*, 4 (1896):424-425; G. Krebs, "Ohren- und Nasenuntersuchungen in der Taubstummen-

anstalt zu Hildesheim," *Archiv für Ohrenheilkunde*, 42 (1897):119–127; G. Krebs, "Was ist Pharyngitis sicca?" *Wiener Klinische Rundschau*, 11 (28 Nov. 1897), 1–2; G. Krebs, "Zur Indicationsstellung der Radicaloperation chronischer Mittelohreiterungen," *Monatsschrift für Ohrenheilkunde*, n.s. 32 (1898):401–403; G. Krebs, "Gesundheitspflege von Ohr und Nase," Blätter für Volksgesundheitspflege, 1 (1901):201–202; G. Krebs, "Trochlearislähmung bei Kieferhöhleneiterung," *Therapeutische Monatshefte*, 17 (1903):461–462; G. Krebs, "Des soins préparatoires et consécutifs aux opérations endo-nasales," *Presse Otolaryngologique Belge*, 2 (1903):535–541; G. Krebs, "Nachbehandlung nach Operation der Rachenmandel," *Centralblatt für Kinderheilkunde*, 10 (1905):207–212; G. Krebs, "Fremdkörper in der Nasenhöhle als Ursache von Kieferhöhlenempyemen," *Zeitschrift für Ohrenheilkunde*, 54 (1907): 141–144; G. Krebs, "Operationslose Behandlung der chronischen Kieferhöhlenempyeme," *Therapeutische Rundschau*, 2 (1908):158–159; G. Krebs, "Operative Heilung der Meningitis diffusa," *Therapeutische Monatshefte*, 24 (1910):239–243. Krebs continued publishing similar articles, at less frequent intervals, through the war years and into the 1920s.

57. Krebs, *Reminiscences*, pp. 12–13; HAK–FLH, Aug. 30, 1976 (Tape 1, pp. 1–3), May 10, 1979 (Tape 88, p. 8, Tape 89, p. 10).

58. *Ibid.*, HAK–FLH, May 14, 1979 (Tape 94, p. 33).

59. Krebs, *Reminiscences*, p. 12; HAK–FLH, Aug. 30, 1976 (Tape 1, pp. 3–4), Dec. 20, 1979 (Tape 110, p. 15), Dec. 22, 1979 (Tape 112, p. 11).

60. *Ibid.*, (Tape 1, p. 17); Wolf Krebs–FLH, Sept. 15, 1986 (Tape 154, pp. 18–19).

61. Krebs, *Reminiscences*, pp. 10–11; HAK–FLH, Feb. 20, 1978 (Tape 56, pp. 13–14), May 12, 1979 (Tape 92, pp. 2–4, 7).

62. Krebs, *Reminiscences*, p. 10; HAK–FLH, May 12, 1979 (Tape 92, p. 6); Wolf Krebs to F.L. Holmes, August 16, 1988.

63. HAK–FLH, Aug. 4, 1977 (Tape 32, pp. 12–13), Feb. 20, 1978 (Tape 57, p. 4).

64. Krebs, *Reminiscences*, pp. 11–12; HAK–FLH, Aug. 11, 1977 (Tape 40, p. 13), May 14, 1979 (Tape 93, pp. 22–24); May 15, 1979 (Tape 94, p. 2); Wolf Krebs–FLH, Sept. 15, 1986 (Tape 155, pp. 41–42).

65. Krebs, *Reminiscences*, p. 11; Wolf Krebs–FLH, Sept. 15, 1986 (Tape 155, p. 41).

66. HAK–FLH, May 11, 1979 (Tape 91, p. 17, Tape 92, pp. 33–34), May 12, 1979 (Tape 92, p. 19); Wolf Krebs–FLH, Sept. 15, 1986, (Tape 154, pp. 26, 28).

67. HAK–FLH, May 12, 1979 (Tape 92, pp. 16–17); Wolf Krebs–FLH, Aug. 3, 1977 (Tape 34, p. 4).

68. Wolf Krebs–FLH, Aug. 3, 1977 (Tape 34, pp. 4, 7–8); HAK–FLH, May 16, 1979 (Tape 96, p. 27), Dec. 20, 1979 (Tape 110, p. 15).

69. HAK–FLH, Aug. 4, 1977 (Tape 32, p. 9), Feb. 21, 1978 (Tape 57, pp. 18–19), Dec. 16, 1979 (Tape 104, pp. 1–2); Krebs, *Reminiscences*, p. 14; Wolf Krebs–FLH, Aug. 3, 1977 (Tape 34, pp. 5, 8).

70. HAK–FLH, May 14, 1979 (Tape 94, p. 28); Königliches Gymnasium Andreanum in Hildesheim, *Zeugnis der Reife: Hans Adolf Krebs*, Sept. 19, 1918, KC.

71. Lise Krebs to HAK, August 24, 1917, A.730, KC; HAK–FLH, Feb. 17, 1978 (Tape 54, p. 19).

72. HAK–FLH, Feb. 17, 1978 (Tape 54, p. 20), May 15, 1979 (Tape 94, p. 5); *Berechtigungsschein zum einjährig - freiwilligen Dienste: Hans Adolf Krebs*, Nov. 10, 1917; Andreanum, *Zeugnis der Reife*, KC.

73. HAK–FLH, Feb. 17, 1978 (Tape 54, p. 20).

74. Krebs, *Reminiscences*, pp. 14–15.

75. HAK–FLH, Feb. 20, 1978 (Tape 56, p. 7).

76. Krebs, *Reminiscences*, p. 15; HAK–FLH, Aug. 4, 1977 (Tape 32, p. 10), Aug. 11, 1977 (Tape 40, p. 13), Aug. 9, 1978 (Tape 81, p. 17).

77. Affidavit signed by Hans Adolf Krebs, September 21, 1918, KC.

Chapter 3

1. HAK–FLH, Feb. 17, 1978, (Tape 54, p. 21).

2. *Ibid.*, pp. 20–21.

3. *Ibid.*, pp. 20–21, Aug. 6, 1981 (Tape 142, p. 8).

4. *Ibid.*, Feb. 17, 1978 (Tape 54, p. 21).

5. Hans Krebs, with Anne Martin, *Reminiscences and Reflections*, (Oxford: Clarendon Press, 1981), p. 15; HAK–FLH, Feb. 18, 1978 (Tape 55, p. 1), Aug. 9, 1978 (Tape 81, pp. 18–19).

6. Erich Stern–FLH, Dec. 14, 1977 (Tape 48, p. 5, Tape 49, p. 20). Krebs recalled the stopping of the train but thought that it had been allowed to continue. HAK–FLH, Feb. 18, 1978 (Tape 55, p. 1). I have followed Erich Stern's version because he appears to have remembered the event more distinctly.

7. Gordon A. Craig, *Germany: 1866-1945* (New York: Oxford University Press, 1980), pp. 402–406; HAK–FLH, Feb. 18, 1978 (Tape 55, pp. 1–2).

8. Krebs, *Reminiscences*, p. 15; HAK–FLH, Aug. 30, 1976 (Tape 1, p. 13), Feb. 18, 1978 (Tape 55, p. 2); Erich Stern–FLH, Dec. 14, 1977 (Tape 48, pp. 4, 6, Tape 49, p. 37).

9. Krebs, *Reminiscences*, p. 16; Erich Stern–FLH, Dec. 14, 1977 (Tape 49, p. 37).

10. Krebs, *Reminiscences*, p. 16.

11. HAK–FLH, Feb. 18, 1978 (Tape 55, pp. 10–11); Erich Stern–FLH, Dec. 14, 1977 (Tape 48, p. 5). When I visited Erich Stern in Decatur, Illinois, I found that he retained the same personal characteristics that had impressed Krebs 60 years earlier.

12. Alma Krebs to HAK, Dec. 19, 1918, A.729, KC.

13. Erich Stern–FLH, Dec. 14, 1977 (Tape 48, pp. 1–2).

14. HAK–FLH, Aug. 30, 1976 (Tape 1, p. 14), Feb. 18, 1978 (Tape 55, pp. 6–7); *Abgangszeugnis, Göttingen* (Hans Krebs, Aug. 6, 1919); *Zeugnis über die Teilnahme an den Präparierübungen bei den Universität zu Göttingen* (Hans Krebs, January 25, 1919), KC.

15. HAK–FLH, Feb. 18, 1978 (Tape 55, p. 10); Alma Krebs to HAK, Dec. 6, 1918, Dec. 19, 1918, Jan. 10, 1919, Jan. 15, 1919, Jan. 19, 1919, Feb. 18, 1919, Feb. 25, 1919, March 1, 1919, A.729, KC.

16. HAK–FLH, Feb. 18, 1978 (Tape 55, pp. 14–15), Feb. 20, 1978 (Tape 56, p. 9); Alma Krebs to HAK, Jan. 10, 1919, Feb. 25, 1919, A.729, KC.

17. HAK–FLH, Feb. 18, 1978 (Tape 55, p. 14), Feb. 20, 1978 (Tape 56, p. 8); Erichh Stern–FLH, Dec. 14, 1977 (Tape 48, p. 6, Tape 49, pp. 31, 38); *Abgangszeugnis Göttingen* (Krebs).

18. Alma Krebs to HAK, Feb. 18, 1919, A.729, KC; HAK–FLH, Feb. 18, 1978 (Tape 55, pp. 15, 18).

19. HAK–FLH, Feb. 18, 1978 (Tape 55, pp. 4–5), May 15, 1979 (Tape 95, pp. 20–21); Alma Krebs to HAK, March 4, 1919, A.729, KC.

20. Alma Krebs to HAK, Jan. 19, 1919, March 1, 1919, A.729, KC.

21. HAK–FLH, Feb. 18, 1978 (Tape 55, p. 2); Krebs, *Reminiscences*, p. 18.

22. Erich Stern–FLH, Dec. 14, 1977 (Tape 48, pp. 4–6, Tape 49, p. 34); HAK–FLH, Feb. 18, 1978 (Tape 55, p. 8).

23. Krebs, *Reminiscences*, p. 18; HAK–FLH, Aug. 5, 1977 (Tape 32, pp. 18–19), Feb. 18, 1978 (Tape 55, p. 9), May 18, 1979 (Tape 97, p. 9); *Abgangszeugnis* (Krebs).

24. HAK–FLH, Feb. 18, 1978 (Tape 55, pp. 11–12); Erich Stern–FLH, Dec. 14, 1977 (Tape 49, p. 38).

25. Lise Krebs to HAK, May 24, 1919, A.730, KC.

26. HAK–FLH, Feb. 18, 1978 (Tape 55, pp. 19–20); Lise Krebs to HAK, April 3, 1919, A.730, KC.

27. HAK–FLH, Feb. 18, 1978 (Tape 55, p. 16).

28. Alma Krebs to HAK, July 3, 1919, A.729, KC.

29. Wolf Krebs–FLH, Aug. 3, 1977 (Tape 35, p. 25); notes on telephone conversation, Dec. 22, 1979.

30. Craig, *Germany*, pp. 397-430; Erich Eyck, *A History of the Weimar Republic*, tr. H.P. Hanson and R.G.L. Waite (New York: Atheneum, 1970), 1:64–142.

31. Krebs, *Reminiscences*, p. 18.

32. Erich Stern–FLH, Dec. 14, 1977 (Tape 48, p. 6).
33. HAK–FLH, Feb. 20, 1978 (Tape 56, p. 10).
34. HAK–FLH, Aug. 30, 1976 (Tape 1, pp. 14–15); Feb. 18, 1978 (Tape 55, p. 8).
35. (N. < ... >) to HAK, Sept. 13, 1919, A.1014, KC; HAK–FLH, Aug. 11, 1977 (Tape 40, p. 15).
36. HAK–FLH, Aug. 11, 1977 (Tape 40, pp. 11–12), March 20, 1980 (Tape 118, pp. 1–5). In discussing Faust, in 1977, Krebs said that he had "read it hundreds of times." For the passages quoted, see *Goethes Werke*, ed. Heinrich Kurz (Leipzig: Bibliographisches Institut, n.d.), 4: 19, 361.
37. HAK–FLH, Feb. 18, 1978 (Tape 55, p. 17), May 18, 1979 (Tape 97, p. 7); Wolf Krebs–FLH, notes of telephone conversation, Dec. 11, 1979.
38. HAK–FLH, Feb. 18, 1978 (Tape 55, p. 20); Dec. 17, 1979 (Tape 106, p. 2).
39. Typewritten (untitled) list of courses for winter semester 1919 through summer semester 1921, KC; HAK–FLH, Feb. 21, 1978 (Tape 58, pp. 9, 14), Jan. 10, 1981 (Tape 130, p. 17); "Kries, Johannes Adolf von," in I. Fischer, *Biographisches Lexikon der hervorragenden Ärzte der letzten fünfzig Jahre* (Berlin: Urban and Schwarzenberg, 1932–1933) 2: 821–822.
40. Typed course list; HAK–FLH, Feb. 21, 1978 (Tape 57, p. 9).
41. *Ibid.*; C.H. Waddington, "Spemann, Hans," *Dictionary of Scientific Biography*, ed. C.C. Gillispie (New York: Charles Scribner's, 1970–80) 12: 567–569; Fritz Baltzer, "Zum Gedächtnis Hans Spemanns," *Die Naturwissenschaften*, 30 (1942): 229–239.
42. HAK–FLH, Feb. 18, 1978 (Tape 55, p. 17); Wolf Krebs–FLH, notes of telephone conversation, Dec. 22, 1979.
43. HAK–FLH, Feb. 18, 1978 (Tape 55, pp. 17–18); Dec. 17, 1979 (Tape 106, p. 2).
44. Wolf Krebs–FLH, Aug. 3, 1977 (Tape 34, p. 25), notes of telephone conversation, Dec. 22, 1979.
45. Krebs, *Reminiscences*, pp. 18–19.
46. HAK–FLH, Sept. 7, 1976 (Tape 4, p. 29), Feb. 17, 1978 (Tape 54, p. 5).
47. *Ibid.*, Feb. 18, 1978 (Tape 55, p. 18); Erich Stern–FLH, Dec. 14, 1977 (Tape 48, p. 9)
48. Wolf Krebs–FLH, notes of telephone conversation, Dec. 22, 1979; May 4, 1988 (Tape 160, p. 10).
49. Erich Stern–FLH, Dec. 15, 1977 (Tape 50, p. 1).
50. HAK–FLH, Aug. 5, 1977 (Tape 36, p. 2).
51. *Ibid.*, Aug. 30, 1976 (Tape 1, p. 7), Feb. 21, 1978 (Tape 57, p. 8).
52. *Ibid.*, Feb. 20, 1978 (Tape 56, p. 11).
53. Wolf Krebs–FLH, Aug. 3, 1977 (Tape 34, p. 11, Tape 35, p. 25); HAK–FLH, Aug. 11, 1977 (Tape 40, p. 14), Feb. 20, 1978 (Tape 56, p. 19); Volkshochschule der Stadt Hildesheim, "Hörerkarte Nr. 785," Feb. 2, 1920, KC.
54. Lise Krebs to HAK, March 4, 1919, A.730, KC.
55. Craig, *Germany*, pp. 429–432; Eyck, *Weimar*, pp. 147–160.
56. H.M. Humberg, "Der Kapp-Putsch in Hildesheim," in *Hildesheim: so wie es war*, ed. Jens-Uwe Brinkmann, (Düsseldorf: Droste, 1976), pp. 65–66.
57. HAK–FLH, Feb. 18, 1978 (Tape 55, pp. 3, 19), Feb. 20, 1978 (Tape 56, p. 8), May 15, 1979 (Tape 94, pp. 3–4); Wolf Krebs to F.L. Holmes, January 2, 1989.
58. HAK–FLH, Feb. 18, 1978, (Tape 94, p. 4).
59. Typed course list, KC; W. Bargmann, "Wilhelm v. Möllendorff," *Zeitschrift für Zellforschung und Mikroskopische Anatomie*, 33 (1943): 167–186.
60. Hermann K.F. Blaschko, "My Path to Pharmacology," *Annual Review of Pharmacology and Toxicology*, 20 (1980): 1–3; Blaschko, "Hans Krebs: Nineteen Nineteen and After," *FEBS Letters*, 117 Suppl. (1980), p. Kll; Hermann Blaschko–FLH, Sept. 10, 1976 (Tape 6, p. 1), Aug. 21, 1977 (Tape 43, p. 14), HAK–FLH, Aug. 5, 1977 (Tape 36, p. 1). Blaschko remembered their meeting as having taken place late in 1919, Krebs remembered the year as 1920. The fact that Krebs took Möllendorff's course in the summer semester of 1920 confirms his recollection in this regard. For the circumstances of their meeting, I have followed Blaschko's account because it appears definite enough to be convincing, even though Krebs remembered only that they had met "when we were both dissecting in the anatomy department," HAK–FLH, Aug. 5, 1977 (Tape 32, p. 18).

61. Blaschko, "My Path," p. 3; K. Th[omas], "Franz Knoop zum Gedächtnis," *Z. physiol. Chem.*, 283 (1948): 1–2.

62. Franz Knoop, *Lebenserscheinungen und Chemie: öffentliche Antrittsrede* (Freiburg: Speyer and Kaerner, 1921), pp. 10–11.

63. *Ibid.*, p. 14.

64. L. Landois, *Lehrbuch der Physiologie des Menschen*, ed. R. Rosenman, 16th ed. (Berlin: Urban and Schwarzenberg, 1919), pp. 341–366; HAK–FLH, Aug. 30, 1976 (Tape 1, p. 25), Feb. 21, 1978 (Tape 58, pp. 14–15).

65. Knoop, *Lebenserscheinungen*, p. 11.

66. HAK–FLH, Aug. 30, 1976 (Tape 1, p. 7), Feb. 20, 1978 (Tape 57, p. 6).

67. Knoop, *Lebenserscheinungen*, pp. 14–17.

68. HAK–FLH, Aug. 30, 1976 (Tape 1, p. 24).

69. Ministerium des Kultus und Unterrichts, Republik Baden, "Universität Freiburg: Dr. Knoop, Georg Franz," series of official documents, including numerous letters from Knoop to various ministers, 1904–1920, G.L.A. 235, No. 8876, Generallandesarchiv, Karlsruhe.

70. *Ibid.*, Ministerium für Landwirtschaft, Domänen und Forsten, July 15, 1911.

71. Robert E. Kohler, *From Medical Chemistry to Biochemistry: The Making of a Biomedical Discipline* (Cambridge: Cambridge University Press, 1982), pp. 25–32; Joseph S. Fruton, *Contrasts in Scientific Style: Research Groups in the Chemical and Biochemical Sciences* (Philadelphia: American Philosophical Society, 1990), p. 179.

72. Franz Knoop to Ministerial Councilor Schwoerer, June 18, 1913, June 23, 1913, *Ministerium des Kultus und Unterricht*, G.L.A. 235, No. 8876, Karlsruhe.

73. Krebs, *Reminiscences*, p. 19.

74. HAK–FLH, Feb. 20, 1978 (Tape 56, p. 15, Tape 57, p. 1); Krebs, *Reminiscences*, p. 19.

75. Bargmann, "Möllendorff," p. 167; Wilhelm von Möllendorff, "Die Dispersität der Farbstoffe, ihre Beziehungen zu Ausscheidung und Speicherung in der Niere," *Anatomische Hefte*, (Erste Abteilung), 53 (1915/16): 87–323.

76. *Ibid.*, pp. 136–137; W. v. Möllendorff, "Methoden zu Studien über vitale Färbungen an Tierzellen," in *Handbuch der biologischen Arbeitsmethoden*, ed. Emil Abderhalden, Abt. V, Teil 2, Heft 2 (Berlin: Urban and Schwarzenberg, 1921), pp. 100–115.

77. Möllendorff, "Methoden," pp. 97–98, 102–103; Wilhelm v. Möllendorff, "Untersuchungen zur Theorie der Färbung fixierter Präparate," *Arch. mikros. Anat.*, 97 (1923): 554–557.

78. HAK–FLH, Sept. 2, 1976 (Tape 2, pp. 12–15), Feb. 20, 1978 (Tape 57, pp. 2–3); Möllendorff, "Dispersität der Farbstoffe," p. 88; Hans Adolf Krebs, "Ueber die Färbbarkeit des Skelettmuskels," *Arch. mikros. Anat.*, 97 (1923): 557; Martin Heidenhahn, *Plasma und Zelle* (Jena: G. Fischer, 1907–1910).

79. Krebs, "Färbbarkeit des Skelettmuskels," pp. 557–558.

80. HAK–FLH, Sept. 2, 1976 (Tape 2, pp. 12–13), Feb. 20, 1978 (Tape 56, pp. 16–17).

81. HAK–FLH, Aug. 11, 1977 (Tape 40, p. 15), Aug. 7, 1981 (Tape 150, p. 3).

82. HAK–FLH, Dec. 20, 1979 (Tape 110, pp. 16–17); Wolf Krebs-HAK, Sept. 15, 1986 (Tape 155, p. 42); Richard Gerlt to HAK, Sept. 19, 1920, KC. Here, I am projecting backward attitudes toward these works expressed by Hans and Wolf Krebs much later in conversations with me. Neither may have articulated such views as clearly at the time; but the stability of their temperaments makes it seem plausible that both would have responded from the start in a manner consistent with their later descriptions of these works. My brief descriptions of the two sonatas draw also on a conversation on Dec. 11, 1988 with Leon Plantinga, professor of the History of Music at Yale University and a Beethoven scholar.

83. Typed course list 1919–1921, KC.

84. Krebs, "Färbbarkeit des Skelettmuskels," pp. 558–564.

85. *Ibid.*, pp. 564–579.

86. *Ibid.*, pp. 568–571.

87. HAK–FLH, Feb. 20, 1978 (Tape 57, p. 1).

88. HAK–FLH, Aug. 30, 1976 (Tape 1, pp. 14–15); Badische Albert Ludwigs=Universität Freiburg, "Herrn Hans-Adolf Krebs," Aug. 9, 1921; Zeugnis, Prüfungskommission zu Freiburg

über die ärtzliche Vorprüfung der Studierenden der Medizin Hans Adolf Krebs, March 7, 1921, KC.

Chapter 4

1. HAK-FLH, Dec. 17, 1979 (Tape 106, pp. 3-4); Wolf Krebs-FLH, Sept. 15, 1986 (Tape 153, pp. 6-7, Tape 155, pp. 33-34).
2. *Ibid.* For an example in which Hans designated himself as *freireligiös*, see *Standes-Liste*, Krebs, Hans Adolf, G.L.A. 235, No. 8893, Generallandesarchiv, Karlsruhe. This document was a questionnaire that Krebs was required to fill out in 1933. The last sentences in the above paragraph draw upon a conversation with Peter Gay.
3. Hans Krebs, with Anne Martin, *Reminiscences and Reflections*, (Oxford: Oxford University Press, 1981), p. 20; John H. Talbott, *A Biographical History of Medicine: Excerpts and Essays on the Men and their Work*, (New York: Grune & Stratton, 1970), pp. 916-918.
4. Ludwig Aschoff, *Lectures on Pathology* (New York: Paul Hoeber, 1924), p. 59.
5. *Ibid.*, pp. 59-82, 131-153.
6. [H.A. Krebs], "Introduction to Aschoff Memorial Lecture," typewritten manuscript, dated July 5, 1955, p. 1, KC; HAK-FLH, Aug. 30, 1976 (Tape 1, p. 6).
7. [Krebs]. "Aschoff Memorial Lecture," p. 1.
8. Ludwig Aschoff, *Ein Gelehrtenleben in Briefen an die Familie* (Freiburg: Hans Ferdinand Schulz Verlag, 1966), pp. 295-298.
9. HAK-FLH, Feb. 21, 1978 (Tape 57, p. 8).
10. Typewritten (untitled) list of courses for winter semester 1919 through Summer Semester 1921, KC.
11. HAK-FLH, Aug. 30, 1976 (Tape 1, p. 15), Aug. 5, 1977 (Tape 32, p. 19), Dec. 15, 1979 (Tape 103, pp. 14-15).
12. *Ibid.*
13. HAK-FLH, Feb. 20, 1978 (Tape 57, pp. 1-2, 7).
14. *Ibid.*, p. 1.
15. For general introductory contemporary discussions of the subject see especially Herbert Freundlich, *Kapillarchemie: Eine Darstellung der Chemie der Kolloide und verwandter Gebiete*, 2d. ed. (Leipzig: Akademische Verlagsgesellschaft, 1922), pp. 1-6; and Richard Zsigmondy, *Kolloidchemie: ein Lehrbuch*, 3d. ed. (Leipzig: Otto Spamer, 1920), pp. 1-20.
16. HAK-FLH, Feb. 21, 1978 (Tape 57, pp. 22-23, Tape 58, p. 1); Leonor Michaelis, *Praktikum der physikalischen Chemie, insbesondere der Kolloidchemie für Mediziner und Biologen*, (Berlin: Julius Springer, 1921); Rudolf Höber, *Physikalische chemie der Zelle und der Gewebe*, 4th ed. (Leipzig: Engelmann, 1914).
17. HAK-FLH, Aug. 11, 1977 (Tape 40, p. 15), Feb. 21, 1978 (Tape 58, p. 7), Dec. 16, 1979 (Tape 104, pp. 3-4).
18. HAK-FLH, Jan. 9, 1981 (Tape 129, p. 5).
19. Wolf Krebs-FLH, May 4, 1988 (Tape 161, p. 23); HAK-FLH, Dec. 17, 1979 (Tape 106, p. 2).
20. Krebs, *Reminiscences*, p. 20; HAK-FLH, Aug. 30, 1976 (Tape 1, p. 14), Aug. 5, 1977 (Tape 36, p. 1), Feb. 21, 1978 (Tape 58, p. 2), May 19, 1979 (Tape 97, pp. 1-2); Erich Stern-FLH, Dec. 14, 1977 (Tape 48, p. 12), Dec. 15, 1977 (Tape 50, p. 3).
21. Wolf Krebs-FLH, Aug. 3, 1977 (Tape 34, p. 9), May 4, 1988 (Tape 162, p. 43).
22. HAK-FLH, Feb. 21, 1978 (Tape 58, p. 2).
23. Wolf Krebs-FLH, Sept. 15, 1986 (Tape 154, p. 30).
24. HAK-FLH, Aug. 4, 1977 (Tape 32, p. 15); Wolf Krebs-FLH, Aug. 3, 1977 (Tape 34, p. 12). Wolf believed that their first landlady was anti-Semitic. Hans, however, did not think her hostility "had anything to do with anti-Semitism."
25. Praktikantenschein nos. 159, 222, 388, Munich, 1922, KC; "Döderlein, Albert," in I. Fischer, *Biographisches Lexikon der hervorragenden Ärzte der letzten fünfzig Jahre* (Berlin: Urban and Schwarzenberg, 1932-1933), 1: 321.

26. Talbott, *Biographical History*, pp. 1034–1036; Ferdinand Sauerbruch, *Das War Mein Leben* (Badwörishofen: Kindler and Schiermeyer, 1951), pp. 340–358; Wolfgang Genschorek, *Ferdinand Sauerbruch: Ein Leben für die Chirurgie* (Leipzig: S. Hirzel, 1978), pp. 92–99, 222.

27. Friedrich von Müller, *Lebenserinnerungen* (Munich: J.F. Lehmanns, 1953), pp. 125–141, 248–251; A. von Domarus, "Epilog," in *Ibid.*, p. 255.

28. HAK–FLH, Feb. 21, 1978 (Tape 58, p. 3), May 19, 1979 (Tape 98, p. 14); Erich Stern–FLH, Dec. 14, 1977 (Tape 48, pp. 7, 18).

29. Müller, *Lebenserinnerungen*, p. 132.

30. HAK–FLH, May 19, 1979 (Tape 98, pp. 14–15).

31. Müller, *Lebenserinnerungen*, pp. 45–66, 130–131; Angelika Pfarrwaller-Stieve, *Friedrich von Müller (1858–1941) und seine Stoffwechseluntersuchungen* (Zürich: Juris, 1983).

32. Georg Hohmann, "Zum Andenken an Professor Dr. Siegfried Thannhauser," *Münchener Medizinische Wochenschrift*, 105 (1963): 357–359.

33. HAK–FLH, Feb. 21, 1978 (Tape 58, pp. 3–4).

34. *Ibid.*, Feb. 20, 1978 (Tape 56, p. 16); H.A. Krebs, "Die Färbung des Skelettmuskels mit Anilinfarbstoffen," *Arch. mikros. Anat.*, 97 (1923): 557–580.

35. Krebs, "Farbung," p. 564.

36. *Ibid.*, p. 579.

37. *Ibid.*, pp. 561–579.

38. HAK–FLH, Sept. 2, 1976 (Tape 2, p. 12), Feb. 20, 1978 (Tape 56, p. 16, Tape 57, p. 2).

39. Wilh. v. Möllendorff to HAK, Mar. 19, 1922, KC.

40. HAK–FLH, Sept. 2, 1976 (Tape 2, p. 12).

41. *Ibid.*; HAK–FLH, Feb. 21, 1978 (Tape 58, p. 2), Aug. 9, 1978 (Tape 81, p. 16); Wolf Krebs–FLH, Aug. 3, 1978 (Tape 35, p. 16); Erich Stern–FLH, Dec. 14, 1978 (Tape 48, p. 11).

42. Erich Stern–FLH, Dec. 15, 1978 (Tape 50, pp. 3–4); Wolf Krebs–FLH, Aug. 3, 1978 (Tape 34, p. 14), May 4, 1988 (Tape 160, p. 14).

43. Wolf Krebs–FLH, Aug. 3, 1978 (Tape 34, p. 12).

44. *Praktikantenschein* nos. 81, 122, 127, 165, unnumb., Munich, 1922, KC; "Hess, Carl von," "Pfaundler, Meinhard von," "Zumbusch, Leo Ritter von", Fischer, *Biographisches Lexikon*, 1:621–622, 2:1204, 1317, 1731; Müller, *Lebenserinnerungen*, p. 175; Ludwig-Maximilians-Universität, *Verzeichnis der Vorlesungen*, Sommerhalbjahr 1922, pp. 10–19.

45. HAK–FLH, Aug. 30, 1976 (Tape 1, p. 5), Aug. 4, 1977 (Tape 32, p. 15); Wolf Krebs–FLH, Aug. 3, 1978 (Tape 34, p. 9).

46. HAK–FLH, Aug. 30, 1976 (Tape 1, pp. 4–9), Aug. 4, 1977 (Tape 32, pp. 13–15); Wolf Krebs–FLH, Aug. 3, 1978 (Tape 34, pp. 9–10); Hans Driesch, *The Science and Philosophy of the Organism* (London: Adam and Charles Black, 1908). Driesch wrote the Gifford Lectures in English, and they were originally published in that language. Krebs probably read a German translation, entitled *Philosophie des Organischen*.

47. HAK–FLH, Feb. 21, 1978 (Tape 57, pp. 9–13); Oscar Hertwig, *Lehrbuch der Entwicklungsgeschichte des Menschen und der Wirbeltiere*, 10th ed. (Jena: Fischer, 1915).

48. Wolf Krebs–FLH, Aug. 3, 1977 (Tape 34, p. 10).

49. HAK–FLH, Feb. 21, 1978 (Tape 58, pp. 12–13); Wolf Krebs–FLH, Sept. 15, 1986 (Tape 154, p. 29).

50. Wolf Krebs–FLH, Sept. 15, 1986, (Tape 153, p. 1), May 4, 1988 (Tape 160, p. 12).

51. *Ibid.*, Aug. 3, 1977 (Tape 34, p. 14); Krebs, *Reminiscences*, p. 7; William Guttmann and Patricia Meehan, *The Great Inflation* (London: Gordon and Cremonesi, 1976), pp. 128–129.

52. Guttmann and Meehan, *Inflation*, p. 86.

53. *Ibid.*, pp. 61–87; Gordon Craig, *Germany: 1866–1945* (New York: Oxford University Press, 1980), pp. 450–456.

54. Wolf Krebs–FLH, Aug. 3, 1977 (Tape 34, p. 14).

55. *Ibid.*, pp. 14-15; Erich Stern–FLH, Dec. 14, 1977 (Tape 48, p. 19).

56. Guttmann and Meehan, *Inflation*, pp. 121–141.

57. Krebs, *Reminiscences*, p. 20–21; Wolf Krebs–FLH, Aug. 3, 1977 (Tape 34, p. 15).

58. HAK–FLH, Feb. 21, 1978 (Tape 58, p. 13), Aug. 9, 1978 (Tape 81, p. 24). For a characterization of the spirit of Berlin that Krebs thought quite apt when I discussed it with him, see

Peter Gay, *Freud, Jews and other Germans: Masters and Victims in Modernist Culture* (Oxford: Oxford University Press, 1978), pp. 169–188; HAK–FLH, Dec. 21, 1979 (Tape 111, p. 4).

59. Praktikantenschein, "Hans Adolf Krebs," Berlin, 1923, KC; HAK–FLH, Feb. 21, 1978 (Tape 58, p. 13); "Bier, August," "Kraus, Friedrich," Fischer, *Biographisches Lexikon*, 1: 116, 2: 815–816.

60. Krebs, *Reminiscences*, p. 21; Guttmann and Meehan, *Inflation*, pp. 64–65.

61. HAK–FLH, Feb. 20, 1978 (Tape 56, pp. 12–14).

62. *Ibid.*, Feb. 21, 1978 (Tape 58, pp. 14–16).

63. Praktikantenschein, "Hans Adolf Krebs," Munich, 1923, KC; HAK–FLH, Feb. 21, 1978 (Tape 58, p. 12); Wolf Krebs–FLH, Sept. 15, 1986 (Tape 154, p. 29).

64. HAK–FLH, Feb. 21, 1978 (Tape 58, pp. 9-10); Erich Stern–FLH, Dec. 14, 1977 (Tape 48, pp. 13–15).

65. *Ibid.*

66. Craig, *Germany*, pp. 435–468.

67. HAK–FLH, Feb. 18, 1978 (Tape 55, pp. 5–6), Feb. 21, 1978 (Tape 57, p. 8); Erichh Stern–FLH, Dec. 14, 1978 (Tape 49, p. 21).

68. Bayerischen Staatsministerien des Innern und für Unterricht und Kultus, "Approbation für Herrn Hans Adolf Krebs als Arzt," Munich, July 7, 1925, KC.

69. Erich Stern–FLH, Dec. 14, 1977 (Tape 48, pp. 17–18); HAK–FLH, Feb. 21, 1978 (Tape 58, pp. 4–9). On the impact of insulin, see Michael Bliss, *The Discovery of Insulin* (Chicago: The University of Chicago Press, 1982), pp. 131–188.

70. HAK–FLH, Aug. 30, 1976 (Tape 1, p. 16).

71. Wolf Krebs–FLH, May 4, 1988 (Tape 161, pp. 19, 24); HAK–FLH, Feb. 21, 1978 (Tape 58, p. 2).

72. HAK–FLH, Feb. 21, 1978 (Tape 58, p. 17), Dec. 21, 1979 (Tape 111, pp. 11–12).

73. *Ibid.*, Feb. 23, 1978 (Tape 60, pp. 8–9); Fischer, *Biographisches Lexikon*, 1:513.

74. HAK–FLH, Feb. 21, 1978 (Tape 58, p. 17).

75. *Ibid.*, Feb. 23, 1978 (Tape 60, p. 3).

76. *Ibid.*, Feb. 21, 1978 (Tape 58, p. 17), Feb. 23, 1978 (Tape 60, p. 8).

77. See, for example, O. Grütz, "Untersuchungen über die Methodik und den klinischen Wert der Goldsolreaktion im syphilitischen Liquor cerobrospinalis," *Archiv für Dermatologie und Syphilis*, 139 (1922): 469.

78. For a succinct summary of contemporary medical views of syphilis, see Sir William Osler, *The Principles and Practice of Medicine*, 10th ed., rev. Thomas McCrae (New York: D. Appleton, 1925), pp. 269–291, 935–948.

79. See Ludwik Fleck, *Genesis and Development of a Scientific Fact*, eds. Thaddeus J. Trenn and Robert K. Merton (Chicago: University of Chicago Press, 1979), pp. 52–81.

80. Zsigmondy, *Kolloidchemie*, pp. 12–14, 149–178.

81. *Ibid.*, pp. 149–178.

82. *Ibid.*, pp. 169–172, 346–351; R. Zsigmondy and E. Joël, "Goldschutz und Fällung durch Eiweisskörper," *Zeitschrift für physikalische Chemie*, 113 (1924): 299–312.

83. Carl Lange, "Die Ausflockung kolloidalen Goldes durch Zerebrospinalflüssigkeit bei luetischen Affektionen des Zentralnervensystems," *Zeitschrift für Chemotherapie*, 1 (1913): 44–50; Walther Weigeldt, "Die Goldsolreaktion im Liquor cerebrospinalis," *Deutsche Zeitschrift für Nervenheilkunde*, 67 (1921): 290.

84. Lange, "Ausflockung," pp. 50–78.

85. Weigeldt, "Goldsolreaktion," pp. 290–291.

86. Grütz, "Goldsolreaktion im syphilitischen Liquor cerebrospinalis," pp. 426–433.

87. Weigeldt, "Goldsolreaktion," pp. 293–297; Heinrich Fischer, "Über den Mechanismus der Goldsolreaktion im Liquor cerebrospinalis," *Z. exp. Med.*, 14 (1921): 60–112.

88. Julius K. Mayr, "Zur Theorie und Praxis der Kolloidreaktionen, mit besonderer Berücksichtigung der Goldsolreaktion," *Archiv für Dermatologie und Syphilis*, 144 (1923): 200–236; Karl Hermann Voitel, "Die Theorie der Langeschen Goldsolreaktion," *Deutsche Zeitschrift für Nervenheilkunde*, 85 (1925): 180–185.

89. Fischer, "Goldsolreaktion," pp. 61–62; Weigeldt, "Goldsolreaktion," p. 309.

90. Zsigmondy, *Kolloidchemie*; H. Freundlich, *Kapillarchemie*; Leonor Michaelis, *Die Wasserstoff-ionen-Konzentration: ihre Bedeutung für die Biologie und die Methoden ihrer Messung*, Pt. 1 (Berlin: Julius Springer, 1922); HAK–FLH, Aug. 30, 1976 (Tape 1, pp. 10–11), Feb. 22, 1978 (Tape 59, p. 2), Feb. 23, 1978 (Tape 60, p. 8).

91. HAK–FLH, Feb. 21, 1981 (Tape 58, pp. 19–20); Hans Adolf Krebs, "Zur Goldsolreaktion im Liquor Cerebrospinalis," *Klin. Woch.*, 4 (1925): 1309.

92. Mayr, "Kolloidreaktionen," p. 212; HAK–FLH, Feb. 21, 1978 (Tape 58, p. 20).

93. Krebs, "Goldsolreaktion," pp. 1309–1311.

94. *Ibid.*, p. 1309.

95. Hans Adolf Krebs, "Die Flockung des kolloidalen Goldes durch Eiweißkörper," *Biochem. Z.*, 159 (1925): 312–313; HAK–FLH, Feb. 21, 1978 (Tape 58, pp. 19–20). Krebs's recollection in 1978 was uncertain. At one point he stated that he saw the gold sol reaction already in use in the clinic. But the weight of his statements favors the view that there was no one present with the skills to perform it and that he introduced the clinical procedure in the III Medical Clinic.

96. David Nachmansohn, "Biochemistry as Part of My Life," *Annual Review of Biochemistry*, 41 (1972): 2–3; HAK–FLH, Feb. 23, 1978 (Tape 60, p. 9); David Nachmansohn-FLH, March 12, 1977 (Tape 8, p. 1).

97. Nachmansohn, "Biochemistry," pp. 2–3; HAK–FLH, Feb. 23, 1978 (Tape 60, p. 10); Nachmansohn-FLH, March 12, 1977 (Tape 8, p. 12).

98. HAK–FLH, Feb. 23, 1978 (Tape 60, pp. 10–11). The treatment was later abandoned, because over the long term it caused dangerous damage to bone marrow.

99. *Ibid.*, p. 12.

100. Bruno Mendel, Werner Engel, and Ingeborg Goldscheider, "Über den Milchsäuregehalt des Blutes unter physiologischen und pathologischen Bedingungen," *Klin. Woch.*, 4 (1925): 262–263.

101. *Ibid.*; Bruno Mendel and Ingeborg Goldscheider, "Eine kolorimetrische Mikromethode zur quantitativen Bestimmung der Milchsäure im Blut," *Biochem. Z.*, 164 (1925): 163–174; HAK–FLH, Feb. 23, 1978 (Tape 60, pp. 12–13).

102. HAK–FLH, Feb. 23, 1978 (Tape 60, p. 13).

103. *Ibid.*, Feb. 22, 1978 (Tape 59, pp. 1, 3–4); Krebs, *Reminiscences*, p. 22.

104. Craig, *Germany*, pp. 467–468.

105. *Ibid.*, pp. 469–497; Otto Friedrich, *Before the Deluge: A Portrait of Berlin in the 1920s* (New York: Harper & Row, 1972); HAK–FLH, Aug. 9, 1978 (Tape 81, p. 24), Dec. 21, 1979 (Tape 111, pp. 4–7).

106. HAK–FLH, Dec. 21, 1979 (Tape 111, p. 4); Ursula Leitner-FLH, June 11, 1986 (Tape 165, pp. 2, 6).

107. Wolf Krebs–FLH, Sept. 15, 1986 (Tape 153, p. 4), May 4, 1988 (Tape 161, pp. 19, 21–22); Wolf Krebs to F.L. Holmes, April 25, 1989.

108. Hans Adolf Krebs, "Die Flockung des kolloidalen Goldes durch Eiweißkörper," *Biochem. Z.*, 159 (1925): 311–314.

109. *Ibid.*, pp. 315–317.

110. *Ibid.*, pp. 316–322.

111. *Ibid.*, p. 312; Lange, "Ausflockung," p. 51.

112. HAK–FLH, Aug. 30, 1976 (Tape 1, pp. 8-9), Feb. 23, 1978 (Tape 59, p. 13).

113. *Ibid.* It should be clear that this was Krebs's subjective view of Wittgenstein. I have not searched for an independent assessment.

114. M. Lewandowsky, "Zur Lehre von der Cerebrospinalflüssigkeit," *Zeitschrift für klinische Medizin*, 40 (1900): 494.

115. L. Stern and R. Gautier, "Les rapports entre le liquide céphalo-rachidien et la circulation sanguine," *Archives internationales de physiologie* 17 (1921–1922): 138–192.

116. *Ibid.*, p. 175.

117. *Ibid.*, pp. 139, 185, 186.

118. Annelise Wittgenstein and Hans Adolf Krebs, "Studien zur Permeabilität der Meningen unter besonderer Berücksichtigung physikalisch-chemischer Gesichtspunkte," *Z. exp. Med.*, 49 (1926): 555.

119. Günther Lehmann and A. Meesmann, "Über das Bestehen eines Donnangleichgewichtes zwischen Blut and Kammerwasser bzw. Liquor cerebrospinalis," *Arch. ges. Physiol.*, 205 (1924): 210–232.

120. Wittgenstein and Krebs, "Permeabilität der Meningen," pp. 556–557; HAK–FLH, Aug. 30, 1976 (Tape 1, pp. 8–9), Feb. 23, 1978 (Tape 59, pp. 16–17); W.V. Farrar, "Donnan, Frederick George," *Dictionary of Scientific Biography*, ed. C.C. Gillispie, (New York: Charles Scribner's Sons, 1970–1980), 4: 165.

121. Quoted in Wittgenstein and Krebs, "Permeabilität der Meningen," p. 557.

122. *Ibid.*, p. 558.

123. HAK–FLH, Feb. 23, 1978 (Tape 59, p. 16).

124. *Ibid.*, Aug. 30, 1976 (Tape 1, p. 9), Feb. 23, 1978 (Tape 59, p. 22).

125. HAK–FLH, July 20, 1980, Tape 120, pp. 1–2; "Allgemeiner Bericht über die 88. Versammlung Deutscher Naturforscher und Ärzte, *Mitteilungen der Gessellschaft Deutscher Naturforscher und Ärzte*, 1 (1924)34–35; *Reisepass* Nr. 9360/24, Dr. Hans Adolf Krebs, pp. 6–9.

126. "88. Versammlung," pp. 48–49, 51–52; HAK–FLH, July 20, 1980, Tape 120, p. 2.

127. Reisepass Nr. 9360/24, pp. 8–9.

128. Hans Adolf Krebs and Annelise Wittgenstein, "Die Permeabilität der Meningen für diffusible Anionen," *Z. exp. Med.*, 49 (1926): 563–566.

129. *Ibid.*, pp. 567–602. This article includes the full, dated protocols for most of the experiments performed.

130. HAK–FLH, Aug. 30, 1976 (Tape 1, p. 9), Feb. 23, 1978 (Tape 60, pp. 8, 15).

131. Krebs, *Reminiscences*, pp. 24–25; David Nachmansohn-FLH, Mar. 12, 1977 (Tape 8, p. 1); HAK–FLH, Aug. 30, 1976 (Tape 1, p. 12)

132. HAK–FLH, Feb. 22, 1978 (Tape 59, pp. 10–11); Krebs, *Reminiscences*, pp. 24–25.

Chapter 5

1. R. Ammon, "In Memoriam Peter Rona," *Arzneimittelforschung*, 10 (1960): 321–324; David Nachmansohn–FLH, March 12, 1977 (Tape 8, p. 1).

2. Ammon, "Rona," pp. 322–326.

3. *Ibid.*, p. 324.

4. *Ibid.*, p. 323.

5. Nachmansohn–FLH, March 11, 1977 (Tape 7, p. 3); HAK–FLH, Aug. 30, 1976 (Tape 1, p. 12), Aug. 5, 1977 (Tape 36, p. 3).

6. HAK–FLH, *Ibid.*, and Feb. 24, 1978 (Tape 62, pp. 1–3).

7. *Ibid.*, Feb. 23, 1978 (Tape 59, p. 23).

8. Annelise Wittgenstein and Hans Adolf Krebs, "Studien zur Permeabilität der Meningen unter besonderer Berücksichtigung physikalisch-chemischer Gesichtspunkte," *Z. exp. Med.*, 49 (1926): 569–597.

9. *Ibid.*, pp. 560, 619–620.

10. HAK–FLH, Feb. 22, 1978 (Tape 59, p. 3).

11. Hans Adolf Krebs, "Zur Goldsolreaktion im Liquor Cerebrospinalis," *Klin. Woch.*, 4 (1925): 1309–1312; Krebs, "Die Flockung des kolloidalen Goldes durch Eiweißkörper," *Biochem. Z.*, 159 (1925): 311–324; Krebs, "Die Theorie der Kolloidreaktionen im Liquor cerebrospinalis," *Zeitschrift für Immunitäts Forschung*, 44 (1925): 75–104.

12. Krebs, "Goldsolreaktion," p. 1310.

13. Krebs, "Flockung," p. 320.

14. Krebs, "Theorie der Kolloidreaktionen," pp. 75–101.

15. *Ibid.*, p. 101.

16. HAK–FLH, Feb. 22, 1978 (Tape 59, p. 3).

17. Krebs, "Goldsolreaktion," p. 1309.

18. HAK–FLH, Feb. 22, 1978 (Tape 59, p. 8).

19. Wittgenstein and Krebs, "Permeabilität der Meningen," pp. 579–597; Wittgenstein and Krebs, "Die Abwanderung intravenös eingeführter Substanzen aus dem Blutplasma," *Arch. ges. Physiol.*, 212 (1926): 270–279.

20. P. Rona and H.A. Krebs, "Physikalisch-chemische Untersuchungen über die Isohämagglutination," *Biochem. Z.*, 169 (1926): 266–280; HAK–FLH, Feb. 24, 1978 (Tape 60, p. 18).

21. Hans Adolf Krebs and David Nachmansohn, "Vitalfärbung und Adsorption," *Biochem. Z.*, 186 (1927): 478–484; David Nachmansohn-FLH, March 12, 1977 (Tape 8, p. 1); HAK–FLH, Aug. 5, 1977 (Tape 36, p. 4).

22. Hans Krebs, *Reminiscences and Reflections*, with Anne Martin, (Oxford: Clarendon Press, 1981), p. 25; HAK–FLH, Feb. 23, 1978 (Tape 60, p. 8), Feb. 24, 1978 (Tape 62, p. 2).

23. Krebs, *Reminiscences*, p. 26; Hans Krebs, with Roswitha Schmid, *Otto Warburg: Cell Physiologist, Biochemist, and Eccentric* (Oxford: Clarendon Press, 1981), p. 80; Hermann Blaschko–FLH, Sept. 10, 1976 (Tape 6, p. 1); HAK–FLH, Aug. 31, 1976 (Tape 2, pp. 2–3), Feb. 23, 1978 (Tape 60, p. 8). Subsequent to the latter conversation of 1978, Krebs learned from the widow of Mendel the way in which the post had originated and told the story in his autobiography.

24. HAK–FLH, Feb. 22, 1978 (Tape 59, p. 10).

25. Krebs, *Reminiscences*, p. 25.

26. HAK–FLH, Feb. 23, 1978 (Tape 59, p. 19).

27. *Ibid.*, (Tape 59, p. 23).

28. Annelise Wittgenstein and Hans Adolf Krebs, "Über die Abwanderung intravenös eingeführter Farbstoffe aus dem Blutplasma," *Klin. Woch.*, 5 (1926): 320; Wittgenstein and Krebs, "Untersuchungen über die Permeabilität der Meningen," *Deutschen Medizinischen Wochenschrift*, 28 (1926): 1161; Wittgenstein and Krebs, "Die Abwanderung," *Arch. ges. Physiol.*, 212 (1926): "I Mitteilung," 268–281; Krebs and Wittgenstein, "II Mitteilung," *Ibid.*, pp. 282–299; Wittgenstein and Krebs, "Permeabilität der Meningen," *Z. exp. Med.*, 49 (1926), "I Mitteilung," 554–562; Krebs and Wittgenstein, "II Mitteilung. Die Permeabilität der Meningen für diffusible Anionen," *Ibid.*, pp. 563–586; Wittgenstein and Krebs, "III Mitteilung. Die Permeabilität der Meningen für diffusible Kationen," *Ibid.*, pp. 587–614; Krebs and Wittgenstein, "IV Mitteilung. Die Impermeabilität der Meningen für Kolloide," *Ibid.*, pp. 615–622.

29. Wittgenstein and Krebs, "Die Abwanderung. I Mitteilung," pp. 280–281; Krebs and Wittgenstein, "Permeabilität der Meningen: II Mitteilung," pp. 606–609; "III Mitteilung," pp. 613–614; "IV Mitteilung," pp. 621–622.

30. Wittgenstein and Krebs, "Permeabilität der Meningen: I Mitteilung," pp. 556, 560–561.

31. *Ibid.*, p. 561.

32. Wittgenstein and Krebs, "Untersuchungen über die Permeabilität," p. 1162.

33. HAK–FLH, Aug. 30 1976 (Tape 1, p. 10), Feb. 23, 1978 (Tape 59, p. 20); Wolf Krebs–FLH, Sept. 15, 1986 (Tape 154, p. 27).

34. Krebs, *Reminiscences*, p. 29; HAK–FLH, Aug. 31, 1976 (Tape 2, p. 3), Feb. 24, 1978 (Tape 62, p. 10).

35. Krebs, *Reminiscences*, pp. 30–31; HAK–FLH, Feb. 24, 1978 (Tape 62, pp. 4–5).

36. Krebs, *Reminiscences*, pp. 30–31; Krebs, *Warburg*, p. 57; HAK–FLH, Feb. 24, 1978 (Tape 62, p. 14), Aug. 4, 1981 (Tape 142, p. 14).

37. Krebs, *Reminiscences*, p. 32; HAK–FLH, Feb. 24, 1978 (Tape 62, p. 7), Aug. 4, 1981 (Tape 143, p. 2).

38. HAK–FLH, Aug. 31, 1976 (Tape 2, p. 4), Feb. 24, 1978 (Tape 62, p. 4).

39. For this and the two following paragraphs, see Krebs, *Warburg*, pp. 13–16; Joseph Barcroft, "Zur Lehre vom Blutgaswechsel in den verschiedenen Organen," *Erg. Physiol.*, 7 (1908): 772–775; T.G. Brodie, "Some New Forms of Apparatus for the Analysis of the Gases of the Blood by the Chemical Method," *J. Physiol.*, 39 (1910): 391–396; Otto Warburg, "Über Beeinflussung der Oxydationen in lebenden Zellen nach Versuchen an roten Blutkörperchen," *Z. physiol. Chem.*, 69 (1910): 452–462; H.A. Krebs, "Stoffwechsel der Zellen und Gewebe," *Methoden der wissenschaftlichen Biologie*, 2 (1929): 1048–1054; Theodore L. Sourkes, "Historical Note on the Warburg Constant-Volume Respirometer," *Journal of Chemical Education*, 29 (1952): 383–384.

40. For this and following paragraphs, see H.A. Krebs, "Stoffwechsel der Zellen, pp. 1048–1084.

41. HAK–FLH, Aug. 4, 1981 (Tape 143, p. 3).

42. *Ibid.*, Feb. 24, 1978 (Tape 62, p. 6).

43. I have inferred Krebs's habits here partly from a comment he made to me after I had watched one of his technicians carry out a set of manometer readings in his laboratory, on how difficult it was to teach technicians to occupy themselves effectively between readings, and that they tended to waste those time intervals.

44. The formulas and procedures involved are described in Krebs, "Stoffwechsel," pp. 1058–1061.

45. HAK–FLH, Feb. 24, 1978 (Tape 62, pp. 6–7).

46. *Ibid.*, Aug. 31, 1976 (Tape 2, p. 4), Feb. 24, 1978 (Tape 62, p. 10).

47. Otto Warburg, "Versuche an überlebendem Carcinomgewebe," *Biochem.Z.*, 142 (1923): 68–84.

48. Otto Warburg, "Über Eisen, den sauerstoffübertragenden Bestandteil des Atmungsferments," *Ibid.*, 152 (1924): 479–482.

49. *Ibid.*, pp. 483–484.

50. *Ibid.*, pp. 484–487.

51. *Ibid.*, pp. 489–491.

52. *Ibid.*, pp. 492–493.

53. Muneo Yabusoe, "Über Eisen- und Blutfarbstoffbestimmungen in normalen Geweben und in Tumorgewebe," *Ibid.*, 157 (1925): 150–157.

54. Franz Wind, "Über die Oxydation von Dioxyaceton und Glycerinaldehyd in Phosphatlösungen und die Beschleunigung der Oxydation durch Schwermetalle," *Ibid.*, 159 (1925): 58–67.

55. Erwin Negelein, "Über die Wirkung des Schwefelwasserstoffs auf chemische Vorgänge in Zellen," *Ibid.*, 165 (1925): 203–213.

56. *Ibid.*, p. 204.

57. Otto Warburg, "Über die Wirkung des Kohlenoxyds auf den Stoffwechsel der Hefe," *Ibid.*, 177 (1926): 471–473.

58. HAK–FLH, Feb. 24, 1978 (Tape 62, pp. 18–19).

59. *Ibid.*, Feb. 25, 1978 (Tape 64, pp. 1–2); Warburg, "Wirkung des Kohlenoxyds," p. 476; Krebs, *Warburg*, p. 26. Krebs mentioned the event here as occurring "in the winter of 1927–1928," but was mistaken about the year, since Warburg mentioned it in the above paper, which was submitted for publication in August 1926.

60. Hans Adolf Krebs, "Über die Rolle der Schwermetalle bei der Autoxydation von Zuckerlösungen," *Biochem. Z.*, 180 (1927): 377; HAK–FLH, Aug. 31, 1976 (Tape 2, p. 4), Sept. 2, 1976 (Tape 2, p. 17).

61. Otto Warburg and Muneo Yabusoe, "Über die Oxydation von Fructose in Phosphatlösungen," *Biochem. Z.*, 146 (1924): 380.

62. Krebs, "Schwermetalle," p. 379; HAK–FLH, Feb. 24, 1978 (Tape 62, p. 4).

63. The original record of this and the experiments described in the next two paragraphs has not survived. I have reconstructed the probable course of this first phase in the investigation from the experiments reported in Krebs, "Schwermetalle," pp. 377–394 that are *not* recorded in the laboratory notebook begun on May 7, 1926, and from Warburg and Yabusoe, "Oxydation von Fructose," pp. 380–386.

64. Krebs, "Schwermetalle," pp. 378, 380–382.

65. *Ibid.*, pp. 384, 386–389.

66. *Ibid.*, p. 378.

67. HAK–FLH, Aug. 31, 1976 (Tape 2, pp. 4–5); Feb. 24, 1978 (Tape 62, pp. 4, 11).

68. Krebs, *Reminiscences*, pp. 32–33.

69. HAK–FLH, Feb. 22, 1978 (Tape 59, p. 8), July 31, 1978 (Tape 69, pp. 12, 14); Krebs, *Warburg*, p. 61.

70. HAK–FLH, Feb. 24, 1978 (Tape 62, pp. 8, 13). Although Hans Krebs believed that he had missed calculus by missing his last year at the Andreanum, Wolf Krebs, who completed his education there in the normal time, did not have calculus either. Wolf Krebs to F.L. Holmes, July 9, 1989.

71. For further details of such encounters, see Krebs, *Warburg*, p. 56. I have translated Krebs's German rendition of Warburg's retort from the German edition of his biography: Hans Krebs, *Otto Warburg: Zellphysiologe, Biochemiker, Mediziner* ("Grosse Naturforscher, vol. 41") (Stuttgart: Wissenschaftliche Verlagsgesellschaft, 1979), p. 77.

72. HAK–FLH, Feb. 24, 1978 (Tape 62, p. 11), March 1, 1978 (Tape 66, p. 17), Dec. 20, 1979 (Tape 110, p. 18), Dec. 21, 1979 (Tape 110, p. 20), Aug. 4, 1981 (Tape 142, p. 6).

73. *Ibid.*, Feb. 24, 1978 (Tape 62, p. 11), Feb. 25, 1978 (Tape 64, p. 1), Dec. 15, 1979 (Tape 103, p. 4). For typical published examples see *Warburg*, "Über die Grundlagen der Wielandschen Atmungstheorie," *Biochem. Z.*, 142 (1923): 518–523; "Bemerkung über das Kohlemodell," *Ibid.*, 152 (1924): 191–192; "Bemerkung zu einer Arbeit von D. Keilin," *Ibid.*, 207 (1929): 494–495; "The Enzyme Problem and Biological Oxidations," *The Johns Hopkins Hospital Bulletin*, 46 (1930): 341–358, on 357.

74. HAK–FLH, Feb. 24, 1978 (Tape 62, p. 5), Aug. 9, 1978 (Tape 80, p. 12), Aug. 4, 1981 (Tape 142, p. 6).

75. *Ibid.*, Feb. 23, 1978 (Tape 59, pp. 14–15, Tape 60, p. 14); Krebs, *Reminiscences*, pp. 23–24.

76. HAK–FLH, Feb. 24, 1978 (Tape 62, p. 5).

77. *Ibid.*, Sept. 3, 1976 (Tape 3, p. 9), Jan. 7, 1981 (Tape 126, p. 8), Aug. 4, 1981 (Tape 143, p. 2).

78. See Krebs's discussion of Warburg's personality in Krebs, *Warburg*, (English ed.), pp. 52–81. For other views of Warburg, see Theodor Bücher, "Otto Warburg: A Personal Recollection," in *Biological Oxidations*, Colloquium-Mosbach (Berlin: Springer Verlag, 1983), pp. 1–29; and Petra Werner, *Otto Warburg: Von der Zellphysiologie zur Krebsforschung* (Berlin: Verlag Neues Leben, 1988).

79. Krebs, *Reminiscences*, pp. 31, 33; Morris Goran, "Haber, Fritz," *Dictionary of Scientific Biography*, ed. C.C. Gillispie (New York: Charles Scribner's Sons, 1970–1980), 5: 620–623; Fritz Lipmann, *Wanderings of a Biochemist* (New York: Wiley-Interscience, 1971), p. 7; HAK–FLH, Aug. 9, 1978 (Tape 81, pp. 20–21), Aug. 4, 1981 (Tape 143, p. 3).

80. Krebs, "Schwermetalle," pp. 390–392; Krebs, Notebook "2," pp. 2–18.

81. Krebs, Notebook "2," pp. 19–27.

82. *Ibid.*, p. 32.

83. *Ibid.*, pp. 33–39.

84. *Ibid.*, pp. 42–44. See Krebs, "Schwermetalle," pp. 387–388.

85. Krebs, Notebook "2," pp. 45–76.

86. *Ibid.*, pp. 80–85.

87. Krebs, "Schwermetalle," p. 384.

88. Krebs, Notebook "2," pp. 87–90.

89. *Ibid.*, pp. 91–93.

90. *Ibid.*, pp. 95, 99.

91. *Ibid.*, pp. 102–118; HAK–FLH, Sept. 2, 1976 (Tape 2, p. 17).

92. Krebs, Notebook "2," pp. 121–130.

93. *Ibid.*, pp. 124–127; HAK–FLH, Sept. 2, 1976 (Tape 2, p. 17).

94. Krebs, Notebook "2," pp. 131–136.

95. HAK–FLH, March 1, 1978 (Tape 67, p. 5), Aug. 9, 1978 (Tape 81, p. 20), Dec. 21, 1979 (Tape 111, p. 13), Aug. 4, 1981 (Tape 143, p. 8).

96. HAK–FLH, Feb. 17, 1978 (Tape 54, p. 17), Mar. 1, 1978 (Tape 67, p. 7).

97. Krebs, *Warburg*, p. 52.

98. Krebs, *Reminiscences*, p. 37; *Deutsches Reich Reisepass*, Nr. 9360/24, "Dr Hans Adolf Krebs," pp. 10–11.

99. Krebs, "Stoffwechsel der Zellen," pp. 1048–1084; HAK–FLH, Aug. 4, 1978 (Tape 75, pp. 21–22). The dependence of Krebs's text on those of Warburg is inferred from a direct comparison with the sources cited by Krebs.

100. Heinrich Wieland and F.G. Fischer, "Oxydationswirkung der Iodsäure und ihre Hemmung," *Berichte der Deutschen chemische Gesellschaft*, 59 (1926): 1571–1581; Krebs, typewritten manuscript fragment, p. 23, KC.

101. Krebs, Notebook "2," pp. 140–145.

102. *Ibid.*, p. 146.

103. *Ibid.*, pp. 147–150.

104. HAK–FLH, Sept. 2, 1976 (Tape 2, p. 15); Krebs, *Warburg*, p. 63.

105. Hans Adolf Krebs, "Ueber die Autoxydation von Kohlenhydraten in ammoniak und in bikarbonathaltigen Salzlösungen," typewritten manuscript fragments, KC.
106. *Ibid.*
107. Krebs, Notebook "2," inserted at pp. 147–148.
108. Krebs, typewritten manuscript fragment, pp. 23–[24].
109. *Ibid.*
110. Krebs, handwritten, untitled manuscript, pp. [1–3], KC.
111. *Ibid.*
112. Krebs, Notebook "2," pp. 154–182.
113. Krebs, "Schwermetalle," pp. 378–394.
114. HAK–FLH, Sept. 2, 1976 (Tape 2, p. 13); Krebs, penciled notes for autobiography, KC.
115. HAK–FLH, Dec. 15, 1979 (Tape 103, pp. 1–2).

Chapter 6

1. Gordon A. Craig, *Germany: 1866-1945* (New York: Oxford University Press, 1980), pp. 498–533; Hajo Holborn, *A History of Modern Germany: 1840-1945* (Princeton: Princeton University Press, 1969), pp. 615–640; HAK–FLH, Dec. 21, 1979 (Tape 111, p. 11).
2. Wolf Krebs–FLH, May 4, 1988 (Tape 161, p. 20), July 3, 1989 (Tape 163, p. 21, Tape 164, p. 43).
3. Hans Krebs, with Anne Martin, *Reminiscences and Reflections*, (Oxford: Clarendon Press, 1981), p. 33; HAK–FLH, Dec. 21, 1979 (Tape 111, p. 17).
4. Otto Friedrich, *Before the Deluge: A Portrait of Berlin in the 1920's* (New York: Harper & Row, 1972), pp. 189–211; HAK–FLH, Dec. 21, 1979 (Tape 111, p. 15).
5. Hans Krebs, with Roswitha Schmid, *Otto Warburg: Cell Physiologist, Biochemist and Eccentric* (Oxford: Clarendon Press, 1981), pp. 4, 18–19; Otto Warburg, "Versuche an überlebendem Carcinomgewebe," *Biochem. Z.*, 142 (1923): 317–323; Krebs, Notebook "1," p. 1; HAK–FLH, Feb. 24, 1978 (Tape 63, pp. 3–4).
6. Warburg, "Überlebendem Carcinomgewebe," pp. 328–333.
7. Seigo Minami, "Versuche on überlebendem Carcinomgewebe," *Biochem. Z.*, 142 (1923): 334–350.
8. Otto Warburg, "Verbesserte Methode zur Messung der Atmung und Glykolyse," *Ibid.*, 152 (1924): 51–63.
9. Otto Warburg, Karl Posener, and Erwin Negelein, "Über den Stoffwechsel der Carcinomzelle," *Ibid.*, 152 (1924): 309–344.
10. *Ibid.*, pp. 317–320.
11. *Ibid.*, pp. 324–326.
12. *Ibid.*, pp. 309, 320–324, 329–330.
13. *Ibid.*, p. 330.
14. *Ibid.*, pp. 331–334.
15. Otto Warburg, "Über die Wirkung von Blausäureäthylester (Äthylcarbylamin) auf die Pasteurische Reaktion," *Ibid.*, 172 (1926): 435.
16. Otto Warburg, *Über den Stoffwechsel der Tumoren* (Berlin: Springer Verlag, 1926); Hans Adolf Krebs and Fritz Kubowitz, "Über den Stoffwechsel von Carcinomzellen in Carcinomserum und Normalserum," *Biochem. Z.*, 189 (1927): 194 n.3; HAK–FLH, Feb. 25, 1978 (Tape 63, p. 6).
17. Warburg, "Überlebende Carcinomgewebe," p. 323; HAK–FLH, Aug. 4, 1981 (Tape 143, pp. 3–4).
18. Krebs, Notebook "1," pp. 1–38; Krebs and Kubowitz, "Stoffwechsel von Carcinomzellen," p. 194; HAK–FLH, Feb. 25, 1978 (Tape 63, pp. 14–17).
19. Krebs, *Reminiscences*, p. 33; HAK–FLH, Sept. 4, 1976, (Tape 3, p. 23), Feb. 24, 1978 (Tape 62, p. 11).
20. Krebs and Kubowitz, "Stoffwechsel von Carcinomzellen," p. 195 n.1; HAK–FLH, Feb. 25, 1978 (Tape 63, pp. 6–7).
21. Krebs, Notebook "1," pp. 40–50; HAK–FLH, Feb. 25, 1978 (Tape 63, pp. 18–19).

22. Krebs, Notebook "1," pp. 51–151; Notebook "3," pp. 1–12.

23. Wolf Krebs–FLH, May 4, 1988 (Tape 161, p. 24), July 3, 1989 (Tape 163, pp. 1–5).

24. *Ibid.*, July 3, 1989 (Tape 163, p. 5).

25. *Ibid.* (Tape 163, pp. 14–15).

26. *Ibid.* (Tape 163, pp. 9–12).

27. Krebs, Notebook "3," pp. 13–34.

28. *Ibid.*, pp. 36–64.

29. *Ibid.*, pp. 66–87.

30. HAK–FLH, Sept. 2, 1976 (Tape 2, p. 23).

31. Krebs, Notebook "3," pp. 90–92.

32. In the paper he subsequently published on the experiments begun here [Hans Adolf Krebs, "Über den Stoffwechsel der Netzhaut," *Biochem. Z.*, 189 (1927): 57–59]; he omitted the customary acknowledgment that the work had been suggested by Warburg, a circumstance that led him, when I drew this to his attention, to comment, "If I had not mentioned him then…it means that he hadn't actually suggested it"; HAK–FLH, Sept. 2, 1976 (Tape 2, p. 21).

33. *Ibid.*, p. 24.

34. *Ibid.*

35. Krebs, Notebook "3," pp. 93–94.

36. O. Meyerhof and K. Lohmann, "Milchsäurebildung und Milchsäureschwund in tierischen Geweben," *Biochem. Z.*, 171 (1926): 383.

37. Otto Warburg, "Manometrische Messung des Zellstoffwechsels in Serum," *Ibid.*, 164 (1925): 481–503.

38. Meyerhof and Lohmann, "Milchsäurebildung," pp. 385–402.

39. Krebs, Notebook "3," pp. 97–98.

40. Warburg, "Zellstoffwechsels in Serum," p. 501.

41. Krebs, Notebook "3," p. 98.

42. *Ibid.*, p. 99.

43. *Ibid.*

44. Otto Warburg, Franz Wind, and Erwin Negelein, "Über den Stoffwechsel von Tumoren im Körper," *Klin. Woch.*, 5 (1926): 829–832.

45. Krebs, Notebook "3," pp. 99–100.

46. *Ibid.*, pp. 101–107.

47. *Ibid.*, pp. 108–115.

48. *Ibid.*, pp. 116–138.

49. *Ibid.*, pp. 140–157.

50. *Ibid.*, p. 148.

51. *Ibid.*, pp. 158–160.

52. HAK–FLH, Sept. 2, 1976 (Tape 2, p. 7), Sept. 2, 1976 (Tape 2, p. 10).

53. *Ibid.*, May 2, 1977 (Tape 12, p. 2), July 20, 1980 (Tape 120, p. 2).

54. *Ibid.*, Sept. 1, 1976 (Tape 2, p. 7).

55. Meyerhof and Lohmann, "Milchsäurebildung," pp. 399–400.

56. Warburg, Posener and Negelein, "Stoffwechsel der Carzinomzelle," p. 318 n.2.

57. HAK–FLH, Aug. 31, 1976 (Tape 2, p. 6); see also Otto Warburg, "Wie viele Atmungsfermente gibt es?" *Biochem. Z.*, 201 (1928): 486–488.

58. Krebs, *Warburg*, p. 16; Otto Warburg and H.A. Krebs, "Über locker gebundenes Kupfer und Eisen im Blutserum," *Bioch. Z.*, 190 (1927): 143–149.

59. Krebs, Notebook "3," pp. 166–268; HAK–FLH, Sept. 2, 1976 (Tape 2, p. 25).

60. Krebs, "Stoffwechsel der Netzhaut," p. 57; H.A. Krebs, "Ueber den Stoffwechsel der Vogelnetzhaut," handwritten and typewritten manuscript, KC. Warburg broadened the scope of the subject treated by eliminating the word "Vogel" from the title.

61. Krebs, "Stoffwechsel der Vogelnetzhaut," pp. [3–4].

62. Krebs and Kubowitz, "Stoffwechsel von Carcinomzellen," pp. 194–202; HAK–FLH, Feb. 25, 1978 (Tape 63, pp. 6–7).

63. Krebs, *Reminiscences*, p. 37; *Deutschen Reich Reisepass*, Nr. 9360/24, "Dr. Hans Adolf Krebs," p. 13.

64. Wolf Krebs–FLH, July 3, 1989 (Tape 163, pp. 6–9); Wolf Krebs to F.L. Holmes, Oct. 10, 1989.

65. Krebs, *Reminiscences*, pp. 33–34; HAK–FLH, March 1, 1978 (Tape 67, p. 7); Wolf Krebs–FLH, July 3, 1989 (Tape 163, pp. 13–14). This English translation of the verse was given by Krebs spontaneously during our conversations. The original German is quoted in *Reminiscences*, p. 34.

66. Wolf Krebs–FLH, Sept. 15, 1986 (Tape 155, p. 35).

67. This statement is contained in a note pasted into a red "Exercise Book" with the word "Autobiography" handwritten on the cover. The note is dated 8/6/73. KC.

68. Krebs, *Reminiscences*, p. 34.

69. Ursula Leitner–FLH, June 11, 1986 (Tape 165, pp. 2–3).

70. Wolf Krebs–FLH, July 3, 1989 (Tape 163, pp. 15–17).

71. HAK–FLH, Dec. 21, 1979 (Tape 111, pp. 7–9), Jan. 10, 1981 (Tape 130, pp. 9–12), Aug. 4, 1981 (Tape 143, pp. 8–9).

72. Warburg and Krebs, "Über locker gebundenes Kupfer," pp. 143–149; Krebs, Notebook "3," pp. 270–359.

73. D. Keilin, "On Cytochrome, a Respiratory Pigment, Common to Animals, Yeast, and Higher Plants," *Proceedings of the Royal Society ser. B*, 98 (1925): 312–339. See also David Keilin, *The History of Cell Respiration and Cytochrome* (Cambridge: Cambridge University Press, 1966), pp. 140–174.

74. Otto Warburg, "Über Kohlenoxydwirkung ohne Hämoglobin und einige Eigenschaften des Atmungsferments," *Die Naturwissenschaften*, 15 (1927): 546.

75. HAK–FLH, Feb. 25, 1978 (Tape 64, p. 2).

76. Otto Warburg, "Über die Wirkung von Kohlenoxyd und Stickoxyd auf Atmung und Gährung," *Biochem. Z.*, 189 (1927): 370.

77. HAK–FLH, Sept. 4, 1976 (Tape 3, p. 11).

78. Krebs, Notebook "3," pp. 363–364, Notebook "4," pp. 7–8, 46.

79. Krebs, Notebook "4," p. 9.

80. Warburg, "Wirkung von Kohlenoxyd," pp. 354–362.

81. Krebs, Notebook "4," p. 9.

82. Krebs, Notebook "4,", pp. 10–27; HAK–FLH, Feb. 27, 1978 (Tape 64, pp. 11–15).

83. Krebs, Notebook "4,", pp. 28–31; HAK–FLH, Feb. 27, 1978 (Tape 64, p. 8).

84. Krebs, Notebook "4," pp. 35–56.

85. *Ibid.*, pp. 57–61; HAK–FLH, Feb. 27, 1978 (Tape 65, pp. 5–8).

86. Krebs, Notebook "4," pp. 65–116.

87. *Ibid.*, p. 119; M.L. Anson and A.E. Mirsky, "On Haemochromogen and the Relation of Protein to the Properties of the Haemoglobin Molecule," *J. Physiol.*, 60 (1925): 54; HAK–FLH, Feb. 27, 1978 (Tape 64, pp. 22–23).

88. Krebs, Notebook "4," pp. 120–139; HAK–FLH, Feb. 28, 1978 (Tape 65, pp. 22–24).

89. Krebs, Notebook "4," pp. 140–147; HAK–FLH, Feb. 28, 1978 (Tape 66, pp. 2–3).

90. Krebs, Notebook "4," pp. 148–168.

91. *Ibid.*, p. 169; Hans Adolf Krebs, "Über die Wirkung von Kohlenoxyd und Licht auf Häminkatalysen," *Biochem. Z.*, 193 (1928): 347–349.

92. Otto Warburg, "Über die chemische Konstitution des Atmungsferments," *Die Naturwissenschaften*, 20 (1928): 345–347.

93. *Ibid.*, pp. 348–350.

94. *Ibid.*, p. 350.

95. HAK–FLH, Feb. 25, 1978 (Tape 64, pp. 2–3).

96. Krebs, Notebook "4," pp. 183–265; Hans Adolf Krebs, "Über die Wirkung von Kohlenoxyd und Blausäure auf Hämatinkatalysen," *Biochem. Z.*, 204 (1928): 323, 340–341; Hans Adolf Krebs, "Über die Wirkung des Schwermetalle auf die Autoxidation der Alkalisulfide und des Schwefelwasserstoffs," *Ibid.*, pp. 343–346.

97. Krebs, Notebook "4," p. 267; Deutsches Reich Reisepass Nr. 9360/24, Hans Adolf Krebs, pp. 16–17.

98. HAK–FLH, March 1, 1978 (Tape 67, p. 6), May 18, 1979 (Tape 97, pp. 5–6), Dec. 21, 1979 (Tape 111, p. 5); Wolf Krebs–FLH, July 3, 1989 (Tape 163, p. 12).

99. HAK to Direktion der städtischen Krankenanstalten, Mannheim, May 10, 1928, KC.

100. Krebs, Notebook "4," pp. 267–383, Notebook "6," pp. 1–84; Krebs, "Wirkung von Kohlenoxyd und Blausäure," pp. 322–342.

101. Krebs, *Reminiscences*, pp. 37–38; Reisepass Nr. 9360/24, p. 14.

102. Krebs, Notebook "6," pp. 85–94.

103. Malcolm Dixon, "The Action of Carbon Monoxide on the Autoxidation of Sulphydryl Compounds," *Biochem. J.*, 22 (1928): 902–908.

104. Krebs, Notebook "6," p. 91; HAK–FLH, Sept. 3, 1976 (Tape 3, pp. 2–5).

105. H.A. Krebs, "Über die Wirkung des Kohlenoxyds auf Hämatinkatalyse nach M. Dixon," *Biochem. Z.*, 201 (1928): 489.

106. Krebs, Notebook "6," p. 91.

107. HAK–FLH, Sept. 3, 1976 (Tape 3, pp. 4–5).

108. See Krebs, *Warburg*, pp. 63–68.

109. Krebs, "Wirkung von Kohlenoxyd und Blausäure," pp. 322–342; Krebs, "Wirkung des Schwermetalle," pp. 343–346.

110. HAK–FLH, Aug. 31, 1976 (Tape 2, p. 5), Sept. 4, 1976 (Tape 3, p. 14).

111. Joseph C. Aub, Elizabeth M. Bright, and Joseph Uridil, "Studies upon the Mechanism of the Increased Metabolism in Hyperthyroidism," *The American Journal of Physiology*, 61 (1922): 300–310, on 309.

112. M. Tomita, "Über den Einfluß des Thyroxins auf die alkoholische Gärung," *Biochem. Z.*, 131 (1922): 175–177; Walter Horrisberger, "Die Wirkung des Schilddrüsenhormons bei gestörtem Kohlehydratstoffwechsel durch Phlorrhizindiabetes," *Ibid.*, 121 (1921): 64–75; F. Haffner, "Pharmakologische Untersuchungen mit einem deutschen Thyroxin," *Klin. Woch.*, 6 (1927): 1932–1935.

113. W. Schoeller and M. Gehrke, "Zur Kenntnis der Thyroxinwirkung," *Klin. Woch.*, 6 (1927): 1938–1939.

114. Krebs, Notebook "6," pp. 96–127; Haffner, "Pharmakologische Untersuchungen," p. 1932.

115. Krebs, Notebook "6," pp. 128–181.

116. HAK–FLH, Aug. 31, 1976 (Tape 2, p. 5), Sept. 4, 1976 (Tape 3, pp. 14–15); Hans Adolf Krebs and J.F. Donegan, "Manometrische Messung der Peptidspaltung," *Biochem. Z.*, 210 (1929):7.

117. Krebs, Notebook "6," pp. 185–278; Krebs and Donegan, "Peptidspaltung," pp. 8–23.

118. HAK–FLH, Sept. 4, 1976 (Tape 3, pp. 15–16).

119. HAK–FLH, Feb. 24, 1978 (Tape 62, p. 12).

120. Untitled typewritten manuscript, dated Jan. 2, 1929, KC.

121. *Ibid.*, dated Feb. 26, 1929.

122. *Ibid.*, dated May 29, 1929.

123. HAK–FLH, Aug. 31, 1976 (Tape 2, p. 6).

124. HAK–FLH, March 1, 1978 (Tape 67, pp. 1–3).

125. HAK–FLH, Dec. 21, 1979 (Tape 111, p. 8).

126. Wolf Krebs–FLH, Sept. 15, 1986 (Tape 153, p. 1).

127. Krebs, Notebook "5," pp. 14–33; Hans Adolf Krebs, "Über Hemmung einer Hämatinkatalyse durch Schwefelwasserstoff," *Bioch. Z.*, 209 (1929): 32–33.

128. Krebs, Notebook "5," pp. 51–173; Hans Adolf Krebs, "Manometrische Messung des Kohlensäuregehaltes von Gasgemischen," *Biochem. Z.*, 220 (1929): 250–252.

129. Krebs, *Reminiscences*, p. 38; HAK–FLH, Sept. 5, 1976 (Tape 3, p. 25), May 16, 1979 (Tape 96, p. 16).

130. HAK–FLH, Sept. 5, 1976 (Tape 3, p. 26).

131. "The Nineteenth International Congress of Physiology," *Science*, 70 (1929): 187.

132. *Ibid.*

133. Quoted in Hans A. Krebs, "The August Krogh Principle: 'For Many Problems there is an Animal on Which it can be most Conveniently Studied'", *The Journal of Experimental Zoology*, 194 (1975): 221.

134. Krebs, *Reminiscences*, p. 38; HAK-FLH, Sept. 6, 1976 (Tape 4, p. 5).
135. Hedwig Michaelis to HAK, Aug. 14, 1929, KC; Krebs, *Reminiscences*, p. 39; HAK-FLH, Sept. 5, 1976 (Tape 3, p. 25).
136. Krebs, *Reminiscences*, p. 39; HAK-FLH, Feb. 27, 1978 (Tape 64, p. 23), Aug. 3, 1978 (Tape 74, p. 11), Aug. 4, 1981 (Tape 142, p. 2).
137. HAK-FLH, Aug. 9, 1978 (Tape 81, p. 19).
138. Krebs, *Reminiscences*, p. 39; HAK-FLH, Feb. 24, 1978 (Tape 62, p. 12).
139. Krebs, *Reminiscences*, pp. 38-39.
140. HAK-FLH, Sept. 5, 1976 (Tape 3, p. 26), Aug. 2, 1978 (Tape 73, p. 10).
141. HAK-FLH, Feb. 24, 1978 (Tape 62, p. 12); Krebs, *Reminiscences*, p. 40.
142. Krebs, *Reminiscences*, p. 40; HAK-FLH, Sept. 2, 1976 (Tape 2, p. 8).
143. Craig, *Germany*, pp. 524-528; It is possible that Krebs attended Stresemann's final conference just 5 days before Stresemann's death; HAK-FLH, Dec. 21, 1979 (Tape 111, p. 11).
144. HAK-FLH, July 31, 1978 (Tape 69, p. 2).
145. Hans Adolf Krebs, "Manometrische Messung der fermentativen Eiweißspaltung," *Biochem. Z.*, 220 (1930): 283-288; "Versuche über die proteolytische Wirkung des Papains," *Ibid.*, pp. 289-303; Krebs, Notebook "5," pp. 188-279, Notebook "7," pp. 2-165.
146. Krebs, *Reminiscences*, pp. 41-42.
147. *Ibid.*, p. 40.
148. Undated, handwritten note, entitled "Autobiography," KC.

Chapter 7

1. Erich Eyck, *A History of the Weimar Republic*, trans. H.P. Hanson and R.G.L. Waite, (New York: Atheneum, 1970), 2:226-241.
2. E. Grafe to HAK, Wurzburg, March 13, 1930, KC.
3. G. von Bergmann to HAK, Berlin, March 28, 1930, KC.
4. Hans Krebs, with Anne Martin, *Reminiscences and Reflections* (Oxford: Clarendon Press, 1981), p. 43; Hans Schaefer, "Klothilde Gollwitzer-Meier," *Deutsche Medezinische Wochenschrift*, 79 (1954): 1908-1909; HAK-FLH, Sept. 5, 1976 (Tape 3, p. 27), July 9, 1977 (Tape 19, pp. 10-11); K. Gollwitzer-Meier to HAK, July 5, [1930], KC.
5. Krebs, *Reminiscences*, p. 43; HAK-FLH, April 27, 1977 (Tape 9, p. 8), August 1, 1978 (Tape 71, p. 19); S.J. Thannhauser to HAK, Feb. 27, 1930, KC.
6. HAK-FLH, April 27, 1977 (Tape 9, pp. 8-10). The young woman lived at the time in Dresden. Krebs did not meet her again for many years, but they maintained a long-lasting friendship through letters.
7. HAK-FLH, Sept. 5, 1976 (Tape 3, p. 29), Feb. 22, 1978 (Tape 59, pp. 5-6); Krebs, *Reminiscences*, p. 44; HAK to *Notgemeinschaft der Deutschen Wissenschaft*, April 28, 1930; Otto Warburg to HAK, May 3, 1930, KC.
8. Krebs, *Reminiscences*, pp. 43-44; HAK-FLH, Sept. 4, 1976 (Tape 3, p. 23), Sept. 5, 1976 (Tape 3, pp. 27-29), Aug. 4, 1981 (Tape 143, p. 9); Krebs, Notebook "7," pp. 170-173; Geh. Oberregierungsrat, *Notgemeinschaft der Deutschen Wissenschaft* to HAK, May 15, 1930, KC.
9. J.F. Donegan to HAK, July 7, 1930, KC.
10. *Ibid.*, Oct. 25, 1930.
11. HAK-FLH, Sept. 5, 1976 (Tape 3, pp. 28-29); Krebs, *Reminiscences*, p. 50.
12. Klothilde Gollwitzer-Meier to HAK, July 5 [1930], KC.; S. Lauter to HAK, July 23, 1930, KC.
13. HAK-FLH, Sept. 5, 1976, (Tape 3, p. 28), Aug. 4, 1981 (Tape 143, p. 9).
14. The most prominent argument for this viewpoint is in Robert Kohler, *From Medical Chemistry to Biochemistry* (Cambridge: Cambridge University Press, 1982), see especially p. 7.
15. Hans Adolf Krebs and J.F. Donegan, "Manometrische Messung der Peptidspaltung," *Biochem. Z.*, 210 (1929): 7-23.
16. Hans Adolf Krebs, "Manometrische Messung der fermentativen Eiweißspaltung," *Ibid.*, 220 (1930): 283-288; "Versuche über die proteolytische Wirkung des Papains," *Ibid.*, pp. 289-303.
17. Krebs, Notebook "8," pp. 1-7.

18. W.B. Wendel and Philip A. Shaffer, "Induced Oxidations in Blood. Oxidation of Lactic Acid to Pyruvic Acid by Methylene Blue," *J. Biol. Chem.*, 87 (1930): xx–xxi.

19. Otto Warburg, Fritz Kubowitz, and Walter Christian, "Kohlenhydratverbrennung durch Methämoglobin (Über den Mechanismus einer Methylenblaukatalyse)" *Biochem. Z.*, 221 (1930): 494–497.

20. Untitled manuscript, dated Jan. 2, 1929, KC.

21. Hans Krebs, with Roswitha Schmid, *Otto Warburg: Cell Physiologist, Biochemist and Eccentric* (Oxford: Clarendon Press, 1981), p. 30; Otto Warburg, "The Enzyme Problem and Biological Oxidations," *The Johns Hopkins Hospital Bulletin*, 46 (1930): 357.

22. Warburg, Kubowitz, and Christian, "Kohlenhydratverbrennung," pp. 494–497.

23. Krebs, Notebook "8," pp. 7–8.

24. Warburg, "The Enzyme Problem," pp. 357–358.

25. See Otto Meyerhof, *Die chemischen Vorgänge im Muskel* (Berlin: Springer, 1930), pp. 17, 110–124, 140–166.

26. Krebs, Notebook "8," p. 26.

27. *Ibid.*, pp. 11–169.

28. *Ibid.*, pp. 45–47, 106–110, 118–123, 130–131, 135–141, 150–158, 162–163, 173–179, 184–189, 194–195, 207–212.

29. *Ibid.*, p. 208.

30. Einar Lundsgaard, "Untersuchungen über Muskelkontraktionen ohne Milchsäurebildung," *Biochem. Z.*, 217 (1930): 162–177.

31. *Ibid.*, pp. 169–176.

32. Paul Kruhøffer and Christian Crone, "Einar Lundsgaard, 1899–1968," *Erg. Physiol.*, 65 (1972): 5; Fritz Lipmann, *Wanderings of a Biochemist* (New York: Wiley Interscience, 1971), p. 17.

33. HAK–FLH, Sept. 5, 1976 (Tape 3, p. 31).

34. Hermann Blaschko–FLH, August 12, 1977 (Tape 43, pp. 1–3). For general accounts of Lundsgaard's investigation and its consequences, see A.V. Hill, "The Revolution in Muscle Physiology," *Physiological Reviews*, 12 (1932): 56–67; Dorothy M. Needham, *Machina Carnis: The Biochemistry of Muscular Contraction in its Historical Development* (Cambridge: Cambridge University Press, 1971), pp. 84–97; and Marcel Florkin, *A History of Biochemistry: Part III, History of the Identification of the Sources of Free Energy in Organisms* (Amsterdam: Elsevier, 1975), pp. 168–173.

35. Einar Lundsgaard, "Die Monojodessigsäurewirkung auf die enzymatische Kohlenhydratspaltung," *Biochem. Z.*, 220 (1930): 1–7.

36. Einar Lundsgaard, "Über die Einwirkung der Monojodessigsäure auf den Spaltungs- und Oxydationsstoffwechsel," *Ibid.*, pp. 8–18.

37. *Ibid.*, 8–9.

38. *Idem.*

39. This incident was recalled by Hermann Blaschko, who was present. Hermann Blaschko–FLH, July 10, 1984 (Tape 166, p. 3). Blaschko related the story in more coherent form before the taping of my conversation with him began.

40. Summarized in Meyerhof, *Die chemischen Vorgänge*, pp. 112–113.

41. Eric Gordon Holmes, "Oxidations in Central and Peripheral Nervous Tissue," *Biochem. J.*, 24 (1930): 914–925.

42. Eric Gordon Holmes and Charles Amos Ashford, "Lactic Acid Oxidation in Brain with reference to the 'Meyerhof Cycle'", *Ibid.*, pp. 1119–1127.

43. HAK–FLH, July 31, 1978 (Tape 69, p. 6); Hermann Blaschko–FLH, Aug. 12, 1977 (Tape 43, pp. 1–3).

44. Krebs, Notebook "8," p. 213; Lundsgaard, "Untersuchungen über Muskelcontraktionen," p. 164.

45. Krebs, Notebook "8," pp. 213–215. As is evident, Krebs used "Normal" and "Molar" interchangeably in identifyng the concentrations of monoiodoacetate. Since the acid is monobasic, his casual habit does not imply confusion.

46. *Ibid.*, p. 214.

47. *Ibid.*, p. 220.

48. *Ibid.*, p. 221.

49. *Ibid.*, pp. 222–223.

50. *Ibid.*, pp. 228, 232–233.

51. *Ibid.*, p. 239.

52. HAK–FLH, Sept. 5, 1976 (Tape 3, pp. 32–33). In retrospect Krebs explained his difficulties as due to the fact that some yeasts produce lactate aerobically.

53. Krebs, Notebook "8," pp. 240–254; HAK–FLH, Sept. 5, 1976 (Tape 3, pp. 29–30); Hans Adolf Krebs, "Über die Proteolyse der Tumoren," *Biochem. Z.*, 238 (1931): 192.

54. Krebs, Notebook "8," pp. 255–257; HAK–FLH, Sept. 6, 1976 (Tape 4, p. 1); Hans Adolf Krebs and Hans Rosenhagen, "Über den Stoffwechsel des Plexus chorioidens," *Zeitschrift für der gesammte Neurologie und Psychologie*, 134 (1931): 643.

55. HAK–FLH, Sept. 6, 1976 (Tape 4, p. 1).

56. Krebs, Notebook "8," p. 258.

57. *Ibid.*, pp. 267–269, 273.

58. *Ibid.*, pp. 274–275.

59. *Ibid.*, p. 278.

60. *Ibid.*, p. 279.

61. *Ibid.*, pp. 282–287. If the dates indicated at the heads of these experiments are correct, then their order in the notebook is inverted.

62. *Ibid.*, pp. 290–292.

63. *Ibid.*, pp. 293–295.

64. *Ibid.*, pp. 296–312.

65. *Ibid.*, pp. 313–315.

66. HAK–FLH, July 20, 1980 (Tape 120, p. 2).

67. Quoted in Hans Krebs, *Otto Warburg*, p. 61.

68. Krebs recalled having made a point, from 1924 onward, of periodically scanning current biochemical, physiological, and medical journals. HAK–FLH, April 26, 1927 (Tape 9, p. 3).

69. Krebs, Notebook "8," pp. 325–327.

70. Ragnar Nilsson, Karl Zeile, and Hans v. Euler, "Zur Kenntis der Monojod- und Monobromessigsäure vergiftungen beim Kohlenhydratabbau," *Z. physiol. Chem.*, 194 (1931): 53–68.

71. Krebs, Notebook "8," pp. 316–317.

72. *Ibid.*, p. 328.

73. *Ibid.*, p. 330.

74. *Ibid.*, p. 480.

75. Hans Adolf Krebs, "Über die Wirkung der Monojodessigsäure auf den Zellstoffwechsel," *Biochem. Z.*, 234 (1931): 278–279.

76. *Ibid.*, pp. 280–282.

77. *Ibid.*, p. 281.

78. *Ibid.*, p. 279.

79. HAK–FLH, Sept. 5, 1976 (Tape 3, p. 31).

80. Krebs and Rosenhagen, "Stoffwechsel des Plexus choroidens," p. 643.

81. Hans Krebs, "Über die Proteolyse der Tumoren," *Biochem. Z.*, 238 (1931): 174–196; HAK–FLH, Sept. 5, 1976 (Tape 3, pp. 29–30).

82. HAK–FLH, Jan. 9, 1981 (Tape 129, p. 5); Wolf Krebs–FLH, July 3, 1989 (Tape 164, pp. 33–34).

83. Krebs, *Reminiscences*, p. 44; HAK–FLH, Sept. 5, 1976 (Tape 3, pp. 28–29).

84. HAK–FLH, Sept. 6, 1976 (Tape 4, p. 2).

85. *Ibid.*, Feb. 21, 1978 (Tape 58, p. 8).

86. *Ibid.*, Sept. 5, 1976 (Tape 3, p. 29); Katherina Holsten to HAK, January 14, 1934, A.993, KC.

87. Katherina Holsten to HAK, May 5, 1934, A.993, KC.

Chapter 8

1. Hans Krebs, with Anne Martin, *Reminiscences and Reflections* (Oxford: Clarendon Press, 1981), pp. 44, 46.

2. *Ibid.*, p. 45; HAK–FLH, Aug. 4, 1981 (Tape 143, p. 10).

3. Krebs, *Reminiscences*, p. 46.

4. *Idem.*; HAK–FLH, May 2, 1977 (Tape 12, p. 1).

5. Theodor Benzinger-FLH, Sept. 3, 1977 (Tape 46, p. 11); Heinz Fuld-FLH, Feb. 24, 1978 (Tape 61, p. 7).

6. Krebs, Notebook "9," pp. 1–16.

7. Richard Kuhn and Rudolf Heckscher, "Über die enzymatische Bildung der Milchsäure aus Methylglyoxal," *Z. physiol. Chem.*, 160 (1926): 116–153.

8. Carl Neuberg and Maria Kobel, "Die desmolytische Bildung von Methylglyoxal durch Hefenenzym," *Biochem. Z.*, 203 (1928): 463–468; Neuberg and Kobel, "Die Isolierung von Methylglyoxal bei der Milchsäuregärung," *Ibid.*, 207 (1929): 232–262.

9. Marthe Vogt, "Die Isolierung von Methylglyoxal als Zwischensubstanz bei der Glykolyse," *Klin. Woch.*, 8 (1929): 793–794.

10. H.K. Barrenscheen, Karl Braun, and Miklos Dreguss, "Glykolysehemmung und Methylglyoxalanhäufung," *Biochem. Z.*, 232 (1931): 165–180.

11. Harold Ward Dudley, "The Effect of Sodium Iodoacetate on Glyoxalase," *Biochem. J.*, 25 (1931): 439–445.

12. Neuberg and Kobel, "Isolierung von Methylglyoxal," p. 240.

13. Krebs, Notebook "9," pp. 6, 11.

14. *Ibid.*, pp. 1–3.

15. *Ibid.*, pp. 4–5.

16. *Ibid.*, pp. 7–9.

17. Büchner, "Medizinische Gesellschaft Freiburg, 1. Br. Sitzung vom 2 Juni 1931," *Klin. Woch.*, 10 (1931): 1786–1788.

18. Krebs, Notebook "9," pp. 12–25; HAK–FLH, Sept. 6, 1976 (Tape 4, pp. 6–7).

19. Krebs, Notebook "9," pp. 26–28.

20. *Ibid.*, pp. 30–32.

21. *Ibid.*, p. 33.

22. M. Henze and R. Müller, "Die Umwandlung der Acetessigsäure durch Methylglyoxal," *Z. physiol. Chem.*, 193 (1930): 88–96.

23. Franz Knoop, *Oxydationen im Tierkörper* (Stuttgart: Ferdinand Enke, 1931), p. 7.

24. Krebs, Notebook "9," pp. 34–37.

25. *Ibid.*, pp. 41–43.

26. HAK–FLH, April 27, 1977 (Tape 9, p. 5).

27. *Idem.*

28. *Idem.*

29. Krebs, *Reminiscences*, pp. 44–46.

30. H.A. Krebs, "The Discovery of the Ornithine Cycle of Urea Synthesis," *Biomedical Education*, 1 (1973): 19–20; HAK–FLH, July 31, 1978 (Tape 69, pp. 11–12).

31. Krebs, "Ornithine Cycle," pp. 19–20.

32. Frederic L. Holmes, "Hans Krebs and the Origin of the Urea Cycle," typewritten manuscript, pp. 38–39 (copy annotated by Krebs).

33. HAK–FLH, July 31, 1978 (Tape 69, p. 13).

34. Kyoji Kase, "Untersuchungen über die Harnstoffbildung" (II, III), *Biochem. Z.*, 233 (1931): 258–282.

35. O. Schultzen and M. Nencki, "Die Vorstufen des Harnstoffs im thierischen Organismus," *Z. Biol.*, 8 (1872): 124–138.

36. W. von Knieriem, "Beiträge zur Kenntniss der Bildung des Harnstoffs im thierischen Organismus," *Ibid.*, 10 (1873): 263–294.

37. E. Salkowski, "Ueber den Vorgang der Harnstoffbildung im Thierkörper und den Einfluss der Ammoniaksalze auf denselben," *Z. physiol. Chem.*, 1 (1877): 1–59.

38. Joseph S. Fruton, *Molecules and Life* (New York: Wiley-Interscience, 1972), p. 434.

39. *Ibid.*, pp. 430–431.

40. Sergej Salaskin, "Ueber die Bildung von Harnstoff in der Leber der Säugethiere aus Amidosäure der Fettreihe," *Z. physiol. Chem.*, 25 (1898): 128–151.

41. Cyrus H. Fiske and Howard T. Karsner, "Urea Formation in the Liver," *J. Biol. Chem.*, 16 (1913): 399–415.

42. B.C.P. Jansen, "The Function of the Liver in Urea Formation from Amino-acids," *Ibid.*, 21 (1915): 557–561.

43. Fruton, *Molecules*, pp. 112–119.

44. E.P. Cathcart, *The Physiology of Protein Metabolism* (New York: Longmans, Green, 1921), pp. 38–55.

45. For a retrospective comment on this change see R.A. McCance, "The Chemistry of the Degradation of Protein Nitrogen," *Physiol. Rev.*, 10 (1930): 1.

46. Wilhelm Löffler, "Desaminierung und Harnstoffbildung im Thierkörper," *Biochem. Z.*, 85, (1917): 233.

47. *Ibid.*, 1917, 85: 230–294.

48. *Ibid.*, p. 291.

49. Wilhelm Löffler, "Zur Kenntnis der Leberfunktion unter experimentell pathologischen Bedingungen," *Biochem. Z.*, 112, (1920): 164–187.

50. Löffler, "Desaminierung," p. 232.

51. For example, see S. Salaskin and J.K. Kriwsky, "Untersuchungen über die Harnstoffbildung im Thierkörper," *Z. physiol. Chem.*, 196, (1931): 121–139.

52. Kase, "Untersuchungen," pp. 258–270.

53. Fruton, *Molecules*, p. 436.

54. *Ibid.*, p. 433; Löffler, "Desaminierung," p. 233.

55. Emil A. Werner, *The Chemistry of Urea* (London: Longmans, Green, 1923), pp. 123–127.

56. Fruton, *Molecules*, p. 436. See William Robert Fearon, "The Biochemistry of Urea," *Physiol. Rev.*, 6, (1926): 409–411, 421; McCance, "Degradation of Protein Nitrogen," p. 27.

57. H.H. Mitchell and T.S. Hamilton, *The Biochemistry of the Amino Acids* (New York: Chemical Catalogue Co., 1929), pp. 282–283.

58. McCance, "Degradation of Protein Nitrogen," p. 2.

59. Fruton, *Molecules*, p. 434.

60. A. Kossel and H. Dakin, "Über die Arginase," *Z. physiol. Chem.*, 41 (1904): 321–331; Kossel and Dakin, "Weitere Untersuchungen über fermentative Harnstoffbildung," *Ibid.*, 42, (1904): 181–188.

61. Löffler, "Desaminierung," p. 234.

62. HAK–FLH, July 31, 1978 (Tape 69, pp. 10–11); Krebs, Notebook "9," p. 96.

63. Donald D. Van Slyke, "Determination of Urea by Gasometric Measurement of the Carbon Dioxide formed by the Action of Urease," *J. Biol. Chem.*, 73 (1927): 695–723.

64. Krebs, Notebook "9," pp. 44–45; HAK–FLH, July 31, 1978 (Tape 69, pp. 15–17, Tape 70, pp. 1–4).

65. Van Slyke, "Determination of Urea," pp. 703–705; Krebs, Notebook "9," pp. 44–48; HAK–FLH, April 28, 1977, (Tape 9, pp. 29–30), July 31, 1978, (Tape 70, pp. 2–3).

66. Krebs, "Discovery of the Ornithine Cycle," p. 20.

67. Krebs, Notebook, "9," pp. 49–53; HAK–FLH, July 31, 1978 (Tape 70, p. 7). Krebs made the cogent point concerning this calculation, that "when one gets some data one tries all sorts of things which could be fit in, without implying that...the calculation is actually valid."

68. *Ibid.*, pp. 54–56; HAK–FLH, Aug. 1, 1978 (Tape 71, p. 1).

69. HAK–FLH, *Ibid.*

70. Krebs, Notebook "9," p. 57.

71. Otto Warburg, Karl Posener, and Erwin Negelein, "Über den Stoffwechsel der Carcinomzelle," *Biochem. Z.*, 152 (1924): 334–335.

72. See Fruton, *Molecules*, pp. 271–272; HAK–FLH, July 31, 1978 (Tape 70, p. 7).

73. Thomas P. Nash, Jr., "Phlorhizin Diabetes," *Physiol. Rev.*, 7 (1927): 385–430.

74. The article was by Robert Daniel Lawrence and Robert Alexander McCance, "The Effect of Starvation, Phloridizin, Thyroid, Adrenaline, Insulin and Pituitrin on the Distribution of Glycogen in the Rat," *Biochem. J.*, 25 (1931): 571–578. On June 23, 1931, under the heading "Phlorizin literature," Krebs had listed in his laboratory notebook this article, and two review articles cited in this article. One of the reviews was the preceding reference (f.n. 73), the other was written in 1912 by Graham Lusk, an earlier pioneer in phlorizin research.

75. Krebs, Notebook "9," pp. 58–59.

76. *Ibid.*, pp. 62–65. See also Krebs, "Discovery of the Ornithine Cycle," pp. 19–20.

77. Krebs, "Discovery of the Ornithine Cycle," p. 20; Krebs, *Reminiscences*, p. 47; Kurt Henseleit, Laboratory Notebook, pp. 1–5 (The original of this notebook was in possession of Mrs. Rosa Henseleit, Kurt Henseleit's widow, in Friedrichshafen, Germany, in 1978, when Hans Krebs obtained a xerox copy of it from her. The xerox copy he gave to me, and it is presently in my collection of research materials concerning Krebs.); Krebs, Notebook "9," p. 70.

78. Henseleit, Notebook, pp. 6–7; Krebs, Notebook "9," p. 71.

79. HAK–FLH, April 27, 1977 (Tape 9, p. 12).

80. Henseleit, Notebook, pp. 8–13; Krebs, Notebook "9," pp. 72–75.

81. Henseleit, Notebook, pp. 14–16; Krebs, Notebook "9," p. 79.

82. HAK–FLH, July 31, 1978 (Tape 70, pp. 12–13).

83. Henseleit, Notebook, pp. 17–18; Krebs, Notebook "9," pp. 81–82.

84. HAK–FLH, Sept. 6, 1976 (Tape 4, p. 7).

85. Henseleit, Notebook, pp. 19–21; Krebs, Notebook "9," pp. 85–87.

86. Henseleit, Notebook, pp. 22–23; Krebs, Notebook "9," pp. 88–89; Krebs, *Reminiscences*, p. 55; HAK–FLH, July 31, 1978 (Tape 70, p. 17).

87. Krebs, Notebook "9," pp. 66–67.

88. *Ibid.*, pp. 68–69.

89. See this volume, Chapter 7, p. 226.

90. Krebs, Notebook "9," pp. 76–77, 83–84.

91. *Ibid.*, pp. 90–92.

92. *Ibid.*, pp. 94–95, 98–99.

93. Henseleit, Notebook, pp. 25, 27.

94. *Ibid.*, pp. 28–68.

95. *Ibid.*, pp. 40–41, 47–48, 64.

96. HAK–FLH, July 31, 1978, (Tape 70, p. 12).

97. Krebs, *Reminiscences*, pp. 45, 47; HAK–FLH, Sept. 6, 1976 (Tape 4, p. 14). Krebs also had "during one term" heavy additional duties as assistant to Thannhauser's demonstration lectures. He did not specify, however, the term in which he did so.

98. Henseleit, Notebook, p. 69.

99. See this volume, Chapter 7, pp. 217, 221–224.

100. Krebs, Notebook "9," pp. 122–123.

101. P. Boysen Jensen, "Über die Einwirkung der Monojodessigsäure auf Atmung and Gärung," *Biochem. Z.*, 236 (1931): 211–218; Fritz Zuckerkandl and Luise Messiner-Klebermass, "Über die Einwirkung Imingruppen bildender Substanzen auf den Zuckerabbau durch Hefe," *Ibid.*, 239 (1931): 174; Krebs, Notebook "9," pp. 97, 118.

102. Hans Adolf Krebs, "Über die Proteolyse der Tumoren," *Biochem. Z.*, 238 (1931): 194; P. Waldschmidt-Leitz to HAK, Jan. 14, 1931, KC; Krebs, Notebook "9," pp. 130–150.

103. HAK–FLH, July 31, 1978 (Tape 69, p. 2).

104. *Ibid.*, Aug. 1, 1978 (Tape 71, pp. 17–18).

105. See the discussions of problem spaces, heuristics, and inductive search in Chapter One of Pat Langley, Herbert A. Simon, Gary L. Bradshaw, and Jan M. Zytkow, *Scientific Discovery: Computational Explorations of the Creative Process*, (Cambridge, Mass.: The MIT Press, 1987), pp. 7–18.

106. HAK–FLH, April 26, 27, 1977 (Tape 9, pp. 6, 16).

107. Krebs, *Reminiscences*, pp. 45–46; Salome Waelsch–FLH, Oct. 18, 1989 (Tape 167, p. 1).

108. Krebs, *Reminiscences*, pp. 45–46.

109. My portrait of Krebs's personality at this time is a composite impression, based in part on my own familiarity with him in the last years of his life, in part on the testimony of those who knew him in Freiburg or who commented that his personality had remained remarkably stable over his adult life, in part on personal letters to him during the Freiburg years, and in part on photographs in his possession from that period. The description of hiking in the Black Forest is based on a visit of my own there, and subsequent conversations with Krebs about it. HAK–FLH, May 9, 1979 (Tape 87, p. 10).

110. Krebs, *Reminiscences*, p. 46.

Chapter 9

1. Henseleit, Notebook, pp. 76–78; HAK–FLH, Aug. 1, 1978 (Tape 75, p. 3).

2. Henseleit, Notebook, pp. 80–82. We may note that Schultzen and Nencki had fed methylamine to rabbits in 1869. It is unlikely, however, that Krebs was intending to repeat their experiment, because he did not look for a monomethyl-substituted urea.

3. *Ibid.*, pp. 83–84; HAK–FLH, Sept. 6, 1976 (Tape 4, p. 8).

4. I. Banga, L. Schneider, and A. Szent-Györgyi, "Über die Bedeutung der Milchsäure für die Atmung des zerkleinerten Herzmuskelgewebes," *Biochem. Z.*, 240 (1931): 478–479; Banga, Schneider, and Szent-Györgyi, "Über den Einfluß der Blausäure auf die Gewebsatmung," *Ibid.*, pp. 454–455.

5. Banga, Schneider, and Szent-Györgyi, "Die Bedeutung der Milchäure," pp. 478–479.

6. O. Meyerhof and E. Boyland, "Über den Atmungsvorgang jodessigsäurevergifteter Muskeln," *Biochem. Z.*, 237 (1931): 406–417.

7. Krebs, Notebook "9," p. 159.

8. Henseleit, Notebook, pp. 85–86.

9. HAK–FLH, Sept. 7, 1976 (Tape 4, p. 15).

10. Henseleit, Notebook, p. 88.

11. See Joseph S. Fruton and Sofia Simmonds, *General Biochemistry*, 2nd ed. (New York: Wiley, 1958), p. 62.

12. Joseph Fruton, *Molecules and Life* (New York: Wiley-Interscience, 1972), p. 434.

13. Henseleit, Notebook, p. 89. See Fruton and Simmonds, *Biochemistry*, pp. 800–801.

14. HAK–FLH, Sept. 6, 1976 (Tape 4, p. 14).

15. Henseleit, Notebook, p. 89.

16. *Ibid.*, pp. 90–92.

17. *Ibid.*, pp. 94–95.

18. *Ibid.*, pp. 96–102.

19. *Ibid.*, pp. 104–108.

20. Krebs, Notebook "9," pp. 165–171.

21. Henseleit, Notebook, pp. 110–112.

22. *Ibid.*, p. 112.

23. H.A. Krebs and K. Henseleit, "Untersuchungen über die Harnstoffbildung im Tierkörper," *Klin. Woch.*, 11 (1932): 758.

24. H.A. Krebs, "The Discovery of the Ornithine Cycle of Urea Synthesis," *Biochemical Education*, 1 (1973): 20.

25. HAK–FLH, Aug. 4, 1978 (Tape 75, p. 3).

26. *Biochemica "Roche"* (Basel: F. Hoffmann-LaRoche, 1930), pp. 4–13. I wish to thank Dr. E.G. Herzog and H.W. Roth, of Hoffmann-LaRoche and Co., for supplying me with a copy of this catalogue; HAK–FLH, Aug. 1, 1978 (Tape 75, p. 3).

27. HAK–FLH, Aug. 4, 1978 (Tape 75, p. 5).

28. K. Felix and H. Röthler, "Das Verhalten von Ornithin, Lysin und Putrescin in der überlebenden Leber," *Z. physiol. Chem.*, 143 (1925): 133–140.

29. HAK–FLH, May 9, 1979 (Tape 87, pp. 12, 15).

30. Krebs, "Discovery of the Ornithine Cycle," p. 20.

31. Ian Hacking, *Representing and Intervening: Introductory Topics in the Philosophy of Natural Science* (Cambridge: Cambridge University Press, 1983), pp. 224-225.

32. HAK-FLH, Sept. 7, 1976 (Tape 4, p. 17).

33. Krebs, "Discovery of the Ornithine Cycle," p. 20; HAK-FLH, Aug. 4, 1978 (Tape 75, p. 29).

34. Henseleit, Notebook, pp. 114-117.

35. *Ibid.*, pp. 117-118.

36. Krebs, "Discovery of the Ornithine Cycle," p. 20.

37. Henseleit, Notebook, p. 114.

38. HAK-FLH, Sept. 6, 1976 (Tape 4, p. 13). On the basis of an earlier gap in his notebook record, Krebs incorrectly recalled the move to new quarters in this conversation as having occurred in September 1931. The source for the date and events of the opening is from an invitation to the celebration contained in KC.

39. Description from photographs and personal visit to the Clinic buildings.

40. *Biochemica "Roche"*, pp. 6, 10, 12; HAK-FLH, Aug. 4, 1978 (Tape 75, pp. 7-9). I owe this commentary in part to suggestions made by Joseph S. Fruton.

41. Henseleit, Notebook, pp. 120-124.

42. Krebs, Notebook "9," pp. 174-177. For the description of the Parnas-Heller method, see J.K. Parnas and J. Heller, "Über den Ammoniakgehalt und über die Ammoniakbildung im Blute," *Biochem. Z.*, 152 (1924): 5-13.

43. Henseleit, Notebook, p. 125.

44. *Ibid.*, pp. 126-129.

45. HAK-FLH, Aug. 4, 1978 (Tape 75, pp. 9-10).

46. Krebs, Notebook "9," pp. 178-179.

47. HAK-FLH, Aug. 1, 1978 (Tape 75, p. 5). If "the experiment was completely negative, then that's that. There's no need to repeat it, especially as these were duplicates."

48. Krebs, "Discovery of the Ornithine Cycle," p. 20. When he incorporated this account into his autobiography, Krebs modified this sentence to read "The significance of this result was not immediately obvious...." Hans Krebs, *Reminiscences and Reflections* (Oxford: Clarendon Press, 1981), p. 55.

49. HAK-FLH, Aug. 4, 1978 (Tape 75, p. 19).

50. Krebs, "Discovery of the Ornithine Cycle," p. 20.

51. HAK-FLH, Aug. 4, 1978 (Tape 75, pp. 8-9).

52. Hans Adolf Krebs and Kurt Henseleit, "Untersuchungen über die Harnstoffbildung im Tierkörper," *Z. physiol. Chem.*, 210 (1932): 35-36.

53. HAK-FLH, Aug. 1, 1978 (Tape 71, pp. 3-4).

54. Krebs and Henseleit, "Harnstoffbildung," p. 56.

55. *Ibid.*, p. 36; Krebs, Notebook "9," pp. 184-185; HAK-FLH, April 28, 1977 (Tape 9, pp. 26-27), July 31, 1978 (Tape 70, pp. 3-4).

56. On contemporary knowledge of asparaginase, see W.F. Geddes and Andrew Hunter, "Observations upon the Enzyme Asparaginase," *J. Biol. Chem.*, 77 (1928): 197-229. Krebs referred to this article in his notebook; Krebs, Notebook "9," p. 191. For the theoretical possibility, as Krebs later reconstructed it, see HAK-FLH, Aug. 4, 1978 (Tape 75, pp. 18-19).

57. Krebs, Notebook "9," pp. 187-192; HAK-FLH, April 29, 1977 (Tape 10, p. 6), Aug. 4, 1978 (Tape 75, pp. 13, 16-17).

58. HAK-FLH, April 29, 1977 (Tape 10, p. 6).

59. Henseleit, Notebook, pp. 134-141; HAK-FLH, Aug. 4, 1978 (Tape 75, pp. 20-21).

60. Henseleit, Notebook, pp. 142-146.

61. *Ibid.*, pp. 147-152.

62. See O. Neubauer, "Intermediärer Eisweißstoffwechsel," in Albrecht Bethe, et al, *Handbuch der Normalen und pathologischen Physiologie*, (Berlin: Springer, 1925-1932), 5:834-839.

63. Henseleit, Notebook, pp. 153-155.

64. HAK-FLH, Aug. 4, 1978 (Tape 75, pp. 11-12).

65. Henseleit, Notebook, pp. 156-163; HAK-FLH, Aug. 4, 1978 (Tape 75, pp. 27-29).

66. Henseleit, Notebook, p. 162.

67. HAK-FLH, Aug. 4, 1978 (Tape 75, pp. 29-35).

68. *Ibid.*, p. 34.

69. *Ibid.*, p. 11.

70. Krebs, "Discovery of the Ornithine Cycle," p. 20.

71. Henseleit, Notebook, pp. 174-183; Hans Adolf Krebs, "Über den Stoffwechsel der Aminosäuren im Tierkörper," *Klin. Woch.*, 11 (1932): 1745.

72. Krebs, Notebook "9," pp. 194-199.

73. Krebs, "Discovery of the Ornithine Cycle," p. 22.

74. *Ibid.*, p. 20.

75. Felix and Röthler, "Verhalten von Ornithin," p. 139.

76. HAK-FLH, Sept. 6, 1976 (Tape 4, p. 12), April 27, 1977 (Tape 9, p. 13), Aug. 7, 1978 (Tape 78, p. 5).

77. Karl Thomas, "Über die Herkunft des Kreatins im tierischen Organismus," *Z. physiol. Chem.*, 88 (1913): 465-477; Junji Karashima, "Über die Glykocyamase," *Ibid.*, 177 (1928): 42-46; Krebs, Notebook "9," pp. 193, 200.

78. Henseleit, Notebook, pp. 184-187.

Chapter 10

1. Henseleit, Notebook, pp. 182, 194-202.

2. Krebs, Notebook "9," pp. 205-208; HAK-FLH, Aug. 4, 1978 (Tape 75, p. 19).

3. Krebs, Notebook "9," pp. 211-218.

4. Henseleit, Notebook, pp. 204-207.

5. HAK-FLH, Aug. 4, 1978 (Tape 75, pp. 37-38).

6. Henseleit, Notebook, pp. 208-210; K. Felix, H. Müller, and K. Dirr, "Über den Argininstoffwechsel," *Z. physiol. Chem.*, 178 (1928): 193.

7. K. Felix and H. Röthler, "Das Verhalten von Ornithin, Lysin und Putrescin in der überlebenden Leber," *Ibid.*, 143 (1925): 136-139; Donald D. Van Slyke, "Manometric Determination of Primary Amino Nitrogen and its Application to Blood Analysis," *J. Biol. Chem.*, 83 (1929): 425-447; S. Edlbacher and H. Burchard, "Zur Kenntnis der Arginasewirkung," *Z. physiol. Chem.*, 194 (1931): 72; Krebs, Notebook "9," p. 219.

8. Henseleit, Notebook, pp. 212-217; HAK-FLH, Aug. 4, 1978 (Tape 75, p. 23).

9. Henseleit, Notebook, pp. 216-217; HAK-FLH, Aug. 5, 1978 (Tape 76, p. 4).

10. Henseleit, Notebook, pp. 220-223.

11. HAK-FLH, Aug. 5, 1978 (Tape 77, p. 5).

12. Krebs, Notebook "9," pp. 220-221.

13. For a thorough and authoritative review of the contemporary state of these questions, see Otto Neubauer, "Intermediärer Eiweißstoffwechsel," in Albrecht Bethe et al., *Handbuch der Normalen und Pathologischen Physiologie*, (Berlin: Springer, 1925-1932), 5: 773-808.

14. Krebs, Notebook "9," pp. 222-223.

15. Neubauer, "Eiweißstoffwechsel," p. 808.

16. Krebs, Notebook "9," pp. 224-225.

17. Neubauer, "Eiweißstoffwechsel," pp. 779-785.

18. Henseleit, Notebook, pp. 232-234.

19. *Ibid.*, pp. 236-245.

20. Henseleit, Notebook, pp. 246-303. This is not an exhaustive list of the experiments Henseleit performed in March, but is representative of their character.

21. *Ibid.*, p. 258.

22. Krebs, Notebook "9," p. 228.

23. *Ibid.*, p. 229.

24. See Hans Adolf Krebs, "Untersuchungen über den Stoffwechsel der Aminosäuren im Tierkörper," *Z. physiol. Chem.*, 217 (1933): 195-196.

25. Neubauer, "Eiweißstoffwechsel," p. 779. It was assumed that at some stage amino acids were also decarboxylated, because in some situations they yielded metabolic partial decomposition products corresponding to those of fatty acids containing one less carbon atom. Neubauer argued

against the possibility that the decarboxylation could precede the deamination. HAK–FLH, April 29, 1977 (Tape 10, pp. 10–12).

26. Krebs, Notebook "9," pp. 231–233.

27. *Ibid.*, pp. 234–237.

28. *Ibid.*, p. 238; HAK–FLH, April 29, 1977 (Tape 10–11, p. 13); Krebs, "Stoffwechsel der Aminosäuren," *Z. physiol. Chem.*, 217 (1933): 196, 216; Charles F.H. Allen, "The Identification of Carbonyl Compounds by Use of Dinitrophenylhydrazine," *Journal of the American Chemical Society*, 52 (1930): 2955–2959.

29. Krebs, Notebook "9," p. 239.

30. Krebs, "Über den Stoffwechsel der Aminosäuren im Tierkörper," *Klin. Woch.*, 11 (1932): 1748.

31. Krebs, Notebook "9," pp. 240–242.

32. *Ibid.*, pp. 240–245; HAK–FLH, April 29, 1977 (Tape 10–11, p. 14).

33. Krebs, Notebook "9," pp. 246–249.

34. *Ibid.*, pp. 250–251.

35. *Ibid.*, pp. 252–259.

36. *Ibid.*, pp. 260–263.

37. *Ibid.*, pp. 264–267.

38. *Ibid.*, pp. 269–270.

39. *Ibid.*, pp. 268–271.

40. *Ibid.*, pp. 272–273.

41. Hans Krebs, "The Discovery of the Ornithine Cycle of Urea Synthesis," *Biochemical Education*, 1 (1973): 20. The above quotation is actually a slightly revised version of the statement of 1973, as it appeared in Hans Krebs, with Anne Martin, *Reminiscences and Reflections* (Oxford: Clarendon Press, 1981), pp. 56–57.

42. HAK–FLH, Sept. 7, 1976 (Tape 4, p. 20), Aug. 1, 1978 (Tape 71, pp. 12–13). See L. Michaelis and Maud L. Menten, "Die Kinetik der Invertinwirkung," *Biochem. Z.*, 49 (1913): 333–369. Michaelis and Menten's equation was an improved version of the one that Victor Henri had derived 10 years earlier using the same assumption. J.B.S. Haldane *Enzymes* (London: Longmans, Green, 1930).

43. HAK–FLH, Aug. 4, 1978 (Tape 75, pp. 25–26). During another conversation on the same topic, Krebs said "...There must be a point which I cannot identify, when this idea occurred to me that ornithine makes arginine." HAK–FLH, Aug. 5, 1978 (Tape 77, p. 14).

44. *Ibid.*, Aug. 1, 1978 (Tape 72, p. 1).

45. Hans Adolf Krebs and Kurt Henseleit, "Untersuchungen über die Harnstoffbildung im Tierkörper," *Klin. Woch.*, 11 (1932): 759.

46. Krebs, "Discovery of the Ornithine Cycle," pp. 20–21.

47. Krebs and Henseleit, "Harnstoffbildung," p. 759.

48. Krebs, "Discovery of the Ornithine Cycle," p. 20.

49. HAK–FLH, Aug. 1, 1978 (Tape 71, pp. 14–16).

50. *Ibid.*, (Tape 72, p. 5).

51. *Ibid.*, Sept. 7, 1976 (Tape 4, p. 22).

52. Howard E. Gruber, *Darwin on Man: A Psychological Study of Scientific Creativity*, 2d. ed. (Chicago: University of Chicago Press, 1981): Gruber, "On the Relation between 'Aha Experiences' and the Construction of Ideas," *History of Science*, 19 (1981): 41–59; Vera John-Steiner, *Notebooks of the Mind: Explorations of Thinking* (Albuquerque: University of New Mexico Press, 1985), especially pp. 7–8.

53. HAK–FLH, Aug. 1, 1978 (Tape 71, pp. 16, 17).

54. Sir Hans Kornberg and D.H. Williamson, "Hans Adolf Krebs: 1900–1981," *Biographical Memoirs of Fellows of the Royal Society*, 30 (1984): 379.

55. Krebs and Henseleit, "Harnstoffbildung," pp. 757–759.

56. For an analogous, but far more profound argument concerning William Harvey and the discovery of the circulation of the blood, see Jerome Bylebyl, "The Growth of Harvey's *De Motu Cordis*," *Bulletin of the History of Medicine*, 47 (1973): 427–470.

57. HAK–FLH, April 29, 1977 (Tape 10–11, p. 21).

58. Henseleit, Notebook, pp. 292–301, 305.
59. *Ibid.*, pp. 306–307.
60. *Ibid.*, p. 308.
61. *Ibid.*, pp. 312, 317, 322.
62. *Ibid.*, pp. 320–321.
63. Krebs and Henseleit, "Harnstoffbildung," p. 758.
64. Joseph S. Fruton and Sofia Simmonds, *General Biochemistry*, 2d. ed. (New York: Wiley, 1958), p. 850.
65. Krebs and Henseleit, "Harnstoffbildung," pp. 758–759.
66. Krebs, "Discovery of the Ornithine Cycle," pp. 20–21.
67. HAK–FLH, Aug. 2, 1978 (Tape 72, pp. 9–10).
68. *Idem*; Mitsunora Wada, "Über Citrullin, eine neue Aminosäure im Preßsaft der Wassermelone, Citrullis vulgaris schrad.," *Biochem. Z.*, 224 (1930): 420–429; D. Ackermann, "Über den biologischen Abbau des Arginins zu Citrullin," *Z. physiol. Chem.*, 203 (1931): 66–69.
69. This and the following equation are reproduced from Hans Adolf Krebs and Kurt Henseleit, "Untersuchungen über die Harnstoffbildung im Tierkörper. II," *Klin. Woch.*, 11 (1932): 1138.
70. Krebs, Notebook "9," p. 282.
71. HAK–FLH, Aug. 3, 1978 (Tape 73, p. 2).
72. Krebs, Notebook "9," pp. 297–298.
73. *Ibid.*, p. 299.
74. Bruno Mendel to HAK, Telegram, April 30, 1932, KC.
75. Krebs, "The Discovery of the Ornithine Cycle," pp. 19–21.
76. HAK–FLH, July 30, 1978 (Tape 68, p. 1).

Chapter 11

1. Krebs, Notebook "9," pp. 283–291.
2. Kurt Dresel, "Über die Wirkung der arsenigen Säure auf Atmung und Gärung," *Biochem. Z.*, 178 (1926): 70–74.
3. I. Banga, L. Schneider, and A. Szent-Györgyi, "Über den Einfluß der arsenigen Säure auf die Gewebsatmung," *Ibid.*, 240 (1931): 466.
4. *Ibid.*, pp. 462–472; I. Banga and A. Szent-Györgyi, "Über Co-Fermente, Wasserstoffdonatoren und Arsenvergiftung der Zellatmung," *Ibid.*, 246 (1932): 203–214.
5. Krebs, Notebook "9," pp. 292–296.
6. *Ibid.*, pp. 302–307. See also, HAK–FLH, April 30, 1977 (Tape 10-11, pp. 23–26).
7. Krebs, Notebook, "9," p. 308.
8. HAK–FLH, April 30, 1978 (Tape 10–11, pp. 27–28). For a succinct discussion of the optical isomers of amino acids, see Joseph S. Fruton and Sofia Simmonds, *General Biochemistry*, 2d. ed. (New York: John Wiley, 1958), pp. 74–84.
9. *Biochemica "Roche,"* (Basel: F. Hoffmann-La Roche, 1930), pp. 4, 10.
10. Krebs, Notebook "9," pp. 310–328.
11. Henseleit, Notebook, pp. 347–348.
12. Krebs, Notebook "9," pp. 329–332.
13. Gustav Embden, "Über das Verhalten der optisch-isomeren Leucine in der Leber," *Beiträge zur chemischen Physiologie und Pathologie*, 11 (1908): 348–355; Krebs, Notebook "9," p. 334.
14. Felix Ehrlich to HAK, May 11, 1932, KC.
15. Krebs, Notebook "9," pp. 337–339; Hans Adolf Krebs, "Über den Stoffwechsel der Aminosäuren im Tierkörper," *Klin. Woch.*, 11 (1932): 1747.
16. Krebs, Notebook "9," pp. 340–341.
17. Henseleit, Notebook, pp. 349–350.
18. See Kurt Henseleit, "Lebenslauf," in *Versuche über die Wirkung von Ornithin und Citrulline auf die Harnstoffbildung in der Leber*, (Berlin: De Gruyter, 1934), p. 15. Henseleit wrote there that "I matriculated at the Albert-Ludwig University in Freiburg from the winter semester of 1930 up

until the summer semester of 1932." There is one further experiment recorded in the notebook, on "ornithine anaerobically," that is dated January 6, 1933. Henseleit, Notebook, p. 351.

19. Hans Adolf Krebs and Kurt Henseleit, "Untersuchungen über die Harnstoffbildung im Tierkörper. II," *Klin. Woch.*, 11 (1932): 1138.

20. *Ibid.*

21. *Ibid.*, pp. 1138–1139.

22. HAK–FLH, Sept. 7, 1976 (Tape 4, p. 27).

23. See this volume, Chapter 6, p. 208.

24. "Medizinische Gesellschaft Freiburg 1. Br. Sitzung vom 10 Mai 1932," *Klin. Woch.*, 11 (1932): 1692–1693.

25. *Ibid.*, p. 1693.

26. *Ibid.*

27. HAK–FLH, Sept. 7, 1976 (Tape 4, pp. 15–16), July 9, 1977 (Tape 19, p. 7), Aug. 2, 1978 (Tape 73, pp. 1–2), May 9, 1979 (Tape 87, pp. 12–14). In several accounts of this incident Krebs gave slightly variant versions of Kapfhammer's comment and of Schoenheimer's reply.

28. Meyerhof to HAK, May 18, 1932; HAK to Meyerhof, May 19, 1932; Franz Knoop to HAK, June 17, 1932, KC.

29. HAK–FLH, Sept. 7, 1976 (Tape 4, p. 16); Krebs, Notebook "9," p. 365; Chemische Gesellschaft Freiburg, announcement for meeting of June 6, 1932, KC.

30. HAK–FLH, April 27, 1977 (Tape 9, p. 14); Aug. 2, 1978 (Tape 73, pp. 5–7; Siegfried Thannhauser, "Zeugnis," May 1, 1933, KC. In Aug. 1978 I took the same cable lift to Schauinland.

31. Hans Adolf Krebs and Kurt Henseleit, "Untersuchungen über die Harnstoffbildung im Tierkörper," *Z. physiol. Chem.*, 210 (1932): 33–66.

32. *Ibid.*, pp. 34–43, 47–51.

33. *Ibid.*, p. 55.

34. *Ibid.*, p. 49; Krebs and Henseleit, "Harnstoffbildung," *Klin. Woch.*, 11 (1932): 758.

35. F. Knoop to HAK, June 17, 1932, KC.

36. C. Neuberg to HAK, July 5, 1932, KC.

37. W. Lipschitz to HAK, July 6, 1932, KC.

38. W. Schoeller to HAK, July 5, 1932, KC.

39. P. Rona to HAK, July 11, 1932, KC.

40. Hans Adolf Krebs and Kurt Henseleit, "Untersuchungen über die Harnstoffbildung im Tierkörper," *Klin. Woch.*, 11 (1932): 758.

41. M. Anson to HAK, June 13, 1932, KC.

42. HAK–FLH, Sept. 7, 1976 (Tape 4, p. 26), Aug. 3, 1978 (Tape 74, p. 11); M. Anson to HAK, Sept. 16, 1931, KC.

43. HAK–FLH, Sept. 7, 1976 (Tape 4, p. 26).

44. *Ibid.*, Sept. 7, 1976 (Tape 4, pp. 25–26); April 28, 1977 (Tape 9, pp. 25–26).

45. Krebs and Henseleit, "Harnstoffbildung," *Z. physiol. Chemie.*, 210 (1932): 35.

46. *Ibid.*, p. 53.

47. Joseph S. Fruton, "Claude Bernard the Scientist," in Eugene Debs Robin, ed., *Claude Bernard and the Internal Environment: A Memorial Symposium* (New York: Marcel Dekker, 1979), pp. 38–39.

48. HAK–FLH, Aug. 3, 1978 (Tape 73, p. 7).

49. For some of these experiments Warburg collaborated with Otto Meyerhof. O. Warburg and O. Meyerhof, "Über Atmung in abgetöteten Zellen und in Zellfragmenten," *Arch. ges. Physiol.*, 148 (1912): 295–310; Otto Warburg, "Beiträge zur Physiologie der Zelle, insbesondere über die Oxydationsgeschwindigkeit in Zellen," *Erg. Physiol.*, 14 (1914): 259. See also Robert E. Kohler, "The Background to Otto Warburg's Conception of the *Atmungsferment*," *Journal of the History of Biology*, 6 (1973): 171–192.

50. Otto Warburg, "The Enzyme Problem and Biological Oxidations," *The Johns Hopkins Hospital Bulletin*, 46 (1930): 349, 357. The main lines of this paragraph were suggested to me by Joseph S. Fruton, conversation, Aug. 27, 1985.

51. Krebs, Notebook "9," pp. 345-353; Krebs, "Stoffwechsel der Aminosäuren," pp. 1747, 1748. My interpretation that Krebs was satisfied that the above experiment established the reaction quantitatively is based on the fact that he did not repeat this experiment again, and he utilized this result in his first published article on the subject.

52. Krebs, Notebook "9," pp. 354-359, 366-375.

53. *Ibid.*, pp. 378-381; Krebs, "Stoffwechsel der Aminosäuren," p. 1747, Table 9.

54. Krebs, Notebook "9," pp. 382-383.

55. *Ibid.*, pp. 386-391.

56. *Ibid.*, pp. 394-404.

57. *Ibid.*, pp. 408-409; Krebs, "Stoffwechsel der Aminosäuren," p. 1745, Table 2; Announcement of Medizinisch-biologischer Abend der Universität Frankfurt, for 18 July, 1932. KC.

58. Krebs, Notebook "9," pp. 423-424; "Stoffwechsel der Aminosäuren," p. 1747, Table 8.

59. Krebs, Notebook "9," p. 440; "Stoffwechsel der Aminosäuren," p. 1747.

60. Krebs, Notebook "9," pp. 430-470.

61. *Ibid.*, pp. 451-454; Max Bergmann, "Neue Synthesen und Enzymversuche im Eiweissgebiet," *Klin. Woch.*, 11 (1932): 1569-1572.

62. Krebs, Notebook "9," pp. 456-476.

63. *Ibid.*, p. 477. On this page is entered one word, "*Sommerferien.*"

64. Krebs, "Stoffwechsel der Aminosäuren," pp. 1744-1745. The article appeared in the *Klinische Wochenschrift* on October 15, 1932, and the usual time between submission and publication was about 8 weeks. The paper included data gathered up through the middle of July. Among the references was one to Max Bergmann's article appearing in the *Klin. Woch.* for September 17, 1932, but the footnote was conspicuously out of order, suggesting that it may have been added at the last minute.

65. *Ibid.*, pp. 1745-1746.

66. *Ibid.*, pp. 1746-1747.

67. *Ibid.*, pp. 1747-1748.

68. *Ibid.*, p. 1748.

69. H.A. Krebs, "The History of the Tricarboxylic Acid Cycle," *Perspectives in Biology and Medicine*, 14 (1970): 167.

70. HAK-FLH, July 9, 1977 (Tape 20, pp. 7-8).

71. Krebs, "Tricarboxylic Acid Cycle," p. 167.

72. On the inevitability of competition and the role of recognition in science, see Warren O. Hagstrom, *The Scientific Community* (New York: Basic Books, 1965), pp. 9-104.

73. Gordon A. Craig, *Germany 1866-1945* (New York: Oxford University Press, 1980), pp. 559-563.

74. Hans Krebs, with Anne Martin, *Reminiscences and Reflections*, (Oxford: Clarendon Press, 1981), p. 50; W. Schoeller to HAK, July 5, 1932, KC; HAK-FLH, April 28, 1977 (Tape 9, pp. 9-10), May 2, 1977 (Tape 12, p. 5), July 9, 1977 (Tape 19, p. 6). See also Hans Bach, *The German Jew: A Synthesis of Judaism and Western Civilization 1730-1930* (New York: The Oxford University Press, 1984), pp. 212-239.

75. HAK-FLH, May 2, 1977 (Tape 12, p. 1).

76. *Ibid.*, HAK-FLH, May 16, 1979 (Tape 96, p. 10); Hermann Blaschko-FLH, Sept. 10, 1976 (Tape 6, p. 4); *Sunti Delle Comunicazioni Scientifiche*, xiv Congresso Internazionale di Fisiologia, Roma: 29 Agosto -3 Settembre 1932 (Rome: Casciano, 1932), pp. 143-144, 247; Carl F. Cori to HAK, Oct. 6, 1932, KC.

77. HAK-FLH, July 30, 1978 (Tape 68, pp. 3-4).

78. Krebs, Notebook "9," pp. 484-487, 498-505, 511-528.

79. *Ibid.*, pp. 529-570.

80. Bergmann, "Neue Synthesen," pp. 1569-1572.

81. M. Bergmann to HAK, Oct. 19, 1932, KC.

82. HAK to M. Bergmann, Oct. 29, 1932, KC.

83. M. Bergmann to HAK, Nov. 1, 1932, KC.

84. Krebs, "Stoffwechsel der Aminosäuren," pp. 1745, 1748.

85. Bergmann, "Neue Synthesen," p. 1572.

86. HAK to M. Bergmann, Nov. 28, 1932, KC.

87. Hans Adolf Krebs, "Untersuchungen über den Stoffwechsel der Aminosäuren im Tierkörper," *Z. physiol. Chem.*, 217 (1933): 205–207.

88. For a general discussion of cooperation and competition in science, see Hagstrom, *Scientific Community*, pp. 69–158.

89. C. Neuberg to HAK, Oct. 21 and 24, 1932, KC.

90. Krebs, "Stoffwechsel der Aminosäuren," *Z. physiol. Chem.*, p. 196.

91. Antoinette Patey and Barbara Elizabeth Holmes, "The Production of Ammonia by Surviving Kidney Tissue," *Biochem. J.*, 23 (1929): 760–766; *Ibid.*, 24 (1930): 1564–1571.

92. Krebs, Notebook "9," p. 278.

93. Krebs, "Stoffwechsel der Aminosäuren," *Klin. Woch.*, p. 1746.

94. Barbara Holmes to HAK, Oct. 26, 1932, KC.

95. HAK to Barbara Holmes, Nov. 6, 1932, KC.

96. Hans Krebs, Notebook "10," pp. 1–4.

97. *Ibid.*, pp. 5–62.

98. Max Planck to HAK, Nov. 18, 1932, KC.

99. HAK to President of the Kaiser Wilhelm-Gesellschaft, Nov. 22, 1932, KC.

100. HAK–FLH, July 31, 1978 (Tape 69, p. 2).

101. F. Gowland Hopkins, "Atomic Physics and Vital Activities," *Nature*, 130 (1932): 869–871.

102. HAK–FLH, May 2, 1977 (Tape 12, p. 10).

103. Albert Ludwigs-Universität, Akademisches Rektorat, Freiburg, Dec. 16, 1932, Nr. 14439, "Habilitation des Dr. med. Hans Adolf Krebs," G.L.A. 235/8893; "Habilitation des Dr. med. Franz Bielschowsky", 235/8681, Generallandesarchiv, Karlsruhe.

104. HAK–FLH, Sept. 7, 1976 (Tape 4, p. 27); Kaiser Wilhelm-Gesellscheft, "Einladung zum 22. Dahlemer Medizinischen Abend," KC.

105. HAK–FLH, Sept. 7, 1976 (Tape 4, p. 27).

106. *Ibid.*, Aug. 31, 1978 (Tape 69, p. 2).

107. Otto Warburg and Walter Christian, "Über ein neues Oxydationsferment und sein Absorptionsspektrum," *Biochem. Z.*, 254 (1932): 438–458; Joseph S. Fruton, *Molecules and Life* (New York: Wiley-Interscience, 1972), pp. 334–335.

108. Krebs, *Reminiscences*, p. 80; HAK–FLH, Jan. 9, 1981 (Tape 129, pp. 5–6).

109. Krebs, Notebook "10," pp. 68–71.

110. Krebs, *Reminiscences*, p. 50.

111. Minister des Kultus und Unterrichts, Nr. A.27329, Karlsruhe, Dec. 22, 1932 Generallandes-archiv, Karlsruhe; Akademisches Rektorat Nr. 14994, Freiburg, Dec. 28, 1932, KC.

112. Thomas S. Kuhn, *The Structure of Scientific Revolutions*, 2d. ed. (Chicago: University of Chicago Press, 1970), p. 24. For Krebs privately, the ornithine effect was, of course, an anomaly, which his theory resolved. Anomalies in the framework of Kuhn's analysis, however, are generally understood to be those that become part of the public domain of a scientific area of investigation.

In 1978 Krebs, who was by then well aware of recent discussions about the nature of scientific revolutions, commented

> My feeling is that the whole development was evolutionary, not revolutionary. Perhaps it was a revolution when the geocentric concept of the world was replaced by the heliocentric. That was Copernicus. I think it was very unfortunate that Kuhn spoke of 'revolutions' on so many occasions, especially as it is confusing with the revolution of the earth around the sun.
>
> [Carl] Popper has recently mentioned that one can enumerate a large number of events that one would call...revolutions. That depends on the definition. But...I think...a revolution is something which occurs suddenly and involves some force. I felt that this was a gradual evolutionary develop-ment.... It was an important, new, and in fact entirely new concept; but that doesn't mean it was revolutionary. I think revolutionary means you remove

some old concepts. I don't think I removed old concepts. I added to them.
HAK-FLH, Aug. 7, 1978 (Tape 77, p. 8).
113. Krebs, *Reminiscences*, pp. 48-49.
114. *Ibid.*, p. 48.
115. HAK-FLH, Sept. 7, 1976 (Tape 4, p. 27); see also, July 9, 1977 (Tape 19, p. 12).

Chapter 12

1. Theodor Benzinger, "Sketch of a Scientific Autobiography," unpublished manuscript, obtained form author; Theodor Benzinger-FLH, Sept. 3, 1977 (Tape 46, pp. 11-12, 16-17). The conversations quoted here and in the following discussion of Benzinger's *Research* are from Benzinger's recollections of what was said.
2. Benzinger-FLH, Sept. 3, 1977 (Tape 46, p. 1); HAK-FLH, May 2, 1977 (Tape 12, pp. 7-9).
3. This summary of the history of the problem up until 1928 is based on Otto Neubauer, "Intermediärer Eiweißstoffwechsel," in Albrecht Bethe et al., *Handbuch der Normalen und Pathologischen Physiologie*, (Berlin: Springer, 1925-1932), 5: 964-967. For Clementi I have relied on the summary in Th. Benzinger and H.A. Krebs, "Über die Harnsäuresynthese im Vogelorganismus," *Klin. Woch.*, 12 (1933): 1207.
4. Benzinger-FLH, Sept. 3, 1977 (Tape 46, p. 1).
5. *Ibid.*, pp. 1-2; HAK-FLH, Aug. 10, 1978 (Tape 81, p. 7).
6. Benzinger-FLH, Sept. 3, 1977 (Tape 46, p. 2). Protocols, dated "Aug. 8, Aug. 30," [30 viii, 8 viii), in Benzinger dossier, KC.
7. S.J. Thannhauser, "Die chemischen Leistungen der normalen Leber für die Vorgänge des intermediären Stoffwechsels," *Klin. Woch.*, 12 (1933): 51.
8. Benzinger-FLH; Sept. 3, 1977 (Tape 46, pp. 2-3). Benzinger recalled Krebs's statement vividly, repeating it in German several times, in the midst of a conversation taking place in English.
9. Protocols in Benzinger dossier, KC.
10. Benzinger-FLH, Sept. 3, 1977 (Tape 46, pp. 2, 7-8).
11. *Ibid.*, pp. 3-4, 13.
12. Heinz Fuld, "Re: Professor Sir Hans Krebs," memorandum prepared for FLH, Feb. 1978, p. 1; Heinz Fuld-FLH, Feb. 24, 1978 (Tape 61, pp. 1-2).
13. Fuld, Krebs, pp. 2-3; Fuld-FLH, Feb. 24, 1978 (Tape 61, p. 5); Heinz Fuld, "Über die diagnostische Verwertbarkeit von Ammoniakbestimmungen im Blut," *Klin. Woch.*, 12 (1933): 1364.
14. Fuld-FLH, Feb. 24, 1978 (Tape 61, pp. 4-5, 13).
15. *Ibid.*, p. 12; Fuld, "Ammoniakbestimmungen," pp. 1364-1366.
16. Fuld-FLH, Feb. 24, 1978 (Tape 61, p. 6).
17. *Ibid.*, pp. 5-7, 12, 18-20.
18. J.K. Parnas, "Dr. Paul Ostern," *Nature*, 154 (1944): 695-696; HAK-FLH, May 2, 1977 (Tape 12, p. 16).
19. HAK-FLH, *Ibid*; P. Ostern, "Methode zur Bestimmung von Oxalessigsäure," *Z. physiol. Chem.*, 218 (1933): 160-163.
20. Hildegard Manderscheid, "Über die Harnstoffbildung bei den Wirbeltieren," *Biochem. Z.*, 263 (1933): 245-249. This was the only investigation by a medical student to result in a published article, but others may have done projects that satisfied their MD requirements.
21. Hermann Blaschko-FLH, Sept. 10, 1976 (Tape 6, p. 9).
22. Fuld, "Re: Krebs," p. 2.
23. For a cogent discussion of the general characteristics of a research school, see Gerald L. Geison, "Scientific Change, Emerging Specialties, and Research Schools," *History of Science*, 19 (1981): 20-40.
24. C. Neuberg to Dr. A.V. Szily, Jan. 10, 1933. Neuberg sent Krebs a confidential copy of the letter, commenting that, even if he did not get this job, the circulation of the opinion might help him eventually to receive a professorship. Neuberg to HAK, Jan. 15, 1933, KC.
25. Theodor Benzinger-FLH, Sept. 3, 1977 (Tape 46, pp. 6-7); HAK-FLH, Sept. 3, 1978 (Tape 74, p. 12).

26. E.S. London, "Die Angiostomiemethode und die mit Hilfe derselben erhaltenen Resultate," *Erg. Physiol.*, 26 (1927): 320–369.

27. Claude Bernard, *An Introduction to the Study of Experimental Medicine*, tr. H.C. Green (New York: Dover, 1957), p. 130.

28. London, "Die Angiostomiemethode," pp. 349–353.

29. E.S. London to HAK, Jan. 2, 1933, KC.

30. Hans Krebs, Notebook "10," pp. 72–75.

31. *Ibid.*, p. 77.

32. Benzinger–FLH, Sept. 3, 1977 (Tape 46, p. 7).

33. H.A. Krebs, "Größe der Atmung und Gärung in lebenden Zellen," in *Handbuch der Biochemie des Menschen und der Tiere*, ed. Carl Oppenheimer, 2nd ed., Suppl. vol. 1, part 2 (Jena: Gustav Fischer, 1933), pp. 863–892, quote on p. 880.

34. Krebs, Notebook "10," pp. 78–121.

35. Benzinger to HAK, Jan. 24, 1933 and Feb. 20, 1933; untitled manuscript and data sheets, Benzinger dossier, KC; Benzinger–FLH, Sept. 3, 1977 (Tape 46, p. 4).

36. P.E. Verkade et al., "Untersuchungen über den Fettstoffwechsel. I," *Proceedings, Koninklijke Akademie van Wetenschappen te Amsterdam*, 35 (1932): 251–266.

37. H.A. Krebs, "Abbau der Fettsäuren," in *Handbuch der Biochemie*, ed. Oppenheimer, 2d. ed., Suppl, Vol. 1, Pt. 1, p. 936.

38. P.E. Verkade to HAK, Jan. 20, 1933, (inserted in back of the reprint requested by Krebs), KC.

39. HAK to P.E. Verkade, Jan. 26, 1933, KC. The addressee is not identified on this letter, but from the content it is evidently Verkade.

40. Krebs, "Abbau der Fettsäuren," p. 936.

41. Erich Eyck, *A History of the Weimer Republic*, tr. M. Hanson and R.G.L. White (New York: Atheneum, 1970), 2: 434–435, 486–487; William Sheridan Allen, *The Nazi Seizure of Power: The Experience of a Single German Town 1930–1935* (New York: New Viewpoints, 1973), p. 129; HAK–FLH, April 28, 1977 (Tape 9, p. 9).

42. Hans Krebs, with Anne Martin, *Reminiscences and Reflections* (Oxford: Clarendon Press, 1981), p. 61.

43. Gordon A. Craig, *Germany: 1866–1945* (New York: Oxford University Press, 1980), pp. 567–570; Hans Krebs, untitled handwritten note, KC.

44. Krebs, Notebook "10," pp. 122–131; Krebs, "Größe der Atmung und Gärung," pp. 866, Table 2, 869, Table 8.

45. Krebs, Notebook "10," pp. 133–137.

46. *Ibid.*, pp. 138–141.

47. HAK–FLH, May 2, 1977 (Tape 12, pp. 16–17).

48. *Ibid.*, May 3, 1977 (Tape 12, p. 22).

49. *Ibid.*, pp. 22–23.

50. *Ibid.*, May 2, 1977 (Tape 12, p. 17). Krebs discussed these experiments further in terms of the Thunberg-Knoop-Wieland theory, but always with the same tendency not to dwell on it.

51. *Ibid.*, May 3, 1977 (Tape 12, p. 23).

52. *Ibid.*, p. 30.

53. Krebs, Notebook "10," pp. 142–144; HAK–FLH, May 3, 1977 (Tape 12, p. 26).

54. Krebs, Notebook "10," p. 145.

55. *Ibid.*, pp. 150–151.

56. *Ibid.*, pp. 146–149, 152–157, 163–164. In between the experiment of Feb. 14 and that of Feb. 16 described above, Krebs carried out a deamination reaction in which he placed the slice in a side arm, and only tipped it into the main solution containing the amino acid after the first 30 minutes. I have been unable to interpret this experiment or its place in the above explanation. The reasoning that I have suggested led Krebs to carry out the experiments of Feb. 16 he gave in his subsequent paper, but without specifying whether he thought of it before or after the experiment. I have assumed that he thought of it before, because the design of the experiment seems to depend on the reasoning. See Hans Adolf Krebs, "Untersuchungen über den Stoffwechsel der Aminosäuren im Tierkörper," *Z. physiol. Chem.*, 217 (1933): 213, 217–218.

57. HAK–FLH, May 3, 1977 (Tape 12, p. 27).

58. *Ibid.*

59. Benzinger to HAK, Feb. 20, 1933, Benzinger dossier, KC.

60. Krebs, "Abbau der Fettsäuren," p. 938.

61. Krebs, Notebook "10," pp. 160–162; Juda Hirsch Quastel and Arnold Wheatley, "Biological Oxidations in the Succinic Acid Series," *Biochem. J.*, 25 (1931): 117–119, 123–124.

62. Krebs, Notebook "10," pp. 165–167; HAK–FLH, May 3, 1977 (Tape 12, pp. 29–31).

63. Craig, *Germany*, pp. 571–574.

64. Krebs, Notebook "10," pp. 168–169; HAK–FLH, May 2, 1977 (Tape 12, p. 19).

65. Krebs, Notebook "10," pp. 170–171.

66. *Ibid.*, pp. 172–175.

67. HAK–FLH, May 2, 1977 (Tape 12, pp. 17, 19–20); May 3, 1977 (Tape 12, pp. 32–34). In a recommendation written for Krebs in May, 1933, Thannhauser mentioned Krebs's "work just begun on the connections between fat and carbohydrate metabolism," an indication that Krebs may at that time have regarded his new investigation as a whole as aimed at that question. S.G. Thannhauser, "Zeugnis," May 1, 1933, KC.

68. When Krebs examined these pages with me in 1977, he saw in them a special significance that could only be apparent in retrospect: "I don't think I ever published this, that these acids...are readily oxidized in the kidney. I did later a great deal of work on the fuel of respiration of kidney, and came to the conclusion that what is burned essentially are fatty acids, not carbohydrate, and amino acids only to a limited extent. But the standard fuel of the kidney is fat. And these are really the first indication that this is so." HAK–FLH, May 3, 1977 (Tape 12, p. 32).

69. Krebs, Notebook "10," pp. 176–181.

70. See especially Chapter 1, pp. 4–6.

71. Franz Knoop, *Oxydationen im Tierkörper* (Stuttgart: Enke, 1931), p. 15.

72. Krebs, Notebook "10," pp. 180–183.

73. *Ibid.*, pp. 184–185.

74. *Ibid.*, pp. 192–193. As a result of work done in the 1960s, Krebs could explain this as an *expected* result when we looked back at it in 1977: "That is in accordance with the general principle that most of the ketone bodies are produced in the liver. But in other tissues fatty acids are oxidized completely." HAK–FLH, May 4, 1977 (Tape 13, p. 4).

75. Krebs, Notebook "10," pp. 195–199.

76. *Ibid.*, pp. 201–208; HAK–FLH, May 4, 1977 (Tape 13, pp. 7–9).

77. Krebs, Notebook "10," pp. 209–216.

78. Craig, *Germany*, pp. 575–578; Sheridan, *Nazi Seizure of Power*, pp. 209–214; Krebs, *Reminiscences*, p. 61; HAK to Lowell Weicker, March 29, 1933, KC.; HAK–FLH, Aug. 11, 1977 (Tape 40, pp. 18–19); Heinz Fuld–FLH, Feb. 24, 1978 (Tape 61, p. 6); Hermann Blaschko–FLH, Aug. 12, 1977 (Tape 43, pp. 10–11).

79. Krebs, Notebook "10," pp. 215, 217, 219.

80. *Ibid.*, pp. 224–226; Hans Adolf Krebs, "Weitere Untersuchungen über den Abbau der Aminosäuren im Tierkörper," *Z. physiol. Chem.*, 218 (1933): 158; Hans Weil-Malherbe–FLH, Sept. 2, 1977, (Tape 44, p. 9).

81. Krebs, Notebook "10," pp. 228–233.

82. *Ibid.*, pp. 233–236.

83. See Alan D. Beyerchen, *Scientists Under Hitler: Politics and the Physics Community in the Third Reich* (New Haven: Yale University Press, 1977), pp. 12–13.

84. Krebs, Notebook "10," pp. 237–239.

85. Walter Herkel to HAK, April 8, 1933, KC.; published in Hans Krebs, "Wie ich aus Deutschland vertrieben wurde: Dokumente mit Kommentaren," *Medizin historisches Journal*, 15 (1980): 367–368; trans. in Krebs, *Reminiscences*, p. 64.

86. HAK to Walter Herkel, Freiburg, April 10, 1933, KC.; publ. in Krebs, "Aus Deutschland," p. 368.

87. E. Rehn to HAK, Freiburg, April 12, 1933, KC.

88. Albert-Ludwigs-Universität, Freiburg im Breisgau, *Vorlesungs-Verzeichnis für das Winter-semester 1933/34* (Freiburg: H.M. Muth, 1933), p. 46.

89. HAK–FLH, May 2, 1977 (Tape 12, p. 13).

90. H.A. Krebs, "Abbau der Aminosäuren," in *Handbuch der Biochemie*, ed. Oppenheimer, 2d. ed., Suppl., Vol. 1, pt. 1, pp. 939–947.

91. Krebs, "Abbau der Fettsäuren," *Ibid.*, pp. 936–938.

92. *Ibid.*, p. 937.

93. Carl Neuberg and Ernst Simon, "Die Endoxydation," *Ibid.*, pp. 929–931.

94. Krebs, *Reminiscences*, p. 63; postcard, advertising brochure, and hotel bill inserted in Krebs, Notebook "10," between pp. 244–247; HAK–FLH, Jan. 9, 1981 (Tape 129, pp. 7–8).

95. Description based on my own visit to St. Peter in Aug. 1978.

96. Krebs, "Stoffwechsel der Aminosäuren," pp. 191–227.

97. *Ibid.*, pp. 203–204.

98. *Ibid.*, p. 227.

99. *Ibid.*, p. 226.

100. HAK to Hermann Blaschko, Easter Monday, [April 17], 1933. This and other letters from Krebs to Blaschko were given to me by Blaschko in 1979. After making copies I gave the originals to Hans Krebs. They are now in KC.

101. *Ibid.*, Krebs, *Reminiscences*, p. 67.

102. HAK to Blaschko, *Ibid.*

103. *Badische Verwaltungsdirektion der vereinigten klinischen Anstalten der Universität Freiburg* to HAK, Freiburg, April 18, 1933. KC.; publ. in Krebs, "Aus Deutschland," p. 369.

104. Krebs, "Aus Deutschland," p. 368.

105. Albert Szent-Györgyi to HAK, April 22, 1933, KC.; publ. in Krebs, "Aus Deutschland," pp. 369–370; trans. in Krebs, *Reminiscences*, p. 65; HAK to Hermann Blaschko, April 25, 1933 (see f.n. 100).

106. HAK to Blaschko, April 25, 1933.

107. HAK to F.G. Hopkins, April 26, 1933, KC.; publ. in Krebs, "Aus Deutschland," p. 370; trans. in Krebs, *Reminiscences*, p. 65.

108. Krebs, *Reminiscences*, p. 67.

109. Otto Warburg to HAK, April 26, 1933; HAK to Otto Warburg, April 29, 1933, KC.; publ. in Krebs, "Aus Deutschland," pp. 371–372, trans. Krebs, *Reminiscences*, p. 66.

110. F.G. Hopkins to HAK, April 29, 1933, KC.; publ. in Krebs, "Aus Deutschland," p. 371, and Krebs *Reminiscences*, pp. 65–66.

111. P. Ostern to HAK, April 24, 1933, KC.

112. Heinz Fuld–FLH, Feb. 24, 1978 (Tape 61, pp. 6–9).

113. Sheridan, *Nazi Seizure of Power*, pp. 199–203.

114. Krebs, *Reminiscences*, p. 74; Hans Krebs, "Introduction to Aschoff Memorial Lecture," typewritten manuscript, dated July 5, 1955, KC.

115. Krebs, *Reminiscences*, pp. 68–71.

116. *Ibid.*, p. 74; HAK–FLH, May 2, 1977 (Tape 12, p. 12).

117. HAK–FLH, Sept. 7, 1976 (Tape 4, p. 28).

118. HAK to Hermann Blaschko, May 31, 1933 (see f.n. 100).

119. Franz Knoop to HAK, April 30, 1933, KC.

120. Krebs, "Stoffwechsel der Aminosäuren," p. 210.

121. Krebs, "Weitere Untersuchungen," pp. 157–159.

122. H.A. Krebs, K. Henseleit, and F. Bielschowsky, "Ueber den Abbau der Pyrimidine im Tierkörper," typewritten manuscript, KC. The manuscript is undated, but includes a reference to a 1933 article, is "Aus der Medizinischen Klinik der Universität Freiburg," and refers to Krebs's paper on amino acids for the *Z. physiol. Chem.* as "in press."

123. Manderschied, "Harnstoffbildung," p. 245; HAK–FLH, Sept. 7, 1976 (Tape 4, p. 18).

124. Otto Warburg, "Über Eisen, den sauerstoffübertragenden Bestandteil des Atmungsferments," *Biochem. Z.*, 152 (1924): 479.

125. Otto Warburg, Karl Posener, and Erwin Negelein, "Über den Stoffwechsel der Carcinomzelle," 152 (1924): 317.

126. HAK–FLH, Sept. 7, 1976 (Tape 4, p. 18).

127. See, for example, Arthur I. Miller, *Imagery in Scientific Thought: Creating 20th Century Physics* (Boston, Birkhäuser, 1984).

128. HAK–FLH, July 25, 1977 (Tape 26, p. 1). It might also be interesting to consider the connection between language and imagery in this case. The German word "Kreislauf," which Warburg used and which Krebs used from the beginning, is not precisely equivalent to any of the English translations - "circulation," "circuit," or "cycle." Literally Kreislauf means "running in a circle." Perhaps the word itself then, was suggestive of a circular diagram to depict metaphorically a process that literally was supposed to proceed not through space, but through time.

129. HAK to H. Blaschko, May 4, 1933 (see f.n. 100).

130. HAK to R.A. Lambert, May 13, 1933, copies in KC. and the Rockefeller Foundation Archives, No. 2, 401A.

131. Robert A. Lambert to HAK, May 16, 1933, KC.

132. F.G. Hopkins to HAK, May 15, 1933, KC; publ. in Krebs, *Reminiscences*, p. 67.

133. HAK to F.G. Hopkins, nd., KC.

134. G. Embden, H.J. Deuticke, and Gert Kraft, "Über die intermediären Vorgänge bei der Glykolyse in der Muskulatur," *Klin. Woch.*, 12 (1933): 213–215; Joseph S. Fruton, *Molecules and Life* (New York: Wiley-Interscience, 1972), pp. 349–352; Hermann Fischer to HAK, March 31, 1933, KC.

135. Embden, "Glykolyse," p. 214.

136. HAK–FLH, Aug. 11, 1977 (Tape 40, pp. 24–25).

137. Robert A. Lambert to HAK, May 22, 1933, KC.

138. HAK to R.A. Lambert, nd., KC.

139. HAK to R.A. Lambert, June 1, 1933; H.A. Krebs to Dr. Kreutzberger, June 8, 1933; Zentrastelle für Judische Wirtschaftsstelle to HAK, June 13, 1933; HAK to L. Lichtwitz, May 30, 1933; L. Lichtwitz to HAK, June 23, 1933, KC.; HAK to H. Blaschko, May 31, 1933 (see f.n. 100).

140. Krebs, *Reminiscences*, p. 67.

141. HAK to W. Löffler, June 12, 1933, KC.

142. HAK to H. Blaschko, May 31, 1933 (see f.n. 100).

143. Krebs, *Reminiscences*, pp. 79–82. The invoice for the packages is in KC.

144. Lise Krebs to HAK, June 6, 1933; Fridolin Böhning to HAK, April 24, 1933, KC.; HAK–FLH, Aug. 13, 1977 (Tape 42, p. 2).

145. HAK–FLH, Sept. 7, 1976 (Tape 4, p. 28).

146. HAK to H. Blaschko, May 31, 1933 (See f.n. 100).

147. Krebs, *Reminiscences*, p. 83.

148. These include the autobiographical note about his early opinion of himself (see Chapter 6, p. 183); a wartime diary in which he repeatedly expressed the expectation that Germany would win the war; his mood at the time he faced forced retirement in Oxford, as described to me by his wife; and the attitude toward contemporary social conditions in England that he expressed often during the time that I knew him.

149. HAK to F.G. Hopkins, June 22, 1933, KC.

150. HAK–FLH, July 9, 1977 (Tape 19, p. 6).

151. HAK to F.G. Hopkins, April 24, 1933; publ. in Krebs, "Aus Deutschland," p. 370; HAK to E.J. Allen, nd.; HAK to Frank Dickens, June 8, 1933, HAK to D.D. Van Slyke, June 8, 1933; HAK to R.A. Peters, nd.KC. It is, of course, possible that he was advised by Lambert or someone else to use the phrase "wegen meiner jüdischen Abstammung" in the letters he wrote during June, in place of "weil ich Jude bin," that he had written in April.

INDEX